Mastering
Web Development with
Microsoft Visual Studio 2005

Mastering™
Web Development with
Microsoft® Visual Studio® 2005

John Paul Mueller

Wiley Publishing, Inc.

Acquisitions and Development Editor: Tom Cirtin
Technical Editor: Russ Mullen
Production Editor: Rachel Gunn
Copy Editor: Cheryl Hauser
Production Manager: Tim Tate
Vice President & Executive Group Publisher: Richard Swadley
Vice President and Executive Publisher: Joseph B. Wikert
Vice President and Publisher: Neil Edde
Book Designer: Maureen Forys, Happenstance Type-O-Rama; Judy Fung
Compositor: Chris Gillespie, Happenstance Type-O-Rama
Proofreader: Nancy Riddiough
Indexer: Nancy Guenther
Cover Design: Design Site

Copyright © 2005 by Wiley Publishing, Inc., Indianapolis, IN

Published by Wiley Publishing, Inc., Indianapolis, IN

Published simultaneously in Canada

ISBN-13: 978-0-7821-4439-X
ISBN-10: 0-7821-4439-X

For general information on our other products and services or to obtain technical support, please contact our Customer Care Department within the U.S. at (800) 762-2974, outside the U.S. at (317) 572-3993 or fax (317) 572-4002.

Wiley also publishes its books in a variety of electronic formats. Some content that appears in print may not be available in electronic books.

This book is dedicated to my brother Mark on his 41st birthday;
may all your wishes come true.

Acknowledgments

Thanks to my wife, Rebecca, for working with me to get this book completed. I really don't know what I would have done without her help in researching and compiling some of the information that appears in this book. She also did a fine job of proofreading my rough draft and page proofing the result. Rebecca also helps a great deal with the glossary and keeps the house running while I'm buried in work.

Russ Mullen deserves thanks for his technical edit of this book. He greatly added to the accuracy and depth of the material you see here. Russ is always providing me with great URLs for new products and ideas. However, it's the testing that Russ does that helps most. He's the sanity check for my work and my code.

A number of people read all or part of this book to help me refine the approach, test the coding examples, and generally provide input that every reader wishes they could have. These unpaid volunteers helped in ways too numerous to mention here. I especially appreciate the efforts of Eva Beattie, who read the entire book and selflessly devoted herself to this project. Bill Salkin provided me with a great many ideas and URLs, as well as tested some of the examples for me. A number of other readers tested procedures and helped refine the book in other ways.

Finally, I would like to thank Tom Cirtin, Mae Lum, Rachel Gunn, Cheryl Hauser, and the rest of the editorial and production staff at Sybex for their assistance in bringing this book to print. It's always nice to work with such a great group of professionals and I very much appreciate the friendship we've built over the last five books.

About the Author

John Mueller is a freelance author and technical editor. He has writing in his blood, having produced 68 books and over 300 articles to date. The topics range from networking to artificial intelligence and from database management to heads down programming. Some of his current books include a Windows power optimization book, a book on .NET security, and books on Amazon Web Services, Google Web Services, and eBay Web Services. His technical editing skills have helped over 39 authors refine the content of their manuscripts. John has provided technical editing services to both *Data Based Advisor* and *Coast Compute* magazines. He's also contributed articles to magazines like *DevSource*, *InformIT*, *SQL Server Professional*, *Visual C++ Developer*, *Hard Core Visual Basic*, *asp.netPRO*, *Software Test and Performance*, and *Visual Basic Developer*. He's currently the editor of the .NET electronic newsletter for Pinnacle Publishing (http://www.freeenewsletters.com/).

When John isn't working at the computer, you can find him in his workshop. He's an avid woodworker and candle maker. On any given afternoon, you can find him working at a lathe or putting the finishing touches on a bookcase. He also likes making glycerin soap and candles, which comes in handy for gift baskets. You can reach John on the Internet at JMueller@mwt.net. John is also setting up a Web site at: http://www.mwt.net/~jmueller/; feel free to look and make suggestions on how he can improve it. One of his current projects is creating book FAQ sheets that should help you find the book information you need much faster.

Contents at a Glance

Contents

Introduction

It seems like a very long time since Microsoft first announced Whidbey and eventually delivered the first beta. In fact, it seems like Microsoft is taking a long time to do anything these days. Some people misinterpret these long delays as a lack of enthusiasm or that perhaps the spark has just gone out of Microsoft's development process. One look at the completed Visual Studio and the many topics discussed in this book should convince you otherwise. Microsoft has done one thing more than with any other previous release of Visual Studio—they've listened. I won't go so far as to say that you'll find every feature of your dreams, but Microsoft has gone a long way toward making Visual Studio the kind of product that developers will enjoy using.

Mastering Web Development with Microsoft Visual Studio 2005 makes the inevitable transition easier by pointing out details of all these changes and then providing code to show you how to use them. Unlike a pure ASP.NET book, you'll also discover a wealth of techniques for combining coding methods you use at the desktop with those that you now need to use on the Web site. While reading and using *Mastering Web Development with Microsoft Visual Studio 2005*, you'll create a large-scale corporate Web site for ABC, Incorporated. In short, instead of simply discovering what ASP.NET provides, you'll actually put this information into action by building a complex Web site.

So What's in Visual Studio for Me?

If you like going home on weekends and don't like banging your head against the proverbial brick wall, Visual Studio 2005 has a lot to offer you. Every developer is going to love working with master pages and themes. The current development process often has developers looking for odd techniques to get repeated content onto a page. Master pages make the process extremely fast and easy. The ABC Incorporated Web example used in the majority of this book demonstrates the full effect of master pages on development. You'll find that the pages look very consistent, yet the book will show you that the repeated material is included only once. Themes add to master pages by letting you give your Web site a consistent feel. Every page uses the same colors automatically. Of course, you might want to give your users a choice. The ABC Incorporated Web example that runs through much of this book shows you how to do that too. A simple change on the main page lets a user switch between any number of themes.

You'll find the amount of drag-and-drop functionality has increased as well. For example, you'll be amazed at how fast you can create complex pages that rely on database input using drag-and-drop techniques. *Mastering Web Development with Microsoft Visual Studio 2005* shows you how to improve on drag and drop using SmartTag technology. Simply click an arrow next to a control to see a SmartTag you can use to configure it. This feature is especially helpful in getting database applications put together quickly. The ABC Incorporated Web site example includes a number of database examples—everything from a shopping cart to a beneficial suggestions Web application. In fact, you'll see just how easy it is to use XML for database purposes in this example—one of the database examples relies on XML instead of SQL Server.

This book also examines new uses for some existing tools. Many developers aren't familiar with everything that Server Explorer can do. Microsoft has made improvements to Server Explorer that make it a must-use tool for development. You'll find an entire chapter on this important topic. By using Server Explorer effectively, you can cut the time required to create any application significantly.

One of the most interesting new features in Visual Studio is WebParts. Imagine providing a little extra code that lets users move items around, get rid of items they don't want, and add items back in when they remove too much—all without bothering you. That's the beauty of WebParts. You provide all of the content that anyone will need and the individual users choose what they want. No longer do you have to contend with requests for little time-consuming tweaks to your Web page design that someone else will want changed.

I could go on—Visual Studio has a wealth of impressive new Web development features and you'll find the majority of them discussed in the book. One of Microsoft's apparent, less stressed, goals was obviously to simplify things for the developer. Let's face it, most developers don't have time any longer to fiddle with poorly implemented features. *Mastering Web Development with Microsoft Visual Studio 2005* helps you understand these new features and get to work quickly using all of the Visual Studio 2005 functionality.

Goals for Writing this Book

One of the major goals for writing this book is to discover the real world functionality of ASP.NET 2.0. Rather than simply assume that something probably wouldn't work or that Visual Studio had a limitation I couldn't overcome, I assaulted all of the boundaries. The result is this book, which discusses a broad range of programming topics. In fact, you'll be surprised at the number of things that Visual Studio can do—I know that I was pretty amazed by the time I completed this project.

Of course, testing the boundaries is nice, but you need practical examples too. You've seen many examples designed for the corporate market in the past and frankly, at least according to the email messages I receive, most of them are so hard to understand that it's a wonder anyone gets anything out of them at all. Consequently, one of the goals for this book was to create a large-scale example that anyone can understand. The ABC Incorporated example breaks all of the complex code down into easily understood parts. The main menu tells you precisely where to find a particular piece of the puzzle in the book—no guesswork involved. All you need to do is play around with the example, determine what you'd like to do, and go to that part of the book. It's really that simple.

Finally, this book helps you discover whether Microsoft is telling the truth about the usefulness and effectiveness of this product. Is Visual Studio really a good tool for creating Web sites? After all, you have a lot of tools from which to choose. I think you'll be surprised at just how easy it is to create Web sites that not only look professional, but don't require a lot of time to build. This book demonstrates that Visual Studio can help you create Web sites of moderate size without the usual array of widgets and lost time of other products. You can get to work almost immediately and use this book as a guide while you create the masterpiece that is your Web site.

Who Should Read This Book?

This book isn't for everyone. I created a book for someone who wants to see what ASP.NET 2.0 and the .NET Framework 2.0 provide, but who doesn't want to spend a lot of time and effort doing it. This doesn't mean, however, that you won't get highly developed, large-scale results: I targeted all of the examples toward the needs of an enterprise developer. All of the discussion considers this audience too. You won't find a small, flimsy home network example in this book. All of the applications are robust and designed to show specific Visual Studio Web development features. This book even includes sections on design strategies for larger application.

NOTE Don't get the idea that I didn't think about the small business or hobbyist developer. My book, *Mastering Microsoft Visual Web Developer 2005 Express Edition* (Sybex 2006), discusses ASP.NET from a small-scale development perspective.

You do need to have certain knowledge to use this book. I'm assuming that you've worked with your computer long enough to understand how it works—you won't find any button clicking exercises in this book. It's also important that you know a programming language at least a little bit. This book doesn't provide basic instruction on either Visual Basic or C#; the two languages used for the examples. Consequently, if you don't know a loop from an object, you probably need to look through a language book before getting this one, such as *Mastering Visual Basic 2005* by Evangelos Petroutsos (Sybex, 2006).

Getting the Source Code

This book contains a wealth of programming examples that you'll want to review as part of learning to use Visual Studio. You're free to type the code in from the book, but you do have an easier means at your disposal for getting the source code. Simply go to the Sybex Web site at `http://www.sybex.com/`, type the last five digits of the ISBN, **4439x**, in the search field, and click Go. Click the link for this book and you'll arrive at the book page. Click the Download link and follow the instructions to download the source code for this book. That's all there is to it and you'll save yourself a lot of time typing everything from scratch.

Conventions Used in This Book

It always helps to know what the special text means in a book. The following table provides a list of standard usage conventions. These conventions make it easier for you to understand what a particular text element means.

Convention	Explanation
`Inline Code`	Some code will appear in the text of the book to help explain application functionality. The code appears in a special font that makes it easy to see. This monospaced font also makes the code easier to read.

Convention	Explanation
`Inline Variable`	As with source code, variable source code information that appears inline will also appear in a special font that makes them stand out from the rest of the text. When you see monospaced text in an italic typeface, you can be sure it's a variable of some type. Replace this variable with a specific value. The text will always provide examples of specific values that you might use.
`User Input`	Sometimes I'll ask you to type something. For example, you might need to type a particular value into the field of a dialog box. This special font helps you see what you need to type.
`Filename`	A variable name is a value that you need to replace with something else. For example, you might need to provide the name of your server as part of a command line argument. Because I don't know the name of your server, I'll provide a variable name instead. The variable name you'll see usually provides a clue as to what kind of information you need to supply. In this case, you'll need to provide a filename. Although the book doesn't provide examples of every variable that you might encounter, it does provide enough so that you know how to use them with a particular command.
`[Filename]`	When you see square brackets around a value, switch, or command, it means that this is an optional component. You don't have to include it as part of the command line or dialog field unless you want the additional functionality that the value, switch, or command provides.
File ➢ Open	Menus and the selections on them appear with a special menu arrow symbol. "File ➢ Open" means "Access the File menu and choose Open."
italic	You'll normally see words in italic if they have special meaning or if this is the first use of the term and the text provides a definition for it. Always pay special attention to words in italic because they're unique in some way. When you see a term that you don't understand, make sure you check the glossary for the meaning of the term as well. The glossary also includes definitions for every acronym in the book.
`monospace`	Some words appear in a monospace font because they're easier to see or require emphasis of some type. For example, all filenames in the book appear in a monospace font to make them easier to read.
URLs	URLs will normally appear in a monospace font so that you can see them with greater ease. The URLs in this book provide sources of additional information designed to make your development experience better. URLs often provide sources of interesting information as well.

Part 1

Discovering Visual Web Developer

In this part:

Chapter 1

Working with Visual Web Developer

When you installed Visual Studio .NET 2005, you might have been surprised to find a bonus—Visual Web Developer. This new product fills a gap in the Visual Studio product line and is Microsoft's recognition that Web development has become a major part of the application market. In many respects, Visual Web Developer is simply a combination of older technologies such as FrontPage, mixed with the Visual Studio projects, and all of the new features found in ASP.NET 2.0. However, it's more than just the combination of those features, as you'll see in this chapter and as the book progresses. Visual Web Developer is a full-fledged development environment capable of creating enterprise-level applications of any complexity.

The focus of this chapter is introducing you to the Visual Web Developer environment, which means discussing ASP.NET 2.0 to an extent, discussing installation requirements, and looking at the IDE. However, you really won't get to know Visual Web Developer until you work through a project or two. Consequently, the chapter also delves into the sample application project that comes with Visual Web Developer—a personal Web site. It's not a big project nor is it something that you're likely to use as an enterprise developer, but it does provide a great view of Visual Web Developer features and that's how this chapter uses it.

This book does consider enterprise-programming needs. Instead of working with a number of individual projects, this book discusses several major projects that demonstrate the complex environment that many enterprise developers encounter every day. The final section of this chapter describes the enterprise project presented in this book. When you're done with this project, you'll have a resource you can use for reference in your own projects and some source code that you can borrow as well.

Introducing Visual Web Developer

Microsoft designed Visual Web Developer to provide complete Web development support. This new product is a combination of development products that Microsoft introduced in the past, along with some new ideas that make Visual Web Developer unique. Don't confuse this product with another version of Visual InterDev or Web Matrix. It's more a combination of the features provided with previous versions of Visual Studio and FrontPage, along with new functionality that only ASP.NET 2.0 provides, including new technologies such as WebParts. (You can find WebParts described in detail in several places in this book, starting with the "Using WebParts to Automate User Customizations" section of Chapter 6.)

Understanding What Visual Web Developer Provides

You can create Web applications and Web services using C#, Visual Basic, and Visual J#. This book concentrates on providing examples in C# and Visual Basic. The idea is that Visual Web Developer is a separate environment for creating Web resources. It even includes a special project that generates a fully functional personal Web site that you can use for experimentation. The "Working with the Personal Web Site Starter Kit" section discusses many of the elements of this sample application and helps you understand how to use it to your benefit.

Fortunately, you don't have to rely only on special technologies to use Visual Web Developer. You can create standard Web pages as well, using common tags and scripts. Chapter 6 shows how you can perform this type of development. The idea is that sometimes simple is better when it comes to certain page types. For example, you might find yourself using some of these techniques to ensure a page remains accessible, as described in Chapter 21.

One of the best features of Visual Web Developer is that you can move any Web application you create from your local drive to the server using the Copy Web tool shown in Figure 1.1. For those familiar with FrontPage 2003 (see Figure 1.2), this feature looks very familiar. The two products use a similar—but not precisely the same—interface for remote connectivity. Microsoft has focused on using FrontPage technology and then improving it in Visual Web Developer. You can learn more about this feature in the "Using the Copy Web Site Tool" section of Chapter 2.

The reason that the FrontPage 2003 connection is so important is that Microsoft did borrow some ideas from FrontPage for Visual Web Developer. For example, the concept of master pages started with FrontPage, but you'll see them developed more fully in Visual Web Developer as Microsoft stretches the technology to meet new needs. You'll first encounter master pages and themes in Chapter 4 of the book. These interface elements make Visual Web Developer easier to use and are consistent with Microsoft's goal for this product of creating a great programming environment for businesses of any size. FrontPage includes functionality that emphasizes simplicity over a heavy-duty programming environment.

FIGURE 1.1

Use Visual Web Developer to interact with both local and remote sites.

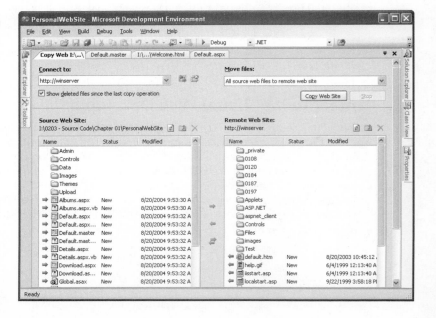

Visual Web Developer also supports many features that reduce programming complexity. For example, you have full access to the SmartTags that appear with many Microsoft products today. SmartTags reduce complexity by limiting the amount of custom code you must create. At the same time, the user gains full access to the functionality a SmartTag can provide. For example, when a Web page contains a stock symbol, a special SmartTag provides information about the stock symbol, such as the number of shares traded. SmartTags also affect the development environment, as shown in Figure 1.3. This SmartTag helps you configure a FormView control. You'll discover more about using SmartTags in the "Working with Control SmartTags" section of Chapter 2. You'll see how to add your own SmartTags to Web pages in the "Designing Custom SmartTags" section of Chapter 20.

Most developers will also appreciate the save/refresh style of working with Web pages that Visual Web Developer provides. In the past, you often had to close the browser, make any required changes to your code, and reopen the browser to see the effects. In a worst-case scenario, you might have to restart Internet Information Server (IIS) to see the change. With Visual Web Developer, all you need to do is make the change, save and compile the code in the IDE, and then click Refresh on the browser to see the change. The "Understanding Save/Refresh Style Page Development" section of Chapter 2 describes this technique in detail.

FIGURE 1.2
Visual Web Developer borrows some ideas from FrontPage 2003.

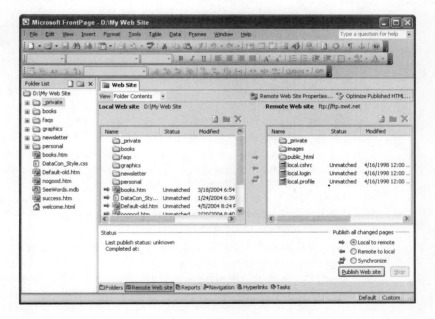

FIGURE 1.3
Using SmartTags reduces end user interface and other development complexity.

Developers have complained that using the debugger for Web pages in previous versions of Visual Studio .NET was difficult. In fact, Microsoft has an entire range of Knowledge Base (`http://support.microsoft.com/default.aspx?scid=fh;EN-US;KBHOWTO`) articles designed to make this process easier, but sometimes the solutions don't work as expected. Because debugging Web pages is difficult, the inclusion of a complete debugger optimized for Web development is important from a productivity perspective. Visual Web Developer includes such a debugger. Chapter 16 tells you more about debugging your applications.

Understanding How Visual Web Developer Differs from Visual Web Developer Express Edition

You might have seen the Visual Web Developer Express Edition offering on Microsoft's Express product Web site at `http://lab.msdn.microsoft.com/express/` and thought that Microsoft might be offering the full product free. Besides the fact that Microsoft didn't integrate Visual Web Developer Express Edition with the rest of the Express product line, it also lacks a number of important features for the enterprise developer. Consequently, although you can use the Express products to experiment and to learn about new .NET Framework features, it isn't the correct environment in which to build full-fledged applications of any size. In fact, the full version of Visual Web Developer found in Visual Studio .NET offers these features—all of which appear throughout the book as part of the enterprise application described in the "Defining the Enterprise Web Project" section of the chapter.

Server Explorer   This feature lets the developer interact with the majority of the server functionality directly. It includes support for performance counters, event log, message queues, services, and any installed copies of SQL Server. Server Explorer can also provide access to special features when installed. For example, when you install Crystal Reports, you can access any Crystal Services features from Server Explorer. Other vendors can provide similar access for server-level features. Chapter 3 helps you understand Server Explorer better.

Team Support   Team development is extremely important. Without team development support, developers can overwrite each other's code and it's impossible to manage a project. Visual Web Developer 2005 provides full team development support through an updated version of Visual Source Safe. It also includes a new tool called Visual Studio Team System. You can also add team development support using third party packages. Chapter 23 helps you understand the team development support in Visual Web Developer better.

Crystal Reports   Building a report by hand is time consuming with .NET because you have to construct the report as a graphic image. A better solution is to rely on a third party offering such as Crystal Reports. The Crystal Reports designer lets you create a report graphically and let the Crystal Reports engine determine how to get the report onto paper. Even though Visual Web Developer doesn't include the full Crystal Reports product, it includes enough functionality to create basic reports without any problem. You can see an overview of Crystal Reports functionality in the "An overview of Crystal Reports Services" section of Chapter 3. An example of using Crystal Reports in an application appears in Chapter 12.

Additional Controls   Visual Web Developer includes a number of controls not found in the Express product. For example, it includes a ConnectionsZone Web part that makes creating connections a lot easier. All of the additional controls relate to some type of enterprise-level functionality. You can find WebParts specific discussions in the "Using WebParts to Automate User Customizations" section of Chapter 6 and the "Working with WebParts" section of Chapter 14.

Additional Projects   Visual Web Developer includes the full set of projects that come with Visual Studio .NET. The projects include a number of control, component, and Web site projects that don't appear in the Express product. You'll see these projects in use throughout the book.

Additional Development Windows   Visual Web Developer includes a number of additional development windows. Some of these windows are related to debugging features—such as the inclusion of additional watch and local windows. The most important window is the browser emulator. It lets a developer test various browser environments with the application to see how the application will appear to the user. The various windows appear in different sections of the book. You can find the common windows described in the "An Overview of the IDE Elements" section of this chapter. The browser emulator appears in the "Working with the Browser Emulator" section of Chapter 2. All of the debugging information appears in Chapter 17.

Design Tools   Microsoft is placing increased emphasis on application design. Visual Web Developer includes a copy of Visio for creating an application design. Even though it isn't the best tool, it does work well enough to create fairly complex designs with little trouble. You'll find a brief overview of Visio in the "Designing Your Application Using Visio" section of Chapter 2. The developer also has access to several built-in controls including Class Diagram (Chapter 21), Application Connection Diagram (Chapter 23), System Diagram (Chapter 23), and Logical Datacenter Diagram (Chapter 23).

Optimization Tools   Creating an optimized application environment is especially important for commercial Web sites. Not only does Visual Web Developer provide access to performance counters and specialized optimization controls (Chapters 3 and 19), but it also provides support for Analysis Server, which allows a developer to profile an application and locate problem areas quickly. You'll find a complete discussion of Analysis server in the "Using Analysis Server Counters" and "Using Analysis Server" sections of Chapter 19. Other profiling and optimization tools appear throughout the book. Of course, you'll also find the add-on servers that Microsoft has provided with every other version of Visual Studio .NET.

Development Tools   The developer will have full access to all of the Visual Studio .NET development tools including ActiveX Control Test Container, Create GUID, Error Lookup, ATL/MFC Trace Tool, OLE/COM Object Viewer, and Spy++. You'll find these tools discussed throughout the book. For example, you'll find the ActiveX Control Test Container described in the "Working with the ActiveX Control Test Container" section of Chapter 15. The Error Lookup utility appears in the "Using the Error Lookup Utility" section of Chapter 17.

Additional Configuration Options   Many of the additional configuration options relate to special project capabilities that Visual Web Developer provides that don't appear in Visual Web Developer Express. For example, the developer will find settings that modify how the keyboard reacts when accessing either Word 2003 or Excel 2003 from within the Visual Studio IDE. A special Device Tools folder contains all of the settings for working with emulators for applications on other devices, such as cellular telephones and the Pocket PC. The "Modifying the Visual Web Developer Options" section of the chapter discusses configuration option access in detail.

Full Version of MSDN   Even though a developer can use the online version of Microsoft Developer Network (MSDN), it's a pain. Having the full version of MSDN available right at your desktop makes working with this important resource fast. In addition, it's possible to customize the local copy of MSDN with notes and to flag local MSDN pages. You can't easily do this with the online version.

Understanding the ASP.NET 2.0 Difference

One of the essential new features for .NET is the introduction of ASP.NET 2.0. The features included with ASP.NET determine what you can do with Web pages and how these pages appear to the end user. The latest version of ASP.NET also promises better performance and security, which is good news for enterprise developers who have often complained about too little of both in ASP.NET. Of course, only time will tell just how well Microsoft integrated these new features into the old product and whether those old security holes are really gone.

The move from older versions of ASP.NET might not be as seamless as you'd like. Enterprise developers will probably want to target new ASP.NET applications first, and then think about moving older applications. As Microsoft begins to overcome security, reliability, and performance issues with Windows and other products, ASP.NET has to change as well. One of the better places to obtain the insights of developers that have made the move is the ASP.NET 2.0 and Visual Studio 2005 Tips and Tricks forum at `http://forums.asp.net/134/ShowForum.aspx`.

Enterprise developers have learned the hard way that previous versions of ASP.NET could deliver a good partial solution, but a full solution often required jumping through hoops and using fancy code fixes. The repetitive code required for these tricks was hard to manage and it could be inconvenient to apply the fixes. ASP.NET 2.0 fixes many of the fit-and-finish problems by adding features to existing controls. In addition, Microsoft has improved the convenience factor for developers by incorporating a new concept borrowed from FrontPage 2003—master pages and themes.

A master page lets you create a Web page that contains elements that all or a group of Web pages must have and then use that page as a means of starting all of the pages on a Web site. A theme contains graphical and structural elements that define a basic concept for your Web site, such as using red for all title text. Figure 1.4 shows a typical example of a master page (note that it has a MASTER file extension). You'll learn more about working with master pages and themes in Chapter 4.

FIGURE 1.4
Master pages give a Web site a consistent look and greatly reduce development time.

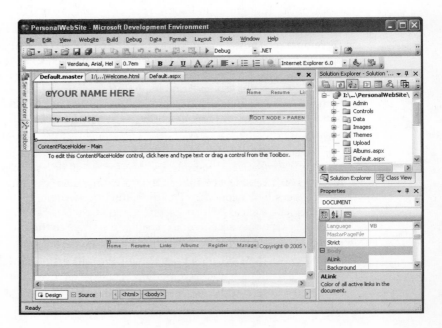

You'll also find many new developer productivity features in ASP.NET 2.0. For example, Microsoft has made it easier to add security to your Web application. ASP.NET 2.0 includes both credential storage and role management support without adding a lot of additional code. Chapter 18 tells you more about creating secure applications using Visual Web Developer. Personalization services (discussed in Chapter 14) make it easier to store user information so that every user has a custom experience. The use of site navigation to provide better access to Web pages and site counters to measure performance ensure that you can manage a site with greater ease. Both features appear in the "Creating a Custom Site Search" section of Chapter 8.

Part of the personalization functionality comes with a new technology called WebParts. This technology includes a number of controls that let the user change the content, appearance, and behavior of a Web page directly from a browser. You can use this technology to ensure that a Web page meets specific user needs such as accessibility or to allow the user to view content in another way (see the "Using WebParts to Automate User Customizations" section of Chapter 6).

NOTE   ASP.NET 2.0 supports 64-bit computing. Generally, working with a 64-bit application in .NET isn't any different from working with a 32-bit application from a coding perspective. However, you'll need to change the project settings and recompile the application.

ASP.NET 2.0 comes with 45 new controls that make creating applications a lot easier. Many of these controls are encapsulations of features developers requested and many had to be created by hand previously. You'll find examples of these new controls in many places in the book. However, the new controls are so important that you'll find many of them described in the "Working with Forms" section of Chapter 5. These controls also support multiple device types now so you don't have to do anything special to serve up a Web page to someone with a handheld device. The "Working with Multiple Device Types" section of Chapter 13 describes this feature in detail.

Management is a big issue because the Webmaster or network administrator usually performs the task, rather than the developer who created the application. Microsoft has made management easier by better documenting the `WEB.CONFIG` and `MACHINE.CONFIG` files. In addition, you'll find scripts for managing these files as part of the ASP.NET 2.0 installation. You can find out more about these features in the "Employing Server Side Redirection" section of Chapter 9.

There are a number of places online to learn more about ASP.NET 2.0. Of course, you'll discover a lot more about ASP.NET 2.0 functionality as this book progresses. Beginning with Chapter 7, the examples in the book demonstrate various ASP.NET 2.0 features that you get with Visual Web Developer. For example, the "Targeting Feedback Forms to Meet Specific Needs" section of Chapter 7 describes how you can use a master page to develop multiple feedback form types so that ad hoc surveys are much easier to implement. Besides the resources in the book, however, you might also want to obtain *Introducing ASP.NET 2.0* by Dino Esposito (Microsoft Press, 2004), and view these Web sites.

Basic ASP.NET 2.0 Overview   `http://www.asp.net/whidbey/whitepapers/ AspNetOverview.aspx`

MSDN ASP.NET 2.0 Topics   `http://msdn.microsoft.com/asp.net/default.aspx`

ASP.NET Security Article   `http://www.sitepoint.com/article/asp-net-2-security`

Master Pages in ASP.NET 2.0   `http://www.c-sharpcorner.com/Code/2004/May/ MasterPages.asp`

New Features of ASP.NET 2.0   `http://www.c-sharpcorner.com/Code/2004/July/ NewFeaturesASPNET.asp`

Performing the Visual Web Developer Setup

Now that you've seen what Visual Web Developer can do for you as a developer, you might be wondering how you can get a copy of this amazing product for your own. You might already have it installed on your machine. When you choose a default setup for any Visual Studio .NET 2005 language product, you also get Visual Web Developer. The only time you won't get Visual Web Developer is when you choose a custom setup and specifically clear the Visual Web Developer selection in the Language Tools folder of the Setup application.

Theoretically, you can install Visual Web Developer as a stand-alone product. In reality, you'll want to combine it with another language product such as Visual Basic or C# so that you can create components and perform other tasks that Visual Web Developer can't perform because it lacks that desktop environment projects. This book assumes that your setup includes Visual Web Developer and another language product in order to create a complete development environment.

Microsoft provides a basic set of requirements for Visual Web Developer, but these assumptions aren't very realistic for the enterprise developer. Table 1.1 provides a more realistic set of requirements that depend on the kind of applications you want to create. When you want to create a small Web site for the LAN, you can get by with the Simple Setup options. Most developers require the Average Setup options. Any developer performing extensive database management tasks or working with large applications will want system that meets the Complex Setup options.

It's important to remember that Visual Studio .NET requires a minimum of 600 MB to install, you need a minimum of 566 MB extra for MSDN, and the .NET Framework requires 264 MB of drive space. In short, you need to consider all of your needs before you begin the installation. At one time, developers considered a 30 GB drive huge; it might not seem so large with the requirements of this latest version of Visual Studio, especially if you also have SQL Server 2005 installed on the same system.

TABLE 1.1: Visual Web Developer Minimum System Requirements

REQUIREMENT	SIMPLE SETUP	AVERAGE SETUP	COMPLEX SETUP
Processor Speed	600 MHz	1.3 GHz	2.6 GHz
RAM	256 MB	512 MB	2 GB
Hard Disk	5 GB	20 GB	30 GB
Display	800 × 600 16-bit Color	1024 × 768 × 16-bit Color	1024 × 768 × 16-bit Color
CD or DVD Drive for CD Installation	X	X	X

Using the IDE

The focus of development language products today is the IDE because the IDE determines how fast and defines how well a developer can write the application. The IDE includes the actual development interface, provides access to components and controls, lets the developer debug the application, and includes the projects and wizards used to create both applications and application elements. You'll find the code used to explore the various view in the \Chapter 01\Views folder of the source code on the Sybex Web site.

NOTE You could write a .NET Framework application using nothing more than a text editor such as Notepad. The ILASM.EXE file in the \WINDOWS\Microsoft.NET\Framework\v2.0.50215 folder will compile the information you provide into a .NET application. However, working with .NET this way would be one of the most time-consuming and error-prone ways of creating an application imaginable. In short, don't get the idea that the IDE provides the language features—it provides the capability to work with the language in an efficient manner. The .NET Framework provides the language features.

An Overview of the IDE Elements

When you first open Visual Web Developer, you'll see what seems like a confusing array of panes in a main window, as shown in Figure 1.5. However, far from being a confusing array of panes, each one of these client windows is actually a part of the development environment. Figure 1.5 provides a label for each one of the major windows that Visual Web Developer opens. If you don't see one or more of these windows, you can always open it by using the options on the View menu. For example, to open the Solution Explorer window, select View ➤ Solution Explorer.

Each of these windows has a special purpose in helping you create applications faster. The following list provides an overview of each of the windows and tells how you'd use the window. You'll obtain additional information about the windows as the book progresses.

Standard Toolbar The Standard toolbar contains common buttons that let you create a new project; add items to a project; save a single or multiple files; cut, copy, or paste items; undo or redo actions; start an application; or find information in the project files. These tasks are common to most file types, so Visual Web Developer normally displays the Standard toolbar.

FIGURE 1.5
The Visual Web Developer IDE provides a number of features for creating applications quickly.

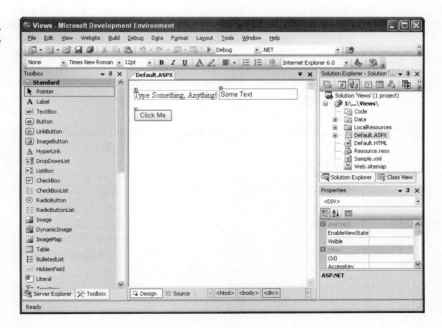

Formatting Toolbar   The Formatting toolbar lets you perform a range of text and object configuration tasks. For example, you can choose the style used to display text on screen (a style defines how similar text should look). You can also augment existing text by modifying the font, font size, and attributes. Any object can receive a foreground or background color change. You use the justification options on paragraphs to determine the text alignment. Individual text elements can also include bullets or numbers. Finally, you can convert an URL into a hyperlink that the user clicks to go to a different Web page or download a resource.

Other Toolbars   Not shown in Figure 1.5 is the wealth of other toolbars. For example, the Build toolbar contains options that help you compile the application. These toolbars appear in other sections of the book.

Solution Explorer   Solution Explorer is a kind of outline of your entire project. It shows which files and references your project includes. You can also use Solution Explorer to access the project settings and add new items. Finally, Solution Explorer can help you organize your project to make it easier to work with.

Class View   The Class View contains an outline of your project from an Object Oriented Programming (OOP) perspective. You can see the classes your application contains. Within the classes, you'll find the methods, events, and properties that your application contains. The Class View contains information about the visibility of application elements and helps you understand the organization of your application better.

Properties Window   The Properties window contains three elements. At the top, you see the selected item. You can select a new item from the drop-down list. The middle of the Properties window contains the properties for the selected item. Every item contains unique properties based on its object type. The bottom of the Properties window contains an explanation of the selected property when an explanation is available.

Editing/Design Area   This is the place where you actually edit or design a Web page. The content changes to reflect the currently selected window tab. For example, when working with a HyperText Markup Language (HTML) document, you'll see tabs for a Source view and a Design view. The Design view lets you modify the graphic elements of the Web page, while the Source view lets you change the code used to create the graphic elements. One or more tabs at the top of the editing/design area let you choose the file you want to work with when multiple files are open. Figure 1.5 shows the Design window (view)—this book examines many other views that Visual Web Developer provides.

Source Window Tab   Selecting the Source tab displays the Source window where you edit code used to create an application. The Source window lets you edit multiple languages—everything from C# and Visual Basic .NET to HTML and eXtensible Markup Language (XML). The Source window can even appear when there isn't any design to perform. In some cases, you'll create data files using the Source window that provides input to your application. In sum, the Source window is the most common window that you'll see when using Visual Web Developer.

Design Window Tab   Whenever a file offers a visual element—something the user can interact with—you'll see the Design tab—selecting this tab displays the Design window shown in Figure 1.5. In this case, the display is showing a standard Active Server Pages eXtended (ASPX) file, the kind that you work with most often.

Server Explorer Tab   Server Explorer is one of the most important, yet least used, features of Visual Studio .NET. Many developers haven't transitioned to using this tool very well and still code application elements by hand. Using this one tool, you can drag and drop everything from performance counters to event log elements onto your project. The elements contain all of the basic configuration information, so all you need to do is provide custom settings. You also use Server Explorer to access databases and to create reports. It's easy to create connections to any server that you can access on the network, making this tool an easy means of exploring the network without leaving the IDE. Chapter 3 discusses Server Explorer in detail.

Toolbox Tab   The Toolbox tab selects the Toolbox—a container filled with controls that you use to create the visual elements of an application. Every control has a different purpose and the applications in this book show you how to use many of them. The "Understanding the New ASP.NET 2.0 Controls" section of Chapter 5 also highlights many of the interesting controls in the Toolbox.

TIP   You can click the AutoHide button (the one that looks like a thumbtack) in the upper right corner of any window to hide that window. The window remains accessible—all you need to do is move the cursor over its tab, but the IDE hides the window when you don't need it. To display a window again, simply click the AutoHide button again. The position of the thumbtack on the AutoHide button tells you whether the IDE will hide the window. The IDE always displays the window when the thumbtack points straight down.

Modifying the Visual Web Developer Options

When you first start Visual Web Developer, you'll want to change the IDE options to meet your personal needs. You'll also want to check the settings every time you begin a new project to ensure that the settings meet project needs. To modify the Visual Web Developer settings, select the Tools ➤ Options command and you'll see the Options dialog box shown in Figure 1.6. (The figure shows all of the options expanded—these options aren't visible when you initially open the dialog box.)

FIGURE 1.6
The Options dialog box contains the Visual Web Developer Settings.

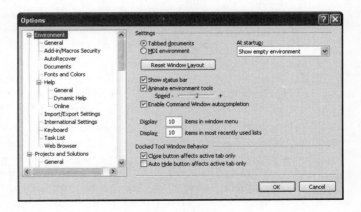

TIP   Most of the dialog boxes in Visual Web Developer include a help button (the one with the question mark in the upper right corner of Figure 1.6). Click the help button and point to an option or field to obtain additional information about it. The first time you use the help feature, Visual Web Developer displays an Online Help Settings dialog box that determines the source of help. Always choose Use Online Help as Primary Source when you know that you'll always have an Internet connection available and don't mind waiting an additional few seconds to receive the latest help that Microsoft can provide. Choose Use Local Help as Primary Source when you aren't sure that you'll have an Internet connection available or prefer not to wait the additional time for online help unless necessary. Select Do Not Use Online Help when you know you won't have an Internet connection available or don't ever want to wait for the latest help information.

Visual Studio provides a wealth of settings that you can use to control how the application environment looks and works. In fact, it's easy to get lost in the myriad of configuration options. The following list provides an overview of the various options at your disposal. The remainder of the book highlights special settings that you need to know about to achieve specific results.

Environment   These options contain settings that affect the IDE as a whole. You'll find settings for everything, from the number of recently used projects that Visual Studio tracks to the colors used to display items on screen. This is the one set of options that you should review one folder at a time when you initial set up Visual Studio .NET. For example, if you're color-blind or have difficulty seeing small type, you'll want to modify the settings in the Fonts and Colors folder. One set of options that you'll want to check for team development is in the Import/Export Settings folder. The Track Team Settings File option lets you choose where Visual Studio stores team settings—an important setting when you want everyone to use the same central storage location.

Projects and Solutions   The options in this folder tell Visual Studio where to store project and solution information for your applications. Generally, you won't want to change these settings unless you work in a team environment and need to store the information in a central location. The folder also contains configuration options that affect what happens when you build and run your application. For example, instead of having Visual Studio ask whether you want to rebuild a project before running it, you can set it to run the old version of the program. This folder also contains a few language-specific settings. As an example, you can set the Visual Basic global options here including Option Explicit, Option Strict, and Option Compare.

Source Control   These options control the source control application you choose for Visual Studio. In general, you'll find some settings for the Visual Studio plug-in and then some source control application specific settings. The plug-in setting controls which source control application you use when you have multiple applications installed.

Text Editor   The Text Editor folder contains one language-specific folder for each language you have installed as part of your Visual Studio setup. The language-specific folders contain two kinds of settings—those shared with all other languages, such as how many spaces to use for task, and those specific to the language, such as the use of outlining for Visual C# developers. You'll also see several common folders of options that affect all languages. The General folder contains options that define text editor behavior as a whole, including the kind of editor that it emulates. You have a choice of Emacs, Brief, or standard Visual Studio emulation. The File Extension folder lets you map nonstandard file extensions to a specific language or editor. For example, you can create special mappings for binary files. The All Languages folder contains general and tab settings for all languages. When you make a change here, it affects all languages unless you provide a language-specific override in one of the language folders.

Database Tools   The options in this folder help you interact with a database more efficiently. You can control everything from the automatic generation of scripts to the default size of data fields. This folder also contains options for managing performance. For example, you can control time-outs and limit the number of rows returned from a query.

Debugging   These options control how the debugger works. Generally, you'll want to maintain the default settings for these options when you begin working with Visual Studio and change them only if you find a particular setting fails to meet your needs. You can modify everything from the messages that the debugger outputs to the way the edit and continue feature works.

Device Tools   The options in this folder help you work with other devices using emulators and direct connections. The default setup includes emulators for the Pocket PC, SmartPhone, and Windows CE 5.0 devices. You can add devices from other vendors as needed for your project. The Form Factors folder lets you configure the specifics for each device (such as screen size and color capabilities) and add new configurations as needed to support your applications.

HTML Designer   The HTML Designer folder options let you change the environment for designing Web pages. For example, you can choose whether the IDE automatically displays the Design view or the Source view. It's also easy to control the use of a grid for placing controls and define whether controls automatically snap to the grid. These settings are relatively important for Visual Web Developer users because they can affect the code that Visual Studio generates in the background. For example, choosing to use a grid means that controls you add automatically have positioning information added to them.

Microsoft Office Keyboard Settings   These settings control how Visual Studio reacts when you load an Excel or Word document into the IDE. The default settings use Visual Studio equivalents for the keyboard commands. You won't have access to custom keyboard schemes. Given that these schemes can be important for the enterprise environment, you'll want to check these settings before you work with Office documents. Otherwise, you might not see the document and work with it using the same methods as the user, resulting in an application that fails to meet goals and expectations.

Windows Forms Designer   These options control the appearance and functionality of the Windows Forms designer. You won't use this feature very often with Visual Web Developer because Visual Web Developer doesn't let you create Windows Forms applications. However, it's important to know about these settings when you use the language products to create a Windows Forms application.

Using the Design View

The Design view is where you use graphical elements to create a user display. To create a display, you select items in the Toolbox and drag them to the form. You can also double-click an item in the Toolbox and the IDE will automatically add it to the form for you. Figure 1.7 shows a simple form containing a Label, Textbox, and a Button control. The Label displays text, "Type Something, Anything!" in this case. The user can't edit the content of a Label. A Textbox control accepts input from the user. You can also provide sample text for the user (always a good idea). After the user interacts with the controls on a form, clicking a Button control performs some action—at least it performs an action when you provide supporting code (see the "Using the Code View" section for details).

FIGURE 1.7
Use Design view to create a user interface for your Web application.

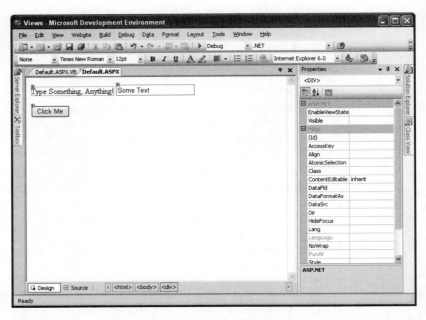

Using Design view isn't simply a matter of placing controls and hoping for the best. You select the controls and organize them in some manner. Normally, you choose an organization that lets the user work without thinking too hard about the organization of the document. For many users, this means placing the controls so they flow from top to bottom and from left to right. You'll see a number of examples of good Web application layouts as the book progresses.

TIP   This book isn't the end-all collection of design ideas. To gain a better appreciation of all of the elements you should consider when designing a great interface, get Mike Gunderloy's *Developer to Designer: GUI Design for the Busy Developer* (Sybex, 2005).

After you place the controls on the form, you'll want to spend a little time configuring them. In all cases, you'll want to provide the control with a meaningful name—one that reflects its use within the application. Every control also has special features that you'll want to configure. For example, when working with a Label control, you'll want to change the Text property so that it includes the text you want to display, as shown in Figure 1.7. The Textbox and Button controls also contain the Text property. While you'll want to change the Text property for the Button control, it's an optional change for the Textbox. You'll gain additional insights about controls and their properties as the book progresses.

It's important to consider what's happening as you work on the interface for your Web application. The Visual Web Developer IDE is adding code to the Web page that reflects the changes you make. In many cases, you don't need to worry much about this code—the IDE maintains it for you automatically. However, should you need to see the code so you can fine-tune it, you can click Source at the bottom of the Design view and you'll see the Source view described in the "Using the Source View" section of the chapter.

Using Source View

Source view shows the code that creates the user interface. Figure 1.8 shows the code used to create the user interface in Figure 1.7. Because Figure 1.8 shows the Label control selected, the IDE highlights that code in Source view. As you work with Visual Web Developer, you can place a control on a form, configure it, and then look at the code the IDE creates in Source view to gain a better understanding of how the process works.

Although Design view is very easy to use, it doesn't provide you with the level of control that Source view does. For example, notice that the IDE created two <br /> tags to create a break on the form. You could replace this code with a <p /> tag if desired to obtain the same result. To test it for yourself, comment out the <br /> tags and replace them with a single <p /> tag, as shown here.

```
<!-- <br /> -->
<!-- <br /> -->
<p />
```

Placing the <br /> tags within a comment <!-- --> means that you can still see the tags and restore them if you wish, but the browser ignores them. More importantly, this example shows how Source view provides you with additional options and greater flexibility in creating a Web page. You can't perform this kind of fine-tuning using Design view.

The best way to use Source view is to create your initial design, including all property settings, using Design view, and then fine-tune the page using Source view. When you want to verify that a control is using optimum code, select the control first so you see its code highlighted in Source view. On the other hand, you might simply want to add specialized code to the page, such as the scripting code described in Chapter 6. In this case, you'll place the cursor where the code needs to go and start typing.

FIGURE 1.8
Use Source view to work directly with tags as needed to create special effects.

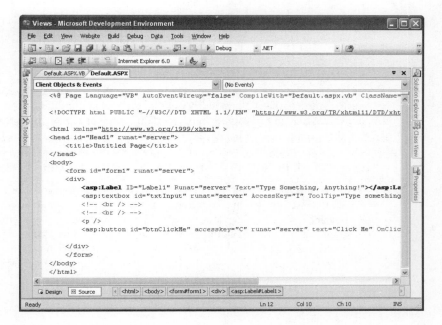

Using the Code View

The Code view is where you edit files that don't include a graphical element, such as the code behind files for your Web pages. Figure 1.9 shows a typical example of the Code view. Notice that the window doesn't include a selection for changing to Design view.

A code behind file contains the code that tells the server what to do when the user performs an action. For example, you might want to calculate an order total when the user clicks Submit to signify that all of the order details are correct. The Code view shown in Figure 1.9 is for the simple Web page shown in Figures 1.7 and 1.8. The act of clicking btnClickMe (the name of the Click Me button in Figures 1.7 and 1.8) is a Click event. The btnClickMe_Click() method is an event handler—it performs a task whenever the Click event for the Click Me button occurs.

You'll also use Code view for other files. For example, whenever you open an XML document, you'll use Code view because XML documents don't have a user interface.

Code view offers two interesting features: IntelliSense (a specialized help system) and Text Editor toolbar support. You can gain limited access to these two features using Source view as well, but they're most useful when working in Code view. The following sections describe these features.

FIGURE 1.9
Use Code view to work with code, such as the code behind, for your Web application.

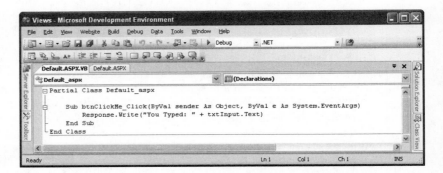

UNDERSTANDING INTELLISENSE

IntelliSense is a special automated help feature that Visual Web Developer provides whenever you write code. The .NET Framework objects can contain methods, properties, events, and even other objects. Whenever you type an object name, such as the Response object shown in Figure 1.10, IntelliSense provides a list of items for that object, as shown in the Object Member List. As you type more information, IntelliSense refines the Object Member List selection. It also provides a tooltip that describes the selection so that you know when you've found the correct object.

TIP Whenever you type code in Code view (and often when you type it in Source view), you'll see IntelliSense support. In fact, the only time you won't see IntelliSense support is when Visual Web Developer doesn't understand something that you're typing. For example, when you make a typographical error in typing the object name, IntelliSense won't appear on screen. Likewise, when you're missing an object reference or using the wrong object, IntelliSense will clue you in by not displaying any information. Use this IntelliSense cue as an indicator that something's wrong.

FIGURE 1.10
IntelliSense provides clues you can use to create code more quickly without accessing help.

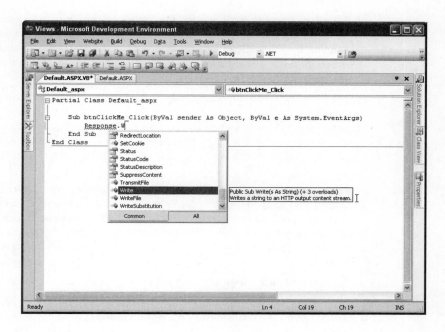

USING THE TEXT EDITOR TOOLBAR

The Text Editor toolbar shown in Figure 1.11 provides a number of features that help you create code with greater ease and precision. Each of these buttons helps you perform a code-related task such as displaying an Object Member List like the one described in the "Understanding IntelliSense" section of the chapter. The following list describes the button purposes in detail.

Clear All Bookmarks   Removes all of the bookmarks in a document. A bookmark in Code view works the same as a bookmark in a book—it helps you get back to a specific location quickly. When you complete a book, you normally remove the bookmark and place the book on the shelf. Likewise, when you complete a code editing process, you can click this button to remove all of the bookmarks.

Move the Caret to the Next Bookmark in the Current Document   Moves the caret (cursor) to the next bookmark in the current document. Even if you have bookmarks set in other documents, the IDE will move between bookmarks in the current document only. When you reach the last bookmark in the document, clicking this button again will move you to the first bookmark in the current document.

FIGURE 1.11
The Text Editor Toolbar helps you work with HTML elements.

Move the Caret to the Previous Bookmark in the Current Document   Moves the caret (cursor) to the previous bookmark in the current document. Even if you have bookmarks set in other documents, the IDE will move between bookmarks in the current document only. When you reach the first bookmark in the document, clicking this button again will move you to the last bookmark in the current document.

Move the Caret to the Next Bookmark   Moves the caret (cursor) to the next bookmark. If the next bookmark appears in a different document, the IDE will display that document. When you reach the last bookmark in the current document, clicking this button again will move you to the first bookmark in the next open document that has bookmarks in it. If there aren't any other documents with bookmarks, the IDE will move the caret to the first bookmark of the current document.

Move the Caret to the Previous Bookmark   Moves the caret (cursor) to the previous bookmark. If the previous bookmark appears in a different document, the IDE will display that document. When you reach the first bookmark in the current document, clicking this button again will move you to the last bookmark in the previous open document that has bookmarks in it. If there aren't any other documents with bookmarks, the IDE will move the caret to the last bookmark of the current document.

Toggle a Bookmark on the Current Line   Creates a bookmark on the current line. The bookmark appears as a square box the left side of the editing area.

Uncomment the Selected Lines   Removes the comment character (if any) from in front of the selected lines of code. This process turns the comments back into code that Visual Web Developer will process when you compile the application.

Comment Out the Selected Lines   Adds comment characters in front of the selected lines of code. This process changes the code into a comment that you can still see and modify, but Visual Web Developer will ignore.

Increase Indent   Increases the space between the left side of the display and the start of the code. Indentation makes code easier to read by showing which code is at the same level of execution. Adding indentation can help you reformat code after you add a new type of processing or processing level.

Decrease Indent   Decreases the space between the left side of the display and the start of the code. As the indentation level increases, the code moves to the right side of the screen and eventually out of view. Removing unneeded indentation can help you see the entire line of code, rather than scrolling back and forth to see it.

Display Word Completion   Displays an Object Member List based on the letters typed to the left of the current cursor position. You can use this feature to help type the names of objects. Normally, method, property, and event values appear automatically when you type the period after an object name, but this feature helps you obtain the initial object name and ensure it appears correctly in the code.

Display Quick Info   Shows a tooltip containing information about the currently selected item. Figure 1.10 shows an example of such a tooltip.

Display Parameter Info   Shows a tooltip containing the parameters for a method or other element that requires input arguments. Figure 1.10 shows a typical example of a tooltip. When a method can accept more than one kind of input argument, the tooltip also includes a method for selecting between the arguments so that you can match the data you want to provide with the arguments the method will accept.

Display an Object Member List   Creates an Object Member List like the one shown in Figure 1.10 for the selected item. You can place the cursor anywhere within the item text and see its entry in the Object Member List. Choosing a new item from the list will replace the selected item in your code.

Working with the Personal Web Site Starter Kit

The Personal Web Starter Kit is a special template that comes with Visual Web Developer. Microsoft included this project to demonstrate the various features that Visual Web Developer provides and help you create a personal Web site very quickly. Although most enterprise developers won't use this project for real world development, it does serve as a great training tool for learning about Visual Web Developer features. The project includes a number of features that you'll want for your personal Web site including a Welcome page and the following features:

- ◆   Administration pages
- ◆   Photo album

The following sections discuss the concept of creating applications using the Personal Web Starter Kit as a starting point. This is actually the first project you'll create with Visual Web Developer. Considering that the project template performs much of the work for you, the project is extremely easy to work with and you'll have a professional-looking project to use for reference later. However, the project in Chapter 2 is more realistic in that it shows how you'll start most projects you create. You'll find this example in the \Chapter 01\PersonalWebSite folder of the source code on the Sybex Web site.

Creating the Application

Before you can begin working with any application, you need to create it. The starting point is a project that defines the parameters of the application and stores any special settings that Visual Web Developer requires. You then begin a process of defining the application. This process includes defining a Web site to act as a container for storing the data you want to display and adding files to the Web site. Each file serves a unique purpose in the overall scheme of creating the Web site you want to design.

The Personal Web Starter Kit is unique in that you define everything in a single step—the project template performs a lot of the work that you normally need to do. The following steps show how to create the Personal Web Starter Kit application.

1. Select File ➢ New Web Site. You'll see the New Web Site dialog box shown in Figure 1.12.

2. Choose the language you want to use from the Language list.

3. Select a location for the project using the options in the Locations list. The example uses the local file system as a storage location.

FIGURE 1.12
The New Web Site dialog box helps you create a Web site to store the applications you create.

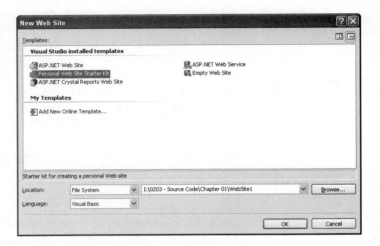

4. Highlight the Personal Web Site Starter Kit project, as shown in Figure 1.12.

5. Type the name and location of the project in the Location field. All projects include these two elements.

TIP   Click Browse to display a Choose Location dialog box. This dialog box lets you find the location you want to use without having to type it. You still need to type a project name after you choose the location.

6. Click OK to create the project or Cancel to close the New Web Site dialog box without creating the project. When you click OK, Visual Web Developer requires several seconds to create the project. Be patient—this process can take a little longer on older machines. Eventually, you'll see the Personal Web Site Starter Kit Design view.

Working with the Application Elements

You have a shiny new Web site filled with pages to work with, but little direction on how to work with them at this point. The `Welcome.HTML` file supplied as part of the kit tells you how to perform tasks such as creating an administrative user who can upload photographs and perform other tasks on the new site. Make sure you review this file as part of learning about the new Personal Web Site Starter Kit project you created. This section starts where the Microsoft supplied documentation leaves off. For example, you'll discover how to modify the content of the Web site.

Begin exploring the application by opening Solution Explorer. You'll see a list of folders and files for this project. Some folders, such as `Themes`, will contain a number of subfolders—one for each theme that the application supports. To see the contents of a folder, click the plus sign next to it; likewise, click the minus sign to hide the content of the folder again. Within each folder, you'll normally find one or more files. For example, the `Images` folder contains a number of placeholder Joint Photographic Experts Group (JPEG) files. These files have either a `JPG` or a `JPEG` file extension.

The actual Web pages for the Personal Web Site Starter Kit have an ASPX file extension. You'll notice a plus sign next to these files—just like the plus signs next to the folders. Click the plus sign and you'll see the code behind file for the Web page. To view the pages in your new Web site, double-click an ASPX entry in Solution Explorer. You'll see the page open in Design view or Source view, depending on how you have your copy of Visual Web Developer configured.

Open the `Links.ASPX` page, which is one of the more typical examples. This page has three major sections. You can edit the About the Links and Some Link Trivia sections, but the banner isn't even selectable. The banner material appears as part of the `Default.MASTER` file. To change the banner, you have to edit this file. However, you have to exercise caution in editing the `Default.MASTER` file because it affects every page that relies on this master page—always put common material—not page-specific material—in `Default.MASTER`.

The two remaining sections of application elements contain three kinds of content. The first kind of content should remain after you perform your edits—it includes headers and other information that you don't need to change. The second kind of content is human readable instructions on how to modify the page. You replace these instructions with content of your own, in most cases, or simply remove the instructions so the Web site users can see them. The third kind of content is unreadable text that takes the place of the content you provide. This is where your main work lies—adding the content you want to provide to site users.

Modifying the Application Template to Meet Specific Needs

At some point, you might find that the Personal Web Site Starter Kit becomes a major asset. Perhaps you want to set up a personal Web site for every sales member of your company. You don't really want to invest in a high-end tool to do it, so Visual Web Developer is the best option, but perhaps not the most time efficient method. You can improve the efficiency of using Visual Web Developer by modifying the application template to meet your specific needs. For example, you might want to add company-specific elements to the template. This section describes how to access the project and modify it to meet your specific needs. It assumes that you're going to create this project more than one time (otherwise, modifying the template doesn't make sense).

WARNING   The procedure in this section is somewhat complicated, and it's going to be a little more than you want to take on if you haven't used .NET in the past. Consider this section food for thought. You might try it now if you've used .NET before, or you might simply decide to come back later after you've gone through more examples in the book. For that matter, you might decide that the projects Microsoft has provided work fine as is and never return to this section.

GETTING STARTED

You'll find the Personal Web Site Starter Kit template in the `\Program Files\Microsoft Visual Studio 8\Common7\IDE\ProjectTemplatesCache\Web\VisualBasic\1033\PersonalWebSite.ZIP` folder of your hard drive. (Users of other languages will find a folder for that language in the Web folder.) Note that even though the folder has a ZIP extension, it's not a ZIP file. Whatever you do, don't modify this project directly—maintain a clean environment by creating a copy of the folder and renaming it for your personal needs. Call it something such as `ABC_Inc.ZIP`.

TIP   The process outlined in this section works with any project template that Microsoft provides. You might decide to customize the standard ASP.NET Web Site project to include custom content or additional files that you always use with this project. The idea behind customization is to tailor Visual Web Developer to meet your needs, rather than work around any limitations Visual Web Developer might have (recreating the same file for every project is a limitation).

The first thing you'll need to do after you copy the ZIP folder is to open it. Inside you'll find all of the files that make up this project. Modify the existing files to meet your needs. For example, you can modify the master template to include your company name or other features you normally use. Another change is the use of a different template or perhaps a larger font for some design elements. The critical concept is to change only those elements that you change every time you use the project.

ADDING FILES TO A TEMPLATE

Adding new files can become a little trickier, but it's quite doable. Begin by adding the new file to the project folder that you created (`ABC_Inc.ZIP` in the case of the example)—not the original `PersonalWebSite.ZIP` project folder. Once you add the new file, you need to decide where it appears in the project. In fact, you can use the same file multiple times in a project should you decide to.

You might wonder how the project template knows what to do with the file you create. The `PersonalWebSite.VSTEMPLATE` file contains all of the required information. Generally, you want to edit this file with extreme care or the project template changes you perform won't work. In fact, the project template might not work at all. This file is in XML format, so you can use your favorite XML editor to work with it or simply open the file in Notepad. Don't use an editor that will add formatting information to the file, such as Microsoft Word.

After you open the file, skip the introductory information—you don't want to edit it in any way. Locate the `<ProjectContents>` tag shown in Figure 1.13. This is where you'll add files to the project.

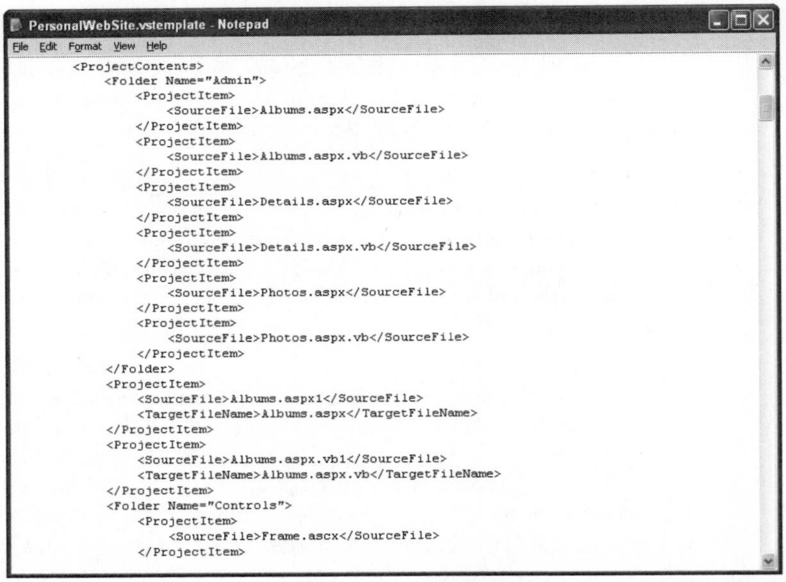


```
<ProjectContents>
    <Folder Name="Admin">
        <ProjectItem>
            <SourceFile>Albums.aspx</SourceFile>
        </ProjectItem>
        <ProjectItem>
            <SourceFile>Albums.aspx.vb</SourceFile>
        </ProjectItem>
        <ProjectItem>
            <SourceFile>Details.aspx</SourceFile>
        </ProjectItem>
        <ProjectItem>
            <SourceFile>Details.aspx.vb</SourceFile>
        </ProjectItem>
        <ProjectItem>
            <SourceFile>Photos.aspx</SourceFile>
        </ProjectItem>
        <ProjectItem>
            <SourceFile>Photos.aspx.vb</SourceFile>
        </ProjectItem>
    </Folder>
    <ProjectItem>
        <SourceFile>Albums.aspx1</SourceFile>
        <TargetFileName>Albums.aspx</TargetFileName>
    </ProjectItem>
    <ProjectItem>
        <SourceFile>Albums.aspx.vb1</SourceFile>
        <TargetFileName>Albums.aspx.vb</TargetFileName>
    </ProjectItem>
    <Folder Name="Controls">
        <ProjectItem>
            <SourceFile>Frame.ascx</SourceFile>
        </ProjectItem>
```

FIGURE 1.13
The <ProjectContents> tag shows the beginning of the template file information.

The `<ProjectContents>` element includes a number of interesting child elements. The following list describes each of the elements and helps you understand where they fit into the project definition.

`<Folder>` The `<Folder>` element defines the name of a folder. It can also hold one or more `<ProjectItem>` elements. Any `<ProjectItem>` elements that appear in the folder also appear in that folder when you create the project. A `<Folder>` element can also contain other `<Folder>` elements (as subdirectories) or it can be blank to create an empty folder.

\<ProjectItem\>   The \<ProjectItem\> element defines a single project item—a file that holds some type of project data. As a minimum, the \<ProjectItem\> element contains a single \<SourceFile\> element. However, it can also include optional elements such as \<TargetFileName\> and \<OpenInEditorPropertyGroup\>. In most cases, a \<ProjectItem\> element appears within a \<Folder\> element. When it doesn't, the file appears in the root directory of the project, such as the Albums.ASPX file that appears in Solution Explorer. Notice that the declaration for this file appears outside a folder.

\<SourceFile\>   The \<SourceFile\> element defines the name of the file within the project template. It usually defines the name of the file as it appears in the project as well. You can modify this behavior using the optional \<TargetFileName\> element. Visual Web Developer copies this file from the project template and places it in the project you create.

\<TargetFileName\>   The \<TargetFileName\> element changes the name of a file copied from the project template. Visual Web Developer normally uses the name of the file as it appears in the project template—using this element lets you change the name so a single source file can appear in the project using several different names.

\<OpenInEditorPropertyGroup\>   The \<OpenInEditorPropertyGroup\> element acts as a container for the \<OpenInEditor\> or \<OpenInWebBrowser\> and \<OpenOrder\> elements. As a whole, the group tells Visual Web Developer to open a source file as soon as it's copied into the project folder.

\<OpenInEditor\>   The \<OpenInEditor\> element tells Visual Web Developer to open a source file in an editor so the developer can modify it. Use this element for standard data files that you expect the developer to modify in some way. In many cases, you'll want to open the file automatically to ensure the developer knows that the file requires change.

\<OpenInWebBrowser\>   The \<OpenInWebBrowser\> element tells Visual Web Developer to open a source file in a browser for viewing. You'll normally use this element with informational files (generally in HTML format).

\<OpenOrder\>   The \<OpenOrder\> element tells Visual Web Developer where to place the source file in the open order. For example, if you provide a value of 1, then this is the first file the developer using your template sees. Make sure that every source file you open as a unique number.

Always remember to place any new entries you create after the opening \<ProjectContents\> element, but before the closing \</ProjectContents\> element. Most of the entries you make are quite simple. For example, to place a file in the root directory, you might include an entry like this:

```
<ProjectItem>
 <SourceFile>SpecialText.TXT</SourceFile>
</ProjectItem>
```

However, let's say you want to rename the file after its copied. To make this change, use the \<TargetFileName\> element like this.

```
<ProjectItem>
 <SourceFile>SpecialText.TXT</SourceFile>
 <TargetFileName>OtherText.TXT</TargetFileName>
</ProjectItem>
```

The file still contains the content of SpecialText.TXT, but now it has a filename of OtherText.TXT. You can also place the file in an existing folder by looking for the appropriate <Folder> element or create a new folder to hold it, as shown here.

```
<Folder Name="Special Folder">
 <ProjectItem>
 <SourceFile>SpecialText.TXT</SourceFile>
 </ProjectItem>
</Folder>
```

In this case, Visual Web Developer creates a new folder named Special Folder before it copies SpecialText.TXT to it. Let's say that you want to open a file automatically for the developer using your template. First, you need to decide whether this is an informational file or a file that you expect the developer to edit. Use the <OpenInEditor> tag for files that you want the developer to edit, as shown here.

```
<Folder Name="Another Folder">
 <ProjectItem>
 <SourceFile>SpecialText.TXT</SourceFile>
 <OpenInEditorPropertyGroup>
 <OpenInEditor>true</OpenInEditor>
 <OpenOrder>11</OpenOrder>
 </OpenInEditorPropertyGroup>
 </ProjectItem>
</Folder>
```

Notice the combination of tags—you must place the <OpenInEditor> element within the <OpenInEditorPropertyGroup> element and tell Visual Web Developer when to open the file using the <OpenOrder> element. The bottom line is that you can add files to an existing template with relative ease and even change the behavior of the template to an extent by carefully editing the VSTEMPLATE file. The important consideration is that you don't want to change any of the operational information, such as any of the package information that appears at the beginning of the file.

COMPLETING THE TEMPLATE FILE CHANGE

At some point, you'll make all of the changes you want to the project template. You still need to get the template ready for use by Visual Web Developer. The following steps tell you how.

1. Use an application such as WinZip (http://www.winzip.com/) to create a ZIP file containing the template. (The built-in Windows XP ZIP file support works fine for reading archives, but not as well for creating them.) What you'll end up with is a file named ABC_Inc.ZIP.ZIP.

2. Copy the file to the \Program Files\Microsoft Visual Studio 8\Common7\IDE\Project-Templates\Web\VisualBasic\1033 folder on your system. (Make sure you copy the file to the correct language folder—the example uses Visual Basic, but you could also use the Visual C# or the Visual J# folders.)

3. Rename the existing PersonalWebSite.ZIP to OldPersonalWebSite.ZIP. Saving the file lets you restore it easily later.

4. Rename the ZIP file you created (`ABC_Inc.ZIP.ZIP` in the case of the example) to `Personal-WebSite.ZIP`. This change forces Visual Web Developer to use the new template.

5. Close and reopen Visual Web Developer if necessary. Otherwise, Visual Web Developer might use an older version of the template loaded into memory.

6. Create a new project with the modified template to test it. If you haven't made any errors, the template will use all of the modified settings.

Defining the Enterprise Web Project

The personal Web site project is interesting and it helps you understand some of the new features of Visual Web Developer, but for the enterprise developer it represents a training tool or a way to set up personal Web sites for people in the company. This project doesn't exercise the full potential of Visual Web Developer, nor does it represent the kind of application that you're most likely to write. Starting with Chapter 4, you'll see how to use Visual Web Developer to create an enterprise-level application. Each chapter will add something to the project. By the time you reach Chapter 23, you'll have a much better idea of how Visual Web Developer can fit in your enterprise project plans.

The example application demonstrates a Web site for ABC, Incorporated—a vendor that specializes in odd devices for the modern person. ABC Inc. could be your company or an example of someone you work with. They stock parts for both corporate and individual sales. This means providing a way to sell products both in bulk and individually. The company also deals with the government, which means meeting government requirements such as the Section 508 accessibility requirements. Naturally, the Web site also has to support a catalog and provide user help as needed.

Because ABC Inc. is a conscientious company, they provide methods for optimizing the Web display to meet specific user needs. In this case, they'll use WebParts, but the book also demonstrates other methods that you can use for your own company's Web site. You'll discover that ABC Inc. provides routine surveys that costumers can fill out to indicate their level of satisfaction with the products the company supplies. Of course, the user can always opt out of these surveys and never see them again.

Like many online vendors, ABC Inc. provides a number of online reports. They use Crystal Reports to perform this task. For example, a customer might want to review previous orders or the status of current orders. The staff might find a use for online reports too in evaluating the health of the Web site or knowing what to sell during client visits.

The example visits developer issues as well. For example, you'll discover how the tools that come with Visual Studio (such as Visio and Visual Source Safe) can help improve the developer experience. In short, the example in this book takes you through the entire development process from an enterprise perspective.

Defining Your Development Goals

This chapter has introduced you to Visual Web Developer. It's important to consider how big a leap Visual Web Developer is when compared to capabilities provided by previous versions of Visual Studio. Using Visual Web Developer lets you create robust Web applications with less effort. In addition, you're using a tool that you have worked with over a number of years, rather than relying on third party development tools to fulfill some needs. Visual Web Developer is a significant change in Microsoft strategy for Web development.

Of course, you'll have to discover how Visual Web Developer fits within your corporate development plans. Make sure you take time to work through the personal Web site project and play with it for a while. It's OK to play when you're discovering something new and exciting, which certainly defines the new capabilities that Visual Web Developer provides. Make sure you check out the IDE features as well and create a few experimental Web sites of your own.

Chapter 2 is another introductory chapter, but it takes a different approach than this chapter did. You'll create a simple application in Chapter 2 to that explores some of the Visual Web Developer and ASP.NET 2.0 features in detail. The goal of Chapter 2 is to help you get ready for the enterprise Web project that appears in the chapters that follow. It helps you work through some of the Visual Web Developer features so that you get more out of the material that follows.

Chapter 2

Creating a Simple Application

Enterprise developers often have to tackle new technologies quickly because time is a significant consideration. This chapter offers a brief look at Visual Web Developer basics and helps you get up to speed with it. You'll create a simple application designed to acquaint you with Visual Web Developer features. If you already know how to work well with Visual Studio .NET, you might want to skip the majority of this chapter. However, even if you skip the rest of the information, make sure you look at the "Designing Your Application Using Visio" section at the end because it provides more information about the enterprise-level application discussed in the rest of the book.

One of the better features of Visual Web Developer is that it provides a built-in Web server. This server isn't accessible to anyone outside your local machine. In fact, the built-in Web server doesn't even run until you tell it to. These features make the built-in Web server very safe to use on just about any machine and very resource friendly, as well, on machines with limitations.

Of course, you'll eventually want to move your application to where someone else can see it. This chapter also discusses how you can use IIS with Visual Web Developer. You'll also discover how to work with other servers, such as Apache, by using techniques such as File Transfer Protocol (FTP). Eventually, you'll want to publish the site using the Copy Web Publishing Tool. It's also easy to use remote development techniques with Visual Web Developer and this chapter shows you how.

This chapter also discusses a few of the features that make Visual Web Developer special. One of the most important features is browser emulation—the ability to create an environment that mimics the environment on another device. (Chapter 13 provides additional information about working with mobile devices.) Another unique feature is the save/refresh style of page development—a real productivity enhancer for any developer.

Because you'll be working with a new project in this chapter, it's also a good time to discuss one of the productivity features that Visual Web Developer provides—control Smart Tags. Using Smart Tags can greatly reduce the time you'll spend trying to configure certain kinds of controls. In some cases, Smart Tags can also provide ideas on how to use the control more efficiently.

Using the Built-in Web Server

Even if you don't have IIS installed on your system, you can test the Web pages you create using Visual Web Developer. The built-in Web server that comes with Visual Web Developer provides everything you need to test a single Web application. You can't use it to build an infrastructure like you can with a full-fledged Web server, but you can use it for local testing. The following sections describe how to work with the built-in Web server so that you can use it to your advantage.

NOTE It's important to think outside the desktop box when you work with Web applications. An application, in this case, can include everything from the code behind on the server used to generate the Web page and interact with the user to the script on the client side used to check the user input. An application is a combination of tags, script, and server-side code, plus components and controls. Web application is a flexible term because the Internet is a flexible environment.

Advantages of Using the Built-in Web Server

The built-in Web server might not sound very exciting at first. In fact, it might sound extremely limited. Before you write it off as something that isn't worth your time though, you need to consider the advantages it provides. The following list provides some ideas why you'll want to use the built-in Web server, even if you have another option at your disposal.

Security No one can access the built-in Web server but you. In fact, you won't access the built-in Web server using the same port twice, making it extremely unlikely that a cracker will gain access. Even if a cracker does gain access, the constantly changing ports means that the cracker will gain access precisely one time before the port changes again. In short, this is an extremely safe way to test your code on the local machine.

Development Speed The built-in Web server is your personal setup. No one else can use it and there aren't any bandwidth concerns. All of your testing happens at the speed of the local machine and there isn't any way to replicate this performance benefit using a remote machine. Even if you use a local copy of IIS, the high degree of connectivity between Visual Web Developer and the built-in Web server means that you don't have to do much to test the application—it all happens at the click of a button.

Testing Reliability Sometimes you can run into errors testing a Web application on an external Web server. For example, a file might not copy or you might forget to set up the project as a Web application. Security can cause problems—you might not have proper access to your own project. Using the built-in Web server eliminates these problems for application testing. Yes, you'll eventually have to face them, but you'll know that the application itself isn't the source of problems when you do. This divide-and-conquer approach to application testing reduces complexity and improves both testing speed and reliability.

Resource Management You don't have to keep the Web server running—not in the same way that you do with other servers such as IIS. Sure, you can stop the other Web servers, too, but it's inconvenient. The built-in Web server creates an icon in the notification area of the Window's Taskbar that you can easily use to stop the server whenever you want. This means that the Web server is only using system resources while you're actually using it.

Disadvantages of Using the Built-in Web Server

Enterprise developers need to consider the number of disadvantages of using the built-in Web server. This tool does provide significant advantages, but there are also significant disadvantages that limit the usefulness of this tool in the enterprise environment. The following list discusses these limitations.

Team Environment The biggest problem with using the built-in Web server is that it impedes interactivity in a team development environment. While it might seem a tad oppressive, a good team environment requires constant communication between team members and the built-in Web server tends to disrupt that communication. If you use the built-in Web server in a team environment, you'll want to set strict guidelines on its use and consider just how it will affect the environment. The question you need to ask is whether the decrease in communication offsets the increase in individual developer productivity. Setting goals can help reduce this effect, but you need to maintain control over built-in Web server use.

Incomplete Testing   Enterprise applications tend to be large—more than one developer can accomplish in many cases. Even if you aren't working in a team environment, but merely coordinating your efforts with other parts of the company, using the built-in Web server can lead to incomplete testing. The developer is working with the application in an isolated environment, which isn't the same environment in which the application will run. Consequently, your organization can encounter significant problems during integration testing if you're not careful in your use of the built-in Web server.

Security   The built-in Web server doesn't incorporate many of the advanced IIS features, including server certificates. This limitation means that you can't test security features in your application, including the use of Secure Sockets Layer (SSL) using the HyperText Transfer Protocol Security (HTTPS) protocol. In short, your shopping cart application might work fine when you test it with the built-in Web server, but due to the lack of security integration and testing, fail completely when you test it on a complete Web server. While you can develop basic application components using the built-in Web server, you'll want to move the application to a full server, at some point, to incorporate and test security features.

Special Settings   The built-in Web server doesn't support special settings. If you need to use a special Internet Server Application Programming Interface (ISAPI) module with your application, you can't test it using the built-in Web server. The built-in Web server also doesn't support specialized mappings or any of the other advanced features that IIS provides. The built-in Web server most definitely won't emulate any third party add-on products you use or provide access to special servers, such as Exchange, that you rely on for the application. The built-in Web server is still useful to perform initial module testing in this case, but is inadequate for any extended testing.

Creating the Application

Your first application doesn't have to be anything complex. In fact, the example is extremely simple because it's important, at this point, to develop the process you'll use to create complex applications later. The following steps will help you get the application set up—I'm assuming that you've already started Visual Web Developer.

1. Select File ➢ New Web Site to display the New Web Site dialog box shown in Figure 2.1.

2. Choose the language you want to use (the example uses Visual Basic). You can choose from Visual Basic, Visual C#, and Visual J#.

3. Choose a location for the application. The example uses the File System option, which relies on a local hard drive. This option assumes that you'll use the built-in Web server for testing. You can also choose to use the HyperText Transfer Protocol (HTTP) or File Transfer Protocol (FTP) options for remote Web server development.

4. Highlight the ASP.NET Web Site project. You could also choose the Empty Web Site project when you need complete control over the project, but that level of flexibility isn't required in this case.

FIGURE 2.1
Create a new Web site by
selecting the ASP.NET
Web Site project.

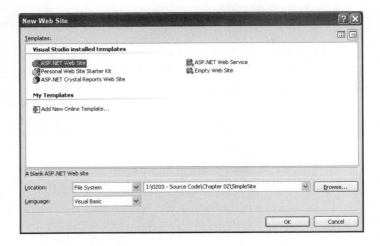

FIGURE 2.1
Create a new Web site by
selecting the ASP.NET
Web Site project.

5. Type the name and location for the Web site on your location hard drive (the example uses `SimpleSite`). Click OK. Visual Web Developer creates a new Web site for you with a single ASPX page open.

6. Click Design to show the Design view. You're ready to create your first project.

TIP As you work with Visual Web Developer, you'll find that windows get moved around—sometimes to the point of making the IDE almost useless. You can return the window setup to its pristine state using the Tools ➤ Options command to display the Options dialog box. Select the General folder and click Reset Window Layout.

The first project won't do very much, but it will introduce you to several important concepts. Begin by opening the Toolbox (if necessary) using the View ➤ Toolbox command. Drag a `Label` control from the Toolbox onto the Design area. The controls always contain an icon that shows their purpose and usually include a text description as well, as shown in Figure 2.2.

TIP You can work with the Toolbox detached from the side of the Visual Web Developer display. Make sure the AutoHide feature is deselected, and then drag the Toolbox where you want to work with it using the title bar. You can even drag the Toolbox outside the IDE area if desired, and drag and drop controls from it to the Design area. To dock the Toolbox back on the side of the IDE, simply drag it to the side—the IDE will highlight the location and the Toolbox will appear when you release the mouse button.

Drag a `Textbox` control from the Toolbox to the Design area. Notice that the IDE places the `Textbox` next to the `Label` control. Press End to place the cursor at the end of the line. Press Enter to move to the next line of the Design area. Pressing Enter places special spacing tags within the page. Drag a `Button` control from the Toolbox to the Design area. Notice that the `Button` appears one line below the two other controls. Unlike desktop applications, you must specifically spell out spaces between controls when working with a Web application.

FIGURE 2.2
The Toolbox provides both an icon and a text description of the controls.

The next step is to add some properties to the application. Begin by selecting the Label control. Display the Properties dialog box (if necessary) using the View ➢ Properties Windows command. Every control you create has a number of properties that define it. Generally, you don't have to change all of the properties. In fact, you'll often change two or three properties out of the many properties the control provides. Figure 2.3 shows properties associated with a Label control. A Textbox or Button control will also have some of these properties but will leave some out and add some of their own as well.

For this example, type **lblInput** in the (ID) property (near the top of Properties window) and **Type some text.** in the Text property. Notice that the text changes in the Design view as well. The reason you want to change the (ID) property is to make it easier to locate controls using the drop-down list at the top of the Properties window (Visual Web Developer lists them alphabetically). Using a specific name also makes the control name easier to remember and the control easier to work with when you write code. You also want to give the control a descriptive name to make it easier to remember the task the control performs.

FIGURE 2.3
Modify a control's features using the entries in the Properties window.

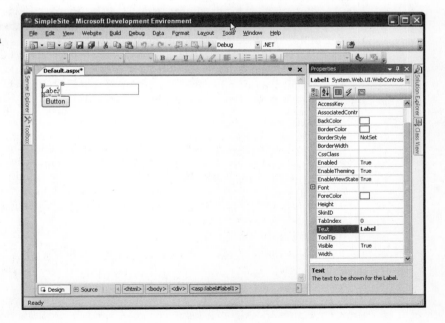

WARNING When you change the name of the text control associated with a label, Visual Web Developer won't update the AssociatedControlID property value automatically. The result is that when you run the application, the Web server will tell you that it can't find the associated control.

Now it's time to change the Textbox control. Type **txtInput** in the (ID) property, **I** in the AccessKey property, **Sample Text** in the Text property, and **Type something interesting.** in the ToolTip property. You make the (ID) property change in the textbox for the same reason that you do with every other control—to make the control easier to locate and work with. The AccessKey property creates a keyboard shortcut for the control so users can access it quickly without removing their hands from the keyboard. The Text property is optional, but you normally want to provide sample text so the user has a better idea of what to type. The ToolTip property tells the application what to display in a tooltip when the user hovers the mouse over the control. Think of tooltips as a form of simplified help.

At this point, you need to go back to lblInput—some property changes require that you move back and forth between controls. The final change for lblInput is to select txtInput in the AssociatedControlID property. This property associates the label with the textbox for accessibility purposes—the association makes it easier to group a textbox or other control with its label—the association connects the label so it properly identifies the textbox. If you try to make this property change before you change the (ID) property of txtInput, the IDE won't make the proper association for you.

It's time to work with the Button control. Type **btnClickMe** in the (ID) property, **C** in the AccessKey property, **Click Me** in the Text property, and **See something happen!** in the ToolTip property. You've configured the form well enough to use now.

The only problem is that clicking btnClickMe won't do anything right now because you haven't told btnClickMe to do anything. Clicking the button is an event and you write an event handler to intercept the event and do something about it. To create an event handler for the Click event of btnClickMe, you need to open Default.ASPX.VB by double-clicking its entry in Solution Explorer. This is the code behind file for Default.ASPX, the file you just configured. The code behind file contains all of the code required to make the ASPX page work.

Select btnClickMe in the Class Name field of the window. Select Click in the Method Name field of the window. The IDE automatically adds the btnClickMe_Click() event handler declaration—the special code that identifies the Click event for btnClickMe. In fact, the cursor's already in the right place to add some code, so type the following code.

```
txtInput.Text = "You clicked Click Me!"
```

You should already have a good idea of what this code does. The txtInput control has a Text property. This code assigns the value You clicked Click Me! to the Text property—changing it on screen. The user sees the new value in place of anything they might have typed. Your code should look like the code in Figure 2.4 at this point. Interestingly enough, you've performed enough work to create your first application. You can run the application by pressing Ctrl+F5.

Using the Build Toolbar

Designing and adding code to your application is only the first step of the process. Once you create an application, you need to build it—change the text you typed into Intermediate Language (IL) code so that the Common Language Runtime (CLR) understands what to do with the application. You can build an application using a number of methods, but the easiest method is to use the Build toolbar shown in Figure 2.5. (Right-click the toolbar area and choose Build from the context menu to display the Build toolbar.) The following list describes the purpose of each button.

FIGURE 2.4
Event handlers hold the code required to make a button do something when you click it.

Class Name   Method Name

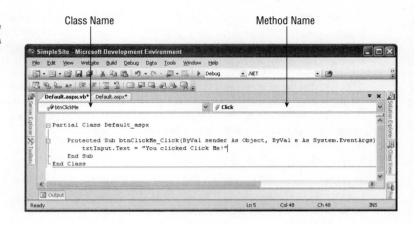

FIGURE 2.5
The Build Toolbar helps you compile your application so you can run it.

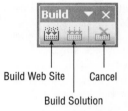

Build Web Site   Cancel

Build Solution

Cancel   Stops the current build action. You can use this option if you suddenly remember that you forgot to do something with the application in the middle of a long build.

Build Solution   Creates an entire solution. A solution usually consists of multiple projects. For example, you might create a solution that includes multiple Web services. Building the solution means creating every project within the solution. Each project will create a separate executable file.

Build Web Site   Creates a Web site. Even if the Web site is part of a larger solution, Visual Web Developer builds only the active project—the current Web site.

To perform the next step in the process, click Build Web Site on the Build toolbar. You'll notice that the IDE saves any files with changes first and then starts building the application. Be patient, the build process can require several seconds to complete, even for a simple project such as this one. When the build process completes, you'll see an Output window at the bottom of the IDE like the one shown in Figure 2.6.

FIGURE 2.6
The Output window tells whether the build process was successful.

The Output window tells you whether the build succeeded. When the build succeeds, you can begin working with the Web site. Otherwise, you need to correct any problems noted during the build and try building the Web site again. Notice, also, that the bar on the left side of the IDE across from the code has changed from yellow to green to signify that the code is ready to use.

TIP Visual Web Developer doesn't display all of the available toolbars—in part, because displaying all toolbars at once would create a cluttered display. You display a toolbar by right-clicking the toolbar area and choosing the toolbar you want to use from the list. To get rid of the toolbar, right-click the toolbar area and choose its entry from the list again.

Using the Standard Toolbar

The Standard toolbar contains a number of buttons that you'll find in any application such as Cut, Copy, and Paste. However, the Visual Web Developer toolbar contains a number of additional options that you need when creating an application. Figure 2.7 shows these special buttons. The following list provides a description of all of the special features on this toolbar.

Add Item   Adds a new item to the project. Whenever you click this button, you'll see the Add New Item dialog box shown in Figure 2.8. Select the item you want to add from the list, change any required settings for that item, and click Add to add it. Notice that you can also download new items from online sources, so you aren't limited to the selection shown in the figure. Next to the button is a down arrow. Click this arrow and you'll see options for adding a new item (which displays the dialog box in Figure 2.8) or adding an existing item. The Add Existing Item dialog box looks like a standard dialog box that you'd use to open any file. Choose the file you want to open and click Add. Visual Web Developer will create a copy of that item and place it in your project folder.

New Project   Adds a new project to the IDE. When you click this button, the IDE will close the old project by default. It will display the New Web Site dialog box shown in Figure 2.1. Choose the kind of Web site you want to create and click OK. The down arrow next to this button includes two options. You can create a new Web site or create a new project. When you select New Project, you'll see the New Project dialog box shown in Figure 2.9. This dialog box lets you create any of the project types supported by the other language products. You can't create a Web project using this dialog box, but you could create a component that you would use on the desktop or a Web site (see the "Using the *<Object>* Tag" section of Chapter 6 for details).

Solution Platform   Defines the type of application and the platform on which it executes. The default setting is the .NET platform for Visual Web Developer. The other options you have depend on the kind of application you create and which language you use. You can also select Configuration Manager to display the Configuration Manager dialog box where you can create new platform definitions. You can learn more about Configuration Manager in the "Working with Configuration Manager" section of Chapter 17.

Solution Configurations   Defines the kind of output for this application. The standard configurations are Debug and Release. You can also select Configuration Manager to display the Configuration Manager dialog box where you can create new output configurations. You can learn more about Configuration Manager in the "Working with Configuration Manager" section of Chapter 17.

FIGURE 2.7

The Standard Toolbar contains a number of helpful buttons, including one that starts the built-in Web server.

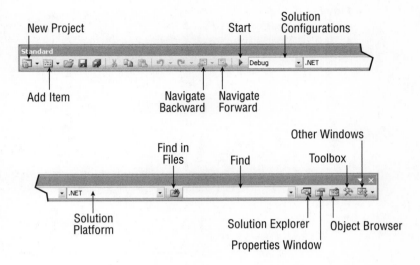

FIGURE 2.8

Create new items for your project using the supplied list or by obtaining new templates online.

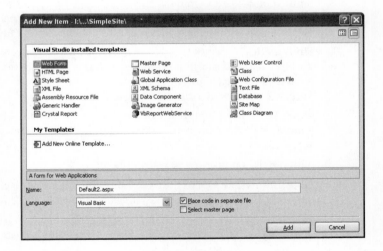

Start   Displays the application in a browser with debugging enabled. You use this feature for testing your application and locating any bugs it might contain. Use this mode as you write your application code to ensure you can troubleshoot any errors as they occur.

Navigate Forward   Changes the cursor position and current page to the next entry in the history list. You use this feature to move between application areas as you perform edits. The Visual Web Developer history list works the same as the one for your browser, except it keeps track of the positions within the project, rather than the places your visit online.

Navigate Backward   Changes the cursor position and current page to the previous entry in the history list.

FIGURE 2.9
Create new standard language projects using this dialog box.

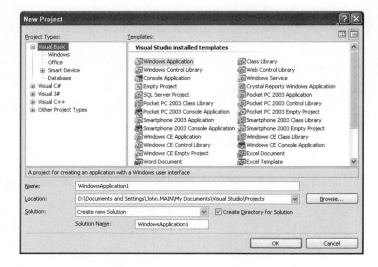

Find   Locates text within the current file. Simply type the text you want to find and press Enter. Press Enter again to find the next location of the word. When you reach the end of the file, the IDE begins again with the first occurrence of the word in the file.

Find in Files   Locates text within all of the files of a project. Type the word you want to locate in the Find field and click this button. You'll see a Find and Replace dialog box. Select the options you want use and click Find. All of the occurrences of the word will appear in the Find Results 1 or Find Results 2 window. See the "Finding and Replacing Text" section for additional details.

Other Windows   Opens any of the standard windows. Click the down arrow and choose the window you want to open. The button defaults to opening the last window that you opened.

Toolbox   Opens the Toolbox when not displayed. If the Toolbox is already open, clicking this button makes it visible and gives it focus.

Object Browser   Opens the Object Browser when not displayed. If the Object Browser is already open, clicking this button makes it visible and gives it focus.

Properties Window   Opens the Properties window when not displayed. If the Properties window is already open, clicking this button makes it visible and gives it focus.

Solution Explorer   Opens Solution Explorer when not displayed. If Solution Explorer is already open, clicking this button makes it visible and gives it focus.

Now that you've built your application, it's time to see how it works. You have two options—you can view the page in your browser without the aid of the debugger or you can start the debugger. For now, choose the Debug ➢ Start Without Debugging command so that you can see what the page looks like. After a few seconds, you'll see the page appear in your browser. Click Click Me and you'll see the text in the `txtInput` control change to match the code you typed earlier. However, the important feature to see is the new Visual Web Developer Web Server icon (see margin icon) at the top of the Notification Area. You can display the menu shown in the figure by right-clicking the icon in the Notification area. Right-click this icon and you'll see the context menu with three items as shown in Figure 2.10.

FIGURE 2.10
The built-in Web server appears as an icon in the Notification Area, shown here with context menu.

Click Stop when you no longer need the built-in Web server. The system releases the resources that the built-in Web server uses. When you want to view the current page in a browser, click Open in Web Browser. Finally, when you click Details, you'll see a Visual Web Developer Web Server dialog box that contains the physical and virtual locations of the current Web site, along with the special port for this application. Click the Stop button on this dialog box to stop the built-in Web server.

Finding and Replacing Text

The Visual Web Developer IDE includes the concept of editing—just as your word processor does. However, you're editing code, in this case, so some of the functionality is a little different from any word processing experience you might have had. Searching and replacing text in a word processed document requires one set of features; performing the same procedure in code requires different features, even though the result is essentially the same. Visual Web Developer actually provides five kinds of find and replace functionality as listed here as part of the Edit ➤ Find and Replace menu.

Quick Find Locates the search text in the current file. You search through the file one occurrence at a time.

Quick Replace Modifies the search text in the current file. You have the option of finding the next occurrence of the search text without replacing the current instance, replacing the current instance and finding the next occurrence of the search text, or replacing all occurrences of the search text.

Find in Files Locates the search text at several levels including the current file, all open documents, the entire solution, or the current project. The results appear in either the Find Results 1 or Find Results 2 window, so you can scroll the returned values and review only those that you need.

Replace in Files Modifies the search text at several levels including the current file, all open documents, the entire solution, or the current project. The results appear in either the Find Results 1 or Find Results 2 window, so you can scroll the returned values and review only those that you need. However, instead of scrolling through the results using the window, you use one of four buttons to locate individual instances and optionally replace the search text. You can choose to find the next instance (meaning you won't replace the current value), replace the current value and look for the next instance, skip the current file completely, and replace all of the values without reviewing them individually.

Find Symbol Locates the specified object (symbol) within the all of the components, the .NET Framework, the current solution, other areas using the Object Browser, or other areas using criteria specified using the Select Component dialog box. The results appear in the Find Symbol Result window. Instead of seeing text as you do with the other searches, you see the actual object and any other objects it contains. You also see a list of applicable methods, properties, and events for the object.

The quick find and replace are easiest to use and provide the least flexibility in performing a search. The Quick Replace dialog box appears in Figure 2.11. The Quick Find dialog box is similar—the only features it lacks are the Replace With field, the Replace button, and Replace All button.

FIGURE 2.11
Use a Quick Find or
Quick Replace to locate
and optionally modify
information in the current file.

The Find What field contains the search text that you want to find. The Replace With field contains the value that will replace the search text. The Look In field tells Visual Web Developer where to look for the information. It defaults to the current document, but you can also choose all of the currently opened documents and the current project. The Find Options group determines how Visual Web Developer searches for the text you provide. Most of these options are self-explanatory, but several options require special emphasis. For example, as your projects become more complex, Visual Web Developer (and you) will hide some of the text to reduce display clutter. Normally, Visual Web Developer only searches visible text—you must specifically check the Search Hidden Text option to look within the hidden areas.

You can also use either wildcards or regular expressions to perform a search. The wildcards work much like those you use at the command prompt with utilities such as Dir. Wildcards to include a few extensions as follow:

◆ * (asterisk) indicates zero or more of any character.

◆ ? (question mark) indicates a single character.

◆ # (number sign) indicates a single digit.

◆ [] (brackets) enclose a series of characters—one of which must be present.

◆ [!] (exclamation mark within the brackets) encloses a series of characters—none of which must be present.

Regular expressions offer more options, but require more work. When you initially click Use, Visual Web Developer enables the Regular Expressions options. Clicking the arrow next to either the Find What or Replace With fields displays a list of regular expressions you can use such as the ones shown in Figure 2.12.

The options for finding and replacing in files are a little different from those shown in Figure 2.11. Again, the Find in Files dialog box is a less complex version of the Replace in Files dialog box shown in Figure 2.13.

The options work much the same as those for the quick find or replace, except you have a few more options in the Look In field. Instead of looking for the entries one at a time, you choose an output location in one of the two results windows. You can even perform two searches using two different output windows and compare the output results. The Look at These File Types field becomes active when you select either Entire Solution or Current Project in the Look In field. This field tells Visual Web Developer to limit its search to specific kinds of files—for example, you might only want to search source code files for a particular string.

A symbol search is inherently different from other kinds of searches because it looks for objects and object components such as methods, events, and properties. Figure 2.14 shows the Find Symbol dialog box. As you can see, it includes the Find What and Look In fields, just like all of the other searches. However, notice that this search also lets you look within project references—you can even look in the .NET Framework when desired.

FIGURE 2.12
Regular expressions
are complex, but
provide extremely
flexible search criteria.

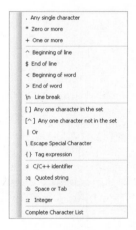

FIGURE 2.13
Use the Find and Replace
in files option to locate
all instances of a search
string within a project.

The Find and Replace options examined in this section produce dramatically different results, as shown in Figure 2.15. The top window shows the results of a quick find—you'll see the item highlighted in the code. The middle window shows the results of a find in file search—you obtain a list of strings that match the criteria. Finally, the bottom window shows the results of a symbol search. In this case, you obtain a list of object elements. The icon next to each entry tells you what type of object element the search has found.

FIGURE 2.14
A symbol search looks for objects and object components.

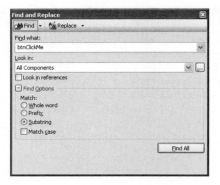

FIGURE 2.15
Make sure you use the correct search to obtain the results you want.

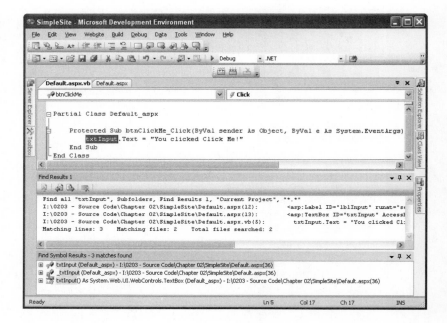

Working with the Browser Emulator

The browser emulator is a Visual Web Developer feature that lets you view your Web page in something other than Internet Explorer—the default browser for Visual Studio when you install it. Using a browser emulator is a simple idea that could go a long way toward enhancing your ability to test Web pages at a lower cost of time. You can start by testing the page in Internet Explorer, and then move on to other browsers.

Actually, the term *emulator* is a misnomer. Yes, you can use emulators, but you can also use full-fledged browser products. In fact, you can use custom applications or anything else that displays Web pages. This new feature helps developers set the IDE to use whatever they need to test a particular application. It's recognition by Microsoft that companies do use products other than Internet Explorer.

Using this feature is easy; simply select the File ➢ Browse With command to display the Browse With dialog box shown in Figure 2.16. Select the browser you want to use and click Browse to display the current project using that browser. You can even set the size of the browser window using the Size of Browser Window field. Common window sizes include 640×480, 800×600, and 1024×768.

FIGURE 2.16
Select any browser you want to use for testing a project using the Browse With dialog box.

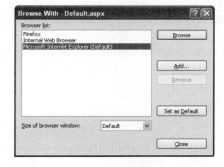

The default setup includes both Internet Explorer and the Internal Web Browser that displays Web pages directly in the IDE. Using the Internal Web Browser can be a real boon to productivity. Not only do you see the Web pages faster, you also don't have to view them outside of the IDE. The Internal Web Browser also saves memory because Windows doesn't have to start the Internet Explorer application. The nicest feature though is that when you right-click a page and choose View Source, you see it within the IDE. Displaying the page in the IDE means that you get all of the color coding that Visual Studio provides, making it easier to see what the output page is actually doing.

Visual Studio defaults to using Internet Explorer as the default browser. Fortunately, you can change this setting by highlighting the browser you want to use and clicking Default. The Browse With dialog box displays (Default) next to the default Web browser so you know which browser Visual Studio will use when you execute the application normally. You can also use the File ➢ View in Browser command to display the Web page using the default browser.

To add a new browser, click Add in the Browse With dialog box. You'll see an Add Program dialog box. Click Browse and use the Browse dialog box to locate the application you want to add to the list of browsers. After you locate the application and click Open in the Browse dialog box, type a friendly name for the application in the `Friendly Name` field of the Add Program dialog box. I found it interesting that you can use a number of applications that developers don't normally associate with debugging an application to view the Web page. For example, it's quite easy to open a Web page up using Word or even Excel. Sending it to FrontPage can be revealing. The only requirement is that the application be able to accept an URL as a command line argument, so you can use a wide variety of applications for testing purposes—applications that would have required extensive setup in the past.

Understanding Save/Refresh Style Page Development

Visual Web Developer includes a new feature that makes it easy to save a change to your application and then simply refresh the browser to see the change. It might seem like an easy concept to include in a development environment, but with older versions of .NET you always needed to close the browser, make your changes, compile the application, reopen the browser, and hope that the server hadn't cached the application (requiring you to reboot IIS). The old way of working with .NET could be frustrating and this new technique is a very welcome change.

Performing Tasks One at a Time

Some developers will create large pieces of code without ever testing them—they keep writing until the code is finished and only then test it out. The result is often a mess because people tend to make the same mistake repeatedly unless corrected. The old way that Visual Studio worked tended to enforce this approach to development. Using the coding save/refresh style means that you can perform one task at a time. The coding cycle works as follows:

1. Divide the code into easily tested pieces called units—a method or property declarations, for example.

2. Write a unit and sight verify that it doesn't contain any errors.

3. Build the code (this step also saves the code to disk) and correct any errors the compiler finds. Repeat as needed until the code builds.

4. Test the code in the browser. If you already have the browser open, click Refresh to load the newly created version of the Web application. Edit the code to fix any errors and repeat step 3 until the browser tests pass.

5. Repeat steps 2 through 4 until you complete the application.

Visual Web Developer helps you create an environment in which you receive constant feedback. Problematic coding techniques become less pronounced over time because you continuously correct them as you create the application. In addition, errors have less of a chance to get buried because unit testing shows the errors in each unit. Part of the debugging cycle takes place as you write the code, which also reduces the complexity of debugging the application later.

Using the Task List Window

One of the hidden gems for developers is the Task List window. This feature can save you considerable time and help you better organize your application development strategy. Adding the appropriate organizational and task-related information can remind you to fix code, add all of the code you need, and better organize the coding tasks by priority and unit. To view the Task List window, select View ≻ Task List. The Task List window normally appears at the bottom of the display, but you can move it anywhere you like or dock it to another area of the display. Figure 2.17 shows a typical view of the Task List window with a user comment entered.

You can add two kinds of entries to the Task List window—user tasks and comments. Enter the user tasks directly into the window. They work best for tasks that affect the application as a whole, such as when you need to add another unit. Enter comments into the code using a special keyword. Generally, you'll use comments for specific kinds of tasks that affect a particular unit.

To add a new user task, click Create User Task on the Task List window toolbar. The Task List window will add a new entry and you can type whatever you want to remind you of the task. Because you can sort the Task List window by the Priority, Completed, or Description fields, it pays to use special keywords at the beginning of your comment such as Add Task. The Task List window adds the comment as normal priority. You can change the priority by clicking in the Priority field of the task that you want to change—you'll see a drop-down list appear with three priority levels: high, normal, and low. When you complete a task, check its entry in the Completed field.

To view the comments tasks for the Web application, select Comments in the Categories drop-down list of the Task List window. Figure 2.18 shows some comments for the example application. In this case, the Task List window sets the priority based on the comments keyword definition, so you can't assign a priority to the task. To show that a task is complete, remove its comment from the code.

All of the comments use special keywords. Visual Web Developer supports four keywords, but you can add more as need. Here are the four keywords and their meanings.

TODO   Defines tasks that you still need to perform. The default setting for this keyword is normal priority.

HACK   Defines code that you created to solve an immediate problem, but isn't good production code. For example, you might directly assign a value to a variable that you actually need to compute. The default setting for this keyword is normal priority.

FIGURE 2.17
Use the Task List window to provide reminders to accomplish specific tasks.

FIGURE 2.18
Use comments to create unit-specific tasks within your Web application.

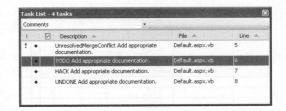

UNDONE   Includes code that you removed to solve a short-term problem. For example, you might comment code out to verify that the application works (up to a point) without it. As another example, you might decide to test two coding techniques to determine which one produces the best result. The default setting for this keyword is normal priority.

UnresolvedMergeConflict   Represents a unit that appears to work find on its own, but doesn't work well with the application as a whole. This comment could also apply to smaller code segments, a partial class, or other coding elements. The idea is that the code should work, but it doesn't when you merge it with something else, so you need to debug the problem. The default setting for this keyword is high priority.

You might have noticed that there's a lack of low-priority keywords and that might not agree with the default settings Microsoft provided. For that matter, you might want to add some keywords of your own because the Microsoft offerings don't do everything you need them to do. Fortunately, you can change both kinds of settings using the Options dialog box (select Tools ➢ Options to display it). Begin by checking the Show All Settings option in the lower left corner. The list of options will grow considerably. Select the `Environment/Task List` folder and you'll see the display shown in Figure 2.19.

To change an existing entry, highlight it in the Token List field, make the required modifications in the Priority and Name fields, and then click Change. The only keyword you can't rename is TODO. The IDE uses this keyword to alert you to changes you need to make after creating a new project or using a wizard. You can change the priority of the TODO keyword.

Adding a new keyword is just as easy. Type the new keyword in the Name field, assign it a priority in the Priority field, and click Add. The IDE will add the new keyword to the list.

The `Environment/Task List` folder also contains two options. The first, Confirm Deletion of Tasks, ensures that you don't remove tasks accidentally when checked. This is a good option to check when you first begin using the IDE, but the confirmation messages can become annoying when your skill level increases. The second, Show Only the File Name, Without the File Path, reduces Task List window clutter by removing the path information when checked. This setting works fine for simple projects, but can become a problem when you work with complex projects that span multiple folders. Generally, you'll keep this option checked when using Visual Web Developer.

FIGURE 2.19
Create new task list keywords or edit existing keywords using this display.

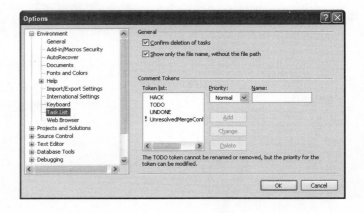

Using the HTML Source Edit Toolbar

The HTML Source Editing toolbar provides quick access some of the HTML editing features provided by Visual Web Developer. You access this toolbar by right-clicking the toolbar area and choosing HTML Source Editing from the context menu. Figure 2.20 shows the HTML Source Editing toolbar. The following list describes each of the buttons in detail.

Navigate Backward   Changes the cursor position and current page to the previous entry in the history list. You use this feature to move between application areas as you perform edits. The Visual Web Developer history list works the same as the one for your browser, except it keeps track of the positions within the project, rather than the places you visit online.

Navigate Forward   Changes the cursor position and current page to the next entry in the history list.

Format the Whole Document   Modifies the text so it fits within the line length you choose and observes any formatting criteria (such as the use of uppercase or lowercase characters) you choose. This feature doesn't check spelling or the usability of the code—it simply formats it.

Decrease Indent   Decreases the space between the left side of the display and the start of the code. As the indentation level increases, the code moves to the right side of the screen and eventually out of view. Removing unneeded indentation can help you see the entire line of code, rather than scrolling back and forth to see it.

Increase Indent   Increases the space between the left side of the display and the start of the code. Indentation makes code easier to read by showing which code is at the same level of execution. Adding indentation can help you reformat code after you add a new type of processing or processing level.

Comment Out the Selected Lines   Adds comment characters in front of the selected lines of code. This process changes the code into a comment that you can still see and modify, but Visual Web Developer will ignore. Visual Web Developer only enables this feature when working with code behind files.

FIGURE 2.20
The HTML Source Editing toolbar makes you more efficient when editing HTML.

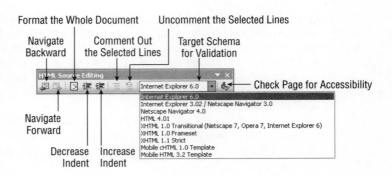

Uncomment the Selected Lines Removes the comment character (if any) from in front of the selected lines of code. This process turns the comments back into code that Visual Web Developer will process when you compile the application. Visual Web Developer only enables this feature when working with code behind files.

Target Schema for Validation Selects the kind of browser the current Web page services. Figure 2.20 shows the options that are accessible from this toolbar. Visual Web Developer only enables this feature when working with Web pages (ASPX or HTML) files.

Check Page for Accessibility Performs an accessibility check on your Web page to ensure it contains the features needed to let people with special needs use it. When you click this button, you see the Accessibility Validation dialog box shown in Figure 2.21 where you can choose the level of validation checks to perform. Accessibility validation includes checking whether people who use screen readers can interact with your display and other important checks that ensure everyone can work with your Web site. Chapter 21 discusses this issue in detail.

FIGURE 2.21
Perform accessibility validation checks on your Web pages to ensure everyone can use them.

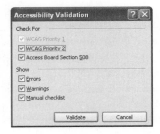

Working with Control SmartTags

Microsoft has incorporated Smart Tag technology into many of its products. This technology first appeared in Microsoft Office and now appears in Visual Web Developer as part of the control technology. Not every control has a Smart Tag, but many do. Any time you might benefit from a little extra formatting assistance, Microsoft includes a Smart Tag with the control.

To see this technology for yourself, add two new lines after the btnClickMe control (the one labeled Button) shown in Figure 2.3. Double-click the DropDownList control in the Toolbox. Visual Web Developer adds the new control to the Web page. Select this control and you'll see an arrow appear in the upper right corner. Click this arrow and you'll see the Smart Tag shown in Figure 2.22. As you can see, a Smart Tag is essentially a specialized context menu with a list of tasks you can perform with the control.

Notice that this Smart Tag contains two kinds of configuration. The first is a link such as Choose Data Source. Click a link and you'll see a dialog box containing configuration items. The second is a checkbox—Enable AutoPostBack in this case. Click this item and the IDE will either enable or disable to the feature.

The Smart Tag for a drop-down list box is relatively simple. You'll see more complex Smart Tags as the book progresses. However, it's important to remember that Smart Tags only gather settings that you could change in other areas of the IDE and make them easier to access. None of the settings on a Smart Tag are unique—they all appear somewhere else, so you can ignore the Smart Tags if you want.

FIGURE 2.22
Use Smart Tags to help
manage the controls in
your application.

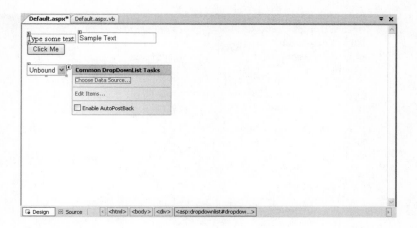

Using Internet Information Server

Many enterprise developers won't want to use the built-in Web server because it interferes with team projects. In this case, you'll want to set your project up to use a remote server from the beginning. Visual Web Developer doesn't do this automatically—the default setup relies on the built-in Web server.

Other developers will use the built-in Web server for experimenting and beginning projects that they eventually plan to deploy, but, at some point, they have to move their application to IIS so that other people can use it. You can accomplish this task using several techniques. The following sections examine several ways to move from the built-in Web server to IIS or another Web server such as Apache. In addition, you'll discover how to set up your system to use a remote connection from the outset.

NOTE   Not all of the techniques in this section will work with every Web server. In fact, Microsoft has every reason to ensure you don't create Web applications for servers other than IIS. However, you can use the Empty Web Site project to create a project devoid of .NET encumbrances. When you use standard HTML, CSS, XML, and other Web files for your application, you can typically deploy it anywhere—to any server. Of course, taking this approach means that you don't get to use many of the great features that ASP.NET 2.0 provides—it's a trade-off and you need to consider how the trade-off affects your application development plans.

Working with Local IIS

You don't have to use the built-in Web server—you can use a local copy of IIS to create applications with Visual Web Developer. The rules are a little different when you use this technique, however, because you already have IIS installed and running. Instead of creating a new Web site, you're opening an existing Web site.

To create a new project using a local copy of IIS, select the File ➢ Open Web Site command. Choose the Local IIS option and you'll see display similar to the one shown in Figure 2.23.

FIGURE 2.23
Open Web applications
found on the local
copy IIS for testing or
modification.

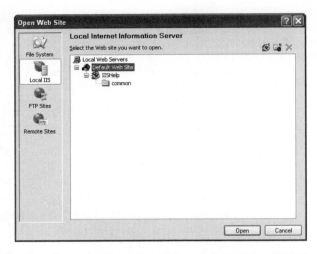

In the upper right corner of the dialog box, you'll see three buttons: Create New Web Application, Create New Virtual Directory, and Delete. Place the cursor where you want to create a new Web application and click Create New Web Application. Type a name for the Web application and you're ready to go. Click Open and Visual Web developer will open the Web site for you.

NOTE   If you install IIS after you install Visual Web Developer, IIS won't have the proper configuration settings for working with ASP.NET 2.0. Visual Web Developer detects this problem and displays a dialog box telling you about the problem. Click Yes to install ASP.NET 2.0 support so that you can begin working with the new Web application. The configuration can take a few minutes to complete.

Sometimes you don't want to place the Web application in the IIS folder or you might create an application using the built-in Web server and want to test it using IIS. In either case, you can create a virtual directory—a directory that appears to reside in the IIS folder but really doesn't. To perform this task, choose a location for the folder and click Create New Virtual Directory. Type the name you want to use for the Web site in the Alias Name field and the location of the actual directory on your machine in the Folder field (you can also find the folder by clicking Browse). Click OK and Visual Web Developer will not only create a virtual directory, but it will automatically set it up as a Web application for you as well.

Creating New Projects with IIS

Generally, when you want to work on team projects, you'll want to create and use a central Web site on a test server, rather than use the built-in Web server. You want the various team members to work together, so the built-in Web server isn't a usable solution in many cases. In these cases, you'll create your project on a remote copy of IIS (or some other Web server) rather than use a local copy of IIS.

In addition to team projects, you'll want to use either a local or a remote copy of IIS when testing some types of applications. For example, you can't test secure applications with the built-in Web server because you can't install a server certificate with it. You also can't test anything that relies on

ISAPI using the built-in Web server and some third party solutions, such as Visual MainWin (a product that lets .NET and Java developers work together) won't work with the built-in Web server either. In short, the enterprise developer has many reasons to skip the built-in Web server and go directly for a full-fledged testing environment.

You have two solutions to create a new project that resides on IIS (or another server), rather than using the built-in Web server. The first is to use FTP to create the project and the second is to use HTTP. The option you select depends on your server setup. Display the New Web Site dialog box shown in Figure 2.24 using the File ➤ New ➤ Web Site command. Choose a language and then a project type. Select either Http or FTP in the Location field, and then type the location of the new project as shown in the figure. Click OK to complete the action. You'll see a Creating New Web Site dialog box for a few moments as Visual Web Developer makes the connection and creates the required files on the server.

NOTE   When using a remote server, you must include all of the proper setup items. For example, the remote server must have the proper .NET Framework support installed and all of the required IIS entries for ASP.NET 2.0. You also need to add the correct security for accessing the server with Visual Studio .NET. Even though Microsoft has made this process a little less difficult, you still must have the proper access to the Web server and rights to perform tasks such as creating files to make the product work.

Using a remote setup works best when you create major new applications where moving the application to a testing location later would prove inconvenient. Unfortunately, you lose a few things when using this solution. The most important issue is that you lose the security features that the built-in Web server provides. Using the built-in Web server really does keep your code safer than working with a centralized test server, so you might consider using it when you begin a new secret project for the company. You also lose the nearly instantaneous starts that the built-in Web server provides because now everything has to travel across the network or a loop back with the local server. Finally, there's some loss of reliability. You can't be sure that the remote connection will prove reliable—even if it does, you'll lose the connection periodically, which means a loss of work efficiency.

FIGURE 2.24
Begin remote projects on the server as a default, rather than copying them later.

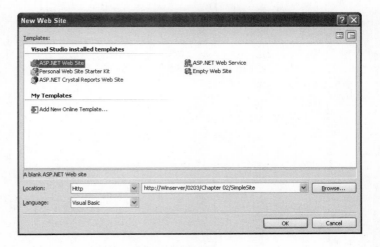

Using the Copy Web Site Tool

Sometimes you do want to start a project using the built-in Web server even in the enterprise environment. For example, you might perform tests to ascertain the viability of developing a certain project in house; using the built-in Web server works perfectly for this need. Of course, when the project proves viable, you'll need to move it to a central Web site so your team can work on it. That's where the Copy Web Site tool comes into play.

The Copy Web Site tool lets you move files to different locations. Visual Web Developer doesn't care where you move the files and it doesn't necessarily care about the kind of server you use. Of course, when you choose something other than IIS, such as Apache, the files you move must work on that server. Microsoft doesn't make it as easy as it could to create applications that don't rely on ASP.NET, but you can do it if you think about the application before you spend time developing it.

Select Website ➢ Copy Web Site to access the Copy Web Site tool. Figure 2.25 shows a typical view of the Copy Web Site tool after you've created a connection to a remote Web site.

To create a connection to another location (either local or remote), click Connect to a Remote Site. You'll see an Open Web Site dialog box like the one shown in Figure 2.26.

You have four techniques to choose from including: File System, Local IIS, FTP Sites, and Remote Sites. Use the File System, Local IIS, and FTP Sites options for local file copying. The FTP Sites and Remote Sites options work for remote connections. The information you provide depends on the site type. For example, an FTP site requires that you provide the FTP URL, the port, the directory, and any required login information as shown in Figure 2.26. The Remote Sites option only requires that you provide an URL, but the remote server may display a dialog box asking for a username and password (assuming the remote server understands this form of communication). Figure 2.23 shows what you need to enter when working with the Local IIS option. The File System option used a Windows Explorer interface, and you can use it to communicate with both local and networked drives.

FIGURE 2.25
Once you open a remote Web site, you can move your project to it.

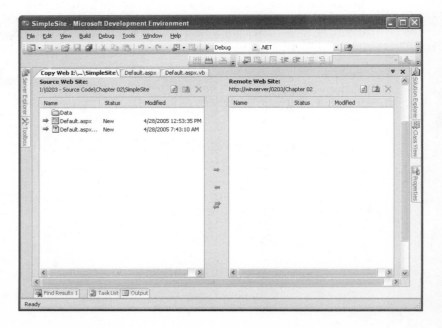

FIGURE 2.26
Use any of four methods to connect to a local or remote file transfer location.

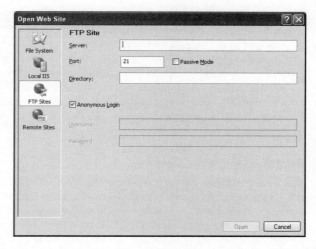

Once you choose a connection type and provide the required information, click Open and you'll see the remote Web site appear on the right side of the display as shown in Figure 2.25. You now have several options for copying files. The Move Files drop-down list includes three options: move the files from the source Web site to the remote site, move the files from the remote Web site to the source Web site, or synchronize the files. After you select any of these options, you click Copy Web Site to move all of the files. The synchronize option is the most interesting because the IDE looks at each file in turn and moves the newest file from each site to the other site. This feature means that some files might move from the source Web site to the remote Web site, while others move from the remote Web site to the source Web site in the same move. When the timestamp on the files on both sites match, then the IDE doesn't move files from either location.

You can also move individual files. Simply highlight the file in the source Web site or remote Web site list and click one of the three movement buttons (only two of which are active). It's possible to move the file or synchronize it. The same synchronization rules apply—the file only moves when it's newer than the one on the other site. Selecting multiple files also works. Choose a starting file, press Shift, and click an ending file to choose files that appear together. Likewise, you can Ctrl+Click to choose individual files without deselecting previous selections.

Designing Your Application Using Visio

Enterprise developers work on large projects that usually involve the efforts of a team of developers, rather than one or two, as small projects require. Large applications require more planning than pen and paper will accommodate—you need some type of design tool. This book doesn't show you all of the details of designing an application. In fact, you'd need several books on the topic. However, this section does discuss Visio, the product the Microsoft supplies as part of Visual Studio Enterprise Edition for addressing application design.

TIP There are many design books on the market. However, the three books that every developer needs to have a complete set of design books are *Coder to Developer*, Mike Gunderloy (Sybex, 2004), *Developer to Designer*, Mike Gunderloy (Sybex, 2005), and *Designing Highly Useable Software*, Jeff Cogswell (Sybex, 2004). Reading *Coder to Developer* helps you understand which tools work best for designing your application and how to use those tools effectively. Mike provides you with great coding examples that demonstrate principles, rather than simply talk about them in theory. Move to *Developer to Designer* next to gain insights into how to put a user interface together that really works. Finally, reading *Designing Highly Useable Software* gives you the final piece of the puzzle, understanding how to create software that really works.

Deciding What to Create

Visio lets you create designs for more than just software. In fact, you can use it to define everything from the layout of a building to the electronics that it contains. Most developers will focus on the software and Web design aids that Visio provides as shown in Figure 2.27. In this case, you're viewing the two Web design projects that Visio provides. The Software category provides templates for designing a number of software elements including COM and OLE, Data Flow Model Diagram, Enterprise Application, Jackson, Program Structure, ROOM, UML Model Diagram, and Windows User Interface.

Designing a Site Map

Most developers begin by creating a new Web site design. To perform this task, select the Conceptual Web Site template shown in Figure 2.28. You'll see a blank design area like the one shown in Figure 2.28. The design area on the right side of the display contains the drawing you create depicting your Web site, while the left side of the display contains a toolbox full of icons you can use to depict Web site elements. You can make the diagram specific to your Web site needs. The point is that you can create a design, move things around, create new connections, and make changes without writing a single line of code.

Visio provides a number of drawing tools you can use. Figure 2.28 shows some of the conceptual icons at work. In this case, Default.ASPX is a main entry point to the Web site. It contains links to AboutUs.ASPX and Help.ASPX, two standard pages that the Web site contains. The Web site contains a series of surveys as well, which the design shows as a page group. You don't necessarily have to define every page immediately, but it helps to define as much as you can.

The Web Site Map Shapes tab of the toolbox contains icons for specific page types. For example, you can differentiate between an HTML page and an ASPX page. You use these shapes after you have a basic design worked out for your Web site. These shapes help you conceptualize the kind of coding the Web site will require and assign the people who are most qualified to perform a given task.

Sometimes you'll want to annotate the drawings you create for your Web site. The Callouts tab shown in Figure 2.28 contains a number of callouts that you can use. Each callout has a different representation on screen, so you can use different callouts for different tasks. For example, you might want to use one callout for items that you still need to design and another callout to list the people who will complete a particular Web site element.

FIGURE 2.27
Visio helps you design
your Web site, rather
than just let it happen.

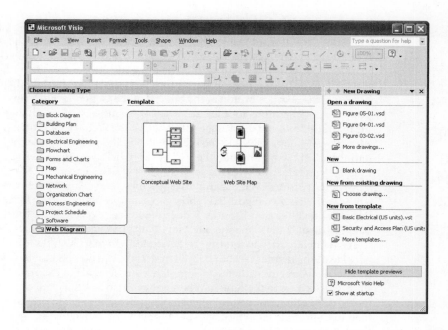

FIGURE 2.28
Define a layout for your
Web site using the Web
Site Map template.

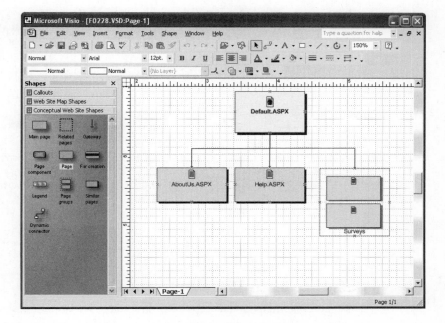

Working with Existing Web Sites

Sometimes you'll want to use Visio to diagnose an existing Web site. To perform this task, select the Web Site Map template shown in Figure 2.27. When you select this option, Visio displays a Generate Site Map dialog box (see Figure 2.29) that includes an Address field that contains the address to the Web site. Type the address of the existing Web site in the Address field.

Notice the Settings button at the bottom of the Generate Site Map dialog box. Click this button to display a list of options for the site map. For example, you can change the number of levels that the site map supports and the number of links that the Web site can contain. You modify the style and layout of the site map, as well as the file extensions and protocols that the Web site supports. All of these settings affect the automation the Visio uses to help you create a site map with greater ease.

Once you're happy with the settings, click OK twice to create the site map. Visio will create a site map for the existing Web site and display it on screen using the rules that you defined in the Generate Site Map dialog box. Figure 2.30 shows an example of the output from a sample Web site. If you find that you don't like the output or it doesn't work as expected, use the Web ➢ Generate Site Map command to display the Generate Site Map dialog box again.

It's relatively easy to modify the generated site map. You'll see a list of drawing elements on the left side of the display as shown in Figure 2.30. All you need to do is drag and drop the elements where needed on the drawing to complete your design. For example, if you want to add a document, simply drag it on to the screen. When you want to create document connections, use the connector tool to draw a line from one element to the other. It's easier to design a Web site using this technique, than to try to code it from scratch because you can move things around and change connections as needed to complete the application without touching a single line of code.

The biggest benefit of using Visio in this manner is the reports it provides. The Web ➢ Reports menu contains a number of reports that you can use to analyze your Web site. For example, you can quickly use Visio to track down broken hyperlinks, even those that are external to the Web site. Another report helps you categorize Web site content by category. All of these reports help you design a better Web site by viewing the Web site in a particular way and verifying the assumptions you have made about it.

FIGURE 2.29

Generate a site map for your existing Web site using the Generate Site Map dialog box.

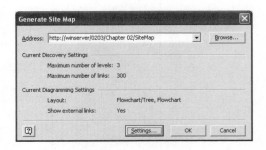

Defining Your Development Goals

This chapter has helped you accomplish a number of important goals, but the most important is taking that first step into creating applications with Visual Web Developer. Even though the project in this chapter is simple, it helps you understand important design and usage principles when you work with Visual Web Developer. This chapter has also shown you how to work with several Web servers. Having a local Web server for testing is great—especially when it's a secure setup. However, at some point, you need to upload your Web application to a production Web server so other people can use it. Finally, you discovered the value of control Smart Tags. This feature is so important that you'll see other uses for it as the book progresses. Most importantly, this chapter has moved you another step in the task of building the enterprise application discussed throughout the rest of the book by considering design issues using Visio.

Now it's time to play. That's right; developers are allowed to play, just like everyone else. Spend some time creating new projects, adding simple controls, and trying the result out locally at least. Try uploading your project to a remote Web server and trying it there as well. (Make sure you don't use a production server for experimentation and have permission to use the server for training purposes.) Check out the Smart Tags for various controls to see what they have to offer. Try creating at least one project directly on a remote Web server. Spend a little time working with Visio to see how it can fit in your design plans.

Chapter 3 helps you discover one of the most important features that the Visual Studio IDE provides, Server Explorer. Many developers still create a majority of their code by hand, rather than use the automation that the IDE provides. The concern is that the code the IDE produces automatically is somehow inferior, which is a myth. Using Server Explorer is such a great productivity aid that every developer should at least try using it and seeing the results firsthand. Chapter 3 is your opportunity to test the time-saving features of Server Explorer while you learn more about what it can do for you.

FIGURE 2.30
Use the output that Visio provides to analyze your Web site.

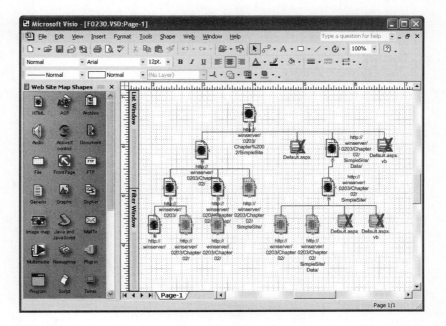

Chapter 3

Using Server Explorer

Server Explorer is more than just a simple aid to programming; it's your window to what's happening on other machines on the network. Using Server Explorer, you can view the status of other machines and gain access to that information in your application. Careful use of Server Explorer greatly reduces programming time because you don't have to guess about server features or configuration requirements. It also reduces debugging time by providing direct access to the correct information about a target machine. It's little wonder then that Server Explorer deserves a separate chapter in the book.

Most developers are aware of the database connections that Server Explorer can provide. However, Server Explorer provides connections to a great deal more information. You can use it to access message queues on any machine that supports them, provide connectivity to performance counters, learn the status of services, and even look through event logs on a machine.

All of the features the Server Explorer provides are important. However, as a Visual Web Developer user, you're more likely to use some features more than you use others. The database connectivity is very important and Part 4 of the book discusses it in detail. However, you'll see an overview of database connectivity in this chapter. In addition to database connectivity, Visual Web Developer users will likely want to access the event logs, use performance counters, and work with both management classes and events. This chapter explores all of these other Server Explorer features in detail.

Understanding Server Explorer

Server Explorer replaces many tools that you used to get as extras on the Visual Studio disk. It also creates new tools for exploring your network in ways that you might not have thought possible in the past. In fact, the term *Server Explorer* is a bit of a misnomer because Server Explorer provides access to any resource on any machine to which you have access. This feature alone makes using the Visual Studio .NET IDE more useful than any previous IDE you might have used. The ability to explore and use resources without leaving the IDE makes application development a lot easier.

Server Explorer shares the same area of your IDE as the Toolbox. Click on the upper icon in the default setup and you'll see Server Explorer; click on the lower icon and the Toolbox appears. Figure 3.1 shows a typical example of the Server Explorer with connections to two machines. Because I have administrator privileges on both machines, all of the resources of both machines are at my disposal.

If you get the idea that you won't need to use the server-side tools much anymore, you'd be correct. You can perform most (but not all) tasks right from Server Explorer. For example, when you want to determine the status of a service on another machine, all you need to do is select it in Server Explorer and look at the Properties window. You can start the service right from Server Explorer by right-clicking the service entry and choosing Start from the context menu.

FIGURE 3.1
Server Explorer gives you the grand view of your network to start and allows you to drill down as needed.

UNDERSTANDING THE NEW MANAGEMENT ENTRIES

Server Explorer includes two new entries that you won't see used in this book simply because they aren't too helpful for Web applications. The first is the Management Classes entry. This entry includes access to all of the system hardware, detailed information about the network connections, processes running on the system, and application installations that the system has recorded. You can even find detailed information about user accounts on the target system. In fact, you'll find a wealth of information not found in any previous version of Visual Studio .NET. Generally, this information is more useful for a local application than it is for a Web application. In fact, you might even consider such information dangerous to expose in a Web application. You can find general information about this feature at http://msdn.microsoft .com/library/en-us/smssdk03/hh/sms/usingsms_csharpServerExplorer.asp.

The second new entry is Management Events. You use this entry to create events that monitor specific Windows events. Generally, the events all relate to Windows Management Instrumentation (WMI), which is a low-level system management tool. Although these events do provide a great deal of functionality for desktop developers, especially for critical operations such as remote application installation, they aren't very useful to Web developer and you should probably avoid using this feature. You can learn more about this feature at http://msdn.microsoft.com/library/default.asp?url=/library/en-us/ wmise/wmioriManagementEventsNode.asp.

You might find that you like the two new management features in Visual Studio .NET 2005 so much that you want them in older versions of the product. Fortunately, Microsoft has made this feature available to users of the older version as well. You can download a Visual Studio .NET 2003 version of the management features at http://www.microsoft.com/downloads/details.aspx?FamilyID=62d91a63-1253-4ea6-8599-68fb3ef77de1&DisplayLang=en.

For those of you who used Server Explorer in the past, you'll notice that Microsoft made some organizational changes. The biggest change is that you no longer can see all that SQL Server has to offer simply by opening the server—you must make a connection to the required database first. However, the functionality is the same as before. If you need to make a new database, reconfigure a table, or create a query, Server Explorer does it all.

Now that you have a basic idea what Server Explorer is all about, it's time to look at it in more detail. The following sections describe Server Explorer in a little more detail and help you work with Server Explorer to perform basic tasks.

Creating a Server Connection

Visual Studio defaults to providing you with a connection to your local machine in Server Explorer. Of course, local connections are only useful when you build applications for the local environment. Generally, you need access to one or more servers. The servers could provide anything from database access to services. It doesn't matter—Server Explorer provides access to them all as long as you have the required rights. Server Explorer won't override server security.

To create a new server connection, right-click the Servers entry in Server Explorer and choose Add Server from the context menu. You'll see the Add Server dialog box shown in Figure 3.2. Type the name of the server that you want to access. You can only access servers on a network that you can contact directly. In other words, you can't use a Virtual Private Network (VPN) across the Internet to contact the server unless you can contact that server by name and not by address or URL. Click OK to create the connection.

This dialog box has a non-obvious feature that you need to know about. Many developers ignore links on dialog boxes because they generally don't provide features—they provide help. In this case, you do need to pay attention to that link at the bottom of the dialog box. Click the Connect Using a Different User Name link and you'll see a Connect as dialog box that requests a username and password. Type the username and password that you want to use to connect to the server and click OK.

After you create a new connection, you'll see a list of entries like those shown in Figure 3.1 for the new server. However, the presence of an entry doesn't necessarily mean that you can do something with it. If you don't have access to a particular feature, Visual Studio will display one of several error messages telling you about the problem. The error could be anything from a lack of rights to the server's refusing the connection. In some cases, the error messages are misleading. For example, you'll often receive a refused connection error message when the server doesn't have a particular feature installed. A few error messages include an error number that you can look up using the Error Lookup tool accessible using the Tools ➤ Error Lookup command.

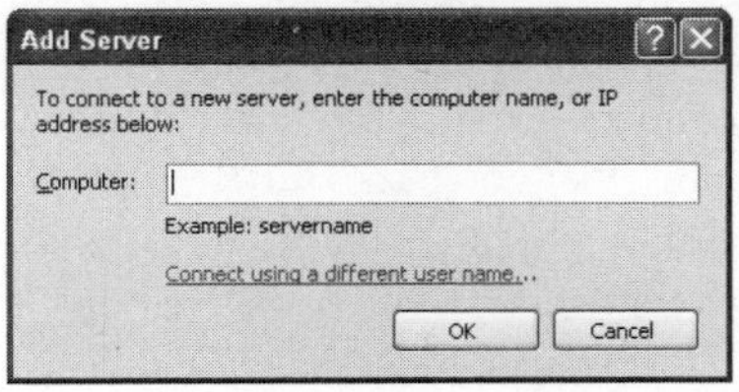

FIGURE 3.2
Use the Add Server dialog box to add a server to the Server Explorer window.

An Overview of Data Connections

Every business maintains databases. In fact, many individuals maintain databases as well. Databases form the most common kind of data storage on computer systems of all types. Database Management Systems (DBMSs) provide the engines that manage the data stored in databases. Server Explorer provides access to a number of common database types. In fact, you can use any database that has direct Visual Studio support or relies on Open Database Connectivity (ODBC).

To create a database connection, right-click the Data Connections icon in Server Explorer and choose Add Connection from the context menu. The first time you perform this task, you'll see the Change Data Source dialog box shown in Figure 3.3. This dialog box contains two fields that provide a broad range of flexibility. For example, when you choose the default Microsoft SQL Server option in the Data Source field, you can still choose between the .NET Framework Data Provider for ODBC, .NET Framework Data Provider for OLE-DB, or .NET Framework Data Provider for SQL Server options in the Data Provider field. However, the most powerful selection is <Unspecified> because it lets you choose from all of the data providers shown in Figure 3.3—you can choose most third party databases using this option.

FIGURE 3.3
Choose the data source you want to use to connect to the database.

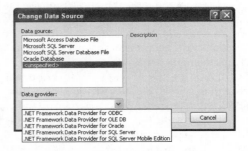

If you plan to use the same database for all of your projects, you'll want to check the Always Use this Selection option at the bottom of the dialog box. When you choose this option, all you really need to do is choose the particular database you want to use from that DBMS the next time you create a connection. Once you choose a data source you want to use, click OK and you'll see the Add Connection dialog box. This dialog box changes appearance based on the kind of data source you use. Figure 3.4 shows how this dialog box looks when you choose Microsoft SQL Server in the Data Source field and .NET Framework Data Provider for SQL Server in the Data Provider field of the Change Data Source dialog box.

When working with SQL Server, you must choose a particular server and a database managed by that server. Click Test Connection to determine whether the connection works. Once you have a working connection, click OK and you'll see the connection added to Server Explorer as shown in Figure 3.5. Notice that you have full access to everything the database has to offer including tables, views, stored procedures, functions, synonyms, types, and assemblies for SQL Server. You can modify all of these elements, delete elements you don't need, and add new elements—all without leaving the Visual Studio IDE.

Visual Studio maintains a connection to the database as long as you use the IDE unless you close the connection by right-clicking it and choosing Close Connection from the context menu. Closing the connection doesn't remove it from Server Explorer and you can easily open it again when needed. When you finally finish using the connection, you can remove it by right-clicking the connection in

Server Explorer and choosing Delete from the context menu. Deleting the connection in Server Explorer doesn't change your ability to access it using code—Server Explorer serves as a tool for creating applications and doesn't maintain the application connection. You'll learn more about working with connections in the "Creating a Database Connection" section of Chapter 10. In fact, all of Part 4 makes heavy use of Server Explorer to work with databases.

FIGURE 3.4
Define a connection to a particular database using the Add Connection dialog box.

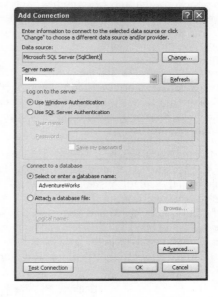

FIGURE 3.5
Server Explorer provides full access to the database once you create a connection to it.

An Overview of Crystal Reports Services

If you've ever had to create a report by hand using the .NET Framework, you know it can be a time-consuming and error-prone process. The problem is that you must manage the printer without really knowing the printer's capabilities in advance unless you're building a custom application for internal company use. Database developers rely heavily on reports to provide a means of accessing the vast information stores that most companies have. Consequently, it's essential to have a good report writer or face the prospect of hand coding reports by hand. Fortunately, Visual Studio .NET comes with Crystal Reports; a report writer you can use to output reports from a variety of sources including databases.

NOTE   The version of Crystal Reports provided with Visual Studio .NET provides limited capability when compared to the full version of the product. Anyone who writes many database reports should consider getting the full version of the product because it contains so many additional features. Not only do you gain access to additional reports, you also gain access to other report sources and some additional automation.

The Crystal Reports Services folder of Visual Studio contains three entries: Crystal Enterprise, Report Application Server, and Server Files Web Service. Unfortunately, the first two entries aren't available with the default Visual Studio setup—you must buy a separate package to use them. When you click on these entries, you'll get the helpful message shown in Figure 3.6 inviting you to learn more about the full version of Crystal Reports. Clicking Yes takes you to the Crystal Reports Web site. You can use the third entry to access reports that you've created. Generally, you'll interact with Crystal Reports using the options in the Add New Item dialog box you access from Solution Explorer. Don't worry too much about this particular feature for now, you'll see it discussed in detail in Chapter 12.

FIGURE 3.6
The Crystal Reports features in Server Explorer border on disappointing because you can't use two of them.

An Overview of Message Queues

Many developers think that COM+ is part of an older technology that doesn't exist in .NET. Actually, COM+ is a very much alive and well. In fact, you can create some amazing applications using .NET with COM+. From a Server Explorer perspective, one of the most prevalent examples of COM+ technology is the message queue. COM+ includes the concept of disconnected applications.

WARNING   You can't add a message queue directly to your Web application because that could expose your server to unacceptable security risks. Instead, you create a standard component that interacts with the Web page through a server-side connection in the background. The "Working with Server-side Components" section of Chapter 20 describes how to work with server-side controls that perform this type of processing.

A disconnected application is a form of asynchronous processing where the client and server don't need to exist at the same time. Messaging, which is a type of email communication, provides the glue required to keep client and server communicating. (The use of message queues isn't precisely the same as email, but the analogy is a good one for understanding how the process works.) The client uploads a message to the server's message queue. A listener application on the server retrieves the message and hands it off to an object that processes the information it contains. When the client expects information back from the server, the object places the response in the client's message queue. The client retrieves the response from the message queue the next time it connects to the server.

The entire process occurs asynchronously and is a good model for some kinds of Web applications. For example, the client need not wait for the server to process yesterday's sales information. The client merely uploads this information to the server's queue. The next day the client can download receipts showing that the server processed the orders and sent the products to the client. Even if the client and server become disconnected, this model works because Microsoft Message Queue Services (MSMQ) handles each message individually and you can use transactions to ensure each message arrives at its destination once and only once.

TIP   I've written a number of articles and books on the topic of COM+, which includes message queuing. You can see a basic article about COM+ as a Web service accessed from .NET at `http://www.devsource.ziffdavis.com/article2/0,1759,1627474,00.asp`. This article also shows you how to create COM+ components using .NET. For a comprehensive view of .NET and COM/COM+ get my book, *COM Programming with Microsoft .NET* (Microsoft Press, 2003).

At the heart of this technology is Queued Components, which in turn uses MSMQ. MSMQ is the base stand-alone technology originally introduced for use within Windows NT for message-based application development. Queued Components are the new COM+ version of MSMQ that offers a true superset of the older technology. All of the older MSMQ interfaces are still in place, but now you also have more automation and integration with COM available in Queued Components. Queued Components provides both an API and component-based interface for developers.

Unlike many of the other services discussed in this chapter, you'll actually use the Computer Management console to manage the queues on a system, unless you choose to create a custom console for the purpose. Figure 3.7 shows an example of the Computer Management console with the Message Queuing folder displayed. Notice that this folder appears in the Services and Applications folder.

FIGURE 3.7
Manage the queues for an application using the Message Queuing folder features.

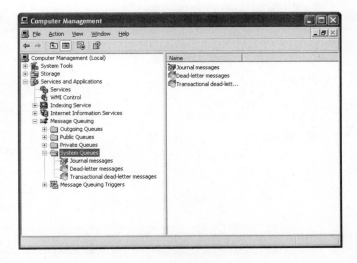

As you can see, MSMQ provides four levels of message queues: Outgoing Queues, Public Queues, Private Queues, and System Queues. The System Queues folder is the only folder that actually contains any queues when you first install Message Queuing (the name of the option found in the Windows Components Wizard for Windows XP). This queue generally contains messages of a system nature, including messages that MSMQ couldn't deliver. The Outgoing Queues folder contains all of the messages that the local computer will send to the server once a connection is established. The Public Queues contain permanent queues that are visible to the public, while the Private Queues folder contains queues that only local applications should see.

Visual Studio .NET makes it almost too easy to use a queue. You can access both local and remote queues using Server Explorer, as shown in Figure 3.8. Notice that you can access all but the Outgoing Queues folder, which makes sense since this folder only contains temporary queues (and only as long as the client lacks a connection to the server).

To add a queue to your application, drag and drop it onto the form. Visual Studio .NET will create a `MessageQueue` object for you. The properties will contain all of the correct pointers for the queue. You can also create and delete message queues in Server Explorer. Right-click one of the main folders and choose Create Queue from the context menu to add a new queue to the folder. Right-click an existing queue and choose Delete to remove it.

Visual Web Developer throws a small wrinkle into using message queuing within an application. The default Windows XP installation won't work. To add Web message queuing capability to Windows XP, you must manually select the MSMQ HTTP Support option in the Message Queuing dialog box shown in Figure 3.9. You access this dialog box by highlighting Message Queuing in the Windows Components Wizard dialog box (displayed from the Add or Remove Programs applet) and then selecting Details. Selecting this option lets you work with message queues using a Web connection. Even with HTTP support added to your application, you must process message queue information indirectly using a server-side component.

FIGURE 3.8
Server Explorer provides easy access to all but the Outgoing Queues folder.

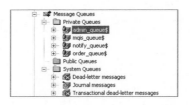

FIGURE 3.9
Add HTTP support so you can use message queuing from Visual Web Developer.

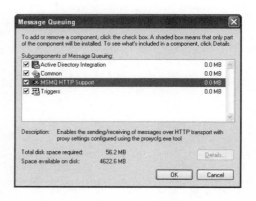

An Overview of Services

You won't ever add services to your Visual Web Developer application. For one thing, you don't really want an outside entity, no matter how benign, to gain access to the services on your server. However, you can still use Server Explorer to manage services on other machines as you develop your application. For example, you can use Server Explorer to check the service status and change it as needed. Figure 3.10 shows how the services appear within Server Explorer.

Services that are stopped use a different icon from those that are started. Right-click any service that you want to start and choose Start from the context menu to start it. You can also stop and pause services by right-clicking them and choosing the correct option on the context menu. Highlight any service to view its current settings in the Properties window. Although you can't change the service settings, you can see how the service is set up to determine whether you need to use the Service console (accessed from the Administrative Tools folder of the Control Panel) to modify them.

FIGURE 3.10
Check and change the status of services on any system you can access.

Working with Event Logs

One of the features that developers come to appreciate about Server Explorer is that it helps you categorize information. You can drill down to the information you need, but ignore everything else. For example, when you open the Application Event Log, you need to connect to the remote server, locate the log, and then search through the list of messages for the particular message you need. Server Explorer categorizes event messages by type, so all you see is the message you want. Figure 3.11 shows a typical example of the Event Log entries provided by Server Explorer. As you can see, this display is almost easier to use than the Event Log console found in the Administrative Tools folder of the Control Panel.

The only control you have over the event log is to clear it. To perform this task, right-click the event log that you want to clear (such as Application) and choose Clear Event Log. You'll see a message box asking you to verify the action. Click Yes to clear the event log. Unfortunately, Server Explorer doesn't provide the opportunity to save the event log to disk—you must use the Event Log console to perform this task. Now that you know the basics of how the event log works, it's time to see how you could interact with it using a Web page. The following sections discuss event logs in detail.

FIGURE 3.11
Server Explorer event log
entries are exceptionally
easy to use.

Using Standard Event Logs

It's relatively easy to work with standard event logs using a Web page. Most people associate this activity with desktop applications, but you shouldn't discount using them for Web needs as well. For example, you could make an event log entry whenever a page fails to load or react as desired. An event log entry could point out database connection overloading or users who leave shopping carts unattended. Listing 3.1 makes a standard event log entry and then lets you read that entry from the same Web page. You'll find this example in the \Chapter 03\EventLog folder of the source code on the Sybex Web site.

As you work with the event log, you'll notice that adding events using the application Test button also changes the content of the Application event log. In fact, the entries appear as part of the Event Log Example category in the list. Remember that ASP.NET hides the code behind for a Web page from the user, so you aren't exposing anything by using this technique. As far as the user is concerned, the event log entry doesn't exist. The call to EventLog.WriteEntry() makes the process simple. All you need to provide is a source, the message, and a type. The event identifier and category provide additional information you can use to sort the event log messages, but you don't have to provide them.

The btnShowResult_Click() event handler shows how you can display the event log to someone using the Web site. The EventLog.GetEventLogs() method returns all of the event logs—to see a specific log you have to locate it in the array. The event logs generally appear in the same order they do in the Event Log console. The application places the Application log into ApplicationEvents and then uses that log to locate application-specific entries.

NOTE You'll see many differences in the way that some .NET Framework features work—the event log is one of them. The EventLog class required that you create objects to perform many of the tasks in the past. The latest version of the .NET Framework lets you perform these actions directly by using static methods.

For this example, the code relies on the Page.Title property to locate the entries because that's how the application records them in the event log. Simply look for the source that you provided to locate the entries specific to a particular Web page. You need to use some other method when looking for entries from other Web pages or from all Web pages as a whole. The application outputs the time the system wrote the event log entry, the entry type (Information, Warning, or Error), and the message. You'll see one entry on the Web page for each entry you create. Figure 3.12 shows typical output for this application.

LISTING 3.1:   Creating an Application Log Entry and Reading It

```
Protected Sub btnTest_Click( _
    ByVal sender As Object, ByVal e As System.EventArgs) _
    Handles btnTest.Click

    ' Create an event entry.
    EventLog.WriteEntry(Page.Title, _
                        "This is a test message", _
                        EventLogEntryType.Information, _
                        1001, _
                        1)

End Sub

Protected Sub btnShowResult_Click( _
    ByVal sender As Object, ByVal e As System.EventArgs)

    Dim AllLogs As EventLog()              ' Contains all the logs.
    Dim ApplicationEvents As EventLog    ' The application event log.

    ' Get all of the event logs and extract the application log.
    AllLogs = EventLog.GetEventLogs()
    ApplicationEvents = AllLogs(0)

    ' Display the content of each event log related to this
    ' application.
    For Each EventMessage As EventLogEntry In ApplicationEvents.Entries

        ' Determine whether this is related to our application.
        If EventMessage.Source = Page.Title Then

            ' Add the message time, type, and content to the list.
            txtOutput.Text = _
                txtOutput.Text + _
                EventMessage.TimeWritten.ToLongTimeString() + " " + _
                EventMessage.EntryType.ToString() + " " + _
                EventMessage.Message + vbCrLf
        End If
    Next
End Sub
```

FIGURE 3.12
Creating and monitoring event log entries is easy using a Web page.

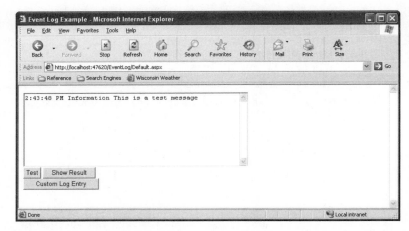

This example demonstrates another important consideration for developers. You can manage a Web site and the applications it hosts from a remote location. However, notice that this application places strict limits on the information it displays as output. You should provide similar limitations for any management tools you build to limit the damage that accidental exposure can cause.

Developing Custom Event Logs

Sometimes you want to place your events in a special log to keep the information separate. In addition, using a separate log tends to reduce any security concerns that you might have about using the event log. The example in this section creates a custom log entry and places an event message in it. After you run the example, you can see the new event log and its entry in Server Explorer. Listing 3.2 shows the code you'll need to use to create the custom log entry. You'll find this example in the \Chapter 03\EventLog folder of the source code on the Sybex Web site.

Before you can use a custom event log, you must create and register it with the server. This application begins by verifying the event log doesn't exist using the EventLog.SourceExists() method. When the event log doesn't exist, the code creates it using the EventLog.CreateEventSource() method. Notice that you must create the new event log by instantiating a new EventSourceCreationData() object that contains the name of the log and the event source. Once you perform this task, the log is ready to use.

Creating a log entry in a custom log is no different from creating the same entry in any other log. The only difference is that you use a different event log entry to hold the data. Figure 3.13 shows the output from this application. Notice that Server Explorer shows the new event log and the message it contains. You might need to right-click the Event Logs entry and choose Refresh from the context menu to display this new addition.

FIGURE 3.13
Use custom event logs to keep your Web page data separate from other applications.

LISTING 3.2:   Creating a Custom Event Log and Associated Entry

```
Protected Sub btnCustomLog_Click( _
    ByVal sender As Object, ByVal e As System.EventArgs)

    ' If you want to create a special log, then you need
    ' to register an event source first (as you already did in your
    ' example code).
    If (Not EventLog.SourceExists("MyEventSource")) Then

        ' Create the new event source.
        EventLog.CreateEventSource( _
            New EventSourceCreationData("MyEventSource", _
                                        "MySpecialLog"))

    End If

    ' Create an entry.
    EventLog.WriteEntry("MyEventSource", _
                        "Special Message", _
                        EventLogEntryType.Information, _
                        12, _
                        22)

End Sub
```

Working with Performance Counters

Most people associate performance counters with a means of tracking application efficiency. However, performance counters can do a lot more work than most people think. For example, you can use performance counters to track user activity and determine when you need more hardware to handle a particular application. It's even possible to use performance counters to monitor unusual Web site activity and associate some types of unusual activity with crackers. Read the "Using Counters Effectively" sidebar to get additional ideas on how you can use performance counters in your application.

The point is that performance counters are essential monitors that count a specific activity—it doesn't matter what activity you choose to monitor. Consequently, if you want to build a special counter to monitor the number of error indications from a Web page, it's perfectly acceptable to do so. The following sections describe performance counters as a piece of software—something you can use to meet your particular needs.

Viewing Performance Counters

While event logs are an essential part of the Windows experience, monitoring them isn't so difficult that you'd want to spend a lot of time doing it. However, one type of monitoring that's a little more difficult involves the performance counters. Working with performance counters has been notoriously difficult in the past. Server Explorer makes it almost too simple to monitor all of the performance counters on your machine. This example uses a `DataSetDataSource` to store the intermediate values and a `GridView` to show the values. You need a timer but can't use the standard timer that a desktop application would use. Instead, the application relies on the `<meta refresh>` tag to provide a 3-second timer as shown here.

```
<meta http-equiv="refresh" content="3">
```

The use of a `<meta refresh>` tag is a bit of a kludge, but it does the job by letting you automatically update the display without a lot of fancy code. All of the remaining tasks occur behind the scenes. Listing 3.3 shows the code you'll need for this example. You'll find this example in the \Chapter 03\ PerformanceCounter folder of the source code on the Sybex Web site.

LISTING 3.3:   Server Explorer Makes It Easy to Use Performance Counters

```
Protected Sub Page_Load( _
    ByVal sender As Object, ByVal e As System.EventArgs) _
    Handles Me.Load

    ' Performance counter.
    Dim UserCounter As _
        New PerformanceCounter("Process", "% User Time", "_Total")

    ' XML Document holding performance data.
    Dim XMLDoc As New XmlDocument()

    ' XML Document elements.
    Dim ProcInst As XmlProcessingInstruction
    Dim Root As XmlNode
    Dim DataEntry As XmlNode
    Dim TimeData As XmlElement
    Dim PerfData As XmlElement

    ' Take action based on the existance of the XML document.
    If File.Exists("Data\PerfData.XML") Then

        ' Load the XML Document.
        XMLDoc.Load("Data\PerfData.XML")

        ' Obtain the document root.
        Root = XMLDoc.ChildNodes(1)

        ' Remove an old entry if there are 10 or more.
        If Root.ChildNodes.Count = 10 Then
            Root.RemoveChild(Root.ChildNodes(0))
        End If

    Else
```

```vb
        ' Create a new root element.
        Root = _
            XMLDoc.CreateNode( _
                XmlNodeType.Element, "PerformanceData", "")

        ' Create the XML processing instruction.
        ProcInst = _
            XMLDoc.CreateProcessingInstruction( _
                "xml", "version='1.0' encoding='utf-8'")
        XMLDoc.AppendChild(ProcInst)
    End If

    ' Create a new data entry.
    DataEntry = XMLDoc.CreateNode(XmlNodeType.Element, "DataEntry", "")

    ' Create the data elements.
    TimeData = XMLDoc.CreateElement("TimeData")
    PerfData = XMLDoc.CreateElement("PerfData")

    ' Get the current time.
    TimeData.InnerText = Date.Now.ToLongTimeString()

    ' Get the next counter value.
    UserCounter.NextValue()
    PerfData.InnerText = UserCounter.NextValue().ToString("0.00")

    ' Add these values to the data entry.
    DataEntry.AppendChild(TimeData)
    DataEntry.AppendChild(PerfData)

    ' Add the data entry to the root node.
    Root.AppendChild(DataEntry)

    ' Place the root in the document.
    XMLDoc.AppendChild(Root)

    ' Save the resulting XML document.
    XMLDoc.Save("Data\PerfData.XML")

    ' Assign the XML document to the DataSetDataSource
    dsPerfData.DataFile = "~\Data\PerfData.XML"
End Sub
```

USING COUNTERS EFFECTIVELY

The term *performance* is stretched when it comes to performance counters. Some developers automatically assume that performance equates to speed, but it doesn't. Performance could relate to resource usage—an application could detect when it's using resources inefficiently or too quickly and adjust its operation, potentially preventing a system crash. Another common use of performance counters is to measure how much or how many of a particular event has occurred, usually within a given time. Tracking network packet usage falls into this category.

In some respects, the term *performance* is a bit of a misnomer because you can use counters to count anything. I prefer to think of performance counters as statistics generators. When you think of them this way, you open up a number of possibilities that didn't exist before. A statistics generator can monitor your system for unexpected events such as a Distributed Denial of Service (DDOS) attack. You can also use them to monitor user events. For example, you can answer questions such as how often users make an error when using a particular dialog box. Opening your mind to the possible uses of statistics generators is the first step to really understanding what they can do for your application.

Unfortunately, some developers learn about performance counters and run amuck with them. A reality of using performance counters is that they affect the performance of the very applications they're supposed to monitor. The performance counter uses some amount of resources including both memory and CPU time to run. Consequently, the measurement isn't precise and it's very hard to compensate for the performance drop in a complex application. Fortunately, the measurement error is extremely small, in most cases, but it's still there. Every counter you add to the application adds to the problem.

A custom application can mitigate the problem of performance-counter drag by making them a configurable option—allowing the administrator to turn the counters on or off as needed. This option still incurs an infinitesimal penalty because the code still needs to check whether the counter is on or off, but the penalty is so small with a modern computer that it doesn't really matter. In general, make all of your counters configurable so the application runs as the fastest possible speed. A problem with many of those high-end applications is that the counters are on all the time, making it impossible to determine how much drag the monitoring system is placing on the application.

It's possible to make a good guess as to how much your performance counter loads the system by placing two copies of the same counter in the code, taking a measurement, and then removing one of the counters to see the effect. The performance difference is the drag placed on the application by that particular counter. This technique isn't foolproof and you do need to monitor the counters individually to obtain an accurate result, but it does work well enough that you can make some determinations on how to advise an administrator who wants to use the counters. Unfortunately, I've yet to see any application documentation that discusses this issue—it's assumed that the counter doesn't load the application at all, which simply isn't true.

Another issue to consider is whether a particular statistic is a good candidate for a performance counter. For example, many applications include one or more memory performance counters. In at least one case, I saw an application where the output of the counter was a straight line—no change at all. The problem is that the application never created any dynamic structures, so its memory footprint didn't change. The memory the application requires is well known, so a performance counter is a waste of time. Using performance counters to measure variable data of consequence is essential.

Notice that the example uses the `Page_Load()` event handler so that every `<meta refresh>` event updates the counter value. Remember that Web pages have no concept of state, so you must provide some means of retaining the state independently of the Web page. This example uses an XML file. The XML file acts as a data source to the `DataSetDataSource` control, `dsPerfData`. Every call to `Page_Load()` refreshes the content of the XML data file.

The code begins by creating the performance counter. You must provide all required data or the `PerformanceCounter` object won't work. In this case, you must provide the `CategoryName`, `CounterName`, and `InstanceName` values found in the Properties window when you select the performance counter in Server Explorer, as shown in Figure 3.14.

The next step is to create the XML document that will hold the performance data values. The example can pursue two courses based on the existence of the document. First, it can create a new document if the `\Data` folder doesn't contain the required information. Second, it can load the existing document into memory. When the document exists, the code creates the `Root` node using the content of the existing document; otherwise, it creates a new `Root` node. The `Root` node in an existing document might have the maximum number of display values, so the code also checks the number of child nodes using the `ChildNodes.Count` property and removes the oldest child using the `RemoveChild()` method when too many children exist.

The XML document in this example contains a maximum of 10 `<DataEntry>` nodes. Each `<DataEntry>` node includes a `<TimeData>` and a `<PerfData>` element that contains the time of the performance counter sample and the value of the sample respectively. The time portion of the sample is in the long time format supplied by the `Date.Now.ToLongTimeString()` method. When you want to retrieve the performance counter value, you must prime the object to get an actual value by calling `UserCounter.NextValue()` at least once before you create the output format using the `UserCounter.NextValue().ToString("0.00")` method. It isn't mandatory to format the string, but the output will have a random number of values after the decimal point if you don't.

The rest of the XML document building process consists of putting together the data entry, placing it in the `Root` node, and placing the entire result in the document. The code then saves the document to disk and assigns the file to `dsPerfData`. At this point, the application automatically displays the output without any additional help as shown in Figure 3.15.

FIGURE 3.14
Server Explorer supplied the values you need for the Performance-Counter constructor.

FIGURE 3.15

This application shows a number of processor values and provides continuous updates.

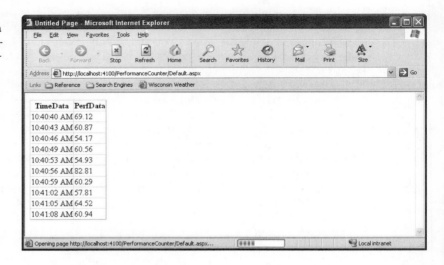

Creating a Simple Counter

Reading performance counters from a Web page is admittedly not a mainstream activity, but it's helpful for the enterprise developer to know that such a technique is possible. Monitoring Web page performance, on the other hand, is a mainstream activity that most developers will perform at some time. Performing this activity means creating one or more custom counters for your application. From a Web page perspective, counters have three phases: creation, updating, and deletion.

The creation phase necessarily begins first. Every counter you create will have certain elements. You must define a container to hold the counters, the actual counter, and instances of that counter. In general, you must create these objects in a specific order to ensure Windows registers them properly. Listing 3.4 shows a typical counter setup. You'll find this example in the \Chapter 03\Performance-Monitor folder of the source code on the Sybex Web site.

The code begins by declaring four global variables. Normally, it's a bad idea to use global variables in a Web application. However, in this case, it's a matter of convenience. The variables get used in more than one place, so it's helpful just to declare them once (not because you're planning on saving them for later).

The btnCreate_Click() method begins by creating a new counter collection. A single category can have more than one counter within it. For example, you might decide to provide a single counter for every Web page on your Web site—each counter tracks a specific Web page event, such as a user request or an error indication.

The next step is to create a single counter using the CounterCreationData() constructor. The definition includes the counter name, a help string that describes the counter, and the counter type. The counter type you choose is important because Windows handles each counter type differently. Once the code defines the counter, it adds the counter to CounterCollect using the Add() method.

It's important that you not attempt to add a category that already exists. The code handles this issue by using the PerformanceCounterCategory.Exists() to determine whether the category already exists. If not, the code uses the PerformanceCounterCategory.Create() method to create the category and add the counter to it.

LISTING 3.4:   Creating a Typical Counter Setup

```
' Contains all of the counters.
Dim CounterCollect as CounterCreationDataCollection

' Information used to create the counter.
Dim CounterData As CounterCreationData

' Performance counter for this application.
Dim LoadEvents As PerformanceCounter

' A random number simulating real data.
Dim EventVal As New Random(DateTime.Now.Second)

Protected Sub btnCreate_Click( _
    ByVal sender As Object, ByVal e As System.EventArgs)

    ' Initialize the counter collection.
    CounterCollect = New CounterCreationDataCollection()

    ' Create a counter.
    CounterData = New CounterCreationData( _
       "Application_Counter", _
       "Demonstrates an application counter.", _
       PerformanceCounterType.NumberOfItems32)

    ' Add the counter to the collection.
    CounterCollect.Add(CounterData)

    ' Add this collection as a new performance counter category.
    If Not PerformanceCounterCategory.Exists(Page.Title) Then
        PerformanceCounterCategory.Create( _
            Page.Title, _
            "Sample Application Counter", _
            PerformanceCounterCategoryType.MultiInstance, _
            CounterCollect)
    End If

    ' Create performance counters.
    LoadEvents = New PerformanceCounter( _
       Page.Title, _
       "Application_Counter", _
       "Load Event Counter", _
       False)
End Sub
```

The counter isn't complete yet because there aren't any counter instances to use for data display. The `PerformanceCounter()` constructor lets you create a new performance counter instance. The code uses the counter category just created, the counter name, and an instance name as input. The fourth argument sets the instance for read-write use.

At this point, you can generate counter events and monitor them using the System Monitor snap-in of the Performance console. You could also build a custom application to monitor the output as shown in Listing 3.3. Generating events with a Web page is different from a desktop application. Remember, Web pages don't provide state, so each call is a new environment. Listing 3.5 shows the code you'll need to generate an event. You'll find this example in the `\Chapter 03\Performance-Monitor` folder of the source code on the Sybex Web site.

LISTING 3.5:   Generating Performance Counter Events

```
Protected Sub btnGenerate_Click( _
    ByVal sender As Object, ByVal e As System.EventArgs)

    ' You must recreate the counter with every click.
    LoadEvents = _
        New PerformanceCounter( _
            Page.Title, "Application_Counter", "Load Event Counter", False)

    ' Generate one event for each click.
    If Not LoadEvents Is Nothing Then
        LoadEvents.RawValue = EventVal.Next(100)
    End If
End Sub
```

Notice that you must recreate the `LoadEvents` performance counter using the `PerformanceCounter()` constructor every time the user generates an event. When the code successfully creates `LoadEvents`, it can then add data to it. In this case, the code adds a random number between 0 and 100 to the display. However, in a real world application, you could register user events, errors, or anything else you want to count and monitor.

Removing a performance counter is relatively easy after all the work of generating one. All you need to do is tell .NET to delete it using the `PerformanceCounterCategory.Delete()` method, as shown here.

```
Protected Sub btnRemove_Click( _
    ByVal sender As Object, ByVal e As System.EventArgs)

    ' Remove the counter category.
    PerformanceCounterCategory.Delete(Page.Title)
End Sub
```

Defining Your Development Goals

This chapter has demonstrated many of the essential features of Server Explorer. This tool is one of the best ideas that Microsoft has ever come up with because it provides you with instant access to everything on the local machine and anything you have rights to access on other machines as well. Server Explorer is an information center that will profoundly affect your programming. The essential concept to remember is that you need to explore to use this tool effectively. The information is there, but you need to know where to find it when you need it.

It's your time to work with Server Explorer. You should take time to investigate your local machine first and then explore the machines around you. Create some simple applications and discover the possibilities that Server Explorer provides. If you're absolutely determined to do things the hard way, try setting up some comparison tests. Track how much time it takes you to replicate the functionality that Server Explorer provides using handwritten code. You might be impressed enough to change your mind.

Chapter 4 shows how to use some new features provided with ASP.NET 2.0. In this case, you'll discover some new visual aids in the form of master pages and themes. The Personal Web Site Startup Kit described in Chapter 1 uses these features, so you've already seen them. However, Chapter 4 provides a hands-on experience where you discover how to implement these features on any Web site you build.

Part 2

Using Built-in Features

In this part:

Chapter 4

Working with ASP.NET 2.0 Master Pages and Themes

ASP.NET 2.0 introduces a number of new features—many of which Microsoft added as part of specific developer requests. Two of the most interesting concepts are master pages and themes. These features are so useful as a means of improving developer efficiency and the overall consistency of a Web site that they merit their own chapter. In fact, enterprise developers will find that these features are essential when working in a team environment because they ensure consistency between team members.

In some respects, master pages and themes accomplish similar goals—they both create a general look and feel for a Web site. However, a master page and a theme differ in their approach to the Web development problem. A master page accomplishes its goal by providing consistent content and, to a certain extent, layout for a Web site. A theme provides consistency through graphical elements, formatting, and layout (among other things).

NOTE   This is the first chapter where we'll begin building a Web site using Visual Web Developer. You'll find all of the files for this project in the \ABC_Inc folder of the source code on the Sybex Web site, along with all of the source code for chapters up to Chapter 23. I'll provide you with specific file-names for specific features as appropriate as the book progresses. The centralized menu on the Default.ASPX page will also help you locate specific features.

Master pages and themes aren't necessarily mutually exclusive—Microsoft designed both technologies to mix in a number of ways. You can create a master page that relies on a theme for its formatting and graphical needs. A Web page can have both a master page (for content and presentation) and a theme (for formatting and graphics). The idea behind these technologies is to help the developer create pages faster by reducing the need to repeat elements that appear on every page. In addition, both master pages and themes reduce update time because you change a single file that affects the entire Web site, rather than make the change one page at a time.

Understanding Master Pages

A master page is a new way of organizing a Web site. It can contain a combination of formatting, graphics, and layout—whatever elements you feel that are common to all Web pages on your site. However, the emphasis is on organization, rather than on content. The idea is to give your Web site a consistent look and reduce the workload on developers. The developer no longer has to create repetitive elements using a number of tried and true methods such as cut and paste. In addition, the developer doesn't have to remember to create the correct elements in the proper order—the master page takes care of everything for the developer.

CSS, THE MASTER PAGE AND THEME ALTERNATIVE

Enterprise developers work with huge Web sites and usually have thousands of lines of code to manage. Even though using a master page or theme is the best solution for enterprise developers, you might not have the option to use this technology in every case. It takes time and coordination to create a master page and theme for your Web site, and then add them to every page. You usually don't have the luxury of completely redesigning a Web site unless someone says you have that luxury. Fortunately, you do have an alternative in the form of Cascading Style Sheets (CSS).

CSS is a good alternative for enterprise developers on a time budget who want to dress up their Web site in the shortest time possible and with the fewest code changes. As you'll discover in this chapter, CSS also provides formatting and, to a lesser degree, some types of layout and graphics. The advantage of CSS is that it's standardized—you can use it on any Web site with any server and expect that any browser with CSS capability will be able to use the page. You might be surprised to learn that you can combine CSS with master pages and themes, so again these options aren't mutually exclusive.

The biggest loss for the enterprise developer using CSS is that you don't get quite the same level of consistency between team members. Even though you can mandate consistency through official documentation, standards, and documentation—these types of control usually prove less effective than using a combination of master pages and themes. You end up spending more time cleaning pages up to make them look consistent. Consequently, the time you spend implementing master pages and themes is more than paid back by reduced clean up time later.

A master page always has a MASTER file extension. In most respects, it looks and acts just like an ASPX Web page. You add content to a master page just as you would for a standard Web page. Of course, it pays to remember that you won't be using this Web page directly—a master page is always an organization tool for other Web pages; no one actually sees it online.

A master page does have two special features that set it apart from other page types. First, it contains a special tag that identifies it as a master page to the Web server like the one shown here.

```
<%@ master Language="VB"
    CompileWith="Default.MASTER.VB"
    ClassName="Default_master" %>
```

This directive tag (a special tag that the server understands and doesn't send to the client) has four important features.

- The word `master` differentiates this page from a standard ASPX page, which uses the word `page`.

- The `Language` attribute tells you that the page uses Visual Basic for coding needs.

- The `CompileWith` attribute tells you that this master page uses code behind and that the code is located in the `Default.MASTER.VB` file.

- The `ClassName` attribute tells you that the default class for this page is `Default_master`, not another class that the `Default.MASTER.VB` file may contain.

Second, a master page contains `ContentPlaceHolder` controls that tell someone using the master page where to add the unique information for the Web page. Using the `ContentPlaceHolder` controls means there isn't any chance for confusion—developers working with a master page can only put content in certain places. Figure 4.1 shows the `Default.MASTER` file from the Personal Web Site Starter Kit example created in Chapter 1.

FIGURE 4.1
Master pages look just like standard Web pages with a few exceptions.

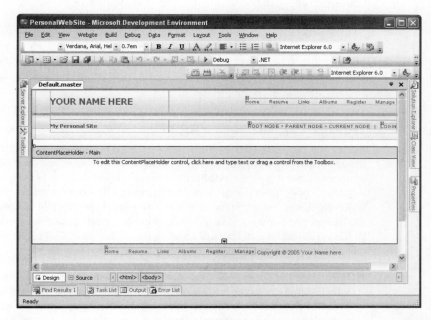

Notice this page contains everything you might expect to see on every page of a Web site including standard links and a link for the site map. All of the identification information also appears on this page. Consequently, when you want to change the name of your Web site or a company wants to change the logo, all you need to do is change the master page, not all of the pages on the Web site.

As previously mentioned, ASPX pages use a directive similar to the one that the master page uses. One big difference is that the ASPX page uses a page directive, not a master directive. This directive also contains a special keyword that links the ASPX page to the master page. You'll find the `MasterPageFile` attribute shown here.

```
MasterPageFile="~/Default.MASTER"
```

When the server sees the `MasterPageFile` attribute, it reads the information found in the associated MASTER file before it reads the content from the ASPX page. It uses the MASTER file content to build a framework for the ASPX page and then places the unique ASPX page content within the framework. Of course, this begs the question of how the server knows where to place the information. The ASPX page contains special container tags that hold the content that the MASTER file describes such as this one.

```
<asp:content id="Content1" contentplaceholderid="Main" runat="server">
```

The <asp:content> tag identifies content information. The id attribute provides local identification that you use to interact with the tag. For example, you might decide to write some code behind to work with the content. The contentplaceholderid attribute identifies the name of the ContentPlaceHolder control in the MASTER file. This value is especially important because it provides the linkage between the ASPX file and the MASTER file—a MASTER file can contain multiple ContentPlaceHolder controls. The runat attribute tells the server that it should process this tag and not send it to the client for processing.

This process might seem long and arduous, but you don't have to worry about it. Using the procedures found in this chapter, the IDE does most of the work for you and you can perform any additional settings changes using simple properties, rather than writing the code. The reason you want to know about these directives is so you understand what's happening and how to fix your pages if they become damaged.

Designing Master Pages

Before you can do anything with a master page, you have to create one. Master pages require a lot more thought than other pages you create because they affect every page on your Web site. It's not simply a matter of creating a great design, but one of determining when content is common to all pages and what type of support the developer using the master page requires. Restricting the master page too much creates an environment where the developer spends a lot of time working around the problems the master page creates. Likewise, developing a generic master page that's completely open to interpretation defeats the purpose of creating the master page in the first place. The following sections discuss these issues and more.

NOTE   Don't be concerned if you receive a script warning message from your antivirus application when adding a master page to a Web site. The error occurs because of the inner workings of Visual Web Developer and not because your machine is suddenly infected with a virus. Of course, you'll still want to react to any warning messages you receive at other times.

Creating the Master Page

Before you can create a master page, you need to create or open a Web site to store it. The "Creating the Application" section of Chapter 1 tells you how to perform this task. The easiest way to add a master page to the Web site is to open Solution Explorer. Right-click the project entry and choose Add New Item from the context menu. You'll see the Add New Item dialog box shown in Figure 4.2. Notice that you can choose to place the code in a separate file—just as you can with a Web Form (ASPX file). In this case, you can't select the Select Master Page option because you can't create a master page based on an existing master page.

Select a language for the master page you want to create. Check the Place Code in Separate File option if you want to store the code behind code in a separate file. Using a separate file is a good idea because doing so helps you create a better development environment—the HTML tags remain separate from the Visual Basic or C# code you write for the code behind. Click Add to add the master page to the project.

Master pages always have to have one content area as a minimum, so you need to add a ContentPlaceHolder control to the master page as shown in Figure 4.3. You should always configure this control before you start adding content to the master page to ensure you provide it with an easily identifiable name and provide everything the developer using the master page will need.

FIGURE 4.2
Select the Master
Page item from the
Add New Item dialog
box to create a
master page.

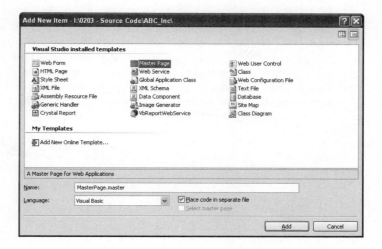

FIGURE 4.3
Configure the default
ContentPlaceHolder
control before you move
on to other tasks.

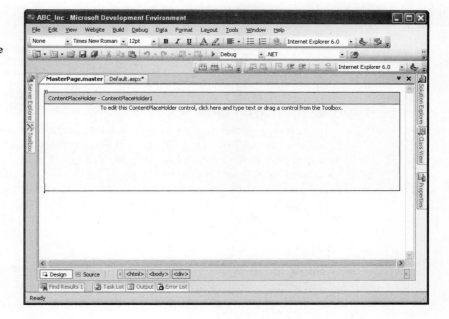

Using Existing Resources

It's quite likely that you'll use the same master page for multiple projects. Once you create the master page, you can make small modifications as needed for other uses. In fact, except for Web Forms, which normally contain unique content, you'll find that many resources you develop are reusable. Consequently, you'll add this existing resource to the project, rather than create a new resource.

To add an existing resource to the current project, open Solution Explorer, right-click the project entry, and choose Add Existing Item from the context menu. You'll see the Add Existing Item dialog box shown in Figure 4.4.

Locate the resource, such as a master page, that you want to use. Don't worry about selecting the code behind page when you select an existing resource because the IDE copies it automatically for you. At this point, you'll see the new file added to Solution Explorer. Look in the project folder and you'll see a copy of the file added there as well. Any changes you make to the resource will affect the local project, but not the project from which you copied the resource.

FIGURE 4.4
Using existing items for your Web site saves time and effort.

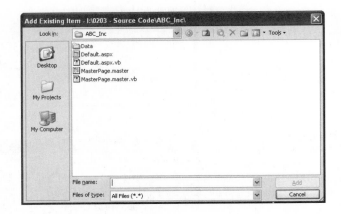

Defining the Master Page

Now that you have a master page to use, you'll want to define some organizational elements for it. The "Creating a Layout" and "Using the Layout Toolbar" sections describe how to add a layout to your master page so that all of the elements you want to add fit nicely.

After you create a layout for your master page, you'll want to add content to it. Generally, you'll want to add basic content to the page, such as a header and footer. This content doesn't have to appear in any special location or rely on complex formatting. Of course, you can always use a theme or CSS to create a specific appearance. The goal is to create a complete page that includes everything that every page on your Web site will need to include. Don't think, however, that these items are limited—consider adding the common elements listed here.

◆ Content

◆ Graphics

◆ Links

◆ Scripts

◆ Controls

◆ Code behind

◆ Anything else common to all pages

That "anything else" element is substantial. If every Web page will include the same sound or other multimedia file, then you should include it as part of the master page and not repeat it for every Web page on your Web site. Of course, you don't want to drown yourself with detail on the first master page. It pays to spend a little time working with the master page and then create a content page or two to see how it works before you move on to the next task.

TIP   Even though you'll still want to maintain corporate policies on content, using a master page can reduce the need for people to spend hours learning every nuance of the policy. A good master page makes it nearly impossible for anyone working on a development team to break the rules for general content structure and placement. Consequently, even semiskilled members will produce Web pages that meet most (or even all) of the requirements every time and with far less effort than before. The result is better Web pages delivered faster by everyone.

Creating a Layout

The Layout toolbar helps you create a well-designed and organized Web page, whether it's a master or a content page. Before you begin using this feature, however, you need to create a layout for your Web page. Layout is actually a fancy term for tables. Just like the tables you create with pen and paper, tables on Web pages let you put anything you want within the rows and columns. With a little effort, tables on Web pages don't have to follow the rigid formatting that you might expect—tables can contain tables, so you can create complex layouts.

To begin the layout process, select the Layout ➤ Insert Table command. You'll see the Insert Table dialog box shown in Figure 4.5. Notice that this dialog box actually contains two methods for creating a table. You can select the Template option to add one of the predefined layouts to your Web page or the Custom option to create a unique layout. Of the two, the Template option is the easiest and you should at least look at the templates to see if any will work for your Web page. In many cases, the template will work, even if you have to make minor modifications. For the purposes of this chapter, choose the Header and Side template.

FIGURE 4.5
Add a table to the master page or content page to organize it.

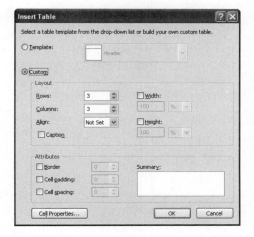

After you choose a template or create a custom table layout, click OK. The example uses the Header and Side template. Something interesting will occur. You'll see the template added immediately before or after the `ContentPlaceHolder` control. To fix this problem, drag the `ContentPlaceHolder` control into the bottom right square. Your display will look similar to the one shown in Figure 4.6.

TIP   It's important to realize that the IDE is creating an enormous amount of code for this master page in the background. All of these HTML tags do exist and you might eventually need to edit them. That's why it's a good idea to click various elements as you create them, click Source, and view the resulting HTML code. In the case of a table, you'll notice it begins with a `<table>` tag, which contains the entire table. Each row within the table is a `<tr>` tag. Rows contain columns—defined by the `<td>` tags. The bottom of the Design view is also helpful in seeing the relationship between tags. Look at the bottom of Figure 4.6 and you'll see that the tag sequence begins with an `<html>` tag (the entire Web page), followed in turn by the `<body>` (all the content), `<div>` (this section of content), the various table tags, and finally, the actual content, which is the `ContentPlaceHolder` control.

Figure 4.6 shows some other interesting layout features. For example, the sizing handles let you change the size of the layout as needed. When you place the cursor over an inner line, you'll notice that it changes into a sizing cursor. Simply move the line to give one cell of the layout more space (and correspondingly less space to the adjoining cell).

It's also possible to add and remove layout elements using the options on the Layout ➢ Insert menu. The only problem is that the options aren't all that clear unless you spend time working with them. Using Figure 4.6 as a starting point, Figure 4.7 shows the results of six different insertions you can make.

FIGURE 4.6
Modify the layout so that the `ContentPlaceHolder` control is in the correct position.

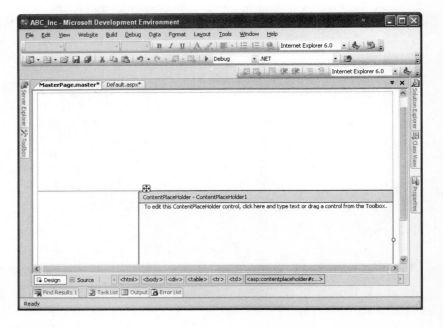

FIGURE 4.7
You can insert new layout features six different ways using the Layout ➤ Insert menu options.

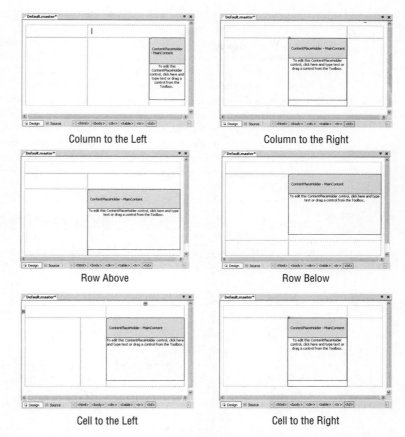

Column to the Left

Column to the Right

Row Above

Row Below

Cell to the Left

Cell to the Right

The various additions follow specific rules. To add a column, you must select a row that spans the entire layout. You can still add a column to a row that doesn't span the entire layout, but you must select the entire row or the column addition looks very much like a cell addition. To make it easier to see the changes, the two column additions use the upper row as a starting point, while the remaining additions use the lower right cell as a starting point (the one with the ContentPlaceHolder control). The positioning of your cursor when you insert a new layout item is just as important as the kind of layout item you choose—different cursor positions have completely different effects because the IDE always adds layout elements relative to the current cursor position. In a few cases, you can obtain the same results using two different cursor positions. For example, inserting a column to the left using the upper row as a starting position produces the same results as inserting a cell from the lower right cell in Figure 4.7.

Sometimes, the visual display just doesn't provide enough information or makes it difficult to select just the item you want. When this problem occurs, you can use the options on the Layout ➤ Select menu to choose the entire table, a column, a row, or a single cell. The IDE shows you which items it selected. For example, when you select a row, the IDE highlights the border of the cell that currently contains the cursor and shows all other affected cells highlighted (usually in blue) as shown in

Figure 4.8. Once you select an element, you can use the options on the Layout menu to resize or delete the elements. There's also an option to merge all of the cells in a selected row or column to produce a single cell. In short, you don't have to perform all of these tasks using just the features that Design view provides.

Once you create a layout, you can begin adding items and additional ContentPlaceHolder controls to the display. It's important to settle on the layout first because it provides the framework for the remaining controls. Figure 4.9 shows the layout and sample content for the example in this chapter.

Notice that the instructions for using the ContentPlaceHolder controls appear within the controls. The developer using the master page you create won't have access to the areas outside the control, so you must put the instructions within the control unless you want the instructions to appear to anyone visiting the page later. The example master page also includes all of the headings, icons, and other resources that appear on every Web page so the content developer performs the minimal amount of work.

FIGURE 4.8
The display uses hints to show the layout selections and make the job of using them easier.

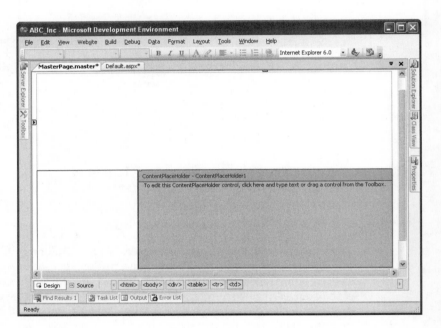

Using the Layout Toolbar

At some point, you'll want to add controls to the Web pages you create. Generally, you'll want to create a nice looking layout—one that looks attractive—without doing a lot of work. That's where the Layout toolbar shown in Figure 4.10 comes into play. You use it to adjust the controls you create on a Web page. For example, you can align a series of controls or resize the controls so they all look the same. The following list describes the purpose and use of each control. It's important to realize that Microsoft is attempting to synchronize control and menu sets across products, so some of the buttons are nonfunctional for Visual Web Developer (even though they are functional for the desktop languages).

FIGURE 4.9
A good layout and well-defined general content make creating content pages easier.

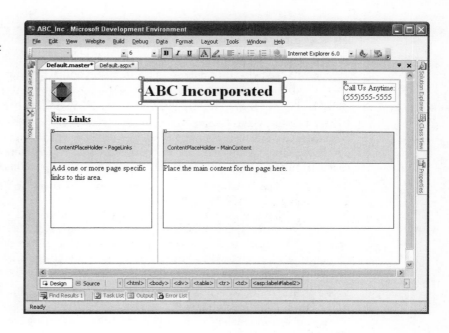

FIGURE 4.10
Use the Layout toolbar to adjust the default layout settings for a Web page.

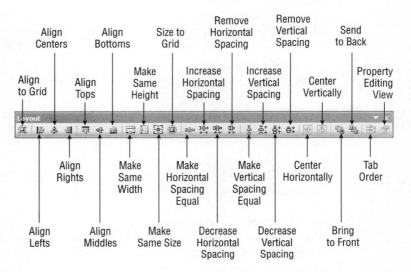

Property Editing View Changes the Design view to include a Quick Edit Mode bar at the top of the display. A dropdown list includes common properties such as Name and Text. You change a property by selecting it from the dropdown list and modifying it directly in Design view, rather than use the Properties window. This feature isn't currently available in Visual Web Developer.

Tab Order   Adds tab order numbers to each of the controls in Design view. Clicking the number lets you edit its tab order. This feature isn't currently available in Visual Web Developer.

Send to Back and Bring to Front   Modifies the stacking order of a series of components. Stacking controls can help you create special effects, but only if the controls appear in the correct order. The last control placed on a form appears in front, while the first control appears behind all other controls. These two buttons let you change the stacking order to achieve specific display results.

Center Vertically and Center Horizontally   Places one or more controls in the center of a form. When you use this feature with all of the controls on a form, you can center the entire display on the form giving it a finished appearance. Unfortunately, browsers don't have a specific form size, so it's no surprise the Visual Web Developer doesn't support this feature.

Remove Vertical Spacing, Decrease Vertical Spacing, Increase Vertical Spacing, and Make Vertical Spacing Equal   Adjusts the vertical placement between selected controls. Use Remove Vertical Spacing to eliminate all of the spacing between controls—they appear one after the other. Decrease Vertical Spacing removes a little of the spacing between controls, while Increase Vertical Spacing adds a little spacing between controls. Select Make Vertical Spacing Equal when you want to make the spacing between controls equal, without changing the starting and ending positions of the controls as a whole.

Remove Horizontal Spacing, Decrease Horizontal Spacing, Increase Horizontal Spacing, and Make Horizontal Spacing Equal   Adjusts the horizontal placement between selected controls. Use Remove Horizontal Spacing to eliminate all of the spacing between controls—they appear one after the other. Decrease Horizontal Spacing removes a little of the spacing between controls, while Increase Horizontal Spacing adds a little spacing between controls. Select Make Horizontal Spacing Equal when you want to make the spacing between controls equal, without changing the starting and ending positions of the controls as a whole.

Size to Grid   Modifies the size of a control to fit within the grid lines provided in Design view. The IDE normally changes the control size based on the proximity of the grid line to the edge of the control. Using a grid helps you create standardized controls and align them with greater ease.

Make Same Size, Make Same Height, and Make Same Width   Modifies the size of a series of controls to have the same size, height, or width. The last control you select in a group defines the standard for all of the other controls. Making all of the text boxes on a form the same size can give your form a more professional appearance. However, you'll also need to consider the data the user will enter—some controls will be larger because they contain more information that the user must see.

Align Bottoms, Align Middles, Align Tops, Align Rights, Align Centers, Align Lefts, and Align to Grid   Changes the alignment of a series of controls depending on the type of alignment selected. The last control you select in a group defines the anchor point for all of the other controls. Aligning the controls on a form gives the form a more professional appearance and helps the user see the anticipated flow from one control to the next.

When you first display this toolbar (right-click the toolbar area and choose Layout from the context menu), you'll notice that the IDE hasn't enabled any of the buttons. A standard Web page doesn't include the concept of layout and positioning except the positioning you can provide using careful component positioning and aids such as tables and frames. Special control attributes let you add specific positioning information. You add this support using either the Layout ➤ Position ➤ Absolute (for absolute positioning explained later in this section) or Layout ➤ Position ➤ Relative command. Here's an example of a label with positioning information added.

```
<asp:Label ID="Label1"
    Style="z-index: 27; left: 600px; position: absolute; top: 24px"
    Runat="server"
    Text="Call Us Anytime: (555)555-5555"
    TabIndex="3
    Width="104px" Height="19px"></asp:Label>
```

This example uses pixels as a unit of measure. Although the correlation of pixels to inches isn't standardized, most developers use a measure of $1/72$ inch per pixel, which means 72 pixels are equivalent to 1 inch.

The IDE creates all of the code shown, but like most automatically generated code, you need to know something about it so you can repair it later if necessary. The `Style` attribute contains the required positioning information. The `z-index` defines this control's position in the list of controls—this list isn't necessarily zero-based, nor is it necessarily continuous. The `left` value tells you that this control appears 600 pixels from the left side of the display, while the `top` value tells you that the control appears 24 pixels from the top. The `position` value tells you that this is an absolute position, rather than a relative position—the information relates to the upper left corner of the browser display. Relative positioning places the control in relation to some other element, such as a table cell, and requires a little more work to get right, but also provides a more flexible display in that the controls remain positioned well even when the user resizes the browser window.

WARNING   Not all browsers can read and understand the styles that Visual Web Developer provides for relative and absolute positioning. Consequently, always assume that some viewers will see a page that uses absolute positioning as if you used relative positioning.

The other attributes for this label help define how it appears on screen and how the user interacts with it. For example, this control runs at the server, so the user sees HTML output based on what the server generates. The `Text` attribute defines the text the user sees on screen. The `TabIndex` attribute describes the selection order for this control when the user presses Tab to move from control to control. Finally, the `Width` and `Height` properties tell you the size of the control.

Many of the layout features rely on the grid displayed in Design view. You can control this feature using the Options dialog box you can access using the Tools ➤ Options command. Select the `Windows Form Designer\General` folder and you'll see the list of grid options shown in Figure 4.11.

The GridSize property defines the number of pixels between grid sections. The LayoutMode determines whether the grid relies on snap lines or actually snaps objects to the grid. (Think of a rubber band—you can place an item outside of the grid lines—the rubber bands, but the grid will snap the item back into place so it lines up with the grid lines.) Set the ShowGrid property to true to see the grid presented on screen. In some cases, developers find this feature helpful because the grid helps the developer place items accurately—other developers find the grid distracting because the form doesn't appear to the developer, as it will to the user. The SnapToGrid property tells the IDE to snap items to the grid automatically when the LayoutMode is SnapToGrid.

FIGURE 4.11
Change the grid characteristics as needed to create a workable and well-designed form.

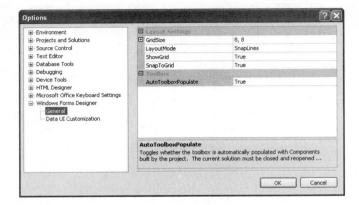

CONSIDERING THE DOWNSIDE OF USING A LAYOUT

Web sites have used tables for many years as an organizational aid. For the most part, it's a natural decision. The only problem is that tables can cause problems for anyone with special needs or less than the optimal display area. For example, a Web page that uses tables for organization might look great on your desktop machine, but someone using a Pocket PC might see just one square (hopefully, the right square). A page that flows well works best because just about any device can see it, even if the viewing experience is lengthy due to the page size. Given that many people use small devices to view Web pages today, the screen real estate question is a very real concern.

Tables can also cause some compatibility problems because not every browser displays tables the same way or uses the same functionality. A special effect that looks great with Internet Explorer might not display well when using Mozilla or Firefox. The problem is that the standards groups have provided general guidelines for tables, but many of the specifics are vendor specific.

Finally, imagine that you're blind and trying to discover the layout of a Web page by listening to a description of its layout. Listening to a description of a table used for layout, rather than content, is akin to listening to four or five radio stations at the same time and trying to enjoy each of the songs. You can do it, but it's difficult and there are possibly better things to do with your time. The problem is that the table doesn't contain descriptive information when used as a layout, so the screen reader moves from topic to topic without informing the listener of the change or making it clear that the change has occurred.

Tables do have some positive points and you don't always have to avoid using them. For one thing, using tables for layout is better than using frames, which have more severe compatibility problems and are an even bigger nightmare for anyone with special needs. Frames can also pose security risks that many users are unwilling to face today. Another potential problem with frames that you can overcome using tables is that search engines usually display the frame page that contains the content—rather than the container page. In some cases, this means the user doesn't have any way to navigate the size because the navigational aids appear in another frame that isn't displayed. Consequently, when you must organize the data on your Web site and none of the organizational techniques in the "Organizing the Web Page" section of Chapter 21 will work, then using a layout is the best alternative.

Creating a Project with Master Pages

Once you have a master page defined, you can use it to create content pages. A content page has all of the content and organization provided by the master page, plus unique content that the individual page provides. You can use master pages to create content pages in a number of ways. The following sections explore the techniques that you'll commonly use.

SELECTING USER INTERFACE DESIGN RESOURCES

Getting great user interface design references helps you get started faster and ensures you won't make as many mistakes during the design process. Typically, you'll find that books are better than Web sites for this kind of information because books have more space to cover contingencies that articles or other online resources can't discuss. However, don't discount Web sites—you might find something that meets a specific need. Newsgroups can help, but you need to state the design issues you want to overcome very clearly and take any advice with a grain of salt because the developer helping you might not have a clear picture of the issues.

You can find a number of good books online. The trick is to find a book that is either completely generic or meets the need of a specific environment. For example, if you want to design a Web application, then you might consider reading *Designing Web Usability : The Practice of Simplicity* by Dr. Jakob Nielsen (New Riders, 1999). Although Web developers could rely on this book, desktop developers can benefit most from *The Humane Interface: New Directions for Designing Interactive Systems* by Jef Raskin (Addison-Wesley, 2000). Good generic books include *Developer to Designer: GUI Design for the Busy Developer* by Mike Gunderloy (Sybex, 2005) and *Designing Highly Useable Software* by Jeff Cogswell (Sybex, 2004).

It's possible to find good help online. For example, the Microsoft User Interface site at `http://msdn.microsoft.com/library/en-us/dnanchor/html/anch_uidesigndev.asp` provides a wealth of information on topics as diverse as accessibility and Microsoft Agent. Dr. Jakob Nielsen presents a number of usability articles at `http://www.useit.com/alertbox/`. This monthly column can provide continuing help with your application as user needs and expectations change. In some cases, you can even find online books such as *Task-Centered User Interface Design* by Clayton Lewis and John Rieman at `http://www.hcibib.org/tcuid/`. The authors offer this book as shareware, so make sure you support them if you use it.

Locating a newsgroup that offers advice on user interfaces isn't hard—it's hard to find good advice. Generally, you'll need to find a newsgroup that caters to your language and choice of device (such as the .NET Compact Framework for mobile devices at `microsoft.public.dotnet.framework.compact framework`). Some newsgroups, such as `comp.human-factors` provide limited generic help should you need it. After many hours of searching, I couldn't find a suitable newsgroup devoted to the topic of user interfaces. Contact me at `JMueller@mwt.net` if you know of such a newsgroup and I'll post it on my Web site with the updates for this book.

Creating a Content Page Using a Master Page

Adding content pages doesn't have to be cumbersome or time consuming. The easiest method for creating a content page based on master page is to open the master page, right-click anywhere on the form in Design view, and choose Add Content Page from the context menu. The IDE creates a new content page that uses default settings and a generic name based on the master page. Figure 4.12

shows typical results of using this method. Notice the grayed out areas—the developer can't modify this information in the content page. However, the developer can interact with the two content areas and remove the instructions as necessary.

NOTE   Most of the ABC Incorporated Web site pages use a master page unless using such a page would interfere with the current example. The Default.ASPX page uses the master page discussed in this section of the chapter, so you can see how the page looks when filled out. The page is fully functional, so you can interact with it as you would any page on a standard Web site.

Another way to create a content page using a master page is to right-click the project entry in Solution Explorer. Choose Add New Item from the context menu and you'll see the Add New Item dialog box. Select the Web Form option, choose a programming language, and type a name for the file. Click the Select Master Page option in this dialog box. Click Add. Normally, you'd see the new page, at this point, but, in this case, you don't—you see the Select a Master Page dialog box shown in Figure 4.13 instead.

As you can see, this is a standard selection dialog box, but it's limited to the current project. You can't choose master pages that reside in other projects because there isn't any guarantee that the other project will even exist on the Web server you use to deploy your project. The limitations of this dialog box are actually a safety feature that ensures your content page has the best possible chance of working. Content pages typically rely on the master page for the <html>, <head>, <body>, and other standard tags, so they might even display without the presence of the master page. Choose a master page from the list and click OK. The IDE creates the required content page for you.

FIGURE 4.12
Content pages are just a few clicks away when you have the master page open.

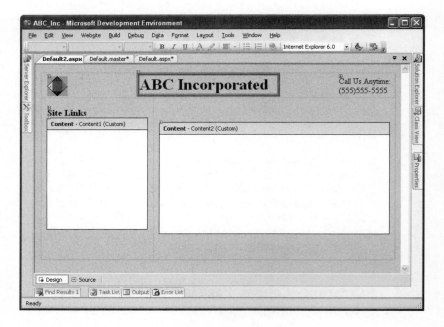

FIGURE 4.13
Choose a master page for
your new Web Form us-
ing any resource in the
current project.

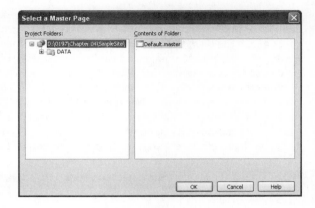

TIP   You can change the master page filename if necessary without resorting to hand editing the code. Open the Properties window and select DOCUMENT from the list of objects. You'll see a list of page-related properties including the `MasterPageFile` property. Change this property to modify the master page that a document uses. Unfortunately, the change in master pages will probably mean hand editing any content areas to match the ID of any `ContentPlaceHolder` controls in the new master page.

Adding a Master Page to an Existing Web Page

You might create a Web page and only then discover that you forgot to attach the master page to it. Theoretically, with careful editing, you can recover from the error, but it's not easy. Generally, if you can recreate the page using one of the techniques in the "Creating a Content Page Using a Master Page" section, you'll save time and effort. If you created the master page as an afterthought, you need to perform the tasks outlined here.

1. Add the appropriate attributes to the page declaration (the `<%@ Page %>` tag) at the top of the file. As a minimum, you need to provide a `MasterPageFile` attribute such as `MasterPageFile="~/Default.master"` and a `Title` attribute such as `title="Untitled Page"`. At this point, you could view the page in Design view and actually see the effect of the master page, but it wouldn't work correctly.

2. Remove the `<!DOCTYPE>`, `<html>`, `<head>`, `<body>`, `<form>`, and `<title>` tags as a minimum (along with the associated closing tags). Any common scripts that normally appear as part of the `<head>` tag should appear in the master page, not the content page, so move the code as needed. At this point, the page should work in a browser, but you won't see your old content—it's not part of an `<asp:Content>` tag.

3. Enclose the existing content in an `<asp:Content>` tag. This tag must include `id`, `Content PlaceHolderID`, and `Runat` attributes. Here's a typical example of an `<asp:Content>` tag for the example master page.

```
<asp:Content ID="Content2"
             ContentPlaceHolderID="MainContent"
             Runat="server">
```

The ID is always unique, but you don't have to provide anything specific. Use a name that you can remember easily in case you have to write code for the content area. The `ContentPlaceHolderID` must match the ID of the `ContentPlaceHolder` control in the master page. This value provides linkage between the content page and the master page. Finally, all pages of this type must run at the server, so you always provide a `Runat="server"` entry.

Sometimes the first conversion attempt fails. In fact, you could experience several failures before you get the page just right. Unfortunately, Visual Web Developer doesn't display a simple message saying you failed—instead you get the odd looking page shown in Figure 4.14. This page does contain useful information that Chapter 17 discusses in detail. For now, all you need to know is that this page tells you that the conversion is incomplete and you need to look again at the changes you made.

FIGURE 4.14
Errors can and will occur when you convert your existing pages to use a master page.

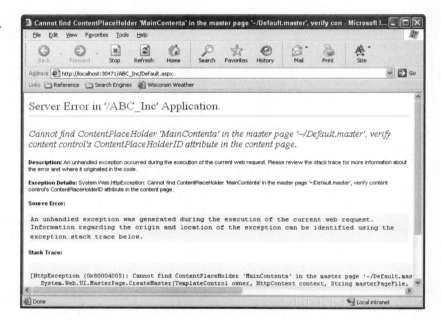

Using Multiple Master Pages in a Project

A Web site can include more than one master page. For example, you might want one look for pages that have static content, another for survey pages, and still another for pages that contain sales figures or other dynamic content. However, it's best to start by creating a simple Web site that contains just one master page. As the Web site grows, you can add other master pages as needed to serve specific needs.

One thing to remember about master pages is that you can't nest them—a master page can't create another master page. Consequently, when you use multiple master pages, you have to update each master page individually. This is the reason that many developers create a single master page and then augment the master page content using themes or other functionality. Of course, then the master page can become quite generic and not very useful in the construction of a Web site. The decision is ultimately yours—you need to consider the trade-offs of the various options at your disposal.

There are a number of reasons to use multiple master pages. The best reason is that you have more kinds of content to cover than a single master page can accommodate. Look again at the example master page in Figure 4.9. While this design works fine for a content page, it wouldn't work very well for a feedback page or an order form. You'd need to create other kinds of master pages to serve those needs.

Understanding Themes

Anyone who's used themes in Windows has a basic understanding of themes in Visual Web Developer. In addition, products such as FrontPage have used themes to good effect. As with Windows and FrontPage themes, Visual Web Developer themes appear in a special folder within the project called Themes. You create a special folder to hold each theme you want to use and place resources within those folders. A theme includes a number of elements such as graphics and formatting information. The idea is to create a concept for your Web page that defines how the page should look. By applying the same theme to every Web page, you can create a consistent look that gives your Web page a professional appearance that users will like.

A theme modifies the appearance of a Web page, but it isn't part of the Web page. Any change you make to the theme will also appear in the Web page. Consequently, if you decide that a font used to display the company's copyright notice is too small, you can change it in the theme and know the change will affect all of the documents that use the theme. Like master pages, themes make it possible to produce global changes that ease development and maintenance requirements.

Like master pages, you must create a link between the theme and any Web pages that rely on it. Unlike master pages, themes are relatively unobtrusive from a coding perspective and you can add them at any time. For that matter, as long as your themes are compatible and provide similar resources, you can switch between themes at any point. Even though you'll define the theme connection using the Theme property of the DOCUMENT object, it's important to know what goes on in the background. All that the IDE does is add a Theme attribute such as the one that follows to the page directive at the top of the coding area.

```
Theme="MyTheme"
```

Once you add this attribute, all of the features of the theme become available to the Web page. Should you decide later not to use the theme, you can simply remove any resources the theme provides from the page (such as special buttons or images) and then remove the Theme attribute from the page declaration.

NOTE   When you want to use the styles and formatting provided by a theme, but not the content, add the theme name to the StylesheetTheme attribute instead of the Theme attribute. All of the SKIN file information is also available when you use this technique—the only thing missing is any content, such as predefined button names. (A SKIN file defines the appearance of the user interface, but not the inner workings of that interface, just as your skin defines your outward appearance.)

The Web page requires a second level of connectivity to make the use of themes complete. You must attach the specific theme entries to the various elements. When working with a SKIN file value, you'll make this entry in the SkinID property for the control. Likewise, when working with a CSS file entry, you'll make the entry in the Class property.

Designing Your Own Themes

Themes can be a little complicated to create, but it's definitely worth the effort. To keep things simple, work on a small portion of the theme at a time. That way you won't get too mired in complexity immediately. You do need to perform four essential steps to create a theme as follow.

1. Create the Themes folder.
2. Define a CSS file for the theme.
3. Define the SKIN file for the theme.
4. Add any required resources.

You won't necessarily perform these steps one time or even in order. Of course, you have to create a Themes folder before you can do anything, but you might find that you need more than one theme and will add to it later. The following sections describe the process for creating a theme.

Creating a Themes Folder

The Themes folder must appear as part of the root directory for your project and it can't include any resources—only subfolders that will act as theme names. To add the new folder to your project, right-click the project entry in Solution Explorer and choose New Folder from the context menu. You'll see a new folder added to the display. Type **Themes** as the new folder name and press Enter.

Now it's time to create the theme. Right-click the Themes folder and choose New Folder from the context menu. Again, you'll see a new folder added to Solution Explorer, but this one will appear in the \Themes folder. Type the name of the theme you want to create, such as **MyTheme**. The \Themes\MyTheme folder will hold all of the resources for the MyTheme theme.

When your theme includes images, you'll want to create an additional subfolder to hold them. Right-click the theme folder (MyTheme for the example) and choose New Folder from the context menu. Type **Images** as the new folder name and press Enter. Copy any resources that the theme will use into the Images folder for that theme.

Defining a CSS File for a Theme

Most themes include a CSS file that defines the formatting characteristics of any tags you want to use. You must add this file to the theme folder. Right-click the theme folder (\Themes\MyTheme in the example) and choose Add New Item from the context menu. You'll see an Add New Item dialog box. Select Style Sheet from the template list. Type a name for the CSS file. You can use any name desired, but it makes sense to give this file the same name as the theme (MyTheme.CSS in the example). Click Add and you'll see the double-sided CSS display.

Make sure you provide formatting for both standard elements and special classes you want to use. The "Creating and Using a CSS File" section of this chapter shows you how to define a CSS file. Once you finish applying the changes, save the file.

Defining the SKIN File and Adding Theme Resources

The SKIN file contains definitions of the various controls. You can approach this task in two ways—create a single SKIN file for all of the controls or create individual SKIN files for each control. Using the single file is the best approach because it's less confusing and you're less likely to lose one of the files.

Unfortunately, you won't find a SKIN file template, so you'll use the Text File template instead. To add the SKIN file, right-click the template folder and choose Add New Item from the context menu. You'll see the Add New Item dialog box. Select the Text File template and type a filename ending with a SKIN extension (MyTheme.SKIN for the example).

Now it's time to create control definitions for the SKIN file. The definition should never include any identifying or unique information such as the ID property or the caption for a button, unless you plan to use that value for every control and the value won't cause a conflict. Here's the easiest way to create these definitions

1. Create a scrap page.

2. Select Design view on the scrap page and place the control you want to create on the scrap page.

3. Configure the control. Make sure you include all common properties but avoid configuring properties that will change from control to control.

4. Type a value in the SkinID property. This value identifies the control within the SKIN file.

5. Select Source view and highlight the line containing the control you want to create. Make sure you copy everything between the beginning and ending tag or the control definition won't work.

6. Click Copy to place the control definition on the clipboard.

7. Select the SKIN file and click Paste. You'll see the control definition displayed in the SKIN file.

8. Repeat steps 2 through 7 for every control you want to add to the SKIN file.

You can add any number and type of controls to the SKIN file. The only requirement is that the control provides some kind of common functionality. For example, if every one of the survey forms you create includes a Submit Survey button, then you should create this button once and place it in the SKIN file, rather than create the button every time you need it. Here's an example of two controls entered in a SKIN file.

```
<asp:Button AccessKey="C"
            Runat="server"
            Text="Click Me"
            ToolTip="Click this button."
            BorderStyle="Ridge"
            BorderWidth="6px"
            SkinID="ClickMeButton" />

<asp:Image Runat="server"
            BorderStyle="Ridge"
            BorderWidth="6px"
            ImageUrl="Images/TestImage.gif"
            AlternateText="A test image."
            Height="50px"
            Width="50px"
            SkinID="LogoIcon" />
```

Notice that neither of the controls contains specific information except the button control. Because this is a specific kind of button—one that always contains the Click Me caption, it includes the Text property value. The AccessKey property lets keyboard users access the button using Alt+C, rather than using the mouse. The ToolTip property provides explanatory information for people who use accessibility devices and helps other users understand the purpose of the button. The BorderStyle and BorderWidth are actually a decorative element in this case. Finally, the SkinID property contains the name that identifies this particular button—every SkinID is unique.

The <asp:Image> tag includes many similar property values such as the border information and SkinID. Notice that the ImageUrl property points to a theme resource without providing a precise theme name. This technique ensures you can use the same SKIN file in multiple themes simply by varying the resources that the theme uses and the kind of formatting it provides. The AlternateText property provides an image description for users who require accessibility aids. Finally, because this is a logo and not an image you might want to resize later, the Height and Width properties contain the logo size.

At this point, you should have a preliminary theme that you'll improve as you test it with your Web site. Figure 4.15 shows a typical simple theme setup. Of course, the theme you create might have multiple SKIN files or it could include other kinds of resource folders (such as Sounds or Multimedia).

FIGURE 4.15
Carefully crafted themes can save the developer time and effort creating consistent pages.

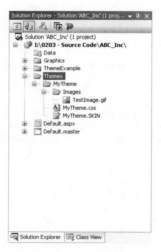

Creating a Simple Project Using Themes

Projects that use themes are similar to those that don't. The only difference is that you have the initial step of creating the theme. This initial step is important because it forces you to think about the project particulars before you begin creating any pages. For example, you must consider how to format the text and how it should appear on screen. A theme helps you consider the functionality of controls and ensures that you've considered all of the resources before you get them on the page. In short, themes aren't just a means of designing pages more efficiently, they're a productivity aid as well. The following sections describe several simple project types you can create using themes.

Applying a Theme to a Page

Once you have a theme created, you need to test it. After all, you might not have thought about everything the first time. The best way to test a theme is to create a test ASPX file using the Web Form template. All you need to do is create an ASPX file using the standard technique since the Add New Item dialog box doesn't offer any special means of connecting the theme file to the Web page. The ABC Incorporated Web site contains an example of a Web page that uses a theme, rather than a master page, in the \ThemeExample folder. You can access this example directly from the main Web site page if desired.

After you create the Web page, open the Properties window. Select DOCUMENT in the list of objects and locate the Theme property, as shown in Figure 4.16. If you configured the directory structure correctly, you'll see a listing of any themes you created in the dropdown list. This is actually the first test of your theme. When you don't see your theme listed, you know that you didn't create the directory structure correctly and need to fix this error. Notice that the dropdown list also includes the standard themes that Microsoft provides. Depending on your installation, you should see at least two standard themes in addition to those provided by your Web application. Enterprise developers might want to choose one of these standard themes for the sake of consistency since they appear on every developer machine.

At this point, you can begin adding controls to your Web page. Whenever you add a control that uses one of the items in the SKIN file, don't make any configuration changes to it. Begin by typing the name of the skin you want to use in the SkinID property for the control. This example only includes two controls in the SKIN file, so the test page uses those two items: ClickMeButton and LogoIcon.

TIP This is one time where using Source view is actually easier than using Design view. Select the control you want to modify in Design view, switch to Source view, and add a new SkinID attribute to the end of the control. As soon as you type the = (equals sign), IntelliSense presents you with a list of SkinID values for that control. You won't see any other SkinID values. This technique ensures you type the SkinID value correctly.

FIGURE 4.16
Verify that Visual Web Developer can locate the themes that you create.

The IDE won't show the changes that the SKIN makes to your page in Design view, but you can see them when you view the page in a browser. To see the changes made to the controls, right-click anywhere on the form and choose View in Browser from the context menu.

You can customize the controls after you create the required layout and assign the `SkinID` values. It's important to remember that you can't change properties that the SKIN file assigns. For example, when you create an `<asp:Button>` tag with a `Text` property value, every control will have that `Text` property value. The only property values that you can change are those that the SKIN file doesn't specify. Consequently, in the case of the example, you could change the width of the `Button` control, but not its caption.

Adding styles to various elements comes next. You work with styles from a theme precisely the way that you use them when working with a style sheet. The "Working with CSS in the Web Page" section of the chapter describes this process in detail.

Applying a Theme to a Web Site

You don't have to apply themes to Web pages one at a time. When you decide to use the same theme for the entire Web site, you can apply it just once by creating a special Web configuration file. To add the Web configuration file, right-click the project entry in Solution Explorer and choose Add New Item from the context menu. You'll see the Add New Item dialog box. Choose the Web Configuration File template and click Add (you can change the filename if desired, but it's not necessary since your Web site only has one configuration file). The IDE creates a new CONFIG file.

The Web configuration file contains a number of entries when you initially create it. You'll find references to these other entries as the book progresses. Locate the `<System.Web>` element. Add a new element to this hierarchy named `<pages>`. This element defines page characteristics for your Web site. In this case, you want to add a `themes` attribute that points to the theme you want to use. Your entry should look similar to the one shown here.

```
<configuration
    xmlns="http://schemas.microsoft.com/.NetConfiguration/v2.0">

    ... Other Entries ...
    <system.web>

        <!-- Tells the System to use MyTheme for all pages. -->
        <pages theme="MyTheme" />

        ... Other Entries ...

    </system.web>
</configuration>
```

Notice that the example includes a comment describing the entry. Always add a comment whenever you make a change to the CONFIG file. Otherwise, you'll look at this file later and wonder what task the entry performs.

Now every Web page you create will use the global theme unless you specifically override the choice by setting the theme for the individual page. A page-level theme declaration always overrides the global theme.

Working with Cascading Style Sheets (CSS)

CSS is perhaps the most useful Web technology that you can learn from an efficiency perspective. Not only will CSS save time and effort formatting the text and controls on your Web site, but it's also a standard technology. You can use CSS on any Web page running from any server and reasonably expect that most people will see the formatting you want to provide—or, at least, a reasonable facsimile. Not every browser renders (interprets and displays) CSS precisely the same, but most do provide an adequate interpretation. The following sections describe how to use CSS.

NOTE Even though Visual Studio doesn't make an issue out of the version of CSS you use for a theme, you might want to know about the different versions and CSS history and part of discovering this very useful technology. You can learn more about CSS on the W3C Web site at http://www.w3.org/Style/CSS/.

Using the Style Sheet Toolbar

The Style Sheet toolbar (access it by right-clicking the toolbar area and choosing Style Sheet from the context menu) contains buttons that make performing most CSS editing tasks easier. Figure 4.17 shows what this toolbar looks like. The following list describes each of the button functions.

Cascading Style Sheet Version for Validation Determines the rules used to validate the CSS file entries. Older versions are more restrictive, but also less liable to create compatibility problems. The list also includes a special Internet Explorer 6.0 entry that helps you tailor the CSS file to this specific browser.

View in Browser Creates a special test page that includes a number of standard tags you can use to verify the appearance of your CSS page. The IDE doesn't actually open an external browser—it uses an internal page instead. Although this is a good way to check your entries quickly, you'll also want to test the CSS entries with your Web site to ensure the entries actually work as intended.

Build Style Displays the Style Builder dialog box you use to define an existing style. See the "Creating and Using a CSS File" section for details.

Add Style Rule Displays the Add Style Rule dialog box you use to add a new style to the CSS file. See the "Creating and Using a CSS File" section for details.

FIGURE 4.17
Quickly edit a CSS file using the features provided on this toolbar.

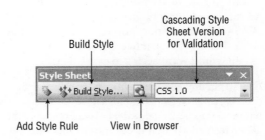

Designing Flexible Interfaces

No matter how well you design your application, someone will complain that some feature doesn't work as expected. During my years of programming, I've personally seen arguments between users about the order of fields on a form. One discussion about a screen degenerated into an intense argument about the order of name elements on the form (one user wanted last name first, the other wanted the first name to appear first). Users will grumble about every aspect of your application given a chance and you'll never satisfy all the users. Some developers solve the problem by giving up and creating the application they want. However, this solution probably works least often because the user's immediate reaction is that the developer isn't listening and lacks any form of human interaction skills.

Flexible user interfaces resolve the user problem by letting each user design the interface that meets their specific needs. Just how flexible you can make the interface depends on a number of factors including the application environment and the programming language you use. Making Web applications flexible is somewhat harder than most desktop applications because many browsers lack the support required to move visual elements around and perform other manipulations the user would like. Depending on your programming skill, schedule, programming language, and patience, you can make some desktop applications so flexible that the user has control over every display element and the application will remember its configuration between sessions.

Let's start with something a little more reasonable than complete application configuration. Even the most mundane Web page allows configuration. For example, you can use Cascading Style Sheets (CSS) to format the Web page. Some browsers let the user substitute their CSS file for the default that you provide on your Web site—making it possible for the user to have complete control over the presentation of information even if you don't provide any other form of programming with the Web page. Some sites extend this principle by providing multiple CSS files. A simple cookie entry controls which CSS file the Web site uses when presenting information to the user. Desktop applications are even easier to control in this area. All you need is an Options dialog box containing the display element settings so the user can change them to meet specific needs. Most desktop applications already provide this feature. Make sure you save the user options in a file or other central location (such as the Windows Registry) if you offer this feature.

The next level of application configuration is component selection. For example, not every user will want to sort the output results. It might seem that simply ignoring the sort field would work, but unnecessary fields are annoying to some users. Again, Web pages can use a cookie to store a list of fields or controls the user doesn't want to see. You'll likely have to provide a configuration page to support this form of configuration—adding a simple link to the page to allow configuration usually works fine. Desktop applications can use an Options dialog box. Most desktop applications don't offer this feature—probably because the developer didn't think to offer the feature or assumed that everyone would want access to every field.

> **NOTE** Don't make every field on a form optional. A user will have to make some entries to perform even basic tasks. For example, a user can't perform an author search without entering an author name, so the author name field isn't optional. However, hiding optional fields can make the application faster and easier to use. You might even find that you want to include some developer-only fields in the list that you control with special entries in the configuration file.

Web applications don't commonly use toolbars or special menus in the same way that desktop applications use them. However, both environments can benefit from some level of customization for both items. Quite a few desktop applications offer this feature. Generally, the user selects a special menu command that allows them to move menu or toolbar elements around, add new menu or toolbar options, or delete options the user feels aren't important. Trying to implement this feature on a Web site would be very hard, but doable, if you use some technologies such as ASP.NET. Make sure you offer a feature that returns everything to its default state in case the user makes a few too many changes.

The ultimate level of interface flexibility lets the user move controls around on screen. This feature lets one user place names in last name order and another user place them in first name order. Complete interface control is difficult to implement on a desktop application and likely impossible for a Web application. Applications that allow complete interface configuration are extremely rare. However, you'll find that some applications don't suffer from the same level of complexity that other applications do, so this might be a viable solution in some cases. At least you can provide the user with enough flexibility to define precisely how the display appears so that your application works as efficiently for that user as possible.

NOTE If you plan to provide complete interface flexibility for your application, you should go all the way by allowing the user to change even mundane features such as font size and typeface. To an extent, you could even let the user change the button captions and control the color of the tiniest text element. It's even possible to let the user add graphics and perform other odd configuration changes given the right programming language, a platform that supports the changes, and enough time.

Creating and Using a CSS File

CSS files aren't very difficult to create—the biggest problem is deciding how to specify in text the formatting options that you normally see graphically on screen. Every CSS file entry consists of three components as follows.

Selector The value that defines how a browser selects a particular formatting definition contained in a Web page.

Property The formatting element that you want to define, such as the font face, color, or size, for a particular selector.

Value The actual formatting information. For example, when working with a color, you might set the value to blue.

Most CSS files use three selector types. The element selector depends on the kind of element. For example, you could define a selector for the <H1> tag. The class selector uses a keyword as a definition. You supply this keyword as part of the element description on a Web page to invoke the selector. The element identifier (ID) relies on the ID value of an element as a selector. This definition will affect one element at most on any Web page because every element has a unique element ID.

When you create a CSS file, the IDE automatically creates a <Body> tag selector for you because most developers create a baseline configuration for the page. The baseline configuration affects all elements contained within the <Body> tag. To configure a tag, place the cursor between the two curly brackets for the body selector in the CSS file. Click Build Style and you'll see the Style Builder dialog box shown in Figure 4.18.

FIGURE 4.18
Use the Style Builder dialog box to add properties and values to a selector.

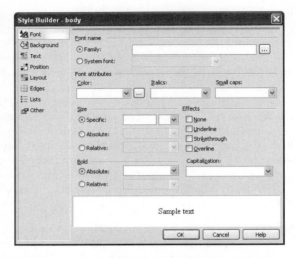

You don't have to fill out every property contained with the Style Builder dialog box—only fill out those properties that you actually want to change. For example, you might decide to change the font color to Blue (on the Font tab), the background color to PaleTurquoise (on the Background tab), the horizontal alignment to justified (on the Text tab), and the indentation to 6 pixels (px). Click OK once you make the changes. Here's what the resulting body selector looks like.

```
body
{
    color: blue;
    text-indent: 6px;
    background-color: paleturquoise;
    text-align: justify;
}
```

Of course, you can't define everything by using a single selector—you'll want specific formatting for other items as well. Most developers begin by defining the formatting for all of the elements they intend to use on a page. To create a new selector, place the cursor on the last empty line (press Enter if necessary to create a new blank line) and click Add Style Rule. You'll see the Add Style Rule dialog box shown in Figure 4.19.

Notice that you can choose from three kinds of selectors: Element, Class Name, and Element ID. When you choose the Element option, you choose the element you want to define from the dropdown list. This list box contains an amazing number of elements—at least most of the comment elements and a few of the uncommon elements as well. When working with the other entry types, simply provide the class name or the ID of the object you want to modify. You don't have to add any special characters to the entries—Visual Web Developer takes care of the special characters for you. After you create the new selector, define its properties just as you did for the <Body> tag earlier.

The CSS file editing display also includes a special view on the left side of the display. This display categorizes the selectors you create and makes it easy to find the one you need. All you have to do is click on the appropriate entry. Figure 4.20 shows the Visual Web Developer CSS editor display. Notice that the highlighting the IDE provides (even though you can't see the color in the figure) makes it very easy to see the selector you've chosen in the left pane on the right side of the display.

FIGURE 4.19
Add new selectors to the
CSS file using the Add
Style Rule dialog box.

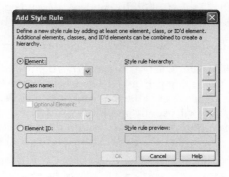

FIGURE 4.20
The use of color coding
makes it easy to see en-
tries—the hierarchical
display makes it easy to
find selectors.

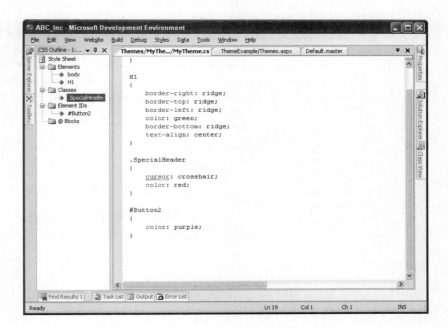

Working with CSS in the Web Page

You'll find it very easy to work with CSS on a Web page because most of the entries are automatic. To begin, you must tell the Web page to use the CSS file. When working with a theme, the theme makes the required entry for you automatically. However, when you use a CSS file by itself, you must add the name of the CSS file to the StyleSheet property of the DOCUMENT object (simply select DOCUMENT in the Properties window). Click the ellipsis next to the field entry and you'll see a Select Stylesheet dialog box that you can use to locate the CSS file on your hard drive.

Most of the entries work automatically. When you create an element or element ID selector, the CSS file works automatically. The class selector requires a little more work. You must select the element that you want to work with and then type the name of the style you want to use in the Class property. This is another case where working in Source view can prove helpful because you can also type the Class attribute by hand and depend on IntelliSense to provide you with useful information. For example, here's <H1> tag with a Class attribute.

```
<H1 Class="SpecialHeader">Header Using CSS</h1>
```

This header will use the properties defined in the .SpecialHeader selector. The interesting thing about CSS is that you only define what you need. If the standard H1 selector provides formatting not found in the .SpecialHeader selector, CSS will continue using the H1 selector formatting. Likewise, all headers will use any properties you define in the Body selector that don't appear in the H1 selector. When working with CSS it's important to remember that a property always has a value once you define it and that you have to override any values you want to change.

Working with Microsoft Using the Web Toolbar

Microsoft provides some help information with Visual Web Developer and you can look at additional resources online. Using the internal help system means that you can find information quickly without leaving the IDE. You can set this option in the Help folder of the Options dialog box you access using the Tools ➢ Options command. Select between the internal and external help format using the Show Help Using field setting. When you do use internal help, you also have access to the Web toolbar for working with help. Figure 4.21 shows this toolbar and the following list describes the various toolbar elements.

FIGURE 4.21
Interact with internal help or directly with Microsoft to learn more about Visual Web Developer.

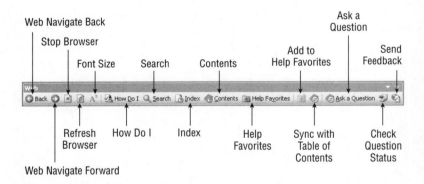

Send Feedback   Sends feedback about the product to Microsoft. When you click this option, the IDE displays a survey type form that you fill out and submit. Someone at Microsoft will review your suggestion and possibly implement it. You generally don't receive feedback when using this option.

Ask a Question and Check Question Status   Accesses the Microsoft newsgroups. When you click Ask a Question, the IDE displays a list of newsgroups where you can ask a question. Click Check Question Status later to determine whether someone has answered your query. This feature relies on a combination of peer and Microsoft help (with a strong emphasis on peer help). When you click Check Question Status, the IDE checks your messages on the newsgroups and provides any feedback you've received.

Sync with Table of Contents   Synchronizes an entry in the Search dialog box or the Index with the table of contents. This feature lets you see where the current topic appears in the hierarchical topic listing. Often, this feature can help you locate related topics that other search techniques might not find. For example, you could use it to locate the next step in a procedure.

Help Favorites and Add to Help Favorites   Displays and adds a topic to the Help Favorites listing in the Help Favorites dialog box. Click Help Favorites to display the Help Favorites dialog box. You can click any of the entries in the Help Topics or Help Searches listings to revisit parts of the help system that you visited previously. Click Add to Help Favorites when you want to add a new topic to the listing. This feature ensures that you can locate hard-to-find topics when you need them.

Contents, Index, and Search   Displays the Contents, Index, or Search features of the help system. You use these three features to locate topics in the help system. Contents provides a hierarchical display of help topics. Index displays an alphabetical list of common help topics. You can perform a word search using the search feature.

How Do I   Displays a list of how to articles for the product. You can select one of these topics to obtain step-by-step procedures for performing a given task.

Font Size   Modifies the font size of the Help view and associated windows. Larger fonts make the display easier to read and smaller fonts present more information in the same space.

Refresh Browser and Stop Browser   Controls the internal browser actions. The Help view is actually a browser and it displays Web pages. Refreshing the browser displays new content that the Web pages might contain after an update. You can click Stop Browser to end a long download.

Web Navigate Forward and Web Navigate Back   Moves to the next or previous page in the Web page history. The IDE maintains a record of the pages you visit, so you can move between pages you have already viewed. Click Forward when you want to move to the next page in the list and Back when you want to see the previous page.

Defining Your Development Goals

This is the first chapter to mention the concepts of layout, formatting, graphics, and design, but it won't be the last. The appearance of your Web application follows closely behind its content and usability. Unfortunately, at least a few Web sites seem to consider appearance as the only goal and fail in both content and usability. This chapter also helps you avoid that problem by keeping the issue of appearance where it belongs—as a means to dress up your content.

Now it's time to try these technologies yourself. The only problem with Microsoft's sample application is that it attempts to do everything. Consequently, it's easy to confuse the roles that the various technologies discussed in this chapter play and hard to see their advantages and disadvantages. A better way to work with these technologies at the outset is to create your own Web applications that use just one technology at first. When you're satisfied that you understand a single technology, move on to using two at a time, and finally try all three at once. Only after you've seen how the technologies work alone and together can you gain a full appreciation of what they can do for your Web application.

Most Web sites contain a mix of static and dynamic (changing) pages. A user might view a historical page about a company that doesn't require anything more than serving up the data. Another page might include a survey that asks the user about the Web experience—this page requires support by the server to process the input the user provides. Still another page could describe the current results of an ongoing event—this is where dynamic content comes into play. You don't know what the page will contain until it's time to serve it up. Chapter 5 helps you discover all of these kinds of interaction and more. It's your next step to creating a truly spectacular Web application.

Chapter 5

Building Intelligent Pages

Enterprise developers recognized long ago that maintaining static pages filled with HTML code isn't a very productive way to work with the Internet. Yes, this technique works fine for a small Web site, but you really need something better. Visual Web Developer provides the kind of page intelligence that enterprise developers need today. In fact, you can choose from several strategies when working with Web pages—everything from hefty content pages created with ASPX to ever changing content pages that rely on XML. This chapter not only points out the various techniques you can use to make your enterprise Web site more efficient, but also recommends strategies that you can mix with your current offerings to make content updates faster and more automatic.

Intelligence can occur in one of two places: the server or the client. This chapter helps you understand server-side intelligence, the kind that's used most often with complex Web development technologies such as database applications or those that have to service a broad range of device types. Chapter 6 discusses client-side intelligence, which offloads part of the processing burden from the server and provides better performance in many cases. The kind of intelligence you use for a Web application depends on the effect you're trying to produce and the level of trust the code must have. In some cases, you'll use both kinds of intelligence in one Web application.

Before you can choose which kind of intelligence to use, you need to know what you can do at each end of the communication. This chapter discusses several kinds of server-side communication that you can perform including such tasks as discovering the client browser and how it's configured, as well as simple form processing.

Finally, this chapter discusses an important user issue—one that's becoming increasingly important. Users have an expectation that you'll protect their identity from anyone outside your organization. They also expect you to keep their email address quiet and want to know precisely how you use any information they do provide. Although an individual Web site can still get by without a privacy policy—your enterprise Web site can't. Not having an enterprise-wide privacy policy in place (one that you actually follow) is an open invitation to lawsuits and legal action. This chapter addresses all of these issues.

NOTE For the purposes of this book, the term *cracker* will refer to an individual that's breaking into a system on an unauthorized basis. It also refers to someone who places software on your system without obtaining your permission first. *Cracking* includes any form of illegal activity on the system such as stealing your identity. On the other hand, the term *hacker* will refer to someone who performs authorized (legal) low-level system activities, including testing system security. Hackers also help find undocumented solutions for many computer needs and create workarounds for both hardware and software problems. In some cases, you need to employ the services of a good hacker to test the security measures you have in place, or suffer the consequences of a break-in.

Understanding Server-side Intelligence

An intelligent Web page includes some type of code—the component that provides the intelligence. Of course, the Web page isn't actually intelligent—it doesn't think or do anything creative, but it does react in a specific way to certain events based on the prerecorded instructions you provide. For example, an intelligent Web page can calculate a total based on the algorithm you provide. The location where the code executes determines certain characteristics of the intelligence. Server-side intelligence means that the server executes the code required to provide Web page intelligence, which provides the following characteristics.

Secure Data Processing   Using server-side processing reduces security risks for the company or individual providing the data because it provides better control over the data. Nothing leaves the server without getting checked and processed first—at least not if the code is written correctly.

Fewer Client Requirements   Clients come in all shapes and sizes, so you can't be sure the client will have the processing power required to perform any work locally. Even when the client has the required processing power, some browsers don't provide all the required support, so you can't tell whether the application will work unless you make a particular browser a requirement. Unfortunately, most browsers include configuration settings that let the user turn off scripting and cookies (with good reason given some of the crackers on the Internet today), so the right browser still doesn't mean that the application will run. In short, clients are unpredictable, so server-side processing is often necessary when you want to make certain that the application will run.

TIP   Make sure you differentiate between public and private Web sites when working in the corporate environment. Although you can't control public Web site participation very well, controlling private Web site participation is both easy and fast. Make sure you configure all systems on the network to use the same browser with the same patches and settings. Using this approach reduces the work required to test the Web site and reduces the support costs of the Web site as well. In addition, you don't expose a private Web site to the Internet, so you can enable features such as cookies and scripting without worry. In short, treat private Web sites differently from public Web sites because they really are different.

Consistent Results   Using server-side processing exclusively means that the client receives only HTML tags. With a little extra effort, you can ensure all of the clients you want to support understand the tags the server sends. The Webmonkey chart at `http://webmonkey.wired.com/webmonkey/reference/browser_chart/index.html` (and associated charts with links on this page) can help you determine the kinds of tags the clients you want to support can understand. For example, if you want to support Internet Explorer 4.0 users, then you can't use eXtensible Markup Language (XML) as an alternative form of data transmission.

Easier Debugging   Because the server sends out completed data and all of the processing occurs on the server, you don't have to worry about what the client is doing. The debugging process is easier because you don't have to consider as many variables when you create the application. All you really need to know is what you expect as input from the client, how the server processes that input, and what the client should get as output.

Better Stability and Reliability   Distributed applications do have many advantages, but they also incur stability and reliability problems. A distributed application—one that relies on a combination of client and server processing—is less stable because both systems must process the data without error and there's less tolerance for even small errors. Reliability also decreases as a factor of the number of failure points—adding client-side processing increases the number of failure points.

Server-side intelligence isn't a one-time process—it's ongoing, just as client-side processing is. The server can process information at several times and in a variety of ways. Here are the most common techniques.

Initial Request   A server can read the client's request header (the part of the message that describes the client and its request) during the initial request. It can then offer a response that better meets client needs or information in certain form.

NOTE   Normally, you don't need to worry much about the request or response headers for messages. Request headers are always part of a request message and describe the client making the request. For example, you can learn that the client can accept text output, but not some forms of graphical output. Response headers always describe the server and the processing it performs to the client. For example, when the server sends one response header, the client knows an error has occurred, but another response header tells the client that the request succeeded.

After Login   The login process, even when you don't see a login screen, requires an initial request, a server response requesting the login information, and a client response with the required login information. At this point, the server knows the identity of the client and can tailor the page content to meet that client's needs. Of course, this assumes there's a login process—many public Web sites don't include one.

Preprocessing   Preprocessing occurs after the server receives the request, but before it does anything with it. In many cases, this is the point in the cycle where the server decides what to do with the request—where to direct it. For example, a request might include invalid data, so the server would send it to an error response, rather than a data processing response. The error response would handle problems such as scripts sent in data fields, rather than the data the server was expecting.

Response   The response is the event that everyone thinks about when it comes to server-side processing. This part of the cycle looks at the input data, decides what to do with it, calculates any results, requests any information from the database, and puts an output page together. The response also considers some special user needs and customizes the output. For example, a potential customer accessing your Web site will require different information than a sales representative on the road.

Postprocessing   Sometimes a response requires additional tweaking or you might need to verify the response in some way. Postprocessing provides a means of looking at the entire message, including response headers, to ensure that the client will react in the right way.

Detecting the Client Configuration

The many charts and graphs available on the Internet depicting various browser capabilities and features point to one conclusion—knowing your client can help you provide a better experience for the user. For example, if you find that a client doesn't support I-frames (inline frames that let you embed data from multiple sources as objects in a Web page, instead of using multiple pages accessed from a master page as standard frames use), you can use standard frames or tables for organizational needs instead. A client that doesn't support graphics could use text descriptions instead. The possibilities are endless. The point is that you have to know something about the client to obtain the information.

The problem is that many users now run special applications that block your access to information about the client. You can't determine anything about the client because the user wants to remain completely anonymous. It's not that the user is being contrary or trying to make your life hard. Many Web sites prey on users by detecting them and following them wherever they go. The user ends up with tons of unwanted spam email, pop-ups, pop-unders (windows that appear under the browser in an attempt to be less intrusive), and, in some cases, even identity theft. For many users, your act of customization is a kind thought, but they'd rather not have it at the cost of their identity.

Developers use several techniques to work around this problem. One of the easiest is to ask the user if their browser supports a specific feature. The user selects an option on the Web page and you can customize the input as needed. The only problem is that this solution relies on the user to have the required knowledge—depending on your Web site, many users won't.

Right after you get over the blank expressions on the faces of some users, you can try another alternative. Many browsers now provide a means to let the user trust just your site, without trusting every site on the Internet. For example, when working with Internet Explorer, you can instruct the user to add your site to their Trusted Site zone. To perform this task, select the Tools ➤ Internet options command. You'll see the Options dialog box. Select the Security tab and highlight the Trusted Site entry to enable the Sites button shown in Figure 5.1.

FIGURE 5.1
Internet Explorer uses the concept of security zones to improve flexibility.

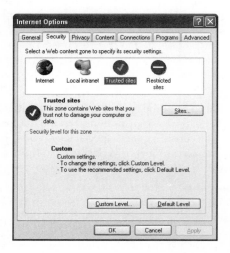

At this point, you can click Sites to display the Trusted Sites dialog box shown in Figure 5.2. Type the URL for the site you want to trust in the Add This Web Site to the Zone field and click Add. Click OK to make the change permanent. Generally, this change lets you detect the user's client configuration.

You can finally detect the client settings without asking the user many questions that the user might not know how to answer. This example uses the Load() event of the form to automatically process the client settings. This event occurs every time you load the form in the browser, so anything you place here happens before you actually see the form on screen. In this case, the form displays the client settings so you can see them, but normally you'll use the code to customize the Web page in some way. Because this example requires a different presentation than the standard Web page, it also uses a different master template. The InfoPage.MASTER page appears in Figure 5.3. You'll find this new master page in the \ABC_Inc folder of the source code on the Sybex Web site.

Listing 5.1 contains the code you need to perform this task. You'll find this example in the \ABC_Inc\ BrowserStats folder of the source code on the Sybex Web site.

FIGURE 5.2

Add the Web site you want to trust to the list of trusted sites.

FIGURE 5.3

Use the right master page for the job—this one provides a lot of display area.

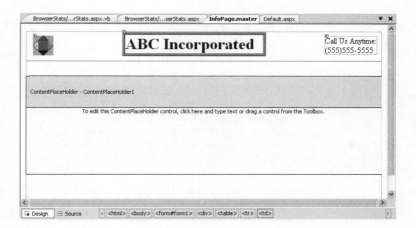

LISTING 5.1: Detecting the Browser Information

```
Private Sub form1_Load(ByVal sender As Object, _
                    ByVal e As System.EventArgs) Handles form1.Load

    Dim Output As New StringBuilder ' Contains the output information.
    Dim Counter As Int32            ' Loop counter variable.
    Dim AgentString As String()     ' A list of user agent values.

    ' Display a heading.
    Output.Append(vbTab + "<h1>Request Header Information</h1>" + _
            vbCrLf)

    ' Get the method used to request the information.
    Output.Append(vbTab + "<h2>Request Type</h2>" + vbCrLf)
    Output.Append(vbTab + vbTab + Request.HttpMethod + vbCrLf)

    ' Get the kind of files the client will accept.
    Output.Append(vbTab + "<h2>Client File Types</h2>" + vbCrLf)

    ' Get the number of file types.
    Output.Append(vbTab + vbTab + "Number of File Types: " + _
            Request.AcceptTypes.Length.ToString() + "</br>" + _
            vbCrLf)

    ' Get the individual file types.
    For Counter = 0 To Request.AcceptTypes.Length - 1
        Output.Append(vbTab + vbTab)
        Output.Append(Request.AcceptTypes.GetValue(Counter).ToString())
        Output.Append("</br>" + vbCrLf)
    Next

    ' Get the User Agent, which includes the browser type.
    AgentString = Request.UserAgent.Split(Convert.ToChar(";"))
    Output.Append(vbTab + "<h2>User Agent Information</h2>" + vbCrLf)
    For Counter = 0 To AgentString.Length - 1
        Output.Append(vbTab + vbTab)
        Output.Append(AgentString.GetValue(Counter).ToString().Trim())
        Output.Append("</br>" + vbCrLf)
    Next

    ' Get the browser capabilities, a special feature available to
    ' ASP.NET developers.
    Output.Append(vbTab + "<h2>Browser Capabilities</h2>" + vbCrLf)
    Output.Append(vbTab + vbTab + "Supports ActiveX Controls: ")
```

```
    Output.Append(IIf(Request.Browser.ActiveXControls, "Yes", "No"))
    Output.Append("</br>" + vbCrLf + vbTab + vbTab + _
                "America Online Browser: ")
    Output.Append(IIf(Request.Browser.AOL, "Yes", "No"))
    Output.Append("</br>" + vbCrLf + vbTab + vbTab + _
                "Plays Background Sounds: ")
    Output.Append(IIf(Request.Browser.BackgroundSounds, "Yes", "No"))

    ' Place the output on the form.
    lblOutput.Text = Output.ToString()
End Sub
```

This example shows a few techniques that can come in very handy when building a Web page using code. One of the techniques you might wonder about at first is the addition of all of the vbTab and vbCrLf constants in the code. You probably won't insert this code when creating a production application because you won't really care about the appearance of the code in the Web page. However, when you create code for testing purposes, the white space does matter. When you view this Web page, right-click the page and choose View Source from the context menu. You'll see the code that the server actually creates for the browser, including the code that you specifically output as shown in Figure 5.4. The highlighted code in Figure 5.4 shows the output that the code in Listing 5.1 produces.

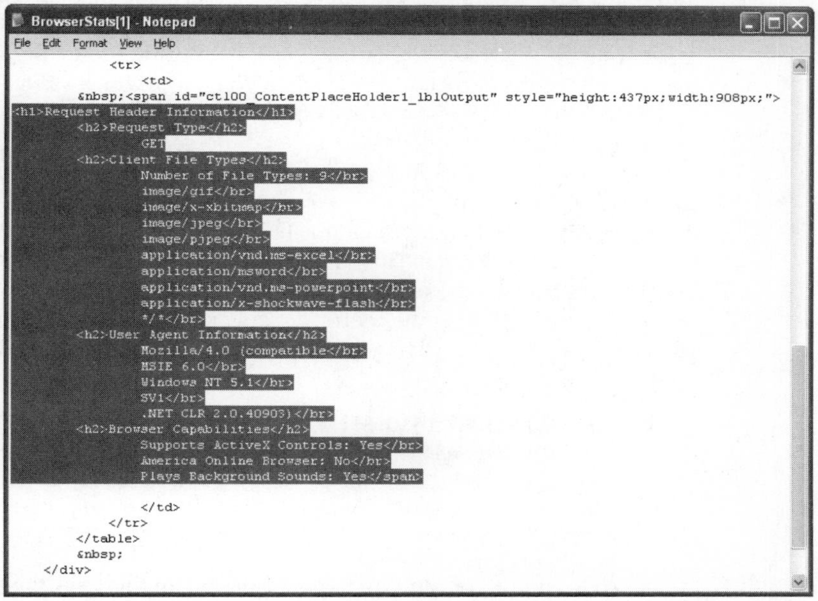

FIGURE 5.4
Adding white space is important when you want to view the code the server outputs.

The next element is the use of the `StringBuilder` control. Relying on the `StringBuilder` control, `Output`, provides a performance boost to the Web application. Standard `String` objects can't grow in Visual Basic, but `StringBuilder` objects can. Whenever you add text to a standard `String` in Visual Basic, CLR actually creates a new `String` object—it doesn't use the old one. Creating the new object takes time that you don't have to expend when using a `StringBuilder`. The downside to using a `StringBuilder` is that it does use more resources than a `String`—essentially, you're trading memory for improved performance in this case.

The example code shows several techniques for gaining access to information the client provides. All of the techniques rely on accessing the `Request` object—an object that you obtain automatically and don't have to create, it contains the request information from the client. A second object, `Response`, defines the information that the server sends to the client. You use the `Response` object to manipulate the output as a whole, rather than affect just a single page features.

The first technique shows how to obtain the request method from the client. The request method determines how the client and server communicate. The "Deciding between the GET and POST Data Handling Methods" section of the chapter describes this issue in more detail. However, look at the code in this case. You can access the `Request.HttpMethod` property directly—no manipulation needed.

The second technique shows that some of the information resides in arrays or collections. In this case, the `AcceptTypes` property is an array where you need to use the `GetValue()` method to obtain a specific element by passing an index (`Counter`). The code obtains the number of elements using the `AcceptTypes.Length` property and used this value to loop through the values.

The third technique shows how to work with encoded data. In this case, `UserAgent` is a string with multiple values separated by a semicolon (;). You could display the string directly, but you wouldn't work with this value as a string in an application. The code shows how to use the `Split()` method to separate the strings so you can examine them using a loop. It's also possible to use the `IndexOf()` method to locate a particular value when you know which value you need.

The fourth technique shows a special capability of ASP.NET. In this case, the code accesses the `Browser` object, which contains a number of Boolean property values. The example shows just a few of these values—there are many others and you should spend some time reviewing them. In this case, the code checks whether the browser supports ActiveX controls (`ActiveXControls` property), is a browser provided by America Online (`AOL` property), and supports background sounds using the `<BGSound>` tag (`BackgroundSounds` property). When a browser supports ActiveX controls but the user has this support turned off, the control appears as a box with a red X through it—you have no way of detecting whether the control actually works or not. You can place a message in the `<Object>` tag so the user sees the message, rather than the nondescript box. Simply type the text within the `<Object>` tag like this.

```
<OBJECT CLASSID="CLSID:812AE312-8B8E-11CF-93C8-00AA00C08FDF"
        ID="MyComponent">
   If you see this message without a corresponding pushbutton, then
   your browser doesn't support ActiveX controls.
</OBJECT>
```

The code ends by outputting the information. In this case, the example uses `lblOutput.Text` as the output. This label appears on the form as part of the standard content area provided by the master page. Figure 5.5 shows the output from this example.

FIGURE 5.5

The client can provide a lot of configuration information you can use to tailor a Web page.

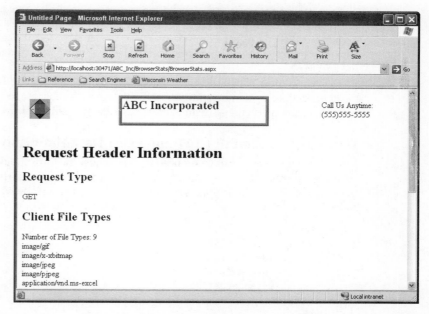

The output tells you a lot about the client. For example, this client used the GET method to access the Web site—this is the most common technique for an initial request unless the client already has intimate knowledge of the server (as when using a Web service). The */* output for file types tells you that this client can accept any file type—at least it will try to. However, this value doesn't necessarily mean that the client will understand the file or that the user can work with it—simply that the browser can accept the file.

The user agent information is especially interesting. Notice that it tells you that this browser is Mozilla compatible—a requirement for non-IIS Web servers in many cases. The next line tells you that the browser is Microsoft Internet Explorer 6.0 and that it's operating on a Windows NT 5.1 (Windows XP) system. The SV1 tells you that the system has Service Pack 2 installed. You can learn more about what this means to the Web application at `http://msdn.microsoft.com/security/default.aspx?pull=/library/en-us/dnwxp/html/xpsp2web.asp`. Finally, the last line tells you that the client is running the .NET Framework 2.0.

ASP.NET does provide you with many advantages in quickly determining the browser status. As previously mentioned, the last section of the output shows various status indicators. In this case, the browser can work with ActiveX components, it isn't an AOL browser, and it can work with background sounds.

Working with Forms

Forms are an essential part of Web page development because they help you exchange information with a user. The <Form> tag in a Web page has the same connotation as a form you use at your desk. Generally, forms let you send a request for information to a user and provide feedback about the information the user provides. In most cases, forms contain a description of the kind of data needed, the reason you need the data, specific descriptions of each data element, and fields the user fills out.

Exchanging data between a client and server isn't quite as easy as giving a form to a supervisor. Forms have specific criteria for exchanging data—a protocol (set of rules) determines how the exchange takes place. For example, you won't place your form in the supervisor's out basket if the supervisor isn't in the office. Likewise, computer forms have rules that the following sections examine and explain.

Of course, there's the little matter of getting the data you want. Fortunately, you have access to a number of useful and interesting ASP.NET 2.0 controls. The last section examines these controls and provides pointers on using them to create extremely flexible forms.

Deciding between the GET and POST Data Handling Methods

Whenever you create a form, you need to decide how the form should interact with the server. For example, you must decide whether the client will use the GET or the POST method to send information to the server. The method appears as part of the `<form>` tag, as shown here. (Note that the use of the term *method* isn't related to objects it in this case—it refers to the technique used to transfer the data.)

```
<body>
    <form name="MySurvey"
          id="MySurvey"
          action="HTMLPage.htm"
          method="get">
    </form>
</body>
```

As you can see, the `<form>` tag normally appears within the `<body>` tag and includes four attributes as a minimum. The `name` attribute defines the form name and is how you reference the form when you receive the data. The `id` attribute identifies the form and lets you interact with it in both code behind (when using ASP.NET) and script (available for both ASP.NET and HTML developers). The `action` attribute defines where the client sends the data. Finally, the `method` attribute defines how the client and server exchange data.

In many cases, it doesn't matter whether you use the GET or POST method for a form. Both techniques send data to the server. However, any server-side coding must know what to expect from the form, so the techniques aren't interchangeable, but the results are the same. The receiving page must use the correct data transmission method. Fortunately, you can use the `Request.HttpMethod` property to determine whether the client used the GET or POST method. In fact, you could provide code that accepts data using either method to ensure the page always works.

The POST method sends the information from the client to the server using the request header. Many developers prefer the POST method because the browser's Address field remains clean and it's less likely that the user will modify the contents of the data sent to the server. Unfortunately, the POST technique really doesn't keep the data that much safer—a determined cracker can still access it. Use the POST technique on sites where you want to maintain some level of data hiding. For example, many sites use it for Web services or confidential information sent using an encryption technique such as Secure Sockets Layer (SSL).

The GET method sends the data as part of the address. For example, you might fill out a form that includes your name and a submission button. The address line could look like this after you submit the data.

```
http://localhost:25860/Forms/HTMLPage.htm?txtName=John&btnSubmit=Send+Data
```

The question mark (?) defines the end of the URL and the beginning of the data. Each entry consists of a control name, such as `txtName`, an equals sign (=) and the data value, such as `John`. Each control is separated by an ampersand (&). Some Web sites actually encourage use of the GET method because they want users to maintain the list of values they sent to the server. For example, search pages often rely on the values stored as part of a URL to return the user to the same place without having the fill out the search form again. In fact, some users rely on this behavior to modify the arguments that appear as part of the URL to obtain better results or even create a list of URLs on a custom Web page. For example, you can store these values as shortcuts in Internet Explorer.

Understanding the Four Levels of Data Processing

You have choices to make when it comes to working with data passed by the client. ASP.NET 2.0 actually supports four levels of data processing—the GET method, the POST method, the control method, and a combination of all three. All of these methods rely on the `Request` object. The property you use determines the data you receive from ASP.NET 2.0. Here are the four processing techniques (including three properties) you need to consider.

`QueryString`   Contains the values passed using the GET method. ASP.NET automatically separates the data into name-value pairs so that you can use the variable name to access its value.

`Form`   Contains the values passed using the POST method. ASP.NET automatically separates the data into name-value pairs so you can easily access the posted data by name.

`Params`   Contains all of the values in the `QueryString`, `Form`, `ServerVariables`, and `Cookies` properties. Because this property combines values from several sources, you can use it to look for data no matter what the source might be. The downside is that you have to sift through a lot of information that you don't need.

Direct Variable Access   Allows direct manipulation of data values. Unlike HTML tags, you can also access ASP.NET controls (`<asp:control>` tags) directly by name. This means that you can control property values directly as well.

Processing Input Using the GET Method

One of the best ways to begin learning how to process information is to use the GET method. All of the information appears as part of the address—the communication technique doesn't hide anything. This example relies on a master page to provide the continuity between pages. Figure 5.6 shows the combination of master page and ASPX page used for this example.

The master page must include the form of processing you want to use. Consequently, you add the `method` attribute to the `<form>` tag to define the processing method you want to use like this.

```
<form id="frmGetForm" runat="server" method="GET">
```

Every page that relies on the master page will use the GET method in this case. However, you'll notice that the master page doesn't include an `action` attribute, which is standard for form processing. To make this page work with ASP.NET, you must set the `UseSubmitBehavior` property true for the submission button. If you don't do anything else, the form automatically posts back to itself. However, if you also set the `PostBackUrl` property, you can send the data to another page for processing. That's what `btnProcessingPage` does in this case. You can either use local or centralized processing depending on the needs of your application.

FIGURE 5.6

This form contains three simple controls: a label, a textbox, and a submit button.

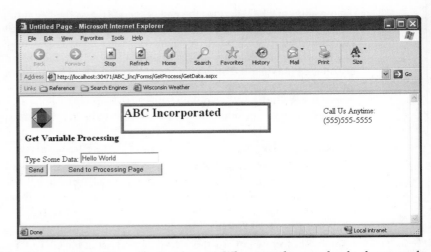

The code behind for this example relies on the Load event. Whenever the page loads, the example looks for a specific set of criteria and processes the Web page. Listing 5.2 shows the code for this example. You'll find this example in the \ABC_Inc\Forms\GetProcess folder of the source code on the Sybex Web site.

LISTING 5.2:   Processing GET Method Input Data Using Code Behind

```
Protected Sub Page_Load( _
    ByVal sender As Object, ByVal e As System.EventArgs) _
    Handles Me.Load

    Dim ProcOut As StringBuilder    ' Individual query string values.
    Dim Variable As String          ' Single query string variable.

    'Perform processing only after the user sees the initial form.
    If Page.IsPostBack Then

        ' Get the input variables, if any, and display them.
        ProcOut = New StringBuilder
        If Request.QueryString.Count > 0 Then

            ' Every variable is a unique entry.
            For Each Variable In Request.QueryString
                ProcOut.Append(Variable)
                ProcOut.Append(" equals ")

                ' Access the variable value by using the variable name.
```

```
            ProcOut.Append( _
                Request.QueryString.GetValues(Variable).GetValue(0))
            ProcOut.Append(vbCrLf)
        Next
    Else
        ProcOut.Append("No Variables")
    End If

    ' Change the page configuration.
    lblInput.Visible = False
    txtInput.Visible = False
    btnSubmit.Visible = False
    btnProcessingPage.Visible = False
    lblOutput.Visible = True
    txtOutput.Visible = True

    ' Output the response.
    txtOutput.Text = ProcOut.ToString()
    End If
End Sub
```

The code begins by declaring variables it needs to process the data. It then checks the Page.IsPostBack property. This Boolean property tells you whether the user has just loaded the page or has clicked Send to transmit the data. (A postback occurs when a control posts information back to the server—it's a communication from the client to the server.) When this value is true, the user has clicked Send and the code can begin processing the data.

The code begins by using the StringBuilder, ProcOut, to hold the processed output. The processing code begins by checking the number of query strings values available using the Request .QueryString.Count property. When there's at least one value to process, the code uses a For Each loop to process the values. Remember that the QueryString property contains data sent using the GET method only, so it won't contain any other values (even if you send them using some other method).

The For Each loop places each member of the Request.QueryString collection into Variable in turn. The code places the variable name into ProcOut, followed by the word equals and the variable value. The Request.QueryString.GetValues(Variable).GetValue(0) property contains the value. It's possible to simply use the Get() method to obtain a value as well (see the "Processing Input Using the POST Method" section for details). This method is convenient when the input has variables with multiple values.

The code ends by placing the result in the txtOutput.Text property. Figure 5.7 shows typical output for this application. The technique shown in this example provides you with complete output, including all of the hidden variables that ASP.NET generates. Interestingly enough, this particular technique is helpful for troubleshooting your Web pages. You can use it to detect problems with inputs as you build and debug the application. It's also possible to view odd problems, such as when you fail to escape a control character such as a space (usually replaced with a plus sign).

FIGURE 5.7
This example processes all of the GET variables, even those that ASP.NET generates automatically.

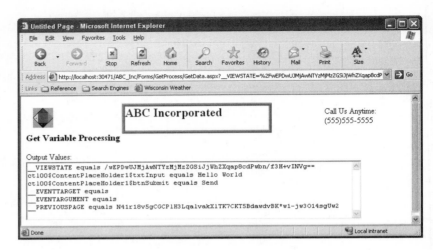

Processing Input Using the POST Method

The POST method places values in the request header, but you can't gain access to the data using the `Request.Headers` property. ASP.NET 2.0 separates this information and places it in the `Request.Form` property instead. However, it's important to know where the data really resides should you ever need to perform low-level troubleshooting.

This example uses the same front-end page shown in Figure 5.6, but processes the information differently, as shown in Listing 5.3. You'll find this example in the `\ABC_Inc\Forms\GetProcess` folder of the source code on the Sybex Web site.

LISTING 5.3:   Processing POST Method Input Data Using Code Behind

```
Protected Sub Page_Load( _
    ByVal sender As Object, ByVal e As System.EventArgs) _
    Handles Me.Load

    Dim DataOut As StringBuilder    ' Output string.
    Dim KeyValue As String          ' Key to control value.

    'Perform processing only after the user sees the initial form.
    If Page.IsPostBack Then

        ' Create the output tags.
        DataOut = New StringBuilder

        ' Locate the key we need.
        KeyValue = ""
        For Each Key As String In Request.Form.AllKeys
            If Key.IndexOf("txtInput") > 0 Then
```

```
            KeyValue = Key
        End If
Next

' Get the input variables, if any, and display them.
If Request.Form.Count > 0 Then

    ' Get the input value directly.
    If Request.Form.Get(KeyValue).Length > 0 Then
        DataOut.Append("'")
        DataOut.Append(Request.Form.Get(KeyValue))
        DataOut.Append("'")
    Else
        DataOut.Append("'Input Value is Blank'")
    End If

Else
    DataOut.Append("No Variables")
End If

' Change the page configuration.
lblInput.Visible = False
txtInput.Visible = False
btnSubmit.Visible = False
btnProcessingPage.Visible = False
lblOutput.Visible = True
txtOutput.Visible = True

' Output the response.
txtOutput.Text = DataOut.ToString()
    End If

End Sub
```

The code still begins by creating a few variables and checking whether the user has clicked Send using the `Page.IsPostBack` property value. However, notice that the code must perform a new task in order to locate the needed data. Although your code has controls with names such as `txtInput`, the actual name of the control changes. Look again at Figure 5.7 and you'll see that the controls are there, but they begin with odd names such as `ct100`. All of the extra text means something to ASP.NET, but it doesn't mean a thing to you (and you don't really need to worry about it). The `AllKeys` property contains a list of all of the values sent using the POST method. The code relies on this fact to locate the particular key that contains the control of interest. Once the code finds the value, it places it in `KeyValue`.

This application uses a standard textbox for output. The code still checks `Request.Form.Count` to verify that there are variables to process. The `Request.Form.Get(KeyValue).Length` check verifies that the `txtInput` variable contains data. If the variable does contain data, the code uses

`Request.Form.Get(KeyValue)` to obtain the value directly. This code assumes that you're working with a single string, not a complex value of some sort.

In this case, the code ends displaying the output textbox and hiding the other controls on the display. Figure 5.8 shows typical results from this example.

FIGURE 5.8
Adding to an existing Web page is relatively easy in most cases.

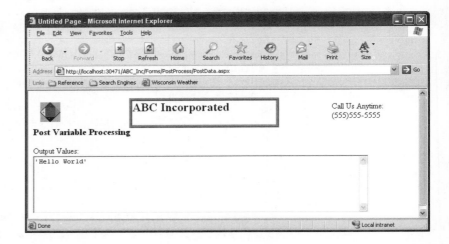

Understanding the New ASP.NET 2.0 Controls

Although you can use standard HTML tags to control input on your Web page, it's a lot easier to use ASP.NET controls. Previous versions of ASP.NET provide a modest assortment of controls that meet most common needs, but developers always find something new to try and Microsoft added new controls to ASP.NET 2.0 to address many of these needs. Figure 5.9 shows the standard preselected controls available to ASP.NET developers.

TIP The Toolbox defaults to a list view of the controls. The list view includes the icon followed by a descriptive name. This view works best when you dock the Toolbox to the side of the IDE and need to locate controls quickly. To see the view shown in Figure 5.9, undock the Toolbox. Right-click anywhere within an area and clear the List View option from the context menu. The descriptive text will disappear and all you'll see is the icon. Hover the mouse over an icon to see the descriptive text.

Some of the controls did appear in previous versions of ASP.NET. For example, if you used previous versions of ASP.NET, you already know about items such as the Textbox control. The controls on the Navigation tab owe their start to FrontPage. Even though these controls aren't a direct copy of the FrontPage equivalents, you'll notice definite similarities if you used FrontPage in the past. The controls on the Login and WebParts tabs are new for ASP.NET 2.0 and you'll use them in several examples in the book. The controls on the HTML tab are the ones that several of the examples in this chapter use.

As you can see from the Toolbox, each group of controls performs a specific task in a particular manner. If you decide that you don't want to use HTML controls, you can simply close the HTML tab or remove the tab from view. To remove a tab from the list, right-click the tab entry and choose Delete Tab from the context menu. Likewise, when you want to add a new tab, right-click within the tab area and choose Add Tab from the context menu. If you end up making a mess of the whole thing, simply right-click the Toolbox and choose Reset Toolbox from the context menu. Of course, using this option resets all of the options and any changes you made are completely reversed (of course, you can always change things back later).

At some point, you might find that you want to use other controls. You can download controls from the Internet, use existing Component Object Model (COM) controls installed on your machine, or create new controls of your own. To add the controls to the Toolbox, right-click the tab where you want the control to appear and select Choose Items from the context menu. You'll see the Choose Toolbox Items dialog box shown in Figure 5.10.

FIGURE 5.9
ASP.NET 2.0 provides myriad controls to address a multitude of needs.

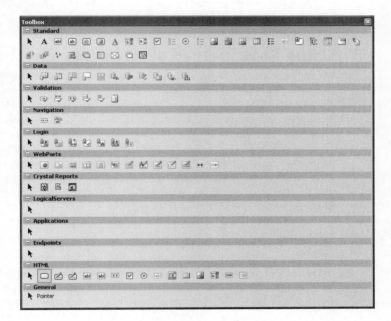

FIGURE 5.10
Add either .NET or COM controls to your Toolbox as needed.

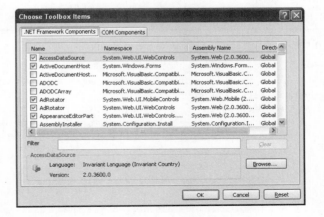

The first thing you'll notice is that even the .NET Framework Components tab contains a number of controls that don't appear in the Toolbox. To add a new item to the Toolbox tab you selected, check the box next to the component name and click OK. The new controls will appear in the Toolbox. Likewise, to remove a control that you no longer want, clear the check box next to the item name. The COM Components tab contains a list of COM components installed on your system. You can select any of the controls that appear in the list.

WARNING   Don't assume that every COM control is going to work with .NET. In fact, some won't because .NET won't be able to build an appropriate compatibility layer. Make sure you run appropriate tests whenever you try to use a COM control in an application. When a control fails in some way, it's usually best to find a .NET alternative if possible.

Using XML Instead of HTML for Web Pages

Many companies have moved to XML for storing data because it's easy to transport and manipulate as needed for various presentations. Even if you haven't personally moved to using XML for data storage, it's quite likely that you'll encounter some form of XML while you work with Web pages. For example, some online media use XML to store the data you read, even though it looks like a standard Web page. In addition, all Web services rely on XML and some databases rely on it too. For example, you can output SQL Server data as XML and process it as a Web page. All of the latest Microsoft Office products read and output XML data too. Consequently, you need to know how to work with XML as a kind of Web page. Although the following sections don't provide a complete tutorial, they do give you a better understanding of the power of XML. (XML does appear in other sections of the book, so this won't be the only time you see it.)

Creating the XML Content

XML is a kind of data storage technology that relies on pure text to store the information. In many respects, XML looks like HTML, but the rules are a lot stricter. For example, an XML tag must always include a closing tag. The example in Listing 5.4 shows two address book records. The listing includes the most common XML information, so it's a good way to work with XML if you haven't done so in the past. You'll find this example in the \ABC_Inc\XMLSample folder of the source code on the Sybex Web site.

LISTING 5.4:   Typical XML Data Example

```
<?xml version="1.0" encoding="utf-8" ?>
<!-- This is a list of my personal names and addresses -->
<AddressBook Version="1.0">
    <!-- Each person record contains the person's name and
         address, as well as one or more telephone numbers. A
         person record can also include special notes and other
         personal data. -->
    <Person>
      <Name>George Smith</Name>
      <Address>
         <AddressLine>1234 West Street</AddressLine>
```

```
            <AddressLine>Suite 20</AddressLine>
        </Address>
        <City>Somewhere</City>
        <State>WI</State>
        <ZIP_Code>54001</ZIP_Code>
        <Telephone>
            <Number Location="Home">(555)555-1212</Number>
        </Telephone>
        <PersonalData>
            <Note Type="TimeToCall" Hour="PM">
                8:30
            </Note>
            <Note Type="SpouseName">
                Nancy
            </Note>
        </PersonalData>
    </Person>
    <Person>
        <Name>Amy Wright</Name>
        <Address>
            <AddressLine>99 Lear Street</AddressLine>
        </Address>
        <City>Edge</City>
        <State>CA</State>
        <ZIP_Code>99122</ZIP_Code>
        <Telephone>
            <Number Location="Office">(555)555-1234</Number>
            <Number Location="Home">(555)555-9876</Number>
        </Telephone>
        <PersonalData />
    </Person>
</AddressBook>
```

The first line of code is an XML processing instruction. Every XML document must contain the <?xml ?> processing instruction. However, you'll encounter other processing instructions in XML documents. An XML processing instruction always includes two angle brackets, with enclosing question marks and the processing instruction name. The <?xml ?> processing instruction normally includes the version and encoding attributes. Attributes always appear as name and value pairs separated by an equals sign as shown in the listing. The values must appear in single or double quotes as shown—the name always appears without quotes.

The second line of code shows a typical comment. Comments always appear within an angle bracket pair that includes an exclamation mark (<!-- -->). The XML parser ignores any text within a comment and a comment can appear on multiple lines.

Every XML document includes a root element that contains all of the other elements in the document. In this case, <AddressBook> is the root element. The <AddressBook> element contains a single attribute, Version, which identifies the version of this document. The version number is optional, but it's a good idea to give your documents version numbers so that you know how to process them as your XML coding technology evolves. You'll find that XML documents do change because the data configuration that looks great today might not work very well tomorrow.

The `<AddressBook>` table consists of `<Person>` element records. This example includes two records, but an XML document can contain any number of records you want. The `<Person>` element is a child of the `<AddressBook>` element, while the `<AddressBook>` element is the parent of all of the `<Person>` elements. XML relies on a hierarchical structure—many developers talk of the child and parent relationships between the various elements as a means of understanding the structure. Although XML doesn't require the use of white space, using line spacing and indentation as shown in Listing 5.4 is very helpful in understanding the various relationships.

UNDERSTANDING THE CORPORATE VIEW OF XML

XML is one of the most popular methods of creating Web pages in the corporate environment for a very good reason—XML is easy to store in a database and even easier to format in any form needed by the end user. Corporations typically don't have time or resources to hire a professional to create every Web page. Yes, some Web pages require special handling and therefore the services of a professional, but many Web pages contain pure content that requires constant update. Consequently, a corporate Web site requires some means of allowing semi-skilled users to provide input and then output the information in a standard format on the corporate Web site.

However, XML has a far more important purpose. You can use XML output from databases to create some types of content automatically so there isn't any human interaction at all. For example, you do need someone to enter orders into the system. However, once the orders are in the system, you can produce a sales report from the data without relying on anyone to interact with it at all. The sales data is already present and the Database Management System (DBMS) can output it automatically as long as the required code is in place.

You need not restrict the use of XML to numeric information either. Most local intranet Web sites include a company directory. Someone is usually responsible for maintaining that information using manual entry techniques. It's easy to automate the output of the data based on the employee database. Just send the required XML data from the database to a file on the server. Not only is this technique faster; it's more accurate as well.

Don't underestimate the importance of XML in interacting with off-site data either. As companies create more connections through Web services, you'll find that XML is the currency of data transfer. In fact, you can see how this works with three public Web services now in existence. Google, Amazon, and eBay all provide Web services where you can download data from their database to your machine—all three rely on XML to perform the data transfer and all three use different techniques to accomplish the task. You can learn more about these three Web services through my books, *Mining Google Web Services*, *Mining Amazon Web Services*, and *Mining eBay Web Services*, (all Sybex, 2004).

Elements that appear at the end of the hierarchy are leaves. For example, `<AddressLine>1234 West Street</AddressLine>` is a leaf element because it appears at the end of the hierarchy. This leaf element includes an address, which is the element data. Elements can also contain other elements as shown in the listing. A leaf element that doesn't include data can include the closing tag at the end of the element like this:

```
<PersonalData />
```

The slash at the end of the tag closes the tag. You don't always need an opening and closing tag pair. Of course, it's legal to use an empty pair like this:

```
<PersonalData></PersonalData>
```

Because XML is hierarchical, it doesn't need to include blank elements unless your application expects a particular element. For example, notice that both records include a `<PersonalData>` element because the application is expecting to see it, but that the second record doesn't include any data for this element. Consequently, the second record doesn't include any `<Note>` elements, even though the first record includes two of them.

As you begin working with XML, you'll find that viewing the XML files in a text editor isn't always easy. You can view them in Visual Web Developer, but the IDE doesn't always provide a quick method of viewing the file and assumes that you have the IDE installed on every machine. Likewise, you can get a high-end XML tool such as XMLSpy (`http://www.xmlspy.com/`), but again, this tool might not always be available. It turns out you can always rely on one tool no matter what machine you decide to use—the browser. Figure 5.11 shows an example of how an XML document appears in Internet Explorer.

Internet Explorer even color codes the XML document for you, making it easy to determine whether a line of text is a comment or an element. If the document lacks white space, Internet Explorer adds it for you. The little dashes next to some of the entries in Figure 5.11 let you collapse a parent element so that the child elements remain hidden. This feature lets you view just the parts of the XML document that you actually want to see.

FIGURE 5.11
Even a standard browser works for viewing XML files in many cases.

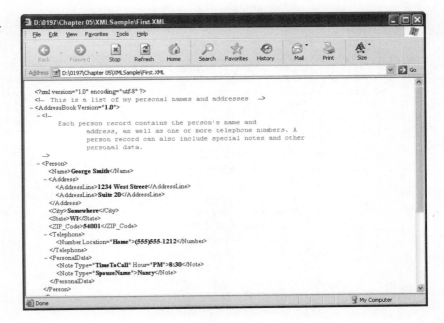

Interpreting the XML Using XSLT

As interesting as XML documents might appear, they really aren't very useful without some kind of interpretation. It turns out that you can create a special kind of XML document that tells a browser or other application how to interpret the XML file you create. The eXtensible Style Language Transformation (XSLT) file is a special kind of XML file that describes how to interpret the XML document. Listing 5.5 shows an example of an XSLT file that interprets the XML document shown in Listing 5.4. You'll find this example in the \ABC_Inc\XMLSample folder of the source code on the Sybex Web site.

LISTING 5.5:   Interpreting XML Data Using XSLT

```
<?xml version="1.0" encoding="utf-8"?>
<xsl:stylesheet version='1.0'
 xmlns:xsl='http://www.w3.org/1999/XSL/Transform'>
<xsl:output method="html" indent="yes" />
<xsl:template match="/AddressBook">

<HTML>
<HEAD>
   <TITLE>Personal Address List</TITLE>
</HEAD>

<BODY>
<H1>Personal Address List</H1>

<!-- Process all of the people in a loop. -->
<xsl:for-each select="Person">

   <!-- Display each record in a separate paragraph. -->
   <p>

   <!-- Get the person's name -->
   <xsl:value-of select="Name" />
   <br />

   <!-- Display the address information. -->
   <xsl:text>Address: </xsl:text>
   <xsl:value-of select="Address" /><br />
   <xsl:value-of select="City" />
   <xsl:text>, </xsl:text>
   <xsl:value-of select="State" />
   <xsl:text>     </xsl:text>
   <xsl:value-of select="ZIP_Code" /><br />
```

```
<!-- Test to see whether the person has an office telephone. -->
<xsl:if test="string(Telephone/Number/@Location) != 'Office'">
    <xsl:text>No Office Phone</xsl:text><br />
</xsl:if>

<!-- Process all of the telephone numbers. -->
<xsl:for-each select="Telephone/Number">

    <!-- Display a telephone number and its length. -->
    <xsl:value-of select="@Location" />
    <xsl:text> Telephone Number: </xsl:text>
    <xsl:value-of select="." /><br />
    <xsl:text>The telephone number is </xsl:text>
    <xsl:value-of select="string-length(.)" />
    <xsl:text> digits long.</xsl:text><br />
</xsl:for-each>

<!-- Test for certain types of personal data and act on it. -->
<xsl:for-each select="PersonalData/Note">
    <xsl:choose>
        <xsl:when test="string(@Type) = 'TimeToCall'">
            <xsl:text>Best Calling Time: </xsl:text>
            <xsl:value-of select="." />
            <xsl:value-of select="@Hour" /><br />
        </xsl:when>
        <xsl:when test="string(@Type) = 'SpouseName'">
            <xsl:text>Spouse Name: </xsl:text>
            <xsl:value-of select="." /><br />
        </xsl:when>
        <xsl:otherwise>
            <xsl:text>Note Type Not Recognized</xsl:text>
        </xsl:otherwise>
    </xsl:choose>
</xsl:for-each>
</p>

<!-- End of person processing. -->
</xsl:for-each>

</BODY>
</HTML>

</xsl:template>

</xsl:stylesheet>
```

The XSLT file starts with the same XML processing instruction as an XML document because it really is an XML document. The next line contains the root element for the document, `<xsl:stylesheet>`. The little "`xsl`" in front of the word stylesheet is a namespace reference. It tells the XML parser that this special kind of element requires instructions from a nonstandard location to understand. The `xmlns:xsl` attribute contains an XML namespace declaration for the `xsl` reference that includes the URL for the instructions.

XSLT files can create a broad range of output types. In fact, you can use them to create any kind of output that you want. Although most XSLT files create some type of text output, it's theoretically possible to create binary output as well. This particular XSLT file creates HTML as output. The `<xsl:output>` element identifies the kind of output, the `method` attribute tells the specific output type, and the `indent` attribute tells the parser to add white space to make the output easier to read. In short, this XSLT file is producing a Web page.

You need to tell the XSLT file where to start processing the input XML file. The `<xsl:template>` element tells the XSLT parser to match the `<AddressBook>` element—the root element of the sample XML file. It's possible to start processing an XML file at any point—you don't have to process the entire document.

At this point, you'll notice that the XSLT file contains standard HTML output. An XSLT file isn't pure XML—it contains a combination of data types. The XSLT parser outputs the HTML directly to the output (no matter what the output might be).

XSLT includes a number of programming instructions. This example shows a few of common instructions, but there are many others. See the "Learning More about XSLT" section of the chapter for resources that tell you about these other programming instructions. The example begins with a loop instruction, the `<xsl:for-each>` element. The `select` attribute tells the parser what kind of element to use as a looping variable. This loop processes every `<Person>` element in the XML file.

The next line of code is another piece of HTML—it's the open paragraph, `<p>`, tag. Within this tag, the XSLT places the extracted values of the `<Name>`, `<Address>`, `<City>`, `<State>`, and `<ZIP_Code>` elements using the `<xsl:value-of>` programming instruction. Notice how the `select` attribute tells the parser which element to work with.

XSLT understands HTML tags and XML elements, but it doesn't understand freestanding text. The `<xsl:text>` programming instruction tells the parser that the included information is text and not something that XSLT has to process. Notice how the example uses these elements to add identifying information to the various XML data entries.

At some point, you'll need to test values in the XML file to determine what course of action to pursue. The `<xsl:if>` programming instruction performs this task by using the value of the `test` attribute. When the test passes, the XSLT file performs any steps contained within the `<xsl:if>` element. Notice that the code uses a special test function to determine whether the `Location` attribute of the `<Number>` element has a value of `Office`. The `<xsl:if>` programming instruction doesn't include the concept of an `else` clause, so you have to perform every test directly.

Some of the XSLT programming instructions become a little complex. For example, many programming languages include a `Select Case` programming structure and XSLT is no exception. The case statements always appear within an `<xsl:choose>` element. Each of the selection criteria appear within a `<xsl:when>` element. Like the `<xsl:if>` programming instruction, you need to provide a test attribute that succeeds or fails. When the test succeeds, the XSLT parser interprets all of the statements within the `<xsl:when>` element. When all of the tests fail, the XSLT parser looks for an optional `<xsl:otherwise>` element that contains alternative instructions.

Now that you have a better idea of how XSLT works, you need to create a connection between the XML file and the XSLT file. Your browser won't know that it's supposed to use this XSLT file unless you provide a processing instruction to that effect in the XML file. The following processing instruction assumes that the XML and XSLT files are in the same folder.

```
<?xml-stylesheet type="text/xsl" href="First.XSLT"?>
```

As with all processing instructions, the `<?xml-stylesheet?>` processing instruction includes the enclosing question marks. The `type` attribute tells the XML parser what kind of information to expect in the stylesheet file. The `href` attribute tells the parser where to find the XSLT file. When you open the XML file in a browser now, the parser sees the processing instruction and interprets the XML file according to the rules in the XSLT file. Figure 5.12 shows the output from this example. As you can see, it's very hard to tell that this is an XML file.

FIGURE 5.12

Using XSLT transforms unreadable XML into something that looks like a regular Web page.

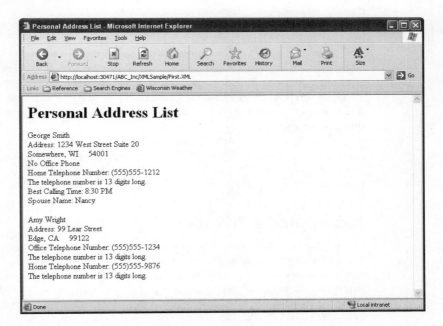

Learning More about XML

Whether you know it or not, you'll run into XML many times during your computer use. The reason is simple—XML makes a great way to exchange data between disparate systems. Fortunately, XML is relatively easy to learn. Visit the W3C Schools site at `http://www.w3schools.com/xml/` to find a complete XML tutorial. You might also want to review the namespace tutorial at `http://www.zvon.org/index.php?nav_id=172&ns=34`.

Unlike many topics discussed in this book, there are multiple versions of XML so you can't rely on just one reference. The most important reference appears at `http://www.zvon.org/xxl/xmlSchema2001Reference/Output/index.html`. However, make sure you also look at the references at `http://www.zvon.org/xxl/xmlSchemaReference/Output/index.html` for complete information. The annotated XML reference at `http://www.xml.com/axml/axml.html` is also handy for seeing the specification and expert commentary side by side.

You can also find a number of good general-purpose XML sites online. For example, the Microsoft XML Developer Center (`http://msdn.microsoft.com/xml/`) is a great place to visit if you use Microsoft products.

Learning More about XSLT

This chapter only skims the surface of what you can do with XSLT. You can perform an incredible number of tasks using this technology. One of the better places to learn about XSLT is `http://www.w3schools.com/xsl/`. You should also view the examples in the XSLT reference at `http://www.zvon.org/xxl/XSLTreference/Output/index.html`. The XSL reference at `http://www.zvon.org/xxl/xslfoReference/Output/index.html` can also come in handy when you begin creating complex XSLT pages. You can also find a good tutorial on the Webmonkey site at `http://hotwired.lycos.com/webmonkey/98/43/index2a.html?tw=authoring`.

Make sure you check out some of the better third party XSLT reference sites. For example, the XSLT.com site at `http://xslt.com/` provides links and resources for XSLT from various vendors (not just Microsoft).

It also helps to have some great books on the topic. Make sure you read books such as *Mastering XSLT* by Chuck White (Sybex, 2002). It also helps to know something about XML schemas, so check out *XML Schemas* by Chelsea Valentine, Lucinda Dykes, and Ed Tittel (Sybex, 2002). (Even though these books have 2002 publication dates, they still contain valuable information.)

Developing a Privacy Policy

Privacy has become a major concern for most people because the news contains numerous stories of personal information misuse. One of the major misuses of personal information is identity theft, but that's by no means the largest misuse. Many users also feel that gathering personal information for marketing purposes without permission and full disclosure of how the requestor will use the information is also a major misuse of personal information. People don't want to suffer through a barrage of unwanted sales calls as witnessed by the proliferation of "No Call" lists both locally and nationally. In fact, many people are taking positive steps to take back their personal information or at least block further attempts to acquire new information.

Personal information covers a range of topics today. Most developers recognize that name, address, telephone number, and other personally identifying information is private. However, users don't want developers to know a lot of other information that some developers see as belonging to the public domain. For example, some developers will try to get the `Referrer` (the previous Web page), `User-Agent` (the browser type, version, and host operating system), and `From` (the user's email address) headers of the user's browser. Brisk sales of products such as Norton Internet Security demonstrate that users don't want developers to collect this information. An interesting side effect of this battle between user and developer is that even though the user is using a new version of products such as Internet Explorer and Mozilla, the Web site often reports the user has an outdated version of the product.

Generally, if your Web site doesn't include a shopping cart application or some other form of transaction that the user wants to participate in, you shouldn't collect any personal information at all. You can also avoid collecting browser information through careful design and by following standards. The Webmonkey chart at `http://hotwired.lycos.com/webmonkey/reference/browser_chart/index.html` helps you understand which design features to avoid based on browser compatibility.

Even with the best design, however, you'll eventually encounter a situation where you want to use cookies (assuming the user has their browser set to accept cookies). Many users realize that cookies aren't inherently evil, but they also realize that a Web site could use cookies for nefarious purposes. All the pop-up ads that you see floating around on your favorite Web site are one reason that people are suspicious. Some of these vendors follow people around to the various sites they visit and keep track of their movements. However, you can overcome the fears of most users by maintaining a privacy policy and including special tags for that policy on your Web site. The most common way to publish and use a privacy policy is Platform for Privacy Preferences (P3P). The World Wide Web Consortium (W3C) sponsors this technique, and you can read about the six easy steps for implementing P3P on your Web site at `http://www.w3.org/P3P/details.html`. The P3P standard (`http://www.w3.org/TR/P3P/`) also contains a wealth of information you should review.

NOTE   The example in this section uses the IBM P3P generator (`http://www.alphaworks.ibm.com/tech/p3peditor`). The W3C site lists several other generators—I chose this particular generator because it comes with a 90-day free trial. Your code might turn out different from mine if you use another generator for your code. For some reason, the IBM P3P generator doesn't work with the current version of the Java Runtime Environment (JRE)—version 1.4.2. IBM recommends using the 1.3.1 version of the JRE that you can download at `http://java.sun.com/j2se/1.3/`.

Your privacy statement will consist of several files, including at least one P3P file that you create using the P3P generator and an XML reference file. A good generator will also help you create a generic privacy summary that you can use for queries from the user and a compact policy statement you can use in the response headers of pages that contain cookies. If you own the server you use for the Web page, you can place the privacy information in the \w3c folder of the Web site. It's also possible to create linkage between the privacy information and your Web page using a `<link>` tag similar to the one shown here.

```
<link rel="P3Pv1" href="http://www.mwt.net/~jmueller/p3p.xml">
```

The problem comes in when you don't own the server that hosts your Web page—the situation for many people, including small business owners. Internet Explorer 6 has several levels of cookie protection built in. The highest level will likely reject your privacy information because Internet Explorer relies exclusively on the compact policy statement supplied as part of the response headers. Adding the compact policy statement is relatively easy if you own the server. Listing 5.6 shows an alternative you can try when you don't own the server, plus some test code you can use to verify the results. You'll find this example in the \ABC_Inc\Privacy folder of the source code on the Sybex Web site.

The `<meta>` tag at the beginning of the code is the essential addition to your application. The `http-equiv` attribute tells the server what kind of response header to add. Some servers don't honor this attribute, so this solution might not work completely in all cases. The `content` attribute tells the client where to locate the privacy policy for your Web site—it works much the same as the `<link>` tag discussed earlier in this section. Finally, the CP attribute defines the compact policy for your server. Most tools, such as the IBM P3P Policy Editor shown in Figure 5.13, tell you what these codes mean and generate a text file containing them for you.

LISTING 5.6: Adding a Compact Policy to a Web Page

```html
<html>
<head>
<meta http-equiv='P3P'
      content='policyref="http://www.mwt.net/~jmueller/p3p.xml",
      CP="NOI DSP COR NID CURa OUR NOR NAV INT TST"'>
<title>Privacy Demonstration</title>
<script>
function SetCookie()
{
    var  UserCookie; // Stores the user name.

    // Create the username cookie.
    UserCookie = "UserName=" + escape(InputVal.value);

    // Add the cookie to the document.
    document.cookie = UserCookie;

    // Tell the user the cookie was saved.
    alert("The cookies were saved.");
}

function ReadCookie()
{
    var  ACookie; // Holds the document cookie.
    var  Parsed;  // Holds the split cookies.
    var  Name;    // The user name.

    // Get the cookie.
    ACookie = unescape(document.cookie);

    // Split the cookie elements.
    Parsed = ACookie.split("=");

    // Get the user name.
    Name = Parsed[1];

    // Display the name.
    alert("Your name is: " + Name);
}
```

FIGURE 5.13
Make sure you generate a compact policy for Web pages that have cookies.

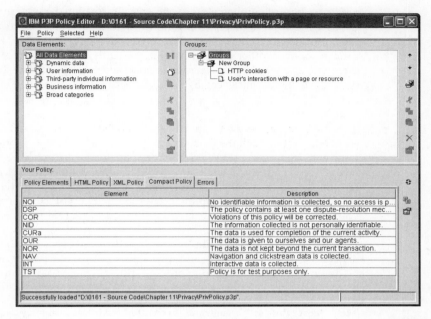

The test code consists of two functions attached to buttons on the example form. The first creates a cookie and attaches it to the document. The second retrieves the cookie stored in the document and displays the results on screen. Neither function is that exciting, but this is enough code to create an error with Internet Explorer 6 if the compact policy isn't accepted. You must have a compact policy in place and Internet Explorer 6 must accept it if you want users to use the high privacy setting. However, even if Internet Explorer 6 decides that it won't accept the compact policy, having a privacy policy in place and set up using the information provided in this section lets the user rely on the medium high privacy setting. Although, the medium high setting isn't quite as comfortable as the high setting, it's much better than the low setting your Web site would require if it didn't have a privacy policy.

Creating a Safe Environment for User Data

Some kinds of user activity on a Web site will require that you know something about the user. For example, when the user requests that you send your newsletter, you'll need an email address. Even if the user provides you with a false name, the email address has to be real or the user won't receive the newsletter. Consequently, the user has to trust you to keep the email address secure and use it only as your privacy statement specifies. Break this trust and you'll find that your Web site is less effective and will have fewer visitors. The first rule of working with user data is to obtain only the user information that you absolutely have to have in order to provide a service.

Sometimes interacting with the user goes far beyond a simple exchange. For example, you might sell products on your Web site. As a minimum, you'll need to know the person's name and address because you need to know where to send items that you sell. However, it's quite likely that you'll know more information than that—a telephone number is likely and you might even need to work with a credit card number or other sensitive information. Because privacy is such an important issue, the user will want to place significant restrictions on what you can do with personal information. Most users won't want you to sell their name or identifying information because they don't want to receive calls from other vendors. More importantly, with identity theft running rampant, you need to safeguard any sensitive information because you might become responsible for its loss. For example, the identity theft experienced by the University of California, Berkeley, caused major waves (see the InfoWorld article at `http://www.infoworld.com/article/04/10/20/HNidtheft_1.html` for details).

Safeguarding user information begins with the lines of communication that you establish. It might seem odd, but some of the worst cracker break-ins begin with an intercepted message. When this information gathering leads to some type of valuable deduction, you have a security leak on your hands. For example, someone can perform a social engineering attack after gathering just enough information about a site visitor to communicate effectively with them directly. Consequently, it's important to keep eavesdropping to a minimum. Encrypt the information before the user sends it to you using a secure setup such as Secure Sockets Layer (SSL)—generally enabled using HyperText Transfer Protocol Secure (HTTPS).

Make sure you protect yourself when you do receive sensitive information from someone else. It's generally a good idea to have an actual agreement page as part of the user sign-up to ensure there's no doubt that the user agreed to provide you with personal information as part of a transaction. In short, make sure you have a strong agreement with the user and stand by that agreement.

TIP Most third party organizations you interact with, such as eBay, require that you use HTTPS and SSL to protect user data you exchange with them. A good application designer will also use HTTPS and SSL for all local user interaction as well. It's important to secure the data stream to reduce the chance of someone peeking at the data. You can learn more about the HTTPS protocol at `http://www.w3.org/Protocols/` and `http://www.faqs.org/rfcs/rfc2818.html`. Learn about the SSL specification at `http://wp.netscape.com/eng/ssl3/`.

You can add a few commonsense principles to ensure your own privacy policy will reduce your liability for user information. For example, many businesses store user information in a database. When crackers breach that database, the information becomes public knowledge and you have a public relations nightmare on your hands. Even if you use stringent methods and encrypt every piece of information in your database, someone with enough time and a good enough reason will likely break through your protections. The best policy is not to store the information at all.

Unfortunately, it's not always possible to get rid of the user data as soon as a transaction is complete. When you need to store user data for a while, make sure you encrypt the database and that you store the information on a server that lacks access to the Internet. Employ automatic aging if, possible, to ensure the system automatically removes the data from the database after a certain time. Keep only the data that you actually need. For example, although you might need to retain the user's name and address, you probably don't have to keep their credit card number on file. Even though it's more convenient to store the credit card information, removing it from your system is safer. Most users won't object to entering their credit card information for every sale if you explain the policy.

WARNING   Always assume that someone's going to feed your application bad data. For example, you'll want to verify that you check data for accuracy before processing it. This means ensuring the data is the proper length and data type, and that it doesn't contain any character data that could cause problems (such as a hidden script). Whenever possible, check the data against a list of acceptable entries and verify that the user has provided complete entries. You can often use regular expressions, a type of check that validates the form of the data, to ensure the data meets a particular requirement, such as a telephone number. In addition, always assume there are going to be security breaches. Maintain a log of access events for your application for 60 days so you can locate, isolate, identify, repair, and hopefully prosecute security breaches. The event log needs to include some type of user identifier, the time of access (including both log on and log off), and the activity the user performed.

You need to consider security for your site when it works with sensitive data from any source. One of the better white papers on how the standards groups are meeting security needs appears on the Microsoft site at `http://msdn.microsoft.com/library/en-us/dnwssecur/html/securitywhitepaper.asp`. Even though this white paper is about Web services, the principles apply to any kind of Web communication. This discussion also provides a road map of security services.

As a final security precaution, you should consider some form of physical security for your system. This could be something as simple as ensuring you lock the system in a room where no one but you can get to it. You could also keep the data held by your system safe by placing the information on a removable disk, removing the disk after each session, and locking it away. There are a number of ways that you can ensure the physical security of your system. For example, companies such as Interface (`http://www.crocodile.de/`) provide physical security add-ons for your computer.

TIP   One requirement that would be easy to miss is to ensure you secure all storage media. This means that you shouldn't expose a system with sensitive data to the Internet if possible and that you must take precautions to safeguard the system when you do. However, the requirement goes further than actual application requirements. Have your system disk securely wiped when you get rid of your current machine. Usually, this means destroying the disk or at least exposing it to a strong enough magnetic force to ensure complete data erasure.

Defining Your Development Goals

This chapter has explored the intelligent Web page from the server perspective. The server has the best control over the flow of data because all of that data resides on its own hard drive. In addition, the server is at a better advantage to implement security and to ensure data receives the proper treatment. Of course, this all comes at a price including additional server loading and loss of user trust in some cases. Generally, server-side intelligence works best for data-gathering projects such as detecting user settings so you can provide a better experience or collecting survey forms. Shopping cart and other financial applications also work best using server-side intelligence.

Now it's time for you to try out server-side processing. Try creating simple applications such as a survey form or an application that collects user data and uses it in a positive manner. The big issue for this chapter is creating a privacy policy. If you don't have a privacy policy defined for your company, create one now—before you write any code or create one Web page design. Far too few Web sites provide a privacy policy and lose both user interest and sales as a result. Make plans now for keeping user data safe (when your Web site stores it) or helping the user understand the need to store the data on their machine. Always use encryption for all storage needs to protect the data from prying eyes (even if the data resides on the user's system).

Chapter 6 considers client-side intelligence. Clients use scripting technology to perform specific tasks, so this chapter also shows how to create and use scripts using one of the most popular languages, JavaScript. You'll find that client-side scripting has many advantages for the developer, but it also comes with problems that you'll need to work around as you create your Web application.

Chapter 6

Working with Scripts

Intelligent pages require code, and that code has to execute somewhere. You have two choices: the client or the server. When you want the code to execute on the server, you create code behind, as shown in Chapter 5, to perform the task. However, when you want the client to perform the work, you need to use scripting. The client's browser sees the script and relies on the local script engine to perform the required tasks. The browser doesn't have a script engine, in most cases—it uses the one supplied by the operating system. For Windows users, this means that you have access to JavaScript or VBScript as scripting languages. The Windows script engine is extensible, so you might have access to other options. However, the important consideration is that other operating systems generally support only JavaScript, so if you want your client-side application to run on the most machines possible, you need to use JavaScript as your scripting language.

Once you have access to the script engine, you need to make other choices. A language like JavaScript can perform a number of standard tasks. For example, you can access any of the controls on the form—HTML as well as ASP.NET controls—so this is a situation where client-side scripting is actually more flexible than working with the server because code behind can't access HTML directly (it's designed to work with ASP.NET controls).

This chapter shows you how to perform a number of other essential tasks using scripts. For example, many scripts perform calculations or perform other behind-the-scenes tasks. These nonvisual tasks are essential to your application. You'll also want to know how to save cookies on the user's machine. The safest place to store user data is on the user's machine where the cookie will eventually expire. You can also combine client and server processing to produce robust applications that serve a variety of complex needs.

The last part of this chapter discusses a new ASP.NET technology called WebParts. The interesting point about WebParts is that this technology lets a user customize a Web application—similar to the customizations that a desktop application can provide. This chapter provides a basic overview and some usage examples. The "Working with WebParts" section of Chapter 14 provides more details.

Understanding Client-side Intelligence

Enterprise developers have to carefully choose between client- and server-side coding. Generally, it's better to err in favor of server-side coding because server-side coding causes fewer problems for the visitor and, therefore, fewer support costs for the company as a whole. A personal Web site usually has greater latitude in this area because the people who visit a personal Web site have targeted needs and are unlikely to have the broad range of devices that an enterprise Web site must support.

An enterprise developer should look at scripting as a means to produce a specific result quickly, rather than a means to reduce the server workload as a smaller Web site would do. It's important to remember that all client-side processing also involves some level of server processing. For example, even though the client can provide a calculated result, the client must still request new data from the server. Consequently, client-side intelligence is actually a hybrid form of processing that provides the following characteristics.

Increased Privacy and Personal Security   Generally, client-side processing reduces privacy problems and increases user security because the server receives less raw data. In fact, a carefully written set of scripts and cookies can keep all personally identifiable information on the client machine so the server doesn't receive anything that a third party could use. For example, instead of receiving a user name, the server would receive a user identifier. The user doesn't even need to send address, telephone, or credit card information for each transaction because the personal identifier locates the user record in the secure storage on the server.

Faster Response Times   Because the client bundles all of the processed data and sends it to the server without intermediate trips, client-side processing tends to produce better response times. Some responses are almost immediate because the client processes them locally. However, even when the client has to request data from the server, the response is likely faster because the server doesn't have to process the raw data first—the client has already performed this task.

Customizable Results   Client-side processing lets the browser perform some analysis of the input and present it to the user in a specific way—independently of the server. The server doesn't have to consider the output as much when using client-side processing—it can provide the same data to everyone. The client can use scripts to manipulate the data and present it the way the user wants.

The enterprise developer also needs to consider the negative effects of using client-side scripts. The issue is one of control—who controls the data stream and the processing of that data. Whenever you use client-side scripting, you give up some of that control to the user. Here are a few issues you should consider.

Security   Every client-side script is a security event waiting to happen. Read the trade press for very long and you'll find that most companies that use some type of client-side scripting eventually end up having to clean up some sort of security mess. The problem is that every possible security opening you can think to close leaves myriad other openings that you didn't consider. Client-side scripting increases you risk considerably.

NOTE   You might think to yourself at this point that some of the issues described in this chapter are contradictory and you'd be correct. A developer often has to consider contradictory goals and assumptions during the development process and find a balance. One of the problematic issues today is improving Web site security, while simultaneously developing new ways to keep user identities safe. In some cases, you have to find a balance point and tweak the application as needed to meet specific goals.

User Headaches   The best page you can present to a user is one that contains plain HTML. The second you add a script, someone's cellular telephone is going to stop working and someone else will have a browser that displays a blank page. Because no one follows the standards completely, even a successful implementation of a page with scripts is going to encounter problems; every browser will interpret those scripts differently.

Team Development Issues   Don't forget that you'll need to add someone to your team who speaks JavaScript when you decide to use scripts. Consequently, the size of your team will grow by at least one person. One person might not seem like much, but now you have one extra line of communication, one more source of bugs, and one more source of problems. Consequently, scripts increase development and support costs while reducing your ability to react to problems quickly.

Client-side intelligence isn't a one-time process—it's ongoing, just as server-side processing is. The client can process information at several times during the request/response cycle and in a variety of ways. Here are the most common techniques.

Form Loading   Use form loading techniques to initialize the client-side environment, create a custom page based on a previous result, or ensure the user environment has specific minimum resources. Form loading is an excellent time to perform any nonvisual tasks you might need to perform to create a good user experience.

Initial Request   Use the initial request to perform processing of basic user input, validation of initial form data, to ensure client meets server-side constraints, or ensure server communication can take place. Performing these tasks at the client means that the data doesn't have to take a round trip across the network. Not only does the server receive less bad data, but the user also gets instant feedback on any problems with the initial request. Of course, you can't perform every task during the initial request. For example, you usually can't perform user validation during the initial request—the server must request the security information during the second request/response cycle.

Automatically   Use automatic processing to ensure the user environment meets user expectations or to ensure that your application meets either client or server processing needs. For example, your Web site might allow a lot of customization, but the initial page won't show the user's preferences unless you use automation to obtain the user's preferences and reconfigure the page as needed. Other forms of automation include client-side setups. For example, a client might need to download a special control or application to ensure that your Web application will work as anticipated.

User Action Response   Whenever possible, perform user action response processing on the client to reduce the time between a user click and the result's appearance on screen. For example, you can always perform calculations locally unless the client is using a resource-poor platform such as a Personal Digital Assistant (PDA) or a cellular telephone. (As these devices gain more intelligence, you'll find that client-side scripts become effective even in these limited environments.)

Timed Response   Rely on timed responses to overcome a variety of error conditions. For example, you might know that the client should receive a response from the server within a specific time frame and that something has gone wrong if this time expires. A timed response can alert the user to the problem and provide a recommended course of action to fix the error. Likewise, some users won't know that you need a particular response from them. A timed response can provide the user with a friendly reminder that they need to provide input. In some cases, you might be able to overcome the problem by performing a default action when the time elapses. Always provide a means for turning off the timer when you take the default action approach because some users with special needs will require additional time.

The most important consideration for client-side scripting is that it can't replace the server. Yes, you can perform many tasks using client-side scripting—some of which you can't perform at the server. However, some developers use extreme programming techniques to try to shoehorn a client-side script to meet a sever-side need. Always review the task you want to perform, attempt to perform it at the location you think works best, and then be willing to change course when it becomes apparent that either the client or the server can't perform the task with ease. Complex scripts that use odd programming techniques usually cause more problems than they solve because many browsers simply won't run them.

Using Basic Scripting Principles

Scripts have some basic properties that you need to consider before using them. For example, it doesn't matter what operating system or browser you use, a script is always interpreted—the script engine runs after the browser hands the script off to it. Because computers interpret scripts, rather than compile them, all scripts incur a performance penalty. Given that most scripts are short, the performance penalty isn't noticeable.

Most operating systems provide a generic scripting engine for several needs, and many operating systems provide a special script debugger. Because Visual Web Developer only runs on Windows, this chapter only considers Windows solutions to the problems of working with the script engine. However, the Web application you create using Visual Web Developer could end up running on just about any operating system and the user might select any of a number of browsers. It's important to at least consider some method of working through problems on other systems (using the feedback form in Chapter 7 is a good start). The following sections discuss basic scripting issues such as performance, scripting engine support, and debugging.

Creating Efficient and Effective Scripts

Scripts provide a wonderful alternative to forcing the server to perform every task needed for intelligent Web pages. Of course, you'll want to create the best scripts possible to reduce support requests for your Web site and enhance the user experience. An efficient script is different from an effective script. Efficient scripts perform fast, reduce network traffic, and use the fewest possible resources. Effective scripts perform the task you want while enhancing the user experience. The best situation is where you create scripts that are both effective and efficient.

The problem is to create an environment where scripting works with the server to provide specific results. Normally, the best approach is to divide whatever task you want to perform into individual steps and then decide where that step will perform best given the available resources. For example, you can't perform a step on the server when the server lacks the required client information. In some cases, you'll have to add another step to move data from one location to the other to garner a boost in performance. Once you create this task list, you can fine-tune it to provide both efficient and effective application performance. Here are some tips you can use to make the task easier.

Use Scripts for Personal Information Processing   Whenever possible, keep the user's personal data on the local machine. Even moving the data from the client to the server for processing is a bad idea. The only exception is when you must have the personal data to complete a server-side task, such as fulfilling an order.

Rely on the Server for Business Processing   Don't expose your business processes to anyone who could use the information to gain entry to your system. Something as simple as a misplaced database name or a special equation used to calculate a price can cause problems for you or your company. Scripting should always focus on the user, never on you or your system.

Make Sure Tasks Are Small Enough   Anytime you find that you have a hard time deciding where to perform a task, it's probably a signal that you haven't made the task small enough. Break the overall task into small enough pieces that your application can perform each subtask in a specific location. It's important to create a task scheme that reflects a reliable order of accomplishing a goal and that means knowing where you can perform the task safely.

Ensure Tasks Are Specific   It's easy to write down a generic description of a task and assume that you know precisely what that task entails. The problem is that a general task description often hides complexity that you won't know about until you actually begin creating the application. You'll save time by creating very specific task descriptions as you think about the application, rather than fixing problems caused by a generalized description later. For example, a task description such as "download the client data" is very generic. Make sure you include details such as the exact client data elements you need. You might find that some of these elements aren't stored on the server and that you'll have to request them from the user.

Track the Precise Location of the Data   You should always know where the data is located. Some developers write code that places some data here and other data there. Eventually, the processing becomes a mess, the data becomes corrupted, or errors occur in the result because it isn't possible to ensure the integrity of the data or even know which data is the newest.

Debugging Your Scripts

At some point, you'll have a Web page that contains a script. You need a debugger that works with the browser so that you can see how the script works in the environment that the user will rely on. To perform debugging, you need to modify a few settings on your machine. First, open Internet Explorer and choose the Tools ➤ Internet Options command. You'll see the Internet Options dialog box. Select the Advanced tab and locate the Disable Script Debugging options shown in Figure 6.1. You'll find the example used for debugging in the \ABC_Inc\Scripts\BrokenScript folder of the source code on the Sybex Web site. Make sure that both options are cleared—checking them will prevent you from debugging the script. Note that not all versions of Internet Explorer have multiple options—you might see a single option for disabling script debugging.

FIGURE 6.1
Make sure you have
debugging enabled in
Internet Explorer.

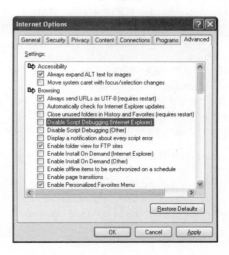

After you check your browser, open the Services console found in the Administrative Tools folder of the Control Panel. Locate the Machine Debug Manager service shown in Figure 6.2. Windows should start the service for you automatically. However, if Windows hasn't started the service, right-click the entry and choose Start from the context menu. The service should start within a few seconds.

Now that you have everything setup, you can start a project that contains a script. After you load the page, three events will trigger the script debugger. The following list describes each option.

An Error Occurs   Whenever the scripting engine experiences an error executing the code, it presents an Error dialog box like the one shown in Figure 6.3 that asks whether you want to start the debugger. The dialog box tells you about the error that the scripting engine encountered so you can determine whether you can fix the error. The error message also includes a line number. The line number isn't always correct, but it will get you close to the line with the problem code. Click Yes to start the debugger.

Open the Debugger Manually   You can load the page and immediately open the script debugger by selecting the View ➢ Script Debugger ➢ Open command.

Open at the Next Statement   Sometimes you don't want to start the debugger until you do something. In this case, select View ➢ Script Debugger ➢ Break at Next Statement command. The browser won't appear to do anything. You can type any data you need to test the page. The debugger starts when you perform an action that executes code, such as clicking the Submit button.

TIP   If you still can't get the script debugger to start, try downloading and installing the Microsoft Script Debugger located at `http://www.microsoft.com/downloads/details.aspx?FamilyID=2f465be0-94fd-4569-b3c4-dffdf19ccd99&displaylang=en`. The debugger should start after you install the Microsoft Script Debugger and restart your system. However, the Visual Web Developer installation should allow you to debug script applications—refusal to start normally indicates there's a problem with your setup.

Whenever the debugger starts, you see the Just-In-Time Debugging dialog box. As a minimum, this dialog box will contain the Microsoft Script Debugger as a debugging option. However, when you have other programming products installed, you should also see them listed. For example, when you have Visual Studio .NET installed, it always appears as one of the debugging options. Visual Web Developer should also appear as one of the debugging options, but may not on certain versions of Windows with specific service packs installed.

Select the debugger you want to use and click Yes. The debugger will start and load the code from the Web page. The fact that the code comes from the Web page and not from the source is an important issue because the Web page might not be the same as your Visual Web Developer code when you create the page using ASP.NET. Because the script has to run in the environment that the user sees, debugging the output, rather than the ASP.NET code, is the best option for scripts. Figure 6.4 shows the Microsoft Script Debugger with the example code loaded.

TIP   Another method you can use to start the script debugger is to load the document you want to debug into your browser. Locate the `MSScrDbg.EXE` file in the `\Program Files\Microsoft Script Debugger` folder. After you start the application, select View ➢ Running Documents. You'll see the Running Documents window. Double-click the running document that you want to debug. The Microsoft Script Debugger will load the document and let you debug it.

The Microsoft Script Debugger isn't fancy, but you can use it to perform basic debugging tasks. The debugger includes a command window where you can test various scripting code while the application runs. You can also view the call stack and set break points. Chapter 17 discusses debugging in detail.

FIGURE 6.2
Start the Machine Debug Manager service when required to ensure the debugger will start.

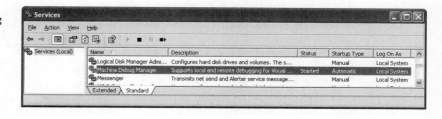

FIGURE 6.3
An error dialog box tells you about the scripting error and describes where to find it.

FIGURE 6.4
Use the Microsoft Script Debugger to locate and fix scripting errors in your code.

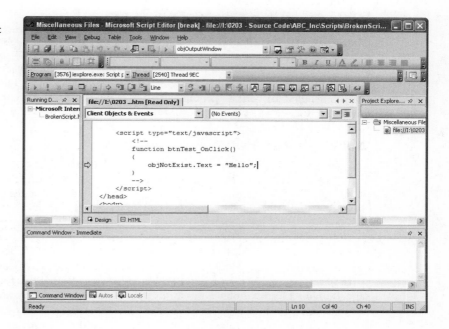

Learning More about JavaScript

Sometimes it's amazing to discover just what you can do with JavaScript because most people don't see JavaScript as a real programming language. However, JavaScript is a very robust language and you can do a lot with it. Not everyone has an eternity, though, to learn a new programming language. One of the best tutorials is the Webmonkey JavaScript Crash Course at `http://webmonkey.wired` `.com/webmonkey/programming/javascript/tutorials/jstutorial_index.html`. This course covers all of the basics including issues such as creating loops and understanding how JavaScript works with variables. Another great tutorial is the one put out by the W3Schools at `http://www` `.w3schools.com/js/`. The W3Schools site also has many excellent coding examples.

Once you get past the basics, you'll want to start looking through a manual that contains all of the JavaScript functions. The best source of information is the ECMAScript site at `http://www` `.ecma-international.org/publications/standards/Ecma-262.htm`. (ECMAScript is a name for standardized JavaScript created by the European Computer Manufacturer's Association.) If you want a strict JavaScript guide, then the JavaScript guide at `http://wp.netscape.com/eng/mozilla/3.0/` `handbook/javascript/` is a good option.

Many people learn best by seeing coding examples. A good source of JavaScript coding examples is Koders as `http://www.koders.com/default.aspx`. Another good place to look for coding examples is JavaScript Source at `http://javascript.internet.com/`. ScriptSearch.com (`http://www` `.scriptsearch.com/`) has many script examples to look at. Finally, you might also want to check out the Microsoft Scripting site at `http://msdn.microsoft.com/scripting/`.

Working with Controls

This section uses the term *control* very loosely because that's how JavaScript treats controls. A control can be anything from an `<Input>` tag to an actual ASP.NET control. You can also create controls on standard HTML pages using the `<Object>` tag. The only problem with this approach is that the client must support ActiveX controls, must allow you to run them on the client system, and must have the control installed (or you can provide a means of downloading the control when required). The following sections describe three kinds of controls that you can work with using scripts.

Working with HTML Tags

You can treat HTML tags as you would controls when working with scripts. For example, Listing 6.1 includes a simple script that works with a control—an `<Input>` tag in this case. You'll find this example in the `\ABC_Inc\Scripts\Controls` folder of the source code on the Sybex Web site. When the user clicks Test, the script displays a dialog box that shows what the `txtMessage` control, the `<Input>` tag, contains.

There's nothing special about this page except that it does use a client-side script to perform work with `btnTest`. The `onclick` attribute connects `btnTest` to the `TestMe()` script. When you begin typing `onclick` in the IDE, you'll notice that IntelliSense even displays it as an event using the event icon.

The browser supplies the `alert()` method for you. All that this function accepts is a simple message, but you'll find it quite useful for diagnosing problems with your applications. The message need not be a string—JavaScript doesn't rely on strict typecasting, so you can supply a string, a number, or an object should you wish to do so. However, the output you receive depends on precisely what you provide as input—an object would display an `[Object]` moniker, rather than a value.

Notice that the actual script appears within a comment (<!-- -->). The reason for this convention is that not all browsers understand scripts. Using the comment keeps browsers that don't understand scripts from choking on the code. Browsers that do understand scripts ignore the comment. Most modern browsers are script friendly, so they'll work with the script without problem. Even so, you should include the comment to ensure that users of older browsers don't experience problems with your Web site.

LISTING 6.1:   Using a Simple Control

```
<!DOCTYPE html PUBLIC "-//W3C//DTD XHTML 1.1//EN"
                   "http://www.w3.org/TR/xhtml11/DTD/xhtml11.dtd">
<html xmlns="http://www.w3.org/1999/xhtml" >
<head>
    <title>Untitled Page</title>
    <script type="text/javascript">
    <!--
        function TestMe()
        {
            // Display a message for the user.
            alert(MyForm.txtMessage.value);
        }
    -->
    </script>
</head>
<body>
    <form id="MyForm" name="MyForm">
        <h1>Control Test Form</h1>
        <div>
            <label id="lblMessage" for="txtMessage">
                Type a Message
            </label>
            <input type="text"
                   id="txtMessage"
                   name="txtMessage"
                   value="Hello" />
        </div>
        <div>
            <input type="button"
                   id="btnTest"
                   name="btnTest"
                   value="Test"
                   onclick="TestMe()" />
        </div>
    </form>
</body>
</html>
```

IntelliSense also plays a role in the use of controls. When you type the name of a control—no matter what kind of control it might be—IntelliSense displays the events, methods, and properties associated with that control. In fact, you can't determine the control type from the IntelliSense display because all controls receive equal treatment. For example, when you type txtMessage, IntelliSense displays a list like the one shown in Figure 6.5 that includes all of the essentials for this control created from a tag.

FIGURE 6.5
IntelliSense helps you access the events, methods, and properties that controls support.

Using the *<Object>* Tag

Most enterprise developers shy away from the <Object> tag because it has caused problems in the past. Microsoft originally introduced the <Object> tag to bring Component Object Model (COM) controls to the Internet. However, many of the issues surrounding the <Object> tag no longer exist. The <Object> tag appears on many Web pages and you'll even find it discussed on the World Wide Web Consortium (W3C) school Web site at http://www.w3schools.com/tags/tag_object.asp. Unfortunately, new issues with the <Object> tag have cropped up. For example, open source browsers such as Firefox tend not to support it.

The <Object> tag works with either standard HTML pages or ASPX pages, so this solution is great for situations where you might have to work in more than one environment. The point is that this is a standard way of adding controls to your Web page. Unfortunately, Visual Web Developer doesn't provide very good support for this essential means of working with controls, so you end up doing extra work to use it. You'll find the examples in this section in the \ABC_Inc\Scripts\Controls folder of the source code on the Sybex Web site.

GETTING THE *<OBJECT>* TAG DATA

Unless you're creating a special control, you'll want to use a control that everyone has on their machine or that they can easily download from the Internet. Otherwise, you need to consider adding the required support to your Web site and have the user download the control. For example, Adobe Reader and Shockwave Flash are both easy to download from the Internet and all Windows users will have some version of the Windows Media Player already installed. With this problem in mind, the example in this section describes how to use the Windows Media Player—a very common and useful control.

NOTE Enterprise developers tend to create more custom controls than individual developers do for a number of reasons. Consider Web sites such as WebEx (http://www.webex.com/) and Microsoft Update (http://windowsupdate.microsoft.com/). In both cases, the custom control provides special functionality that lets the user interact with the Web site in a new way. Both Web sites provide automated techniques for downloading and testing the required custom control. WebEx also provides manual download and customer support specifically devoted to working out problems with their custom control.

The problem is that you don't know anything about this control, other than it exists somewhere on most machines. The Object Browser can prove invaluable in this case. Select View ➢ Object Browser to display the Object Browser. Click Add Other Components and you'll see the Select Component dialog box shown in Figure 6.6. Locate the component you want to use and click Add. Notice that this display tells you the name and location of the component DLL. Click OK to add the component to the Object Browser.

FIGURE 6.6
Use the Object Browser to your advantage when working with the <Object> tag.

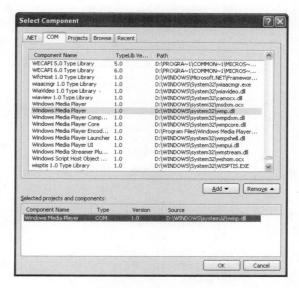

The Object Browser display is very useful because it tells you about the control—how to access its features. The property listing comes in especially helpful later. You need to perform one additional task before you can use the control—you need to learn its class identifier—a special number that uniquely identifies the control. You have two choices for locating this number. The first is to use the OLE/COM Object Viewer utility described in the "Using the OLE/COM Object Viewer to Locate Objects" section of the chapter. The second is to use the Registry Editor to locate the class identifier.

To use the Registry Editor, open a command prompt, type **RegEdit.EXE**, and press Enter to start the Registry Editor. After you open the Registry Editor, choose Edit ➢ Find. Type the path and name of the component DLL and click Find Next. Components can have a lot of property pages and other entries in the registry. Figure 6.7 shows a typical component entry. Notice that it contains the full component name and entries such as the version number. The property page and other entries won't contain this level of detail, so you can easily identify the component entry. The class identifier appears as the key. Right-click the entry and choose Copy Key Name from the context menu.

WARNING   Avoid editing the Registry unless you understand precisely what the change will do. Always create a backup of the Registry before you make any changes to it. You can find an excellent set of utilities for saving and restoring the Registry at http://www.larshederer.homepage. t-online.de/erunt/.

FIGURE 6.7
Using the Registry Editor
lets you copy the class
identifier directly.

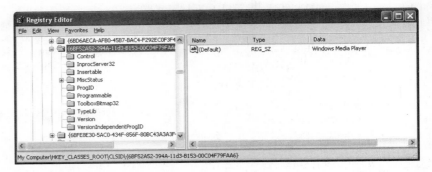

The `<Object>` tag is somewhat self-contained. You can interact with it using a script, but it's best to configure the object as much as possible when you create the `<Object>` tag. Fortunately, the `<Object>` tag is relatively easy to understand. Here's the `<Object>` tag, default parameters, and default values for the Windows Media Player.

```
<OBJECT id=objMediaPlayer
        classid=CLSID:6BF52A52-394A-11d3-B153-00C04F79FAA6>
    <PARAM NAME="URL" VALUE="">
    <PARAM NAME="rate" VALUE="1">
    <PARAM NAME="balance" VALUE="0">
    <PARAM NAME="currentPosition" VALUE="0">
    <PARAM NAME="defaultFrame" VALUE="">
    <PARAM NAME="playCount" VALUE="1">
    <PARAM NAME="autoStart" VALUE="-1">
    <PARAM NAME="currentMarker" VALUE="0">
    <PARAM NAME="invokeURLs" VALUE="-1">
    <PARAM NAME="baseURL" VALUE="">
    <PARAM NAME="volume" VALUE="50">
    <PARAM NAME="mute" VALUE="0">
    <PARAM NAME="uiMode" VALUE="full">
    <PARAM NAME="stretchToFit" VALUE="0">
    <PARAM NAME="windowlessVideo" VALUE="0">
    <PARAM NAME="enabled" VALUE="-1">
    <PARAM NAME="enableContextMenu" VALUE="-1">
    <PARAM NAME="fullScreen" VALUE="0">
    <PARAM NAME="SAMIStyle" VALUE="">
    <PARAM NAME="SAMILang" VALUE="">
    <PARAM NAME="SAMIFilename" VALUE="">
    <PARAM NAME="captioningID" VALUE="">
    <PARAM NAME="enableErrorDialogs" VALUE="0">
    <PARAM NAME="_cx" VALUE="6350">
    <PARAM NAME="_cy" VALUE="6482">
</OBJECT>
```

Just in case you're wondering, unlike some programming languages, the browser doesn't care whether you write your tags in lowercase `<object>`, or initial caps `<Object>`, or uppercase `<OBJECT>`. The reason the code appears as it does, in this case, is this is how the `<Object>` tag stores the data internally using the `outerHTML` property. Listing 6.2 shows a simple page you can use to test various objects and see which `<Param>` tags they support. Notice that I haven't included any `<Param>` tags in order to see the default values the control uses—the control won't actually work this way.

LISTING 6.2:   Testing *<Object>* Tag Parameter Values

```
<!DOCTYPE html PUBLIC "-//W3C//DTD XHTML 1.1//EN" "http://www.w3.org/TR/xhtml11/DTD/
xhtml11.dtd">
<html xmlns="http://www.w3.org/1999/xhtml" >
<head>
    <title>Show the Object Params</title>
    <script type="text/javascript">
    <!--
        function ViewParams()
        {
            txtOutput.value=objMediaPlayer.outerHTML;
        }
    -->
    </script>
</head>
<body>
    <h1>Show the Object Params</h1>
    <object id="objMediaPlayer"
            classid="CLSID:6BF52A52-394A-11d3-B153-00C04F79FAA6" >
    </object><br />
    <input type="button" id="btnTest" value="Test" onclick="ViewParams()" /><br />
    <textarea id="txtOutput" cols="50" rows="10" />
</body>
</html>
```

DEVELOPING WITH THE *<OBJECT>* TAG

Once you know enough about the control you want to use, it's time to begin creating a Web page with it. Depending on the control, the object could be a single part of a much larger design, or it might be the basis of the entire page. For example, an on-screen drawing application would likely have a number of constituent parts. On the other hand, you could create an entire Web page out of the Windows Media Player. The example that appears in Listing 6.3 shows how you can interact with the Windows Media Player as an application.

LISTING 6.3:   Using the Windows Media Player on a Web Page

```
<!DOCTYPE html PUBLIC "-//W3C//DTD XHTML 1.1//EN"
                      "http://www.w3.org/TR/xhtml11/DTD/xhtml11.dtd">
<html xmlns="http://www.w3.org/1999/xhtml" >
<head>
    <title>Play the Windows Media Player</title>
    <script type="text/javascript">
    <!--
        function ChangeTune()
        {
            // Select the desired tune.
            switch (optSelect.selectedIndex)
            {
                case 0:
                    objMediaPlayer.URL = "Bells.WAV";
                    break;
                case 1:
                    objMediaPlayer.URL = "Cuckoo2.WAV";
                    break;
                case 2:
                    objMediaPlayer.URL = "Shred2.WAV";
                    break;
            }

            // Display the effect of the change.
            txtOutput.value = objMediaPlayer.childNodes(0).name +
                            " is set to " +
                            objMediaPlayer.childNodes(0).value;

            // Play the tune.
            objMediaPlayer.controls.play();
        }
    -->
    </script>
</head>
<body>
    <h1>Play the Windows Media Player</h1>
    <p>Click Play to start the sound.</p>

    <!-- The configured Media Player object. -->
    <object id="objMediaPlayer"
            classid="CLSID:6BF52A52-394A-11d3-B153-00C04F79FAA6" >
        <param name="URL" value="Cuckoo2.WAV" />
        <param name="autoStart" value="0" />
    </object><br />
```

```
    <!-- Sound selections from the current project and the
        change button. -->
    <select id="optSelect">
        <option value="Bells.WAV">Bells</option>
        <option value="Cuckoo2.WAV">Cuckoo</option>
        <option value="Shred2.WAV">Shredder</option>
    </select>
    <input type="button"
            id="btnChoose"
            value="Choose"
            onclick="ChangeTune()" /><br />

    <!-- An output area to monitor the status of the Media Player
        object. -->
    <textarea id="txtOutput" cols="50" rows="2" />
</body>
</html>
```

The Web page contains the Windows Media Player control, a sound effect selection, and a button for changing the sound within the Windows Media Player. The example also includes a status window so you can see the effects of the change on the internal Windows Media Player data. The project folder contains three sound files that you can use, or you can create sound files of your own.

When the user clicks Choose, `btnChoose` calls `ChangeTune()`. The `ChangeTune()` function begins by setting the `objMediaPlayer.URL` property to the name of the new sound file. The next step verifies the setting by outputting the `objMediaPlayer.childNodes(0).name` and `objMediaPlayer.childNodes(0).value` properties. The `childNodes` array contains a list of the parameters described in the "Getting the *<Object>* Tag Data" section of the chapter in the order described. Every object you create has the same feature, so you can easily track the status of various elements, even those not accessible through properties.

TIP The Internet provides a number of resources for using the Windows Media Player. One of the best sources is the series of articles that Microsoft provides at `http://msdn.microsoft.com/library/en-us/wmplay10/mmp_sdk/displayingwebpagesinwindowsmediaplayer.asp`. You'll find a streaming media jukebox player application described at `http://www.webreference.com/js/column51/install.html`. The article at `http://cita.rehab.uiuc.edu/mediaplayer/sami-web.html` tells you how to add media with captions to your Web site. In fact, this is one of the few examples that also shows you how to request a download of the Windows Media Player when the client machine doesn't have it installed.

The final step tells the Windows Media Player to play the selected file using the `objMediaPlayer.controls.play()` method. Unfortunately, you won't find either the URL property or the `play()` method listed in IntelliSense—you must know which properties and methods the object supports. That's why it's handy to have a copy of Object Browser open so you can work with the various properties and controls. Figure 6.8 shows typical output from this application. Notice that even though you can't see the object in Visual Web Developer, it displays correctly on the Web page and you even have full access to the various object features.

FIGURE 6.8
The Windows Media
Player and other
objects work great
on Web pages.

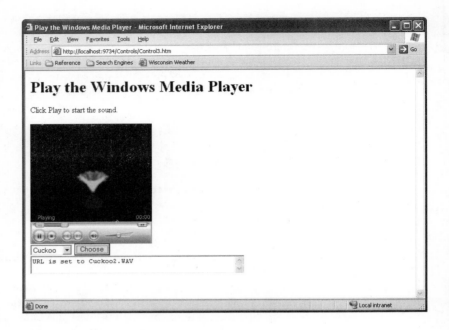

USING THE OLE/COM OBJECT VIEWER TO LOCATE OBJECTS

Visual Studio comes with a wealth of really interesting tools—many of which appear somewhere in this book. Unfortunately, Microsoft hides them from view, so you have to know where to look. For example, check out the `\Program Files\Microsoft Visual Studio 8\Common7\Tools\Bin` folder on your machine and you'll find `OleView.EXE`. The OLE/COM Object Viewer utility can save you considerable time when working with objects of any type.

Because enterprise developers have to work with older applications so often, it's very helpful to have the OLE/COM Object Viewer installed directly in the IDE where you can grab it whenever you want. To add the utility, select the Tools ➢ External Tools command to display the External Tools dialog box shown in Figure 6.9. Click Add to add a new tool entry. The figure shows how to add the OLE/COM Object Viewer to the list of tools.

When you start up the OLE/COM Object Viewer, you'll find that the data appears in a hierarchy. Figure 6.10 shows the main elements of this utility. You can locate objects by category or simply search through the All Object entry for the object you need. This utility makes it easy to learn about the object's type library and interfaces. It's even possible to locate information based on application association.

Lest you think that there's no chance of ever using this utility with a pure .NET application, think again. Every component or control you create with a COM attribute appears in the .NET Category folder shown in Figure 6.11. The highlighted control is one that I use for creating eBay Web Service applications. The point is that you can find .NET controls in the list and use them with a `<Object>` tag (if desired) on a Web page. This technique comes in handy when you want to use a desktop control on a Web page even when the control won't normally work in this scenario.

FIGURE 6.9

Install the tools you need in the IDE to make them accessible without looking for them every time.

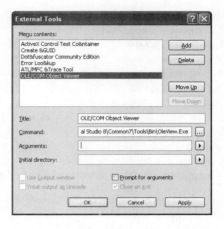

FIGURE 6.10

The OLE/COM Object Viewer makes it easy to locate any object using several techniques.

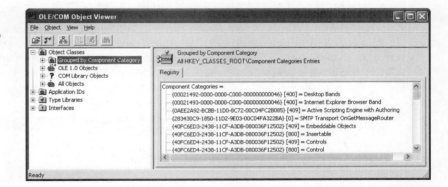

FIGURE 6.11

Even .NET controls and components appear in the list when you use a COM attribute.

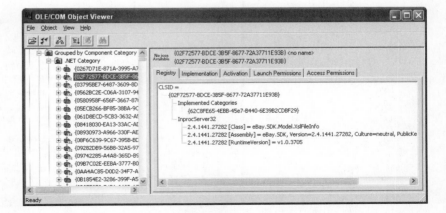

The example in this chapter relies on the Windows Media Player. You can locate the control in the All Objects folder, by application, by interface, or using a number of other means. However, you'll normally to begin looking in the in the Control folder shown in Figure 6.12. To ensure you get the right information for the <Object> tag, right-click the control entry and choose Copy HTML <Object> Tag to Clipboard from the context menu. All you need to do now is paste the tag into Visual Studio. The resulting <Object> tag doesn't include the required <Param> tags, but it's a step in the right direction.

Notice that while the left pane provides an overview of the control, the right pane provides details about the current object. The utility works just like Windows Explorer. Click the plus sign next to the control entry and you'll see the list of interfaces that this control supports. You can select the interfaces to learn more about them. For example, you can determine precisely which DLLs this control needs to function by looking at the interface information in many cases.

TIP Sometimes the OLE/COM Object Viewer will reveal Java classes on the system—an important consideration in some Web development tasks. To determine whether a control relies on Java, select the control entry, choose the Implementation tab, and look at the Java check box. When you see a check in this option, you know that the control relies on Java.

The OLE/COM Object Viewer can help you with a wealth of configuration problems too. For example, select the Launch Permissions tab and you can choose who can launch the control and use it. Likewise, the Access Permissions tab lets you select the access security for the control. You can also control how the control activates—perhaps you want it to activate on the server rather than the client. The Activation tab lets you adjust these features.

FIGURE 6.12
The OLE/COM Object Viewer makes locating controls easy.

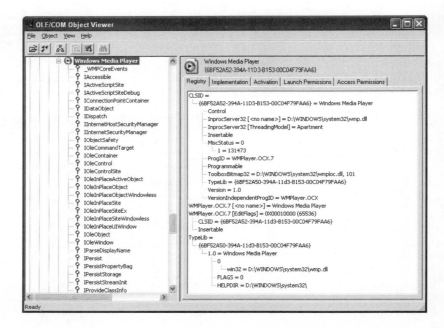

Whenever you finish working with a control, make sure you release it. Otherwise, it just hangs around in memory using up resources. To release the control, right-click its entry and choose Release Instance from the context menu.

Relying on ASP.NET Controls

Of all the controls you can use with Visual Web Developer, ASP.NET controls prove the least cumbersome and difficult to use. Unfortunately, you'll find that using scripts with master pages is very hard when working with ASP.NET. You have to overcome a number of obstacles that include control renaming and the inability to use standard HTML controls within the content areas. Consequently, you'll need to determine whether you want scripts or master pages in most cases.

You have to follow a few odd rules when working with ASP.NET controls, one of which is that you can't always use an ASP.NET control to perform a task. The control that actually interacts with the script must be an HTML control. For example, you can create an entire form using ASP.NET controls as long as the button used to submit the form using a script is an HTML control. ASP.NET controls only support code behind techniques, which means they always require server support. Listing 6.4 shows a simple example of working with ASP.NET controls. You'll find this example in the \ABC_Inc\Scripts\Controls folder of the source code on the Sybex Web site.

LISTING 6.4:   Using Scripts with ASP.NET Controls

```
<%@ Page Language="VB"
        AutoEventWireup="false"
        CompileWith="Control4.aspx.vb"
        ClassName="Control4_aspx" %>

<!DOCTYPE html PUBLIC "-//W3C//DTD XHTML 1.1//EN"
                      "http://www.w3.org/TR/xhtml11/DTD/xhtml11.dtd">

<html xmlns="http://www.w3.org/1999/xhtml" >
<head runat="server">
    <title>Untitled Page</title>
    <script type="text/javascript">
    <!--
        function btnChange_OnClick()
        {
            var InputString;

            // Get the current string value.
            InputString = form1.txtInput.value;

            // Encode it.
            form1.txtOutput.value = escape(InputString);
        }
    -->
    </script>
</head>
```

```
<body>
    <form id="form1" runat="server">
    <div>
        <asp:Label ID="lblGreeting"
                   Runat="server"
                   Text="ASPX Control
                   Demonstration" Font-Bold="True"
                   Font-Size="X-Large"></asp:Label>
        <br />
        <asp:Label ID="lblInput"
                   Runat="server"
                   Text="Type any string: "
                   AssociatedControlID="txtInput"></asp:Label>
        <asp:TextBox ID="txtInput"
                     AccessKey="T"
                     Runat="Server">
            A Sample String
        </asp:TextBox><br />
        <asp:Label ID="lblOutput"
                   Runat="server"
                   Text="Output string: "
                   AssociatedControlID="txtOutput"></asp:Label>
        <asp:TextBox ID="txtOutput" Runat="server"></asp:TextBox>
        <br />
        <input id="btnChange"
               accesskey="C"
               type="button"
               value="Change the Text"
               onclick="btnChange_OnClick()" />

    </div>
    </form>
</body>
</html>
```

Begin by looking at the HTML for this example. All of the controls are ASP.NET controls, not standard HTML controls, except for btnChange. You need to use a standard HTML control here because the standard ASP.NET button doesn't support scripting through the onclick attribute. The HTML in this example demonstrates a perfect mix of ASP.NET and HTML—at least if you want to use client-side processing to reduce the workload on the server.

WARNING The features described in this section only apply to ASP.NET 2.0. Older versions of ASP.NET are extremely painful to work with when using scripts because the server mangles the control names. To learn more about this particular problem, see the WWW Coder article at http://www.wwwcoder.com/main/parentid/261/site/3590/68/default.aspx.

Notice that this code does include the usual <%@ Page> directive. You can create a page where some buttons or other controls with events use client-side processing and other controls rely on the server for processing. The point is that you have the freedom to use whatever kind of processing works best for the particular situation.

When a user clicks Change the Text in this application, btnChange calls the btnChange_OnClick() method. This function begins by obtaining the form1.txtInput.value property. IntelliSense won't tell you that this control is available, nor will it tell you about the full list of properties and objects that form1 possesses. Sometimes you have to work with the script for a while in the debugger to understand fully the properties, methods, and events the various controls support in code. Notice, however, that txtInput is an ASP.NET control and you can access it without error in the script.

Once the code obtains the value of txtInput, it uses the escape() function to modify any characters that could cause problems in HTML so that you can transmit them without error. The code places the result in form1.txtOutput.value (another ASP.NET control) and the user sees the value on screen—without a trip to the server. Figure 6.13 shows typical output from this application.

Notice that the escape() function converts problem characters to other forms. For example, it converts spaces to %20 and the backslash (\) to %5C. This is a standard conversion that all Web servers understand and use. You can find a complete list of these conversions on the User Interface Programming site at http://www.petterhesselberg.com/charcodes.html.

FIGURE 6.13
ASP.NET Web pages can use scripts just as easily as standard HTML.

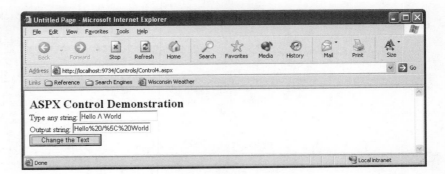

Scripting with Client Callback

An enterprise developer might find that having all of the script on the client isn't that good of an idea and simultaneously want to enhance page performance by reducing network traffic. ASP.NET 2.0 provides an alternative to posting an entire page back every time the user needs an answer in the form of the client callback. This feature assumes you have a server that has the code behind code on it. Therefore, most hobbyist and small company Web sites can't use this technique—especially not on a hosted Web site.

The process relies on a new interface, ICallbackEventHandler that includes one method, RaiseCallbackEvent(). The combination of these two items lets you define a callback in the Web page. ASP.NET actually creates the JavaScript to implement the callback for you. All you need to do is provide a placeholder for the script so ASP.NET knows where to place it. You also need to provide two output scripts. The first defines what to do when the call succeeds and the second defines what to do when it fails. The starting point is the code behind shown in Listing 6.5. You'll find this example in the \ABC_Inc\Scripts\Controls folder of the source code on the Sybex Web site.

LISTING 6.5:　　　Creating an ASP.NET Callback Class

```
Partial Class Control5_aspx
    Implements ICallbackEventHandler

    Public strCallbackFunctionInvoke As String

    Protected Sub Page_Load(ByVal sender As Object, _
        ByVal e As System.EventArgs) Handles Me.Load

        ' Define the event handling information.
        strCallbackFunctionInvoke = _
            Me.GetCallbackEventReference( _
                Me, "Input", "ReverseString", "context", "ShowError")

    End Sub

    Public Function RaiseCallbackEvent(ByVal eventArgument As String) _
        As String Implements _
        System.Web.UI.ICallbackEventHandler.RaiseCallbackEvent

        Dim Output As New StringBuilder()    ' Contains the result.

        ' Verify the string is the proper length.
        If eventArgument.Length = 0 Then
            Throw New ArgumentException("No string provided!")
        End If

        ' Process the characters one at a time.
        For Each Item As Char In eventArgument

            ' Insert the characters at the beginning to reverse the
            ' string.
            Output.Insert(0, Item)
        Next

        ' Return the reversed string.
        Return Output.ToString()
    End Function
End Class
```

The code begins by defining strCallbackFunctionInvoke, which is the placeholder that tells ASP.NET where to place script in the Web page. You'll see this string again in Listing 6.6. However, for now, all you need to know is that it contains the information that the Web page needs to make a callback. The code defines the content of this string in the Page_Load() method. The

GetCallbackEventReference() method returns a specially formatted string containing the callback information. The callback information includes:

◆ A reference to the control that handles the callback

◆ The name of the Web page variable that holds the input data

◆ The name of a function on the Web page that the callback will call when the call succeeds

◆ A variable containing context information for the callback

◆ The name of a function on the Web page that the callback will call when the call fails

The RaiseCallbackEvent() method performs the actual data processing. You can pass a single string to this method—the same string defined as Input in strCallbackFunctionInvoke. In this case, the code simply reverses the content of the string and sends it back to the caller. You can perform any amount of processing in this method, but you only have one method to use, so you'll need to implement selective processing in some cases.

Now that you know what the code behind is doing, it's time to look at the Web page. Listing 6.6 shows the simple Web page used for this example. Notice how the variables and functions defined in Listing 6.5 appear in this listing.

LISTING 6.6:   Creating Callback Linkage Using Client Scripts

```
<head runat="server">
    <title>ASP.NET Client Callback Demonstration</title>

    <script language="javascript">
    <!--
        function SendData()
        {
            var Input = form1.txtInput.value;
            var context = "";

            <%=strCallbackFunctionInvoke%>
        }

        function ReverseString(Output, context)
        {
            // Display the output information.
            form1.txtOutput.value = Output;
        }

        function ShowError(Error, context)
        {
            // Display the error message.
            alert(Error);
        }
    -->
```

```
            </script>
        </head>
        <body>
            <form id="form1" runat="server">
            <div>
                <p>
                    <asp:Label ID="lblGreeting" runat="server"
                            Text="ASP.NET Client Callback Demonstration"
                            Font-Bold="true" Font-Size="Large"></asp:Label>
                </p>
                <p>
                    <asp:Label ID="lblInput" runat="server"
                            AssociatedControlID="txtInput"
                            Text="Type Some Text: "></asp:Label>
                    <asp:TextBox ID="txtInput" runat="server"
                            ToolTip="Data for the server.">
                    </asp:TextBox><br />
                    <asp:Label ID="lblOutput" runat="server"
                            AssociatedControlID="txtOutput"
                            Text="Results: "></asp:Label>
                    <asp:TextBox ID="txtOutput" runat="server"
                            ToolTip="Shows the result of the call.">
                    </asp:TextBox>
                </p>
                <p>
                    <input id="btnTest" type="button" value="Test"
                            accesskey="T" title="Send data to the server."
                            onclick="SendData()" />
                </p>
            </div>
            </form>
        </body>
```

Begin with `btnTest`. The `onclick` event handler for this button is `SendData()`. When you view `SendData()` you see two lines that define variables with very specific names—the same names defined for `strCallbackFunctionInvoke` in Listing 6.5. In this case, Input receives the value from `form1.txtInput`. The only line of code is `<%=strCallbackFunctionInvoke%>`, which tells ASP.NET to replace this entry with the callback information. Figure 6.14 shows how this works in actual practice. The figure shows what you see when you run the application and view the source. Notice that ASP.NET automatically replaces the variable with the code needed to make the callback.

The `WebForm_DoCallback()` method shown in Figure 6.14 calls the `RaiseCallbackEvent()` method shown in Listing 6.5 indirectly using an XMLHTTP object that is hidden from view. The arguments tell the XMLHTTP object how to interact with the Web page. When the call succeeds, the XMLHTTP object passes control back to the `ReverseString()` function, which displays the result in `form1.txtOutput`. On the other hand, when the call fails, the XMLHTTP object passes control back to the `ShowError()` function, which displays an `alert()` with the error message. Figure 6.15 shows typical output from this application.

FIGURE 6.14
You must view the Web site source to see the actual callback script.

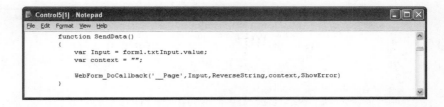

FIGURE 6.15
The application simply reverses a string, but you can build code behind of any complexity.

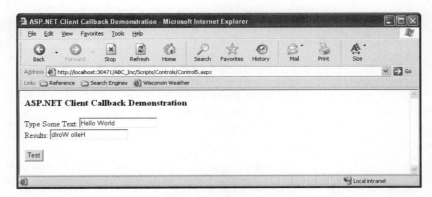

The point of this example is that the majority of the processing took place on the server. This approach reduces security risks. In addition, you can achieve good data hiding so that users don't know the basis for calculations or the source of your information. However, the technique also allows client-side processing. You could check the data for errors before sending it to the server. It's also quite easy to perform postprocessing using this technique. Of course, the most important aspect is that the data flows between client and server without sending the page back. Consequently, this technique conserves systems resources and enhances performance.

Storing and Deleting Cookies

No matter how you try to avoid using them, some applications require the use of cookies. The problem is simple. Web communications are one way. A client makes a request and the server responds. When the client makes a second request, the server views it as a new connection, making Web communications stateless. The only way to add state information (maintain a view of the transactions taking place) is to use cookies in many cases. Cookies store the information needed for the system to keep track of the conversation between the client and the server. The following sections describe the two cookie types: temporary and permanent.

Creating and Reading Temporary Cookies

Always use temporary cookies when you can. A temporary cookie only lasts for the current session, which means that you don't have as many privacy and security concerns when using them. In addition, most users are more willing to allow cookies when they know that the cookie will only last a short time. Listing 6.7 shows how to create a temporary cookie. You'll find this example in the \ABC_Inc\Scripts\Cookies folder of the source code on the Sybex Web site.

LISTING 6.7:   Using Temporary Cookies

```
<!DOCTYPE html PUBLIC "-//W3C//DTD XHTML 1.1//EN"
                      "http://www.w3.org/TR/xhtml11/DTD/xhtml11.dtd">
<html xmlns="http://www.w3.org/1999/xhtml" >
<head>
    <title>Temporary Cookie Demonstration</title>

<script language="javascript">
<!--
   function GetCookie()
   {
      if (clientInformation.cookieEnabled)
      {
         // When there aren't any cookie values, ask
         // for new entries.
         if (document.cookie.length == 0)
         {
            // Get the user name.
            txtUserName.value = prompt("Please type your user name");

            // Get a background color.
            document.bgColor = prompt("Type a background color name");
         }
         else
         {

            // Get the cookie values.
            var aCookies = document.cookie.split("; ");

            // Process each of the cookie values.
            for (Counter = 0; Counter < aCookies.length; Counter++)
            {
               // Divide the cookie into a name and value pair.
               var aCrumb = aCookies[Counter].split("=");

               // Determine the cookie type.
               switch (aCrumb[0])
               {
                  case "UserName":
                     txtUserName.value = unescape(aCrumb[1]);
                     break;
                  case "bgColor":
                     document.bgColor = unescape(aCrumb[1]);
                     break;
               }
            }
         }
```

```
            // Display a personalized greeting.
            txtGreeting.innerText =
                "Hello " + txtUserName.value + ", glad to see you!";
        }
        else
        {
            // Provide a greeting for users who don't have
            // cookies enabled.
            txtGreeting.innerText="Hello stranger, glad to see you!";
        }
    }
    function SaveCookie()
    {
        // Determine whether the user has cookies enabled.
        if (clientInformation.cookieEnabled)
        {
            // Normally you don't display a message, but it's
            // good for testing.
            alert("Saving Cookie");

            // Save the user's name.
            document.cookie =
                "UserName=" + escape(txtUserName.value) + ";";

            // Save the user's background color preference.
            document.cookie = "bgColor=" + escape(document.bgColor);
        }
    }
//-->
</script>

</head>

    <!-- Use one function for loading the cookies and another to save
         them -->
    <body onload="GetCookie()" onunload="SaveCookie()">

    <!-- This input is only used for temporary data storage so it has
         no size. -->
    <input type="hidden" id="txtUserName" visible="false" />

    <!-- Display the customized greeting. -->
    <p id="txtGreeting"></p>

</body>

</html>
```

When the form loads, it calls the GetCookie() function. This code considers three situations.

1. The user has cookie support, but hasn't visited the site before, so there aren't any cookies to read.

2. The user has visited the site before and there are cookies to read.

3. The user's browser doesn't have cookie support.

The first if statement checks the clientInformation.cookieEnabled property to determine whether the user has cookie support enabled. When the user doesn't have cookie support enabled, the code executes the else clause of this if statement to display a generic greeting. The code doesn't change the background color because there isn't any way to determine the user's preference. You could easily add the generic greeting to the form and avoid using scripts at all when the client doesn't support cookies.

NOTE   Checking for client cookie support illustrates an important concept—always provide an alternative for the user that doesn't want to use cookies even if that alternative is inconvenient for you. Most Web sites work with cookies or they don't work at all, which is a very poor way of treating the user. Sometimes you can't provide the requested functionality with cookies, but there's usually an alternative even when using shopping carts. Simply display a message asking the user to call your customer support line to make the order over the telephone. Using this technique means you won't lose out on a sale.

The next step is to determine whether the user has any cookies for your site. When the document. cookie.length property is 0 there aren't any cookies to process and you can assume this is a first-time user. The code prompts for values to store in the cookies, but you can obtain the cookie data using any other technique you want. Notice that the code doesn't store the data in variables—it uses form entries to store the information. This is a common practice because the form entries are global to the entire Web page.

The else clause executes when the user has cookie support enabled and there are cookies to process. The code uses the special split() method to divide the cookie entries. The split() method creates an array that JavaScript stores in aCookies. The array contains one entry for each cookie.

TIP   You might have noticed the use of the escape() and unescape() functions in the example. Always escape (also known as URL encoding) the values you save to a cookie to ensure that the script converts any control characters into a form that the text file can accept. Likewise, unescape the values when you retrieve them from the cookies to ensure the control character data is restored.

Now that the cookies are split, the code uses the aCookies.length property to determine how many cookies there are and processes each cookie in turn using a for loop. To process a cookie, you must break it into crumbs (a name and value pair). The code uses the split() method again to perform this task and places the name and value pair in the aCrumb array.

NOTE   A cookie consists of two crumbs: a name and a value. The name is the identifier you use for the cookie. Listing 6.7 shows two cookies named: UserName and bgColor. Always choose a name that identifies the purpose of the cookie so you can retrieve and understand its purpose later. The value is the information you want to save. You can retrieve any variable or object property you want to save as a value.

The name `crumb` always appears in array element 0, so the code can use a `switch` statement to process it. A `switch` is an extended version of the `if` statement. Every case entry acts as an `if` statement. Therefore, the code asks whether the name equals `UserName` first and `bgColor` second. When the name doesn't match either value, nothing happens.

When the name does match one of the target values, JavaScript follows the code between the case entry and the break entry. For example, when working with the `UserName` crumb, the code places the value, which always appears in `aCrumb` element 1, into the `txtUserName.value` property.

When the form unloads, it calls the `SaveCookie()` function. Notice that this form contains event handlers for two `<body>` tag events—you can assign as many scripts as needed to various tag events to create a complete solution. This function begins by determining whether the client has cookies enabled. If the client doesn't have cookies enabled, the function exits without doing anything. Otherwise, the code displays a message box using the `alert()` function. It then saves the cookie using the `document.cookie` property.

Unlike many properties, the `document.cookie` property is a collection. Every time you supply a new name and value pair, JavaScript creates a new entry for it in the collection. Consequently, when the code assigns the `UserName` value and then the `bgColor` value to the `document.cookie` property, JavaScript actually creates two entries—one for each value.

Creating and Reading Permanent Cookies

Permanent cookies let you save data between sessions. Some less than honorable Web sites use them to do things like track user movements. Fortunately, you have many useful and positive ways to incorporate permanent cookies into your applications too. A common need is saving user configuration information so that you can restore the user experience for each visit. For example, you could use a cookie to store the user's preferred CSS file as suggested in the "Designing Flexible Interfaces" section of Chapter 4. Always make sure that you provide a privacy policy when using cookies as outlined in the "Developing a Privacy Policy" section of Chapter 5. Listing 6.8 shows how to create a permanent cookie. You'll find this example in the `\ABC_Inc\Scripts\Cookies` folder of the source code on the Sybex Web site.

LISTING 6.8:   Using Permanent Cookies

```
<!DOCTYPE html PUBLIC "-//W3C//DTD XHTML 1.1//EN" "http://www.w3.org/TR/xhtml11/DTD/
xhtml11.dtd">
<html xmlns="http://www.w3.org/1999/xhtml" >
<head>
    <title>Permanent Cookie Demonstration</title>

    <script language="javascript">
    <!--
    function btnSave_Click()
    {
        var UserCookie;              // Stores the user name.
        var TheDate = new Date();    // Date object.
        var Expire;                  // Expiration date.

        // Build an expiration date. Begin by getting the day.
```

```
// of the week.
switch (TheDate.getUTCDay() + 2)
{
case 1:
    Expire = "Sun, ";
    break;

... Other Cases ...

case 7:
    Expire = "Sat, ";
    break;

}

// Add the date.
Expire = Expire + (TheDate.getUTCDate() + 1);

// Add the month.
switch (TheDate.getUTCMonth() + 1)
{
case 1:
    Expire = Expire + " Jan ";
    break;

... Other Cases ...

case 12:
    Expire = Expire + " Dec ";
    break;
}

// Add the year.
Expire = Expire + TheDate.getUTCFullYear() + " ";

// Add the time.
Expire = Expire + TheDate.getUTCHours() + ":" +
        TheDate.getUTCMinutes() + ":" +
        TheDate.getUTCSeconds() + " UTC";

// Create the username cookie.
UserCookie = "UserName=" +
            escape(prompt("Type your name")) +
            "; expires=" + Expire + ";";

// Add the cookie to the document.
document.cookie = UserCookie;
```

```
        // Tell the user the cookie was saved.
        alert("The cookies were saved and will expire on: " +
            Expire + ".");
    }

    function btnGet_Click()
    {
        var  ACookie; // Holds the document cookie.
        var  Parsed;  // Holds the split cookies.
        var  Name;    // The username.

        // Get the cookie.
        ACookie = unescape(document.cookie);

        // Split the cookie elements.
        Parsed = ACookie.split("=");

        // Get the username.
        Name = Parsed[1];

        // Display the name.
        alert("Your name is: " + Name);
    }

    //-->
    </script>
</head>
<body>

    <h1>Permanent Cookie Demonstration</h1>
    <p>
        <button id="btnSave" onclick="btnSave_Click()">
            Save Cookie
        </button>
        <button id="btnGet" onclick="btnGet_Click()">
            Get Cookie
        </button>
    </p>

</body>

</html>
```

The actual cookie creation process is the same as Listing 6.7. In this case, you have access to two buttons on the form—one saves the cookie, while the other gets the cookie. Defining the date takes a little more work. You must create a Universal Time Code (UTC) date for your cookie. The date must appear in a very specific format. The code in Listing 6.8 shows how to create such a date. The final date appears like this:

```
Sat, 5 Jun 2004 18:44:53 UTC
```

To begin the process, the code creates a Date object, `TheDate`. This object provides access to a number of date and time functions, including the UTC functions shown in the code. For example, the `getUTCDay()` function retrieves the day of the week as a number between 0 and 6. Because the date must contain the day as a name, the code uses a switch to convert it to text form.

One of the problems with working with the time functions is that you can't retrieve the time directly. You must use the method shown. The `getTime()` method returns the number of milliseconds since midnight January 1, 1970, which isn't particularly helpful in this case.

Notice that adding an expiration is simply adding another cookie to the document. The expiration date relies on the keyword `expires`, which you can't use for any other purpose. When JavaScript sees this keyword, it reads the date supplied and acts according to specific rules. When the date is in the past, JavaScript erases the cookies immediately. On the other hand, when the date is in the future, JavaScript creates a file on disk that holds the information. The precise location varies, but when you use Windows 2000 or Windows XP, the cookie appears in the `\Documents and Settings\<Your Login Name>\Cookies` folder. The cookie has your name and the folder in which the associated Web page appears, along with a TXT extension. You can easily open the file and see what it contains using Notepad.

Using WebParts to Automate User Customizations

WebParts help you create pages that users can customize as desired. One of the interesting features of WebParts is that they rely on a combination of server- and client-side code. When you create a Web page that includes WebParts, you'll find that it contains scripts that the server automatically generates based on the content of the page you design. The server side of the code manages the page, and it stores the changes the user makes in the local Access database. You'll find that this technique eliminates the need for cookies, but it also creates a requirement for a strong privacy policy that users will accept. Note that this chapter only outlines the basic scripting and database considerations for working with WebParts. The "Working with WebParts" section of Chapter 14 provides additional details. You'll find this example in the `\ABC_Inc\WebParts\Simple` folder of the source code on the Sybex Web site.

TIP　WebParts is an exciting new technology and some early adopters have already begun working with them. You can find an interesting tutorial from one of these early adopters at `http://www.carlosag.net/Articles/WebParts/connectionsTutorial.aspx`.

Adding the *WebPartManager*

The `WebPartManager` control is the component that coordinates the efforts of all of the other controls that you add to the Web page. This control doesn't actually create any content and you don't have to do anything to configure it. However, you must have one (and only one) of these controls on the page before you add any other WebPart controls to the page. You can drag and drop this control from the Toolbox or add it to the page in Source view, as shown here.

```
<asp:WebPartManager ID="WebPartManager1" Runat="server">
</asp:WebPartManager>
```

Changing Selections Using a Custom Control

Before the user can work with WebParts, you must provide a means for them to change selections. Theoretically, Microsoft could provide a control to perform this task, but for whatever reason, they decided not to do so. Consequently, you need to create a custom control to perform the task. You begin this task using the Add New Item dialog box to add a Web User Control to your project. This file type has an ASCX file extension.

Custom controls have two parts. The first part is the display you provide to the end user. Figure 6.16 shows the control interface for this product. It includes a drop-down list for selecting the editing mode, a reset link, and two radio buttons that determine the scope of the changes you make. The scope is important. When you choose the user scope, the changes only affect the local user. Choosing the shared scope mean that everyone's affected.

After you create the basic appearance for the control, you need to add code to make it function. The code in Listing 6.9 shows the initialization portion of a very basic control based on the Microsoft example. You can use this code directly or modify it to meet your needs. However, unless you have a pressing reason to change something, you should stick with this basic example.

FIGURE 6.16

Create a control that includes these basic elements to provide an editor menu.

LISTING 6.9: Defining Editor Handling Features for WebParts

```
' Use a field to reference the current WebPartManager control.
Dim WPM As WebPartManager

Sub Page_Init(ByVal sender As Object, ByVal e As EventArgs)
    ' Tell the Web page to use this handler for WebParts.
    AddHandler Page.InitComplete, AddressOf InitComplete
End Sub

Sub InitComplete(ByVal sender As Object, ByVal e As System.EventArgs)
    Dim DisplayMode As WebPartDisplayMode    ' A list of zones.
    Dim ModeName As String                   ' A mode title.
    Dim ddlModeItem As ListItem              ' One mode entry.

    ' Get the current WebPartManager for the page. The WebPart
    ' Manager will know about all of the editor zones for the
    ' current page.
```

```
WPM = WebPartManager.GetCurrentWebPartManager(Page)

' Fill the drop-down list with the names of display modes
' that the page supports.
For Each DisplayMode In WPM.SupportedDisplayModes

    ' Get the current display mode.
    ModeName = DisplayMode.Name

    ' Make sure a mode is enabled before adding it.
    If DisplayMode.IsEnabled(WPM) Then

        ' Define a new mode list item and add it.
        ddlModeItem = New ListItem(ModeName, ModeName)
        ddlMode.Items.Add(ddlModeItem)
    End If
Next DisplayMode

' Determine whether this user can work with shared scope
' items. Only administrators normally have this privilege.
If WPM.Personalization.CanEnterSharedScope Then

    ' Make the personalization scope panel visible.
    pnlPersonalizeMode.Visible = True

    ' Select the correct scope for the current setup.
    If WPM.Personalization.Scope = PersonalizationScope.User Then
        rbUserScope.Checked = True
    Else
        rbSharedScope.Checked = True
    End If
End If
End Sub
```

The central focus of most activities in this custom control is the WebPartManager control that you added to the Web page. The WebPartManager control, WPM, tracks all of the page activity, knows which zones the page contains, and can interact with the various zones you provide. Consequently, the code defines WPM as a global variable to make the process of working with the page easier.

The Web page only calls the custom control during the page initialization process. To make the control active, you must provide one or more event handler additions during the Page_Init() method call performed by the Web page as part of initializing your control. In this case, the only handler that the Page_Init() method adds is one that calls InitComplete() once the page initialization finishes. The reason for using this approach is that WPM won't know about the various zone controls on the page until after the initialization completes, so the code can't create a menu before that time.

The `InitComplete()` method begins by obtaining a copy of the `WebPartManager` for the current page. It then uses `WPM` to obtain the name or title of mode the Web page currently supports. The modes appear in the `WPM.SupportedDisplayModes` collection. The code gets the name for a mode, verifies that the page has the required control for that mode, and then adds the mode name to the list. The `WebPartManager` supports several modes including:

◆ BrowseDisplayMode

◆ CatalogDisplayMode

◆ ConnectDisplayMode

◆ DesignDisplayMode

◆ EditDisplayMode

The initialization ends by verifying the user's capabilities. Administrators can change both their personal settings and the settings for everyone who uses the Web page. The ability to change individual or all settings is called scope and the `WebPartManager` currently supports two scopes: user and shared. The code detects people who can use shared mode (the default is use) and makes the Personalization Scope panel available to those who have the proper credentials.

Once the initialization is complete, you need to add code to handle the individual controls. The only control that you must implement is the drop-down list that lets the user choose an editing mode. Everything else is optional. Here's the code for the drop-down list.

```
Sub ddlMode_SelectedIndexChanged(ByVal sender As Object, _
                            ByVal e As EventArgs)
    Dim SelMode As String                 ' The User Selected Mode.
    Dim DisplayMode As WebPartDisplayMode  ' WebParts Properties.

    ' Get the editor mode that the user selected from the drop-down
    ' list.
    SelMode = ddlMode.SelectedValue

    ' Get the information for that mode from the list of supported
    ' modes.
    DisplayMode = WPM.SupportedDisplayModes(SelMode)

    ' Change the page to the selected display mode.
    If Not (DisplayMode Is Nothing) Then
        WPM.DisplayMode = DisplayMode
    End If
End Sub
```

The code begins by obtaining the mode the user selected from the drop-down list, `ddlMode`. It uses this information to obtain properties for that particular mode from the list of modes that the `WebPartManager` supports using the `SupportedDisplayModes()` method. Finally, the code sets the current `WPM` mode to match the mode the user selected by changing the `WPM.DisplayMode` property.

Users will make mistakes, so it's nice to provide a means for resetting the display. The Reset User State hyperlink performs this function. When the user clicks this link, the following code changes the WPM state.

```
Protected Sub lbtnReset_Click(ByVal sender As Object, _
                              ByVal e As EventArgs)

    ' Reset all of a user's personalization data for the page.
    WPM.Personalization.ResetPersonalizationState()

End Sub
```

Fortunately, the WebPartManager provides everything needed to perform this task, so you don't have to perform any messy state tracking. The ResetPersonalizationState() method call takes care of everything.

The final task is to let an administrator switch from user to shared mode. You only need to implement this feature when the Web site uses shared settings and allows someone to change them. Here's the code you use to perform this task.

```
Protected Sub rbUserScope_CheckedChanged(ByVal sender As Object, _
                                         ByVal e As EventArgs)

    ' Verify the current scope setting.
    If WPM.Personalization.Scope = PersonalizationScope.Shared Then

        ' Change to user scope if necessary.
        WPM.Personalization.ToggleScope()
    End If
End Sub

Protected Sub rbSharedScope_CheckedChanged(ByVal sender As Object, _
                                           ByVal e As EventArgs)
    ' Verify the current scope setting. Make sure the user is allowed
    ' to enter the shared scope.
    If WPM.Personalization.CanEnterSharedScope AndAlso _
       WPM.Personalization.Scope = PersonalizationScope.User Then

        ' Change to the shared scope.
        WPM.Personalization.ToggleScope()
    End If
End Sub
```

The only call of concern, in both cases, is ToggleScope(). Of course, this means that you must verify the current scope before you call the ToggleScope() method. Otherwise, the toggling sequence will get out of order. Notice also that you must verify a user's credentials before switching into the shared scope mode. Otherwise, anyone could change the shared settings.

Once you complete the custom control, drag it from Solution Explorer onto your application form. The control only displays the mode selection and reset options when you add it to the Web page since the personalization scope features are only available at runtime after verification of the user credentials.

Creating Content with the WebPartZone

A WebPart Web page contains two kinds of content. The first kind is content that the user can't modify. For example, you wouldn't want to let the user remove the company logo from a Web page or modify important content such as warnings. The second kind is content that helps the user in some way that you want to allow the user to change as needed. For example, if your Web page includes the local weather and you feel that information is ancillary, you can let the user remove it or at least move it out of the way. The second kind of content appears in a WebPartZone control.

Normally, you'll include several WebPartZone controls on a page so the user can move items around. A page might contain a sidebar for less important information, a main area for important materials, and a lower section for items the user wants, but doesn't use very often. The point of this example is to show the WebPart technology, rather than interesting content, so the two WebPartZone controls shown here contain simple labels and hyperlinks.

```
<asp:WebPartZone ID="wpzTest"
                 Runat="server"
                 HeaderText="Content Selections"
                 EditVerb-Text="Edit">
    <ZoneTemplate>
        <asp:Label Runat="server"
                   Text="Hello the First Time"
                   ID="lblGreeting1" />
        <asp:HyperLink ID="hlNowhere"
                       Runat="server"
                       NavigateUrl="Default.aspx">
            Goes Nowhere
        </asp:HyperLink>
    </ZoneTemplate>
</asp:WebPartZone>
<asp:WebPartZone ID="wpzTest2"
                 Runat="server"
                 HeaderText="Alternate Content Selections"
                 EditVerb-Text="Edit">
    <ZoneTemplate>
        <asp:Label Runat="server"
                   Text="Hello the Second Time"
                   ID="lblGreeting2" />
    </ZoneTemplate>
</asp:WebPartZone>
```

Notice that the controls appear within a `<ZoneTemplate>` tag. You must include this tag as a container for the content. The content itself is relatively simple. The point is that you can include any content you want within the `<ZoneTemplate>` tag.

Modifying the Content with an *EditorZone*

Depending on what you want the user to do with the page, you can provide the design, edit, or both verbs on the WebPartPageMenu control. The design verb only lets the user move things around, while the edit verb allows a lot more. When you include the edit verb, you also need to add an EditorZone control. The Web page automatically displays the content of this control when the user selects the edit verb. Here's an example of an EditorZone control with two kinds of editors.

```
<asp:EditorZone ID="EditorZone1" Runat="server">
    <ZoneTemplate>
        <asp:AppearanceEditorPart Runat="server"
                                ID="AppearanceEditorPart1" />
        <asp:LayoutEditorPart Runat="server" ID="LayoutEditorPart1" />
    </ZoneTemplate>
</asp:EditorZone>
```

As with most zone controls, you must place the EditorZone control content within a <ZoneTemplate> tag. In this case, the application uses an AppearanceEditorPart (changes the appearance of the control) and a LayoutEditorPart (lets the user move the data elements around) control. As you can see from the code, you don't have to perform a lot of work to make these controls functional. Figure 6.17 shows both controls in action.

FIGURE 6.17

Make changes to the appearance (*Appearance EditorPart*) and layout (*LayoutEditorPart*) of the Web page.

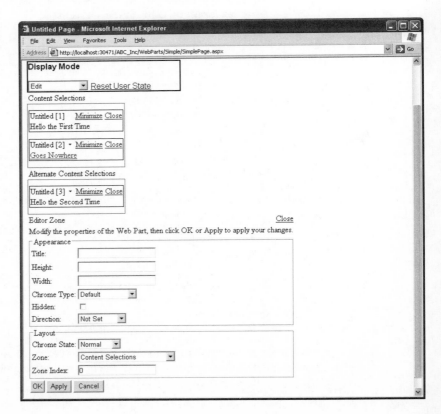

To make this display appear, the user first chooses Edit from the Change the Layout menu. This selection displays the various controls, as shown in Figure 6.17, and makes the Edit selection for each control accessible. Choosing the Edit option for a particular control displays both the Appearance EditorPart and LayoutEditorPart controls. Notice that the AppearanceEditorPart control lets the user change the title for the display element, as well as its width and height. The user can also choose to display the element with a title and border, or without either item. The user can even hide unwanted items from view. The LayoutEditorPart control makes it possible to move Web page elements around and change their state from normal (viewable) to minimized (just the title showing). The Zone Index field changes the control's position within a particular zone.

It's important to note that you can add other controls to the list. The BehaviorEditorPart control lets the user change how the control interacts with the Web page. The PropertyGridEditorPart control lets the user change individual properties for the controls. Both of these controls require special programming, so they appear in the "Working with WebParts" section of Chapter 14.

Adding New Items with the *CatalogZone*

Think of a catalog as something you don't have now, but would like to have on the Web page. For example, when a user closes an element on a Web page and wants it back later, they open the catalog and select the missing item. Visual Web Developer supports three kinds of catalogs through the CatalogZone control. The PageCatalogPart control is the easiest to use and the one that you'll add most often. It lets a user add closed items back onto the page. The DeclarativeCatalogPart and ImportCatalogPart controls provide access to external elements and require special handling, so you'll find them discussed in the "Working with WebParts" section of Chapter 14. Here's a sample of the PageCatalogPart control.

```
<asp:CatalogZone ID="CatalogZone1" Runat="server">
    <ZoneTemplate>
        <asp:PageCatalogPart ID="PageCatalogPart1" Runat="server" />
    </ZoneTemplate>
</asp:CatalogZone>
```

This control becomes active when the user selects the catalog verb from the WebPartPageMenu control. Figure 6.18 shows a typical example of the PageCatalogPart control in action. Notice that it contains the closed element on this Web page. To display the element, the user checks the element option (Untitled [3]), chooses a location from the Add To field, and clicks Add.

Viewing the Script behind the Controls

It's interesting to note that even though you don't write any script to use WebParts, the IDE adds these scripts for you automatically. Right-click the example Web page and choose View Source from the context menu. You'll see the source code for the example Web page as the browser sees it. The first thing you'll notice is that the page contains many scripts sprinkled throughout the page, as shown in Figure 6.19.

Viewing the source for this Web page points out an important reason for learning the scripting language that you choose for Visual Web Developer. Even if you decide not to use scripting for your page, there's a good chance that anything you ask the IDE to perform automatically will produce some client-side code. Knowing how this code works can help you diagnose problems with the Web page. No, you can't modify the code directly, but the code that the IDE produces does help you understand what's going on in the background. In some cases, a change to the settings can make a big difference in the script that you see in the output.

FIGURE 6.18
Add elements back onto the Web page using a *PageCatalogPart*.

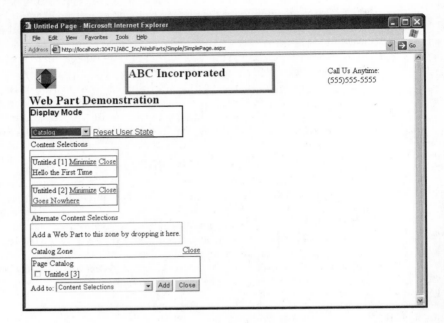

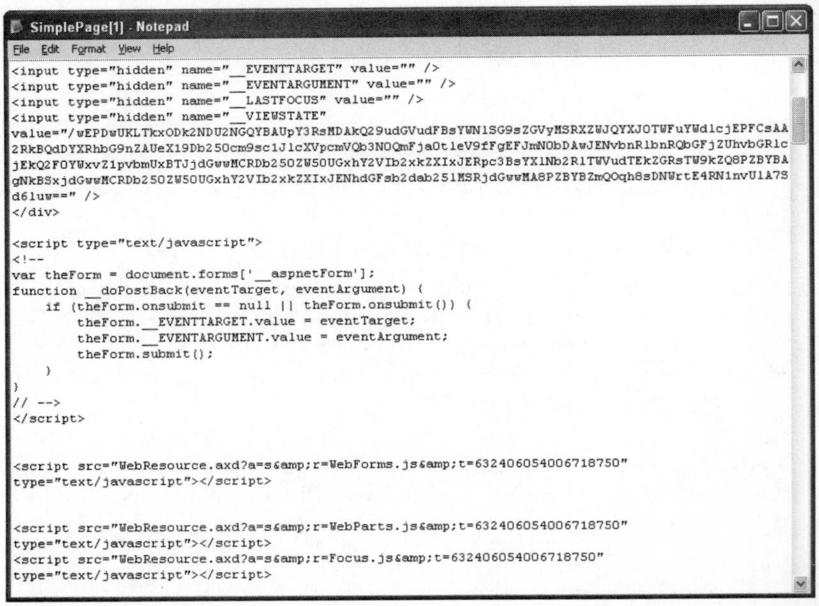

FIGURE 6.19
WebParts really do rely on a combination of client- and server-side scripting.

Keeping Data Safe with Encoding

After you work with the example page for a while, you'll notice that any changes you make appear the next time you start the application—even if you clear all of the cookies from your system. Web-Parts don't rely on cookies to store settings—the settings appear on the server in the `\App_Data` folder in the `ASPNetDB.MDF` database. Look in the `aspnet_PagePersonalizationPerUser` table and you'll see at least one entry like the one shown in Figure 6.20.

The ID field contains the number of the entry. When you find that a page contains errors, it's usually a good idea to delete the personalization settings to avoid creating problems when you test any changes you make. The `PathId` field contains the number of the Web page affected by the settings. You can find this information in the `aspnet_Paths` table. The `UserId` field contains the number of the user that requested the personalization. This value appears in the `aspnet_Users` table. Now, notice the `PageSettings` field. This information is completely encoded. No one can determine what personalization settings the user had made—not even the developer. Only the page user knows which settings are in force, which is the way things should be.

FIGURE 6.20
The WebParts technology automatically makes user selection information safe.

Defining Your Development Goals

This chapter has demonstrated some exciting uses for scripts in your client-side applications. In addition, you've discovered some interesting testing techniques and even learned more about how scripting works on operating systems such as Windows. Of course, it's important to remember that client-side scripting can't solve every problem, not even if you use some of the convoluted and messy scripts that some developers use to work around client-side scripting issues. You also encountered a new user-friendly technology that helps a user develop a better rapport with your applications—WebParts.

Scripts can become a favorite tool or a nightmarish experience—it all depends on how much time you spend working with them. The examples in this chapter provide a good starting point for your scripting experience, but serious developers spend time fine-tuning their scripting knowledge by browsing Web sites that specialize in this particular technology. You'll want to work with as many kinds of scripts as possible so you can truly understand the possibilities. Once you feel you have enough information, try creating some scripting scenarios of your own. Begin by determining whether the task would work better on the client or the server and then test your theory by building the required scripts.

Chapter 7 discusses an essential topic—feedback forms. Many developers (and other people for that matter) view feedback forms as a nuisance. Someone writes in about a problem and makes you look bad. However, properly designed feedback forms are actually resources that make your life easier. A feedback form can provide new ideas for your Web site—ideas that you don't have to think about too hard because someone else has already done the heavy lifting for you. Good feedback forms can also provide a foot in the door. Go ahead, contact the sender, and put them on the hot seat with you. Complaining is easy—figuring out a solution is hard. Perhaps the person who sent you the complaint also has a really interesting and useful way to fix the problem. The point is that feedback forms are great—they let you interact with someone using your Web site and use them as a resource.

Part 3

Creating Simple but Effective Pages

In this part:

Chapter 7

Creating Feedback Forms

Feedback is one of the most miserable forms of Web site interaction for many developers. In fact, entire companies seem adverse to the very notion of feedback because the assumption is that no one fills out feedback forms unless they have an axe to grind. Enterprise developers face the additional burden of trying to figure out how to direct the feedback to the right person. In some cases, a feedback form could go to several people and, in others, the company doesn't provide someone in particular to handle the form.

Unfortunately, my own analysis shows that most people fill out feedback for the sole purpose of complaining about something—very little goes on in the feedback department in the way of thanks or congratulations. Consequently, it's easy to wonder why anyone in their right mind would create not one but several kinds of feedback forms. The answer is simple: You must view feedback forms from a different perspective and manage the information they provide to obtain something of value from them. That's one of the main points of this chapter—discovering why feedback forms are essential to the success of your Web site.

Once you determine that feedback forms are essential, it's time to consider the kinds of forms you should supply. Every Web site should consider three kinds of feedback form as a minimum. The most negative, and yet most essential, feedback form requests user satisfaction information. A second, less negative, form lets the user request help for using your Web site. Finally, a positive feedback form that few Web sites appear to employ is the beneficial suggestion. Generally, providing these three feedback forms help you create a great Web site that meets most users' needs. Of course, adding other specific feedback forms is always helpful and demonstrates that you really do have the user's needs in mind.

Developing great feedback forms doesn't mean you'll actually receive great feedback. In fact, designing a feedback form incorrectly simply opens your Web server to attack by crackers. Consequently, the final portion of this chapter discusses principles you should use when designing forms of any kind. Although the information does center on the feedback form, most of the information provided will help you avoid major problems with form security and lackluster input from the user.

Understanding the Need for Feedback Forms

The first consideration for feedback forms is how to make them into a resource, rather than a major nuisance. A feedback form is someone else's interpretation of your Web site. The interpretation isn't always correct or even warranted—it simply reflects their opinion at that moment in time. In fact, you'll find that the opinions change over time, so the feedback you get today won't be the feedback you receive tomorrow. I've actually had people provide negative feedback one day and retract it the next simply because they were having a bad day and I happened to be an easy target. The important thing to remember is that you can make feedback a resource rather than take it as a personal assault on you or your Web site.

Feedback forms also provide an invaluable method of letting people let you know about Web site issues. The alternatives are that the user will leave your Web site for another one or that your Web site will garner a bad reputation—making it less likely that people will visit in the first place. When people know that you care enough to discuss issues and act on them, it's easier to overlook any problems until you have time to fix them. Generally, the positive attitude that well-designed feedback forms provide creates a better Web site environment. Obviously, you'll run into the person who's having a bad day, but even so, you can normally work around a problem when you know about it—not including feedback forms means you won't ever know about it.

It's not always necessary to focus feedback forms on problems. Sometimes it's better to include a number of positive feedback forms as well. For example, instead of asking the user what's wrong about your Web site, ask them what they like about it instead. In addition, you can seek out the user's opinion—give them a chance to help you design a better Web site by creating a beneficial suggestion form. These positive feedback forms not only give the user a chance to voice an opinion but provide positive feedback to you as well. More importantly, placing the user on the hot seat with you makes it easier for the user to see things from your perspective.

Feedback forms provide an essential service that you must consider in order to have a successful Web site. You need feedback forms to discover more about the user's needs, wants, and desires. In fact, you might even want to classify the feedback you receive on that basis.

Needs   A need is something the user must have to use the Web site at all. For example, if users complain that the color combinations you use make it hard to read the Web site, you should classify that as a need and fix it as soon as possible.

Wants   A want is something that the user requires to enjoy the Web site, but might not need to use it. For example, an "about the company" page is something that helps the user enjoy the site and builds a rapport between your company and the user, but the user doesn't have to have an about the company page in order to obtain good information from the Web site.

Desires   A desire is something that the user doesn't need to either use or enjoy the Web site, but requests anyway. For example, a user might request that you use animated GIFs to dress up the Web site. Although the animation makes the Web site look nicer, it doesn't really affect the user's enjoyment to any degree—it's a bit of extra fluff that you've added.

Targeting Feedback Forms to Meet Specific Needs

In some respects, feedback forms are a kind of marketing. You're marketing the service aspect of your Web site. For this reason, an enterprise developer should get active feedback from the marketing department when creating a Web site. After all, the marketing people are professionals trained to get a specific message across to people no matter what the media might be. In addition, make sure you get the art department involved to dress up the forms and management involved to ensure the form presents the correct company image. Many developers try to take the burden on themselves and that's the wrong approach for feedback forms.

A feedback form tells the user that you value their opinion and plan to do something about it. More importantly, the feedback form itself provides you with the ideas required to do something about the information you receive. Unfortunately, just providing the user with a feedback form that asks, "Yeah, what do you want?" isn't going to do the job. You must target the feedback form to achieve certain goals and may find that you have to tweak the feedback form as you get responses in order to fine-tune the result. The following sections describe some of the methods you can use to target a feedback form.

TIP Don't get the idea that feedback forms always provide two-way communication. In many cases, the user will simply tell you what's wrong and won't want to hear back from you. Of course, this kind of communication is limited in that you can't even ask for additional information. That's why you want to encourage the user to provide some form of two-way communication when you can. Feedback forms can encourage such communication by providing the user with a good reason to continue the conversation. You can offer everything from a pleasant environment to rewards for continuing the conversation so you can obtain all of the information you need. The bottom line is that feedback forms as a resource mean that you must spend some time cultivating the user response.

Considering What You Expect from the Form

Targeting a specific need means creating forms that have fields that answer the questions for a particular requirement. For example, you might create a number of user feedback forms, but each form will answer specific questions. A product feedback form will have part numbers, color, and other product information, while a Web page feedback form will include the URL and the configuration options that the user selected. You might create special user feedback forms for your information page and others for the site search. The idea is to create specific forms for each need so that the user isn't faced with questions that don't make sense, such as asking for the requested URL as part of a product feedback form.

Sometimes you can help yourself by adding hidden fields to the Web page. For example, you don't have to create a special feedback form for every product. However, you also can't assume the user will know the model number of the product they want to ask about, especially if they don't currently own the product. Consequently, you can add hidden fields to the requesting form that include the information you know you'll need, yet can't provide as part of the generic form. Figure 7.1 shows a typical example of hidden fields. In this case, the first hidden field contains the product name, while the second contains the model number. To use a hidden field, all you need to provide is a unique name as part of the (ID) property and the information as part of the Value property.

FIGURE 7.1
Hidden fields make it easier to pass specifics that you can't count on the user providing.

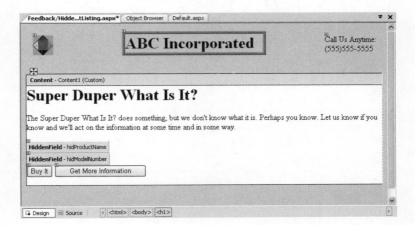

The user won't see the hidden fields when viewing the form using a browser, but the data's there. Notice that this form has a special button for getting more information. The user clicks this button and the Web server passes them along to the generic product request form that you create. However, it won't appear generic—the page actually looks specific because of the hidden fields you provide and even your database will include specific information. Figure 7.2 shows a typical example.

The secret is to modify the form so that the information from the hidden fields configures it as needed. You add this information using the Load event handler shown in Listing 7.1. You'll find the example used for debugging in the \ABC_Inc\Feedback\HiddenFields folder of the source code on the Sybex Web site.

The code begins by retrieving the key values for each of the hidden fields on the parent form. This page relies on a master page, so you can't access the fields directly as you can when using Web pages without the master page connection. Notice that you only need to locate the hidden field within the list of keys—the field name is still there, but it has additional text attached to it. This example also demonstrates the need to provide some type of error trapping. You could provide some means of error handling through the master page to keep the user from seeing the error, but adding this code to the page is a good idea unless you want people prowling around looking for ways onto your enterprise network.

Because the form uses the POST method, you can rely on the `Request.Form.GetValues()` method to retrieve the hidden field information. The code assigns these values to the `txtProductName` and `txtModelNumber` text boxes to create the display in Figure 7.2. The code then makes these fields read-only so the user can't change them.

FIGURE 7.2

Collect and display information from the hidden fields on your generic form.

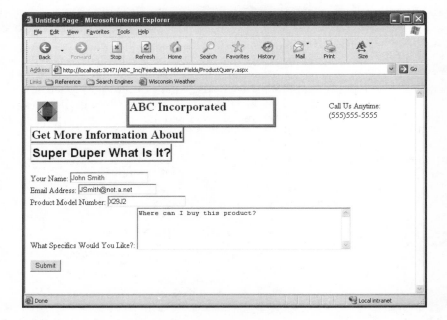

It's interesting to note that the header for the Web page in Figure 7.2 uses two different controls. The "Get More Information About" text appears within a label, so clicking Submit won't send this information to the server. However, the "Super Duper What Is It?" text appears in a textbox, so the form does send this information to the server. As far as the user's concerned, both elements are the same—they look and act the same—only you know the difference.

LISTING 7.1:   Obtaining Feedback Information from Hidden Fields

```
Protected Sub Page_Load(ByVal sender As Object, _
    ByVal e As System.EventArgs) Handles Me.Load

    Dim strProdName As String    ' Key for hidden product name.
    Dim strModNumber As String   ' Key for hidden model number.

    ' Locate the keys we need.
    strProdName = ""
    strModNumber = ""
    For Each Key As String In Request.Form.AllKeys
        If Key.IndexOf("hidProductName") > 0 Then
            strProdName = Key
        End If
        If Key.IndexOf("hidModelNumber") > 0 Then
            strModNumber = Key
        End If
    Next

    ' Verify the information was sent.
    If strProdName.Length = 0 Then

        'Raise an error.
        Throw New ArgumentNullException("hidProductName")
    End If
    If strModNumber.Length = 0 Then

        ' Raise an error.
        Throw New ArgumentNullException("hidModelNumber")
    End If

    ' Get the information from the hidden fields.
    txtProductName.Text = Request.Form.GetValues(strProdName)(0)
    txtModelNumber.Text = Request.Form.GetValues(strModNumber)(0)

    ' Make sure the user can't change it.
    txtProductName.ReadOnly = True
    txtModelNumber.ReadOnly = True
End Sub
```

Defining the Basic User Requirements

Users have specific needs when working with forms. For example, you need to explain how to fill out the form without making the user feel silly or stupid. One of the most effective ways to accomplish this goal is to create questions using sentences that include a description of the information you need. For example, a field that says "Model Number" doesn't really tell the user much, but a field that says "Provide the model number located on the white tag in back of the product." tells the user precisely what you need and where to find it.

Sometimes a good question isn't enough. That's why you should also provide sample information as part of the input. Make sure this information isn't real, but is a good example. Scan the form after the user submits it to ensure the form contains a real model number instead of the example you provided.

Another useful addition to a Web page is to provide entries for every `Title` property. The `Title` property displays a tooltip like the one shown in Figure 7.3. When the user hovers the mouse over this control, the browser displays a tooltip that explains what the user will see after clicking Get More Information. Notice that the questions on this form help the user understand what you need, while the tooltips tell what the user gets for filling out the form.

The concept of telling the user what they receive for providing helpful information is central to designing forms that actually work. In fact, the act of telling the user why they're filling out the form is the only way to ensure that your form will work as anticipated. The user has a need to know why you want the data and how you'll use it. This need goes back to the requirement to provide a privacy policy as explained in the "Developing a Privacy Policy" section of Chapter 5.

FIGURE 7.3
Collect and display information from the hidden fields on your generic form.

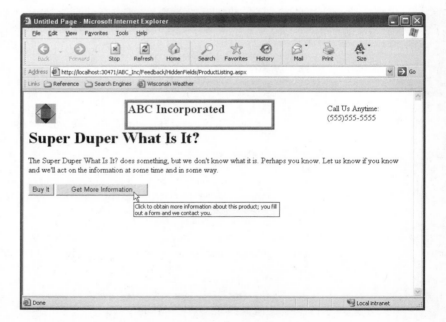

Using a Master Page to Create Multiple Feedback Form Types

At some point, you'll have a list of feedback forms that you want to implement. Depending on how complex your Web site is, you might have several kinds of user feedback forms, a number of product suggestion forms, even several kinds of help forms. The list of forms might seem daunting at first. However, you can dramatically decrease the complexity of the situations by using master pages.

The goal is to find the common areas of each form and then create a master page to address that particular form. For example, you might create a master page for feedback forms. All of the feedback forms would have common elements such as the username and email address, so the master page would include these elements. However, a Web page feedback form might include an URL field while a product feedback form includes a model number field. This special information appears on the individual forms in an area that you designate.

It's unfortunate that you can't create master pages based on other master pages. If this feature were available, you could create a master page with all of the company information. Every feedback form master page could inherit from this beginning page so you would ultimately have just one page with each kind of information. Even so, you can cut and paste the common elements between master pages. Figure 7.4 shows an example of a master page you might create.

The master page uses a layout, but this isn't one of the standard layouts. It contains four sections with very specific purposes. The top is the standard heading found in other master pages for ABC, Incorporated. Every master page should include this common element so a user entering the Web site from another location will instantly recognize it as your Web site. The next section down contains common information such as a greeting and an area where the user can provide a name and email address. The next section contains the form questions—the area the developer will change, two hidden controls that control form functionality, and a submission button. The final area is a footer that contains a copyright notice in this case. The footer could also include a privacy notice, contact information, and other supplementary data when creating a master page for your company.

FIGURE 7.4

Select a master page for the user feedback form you want to create.

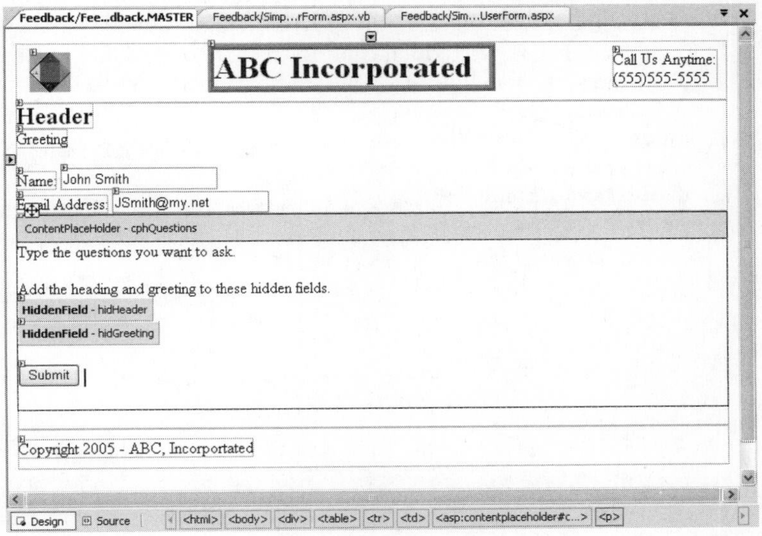

To make this project work better, create the master page first, and then the pages that depend on it. Right-click the project entry in Solution Explorer and choose Add New Item from the context menu. Create a new Master Page. Once you create the master page, start creating the forms you need. Make sure you check Select Master Page on the Add New Item dialog box. Click Add and you'll see the Select a Master Page dialog box shown in Figure 7.5. Notice that the master page appears in a special Feedback folder. Organizing the feedback pages in a special folder can make it easier to create robust Web sites and reduce programming errors. Choose the master page you want to use and click OK.

This is a situation where you'll want to add code in a number of places. First, think about the master page itself. This page contains all of the general elements for the Web page such as the heading. Unfortunately, you don't know the heading name, at this point, and you know that more than one page will use the master page, so you couldn't assign a specific name even if you had one in mind. This is another situation where using hidden controls can be quite helpful. The master page would include a Load event handler like the one shown in Listing 7.2 to ensure the general elements are set. You'll find this example in the `\ABC_Inc\Feedback\FeedbackMaster` folder of the source code on the Sybex Web site.

Using the hidden fields lets the developer implement the form based on the master page. This technique lets the master page change the heading and greeting text without providing access to any other element. Notice that you need to verify that the caller (not the form based on the master page, but the actual caller) passed the required hidden controls. As with all master page setups, you need to check for the keys first, and then obtain the values pointed to by the keys. Error handling is different in this application. You might not want to display a header or greeting on certain pages. This application simply makes the labels invisible when the caller provides a blank value or uses the default provided by the master when the values are missing. The `Request.Form.GetValues("strHeader")` method obtains the values you want to display when the hidden value is available and displays it on screen.

You still have one thing to consider when working with the form based on the master page. It's impossible to edit the two hidden controls supplied as part of the master page in the example. However, the two hidden controls provide default values. The page that calls the form you create will have to include the two hidden controls to change the default text. Figure 7.6 shows a test page that includes the two hidden fields—these values override the defaults provided on the master page.

FIGURE 7.5
Select a master page for the user feedback form you want to create.

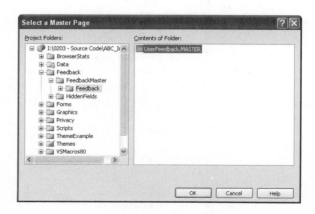

LISTING 7.2:   Handling Content in the Master Page

```
Private Sub frmMaster_Load(ByVal sender As Object, _
                          ByVal e As System.EventArgs) _
                          Handles frmMaster.Load

    Dim strHeader As String     ' Key for hidden product name.
    Dim strGreeting As String   ' Key for hidden model number.

    ' Locate the keys we need.
    strHeader = ""
    strGreeting = ""
    For Each Key As String In Request.Form.AllKeys
        If Key.IndexOf("hidHeader") > 0 Then
            strHeader = Key
        End If
        If Key.IndexOf("hidGreeting") > 0 Then
            strGreeting = Key
        End If
    Next

    ' Replace the standard heading and greeting.
    If strHeader = "" Then
        lblHeader.Visible = False
    Else
        lblHeader.Text = Request.Form.GetValues(strHeader)(0)
    End If
    If strGreeting = "" Then
        lblGreeting.Visible = False
    Else
        lblGreeting.Text = Request.Form.GetValues(strGreeting)(0)
    End If
End Sub
```

This example demonstrates several principles. First, it contains code as part of the master page, so the code affects every page that relies on the master page. Second, it uses hidden values to override the master page default values. Third, it combines all of this master page information with special content provided as part of the page itself. The result appears in Figure 7.7. This page begins to demonstrate some of the power that Visual Web Developer provides to the enterprise developer. Imagine mixing various content sources to create a specific result that makes each page look as if you built it by hand.

FIGURE 7.6
Developers will need to
call the form with the required hidden fields, but
make sure you provide
defaults as well.

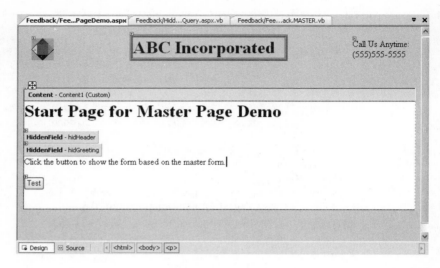

FIGURE 7.7
The content on this
page combines several
sources to create a cohe-
sive whole.

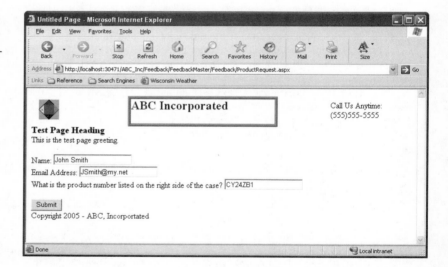

Creating a User Satisfaction Form

Most people have an opinion. The opinion doesn't have a right or wrong value—it's simply how they feel about a particular topic. Getting an honest opinion from people can be difficult, but you can do it. When the topic concerns your application or Web site, the need to get an honest opinion is essential. Otherwise, changes you make to an application or Web site as the result of user feedback is going to be off target—you want to target the users of your site to ensure they have a great experience.

TIP   Don't assume that every positive feedback message you receive means that you're doing everything right with your application. Some people will tell you positive things to obtain benefits they might not normally receive or simply because they don't want to hurt your feelings. Likewise, not every negative message is an indictment against your programming practices. Sometimes a user will have a bad day and decide to take it out on you because you're the nearest target that can't attack back. Deciphering feedback often means reading the message several times and deciding just how it affects your application (or whether it affects your application at all).

The following sections discuss user feedback. This information reflects issues you need to consider when working with your Web site. For example, it discusses some of the problems of sorting information into the right area for consideration.

Designing User Feedback

One of the problems in getting good user feedback is designing the form so that it elicits a response, especially from users who don't normally express themselves well. A nebulous question, such as "How do you feel about this input form?" won't net you a very good response. You need to direct the user to the kind of input you want, without contaminating the user's response. For example, "Does the item search form help you find the information you need to make a purchase, or do you find yourself using alternative search techniques?" offers the user a choice and makes them think about alternatives. The question is still specific enough that even a shy user can provide an answer. Offering yes, no, and other (with a comment field) lets the shy user off the hook, but also lets vocal users state their answers in precise terms.

The problem with most enterprise forms is that committees with varying interests and political motivations design them. It's easy to find examples on most corporate Web sites where the style, content, focus, and methodology for feedback forms changes as you move from area to area. Users often get confused before they even begin working with the form. Consequently, you need to define a style guide for feedback forms for your company as part of the process of creating the first form.

Consider the form shown in Figure 7.8. The form uses a simple mechanism, radio buttons, to help the user make a decision. Users who aren't very vocal can always choose the simple yes or no answers. However, the form also leaves space for vocal users to express an opinion. This form also demonstrates a principle of helping a user use a form by dynamically changing the form to meet specific needs. Only when a user selects the Other option do the spaces for additional information become available. This feature helps users who provide a simple answer know that you aren't requiring anything more from them.

The Web page shown in Figure 7.8 uses the same master page shown in Figure 7.6. In this case, the hidden fields don't contain any information, so the heading and greeting shown in Figure 7.7 don't appear. However, the Name and Email Address fields do appear because they aren't optional. Obviously, you'll need to modify the master page design to allow for any number of scenarios. The point is that this portion of the example does demonstrate the flexibility inherent in master pages.

You need to change some control settings and provide some code behind to make this page function. To make the automation form changes work, you must set the `AutoPostBack` property of each of the `RadioButtonList` controls to `True`. Making this change means that the page posts back to the server every time the user chooses an option. You must also provide a `SelectedIndexChanged()` event handler for both `RadioButtonList` controls. Listing 7.3 shows code you can use to implement the radio button behavior. You'll find this example in the `\ABC_Inc\Feedback\SimpleUserFeedback` folder of the source code on the Sybex Web site.

FIGURE 7.8
Create forms that help
users provide input by
providing default an-
swers and allowing for
additional input.

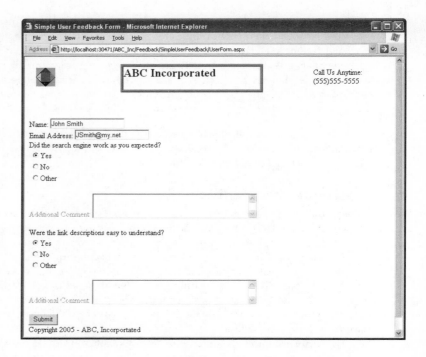

LISTING 7.3:   Handling Feedback Form Events

```
Protected Sub rblQuestion1_SelectedIndexChanged(ByVal sender As Object, _
    ByVal e As System.EventArgs)

    ' Modify the additonal information field as needed.
    If rblQuestion1.SelectedIndex = 2 Then
        lblQuestion1Add.Enabled = True
        txtQuestion1Add.Enabled = True
    Else
        lblQuestion1Add.Enabled = False
        txtQuestion1Add.Enabled = False
    End If
End Sub

Protected Sub btnSubmit_Click(ByVal sender As Object, _
                        ByVal e As System.EventArgs)
    ' Perform any required page processing...

    ' Send the user to the next page.
    Response.Redirect("ThankYou.ASPX")
End Sub
```

The example shows only one of the radio buttons, but both radio buttons require about the same code. In this case, all you need to do is enable the optional input as needed. However, this example demonstrates a need to create responsive forms that lead the user as needed. You could also implement this feature using a client callback. See the "Scripting with Client Callback" section of Chapter 6 for additional details.

Typically, you'll need to perform two tasks when the user clicks Submit on a feedback form. First, you'll need to process the data. Generally, you'll place the data in a database or within an XML file. However, you could just as easily send the information to someone's email account or make it available in other ways. Some companies actually provide feedback on a local intranet as a means of helping employees understand what customers really think. Second, you'll redirect the user to a thank you page of some type. In most cases, this page will include a thank you message and links that take the user to another location on the Web site. This example offers links to go back to the main page or to restart the example.

Developing Automated Feedback

Automated feedback systems accept the forms that users provide, process them, and create reports based on the results. All you have to do once you create the initial form is to wait for the system to receive enough results for a report. This book doesn't delve into automated feedback systems because there are a number of resources you can use for this type of programming. Here are a couple of resources you should consider.

User Feedback HTML Form `http://www.bytesworth.com/learn/html00009.asp`

Creating Feedback Forms for WAP Sites `http://www.aspfree.com/c/a/Code%20Examples/Creating-feedback-forms-for-WAP-sites--By-Michael-Wright`

However, given that many developers want to provide an application that does everything the user could possibly need to do, making the feedback page friendly is critical. In general, the more you automate the feedback to make things easier for your company, the fewer users will be able to use the feedback system. This issue is especially true of form-based Web feedback because many users now turn off scripting, cookies, applets, and plug-ins for fear their systems will download viruses or experience other problems. Automation usually requires some level of client and server scripting, along with cookies and even plug-ins.

The problem even occurs with desktop applications. Some vendors make feedback available as part of a Help menu option. In most cases, the feedback form works and sends the information to the vendor (usually over the Internet). However, problems arise when the vendor assumes the user has a permanent connection to the Internet—many users use dial-up connections. Fortunately, every Web site developer can assume that the user has some kind of Internet connection (even if it's through a proxy server); otherwise, the user wouldn't be able to visit the Web site at all.

Creating a Help Request Form

Help request forms are one of the most important forms you can add to your Web site because they let you interact with the user directly. Of course, simply receiving the request isn't enough to satisfy the user—you have to have someone to answer the query. This application isn't finished to the point where you could use it without some modifications, but it gives you an idea of how you could produce such an application without expending a lot of time or energy.

Designing the Request Page

The example is quite simple, but also quite functional. The request page contains just four fields, yet this information is all you need to answer a help request in many cases (complex forms on most Web sites not withstanding). The form in Figure 7.9 shows a typical example.

What you can't see in the figure are all of the tooltips provided with the input page. You use the `ToolTip` property for ASP.NET controls to add a tooltip to the page. The server automatically converts the `ToolTip` property to the `Title` attribute for the HTML it outputs. The idea is to provide the user with enough extra information to fill out the form. Theoretically, you should also provide default values in the form fields; but, in some cases, this technique actually backfires because the user can't see which fields require additional information.

Notice that this form is almost too simple looking. Part of the reason is that this is an example and I didn't want to clutter it with extra doodads. However, it's always a good rule of thumb to keep things simple when it comes to forms. Use the least possible number of fields. Make sure the fields are always easy to understand. Provide extra help in the form of tooltips so everyone can participate.

Generally, you want the input form to flow from the initial input screen shown in Figure 7.9 to some type of response screen. In most cases, you'll want to give the user a feeling of success as shown in Figure 7.10. Notice that this page also includes a `LinkButton` control that takes the user back to the main page. Always ensure that your forms flow from one place on your Web site to another so the user doesn't have to click the Back button on their browser constantly. Chapter 8 provides a number of other ideas for making movement on your Web site easy.

FIGURE 7.9
Keep your request form simple and easy to understand so users will fill it out.

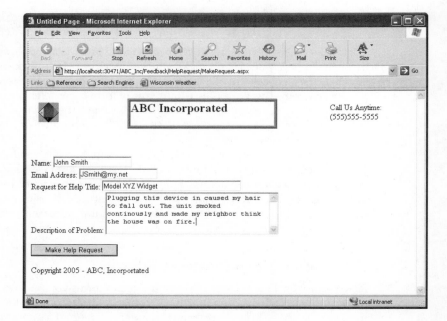

Always provide some form of error trapping for your forms. The example is very simple in that it only checks for fields that the user hasn't filled out. You should also explicitly check for fields with the wrong input data and fields that contain viruses, scripts, or simply odd information that you don't want in your database. Some users appear to have so much time on their hands that they'll test for every kind of odd input they can think of when trying out your Web site. In this case, the example displays a simple message as shown in Figure 7.11.

FIGURE 7.10
The user should be able to move from one location on your site to another without much effort.

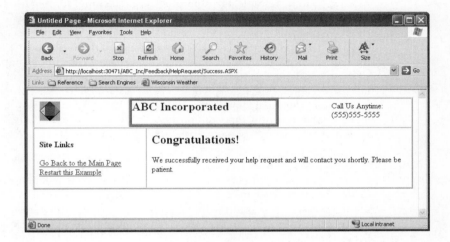

FIGURE 7.11
Always provide some form of error trapping and messaging with your application.

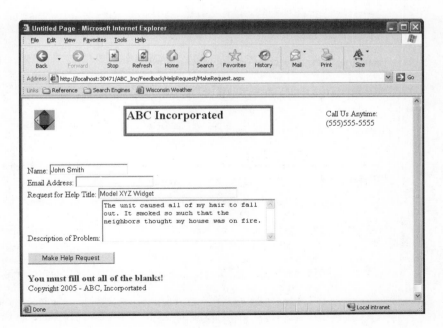

Developing the XML Storage

You have many options at your disposal for processing the forms you receive from users. This example uses a very simple methodology that works quite well. The example relies on an XML file to store the data and XSLT to translate the information into a Web page. The "Transforming the Results with XSLT" section of the chapter tells you more about the XSLT part of the equation. This section concentrates on the XML storage.

To keep things simple, the example stores each input form in a separate file. As the technician answers a request, the application either archives or deletes the file from the drive. A special algorithm ensures that every form has unique name, even when one user submits multiple forms. The XML file requires the usual <?xml?> processing instruction, a root node, and child nodes for holding the data. Figure 7.12 shows the essential data structure for this example.

As you can see, this XML is very simple. It stores the data items shown in the form in Figure 7.9 in a direct correspondence. Anyone looking at the XML could see how the user provided all of the required information. However, viewing XML directly isn't pleasant, no matter how simple you make it. Consequently, this example also includes the <?xml-stylesheet> processing instruction shown here. Whenever someone opens the XML file, they'll see a Web page created by the XSLT file.

```
<?xml-stylesheet type='text/xsl' href='DisplayReport.XSLT'?>
```

Now that you have a better idea of what tasks the code will perform, it's time to review the code. Listing 7.4 shows how to create and save an XML file based on the contents of a form. You could use this technique for any form, but the code provides specific formatting for the example form in Figure 7.9. You'll find this example in the \ABC_Inc\Feedback\HelpRequest folder of the source code on the Sybex Web site.

FIGURE 7.12

Use a simple data structure to store the information so you can process it easily.

LISTING 7.4: Creating an XML Storage File

```
Protected Sub btnSubmit_Click(ByVal sender As Object, _
                           ByVal e As System.EventArgs)
    Dim strUserName As String          ' Key for user's name.
    Dim strUserEmail As String         ' Key for user email.
    Dim strName As String              ' User's name.
    Dim strEmail As String             ' User's email address.
    Dim Output As XmlDocument          ' All of the input.
    Dim PInst As XmlProcessingInstruction   ' A processing instruction.
    Dim Attr As XmlAttribute           ' A node attribute.
```

```vb
Dim RootNode As XmlElement                    ' The root node.
Dim DataNode As XmlElement                    ' Individual data element.
Dim ThisPath As String                        ' Mapped application path.
Dim Filename As String                        ' Path to the data store.

' Locate the keys we need.
strUserName = ""
strUserEmail = ""
For Each Key As String In Request.Form.AllKeys
    If Key.IndexOf("txtName") > 0 Then
        strUserName = Key
    End If
    If Key.IndexOf("txtEmail") > 0 Then
        strUserEmail = Key
    End If
Next

' Verify the information was sent.
If strUserName.Length = 0 Then

    'Raise an error.
    Throw New ArgumentNullException("hidProductName")
End If
If strUserEmail.Length = 0 Then

    ' Raise an error.
    Throw New ArgumentNullException("hidModelNumber")
End If

' Get the information from the hidden fields.
strName = Request.Form.GetValues(strUserName)(0)
strEmail = Request.Form.GetValues(strUserEmail)(0)

' Verify that the data fields have all of the required information.
If strName.Length = 0 Or _
   strEmail.Length = 0 Or _
   txtTitle.Text.Length = 0 Or _
   txtDescription.Text.Length = 0 Then

    lblErrorMessage.Visible = True
    Return
End If

' Create the XML document.
Output = New XmlDocument()

' Define the XML processing directive.
```

```
PInst = Output.CreateProcessingInstruction( _
    "xml", "version='1.0' encoding='utf-8'")

' Add the XML processing directive to the document.
Output.AppendChild(PInst)

' Define the XSLT processing directive.
PInst = Output.CreateProcessingInstruction( _
    "xml-stylesheet", "type='text/xsl' href='DisplayReport.XSLT'")

' Add the XSLT processing directive to the document.
Output.AppendChild(PInst)

' Create the root node that holds all of the other data.
RootNode = Output.CreateElement("HelpRequest")
Attr = Output.CreateAttribute("TimeIn")
Attr.Value = DateTime.Now.ToString()
RootNode.Attributes.SetNamedItem(Attr)

' Create the name node and add it to the root node.
DataNode = Output.CreateElement("Name")
DataNode.InnerXml = strName
RootNode.AppendChild(DataNode)

' Create the email node and add it to the root node.
DataNode = Output.CreateElement("Email")
DataNode.InnerXml = strEmail
RootNode.AppendChild(DataNode)

' Create the request title node and add it to the root node.
DataNode = Output.CreateElement("Title")
DataNode.InnerXml = txtTitle.Text
RootNode.AppendChild(DataNode)

' Create the description node and add it to the root node.
DataNode = Output.CreateElement("Description")
DataNode.InnerXml = txtDescription.Text
RootNode.AppendChild(DataNode)

' Add the root node to the document.
Output.AppendChild(RootNode)

' Determine the path for this application.
ThisPath = Page.MapPath(Page.AppRelativeVirtualPath)
ThisPath = ThisPath.Replace("\MakeRequest.aspx", "\")

' Create the filename. Build a unique name first and then remove
' any elements that might cause problems. Finally, include the
' destination folder.
```

```
        Filename = strName + "_" + DateTime.Now.ToString() + ".XML"
        Filename = Filename.Replace(" ", "_")
        Filename = Filename.Replace(":", "_")
        Filename = Filename.Replace("/", "_")
        Filename = ThisPath + "HelpRequests\" + Filename

        ' Save the document to disk.
        Output.Save(Filename)

        ' Send the user to the success page.
        Response.Redirect("Success.ASPX")
    End Sub
```

The code begins by verifying the input data. This example is unique in that some of the data resides on the master page and other data resides on the local form, so you must use two different techniques to recover the data. In this case, the code ensures that the user has entered information in all of the fields. You can provide any level of error checking—the important thing is to provide some level of error checking and ensure it meets your data processing needs. When the user doesn't enter the proper information, the example displays a label on screen, as shown in Figure 7.11. The label is always there, but the server only outputs it when the user makes a mistake.

The center of the XML processing universe is the XmlDocument component, which is Output in this case. The XmlDocument component holds the data, lets you save it, and helps you create new elements as you need them. This example only uses a few of the common elements—the .NET Framework provides a host of useful components for creating the XML document you need.

Once you create a document, you begin filling it from top to bottom. Yes, you can fill it in any order you want, but using the top to bottom order greatly reduces the amount of code you must write and debugging time as well. Consequently, the code begins by creating an XmlProcessingInstruction component that contains the <?xml?> processing instruction. Notice that you don't create this element (or any other element) directly—you must rely on Output to do it for you using the Create ProcessingInstruction() method.

The CreateProcessingInstruction() method is a little odd. Most elements require that you add attributes separately, as you'll see with the <HelpRequest> element later in this section. When working with a processing instruction, you always include the attributes as data. In fact, if you look at this object in the debugger, you'll see that the Attributes property is Nothing (null)—you couldn't add anything to it even if you wanted to. After the code creates the <?xml?> processing instruction, it uses the Output.AppendChild() method to add the processing instruction to the document. As far as Output is concerned, the processing instruction doesn't exist until the code performs this step. The code performs the same sequence of events for the <?xml-stylesheet?> processing instruction used to link the XML page to the XSLT file.

The next step creates the root node using the Output.CreateElement() method. Remember that the root node in XML acts as a container for all of the data. This root note also includes an attribute called TimeIn that lets the support person know when the user sent the help request. Notice how the code creates the root node, <HelpRequest>, and then adds the TimeIn attribute to it. Even though you use Output to create the various pieces of the element, the element is a stand-alone portion of the document.

Now it's time to add the data elements. Again, the code uses `Output` to create the elements. In this case, the code creates leaf nodes, so they have a `Value` property entry. However, to make adding this information easier, the code actually uses the `InnerXml` property to add the data (using the `Value` property directly will display an error message). The code then uses the `RootNode.AppendChild()` method to add the data node to the root node—you don't add this data directly to the document because the document can't see it—only the root node can see it.

This code brings up an important issue. XML uses the concept of data levels. Every time you want to create a new level, you must work directly with the level to ensure the data is added correctly. Creating a complex XML data storage structure tends to complicate the code and increase the potential for errors. Always create a simple data structure when you can.

At this point, the `RootNode` is complete, so the code uses the `Output.AppendChild()` method to add the `RootNode` to the document. You can output the document, at this point, and it will look like the presentation shown in Figure 7.12 (with the XSLT processing instruction added).

Depending on how you set up your application, you'll want to create some way to store the data so that multiple requests don't interfere with each other. Although the example could use a single XML document to store the data—using a single document would limit the application to processing one request at a time. Therefore, the example uses a separate file for each request. However, now you have to create a unique name for the file to ensure that one request doesn't overwrite another. The next series of coding steps performs this task beginning with locating the application folder so the support personnel know where to find the data. Interestingly enough, if you don't perform this first step, the application attempts to write the data in the `\Program Files\Microsoft Visual Studio 8\Common7\IDE` folder of your hard drive.

The code begins by getting the current path for the Web page using the `Page.MapPath()` method. The page supplies this information as part of the `Page.AppRelativeVirtualPath` property. Unfortunately, the path contains the name of the file. You can use a number of techniques to separate the filename from the path, but the example uses a simple string replacement through the `ThisPath.Replace()` method to create the path.

Knowing where to place the file is only part of the answer. The code now creates a unique filename using the user's name and the current time. This technique ensures that even if the same user submits more than one form, each form will reside in a unique file. Of course, the string form of the time includes colons (:) and the date includes slashes (/). In addition, the space in the name might make it more difficult to locate the file. The code uses the `Replace()` method to replace the potential problem character with underscores. It then adds the path and filename together. The final XML processing step uses the `Output.Save()` method to send the data to disk.

If the code exited now, the user's data would appear on the hard drive, but the user wouldn't know whether the server saved it. The code uses the `Response.Redirect()` method to redirect the user to the success Web page shown in Figure 7.10.

Transforming the Results with XSLT

At this point, the example application has addressed the needs of user, but hasn't provided a means to process the data. It's tempting to create a special ASP.NET page, load the XML data, and process it using code similar to that shown in Listing 7.2 to gain a little flexibility. However, if you want to save time, then processing the file using XSLT works just fine and you really won't notice much loss in the way of flexibility. Listing 7.5 shows the XSLT used to process the example code.

LISTING 7.5:   Parsing the Output Data

```xml
<?xml version="1.0" encoding="utf-8" ?>
<xsl:stylesheet version='1.0'
 xmlns:xsl='http://www.w3.org/1999/XSL/Transform'>
<xsl:output method="html" indent="yes" />
    <xsl:template match="/HelpRequest">

    <HTML>
    <HEAD>
        <TITLE>Help Request</TITLE>
    </HEAD>

    <BODY>
        <h1>Help Request</h1>

        <!-- Display the title of the request. -->
        <h2><xsl:value-of select="Title" /></h2>

        <!-- Display the name. -->
        <p>Name:
        <xsl:value-of select="Name" /></p>

        <!-- Display the time the request was received. -->
        <p>Time Received: <xsl:value-of select="@TimeIn" /></p>

        <!-- Display the description of the help need. -->
        <p>Description: <xsl:value-of select="Description" /></p>

        <!-- Display the email address. -->
        <xsl:text disable-output-escaping="yes">
            &lt;a href="mailto:
        </xsl:text>
        <xsl:value-of select="Email" />
        <xsl:text>?subject=</xsl:text>
        <xsl:value-of select="Title" />
        <xsl:text disable-output-escaping="yes">
            "&gt;Contact User&lt;/a&gt;
        </xsl:text>
        <br />
    </BODY>
    </HTML>

    </xsl:template>

</xsl:stylesheet>
```

The code begins with the usual declarations required for an XSLT file. It then selects the root node of the XML document, which is always the same because of the way the application creates the XML document. All processing revolves around the `<HelpRequest>` node.

The example displays the data in a different order than it appears in the XML form. You don't have to display the data in any specific order and can, in fact, use the same data more than one time. For instance, you'll find the `<Title>` node used twice in this example. Figure 7.13 shows how the output looks so you can compare it to the appearance of elements within the XSLT file.

The first processing step displays the `<Title>` element as a heading on the Web page using the `<xsl:value-of>` element. The user's name appears next using the same technique, but within a paragraph this time. Notice how the code retrieves the `TimeIn` attribute and displays it on screen. Always precede attribute names with the at (@) symbol. Processing the `<Description>` element is the same as the `<Name>` element.

The email address presents a bit of a problem. You don't want to force the support person to type the email address into a response by hand. In addition, adding the title to the response automatically saves the support person time. Consequently, what you need is a link that includes the `mailto href` and a subject variable like this:

```
<a href="mailto:JMueller@mwt.net?subject=My Title">
```

Because you have to include variable information as part of the tag, you can't just construct it as you would a header or paragraph tag. The code uses the `<xsl:text>` element to include the less than (<) and greater than (>) symbols in the tag. However, notice that the `<xsl:text>` element also includes an `disable-output-escaping="yes"` attribute that tells the XML parser to output this data as a tag, not as an actual less than or greater than symbol. The code uses the `<xsl:value-of>` element and a plain `<xsl:text>` element to construct the rest of the tag. As this example shows, you can create complex Web page elements using XSLT as long as you think them through. When the support person clicks the link shown in Figure 7.13, they'll see an email response similar to the one shown in Figure 7.14. Notice that the email response already has the correct email address and subject filled out.

FIGURE 7.13
The output from the XSLT file is easy to read, understand, and use.

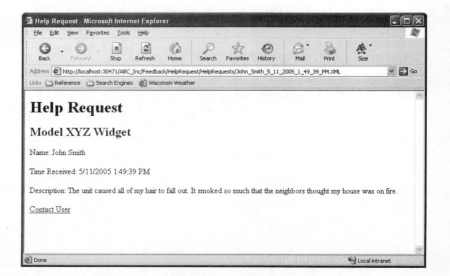

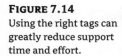

FIGURE 7.14
Using the right tags can greatly reduce support time and effort.

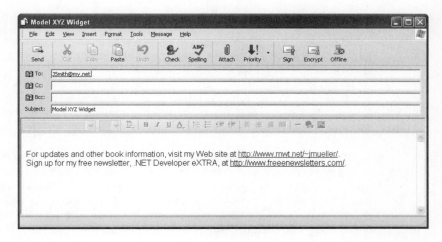

Developing a Beneficial Suggestion Form

Any Web site can benefit from a beneficial suggestion form. You could model it after the help request form described in the "Creating a Help Request Form" section of the chapter. The user would need to provide a name for the idea and an appropriate description as a minimum. However, because there isn't any way to go back and ask who generated an idea later when working on the Internet, you'll probably want to include the user's name and email as well—hoping that the user will provide valid entries so you can contact them later.

The problem with just sticking a beneficial suggestion form on your Web site is very few people are going to fill it out. Consequently, you need some type of reward for filling the form out, but make it contingent on providing a good idea—one that you can really use to improve the Web site. Other-wise, you'll end up with a ton of useless ideas and people with their hands out expecting the promised reward. The reward also makes it more likely that you'll get a valid username and email address so that you can contact them later, discuss the idea, and get enough details to implement it.

TIP   Rewards don't have to have monetary value or cost very much to make an impact. Giving the user a public forum—some type of public recognition for the input—is often enough to garner at least some beneficial suggestions. However, even low-cost ideas work. One developer offered gift certificates at Amazon in lieu of cash or products. Another developer offers free consulting time and others offer free products created by their company. You don't have to make the reward expensive—it simply has to have sufficient value in the eyes of the user to make it worthwhile to come up with ideas and submit them.

This kind of form benefits from directed questions. Sometimes a user has a great idea that they don't know how to express. A smart developer knows how to draw the information out of the user. It's easier to discover great communication techniques, rather than reinvent every idea that comes your way. For example, many developers include a list of categories for the beneficial suggestions. The very act of categorizing the idea helps the user articulate it with greater accuracy. A few developers will ask the user to quantify the idea. For example, determining how much of the Web site the idea impacts will give the user a better idea of its usefulness.

Deciding between Required and Optional Data

Most users aren't going to supply every piece of information you request—no matter how aggressively you request it. Some Web sites get around this problem by making their forms obnoxious and persistent. The form keeps returning with all of the cheer of an unloved relative pointing out the fault in every move. Red stars or text describing the stupidity of the form submitter shows the glaring hole in the information coverage—the information the user won't provide under any circumstance. Users commonly take care of the problem by either refusing the fill the form out at all or providing false information. In either case, you lose. Either you lose the user's feedback or you lose the integrity of your database.

A positive way to avoid this problem is to make an honest determination of the information you really need. Yes, it's nice to know whom you're dealing with, but let's face it: the Internet is all about getting what you need using an anonymous face and most users aren't going to give up that privilege unless you give them a very good reason to do so. For example, a user feedback form is equally valid whether you know the user's name or not. It's true that getting the user's email address will let you ask the user additional questions and ask opinions about the resolution of a problem, but getting the initial feedback is valuable enough that you don't want to create an environment where the user doesn't provide the information at all. Consequently, all you really need is a title for the feedback along with the feedback itself. You should also request amplifying information as needed, but make sure you really need the amplifying information.

TIP   Some kinds of feedback form information are ambiguous. For example, a general comment about your Web site need not include a part number, but a comment about a specific piece of equipment that you sell probably should have the part number. Consequently, you might need to create multiple feedback forms with a number of amplifying fields that include required information. Tailoring a form to meet specific needs makes it more likely that the user will fill the form out completely.

Some forms do require interaction. For example, a help request form requires some level of interactivity to be effective. In this case, you can explain to the user that you must have an email address in order to respond to their question. Failure to provide the information, in this case, means that you can't complete the request for help. The lack of an email address or other means of communication, in this case, really does mean that the form is useless. However, don't limit the user to one kind of input. The required field can include a number of alternatives. Perhaps you can provide places for an email address, written response, or telephone number. Yes, it requires an extra effort on your part, but that's how people develop reputations for providing superior service. You'll have to decide just how much service you can afford to provide, but this is one case where users will understand the need for additional information.

It's possible to coax additional information out of users, in many cases, even when a user could argue that the information isn't essential. For example, a beneficial suggestion form works just fine whether the user provides a name and email address or not. Of course, a beneficial suggestion that isn't complete or doesn't provide some kind of interactivity might not be very useful—perhaps it simply isn't complete and you need more information. Rather than waste a perfectly good idea, try to convince the user to supply the information you need. For example, you could provide some form of gratuity in exchange for the user input. A small token of your appreciation not only makes it more likely that someone will come up with an idea, but that they'll also provide the extra information you need such as a name and email address.

Some Web sites provide registration or other forms full of dubious requirements for information. At least a few users will provide all of the requested information because they just don't know how to say no, but many will provide purposely misleading or false information just to get past the form. According to a number of trade press articles, interviews with users, newsgroup entries, and other sources of information, here are a few of the most common requests for information that go unheeded.

Email Address   The only time you should request an email address is when you have to send the user some kind of response to a question. Sometimes you'll want to request an email address as an optional input—such as when the user provides input that could require additional discussion. In many cases, you can avoid the problem by not requesting the user's email address at all.

Address   The only time you should request an address is when you need to send the user a product. Given the nearly constant appearance in the news of stalkers and other nefarious individuals misusing address information, many users are wary about giving out this information. Generally, the address you receive is going to be fake unless the user has a very good reason to give it to you.

Telephone Number   Never request a telephone number as a required input—you should always make this information optional. It's unlikely that you'll spend the money to call the user if they supply an email address anyway. Even when a user orders a product from you, you have the option of verifying that their form of payment is valid before you ship the product.

Personal Information   Never request personal information such as age, sex, nationality, or religion. With identity theft running rampant, most users are unlikely to provide you with valid information. Invalid personal information could color a survey you make by providing useless demographics. Likewise, many users are going to provide false information because they fear prejudice. The anonymity of the Internet makes it impossible to verify anything other than the answers the user wants you to have.

Preferences   The only time you should ask about preferences is when you're conducting a survey or trying to fulfill a user need such as selling them a product or providing help. Make sure the preferences you request are important. For example, you can't sell the user a product without knowing the color in some cases—users understand this requirement and will provide you with good information. However, users are less likely to answer a request for information that has nothing to do with the current topic, such as whether they like men with green or orange hair better.

The main reason that most of these information requests go unheeded is that users value their privacy. They don't want to provide an address because they fear you'll sell their name and address to a marketing firm that will promptly bombard them with home loan advertisements. The user doesn't really care that you think they need a particular service and have an aching desire to buy a new product, so many of them will provide you with what you want least—bad information. The bottom line is that users are more likely provide you with everything you really need when you consider optional versus required information carefully.

Devising Methods of Reducing Repeat Input

Some feedback forms ask the same question in more than one way, supposedly to force the user to provide more information or at least validate the user's assertions. The result of this kind of feedback is repetition. The repeated data consumes more space in your database, requires additional processing time without providing any significant gain in information, and frustrates the user. The user frustration part is especially important because a frustrated user provides less useful information.

The problem for many developers is that it's easy to become engulfed in details rather than look at the overall picture. For example, you could begin the user help form by asking for a general description of the problem. The next question might ask for a list of steps required to reproduce the problem. Even though they appear as two different questions, many users will answer them the same way. In fact, some users will go so far as to cut and paste the two answers, so you get precisely the same answer for both. A great way to avoid this problem is to have several people from varied backgrounds test the form. Make sure they haven't seen the form before. When you receive the results, you'll start to notice similarities in the answers and that information will help you prevent some of the repetition.

In some cases, a user will provide a standard "non-answer" in place of real information because they're simply too lazy to provide the information you want. Their goal is to answer the questions as quickly as possible and still receive what they want back from you. Answering the questions quickly, rather than correctly is a problem that you have to address. You could process the form using some type of string comparison. For example, you could look for duplicate strings, flag them on the form, and ask the user whether they really intended to provide the duplicate answers. Often, this little check is all that you need to get rid of the non-answers. Of course, you have to ask why the user didn't provide the information you need in the first place. Redirecting the questions so the user can see the need to answer them often helps, but won't solve the problem in every case.

VALIDATING REQUIRED INPUT

Once you decide that the user must provide some input to satisfy the basic requirements of a form, you need to validate that input. Chapter 17 provides details on creating secure forms, but you need to perform validation on the form as well. For example, many Web pages fail to verify that the user has entered any information at all until the form goes all the way back to the server. A local script can ensure that the user has provided input in the required spaces. You can also verify that the input meets length requirements and that it doesn't include any special characters that might indicate a virus, rather than useful information.

Validation also means adding some intelligence to the checks. For example, you could parse the input to ensure it contains a part number as part of the explanation of a hardware failure. You can also verify that the input includes special terms. Input about an application might require some mention of settings, so you can check the input for this term to ensure the user has included the settings. Of course, you don't want to go too far—language provides myriad ways to express the same idea so you'll want to ensure that you look for reasonable input rather than every specific word you think should appear in the text.

Make sure you also look for potential errors in the input. For example, if some percentage of the input you receive contains two words that users often confuse, you might want to verify that the user actually meant to use the term in the feedback. Some terms are confusing enough that there's an entire Web site devoted to the topic—Confusing Words at http://www.confusingwords.com/index.php. In short, always provide the user with helpful assistance.

Another potential problem is that your form isn't accessible. Perhaps the questions are worded in such a way that the user can't understand them and provided replicated input as a show of frustration. Avoid using jargon and abbreviations whenever possible—have a nontechnical person review the form for potential problems before you make it available on the Web site. Accessibility problems come in a number of forms and you can discover more of them in Chapter 21.

Defining Your Development Goals

This chapter helps answer some general questions about forms, such as discussing some simple techniques for securing them. However, it also discusses a specific kind of form—the feedback form you should consider standard fare on your Web site. When a user sees that you care enough to request their input constantly, it's hard for them to go somewhere else and tell other people that you're just missing the point. Most people will take you up on your offer to let them complain and a few will end up providing something much more—good input on how you can create a better Web site. The best part about this kind of input is that it's from the very people who are using your Web site, so it's always pertinent—always right on the mark. Best of all, you don't have to pay anyone to provide the input to you.

At this point, you can build the feedback forms for your Web site. Make sure you create specific feedback forms and change the content as needed to reflect the changing Web site scenery. As you make changes, ask people specific questions about those changes. Not only will asking specific questions help the people who didn't see the changes recognize them, but you'll discover whether the input you received from a boisterous user last week really does reflect the opinion of most of the Web site users. In addition to the three forms described in this chapter, make sure you create some special forms for your Web site as well. For example, if your Web site specializes in greeting cards, ask users what kinds of greetings they'd like to see in the future.

Chapter 8 discusses another important feature that every Web site should include—a site search. Helping people locate essential information on your Web site is just as important as the feedback forms described in this chapter. Unfortunately, creating a great site search is not only time consuming and error prone, but open to interpretation by the people using your Web site. A site search that works great for you and even the majority of the people using your site might not work well for those who need the site search the most. This chapter helps clear some of the ambiguities you have to consider and provides more than one technique for solving everyone's search needs.

Chapter 8

Developing a Site Search

Unless your Web site is extremely small, users will occasionally experience problems finding something. They might know that you have pictures on your Web site, but might not know where to find them. A link from someone else's Web site might provide a tantalizing clue as to what your Web site contains, but the user might not get a good idea until they search your site. In short, most Web sites require at least one, and perhaps several, ways to search for information.

This chapter begins by examining the kinds of searches you can create and then demonstrating how to create those searches using the custom techniques that Visual Web Developer provides. Although the custom search isn't perfect, you gain flexibility in how the search is weighted and what the user sees. You'll normally use custom searches when your Web site includes data that's unusual in some way or when you're running a private Web site.

Enterprise developers have access to a wealth of resources and normally don't have to worry about the issues surrounding hosted servers. However, having access to all of the resources doesn't mean you can come up with a perfect search routine. Sometimes it's smarter to have someone else do all of the work. An alternative to writing your own search routine is to use Google for searching. Google provides several methods that let you incorporate its search engine into your Web site. In fact, some of these techniques rely on simple HTML that you add to your Web page. Other techniques require a little more work, but offer greater flexibility.

You might not want to restrict searches to your own Web site. Sometimes you want to provide the capability of searching other Web sites or having those Web sites provide search results for your site. This chapter also examines techniques you can use to make these cross-site searches more efficient.

Finally, this chapter discusses the topic of site maps. A site map is a kind of picture of the layout of your Web site. Users like site maps because site maps help them find information by topic, rather than using a specific search. You should combine site maps with searches on larger Web sites. Site maps also work with smaller Web sites, but have a reduced effect on usability because the Web site is easier to navigate.

TIP   It isn't always necessary to write a search routine for your Web site from scratch. Third party vendors such as Wrensoft produce search engines to make the job easier. The Zoom Search Engine (`http://www.wrensoft.com/zoom/index.html`) is one such offering. You don't need to do much to make these products work. Of course, the speed you gain is offset by the flexibility you lose—a third party vendor will provide you with a generic solution—not the specific solution you can create using hand coding techniques.

Understanding the Site Search Types

Before you can create any kind of search for your Web site, you need to consider what kind of search you need. In some cases, you'll need multiple search engines to address every need, but it pays to start with the one that you need most. Not every Web site relies on precisely the same search. The following list provides the basic kinds of search engines that you'll find on the Internet, but you'll want to note any special search engines you run across because these special engines provide you with great ideas for upgrades of your own. One of the more interesting places to see side-by-side comparisons of search engine output is Dogpile at `http://www.dogpile.com/`.

Specific Page   The specific page search is the most common. The search engine returns one or more pages that contain keywords or fit within other criteria for the search term that the user provides. Indexing technique (whole page, `<meta>` tags, or some other method), indexing criteria (which words the search engine indexes), and weighting (how much value each word has in determining the search score) all play an important part in determining the results you obtain from a specific page search engine.

Informational   An informational search can retrieve whole Web pages, snippets, or specific page elements depending on how the developer constructs the search engine. In many cases, the search engine provides options for fine-tuning the search based on the content of a single return. The search engine may or may not provide a link for the Web page itself since the user relies on this kind of search to quickly research specific bits of information.

Downloads   Instead of locating Web pages, this kind of search locates files. Most search engines specify a file type, such as graphics or audio. You could use this kind of search engine to locate a missing DLL on your machine or to find an updated driver for your network printer. Download searches always provide a direct link to the file—clicking the link normally starts the download process.

Corporate Data   Sometimes a corporation has to provide a data mining search engine—one that looks for the information particular to your particular company. A data mining operation normally doesn't occur on a public Web site. You normally keep this kind of information secret. The search could be for anything. For example, if you're a member of an engineering company, you might need to search for drawings of a certain kind of cable or a circuit board that performs a particular task. The idea is to make the most out of the information you already have so you don't have to reinvent the wheel.

Creating a Custom Site Search

Visual Web Developer provides the means for creating a custom site search. A custom site search depends on your ability to describe your Web site and define the criteria that you think users will need. The following sections describe the tools that Visual Web Developer provides for creating a custom site search.

Developing a Simple Site Search

Searching a Web site comes down to figuring out how to index the pages and then determining how to use that index to locate content. Although the example in this section only lets you search for one word at a time, it does provide you with the basic principles for creating a custom search. The following sections address both the indexing and the index searching requirements.

OVERRIDING MASTER PAGE CONTENT

Master pages can introduce some interesting programming problems. For example, you'll run into a problem indexing content on your pages because the master page hides some of the information from view. You need to consider how to index a Web page carefully. Making the index too small or confined means that users won't be able to search your site completely, reducing the usefulness of the search engine you create. On the other hand, making the index too comprehensive increases search times to the point that no one will want to wait for the search to complete. Consequently, you need to choose a middle ground for the index.

The technique that works best, in many cases, requires that you perform some additional work for each Web page. It relies on the use of special <meta> (or informational) tags. A <meta> tag always contains a name and content attribute pair. This example uses three common <meta> tags, but you can learn about others at http://www.theemiratesnetwork.com/computers/webmaster/metatag1.htm. Here are the three <meta> tags that appear in the <head> tag area of each Web page.

```
<meta name="title" content="Custom Site Search Example">
<meta name="description"
      content="Discover how to create a site search.">
<meta name="keywords" content="Custom Site Search Find Keyword">
```

The title <meta> tag provides the title that you want to appear on the search page. Many search engines use the <meta> tag version of the title, rather than the actual <title> tag information. Supplying both the <meta> tag and the <title> tag ensures that your Web page is always listed using the title you want. The description <meta> tag contains a description of the services that a Web page provides. Shorter descriptions normally work best, but be sure you describe that particular page fully (in other words, don't use the same description for every page on your Web site). The keyword <meta> tag is the most important because it contains the list of words that most search engines use to locate content on your site.

Unfortunately, because a content page can't have a <head> tag, it would seem unlikely that you can add a <meta> tag to the page. It's easy to add common <meta> tags to the master page, but adding them to the content page directly is impossible. Fortunately, you have another technique at your disposal. You can override the master page as part of the Page.Load() event, as shown here.

```
Protected Sub Page_Load(ByVal sender As Object, _
                        ByVal e As System.EventArgs) Handles Me.Load

    ' Set the <meta> tags for this page.
    Master.Page.Header.Metadata.Add( _
        "title", "Custom Site Search Example")
    Master.Page.Header.Metadata.Add( _
        "description", "Discover how to create a site search.")
    Master.Page.Header.Metadata.Add( _
        "keywords", "Custom Site Search Find Keyword")
End Sub
```

The result of adding the <meta> tag using this technique is the same as adding it directly to the <head> tag from the user's perspective. Figure 8.1 shows what the user will see when looking at the page source. The only problem is that the ASPX file doesn't include this information—it only appears in the source code file. Consequently, when indexing the Web site, you can't simply look at the ASPX pages and hope for the best. What you really need to do is load the page as the user sees it, grab the actual information from the Web page, and then close it.

FIGURE 8.1

The user sees the result of code, master page, and ASPX file combined.

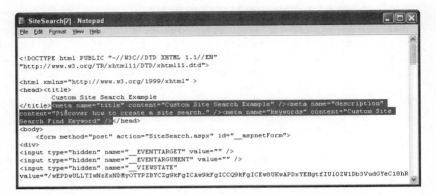

The `Master.Page.Header` collection is actually quite handy. It contains properties that let you override the following items.

◆ `LinkedStyleSheets`

◆ `Metadata`

◆ `StyleSheets`

◆ `Title`

It's possible to override a number of other master page features as well. For example, you can override control settings as needed. A title label that you add to the master page can have any text that a particular page requires. In addition, you can define custom properties for the master page. The content page can set these properties as needed to achieve a particular effect. In short, even though master pages provide a particular structure, they're also flexible enough for you to modify through code to meet specific client needs.

GETTING A LIST OF PAGES FROM THE SITE MAP

Most Web sites in existence today have a site map. The site map is a means of describing the organization of a Web site using some type of database. ABC Incorporated relies on the site map controls described in the "Using the Site Navigation Features" section of the chapter. These features let a user move from area to area with few problems and display a map back to the Web site's home page. Most of the navigation features depend on a specially formatted XML file named `Web.SITEMAP`. You'll find a description of this special file in the "Creating a Site Map" section of the chapter. Of course, by now you're wondering what all this has to do with creating a custom search program.

Just like any user, a search program has to know about and understand the organization of a Web site in order to locate the pages it contains. Although Microsoft never envisioned anyone using the `Web.SITEMAP` file to create a search routine, it actually works quite well. Because this file has to be up-to-date in order for the navigation features to work, it also provides a verifiable source of information to use when constructing an index of terms for a Web site. What the search routine needs is a list of Web pages and their relative location on the Web site for processing—the `Web.SITEMAP` file can provide this information with only a little effort on your part. Listing 8.1 shows the code used to change the `Web.SITEMAP` file into an array of relative Web page locations. You'll find this example in the `\ABC_Inc\Searches\CustomSearch` folder of the source code on the Sybex Web site.

LISTING 8.1:   Creating a List of Page Locations from a Site Map

```
Function GetSiteMapPageList() As String()
    ... Variable Declarations ...

    ' Determine the path for this application.
    ThisPath = Page.MapPath(Page.AppRelativeVirtualPath)
    ThisPath = _
        ThisPath.Replace("\\Searches\CustomSearch\IndexPages.aspx", "\")

    ' Obtain a list of all of the files to index.
    TheFiles = Directory.GetFiles(ThisPath, "*.SITEMAP")

    ' Determine whether the sitemap exists.
    If TheFiles.Length = 0 Then
        Return Nothing
    End If

    ' Open the file for reading.
    FileRead = New StreamReader(TheFiles(0))

    ' Load the XML document.
    SiteMap = New XmlDocument()
    SiteMap.LoadXml(FileRead.ReadToEnd())

    ' Process each Web page in turn.
    Output = New ArrayList()
    For Each SiteNode As XmlNode In SiteMap.ChildNodes(1)

        ' A well-formed Web.SITEMAP file could have multiple
        ' comment entries, but will have only one top level
        ' siteMapNode entry.
        If SiteNode.Name = "siteMapNode" Then
            Output = ProcessSiteMapElements(SiteNode)
        End If
    Next

    ' Convert the ArrayList to a String()
    ReDim StrOut(Output.Count - 1)
    For Count As Int32 = 0 To Output.Count - 1
        StrOut(Count) = CType(Output(Count), String)
    Next

    ' Return the data.
    Return StrOut

End Function
```

```
Function ProcessSiteMapElements(ByVal Element As XmlNode) As ArrayList
    Dim Output As ArrayList      ' The list of URLs
    Dim ChildOut As ArrayList  ' A child element.

    ' Get the information for this element.
    Output = New ArrayList
    Output.Add(Element.Attributes("url").InnerText)

    ' Determine whether the node has children.
    If Element.HasChildNodes Then

        ' If so, process each child in turn.
        For Each Child As XmlNode In Element

            ' Verify this isn't a comment or other element.
            If Child.Name = "siteMapNode" Then

                ' Get the child information.
                ChildOut = ProcessSiteMapElements(Child)

                ' Place the nodes it contains in the current ArrayList.
                For Counter As Int32 = 0 To ChildOut.Count - 1
                    Output.Add(ChildOut(Counter))
                Next
            End If
        Next
    End If

    ' Return the output.
    Return Output
End Function
```

The code consists of two functions. The caller invokes GetSiteMapPageList() to begin the process. The output of this function is a String array containing a list of relative page locations in the Web.SITEMAP file. The code begins by creating a path to the root of the Web site. Because you know the location of the current Web page, but not necessarily the storage location of the Web site on the host system, you use can use the Page.MapPath() method to map the relative virtual path of the current Web page to a fully qualified physical path. Unfortunately, this path points to the current page, not to the root directory of the Web site. Replacing the extra path information with a simple backslash resolves the problem.

Now that the code knows the location of the root directory for the Web site, it uses the Directory.GetFiles() method to retrieve what should be the only SITEMAP file in that folder. When this file is missing, the code returns without performing any processing (since there's nothing to process). Most corporate Web sites will have this file so the code continues by opening the file using a TextReader object and the Streamreader() constructor. It reads the data into an XML document using the LoadXml() method.

You can use the debugger to view the resulting XML file. Simply select the XML Visualizer for the `SiteMap.OuterXml` property, as shown in Figure 8.2. Visualizers are a new feature for Visual Web Developer that greatly reduce the complexity of working with XML files. You select a Visualizer by clicking the down arrow next to the magnifying glass, as shown in Figure 8.2. The IDE presents choices based on the kind of data that you selected. In this case, the choices are XML Visualizer, Text Visualizer, and HTML Visualizer.

NOTE   You should read the entire file in one pass, as shown in the example using the `FileRead.ReadToEnd()` method. Reading a SITEMAP file in increments can become quite messy and code intensive.

As this point, you have an XML document containing two nodes. The first is an XML processing instruction. The second node, `SiteMap.ChildNodes(1)`, contains the `<siteMap>` element, which in turn contains the first `<siteMapNode>` element. The example assumes that you have one root page, but some Web sites have more and you could easily change the code to accommodate them by expanding the root node processing, as shown in later parts of the example. The `ProcessSiteMap Elements()` method returns an `ArrayList` containing the pages for the Web site.

It's important to convert the `ArrayList`, essentially an array of type `Object`, to an array of type `String`. The code performs this task using a simple loop. Notice the use of `CType()` to perform the conversion. The `GetSiteMapPageList()` method ends by returning the `String` array to the caller.

Now it's time to look at the `ProcessSiteMapElements()` method, which accepts an `XmlNode` as input and returns an `ArrayList`. This simple method actually performs a complex job because you don't know how your Web site is set up at any given time. The method relies on recursion to process any number of nodes at any depth based on the site map information provided.

The code begins by adding its own URL to the `ArrayList`, `Output`. Notice that the code uses the attribute name as an index and selects the information from the `InnerText` property. When a child has nodes, the code begins processing them next. Of course, you don't know what kind of node the child contains—it could be a comment or even an incorrect entry. The code verifies the node type using the `Child.Name` property.

This is where the logic for processing the nodes can get tricky. The example uses recursion to call `ProcessSiteMapElements()` with the child node. On return from the call, `ChildOut` contains an `ArrayList`. You have no idea of how many items `ChildOut` contains, so you can't simply add `ChildOut` to `Output`. The code must instead use a `For...Next` loop to process the `ChildOut` entries individually.

FIGURE 8.2
View the content of the Web.SITEMAP file once you load it into memory.

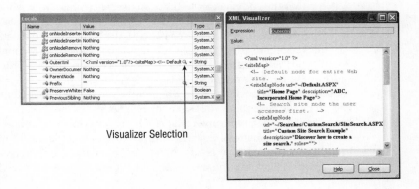

Visualizer Selection

The code ends by returning the current value of Output. Because this is a recursive function, the caller can be another copy of the `ProcessSiteMapElements()` method or the `GetSiteMapPageList()` method. The important consideration is that you eventually end up with a `String` array containing the list of Web pages in the `Web.SITEMAP` file.

TIP   Using the `Web.SITEMAP` file as a source for the Web pages to add to your search index has the advantage of not exposing hidden pages. When a page doesn't appear in the `Web.SITEMAP` file, it won't appear in the search either. Although a user could rely on other methods for finding hidden pages (such as a custom Google search), the absence of hidden Web pages from your custom search does increase security a little.

OPENING WEB PAGES FOR PROCESSING

The Web pages that ABC Incorporated and most other corporations use today come from a number of sources. In fact, the page might not physically exist on the Web site in many cases—the Web application generates the page as needed from information the developer provides. Consequently, a search indexing routine can't simply load the page from the Web site to index its content. Without an index, there's no search routine for the user, so the developer must have a means for viewing the Web page as the user will see it.

The "Getting a List of Pages from the Site Map" section of the chapter demonstrates the code to begin the process of viewing the individual Web pages. You need a list of pages to load and index. This section shows how to obtain the page and load it into memory as a `String`. Listing 8.2 shows the code you'll need to build an URL without knowing the base address of the Web site at the outset and then load the Web page into memory. You'll find this example in the `\ABC_Inc\Searches\CustomSearch` folder of the source code on the Sybex Web site.

The code begins by creating an URL for loading the Web page. You might think that the .NET Framework provides this information in an easily accessible form, but it doesn't—you must build the information up from bits and pieces that the .NET Framework provides. The URL always begins with a protocol, which you provide as a string. The `Request.ServerVariables("SERVER_NAME")` method obtains the name of the server for the current Web site, while the SERVER_PORT variable obtains the port number for the Web site. You can't assume the Web site is using port 80 because some Web sites don't use the common port today and the testing environment for the built-in server certainly doesn't use port 80. The list of URLs the code created earlier are relative URLs provided in the `Web.SITEMAP` file. You must use the `Page.ResolveUrl(RelativeUrl)` method to resolve the URL into a form that you can use as part of a complete URL.

Now that the code has an URL it can use, it creates a `WebRequest` from it using `WebRequest.Create()`. This is a general method for creating a Web request of any type. However, the code needs an `HttpWebRequest` to load a Web page, so the code wraps the entire package into a `CType()` to convert the `WebRequest` in an `HttpWebRequest`. `PgRequest` now contains a request for a Web page—it doesn't contain the actual Web page or even a connection with the server.

The next step is to obtain an `HttpWebResponse` from the server. Essentially, this step creates a connection with the server and asks whether the server has a particular resource. The code performs this task using the `PgRequest.GetResponse()` method, which returns a generic `WebResponse`. Again, the code uses a `CType()` to convert the result to an `HttpWebResponse` object.

Once the code has established communication with the server and determined a resource exists (a Web page, in this case), it creates a `Stream` object, `DataOut`, to create a conduit for transmitting data between the client and the server. `DataOut` doesn't contain any data—it simply provides a conduit.

To read the data, the code builds a `StreamReader` object, `ReadMe`. Using the `ReadMe.ReadToEnd()` method, the code finally downloads the Web page as a `String` and places it in `WebPage`. The code ends by sending the Web page back to the caller.

LISTING 8.2:   Loading Web Pages into Memory

```
Function GetWebPage(ByVal RelativeUrl As String) As String
    ... Variable Declarations ...

    ' Verify the Web site has a Web.SITEMAP file and open it as
    ' an XML document.
    PgRequest = CType(WebRequest.Create( _
        "http://" + Request.ServerVariables("SERVER_NAME") + ":" + _
        Request.ServerVariables("SERVER_PORT") + _
        Page.ResolveUrl(RelativeUrl)), HttpWebRequest)

    Try

        ' Get the resulting page from the server.
        PgResponse = CType(PgRequest.GetResponse(), HttpWebResponse)

        ' Place the data in a data stream for processing.
        DataOut = PgResponse.GetResponseStream()

        ' Read the data.
        ReadMe = New StreamReader(DataOut)

        ' Create the Web page.
        WebPage = ReadMe.ReadToEnd()

        ' Close the data stream.
        DataOut.Close()

    Catch WE As WebException
        ' Display the server's error message if an error occurs.
        lblError.Text = WE.Message
        lblError.Visible = True

        ' Exit the routine.
        Return Nothing

    End Try

    ' Return the resulting Web page to the caller.
    Return WebPage
End Function
```

CREATING A KEYWORD DATABASE

You need to create and then store the index in some way. Many commercial Web sites use a special database application to perform the task. However, someone creating a simple search doesn't need anything that complex. You can easily store the information in an XML file and use a standard Web page to create the information. Figure 8.3 shows a single record from the XML file used for this example.

The XML file contains two tables. The first, tblOverview, contains the title, description, and URL for the Web page, while the second, tblKeywords, contains a list of keywords for the Web page. A single Web page can have only one tblOverview entry, but will normally have multiple tblKeywords entries. A special ID field in each table provides a link so you can search the keywords and retrieve the information you want to display on screen. Listing 8.3 shows the code required to create this index. You'll find this example in the \ABC_Inc\Searches\CustomSearch folder of the source code on the Sybex Web site.

FIGURE 8.3

Storing the index for a Web site as XML works fine in many cases.

LISTING 8.3: Indexing the Web Page Data

```
Sub btnStart_Click(ByVal sender As Object, ByVal e As System.EventArgs)
    ... Variable Declarations ...

    ' Get the list of Web pages to process.
    TheFiles = GetSiteMapPageList()

    ' Create the DataSet
    Output = New DataSet("dsOutput")
```

```
' Add the single entry, parent table.
Output.Tables.Add("tblOverview")
Output.Tables("tblOverview").Columns.Add( _
    "ID", GetType(Int32))
Output.Tables("tblOverview").Columns.Add( _
    "Title", GetType(String))
Output.Tables("tblOverview").Columns.Add( _
    "Description", GetType(String))
Output.Tables("tblOverview").Columns.Add( _
    "URL", GetType(String))

' Add the keywords table.
Output.Tables.Add("tblKeywords")
Output.Tables("tblKeywords").Columns.Add( _
    "ID", GetType(Int32))
Output.Tables("tblKeywords").Columns.Add( _
    "Keyword", GetType(String))

' Set a relationship between the tables.
Output.Relations.Add("PageKeywords", _
    Output.Tables("tblOverview").Columns("ID"), _
    Output.Tables("tblKeywords").Columns("ID"))

' Set the record ID
RecordID = 0

' Clear the data entries.
Title = ""
Description = ""
Keyword = ""
ReDim Keywords(0)

' Process one file at a time.
For Each ThisFile In TheFiles

    ' Get the Web page and place the data in a string.
    TheData = GetWebPage(ThisFile)

    ' Skip processing if there aren't any <meta> tags.
    If TheData.IndexOf("<meta") > 0 Then

        ' Keep processing the <meta> data.
        Do Until TheData.IndexOf("<meta") = -1

            ' Locate the <meta> tag.
            TheData = TheData.Substring(TheData.IndexOf("<meta"))

            ' Look for the title <meta> tag.
```

```
If TheData.Substring(12, 5) = "title" Then
    TheData = _
        TheData.Substring(TheData.IndexOf("content"))
    TheData = _
        TheData.Substring(TheData.IndexOf( _
            Convert.ToChar(&H22)) + 1)
    Title = _
        TheData.Substring(0, TheData.IndexOf( _
            Convert.ToChar(&H22)))
End If

' Look for the description <meta> tag.
If TheData.Substring(12, 11) = "description" Then
    TheData = _
        TheData.Substring(TheData.IndexOf("content"))
    TheData = _
        TheData.Substring(TheData.IndexOf( _
            Convert.ToChar(&H22)) + 1)
    Description = _
        TheData.Substring(0, TheData.IndexOf( _
            Convert.ToChar(&H22)))
End If

' Look for the keywords <meta> tag.
If TheData.Substring(12, 8) = "keywords" Then
    TheData = _
        TheData.Substring(TheData.IndexOf("content"))
    TheData = _
        TheData.Substring(TheData.IndexOf( _
            Convert.ToChar(&H22)) + 1)
    Keyword = _
        TheData.Substring(0, TheData.IndexOf( _
            Convert.ToChar(&H22)))

    ' Split the keywords into an array.
    Keywords = Keyword.Split(Convert.ToChar(" "))
End If

' See if we have a complete record.
If (Title.Length > 0) And _
   (Description.Length > 0) And _
   (Keyword.Length > 0) Then

    ' Add the overview data to the DataSet.
    DR = Output.Tables("tblOverview").NewRow()
    DR("ID") = RecordID
    DR("Title") = Title
    DR("Description") = Description
```

```
            DR("URL") = Page.ResolveUrl("/CustomSearch/" + _
                ThisFile.Substring(ThisFile.LastIndexOf("\") + 1))
            Output.Tables("tblOverview").Rows.Add(DR)

            ' Add the keywords.
            For Each Keyword In Keywords
                DR = Output.Tables("tblKeywords").NewRow()
                DR("ID") = RecordID
                DR("Keyword") = Keyword
                Output.Tables("tblKeywords").Rows.Add(DR)
            Next

            ' Clear the data values.
            Title = ""
            Description = ""
            Keyword = ""
            ReDim Keywords(0)

            ' Increment the record identifier.
            RecordID = RecordID + 1
        End If
    Loop

    ' Assign the DataSet to the GridView
    dgResults.DataSource = Output
    dgResults.DataBind()
   End If
Next

' Determine the path for this application.
ThisPath = Page.MapPath(Page.AppRelativeVirtualPath)
ThisPath = ThisPath.Replace("\IndexPages.aspx", "\")

' Write the results to a database.
Output.WriteXml(ThisPath + "Data\Index.XML")
Output.WriteXmlSchema(ThisPath + "Data\Index.XSD")


End Sub
```

The code begins by retrieving a list of Web pages to process and placing them in the TheFiles String array. See the "Getting a List of Pages from the Site Map" section of the chapter for details on how this process works.

The next step is to create the DataSet, Output, used to store the data, which includes two tables, tblOverview and tblKeywords. The Columns.Add() method adds the columns to each of the tables. Notice that you must provide a data type for each column using the GetType() method. Output also defines a relationship between the two tables using the Output.Relations.Add() method. Although you don't necessarily have to define this relationship, it helps reduce the chance of data errors in the index. This first section of code finishes by initializing some of the variables used for processing the data.

The keyword processing loop begins by reading a Web page into memory. The "Opening Web Pages for Processing" section of the chapter describes how to read a Web page into memory. The output of the `GetWebPage(ThisFile)` call is a string containing the complete Web page. You can verify the content of the Web page using the HTML Visualizer shown in Figure 8.4. Although the HTML Visualizer doesn't display some of the details such as graphics, you can see the content of the page as the user will see it. Use the Text Visualizer to see the Web page source.

Once the Web page appears as string, the code can begin processing it. The first task is to locate the first `<meta>` tag using `TheData.IndexOf("<meta>")`. Not every Web page will have `<meta>` tags, so this code prevents the loop from failing. A Web page that does include `<meta>` tags won't have them in any particular order, so the loop must process them one at a time and provide logic that processes just the required `<meta>` tags and knows when the Web page has provided all of the required `<meta>` tags. The example performs these tasks by filling three separate variables with the `<meta>` tag information. Notice the amount of string manipulation you must perform to obtain the `<meta>` tags. The code shown should work reliably with any functional `<meta>` tag combination. Note that &H22 converts to a double quote ("). The keywords require special processing because you need to split them into separate words. The code accomplishes this task by obtaining all of the keywords and then using the `Keyword.Split()` method to place the keywords in a string array.

The code recognizes a complete record by the appearance of text in all three of the `<meta>` tag strings, `Title`, `Description`, and `Keyword`. The code adds the required new rows to the target table using the `NewRow()` method. It fills the resulting `DataRow`, `DR`, with the information obtained from the `<meta>` tags. The data doesn't actually appear in the table, though, until the code calls the `Rows.Add()` method. Notice that the keywords create multiple entries in the associated `tblKeywords` table because there's one entry for each keyword. The table code ends by resetting the various `<meta>` tag variables so the loop can recognize when the next record is ready.

The next task is to display the resulting data on screen. The loop performs this task by assigning `Output` to the `dgResults.DataSource` property. Calling `dgResults.DataBind()` makes the data visible. Figure 8.5 shows typical results of an indexing session.

FIGURE 8.4
Verify the Web page presentation using the HTML Visualizer and content with the Text Visualizer.

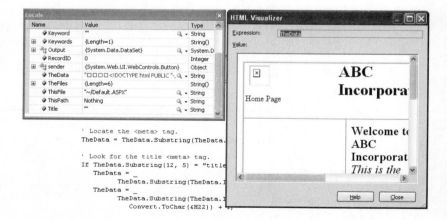

Having a great looking display doesn't do much for the application. The final two lines of code write the data and the associated schema (a description of the database structure) to the application's \Data folder. Figure 8.3 shows typical XML file output. You can view the resulting XML Schema Definition (XSD) file in Visual Web Developer. Figure 8.6 shows the database structure for this application. Notice that the fields are as you expect and that the XSD file shows the relationship between the two tables.

FIGURE 8.5
The Web page output tells you about the index file entries.

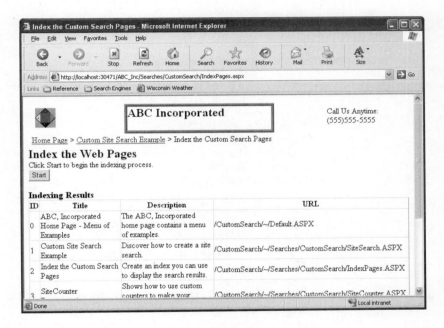

FIGURE 8.6
Use XSD files to describe complex XML table relationships.

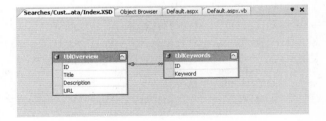

SEARCHING THE INDEX

At this point, you have an index based on the keywords <meta> file to use for the custom search. It's important to note that many search engines today index the entire Web page, so the indexing code in Listing 8.3 is the minimum you can use to obtain a relatively simple search. (Many modern search engines rely on spiders—special applications that constantly look for Web page changes—to ensure that any Web page changes appear in an updated index.) The search in this section only accepts a single keyword. The main reason for this limitation is that adding Boolean searches makes the quote quite complex and tends to hide the basic principle—looking for something in the index. Listing 8.4 shows the code used to search the index. (You'll find this example in the \ABC_Inc\Searches\CustomSearch folder of the source code on the Sybex Web site.)

NOTE Even though the source code shown in this section concentrates on the search specific sections of the ABC Incorporated Web site, the actual code on the Sybex Web site provides entries for all of the Web pages. In short, this search mechanism is functional even though it's simple and you can use it to search for examples.

LISTING 8.4: Getting Data from the Index

```
Sub btnSearch_Click(ByVal sender As Object,
                    ByVal e As System.EventArgs)

    ... Variable Declarations ...

    ' Determine the path for this application.
    ThisPath = Page.MapPath(Page.AppRelativeVirtualPath)
    ThisPath = ThisPath.Replace("\SiteSearch.aspx", "\")

    ' Read the raw DataSet from disk.
    dsInput.ReadXmlSchema(ThisPath + "Data\Index.XSD")
    dsInput.ReadXml(ThisPath + "Data\Index.XML", _
                    XmlReadMode.ReadSchema)

    ' Sort and search the data.
    ThisView = dsInput.Tables("tblKeywords").DefaultView
    ThisView.Sort = "Keyword"
    Hits = ThisView.AddNew().DataView.FindRows(txtSearchTerm.Text)

    ' Define the filtered information DataSet.
    dsFiltered.Tables.Add("tblOutput")
    dsFiltered.Tables("tblOutput").Columns.Add( _
        "Title", GetType(String))
    dsFiltered.Tables("tblOutput").Columns.Add( _
        "Description", GetType(String))
    dsFiltered.Tables("tblOutput").Columns.Add( _
        "URL", GetType(String))

    ' Process the individual records.
    For Counter = 0 To Hits.Length - 1
        SDR = Hits(Counter).Row
        ODR = dsInput.Tables("tblOverview").Rows( _
            Convert.ToInt32(SDR("ID")))
        DR = dsFiltered.Tables("tblOutput").NewRow()
        DR("Title") = ODR("Title")
        DR("Description") = ODR("Description")
```

```
        DR("URL") = ODR("URL")
        dsFiltered.Tables("tblOutput").Rows.Add(DR)
    Next

    ' Display the result.
    gvOutput.DataSource = dsFiltered
    gvOutput.DataBind()
End Sub
```

The code begins by determining the physical path of the data files and using the physical path to read both the schema and index into a `DataSet`, `dsInput`. Notice that the code reads the schema first and then the data to ensure `dsInput` interprets the information correctly. To ensure that the application interprets the schema correctly, use the `XmlReadMode.ReadSchema` constant when reading the data.

Now that `dsInput` has data to work with, the code creates a view of the data. A view doesn't change the data in any way, simply the way that application sees the data. In this case, the code sorts the data by the keyword. Sorting is important to ensure `dsInput` can locate the information you want to find. It then creates the view using `ThisView.AddNew()`. The `DataView.FindRows()` method determines the kind of view—a list of rows that match the search term. The code combines both operations into one statement.

The code has now examined the keywords and obtained a list of rows that contain the search term. These values appear in `Hits`. The row from `tblKeywords` consists of the keyword and the ID field, which has the same number as the ID field in `tblOverview`. It's important to build another `DataSet`, `dsFiltered`, to hold the values from `tblOverview` that match the values in `Hits`. Even though you could build a view using the current dataset, creating the new dataset has two important advantages. First, you don't need the ID field from `tblOverview`—it won't help the user in any way. Second, `dsFiltered` won't require any fancy manipulation to create the required output.

The processing loop comes next. The example relies on three `DataRow` objects to perform the required manipulation: `SDR` (the source data row from `Hits`), `ODR` (the output data row from `tblOverview`), and `DR` (the display data row that contains the manipulated data). The code creates a new `DR` for each iteration of the loop using the `dsFiltered.Tables("tblOutput").NewRow()` method. It then fills `DR` with the data from `ODR` and finally adds it back into `dsFiltered` using the `Rows.Add(DR)` method.

Now that `dsFiltered` contains the final search output, the code displays it on screen using the `GridView`, `gvOutput`. Notice that the code sets the `DataSource` property first and then displays the information by calling `DataBind()`. Figure 8.7 shows the output from the example.

You'll notice that Figure 8.7 shows the URL as a hyperlink. The user can click the hyperlink to move from page to page. The secret of this display is to create custom columns for `gvOutput`. To begin, display the `GridView` SmartTag and choose Edit Columns from the menu. You'll see the Fields dialog box shown in Figure 8.8 (the screenshot shows the fields configured). Clear the Auto-Generate Fields option and then begin adding the fields you need. The example uses two `Bound Field` and one `HyperLink Field` controls. As a minimum, you must provide values for the `HeaderText` and `DataField` properties for each `Bound Field` control. The `DataField` property values must match field names within `dsFiltered`. The `HyperLink Field` control requires three entries. The `HeaderText` property contains the text that appears at the top of the column, the `DataTextField` property contains the text the user sees on screen, and the `DataNavigateUrlFields` property contains the actual navigation URL.

FIGURE 8.7
The simple search only
looks for one keyword,
but demonstrates the
complexity of a custom
search.

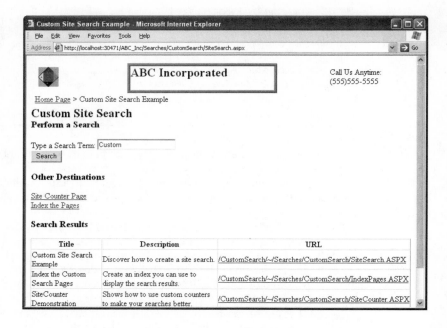

FIGURE 8.8
Configure the *GridView*
control with custom col-
umn entries to ensure
the user sees the correct
display.

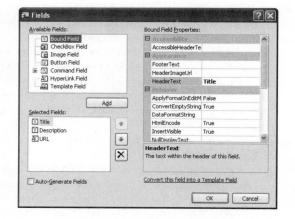

Defining Preferred Links Based on Site Counters

ASP.NET 2.0 contains a wonderful new class called SiteCounters. This class lets you create a
database that tracks how users work with your site. For example, you could track all of the links
that the user clicks. The Microsoft documentation focuses on using the SiteCounters class with
the AdRotator control. Combining the two does make sense because you can easily track the number
of clicks a particular advertisement receives (see the "Using the *AdRotator* Control" section of Chapter 14
for additional details on the AdRotator control), but you can use the SiteCounters class for so many

other purposes. For example, you could use the counters for statistical purposes—to determine which products are most popular. This section concentrates on using the `SiteCounters` class to improve the search results for your Web site. By tracking what users click on most often, you can weight the search results you provide to make it easy for users to locate the most popular choices quickly.

One way to track user access to a Web page is to create a custom site counter for each page. Whenever someone loads the page, the site counter records the information. Later, you can create a report on your findings and manually weight the pages or you can simply include the count in your custom search calculations. To begin, here's the simple code you use to create a custom counter for each page.

```
Sub Page_Load(ByVal sender As Object, _
                ByVal e As System.EventArgs) Handles Me.Load
    ' Provide an application name for the site counters.
    SiteCounters.ApplicationName = "Custom Search"

    ' Add a new entry to the database and store it immediately.
    SiteCounters.Write("Page Changes", _
                    "Custom Search Page", _
                    "PageLoad", _
                    "~/SiteSearch.ASPX")
    SiteCounters.Flush()
End Sub
```

The code begins by assigning an application name to the site using the `SiteCounters` object. You don't have to perform this step, but it helps to add an `ApplicationName` property value when you work with multiple Web sites. This extra field can help you sort through the data based on the particular site, yet create a comprehensive whole view of all the sites.

The `SiteCounters.Write()` method lets you create a custom entry and place it in the database. You can include a number of arguments, including the group name, the name of this particular page, the event that triggered the entry, and URL used to navigate to the page. Theoretically, the application should write this data to the database, but testing shows that it's easy to corrupt the database when you move from page to page. Calling `SiteCounters.Flush()` ensures that the data actually gets to the database.

Once you have the basic code added to the Web pages you want to track, you might want to display some statistics for them on a special administrative page. Listing 8.5 shows typical code for displaying either complete or individual statistics for your custom counters. You'll find this example in the \ABC_Inc\Searches\CustomSearch folder of the source code on the Sybex Web site.

The code begins by writing this page's custom counter to the database. It then begins displaying the statistics. You can choose a number of display scenarios. For example, you could display all of the events for just one page. This example displays the statistics for the entire group because the page statistics use a unique group name. Using a unique name for the group makes sense because you're creating statistics for a search, not for any other purpose. In fact, you can create as many entries in as many groups as you wish in order to keep the data completely separate.

Notice that the code includes a starting and ending time as part of the `SiteCounters.GetGroup Rows()` method. You can use this feature to retrieve a subset of the data—the technique shown retrieves all of the data. Once the code retrieves all of the group data and places it within a `DataSet`, it sets the `DataSource` property of a `DataGrid` control, `dgStatsView`, and then uses the `DataBind()` property to cause `dgStatsView` to display the data on screen.

LISTING 8.5:　　　Tracking Complete or Individual Page Statistics

```
Sub Page_Load(ByVal sender As Object, _
               ByVal e As System.EventArgs) Handles Me.Load

    Dim ClickStats As DataSet    ' Holds the statistics

    ' Add a new entry to the database and store it immediately.
    SiteCounters.Write("Page Changes", _
                        "Site Counter Page", _
                        "PageLoad", _
                        "~/SiteCounter.ASPX")
    SiteCounters.Flush()

    ' Display the current statistics.
    ClickStats = SiteCounters.GetGroupRows(DateTime.MinValue, _
                                            DateTime.MaxValue, _
                                            "Page Changes")

    dgStatsView.DataSource = ClickStats
    dgStatsView.DataBind()

    ' Display individual values.
    txtCustomSearch.Text = _
        SiteCounters.GetTotalCount(DateTime.MinValue, _
                                    DateTime.MaxValue, _
                                    "Page Changes", _
                                    "Custom Search Page").ToString()
    txtSiteCounter.Text = _
        SiteCounters.GetTotalCount(DateTime.MinValue, _
                                    DateTime.MaxValue, _
                                    "Page Changes", _
                                    "Site Counter Page").ToString()
    txtSiteControl1.Text = _
        SiteCounters.GetTotalCount(DateTime.MinValue, _
                                    DateTime.MaxValue, _
                                    "Page Changes", _
                                    "Site Counter Page 1").ToString()
    txtSiteControl2.Text = _
        SiteCounters.GetTotalCount(DateTime.MinValue, _
                                    DateTime.MaxValue, _
                                    "Page Changes", _
                                    "Site Counter Page 2").ToString()
End Sub
```

Obtaining single statistics is a little harder. In this case, the code retrieves a single numeric count using the `GetTotalCount()` method. Again, you can specify a beginning and ending time for the count. In this case, you must specify both the group name and the individual counter name. Figure 8.9 shows the output of this example.

The best solution for working with the `SiteCounters` class would be a way to track unique visits to the page itself, but you can't easily track pages using the `SiteCounters` class and the results can become skewed when users click the Back and Forward buttons on the browser. Consequently, you can track control activity instead—a user has to click something to move from one page to another and have it count toward the total. This technique still has pitfalls, but it could introduce fewer weighting problems for some Web sites. The biggest drawback to this approach is that it can't track the user's initial entry into the Web site because that entry relies on loading the page directly or a click from another site.

When using the `SiteCounters` class to track Web site usage for creating weighted search results, you don't want to track every control—just those that transfer control from one page to another. For this reason, you'll normally track the `Button`, `LinkButton`, and `Hyperlink` controls. Depending on the circumstances, you might track other controls, as well, but these three buttons will normally provide all of the page movement functionality you require.

To start tracking the clicks made by users, you must decide how to organize the database and make three simple changes to each control you want to track. You don't actually have to create the database—Visual Web Developer creates it for you, but you do have to set the appropriate properties shown in Figure 8.10. Begin by setting the `CounterGroup` property to a common value for all page change information, such as Page Changes. The next step is to set the `CounterName` property to the name of the page that the user will go to after clicking the control—make sure each page has a unique name. Once you complete these two steps, set `CountClicks` to true.

FIGURE 8.9
You can retrieve the site counter data individually or work with it as a data set as needed.

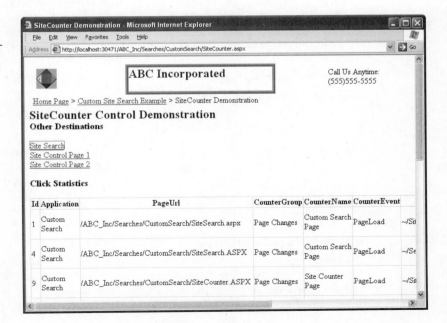

FIGURE 8.10
Setting the *CountClicks*
property to true is
enough to start
counting clicks.

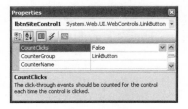

Don't get the idea that the `SiteCounters` class uses a mysterious database located in a hidden location that you'll never find. Like many other Visual Web Developer features, this information appears in the `ASPNetDB.MDF` file found in the `\App_Data` folder for the individual project. When you want to remove old counters or modify existing counters, open the `ASPNetDB.MDF` file and locate the `aspnet_SiteCounters` table. When you open this table, you'll see a list of Web site counter entries. You can easily modify or delete entries as needed. Creating a new entry is a little harder and you should probably rely on code to perform this task.

Using Google to Create a Site Search

Creating a custom site search isn't a minor undertaking—you'll spend a lot of time creating the search engine, deciding how to weight the various search factors, and adding new kinds of searches to satisfy user needs. In fact, if your Web site is large enough, you could conceivably end up hiring multiple developers just to maintain the search engine. In many cases, developers don't feel the effort is worth the results. Fortunately, Google provides a ready-made alternative.

The advantage of using Google as your search engine extends well beyond development time, however. Using Google also makes it possible to shift the processing burden from the server to the client. By using scripting techniques, you can provide a great search engine without incurring much development time and still reduce the costs of running your Web site. The following sections discuss the various techniques you can use to add a Google search to your Web site.

Using the Web Service

Before you begin working with Google Web Services, you need to obtain the kit and a developer license. Once you have the kit, you need to install it and become familiar with its content. The following sections describe the kit-related tasks you need to perform.

TIP   Google lets you perform many different tasks with its Web service, and Google has recently added a few additional search features. I based much of the material in this section of the chapter on my book, *Mining Google Web Services: Building Applications with the Google API* (Sybex, 2004). This book shows you the full extent of the functionality Google Web Services can provide for your Web site.

Performing the Download

Downloading the kit is easy. You'll find the main Web services page at `http://www.google.com/apis/`. Figure 8.11 shows that this page contains some information, along with two important links. Although the steps shown in the figure are numbered, you can perform the first two steps in any order. This chapter assumes that you want to download the Google Web Services Kit first.

FIGURE 8.11
You can obtain both the kit and the developer license on this site.

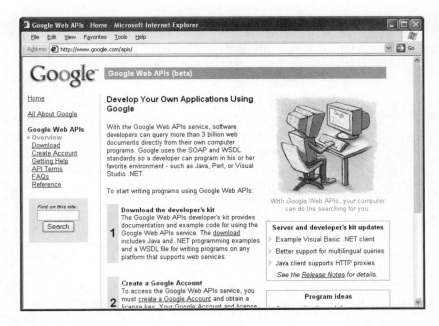

USING THE NON-CODED APPROACH

Before you begin writing code, it's important to understand that Google does provide several free search services that don't require much (if any) coding. All you have to do to use these free services is paste a little HTML on your Web page. You can learn more about these free offerings at http://www.google.com/searchcode.html. The bottom line is that you can gain site-specific access to what many people consider the most powerful search engine in the world with about 10 seconds of work. However, the non-coded approach does come with a few problems and you need to consider whether another approach will work better.

The main problem with the free search that Google provides is that you lose control of the visitor to your site. The search executes on the Google Web site. Consequently, the person that originally came to your Web site for help could literally end up anywhere on the Internet after the search. In addition, a user who has your site set up as a trusted site will suddenly see messages that they're entering an untrusted zone if Google isn't also part of their trusted list. In short, the transfer from your site to the Google site disrupts the smooth Web surfing experience that users expect—not the impression of your site that you want to promote.

Output is also a problem since you can only see the information in one form: the one that Google chooses for you. If Google's idea of what the display should include matches your own, fine, but this is seldom the case. Most Web site owners want a customized display that meets specific requirements. Consequently, even though the easy solution to using Google works well, the inflexibility of this solution runs counter to what most people want.

Click the download link and you'll see a page that describes the kit. This page also includes the licensing agreement for the Google Web Services Kit. Make sure you read the licensing agreement and understand what it means before you proceed. Don't worry about copying the licensing agreement to disk—the kit includes a copy of the licensing agreement you can use for reference purposes later. Check the "I have read and agree with the Google Web APIs license terms." option and then click Download Now. You'll see a File Download dialog box. Click Save and you'll see a Save As dialog box. The default name of the file is `GoogleAPI.ZIP`, but you can save it using another name if desired. Click Save and you'll receive the file—a mere 666 KB in size.

GETTING A LICENSE

Once you complete the download process, click the Create a Google Account link that's available on the same page as the Google Web Services Kit download. You'll see a Web page that requests an email address and password. This page also contains links to Google's terms of service and privacy statements. Make sure you read both before you proceed. The Google Web Services Kit doesn't include copies of either document, so you might want to copy the information and save it on disk for use later. When you finish reading both documents, check the "I have read and accepted the Google Terms of Service above and Privacy Policy." option and click Create My Google Account.

At this point, you'll see a message stating that Google will send a verification message to your email. Click on the link provided by the verification message to activate your account. After you verify your account, Google will send your developer license to your email. The license normally arrives in about an hour—you might need to wait more or less time depending on how busy Google is at the time. Make sure you save the email message containing the developer token because you'll need it for every transaction later.

TIP You can always change the password and other information associated with your account. Simply go to the Google Accounts site at `https://www.google.com/accounts/Login`. Type your name and password to enter the site. Select the My Account link to change the account information.

INSTALLING THE KIT

The kit is actually a Zip file containing examples and documentation. If you're running Windows XP, the operating system provides a program to unpack the file for you. Otherwise, you'll need a special program that reads the compressed file and unpacks it for you such as WinZip (`http://www.winzip.com`).

You won't find any actual developer tools in the Zip file. The file does include complete path information, so you can unpack it in the root folder of your hard drive if you like. I used the D drive on my system, so the Google Web Services Kit appears in the `D:\GoogleAPI` folder.

At this point, the kit is ready for use. However, before you go any further, you need to know about two files in the `\GoogleAPI` folder. The `LICENSE.TXT` file contains a copy of the license agreement that you saw online. Make sure you retain this file so that you can refer back to the usage terms as needed.

The `README.TXT` file contains useful information about the Google Web Services Kit and tells you where you can obtain additional information. This file is very helpful because it contains URLs where you can obtain additional examples. It also has URLs for help sites and additional information. Finally, you'll want to read this file if you want to run the examples because it contains instructions for using them.

Performing a Simple SOAP Call

Google Web Services relies on the use of the Simple Object Access Protocol (SOAP) to make calls. SOAP is yet another form of XML. However, this form of XML provides a means of communication, rather than a means of data storage. As you work with XML, you'll find that it's incredibly flexible and developers use it for many purposes. You get full SOAP support with Visual Studio .NET, and many Windows updates also install it. You can also find the SOAP Toolkit 3.0 at `http://www.microsoft.com/downloads/details.aspx?FamilyId=C943C0DD-CEEC-4088-9753-86F052EC8450&displaylang=en`.

TIP This section of the chapter doesn't provide a complete SOAP tutorial, but it does provide sufficient information for you to use the example code. However, you can find a great SOAP tutorial at `http://www.w3schools.com/soap/`. It's also helpful to study the official SOAP specification (`http://www.w3.org/TR/2001/WD-soap12-20010709/`), primer (`http://www.w3.org/TR/soap12-part0/`), messaging framework (`http://www.w3.org/TR/soap12-part1/`), and adjuncts (`http://www.w3.org/TR/soap12-part2/`).

SOAP is actually incredibly easy to use to access Google once you understand the basic principles. It's time to try the first SOAP call using a technique that many developers will employ for learning Google Web Services—a simple Web page. Listing 8.6 shows how to make a simple SOAP call using JavaScript. You'll find this example in the `\Chapter 08\GoogleSearch` folder of the source code on the Sybex Web site.

The code begins by creating a SOAP client. The client communicates with the server—it ensures that the message traffic flows as anticipated and that the request is formed correctly. The `SoapClient.MSSoapInit()` function creates a connection to the server. This step isn't the same as sending data to the server—all it does is create the connection.

At this point, the code can make a request of Google Web Services. Requests take the form of specially formatted function calls. You must know the name of the function call as well as the variables it requires—all of which appear in the Google Web Services Kit that you install. The code makes the request by sending all of the required arguments as part of the `SoapClient.doGoogleSearch()` function call. The following list defines each of the search request arguments. Your application must provide these arguments in order as part of the search request. Otherwise, Google won't honor the request.

key Every request you make requires the license key you obtained from Google. When you make a request without the license key or using the key found in the Google examples, you'll receive an invalid authorization key message. Google uses a string of zeros (00000000000000000000000000000000) as the sample key—this key looks nothing like the actual key. The examples in this book use "Your-License-Key" as the sample key. In both cases, you must replace the sample key with a real key.

q This string argument contains the search request. Tests indicate that you can make search requests of any length and Google will honor them. This means you can be quite specific in requesting what you want or you can make a general query and filter the data locally. The one caveat you do need to observe is that complex search specifications tend to reduce the number of results to the point that you don't get any results at all. Smart search techniques make the request specific, without attempting to locate the one result that perfectly matches a need. See Chapter 2 for a complete discussion of search request elements.

start This numeric argument contains the 0-based starting point for the search. You must couple this starting point with the number of results you request, with 10 results being the maximum. Consequently, if you want to view the third set of results and you request 10 results for each set, you'd set this argument to 30. An odd problem can occur when working with Google Web Services, however. Although the results you receive are sequential, they aren't necessarily complete. The actual results might start at 1 or skip a similar result. This means you can't use a strict starting point; you must base the starting point on the returned values.

maxResults Google lets you request a maximum of 10 results. However, you can specify less than that amount when you only need a few results. In addition, you may receive fewer results if the search criteria are strict enough. The benefit of requesting fewer results is that you get the response faster, so your application performs better. However, if you plan to request additional results anyway, it's probably better to request the maximum number of results and cache the additional results locally.

filter The documentation doesn't make this particular argument very clear. You provide true or false as the input values—not the values described in the Automatic Filtering section of the Google Web API Reference. Turning on filtering means that Google looks for results that have the same title and snippet. The Web service only returns the first result and eliminates the others. In addition, Google only returns the first two results from a particular Web host. Filtering means that you have to select the start argument value carefully because Google will leave out some of the results.

restrict This argument restricts the results you receive to a particular country of origin. Don't confuse this argument with a language restriction. For example, when you select the United States as the country of origin, you could still receive pages written in Spanish or German. However, you won't receive results from either Spain or Germany. The Restricts section of the Google Web API Reference contains a chart of country codes you must use for this argument. As with most restrictions, this argument will create holes in the result set and affect the start argument value.

safeSearch Generally, you can use this argument to ensure you don't receive any results with pornographic content. However, the filter doesn't work all the time and some search terms will almost certainly retrieve adult content despite the use of this filter. Set the argument to true when you want to avoid adult content. Contact Google at `safesearch@google.com` when you encounter pornographic material that you don't want. Telling Google about the problem will help refine the filter so that others don't encounter the same results.

lr Sometimes you need a result in a specific language. This argument doesn't restrict the country that you get a result from, but it does restrict the language of the result. For example, you could tell Google that you only want results written in Japanese. The Restricts section of the Google Web API Reference contains a chart of country codes you must use for this argument. As with most restrictions, this argument will create holes in the result set and affect the start argument value.

ie This argument is ignored. You still need to provide it as part of the SOAP message, but leave the content blank (an empty string).

oe This argument is ignored. You still need to provide it as part of the SOAP message, but leave the content blank (an empty string).

LISTING 8.6:   Simple JavaScript SOAP Call

```javascript
function CallGoogle()
{
    // Create the SOAP client.
    var SoapClient = new ActiveXObject("MSSOAP.SoapClient30");

    // Initialize the SOAP client so it can access Google
    // Web Services.
    SoapClient.MSSoapInit("http://api.google.com/GoogleSearch.wsdl",
                          "GoogleSearchService",
                          "GoogleSearchPort");

    // Make a search request.
    var ThisResult =
        SoapClient.doGoogleSearch("Your-License-Key",
                                  SubmissionForm.SearchStr.value,
                                  1,
                                  10,
                                  false,
                                  "",
                                  false,
                                  "",
                                  "",
                                  "");

    // Return the results.
    return ThisResult;
}
```

On return from the call, ThisResult contains the return data from Google in the form of a SOAP message. This object isn't an XML document. You must retrieve the XML document using the technique shown in Listing 8.6. However, at this point, you have a pointer to the information you need.

Using a Script to Call an XSLT Page

Google doesn't know how you want to present the data it provides, so the XML you receive doesn't include any form of XSLT declaration. This declaration appears as <?xml-stylesheet type="text/xsl" href="SearchDisplay.xsl"?> in the XML file. The href attribute tells where to find the XSLT file. Without this information, the browser will never display anything but XML on screen. It would seem that the situation is hopeless. However, you have other options, such as writing a script that performs the transformation process using another technique.

The example in Listing 8.7 shows how you can download a response from Google, store the information locally, and translate it using XSLT. The result is the same as modifying the XML file to include the required linkage information, but far more automatic. You'll find this example in the \Chapter 08\GoogleSearch folder of the source code on the Sybex Web site.

LISTING 8.7: Performing a Transformation in JavaScript

```
function GetData(XslFile)
{
   // Get the search data.
   var TheResult = CallGoogle();

   // Place the resulting information in an XML document.
   var ProcDoc = new ActiveXObject("Msxml2.DOMDocument.4.0");
   ProcDoc.async = false;
   ProcDoc.loadXML(TheResult.context.xml);

   // Create an XSLT document and load the transform into it.
   var XSLTData = new ActiveXObject("Msxml2.DOMDocument.4.0");
   XSLTData.async = false;
   XSLTData.load(XslFile);

   // Display the output on screen.
   document.write(ProcDoc.transformNode(XSLTData));
}
```

Before the script can do anything, it must obtain the search results from Google. When using Google Web Services, you must rely on SOAP to perform this task. SOAP is extremely flexible, so you can use a number of techniques to make a request with it. The "Performing a Simple SOAP Call" section of the chapter shows one such technique. All you need to know, for the moment, is that the script obtains search results from Google using the `CallGoogle()` function.

The next step is a little tricky and definitely Windows specific. The code creates an instance of the Microsoft XML component. The `ActiveXObject()` function performs this task. The `Msxml2 .DOMDocument.4.0` string identifies the component. You might have to use `Msxml2.DOMDocument.5.0` on newer machines with Microsoft Office 2003 or another new product loaded—the last part of the string identifies the component version number. Setting the `async` property to false is important because you don't want the call to load the XML to return until the browser actually receives this file. Finally, the `ProcDoc.loadXML()` function loads the response from Google Web Services. Notice that the code uses the `loadXML()` function to load text formatted as XML, rather than XML from a file.

NOTE   Most versions of MSXML work fine for this example. However, you'll probably want to get MSXML Version 4.0 Service Pack 2 (SP2) from `http://www.microsoft.com/downloads/details.aspx?FamilyID=3144b72b-b4f2-46da-b4b6-c5d7485f2b42&DisplayLang=en`. (MSXML Version 5.0 isn't available for download as of this writing.) This latest version includes a number of features that make working with XML documents a lot easier. In addition, you'll find that the latest versions are slightly faster and contain a number of bug fixes that make your application more reliable.

The code now has a local copy of the data from Google. This local copy will disappear as soon as the function ends, so you don't have to worry about update requirements, but it's important to understand that the copy resides in memory on your machine somewhere.

At this point, the code has data to work with, but no XSLT file. The next step loads the XSLT file defined by the `XslFile` variable. Notice that the code uses the `XSLTData.load()` function because the XML appears in a file that the application must load into memory. The coupling between the XML response and the XSLT occurs in the `XMLData.transformNode()` function call. This call produces output that the `document.write()` function then sends to the current page. The result is that you see the transformed XML on screen, as shown in Figure 8.12. Notice that the URL doesn't change, even though the content differs, because you're still theoretically on the same Web page.

FIGURE 8.12
The results of using a script to transform XML data received from Google.

Translating the Result with XSLT

This section describes the XSLT page used with the transformation described in the "Using a Script to Call an XSLT Page" section (see Listing 8.7). Listing 8.8 shows how to create an XSLT page that outputs HTML code. You could use the same technique to create a report or any other form of output based on the XML input received from Google. (You'll find this example in the `\Chapter 08\ GoogleSearch` folder of the source code on the Sybex Web site.)

The code begins with the usual declarations. The `<xsl:output method="xml" indent="yes"/>` tag is important because it determines the kind of output the parser creates. You can also choose text as the output method or tell the parser that you don't want the output indented. Notice that the code also matches the `return` element using the `<xsl:template match="/return">` tag. All of the data appears within this element, so there isn't a good reason to match the root node of the XML document.

LISTING 8.8:   Designing an XSLT Page

```
<?xml version="1.0" encoding="UTF-8"?>
<xsl:stylesheet version="1.0"
    xmlns:xsl="http://www.w3.org/1999/XSL/Transform"
    xmlns:fo="http://www.w3.org/1999/XSL/Format">
<xsl:output method="xml" indent="yes"/>
<xsl:template match="/return">
<html>
<head>
    <title>XSLT Transformation Example</title>
</head>
<body>
    <!-- Display a heading. -->
    <h1 align="center">Translated Google Web Services Results</h1>

    <!-- Display some common information. -->
    <h2>Common Results</h2>
    <label>
        Search request:
        <xsl:value-of select="searchQuery"/>
    </label><br/>
    ... Other Common Results ...

    <!-- Display the search result values. -->
    <table align="center" border="1" width="100%">
        <caption><h2>Results Returned from Query</h2></caption>
        <tbody>
            <tr>
                <th>Site Title</th>
                <th>Snippet</th>
                <th>URL</th>
                <th>Cached Size</th>
            </tr>
            <xsl:for-each select="resultElements/item">
                <tr>
                    <td>
                        <xsl:value-of select="title"
                            disable-output-escaping="yes"/>
                    </td>
                    <td>
                        <xsl:value-of select="snippet"
                            disable-output-escaping="yes"/>
                    </td>
                    <td>
                        <xsl:text disable-output-escaping="yes">
                            &lt;a href='
```

```
            </xsl:text>
            <xsl:value-of select="URL"/>
            <xsl:text disable-output-escaping="yes">
               '&gt;
            </xsl:text>
            <xsl:value-of select="URL"/>
            <xsl:text disable-output-escaping="yes">
               &lt;/a&gt;
            </xsl:text>
         </td>
         <td><xsl:value-of select="cachedSize"/></td>
      </tr>
   </xsl:for-each>
   </tbody>
</table>

</body>
</html>
</xsl:template>
</xsl:stylesheet>
```

The code then outputs the heading. Notice that this is pure HTML and that the code isn't doing anything but outputting this text. The code moves on to the body where it outputs a heading.

The XSLT-specific code begins when the code outputs some of the common information returned by Google. None of this information requires special handling, so the code uses a simple `<xsl:value-of select="searchQuery"/>` tag to retrieve and display the information. The information is surrounded by descriptive text and enclosed within a `<label>` to make it easier to see.

Each return value requires special handling, so the code relies on a table. Notice the head of the table is standard HTML, but that the next selection is an `<xsl:for-each>` element. This statement tells the parser to look at all of the children of the `resultElements/item` node. The system will process each `<item>` element in turn. The next step is to use the `<xsl:value-of>` element to retrieve the name and value attributes of each `<item>` element. Because some of these entries contain the text version of the HTML tags such as `&gt;` for the greater than (>) symbol, you must include `disable-output-escaping="yes"` attribute with the `<xsl:value-of>` element. Otherwise, the code will display the > symbol and not create a tag. The code ends by completing the HTML page, and then completing both the template and the stylesheet.

Discovering Site Maps

Many Web sites now include a site map. In some cases, the Web site relies on a site map in place of a site search, but in most cases, the site map augments any search capability the site search provides. A site map is always some type of text or graphic representation of the site based on the site content. For example, you could create a topical tree that helps the user define the information they need. The following sections discuss site maps and help you create one using the tools that Visual Web Developer provides.

Understanding the Differences between a Site Map and a Site Search

It's important to understand the differences between a site search and a site map—they accomplish similar goals, but use completely different techniques. A site search relies on the user to provide input in the form of keywords. The user must already have some idea of what they are searching for to use this technique. The results the user receives from a site search vary greatly depending on the flexibility and functionality of the search engine.

A site map provides a representation of the Web site as a whole. The user need not know anything about the Web site to use a site map because the site map presents all of the information at one time. The user looks through the list of entries to locate the required information. Clicking a link takes the user to the specified Web page.

Even though a site map may appear superior to a site search at first glance, the site map also suffers from limitations. Using a good search engine, a site search can turn up possible pages that the user might not have originally considered. A site search is also more precise—more targeted—because it presents only the hits that relate to the user's search terms. The targeting is important because the user can choose from known good selections, rather than scan an entire Web page looking potentially good information.

Another point to consider is the number of results that a site search can provide. Even though the user must supply good search terms to begin a site search, a site search ultimately returns more results than a site map can. When creating a site map, the developer must limit the possible search criteria to a topic or other form of descriptive data, rather than a raw collection of words on the page.

Ultimately, it's not a matter of discovering which technique is better. Both a site map and a site search fulfill specific needs for particular users. The choice you make depends partially on who you expect to visit your Web site. A Web site with many first-time novice users generally benefit most from a site map, while a Web site that has a loyal following of advanced users normally does better with a site search. In some cases, providing both search methods is the best choice because a Web site receives a random mix of users.

Using the Site Navigation Features

The site map functionality provided by Visual Web Developer includes a special kind of Web page (described in the "Creating a Site Map" section) and two special controls. These controls appear on the Navigation tab of the Toolbox. The following sections describe the two controls and tell how you can use them to add navigation features to your Web site.

USING THE *SITEMAPPATH* CONTROL

The SiteMapPath control works with the SITEMAP file described in the "Creating a Site Map" section of the chapter. Any site map entries that you place in the SITEMAP file also appear on this control depending on the Web page's position in the site map hierarchy. You use this control when you want a simple path displayed on screen from the current location to the main page on your Web site (also called the root node).

You can control many of the formatting features of this control. For example, you can change the colors or even the appearance of the various links. You can change the order in which the links appear and features such as the display of tooltips when the user hovers the mouse over the control. It's also possible to choose from one of the predefined templates using the Edit Templates option on the `SiteMapPath` SmartTag.

USING THE *MENU* CONTROL

The `Menu` control can also rely on the content of a `SITEMAP` file for a list of links. However, this control is a lot more flexible than the `SiteMapPath` control because you can also use a database as a source of links or you can enter the links manually. In short, you use the `Menu` control when you need additional flexibility and the use of a drop-down list works as well as the map path provided by the `SiteMapPath` control.

Besides the flexibility of data source, you can also choose a static or dynamic view that you select using the Views field on the `Menu` SmartTag. The static view reads the data source or manual entry when the page loads and only updates the display when the user reloads it. The advantage of this approach is that you conserve network bandwidth and improve application performance. The dynamic view updates the information as needed from the data source while the page is loaded. The advantage of this approach is that you can make new options available as the user needs them.

To change the menu items manually, click Edit Menu Items on the `Menu` SmartTag. You'll see the Menu Item Editor shown in Figure 8.13. The figure shows one item added. To add an item, click either Add a Root Item or Add a Child Item (the first two buttons above the Items list). You must define the `NavigateUrl`, `Text`, and `Value` properties as a minimum. It's extremely helpful to include a `ToolTip` property value, as well, so users can obtain additional information about choices they make.

To add a data source, select an existing entry in the Choose Data Source field of the `Menu` SmartTag or choose `<New Data Source...>` to create a new data source. You'll see a Data Source Configuration dialog box. This dialog box lets you choose between a site map and an XML database as a source of entries for your menu. When you select a site map as a data source, you don't have to perform any additional work because the control automatically uses the `SITEMAP` file you define for other purposes. When working with an XML database, you must create the specially formatted XML (see Listing 8.9 for an example). This is a viable option if you store your site map in a database, but isn't especially convenient and you should avoid using it when possible.

FIGURE 8.13
Create menu items manually using the Menu Item Editor.

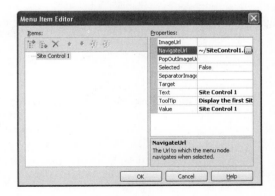

Creating a Site Map

A site map requires a little special programming. Visual Web Developer encapsulates this programming as part of the Site Map template located on the Add New Item dialog box. When you select this template, you'll create a new Web.SITEMAP file. The special SITEMAP extension defines a site map for your Web page. The SITEMAP file is yet another example of XML at work. You define the structure of your Web site using a series of XML entries. Subpages appear as child nodes of the parent used to call them. For example, the "Creating a Custom Site Search" section of the chapter used a number of Web pages to perform its work. The first page you access is SiteSearch.ASPX, so that page acts as the parent for all other nodes, as shown in Listing 8.9. You'll find this example in the \ABC_Inc\Searches\CustomSearch folder of the source code on the Sybex Web site.

LISTING 8.9:   Defining a Site Map Structure for a Web Site

```xml
<?xml version="1.0" encoding="utf-8" ?>
<siteMap>
    <!-- Node the user accesses first. -->
    <siteMapNode url="SiteSearch.ASPX"
                 title="Custom Site Search Example"
                 description="Discover how to create a site search."
                 roles="">

        <!-- Two nodes accessed from SiteSearch.ASPX. -->
        <siteMapNode url="IndexPages.ASPX"
                     title="Index the Custom Search Pages"
                     description="Create a search results index."
                     roles="" />
        <siteMapNode url="SiteCounter.ASPX"
                     title="SiteCounter Demonstration"
                     description="Shows how to use custom counters."
                     roles="">

            <!-- Two nodes accessed from SiteCounter.ASPX. -->
            <siteMapNode url="SiteControl1.ASPX"
                         title="Control Site 1"
                         description="An extra page."
                         roles="" />
            <siteMapNode url="SiteControl2.ASPX"
                         title="Control Site 2"
                         description="An extra page."
                         roles="" />
        </siteMapNode>
    </siteMapNode>
</siteMap>
```

The site map appears as a series of `<siteMapNode>` elements that you can nest as needed to create the hierarchy for your Web site. Each `<siteMapNode>` element contains four attributes.

url   Contains the relative or absolute URL of the target page. Make sure you include the path from the root node when working with relative URLs.

title   Contains the page title. You should use the same title that appears in the `<title>` tag or the title `<meta>` tag when defining this option.

description   Defines the purpose of the Web page. You can use the content of the description `<meta>` tag for this entry. However, if the standard description is too long to create an effective tooltip, you can always shorten the text so it fits on screen.

roles   Creates a security setting for this site map entry. Only users who exist in the appropriate security role can access the entry. Visual Web Developer uses the concept of roles to enforce security—users exist in roles that have specific security access. The user's role can change depending on circumstance—a user with a local connection acting as a manager might have more rights than with a remote connection as a user. See Chapter 17 for a complete description of security issues in Visual Web Developer.

Once you create a `SITEMAP` file, you can add either a `SiteMapPath` or `Menu` control to the pages on your Web site to display its content. Figure 8.14 shows examples of both kinds of output. (You can also see this technique at work on the `Default.ASPX` page of the ABC Incorporated Web site. The `Default.ASPX` page contains references for all of the ABC Incorporated Web site examples, Chapters 4 through 21, in this book.) The `SiteMapPath` appears at the top of the page immediately below the page title, while the `Menu` appears at the bottom of the page. Notice how hovering the mouse displays a tooltip describing the page.

FIGURE 8.14
Use the appropriate control to display your site map.

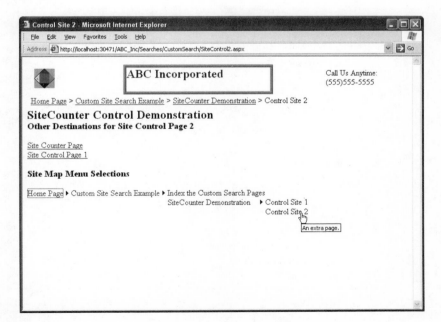

Defining Your Development Goals

This chapter has helped you understand the purpose and effectiveness of site searches using various techniques and under a number of conditions. In some cases, you also need to create a site map to ensure that all users can find everything they need. The choices you make determine how easy your site is to search, which ultimately determines its popularity. Users can't tell other people about great information they can't find.

It's time to determine the search setup for your Web site. You can begin by defining the search elements the user is likely to need. After you decide what kind of search to create, you'll need to determine how to create it. Using a custom search does have significant benefits, but also requires a lot of effort on your part. Many developers rely on Google searches to meet their needs. After you create one or more searches for your Web site, think about creating a site map as well. In fact, you might want to use some of the tips from Chapter 7 to design a form to get user feedback on the kind of site they need as well.

Chapter 9 helps you understand both pop-ups and redirection—two resources that you can use with either forms or searches. Some Web sites use these features to good effect in making the user experience better. Of course, it's always easy to misuse a technology. Pop-ups have become a problem for many people because Web site developers have misused them in the past. Chapter 9 not only shows you great uses for both pop-ups and redirection, but also helps you avoid misusing these technologies.

Chapter 9

Using Pop-ups and Redirection

On the Internet, getting to where you really want to go is half the adventure. Web sites change their domain name, Webmasters move pages around, sometimes a Web site will provide more than one path to the same information, and there are even times when you'll get the wrong URL the first time. No matter how you get to where you're going, pop-ups and redirection both have a role to play in getting you there. This chapter explores legitimate uses of both techniques and exposes some uses that you'll want to avoid to keep Web site visitors happy.

Many people criticize the use of pop-up forms for good reason—most Web sites use them in unappealing ways to try to sell you something or get you to do something that you don't want to do. However, pop-up forms can have many legitimate uses as well. For example, you can provide a pop-up form that reminds a user to perform a specific task or asks the user's opinion about Web site functionality.

NOTE   This chapter doesn't explore a variation of the pop-up, the pop-under. Proponents of the pop-under say that it's less intrusive than the pop-up, but there are few legitimate uses for the technology. A pop-under appears under the main Web page, which means that the user can't even see it immediately. Some Web sites, such as ASAP! A Stand Against Pop-under ads! (http://jenett.org/asap/), speak out against pop-under advertisements.

Like pop-up windows, redirection has a number of legitimate uses. In fact, of the two technologies, redirection probably has the most legitimate use—getting people to the location of a new page on your Web site. Unfortunately, like pop-ups, redirection has a lot of potential for misuse, so users are leery of redirection, in many cases for good reason. You have access to three kinds of redirection when using Visual Web Developer and this chapter explores all three. The kind of redirection you choose depends on the need that your Web site is trying to serve and the security requirements for the redirection. Although using the meta refresh tag is still extremely popular and you can rely on scripted redirection when the client trusts your Web site enough to run scripts, server-side redirection is becoming extremely popular because it's the most secure and reliable method of performing this task.

NOTE   Many corporate Web sites now eschew both pop-ups and redirection because of their association with phishing attacks, viruses, privacy concerns, and other issues. Before you even read this chapter, consider whether you want to use this technology on your Web site. Decide during the course of the chapter which technologies you'll use and provide a corporate policy on this issue. Make sure you provide the Web site user with a policy as well. Tell the user precisely how you use these technologies and provide them with a means to turn it off.

Understanding User Concerns over Pop-ups and Redirection

Most corporate Web sites use pop-ups responsibly, but because users have experienced problems with pop-ups on other Web sites, they want nothing to do with them. The problem with pop-up advertisements has become so severe that even Microsoft has recognized the need for a pop-up blocker (special software that keeps pop-up windows from appearing on screen). You can now get a built-in pop-up blocker as part of Widows XP Service Pack 2 (SP2), which you control using the Privacy tab of the Internet Options dialog box. Click Settings and you'll see the Pop-up Blocker Settings dialog box shown in Figure 9.1. This dialog box has the highest settings enabled (see `http://www.microsoft.com/windowsxp/using/web/sp2_popupblocker.mspx` for additional details).

Quite a few third party vendors also supply pop-up blockers for other versions of Windows, many of which are special toolbars for Internet Explorer. The three most common toolbar options are the MSN toolbar (`http://toolbar.msn.com/`), Google toolbar (`http://toolbar.google.com/`), and the Alexa toolbar (`http://download.alexa.com/index.cgi`). The point is you must provide the user with a good reason to allow your pop-up window other than the fact that you want to sell products.

NOTE It's interesting to note that pop-up blockers can cause problems of their own. A friend recently related that several employees decided to add pop-up blockers to their system without permission. It wasn't long and the users complained of problems with their systems. A specific combination of applications would cause one of the applications to crash—sometimes the cure is worse than the disease.

Redirection hasn't come under the common definition of a plague that pop-up advertisements have, but it can actually be a bigger problem. It's possible for a cracker with the proper tools to redirect a browser from a legitimate Web site to a look-alike that contains viruses, Trojan horses, or other content of dubious quality. Some of this redirection takes place in situations where the user has no idea that the redirection has occurred, such as the cross-site scripting issue described in the US-CERT article at `http://www.us-cert.gov/cas/techalerts/TA04-163A.html`. You can find a concise description of some of the security problems with redirection on the LWN site at `http://lwn.net/2000/features/Redirect.php3`. Redirection can also be regional because of the way the Internet is set up. A user in Washington might experience a redirection problem that a user in Maine doesn't.

Some users respond to the security issues created by redirection by disabling some browser features such as scripting. In fact, Internet Explorer can also disable the meta refresh tag using the settings on the Security Settings dialog box shown in Figure 9.2. (You can access this dialog box by opening the Internet Options dialog, selecting a security zone on the Security tag, and clicking Custom Level.) Consequently, the only sure way to provide redirection on your Web site is to use server-side redirection. Not surprisingly, this is also the safest method of providing redirection and the one that the user is most likely to accept.

Although you know that you have no evil intent in using either pop-ups or redirection, convincing the user is going to be difficult given the problems that both technologies can cause. That's why you need to create a written set of policies for your Web site. A privacy policy assures the user that any information you collect as part of pop-ups and the use of redirection will remain private and describes precisely how you'll use the information. You also need a policy that defines why your site is using these technologies and encourages the user to contact you about the legitimacy of this need. It's also a good idea to be proactive about providing the user with facts about both technologies so the user understands the risks on other Web sites. The goal is to provide the user with the education required to understand your use of these technologies and provide a good reason for the user to allow your use of them.

FIGURE 9.1

Internet Explorer users now have a built-in pop-up blocker in Windows XP SP2.

FIGURE 9.2

Disabling both scripted and meta refresh redirection is easy in Internet Explorer.

Creating a Pop-up Form

The basic pop-up form is easy to create. The technique relies on a little JavaScript to perform the task, and any kind of Web page can support the form. You'll find this example in the \ABC_Inc\Popups\ BasicPopup folder of the source code on the Sybex Web site. To begin creating a pop-up, you'll need a method of displaying the window. The Web page shown in Listing 9.1 shows a simple demonstration form you can use.

WARNING   Never include a pop-up as part of a master page. When you include a pop-up on a master page, everyone who uses that master page will see the pop-up even when it isn't appropriate. Create pop-ups on a page-by-page basis and add them only when it's appropriate to do so. Make sure your corporate policy defines specifically when to use pop-ups.

LISTING 9.1:   Displaying a Pop-up Using JavaScript

```
<asp:Content ID="Content2" ContentPlaceHolderID="MainContent" Runat="Server">
   <script type="text/javascript">
   <!--
      function btnPopup_OnClick()
      {
         var Features;

         // Create a description of the features.
         Features = "height=" + __aspnetForm.txtHeight.value;
         Features = Features + ",width=" + __aspnetForm.txtWidth.value;
         if (__aspnetForm.cbScrollbar.checked)
               Features = Features + ",scrollbars=yes";
         else
               Features = Features + ",scrollbars=no";

         // Display the pop-up.
         window.open('PopupPage.HTM', 'TestWindow', Features);
      }
   -->
   </script>
   <h1>Pop-up Window Demonstration</h1>
   <label>Window Height: </label>
   <input id="txtHeight" type="text" value="200" /><br />
   <label>Window Width: </label>
   <input id="txtWidth" type="text" value="400" /><br />
   <label>Scrollbars: </label>
   <input id="cbScrollbar" type="checkbox" value="Scollbars" /><br />
   <input id="btnPopup"
          title="Displays the popup on screen."
          accesskey="S"
          type="button"
          value="Show Popup"
          onclick="btnPopup_OnClick()"/>

</asp:Content>
```

You should notice two features about this Web page immediately. First, the script appears within the `<asp:Content>` tag. Because the browser doesn't care where the script appears, you can normally use this technique without problem. Second, the page relies on standard HTML controls. This page actually has a mix of ASP.NET and HTML controls on it. Each control type has a specific purpose. In many cases, you'll find using HTML controls works better on pages that use a master page because ASP.NET doesn't scramble the control name—making it easier to access from a script. Of course, you also lose the ability to use ASP.NET code behind features with the controls, so you have to consider the implications of the tradeoff.

The demonstration form lets you try various simple pop-up settings to see how they affect the appearance of the page. Figure 9.3 shows the form along with the associated pop-up. As you can see, you can change the size of the form quite easily, as well as the presence of scrollbars in the resulting form. The resulting form doesn't include any of the normal browser toolbars because it's a pop-up.

The essential part of this page is the `window.open()` method call in the `btnPopup_OnClick()` function. The page calls this method when the user clicks Show Popup. The code builds up a list of comma separated features based on the form content before it calls the `window.open()` method. The `window.open()` method accepts up to four arguments including the pop-up form URL, form name, form feature list, and a Boolean value that replaces the current pop-up window when set to true.

NOTE The features list is optional. If you don't provide a features list, the pop-up form uses the settings the user prefers for the browser. In other words, it looks like another browser window, rather than a pop-up form.

FIGURE 9.3
The demonstration page lets you test various pop-up form features.

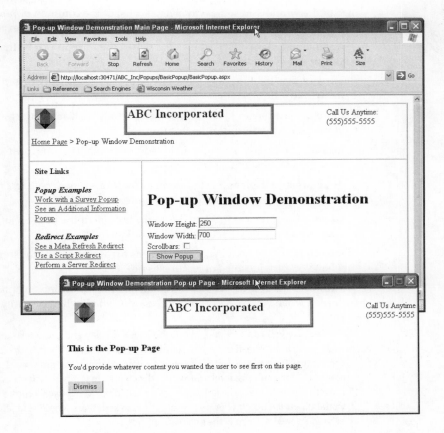

At some point, you'll want to close the window. Most users will figure out that they need to click the close box in the upper right corner of the form. However, your pop-up will have a nicer appearance when you include a button for dismissing the pop-up from the screen. All you need is a simple function to perform the task like the one shown here.

```
<script type="text/javascript">
<!--
    function btnDismiss_OnClick()
    {
        // Close this window.
        window.close();
    }
-->
</script>
```

The features list for a pop-up can include a number of arguments—all of which affect the appearance of the window in some way. Here's a list of the common pop-up window feature arguments. Note that you must include some arguments, such as width and height, together, as shown in the list.

width and height Determines the size of the form in pixels (the default is the same size as the parent window).

left and top Defines the upper left corner of the form on the screen in pixels (the default centers the window on screen).

toolbar Displays a toolbar (standard buttons toolbar) on the form when set to yes (the default when you provide a list of features is no).

location Displays a location field (address toolbar) on the form when set to yes (the default when you provide a list of features is no).

directories Displays a list of popular locations (links toolbar) on the form when set to yes (the default when you provide a list of features is no).

status Displays a status bar across the bottom of the pop-up form when set to yes (the default when you provide a list of features is no).

menubar Displays a list of menu items across the top of the form when set to yes (the default when you provide a list of features is no).

scrollbars Displays a vertical scrollbar as a minimum and an optional horizontal scrollbar when needed when you set this option to yes (the default when you provide a list of features is no).

TIP Because you can't be sure about the user's display and predetermine how the other settings you choose will affect the display, you should either provide scrollbars in the form or allow the user to resize the form as needed to display the content. For example, the user could rely on a large font to display content—you can't predetermine when the change in font size will occur, so letting the user resize the form to accommodate the larger font is a good idea. (Many users require large fonts to address special visual needs such as low or poor vision.) Using scrollbars would also allow the user to move content around as needed to view the entire form.

resizable Allows the user to resize the form when set to yes (the default is no, which means the user can't resize the form).

dependent   Sets the form to automatically close when the parent window closes when set to yes (the default when you provide a list of features is no).

fullscreen   Displays the form full screen, rather than as a smaller dialog box, when set to yes (the default when you provide a list of features is no).

WARNING   The channelmode option doesn't work well with master pages. Avoid using this feature unless you plan to display the Web page without using a master page.

channelmode   Sets the form to use channelmode—a feature that is only available to Internet Explorer users when set to yes. The form displays a specialized menu in full screen mode. In some cases, you'll also see an Explorer Bar on the left side of the display.

Using Pop-up Forms

Pop-up forms or windows have a number of legitimate uses. For example, when you visit the Windows Update site at `http://windowsupdate.microsoft.com/`, you'll notice that Microsoft uses pop-up windows to display status information as the Web site looks for updates on the host machine. Although this isn't the most common use of a pop-up window, it's a legitimate one and a use that you could consider for a custom Web application. The point is that this window doesn't advertise anything—it's there to help the user. The following sections describe other legitimate uses for pop-up forms.

Additional Information

Sometimes a Web site has instructions that it must present to new users. For example, you might require that the user install a kit prior to installing software updates or perform other tasks as part of a setup. The user will visit your Web site many times, but need the instructions only once or twice. When you use a static page to display the required information, the user has to wade through all of the novice-level material before getting to the needed material during each visit. Using a pop-up window for this information means that the Web site can display just the essentials on the main window. A new user will see the pop-up window on the first visit and read through the required material, but an advanced user can simply dismiss the window and get right down to business.

In fact, you can easily extend this idea by creating a check box on the pop-up form that says something like, "Don't display this information in the future." A cookie on the user's machine alerts you to the fact that the user doesn't want to see the information anymore, so your Web page won't even display the pop-up window. Of course, if you take this approach, you'll also want to include an option to display the pop-up window again when the user needs to display the information. Making changes two-way is an important concept.

The example in this section explores a few new concepts. The first is the use of a shared script file. Sharing a script lets you create the code once, yet use it as many times as needed. Script sharing is a common practice on Web sites because it's such a big productivity enhancer. The second is sharing a cookie between Web pages. Once you create a permanent cookie, you can share it with any page on a particular Web site. By adding some special information (the path and domain elements), you can also share the cookie with pages in a particular path or even within the same domain. (You can learn more about the path and domain elements of a permanent cookie at `http://wp.netscape.com/newsref/std/cookie_spec.html`.) The third is creating a null link—one that doesn't actually lead anywhere. This technique lets you execute a script without actually taking the user anywhere.

CREATING THE SHARED JAVASCRIPT FILE

You can store scripts externally and then reference them from more than one page. Unfortunately, Visual Web Developer doesn't provide a template to perform this task, so you'll need to select the Text File template and type a script filename such as SharedScript.JS. Listing 9.2 shows the shared script file used for this example. You'll find this example in the \ABC_Inc\Popups\AddedInformation folder of the source code on the Sybex Web site.

LISTING 9.2:   Placing Cookie Scripts in a Shared File

```javascript
function GetExpireDate(Days, Months, Years)
{
    var TheDate = new Date(); // Date object.
    var Expire;               // Expiration date.

    // Add the required time intervals.
    TheDate.setHours((Days * 24) + TheDate.getHours());
    TheDate.setMonth(TheDate.getMonth() + Months);
    TheDate.setFullYear(Years + TheDate.getFullYear());

    // Build an expiration date. Begin by getting the day
    // of the week.
    switch (TheDate.getUTCDay() + 1)
    {
    case 1:
        Expire = "Sun, ";
        break;

    ... Other Cases ...

    case 7:
        Expire = "Sat, ";
        break;

    }

    // Add the date.
    Expire = Expire + (TheDate.getUTCDate());

    // Add the month.
    switch (TheDate.getUTCMonth() + 1)
    {
    case 1:
        Expire = Expire + " Jan ";
        break;

    ... Other Cases ...

    case 12:
```

```
        Expire = Expire + " Dec ";
        break;
   }

   // Add the year.
   Years = TheDate.getUTCFullYear();
   Expire = Expire + Years + " ";

   // Add the time.
   Expire = Expire + TheDate.getUTCHours() + ":" +
           TheDate.getUTCMinutes() + ":" +
           TheDate.getUTCSeconds() + " UTC";

   // Return the result.
   return Expire
}
```

With careful programming, you can move many of your JavaScript applications to a separate file. In this case, the application accepts the number of days, months, and years that you want to add to the current date. The return value is an expiration date that you can use to create a permanent cookie.

The first task is to add the required time intervals to the current date. When working with days, you must actually add the required hours, rather than the number of days, so the code multiplies Days by 24 to obtain the number hours from the current time, which it obtains using the TheDate .getHours() method. The code then uses the TheDate.setHours() method to change the date. If the number of days changes the month or year, the TheDate.setHours() method automatically accounts for the differences. Adding the Months and Years values is easier because you can add them directly to the date, rather than perform a conversion.

The code creates the expiration date by creating a new string value, Expire. It begins by determining the day of the week using a switch statement. The code then adds the day, the month as a text value (using another switch statement), the year, and finally the time. The function passes this information back to the caller.

Now that you have a file with a number of useful scripts, you need to add it to the Web page that relies on them. All you need to do to perform this task is create a blank script in the Web page like this:

```
<script src="SharedScript.JS" type="text/javascript"></script>
```

When the browser sees a <script> tag like this one, it automatically loads the file along with the Web page. The scripts contained within the source file (defined by the src attribute) become available to any part of the Web page.

HANDLING <BODY ONLOAD="PAGELOAD()"> SCRIPTS

Most developers are aware of how you can use the <body> tag's onload event to execute a script when the page loads. Unfortunately, this technique doesn't work when you're working with master pages because you don't have access to the <body> tag. An alternative that many developers will use at this point is to add the script without a function name directly after the <body> tag. Unfortunately, using this approach will result in an error message—the script won't execute. To make this scenario work, you must inject the script into the Web page using the ASPX page Load() event.

What you'll do is create the script in the event handler and then add it to the Web page indirectly, as shown in Listing 9.3. You'll find this example in the \ABC_Inc\Popups\AddedInformation folder of the source code on the Sybex Web site.

LISTING 9.3:   Creating an Onload Script

```
Protected Sub Page_Load(ByVal sender As Object, _
    ByVal e As System.EventArgs) Handles Me.Load

    Dim TheScript As New StringBuilder   ' Holds the injected script.

    ' Create the script.
    TheScript.Append("<script type='text/javascript'>" + vbCrLf)
    TheScript.Append("var  ACookie; // Holds the document cookie.")
    TheScript.Append(vbCrLf)
    TheScript.Append("var  Parsed;  // Holds the split cookies.")
    TheScript.Append(vbCrLf + vbCrLf)
    TheScript.Append("// Get the cookie." + vbCrLf)
    TheScript.Append("ACookie = unescape(document.cookie);")
    TheScript.Append(vbCrLf + vbCrLf)
    TheScript.Append("// Check the cookie status." + vbCrLf)
    TheScript.Append("if (ACookie == '')" + vbCrLf)
    TheScript.Append("   window.open('AddedInfoPopup.ASPX', " + vbCrLf)
    TheScript.Append("               'AddedInfo', " + vbCrLf)
    TheScript.Append("               'height=300, width=400, ")
    TheScript.Append("resizable=true, dependent=true');")
    TheScript.Append(vbCrLf + vbCrLf)
    TheScript.Append("// Split the cookie elements." + vbCrLf)
    TheScript.Append("Parsed = ACookie.split('=');" + vbCrLf + vbCrLf)
    TheScript.Append("// Determine whether the user wants the ")
    TheScript.Append("additional Information" + vbCrLf)
    TheScript.Append("// displayed on screen." + vbCrLf)
    TheScript.Append("if (Parsed[1] == 'false')" + vbCrLf)
    TheScript.Append("   window.open('AddedInfoPopup.ASPX', " + vbCrLf)
    TheScript.Append("               'AddedInfo', " + vbCrLf)
    TheScript.Append("               'height=300, width=400, ")
    TheScript.Append("resizable=true, dependent=true');")
    TheScript.Append(vbCrLf)
    TheScript.Append("</script>")

    ' Add the script to the Web page.
    Me.ClientScript.RegisterStartupScript( _
        GetType(String), "ShowInfoPage", TheScript.ToString())
End Sub
```

The process is relatively simple. All you need to do is build up a string containing the script you want to execute. Adding white space is extremely helpful when you start debugging the script, so adding the vbCrLf constants is necessary. Once you build up a script, you add it to the Web page using the Me.ClientScript.RegisterStartupScript() method. This method accepts three inputs—the data type of the script, the script identifier, and the script content. When you run the script it looks precisely like a script that you added directly to the Web page. Figure 9.4 shows the actual source code from the AddedInformation.ASXP page.

The injected script begins by loading the cookie created by the added information pop-up form. If the cookie is missing, the code automatically displays the pop-up form because this is the user's first visit to the Web site. This cookie is normally available because it's permanent and the main page is in the same path as the Web page that created the cookie. After the code loads the cookie, it determines whether the user wants the additional information pop-up form loaded. If the user wants to see the additional information, the code uses the window.open() method to open the pop-up window. Notice that this pop-up form depends on the main page, which means it closes automatically when the user closes the main page.

TIP   It's usually easier to build and test the script using a standard Web page than to create it in an ASPX page. Once you perfect the script, you can move it to the code behind page.

The pop-up page also requires a script that automatically executes when the main page opens it. Listing 9.4 shows this script.

As you can see, the technique for creating the injected script is the same, but the results are different. In this case, the script used the content of the cookie to configure the form. When the cookie exists and it contains a value of true, the code checks the check box in the form. This script ensures the user sees the true status of the form when the pop-up displays.

NOTE   You don't have to inject all of the scripts you want on a Web page—only those that will execute when the page loads. Scripts that execute as the result of a button click can appear within the <asp:Content> tag of the content page.

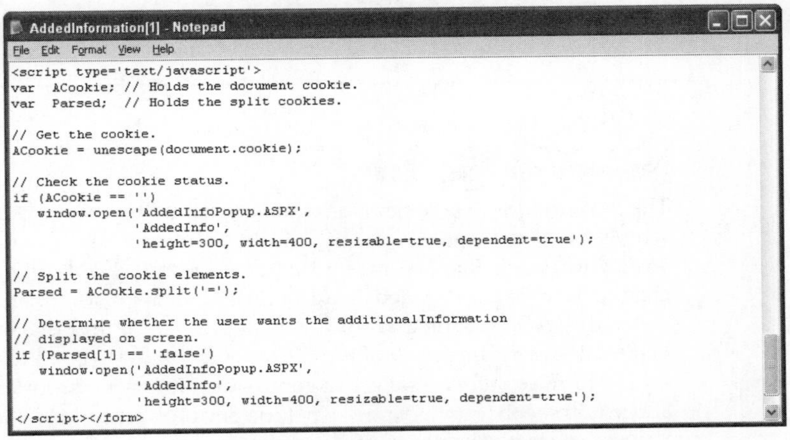

FIGURE 9.4
Injected scripts look like you added them directly to the Web page.

```
AddedInformation[1] - Notepad
File  Edit  Format  View  Help
<script type='text/javascript'>
var  ACookie; // Holds the document cookie.
var  Parsed;  // Holds the split cookies.

// Get the cookie.
ACookie = unescape(document.cookie);

// Check the cookie status.
if (ACookie == '')
    window.open('AddedInfoPopup.ASPX',
              'AddedInfo',
              'height=300, width=400, resizable=true, dependent=true');

// Split the cookie elements.
Parsed = ACookie.split('=');

// Determine whether the user wants the additionalInformation
// displayed on screen.
if (Parsed[1] == 'false')
    window.open('AddedInfoPopup.ASPX',
              'AddedInfo',
              'height=300, width=400, resizable=true, dependent=true');
</script></form>
```

LISTING 9.4: Configuring a Page Based on Cookie Settings

```vb
Protected Sub Page_Load(ByVal sender As Object, _
    ByVal e As System.EventArgs) Handles Me.Load

    Dim TheScript As New StringBuilder   ' Holds the injected script.

    ' Create the script.
    TheScript.Append("<script type='text/javascript'>" + vbCrLf)
    TheScript.Append("   var  ACookie; // Holds the document cookie.")
    TheScript.Append(vbCrLf)
    TheScript.Append("   var  Parsed;  // Holds the split cookies.")
    TheScript.Append(vbCrLf + vbCrLf)
    TheScript.Append("   // Get the cookie." + vbCrLf)
    TheScript.Append("   ACookie = unescape(document.cookie);")
    TheScript.Append(vbCrLf + vbCrLf)
    TheScript.Append("   // Split the cookie elements." + vbCrLf)
    TheScript.Append("   Parsed = ACookie.split('=');")
    TheScript.Append(vbCrLf + vbCrLf)
    TheScript.Append("   // Determined the checked value." + vbCrLf)
    TheScript.Append("   if (Parsed[1] == 'true')" + vbCrLf)
    TheScript.Append("      __aspnetForm.cbDontShow.checked = true;")
    TheScript.Append(vbCrLf)
    TheScript.Append("   else" + vbCrLf)
    TheScript.Append("      __aspnetForm.cbDontShow.checked = false;")
    TheScript.Append(vbCrLf)
    TheScript.Append("</script>" + vbCrLf)

    ' Add the script to the Web page.
    Me.ClientScript.RegisterStartupScript( _
        GetType(String), "ShowInfoPage", TheScript.ToString())
End Sub
```

DESIGNING THE POP-UP FORM

The pop-up form has several tasks to perform in this example. The form stores a cookie that tracks whether the user wants to see the additional information presented by this form, so the form has to work with the cookie. This means that the code must display the current cookie status and let the user change the cookie as needed. In addition, the form must contain some means of dismissal. Listing 9.5 shows the code for this part of the example. You'll find this example in the \ABC_Inc\Popups\ AddedInformation folder of the source code on the Sybex Web site.

The form actually contains two controls, as shown in Figure 9.5. Look at the HTML for this example and you'll see that both controls include onclick attributes. That's right—you can attach a script to a check box just as easily as you can a button, so you can use whatever control makes sense for a particular task. The btnDismiss code simply closes the pop-up form, as you'd expect.

LISTING 9.5:   Displaying and Configuring the Pop-up Form

```
<asp:Content ID="Content1" ContentPlaceHolderID="ContentPlaceHolder1"
            Runat="Server">
    <script src="SharedScript.JS" type="text/javascript"></script>

    <script type="text/javascript">
    <!--
        function btnDismiss_OnClick()
        {
            // Close the window.
            window.close();
        }

        function cbDontShow_OnClick()
        {
            var UserCookie; // Stores the username.
            var Expire;     // Expiration date.

            // Get an expiration date. Set it to expire one year
            // from the current date.
            Expire = GetExpireDate(0, 0, 1);

            // Create the username cookie.
            UserCookie = "AddedInfo=" +
                        escape(__aspnetForm.cbDontShow.checked) +
                        "; expires=" + Expire;

            // Add the cookie to the document.
            document.cookie = UserCookie;
        }
     -->
     </script>
    <asp:Label ID="lblGreeting" runat="server"
            Font-Bold="true" Font-Size="Large"
            Text="Added Information Page">
    </asp:Label>
    <p>
        <asp:Label ID="lblInfo" runat="server"
                Font-Italic="true"
                Text="This section normally contains the instructions
                    that you want the user to see the first few times
                    they open the page.">
        </asp:Label>
    </p>
    <p>
        <label>Don't Show This Window Again</label>
```

```
            <input id="cbDontShow"
                    type="checkbox"
                    accesskey="S"
                    title="Disables additional information display."
                    onclick="cbDontShow_OnClick()" />
        </p>
        <p>
            <input id="btnDismiss"
                    type="button"
                    value="Dismiss"
                    accesskey="D"
                    title="Closes the added information window."
                    onclick="btnDismiss_OnClick()" />
        </p>
    </asp:Content>
```

FIGURE 9.5
The example uses controls to ensure the applications meet user needs.

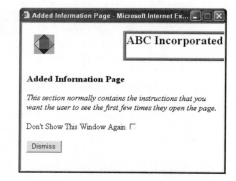

The cbDontShow_OnClick() method uses the GetExpireDate() function to create an expiration date. It then obtains the value of the cbDontShow.checked property and creates a cookie. Because this is a permanent cookie, it appears in the user's \Cookies folder. The example sets the cookie to expire in a year. Consequently, the user will see the additional information pop-up form once a year if the cookie never changes. You could add code to refresh the cookie as needed, but having it pop up occasionally reminds the user that the information is available.

CREATING THE MAIN PAGE

The added information page won't display until the main page—the one the user initially opens—creates it. This fact means that the code for setting the cookie is inaccessible to the user once the user decides to set the form not to display. Since you don't want to display the form unless the user requests it, the main page requires both an automatic and a manual means of displaying the pop-up form. You can learn more about the automatic method in the "Handling <body onload="PageLoad()"> Scripts" section of the chapter. The user relies on the manual method when needed to display the additional information or change the automatic display setting. Listing 9.6 shows the code required for this part of the example.

LISTING 9.6:   Managing the Pop-up Form

```
<asp:Content ID="Content2" ContentPlaceHolderID="MainContent"
            Runat="Server">
  <script type="text/javascript">
  <!--
      function ForceLoad()
      {
          // Force the added information page open.
          window.open("AddedInfoPopup.ASPX",
                      "AddedInfo",
                      "height=300, width=400, resizable=true,
                       dependent=true");
      }
  -->
  </script>
  <asp:Label ID="lblGreeting" runat="server"
            Font-Bold="true" Font-Size="Large"
            Text="Informational Page Demonstration">
  </asp:Label>
  <p>
      <asp:Label ID="lblMessage" runat="server"
                Font-Italic="true"
                Text="This page contains the main Web site content.">
      </asp:Label>
  </p>
  <a href="AddedInformation.ASPX" onclick="ForceLoad()">
      Open the added information page.
  </a>
</asp:Content>
```

Notice the special link near the bottom of the page. As you can see from Figure 9.6, it looks like any other link you might have seen in the past. However, the href attribute points back to the current page. You always have to include the href attribute or the link won't appear as a link—it'll appear as text, but this href attribute won't take the user anywhere. Notice that the <a> tag does include an onclick attribute, which calls the ForceLoad() function when the user clicks the link. The ForceLoad() function simply displays the pop-up form without any intermediate checks. A null link provides the interface the user expects, but performs the task that you need.

Help Pages

Most users like to have help pages side by side with their main page so they can use the two together. Consequently, a help page is an excellent use of a pop-up form. The user can click Help on any given page and get the help required to work with it. This feature gives your Web application a decidedly desktop feel. Besides making the user happy, creating pop-up help pages also reduces support costs for your Web site. You can even add a level of context sensitivity to the help pages by using a different URL for each page or relying on anchors to access a particular portion of a single help page.

Mechanically, help pages are very much like the informational pages described in the "Additional Information" section of the chapter. Of course, you don't need a check box to let the user indicate that they don't want to see the help page because the user will decide when the help page appears. You might want to include the menu bar using the `menubar` feature so the user can add special help pages to their favorites list.

A help page also relies on the fourth `window.open()` method argument. Set the `replace` argument to true to ensure the user doesn't end up with many copies of the same page. Replacing each old request with a new request means the user sees a single main page and just one help page—avoiding confusion that will certainly keep support costs down.

Users naturally want to move between topics, so your help page will include plenty of content links. However, you might also want to include a list of popular links along with the side of the page or even use a `Menu` control (see the "Using the Menu Control" section of Chapter 8 for details) to display a user's favorite links. You could store the links using cookies and then populate the `Menu` control using code during page loading.

Unlike an information page, where scrollbars work fine, you'll want to make help pages resizable so the user can modify the size as needed. In fact, you might want to store these settings as part of a cookie so that you can restore the window to its original size later. In short, even though help pages work very much like informational pages, they have a few bells and whistles you need to add to ensure smooth operation and good user support.

FIGURE 9.6
Use null links as needed to create the proper presentation without compromising functionality.

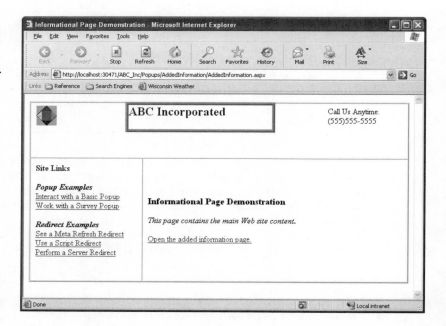

NOTE   You might have noticed that this chapter relies heavily on cookies. As your Web pages increase in complexity, you need some means of storing both temporary and permanent data. When a user doesn't allow cookies, you'll have to convince them to make an exception, use server-side storage if possible, or use a non-scripting solution for the problem. In general, using cookies on a private Web site is never a problem. Using them on a public Web site can be a problem depending on how much trust the user has in your Web site. Given the current Internet environment, it's not too surprising to find users reluctant to allow cookie support so you need to spell out precisely how you plan to use them in order to garner support.

User Survey

User surveys represent another way to use pop-up forms to benefit the user. In this case, however, using pure HTML could be troublesome. Yes, you can definitely do it, but Visual Web developer offers so many interesting ways to work with data that you won't want to use pure HTML. In fact, this is a perfect time to begin using the View and MultiView controls to create a great presentation that all of your users can work with. The interesting part of the View and MultiView controls is that you can present multiple pages of data to the user without leaving the current page.

However, a pure ASP.NET solution doesn't work particularly well either. For example, the very act of presenting the pop-up form is a nightmare when working with ASP.NET. All you need is a few lines of script of accomplish the task. Consequently, this example does use HTML as well. In fact, it demonstrates that you can combine ASP.NET and HTML in one application in a way that the user will never notice or care about. You'll find this example in the \ABC_Inc\Popups\Survey folder of the source code on the Sybex Web site.

USING THE *VIEW* AND *MULTIVIEW* CONTROLS

The View and MultiView controls work together to create what appears to be multiple Web pages from a single Web page. The idea is to create an environment where you get to work with all of the data in one page, but the user sees multiple, less complex, pages that fit on most screens. Each View control can contain a whole page worth of information. You can select each page independently. Therefore, the user seems to move from page to page, but actually stays in place. Figure 9.7 shows a typical example of multiple View controls contained within a MultiView control.

The page shown in Figure 9.7 works as any other ASP.NET page you create. For example, the banner at the top appears on every page because it resides outside of the MultiView control. Nothing stops you from creating common content, and including more than one MultiView control is necessary to display unique content on each page. You could even use the technique to create pages that contain statistics in one MultiView control and one of several graphical representations in another. All the user sees is one of the pages, however, as shown in Figure 9.8.

You use the MultiView control (SurveyForm in the example) to switch between View control outputs (Page1 through Page4 in the example). In fact, the process is incredibly easy, as shown here.

```
Sub Page_Load(ByVal sender As Object, _
              ByVal e As System.EventArgs) Handles Me.Load
    ' Load the first page of the survey.
    SurveyForm.SetActiveView(Page1)
End Sub
```

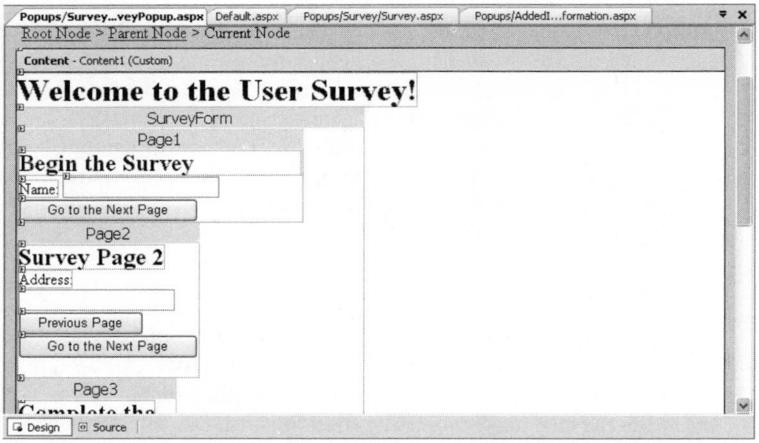

FIGURE 9.7
Each *MultiView* control contains multiple View controls.

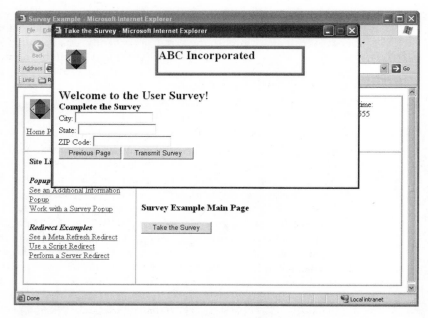

FIGURE 9.8
The user sees only the part of the display that you want them to see.

When the form opens, the code loads the first View control, Page1, using the SurveyForm .SetActiveView() method. You don't need to refresh anything or worry that the user won't gain access to all of the form functionality. The server takes care of everything for you. Consequently, you only create one line of code to display a View control—the IDE creates all other code for you in the background as you lay out the various page elements. The simplicity of this approach is the reason that you want to avoid using HTML, whenever possible, to create this kind of pop-up form.

CREATING THE POP-UP SURVEY FORM

All of the survey coding takes place on the server. However, the actual mechanics of displaying the form should take place on the client. Generally, you won't see developers mix ASP.NET and HTML controls on one form. Fortunately, the technique works extremely well and makes a lot of sense when you can employ it successfully. Figure 9.9 shows the combination of ASP.NET and HTML controls used for this example. Notice that the HTML control (highlighted in the figure) has a very familiar look from the example in the "Additional Information" section of the chapter, even though this is essentially an ASP.NET application.

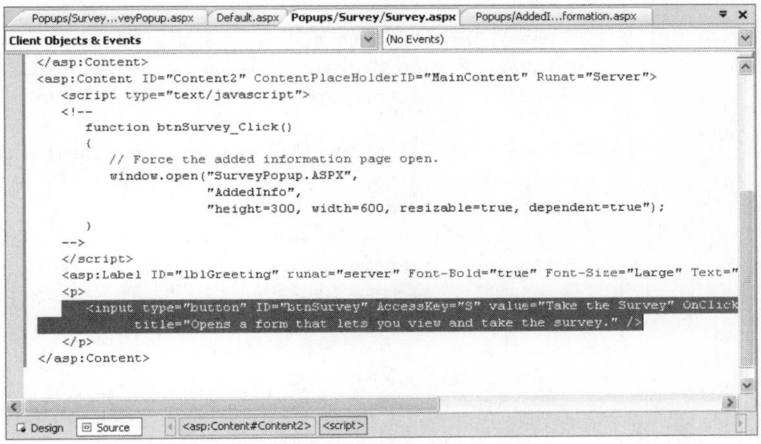

FIGURE 9.9
Mixing ASP.NET and HTML controls really isn't taboo and you should use the technique whenever possible.

```
</asp:Content>
<asp:Content ID="Content2" ContentPlaceHolderID="MainContent" Runat="Server">
    <script type="text/javascript">
    <!--
        function btnSurvey_Click()
        {
            // Force the added information page open.
            window.open("SurveyPopup.ASPX",
                    "AddedInfo",
                    "height=300, width=600, resizable=true, dependent=true");
        }
    -->
    </script>
    <asp:Label ID="lblGreeting" runat="server" Font-Bold="true" Font-Size="Large" Text="
    <p>
        <input type="button" ID="btnSurvey" AccessKey="S" value="Take the Survey" OnClick
                title="Opens a form that lets you view and take the survey." />
    </p>
</asp:Content>
```

The reason that this combination makes sense, in this case, is that you must tell the client to load and unload the pop-up form. Theoretically, you can do this from the server using pure ASP.NET code, but you'll write a lot of code to do it and the resulting application won't perform well. This example uses the same code as the added information example to load and unload the pop-up form.

PROCESSING THE SURVEY

Once you collect all of the survey data, you'll want to process it. Depending on your particular requirements, XML files or a database will work equally well for a smaller organization. Large organizations that expect thousands of survey results will want to use a database. The example relies on an XML file, in this case, that creates a unique entry based on the username and the time, as shown in Listing 9.7.

The code begins by obtaining the application path. It then creates a unique filename based on the username and the current time. The code outputs the filename to `txtMoreInfo.Text` as part of the final page display. Providing the user with a filename not only makes it possible for that user to track the survey, but also gives a feeling of completion that many survey applications lack. Notice that the code doesn't provide the user with a path to the file—this action would represent a security risk. After the code outputs the filename, it creates a complete filename by combining the path with the unique filename.

LISTING 9.7:   Processing the User Input as XML

```
Sub btnSubmit_Click(ByVal sender As Object, ByVal e As System.EventArgs)
    Dim ThisPath As String                   ' Application path.
    Dim Filename As String                   ' Full path to data store.
    Dim Output As XmlDocument                 ' Contains all input.
    Dim PInst As XmlProcessingInstruction     ' A processing instruction.
    Dim RootNode As XmlElement                ' The root node.
    Dim DataNode As XmlElement                ' Individual data element.

    ' Determine the path for this application.
    ThisPath = Page.MapPath(Page.AppRelativeVirtualPath)
    ThisPath = ThisPath.Replace("\IndexPages.aspx", "\")

    ' Create the filename. Build a unique name first and then remove
    ' any elements that might cause problems. Finally, include the
    ' destination folder.
    Filename = txtName.Text + "_" + DateTime.Now.ToString() + ".XML"
    Filename = Filename.Replace(" ", "_")
    Filename = Filename.Replace(":", "_")
    Filename = Filename.Replace("/", "_")

    ' Set the output information.
    txtMoreInfo.Text = Filename

    ' Complete the filename.
    Filename = ThisPath + Filename

    ' Create the XML document.
    Output = New XmlDocument()

    ' Define the XML processing directive.
    PInst = Output.CreateProcessingInstruction( _
        "xml", "version='1.0' encoding='utf-8'")

    ' Add the XML processing directive to the document.
    Output.AppendChild(PInst)

    ' Create the root node that holds all of the other data.
    RootNode = Output.CreateElement("Survey")

    ' Create the Name node and add it to the root node.
    DataNode = Output.CreateElement("Name")
    DataNode.InnerXml = txtName.Text
    RootNode.AppendChild(DataNode)

    ... Other Data Nodes ...
```

```
      ' Add the root node to the document.
      Output.AppendChild(RootNode)

      ' Save the document to disk.
      Output.Save(Filename)

      ' Load the final page.
      SurveyForm.SetActiveView(Page4)
End Sub
```

At this point, the code begins creating an XML document. As normal, the code begins by creating an XML document and placing an XML processing directive within it. The code then begins creating the root node and filling it with the data nodes from the survey form. Finally, the code adds the root node to the XML document, `Output`, and the document is complete. The `Output.Save()` method places the XML file on disk where you can retrieve it later.

The code uses the `SurveyForm.SetActiveView()` method to display the form on screen. However, in this case, the form contains unique data for the user to view. You can perform any code manipulation of the `View` controls necessary during runtime to complete a display. The design time configuration only provides the basic requirements in many cases.

Using Meta Refresh for Redirection

The meta refresh tag is one of the most popular ways of redirecting a Web site user from one page to another. The tag is easy to use and most browsers support it, which means the developer doesn't have to perform any fancy coding or worry about compatibility issues. However, the World Wide Web Consortium (W3C), a standards group that provides information about standardized tag use, does recommend against using this technique in the W3C Recommendation at `http://www.w3.org/TR/html4/struct/global.html#adef-http-equiv`. The fact remains that this is a very easy way to send users to another page and you need to know about it for that reason. Here's an example of a meta refresh tag.

```
<meta http-equiv="refresh" content="3;url=http://www.mysite.com">
```

This tag tells the browser to wait 3 seconds and then redirect the user to `http://www.mysite.com`. The `http-equiv` portion of the tag translates to HyperText Transport Protocol Equivalent. In short, the `<meta>` tag tells the browser that this tag takes the place of an HTTP header that the browser might ordinarily expect to receive from the server. The content contains the number of seconds to wait along with the URL that the browser should load. Notice that you must separate these two arguments by a semicolon (;).

NOTE Don't confuse the meta refresh tag with the completely standard and recommended meta expires tag: `<META http-equiv="Expires" content="Friday, 31 Dec 2004 14:30:00 GMT">`. In this case, the page will expire on Friday, 31 December 2004, at 2:30 in the afternoon. The meta expires tag ensures that the browser always has a fresh copy of the content on your Web site. You set the tag to refresh the page at a reasonable interval to ensure the user doesn't see the cached version of a page that resides on their hard drive. Caching makes Web pages load faster because the browser uses a local copy, rather than download the content from the Internet. However, this performance boost can cause problems by letting the user see old content.

ASP.NET 2.0 doesn't provide a means of creating any form of `<meta>` tag with an `http-equiv` attribute. None of these useful tags are available to you unless you rely on a somewhat non-standard approach to overcome the problem. It turns out that you can manipulate the `Master.Page.Header.Title` property to your advantage, as shown here. You'll find this example in the `\ABC_Inc\Redirection\MetaRefresh` folder of the source code on the Sybex Web site.

```
Protected Sub Page_Load(ByVal sender As Object, _
    ByVal e As System.EventArgs) Handles Me.Load

    ' Create a unique title that includes two tags. You don't
    ' have to limit yourself to just one.
    Master.Page.Header.Title = _
        "Meta Refresh Main Page</title>" + vbCrLf + _
        "<meta http-equiv='refresh' content='4;url=Redirect.ASPX'>"

End Sub
```

This code essentially replaces the `<title>` tag with any number of tags that you need. However, this technique leaves an extra closing `</title>` tag in the header of the Web page. The technique works with every browser tested—the browser simply ignores the extra closing tag. However, if you can use another technique, you'll probably run into fewer problems in the end. Any additional information in a Web page can always turn into a source of problems.

TIP If you have a written redirection policy, you can also include the link on the redirected page. The user can click this link to learn more about the reason for the redirection before committing to clicking the link. The reason for adding a written policy is to ensure the user understands why you move material or use redirection for other purposes.

Unfortunate as it might seem, the meta refresh tag doesn't provide any clues to a user who has the tag disabled. Typically, the user sees a blank page. The only way that a well-informed user knows what to do with this page is to right-click the blank page and choose View Source from the context menu. This action displays the source code for the Web page, where the user can highlight the redirection text and go to the new Web page. A few smart developers have come up with a solution—add a manual tag to the page as well, as shown in this code.

```
<asp:Content ID="Content2" ContentPlaceHolderID="MainContent"
            Runat="Server">
    <asp:Label ID="lblGreeting" runat="server"
                Font-Bold="true" Font-Size="Large"
                Text="Using Meta Refresh"></asp:Label>
    <p>
        <asp:HyperLink
            ID="hlRedirect"
            NavigateUrl="~/Redirection\MetaRefresh/Redirect.aspx"
            runat="server">
                Click this Link to Go to the Page
```

```
    </asp:HyperLink><br />
    <asp:HyperLink
        ID="hlPolicy"
  NavigateUrl="~/Redirection/MetaRefresh/Policies/UsingRedirection.aspx"
        runat="server">
            Discover why we use redirection.
    </asp:HyperLink>
  </p>
</asp:Content>
```

Now users who don't have the meta refresh tag enabled or don't have a browser that supports the tag can click the supplied link. Because this fix is relatively simple, you could even implement it as a master page solution. All the developer would need to do is supply the required links. Using this option also means the user doesn't have to guess about your intentions for the redirection—you simply moved the page and the user needs to click the link to find the new location.

OTHER REDIRECTION ALTERNATIVES

It's possible to use client-side scripting to perform redirection. In fact, you've already seen the required techniques in this chapter. All you need to do is set an automatic selection interval using a feature such as the `self.setTimeout()` function. You can find a simple example of this approach in the `\ABC_Inc\Redirection\Scripted` folder of the source code on the Sybex Web site.

You can find many resources for using scripted redirection on the Internet. For example, you'll find an example that shows how to respond to client differences on the JavaScript Redirection site at `http://www.pageresource.com/jscript/jredir.htm`. ScriptSearch.com (`http://www.scriptsearch.com/JavaScript/Scripts/Redirection/`) includes scripts that a peer group reviews for accuracy and usefulness.

Some of the approaches you'll find combine techniques that you already know. The script at `http://grizzlyweb.com/webmaster/javascripts/redirection.asp#Timed-Redirect` shows how to combine JavaScript and a meta refresh tag to provide scripted and non-scripted solutions to the same problem. In short, the topic of redirection is extremely popular and you can find ready-made resources to perform almost any task.

Employing Server-side Redirection

Server-side redirection is the safest and most flexible means of redirecting a client in many cases. The server receives the request, translates it, and then sends the appropriate page to the user. The whole process takes less than a second, in most cases, yet the server performs a lot of work during that time. Because the entire event occurs at the server, you can maintain an extremely secure environment—no outside force can interfere unless you server is compromised. Of course, nothing comes free—you do pay an additional cost in server performance. Because the server performs additional processing, you'll find that you can't handle quite as many users as before. You'll find this example in the `\ABC_Inc\Redirection\ServerSide` folder of the source code on the Sybex Web site.

Understanding How Server-side Redirection Works

When a server receives a request, it doesn't just fulfill that request immediately. The server first determines where the request is supposed to go and then applies any number of filters to that request. For example, Internet Information Server (IIS) supports a number of filtering features (as do most servers).

An Internet Server Application Programming Interface (ISAPI) filter is a special DLL that you load into the server. The ISAPI filter views the request and performs any required processing on it before passing it to the next ISAPI filter in line or passing it back to the server. You configure the ISAPI filter as part of the Web site or application properties using the Internet Services Manager console located in the Administrative Tools folder of the Control Panel, as shown in Figure 9.10. This particular filter looks for FrontPage Server Extension calls and redirects them as needed—it affects every request for this particular Web site. These filters also apply to your Visual Web Developer projects when using a full version of IIS. The built-in server you use for testing your code doesn't support this kind of filtering, so you might need to move your code to perform full testing.

Filtering affects requests at many levels. For example, filtering can affect some file types or extensions and not others, as shown in Figure 9.11. Click Configuration on the Home Directory tab of a Web site Properties dialog box and you'll see the Application Configuration dialog box shown in Figure 9.11. The Application Configuration dialog box shows the DLL used to handle a particular request based on its file extension. Some DLLs handle entire classes of file types. Notice that IIS handles the ASP file extension directly, but relies on the .NET Framework to handle the ASPX file extension.

The filters appear in a hierarchy, which the Web request visiting the server-side filters first, then the Web site, then the application, and finally the individual page filters. The filters don't all appear in the Internet Services Manager console either. Some of them appear as part of the `Machine.CONFIG` and `Web.CONFIG` files—others appear as code within the individual page. These individual filters appear lower in the hierarchy and have a smaller effect on the Web site as a whole.

FIGURE 9.10
ISAPI filters can redirect requests as needed to a specific server application.

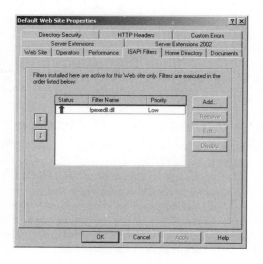

FIGURE 9.11

Filtering also affects requests for specific file types and extensions.

Whatever the level a filter appears at, most filters have the option of performing a redirection of some type. For example, a filter can raise an error and cause the server to display an error message. The filter can directly change the Web page as well. In some cases, a filter can intercept an event caused by another filter and react to it. For example, when the server filter that checks for the presence of the requested file on the machine raises an error because the file isn't present, another filter can intercept the event and react to it. Eventually, the request passes through all of the filters and the server sends a final response to the client.

Using the Coded Method

Any ASPX Web page you create can perform redirection. You can make the redirection part of a button client or in response to an automatic event such as loading the page. No matter how the event occurs, the code for transferring control from one page to another is relatively easy to create, as shown here.

```
Sub btnCodedTest_Click(ByVal sender As Object, _
                       ByVal e As System.EventArgs)

    ' Transfer control to a different page.
    Server.Transfer("NewPage.ASPX", True)
End Sub
```

This feature relies on the `Server` object—a special object that you don't have to create that provides an interface with the server. The `Transfer()` method accepts two arguments. The first contains the URL that you want to use for redirection. The second argument defines whether you want the various arguments, such as the query string, to pass to the redirected page. Setting this value to `True` does incur a small performance penalty, so only pass the information when you actually need it on the redirected page.

You can use this technique for any kind of redirection. However, it only works for one Web page—the one with the code attached. Other techniques described in this book can garner a better response for multiple pages. For example, you can create an HTTP handler using the techniques in the "Working with HTTP Handlers" section of Chapter 18. The "Modifying the *<customErrors>* Element of the *Web.CONFIG* File" section of this chapter also discusses techniques for working with multiple pages.

Modifying the *<customErrors>* Element of the *WEB.CONFIG* File

The Web.CONFIG file contains a wealth of settings that help the developer create a robust Web site. The <customErrors> element of this file contains settings that control how the Web site reacts to errors. The server reports errors in the status member of the header of any response it creates. The status numbers are standard for every Web server, so you don't have to worry about any odd surprises. A successful response always has a status code of 200. Error messages usually have a 400 series error code. You can find a list of these status codes and their meanings at http://www.w3.org/Protocols/rfc2616/rfc2616-sec10.html.

Theoretically, you can handle any status code that you want. However, the error codes are of greatest interest because they affect the client most. Every error that you want to handle requires an <error> element in the <customErrors> node, as shown here.

```
<customErrors mode="RemoteOnly" defaultRedirect="GenericErrorPage.htm">
<!--
    <error statusCode="403" redirect="NoAccess.htm"/>
-->
    <error statusCode="404" redirect="NewPage.ASPX"/>
</customErrors>
```

The default Visual Web Developer Web.CONFIG page includes two error handle entries, both of which are commented out using the <!-- and --> pair. This example enables the Not Found status code of 404 that represents a request for a nonexistent resource on the server. The statusCode attribute of the <error> element tells which status code to detect. The redirect attribute defines which Web page to open when this error occurs.

The only problem with this code is that you can't see the result when working with Visual Web Developer. Even with the error handler enabled, you'll see an error message display. The mode attribute of the <customErrors> element tells the server how to apply the custom error handler. The default value of RemoteOnly is useless for Visual Web Developer users because there isn't any remote access to the server. Always set this value to On to see the custom error handler and Off to see the standard error message.

Whenever the server intercepts an error, it attaches special information for the error handler as part of the query string. You can detect and use this information in the handle page, as shown here.

```
Sub Page_Load(ByVal sender As Object, _
              ByVal e As System.EventArgs) Handles Me.Load

    ' Display the error information, when included.
    txtErrorInfo.Text = Request.QueryString.Get("aspxerrorpath")
End Sub
```

The aspxerrorpath query string variable contains the location of the page that failed. You can use this information to create a log or simply display it on screen. Figure 9.12 shows typical results for this example.

FIGURE 9.12
The server passes the failed page information to the page handling the error.

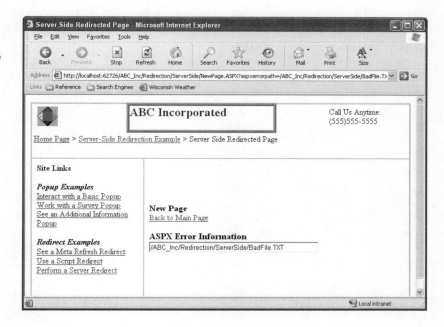

Defining Your Development Goals

This chapter has demonstrated techniques you can use to create pop-up windows and use redirection to help the user find new or existing materials on your Web site. Whether you use these techniques depends on the goals that you want to accomplish. Given the potential for misuse of these technologies, you'll want to exercise care in relying on them and provide the user with good reasons to accommodate these needs. The bottom line is that you have a number of new useful techniques you can use, but you need to use them wisely.

It's time to decide whether your Web site can benefit from either pop-ups or redirection. One of the essentials, especially when working with pop-ups, is to write a policy that explains the use of the technology. Writing the policy is actually a good test of the actual need for these technologies. The act of writing the policy places you in the position of having to explain the use of the technology in terms that the user will accept. A failure to write a good policy, one that you know the user will accept, usually indicates that you don't need to use the technology.

Chapter 10 explores a new area of Visual Web Developer, database applications. Previous chapters have demonstrated a number of uses of XML files as a means of storing critical data for your Web site. However, XML files can't fulfill every need. In many cases, you need to create a formal storage area, which means using a database to accomplish the task. Fortunately, Visual Web Developer makes this task easy using Database Explorer.

Part 4

Working with Dynamic Data

In this part:

Chapter 10

Developing Simple Database Applications

Although generalizing is always dangerous, one generalization you can probably safely make is that all businesses use Database Management Systems (DBMSs) of some sort. Businesses can't operate without some means of storing data and retrieving it quickly when needed. Imagine trying to keep track of employees in your organization or the customers you work with without a database.

A database is the storage container for the data, while the DBMS manages the storage container. The most common DBMS for Visual Studio is SQL Server. Yes, you can also use Microsoft Access or a third party product such as MySQL or Oracle to create applications with Visual Studio. In fact, you can create a connection for any database that supports Open Database Connectivity (ODBC), Object Linking and Embedding–Database (OLE-DB), along with SQL Server and Oracle. Visual Studio is quite flexible.

NOTE　This chapter assumes that you have SQL Server installed on your machine. You'll also find examples that show how to work with Microsoft Access in this basic chapter—the rest of the book relies exclusively on SQL Server. Even if you don't have these products installed, you can follow along with the examples to see some of the techniques you can use with Visual Studio when creating Web applications. For more information, see *Mastering SQL Server 2005* by Mike Gunderloy and Joseph L. Jorden (Sybex, 2006).

This chapter begins by providing a very brief overview of SQL Server. You'll learn about the new features in SQL Server 2005 and explore some of the tools that SQL Server 2005 provides. The new tools are especially important because you won't find the old graphical tools anymore. Microsoft has put a lot of effort into making SQL Server 2005 exceptionally easy to use—or at least easier.

Visual Studio includes a number of features that make working with SQL Server (or any DBMS for that matter) easier. For example, the Server Explorer lets you view the content of a database with relative ease so that you can simply drag and drop items onto the form. You'll also find that the concept of code-free data binding saves you considerable time. The IDE also provides a number of toolbars that reduce the time required to perform tasks. In short, Visual Studio makes it easier to work with databases than ever before.

This chapter does provide you with a number of simple examples that demonstrate how you can add database management to Visual Studio applications. One of the most important examples shows how you can access the ASPNetDB.MDF database, which stores the settings for your application. You'll also discover how to access existing databases, such as those that rely on ODBC connections. All of these short examples help you understand the concepts of working with databases in Visual Studio.

Understanding the New SQL Server 2005 Features

You might begin by asking what isn't new about SQL Server 2005. Microsoft changed a lot of the basic functionality provided by this product. Of course, the most noticeable changes are the new tools that you get. Gone are old standbys such as Enterprise Manager and Query Analyzer. You now have access to better tools that follow the user interface conventions used by Visual Studio—making SQL Server significantly easier to learn and use. The "Using the SQL Server Management Studio" section of the chapter describes the single tool, SQL Server Management Studio, which replaces all of the graphical tools you used in the past.

Another new tool that this chapter discusses is the SQL Computer Manager. You'll find this tool described in the "Working with SQL Computer Manager" section of the chapter. It replaces the Server Network Utility, Service Manager, and Client Network Utility tools used in SQL Server 2000. Consolidating these three utilities means that you can get more work done without having to change tools all of the time. More importantly, you'll find that SQL Computer Manager actually provides more information that you can use to manage your network connections.

One of the big additions that Microsoft has been promoting heavily is the ability to use .NET languages from within SQL Server. Don't get too excited. You'll find limitations to this new technology and it definitely doesn't replace the T-SQL that you've used to create stored procedures in the past. Think of the .NET language functionality as more of a nice addition, rather than as a replacement for any existing technology.

Database applications have always included tools that help you optimize various aspects of using the data. SQL Server 2005 provides a number of tools that do more than help you use data efficiently—they also help you organize the data and even analyze the database itself. Although this book doesn't provide detailed analysis of database construction techniques, you'll learn about the various analysis and performance tools in the "Employing the Profiler" section of this chapter.

This chapter doesn't discuss some of the new SQL Server features. For example, you won't learn how to create a distributed database solution for a multi-terabyte warehouse application. However, you can get an overview of these more exotic features in the Microsoft article provided on the SQL Server Web site at http://www.microsoft.com/sql/2005/productinfo/overview.mspx. The point is that this chapter concentrates on using SQL Server 2005 to do something productive and demonstrates many of the new features to you. The remaining chapters in Part IV help you create applications using SQL Server 2005.

Working with SQL Server 2005

SQL Server does provide a few interesting tools that you'll need to create database applications. The most important tool, in many cases, is SQL Computer Manager because it provides the status information you need. The tool that you'll use most is SQL Server Management Studio (SSMS) because this is where you create queries, design new databases, and perform other management tasks. However, you'll also want to spend time working with the various command line tools that SQL Server provides because they help you perform the actual management tasks. Once you create an application, you'll want to use the tools that Microsoft provides to optimize the database to ensure it works at top efficiency. These tools include Analysis Services, Business Intelligence Development Studio, Database Tuning Advisor, and Profiler. The following sections describe all of these tools.

Working with SQL Computer Manager

The SQL Computer Manager appears as part of SQL Server. You'll find this utility in the Start ➤ Programs ➤ Microsoft SQL Server 2005 menu. This utility is the same as the one that the full version of SQL Server 2005 uses, so you can use it to monitor the full version of the product. The following sections describe essential tasks you can perform using this utility.

GETTING SQL SERVER STATUS INFORMATION

One of the more important tasks you can perform with this utility is to obtain status information. The Services folder shown in Figure 10.1 contains a list of the SQL Server services—not all of these services appear on your machine when you install SQL Server. For example, even though the utility contains an entry for SQL Agent, you won't see an entry in this folder when using SQL Server because this version of the product doesn't support SQL Agent.

The SQL Computer Manager also provides other forms of status information. For example, look at the Server Network Configuration folder and you'll see an entry for each instance of SQL Server on the machine. Within these instance-specific folders, you'll find the protocols that SQL Server supports including shared memory (Sm), named pipes (Np), Transmission Control Protocol/Internet Protocol or TCP/IP (Tcp), and Virtual Interface Architecture or VIA (Via). A status indicator next to each entry shows whether you have this protocol enabled.

The Client Network Configuration folder contains options that the client can use to connect to the server. The Client Protocols folder defines which protocols the client can use to connect to the server. This folder has the same four options that the server provides. The Aliases folder contains a list of alternate identities the client can use to connect to the server. This feature is helpful because you can use it to hide connectivity from the client and redirect the client as needed when the server setup changes. In most cases, you won't need to use an alias when working with SQL Server.

FIGURE 10.1
SQL Computer Manager provides access to a number of SQL Server features.

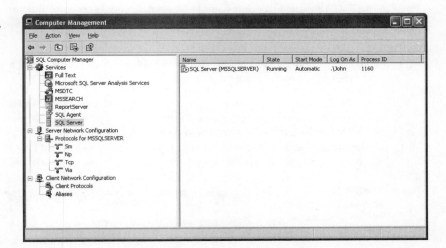

ENABLING AND DISABLING NETWORK SUPPORT

At some point, you'll want to share the data you've created across a network. For example, you might set up a test site for the other developers on your team. SQL Server doesn't enable network support by default so you need to perform some additional work.

The first task is to start the SQL Browser service so that client computers can locate the instance of SQL Server on your system. When you want this feature enabled every time you start the system, you'll want to set the SQL Browser service to start automatically. The downside of starting this service is that viruses and other unappealing intruders can also find your setup. Consequently, you don't want to enable other network connections unless you actually need them. Open the Services console found the in the `Administrative Tools` folder of the Control Panel to start the SQL Browser service. When you want to start the service for a short connection, right-click the SQL Browser service entry and choose Start from the context menu. Otherwise, double-click the entry to open the SQL Browser Properties dialog box. Set the Startup Type field to Automatic and click Start. Click OK to close the SQL Browser Properties dialog box. The Services console will appear, as shown in Figure 10.2, when you finish.

Now you need to enable the desired protocols on the client and server. Begin with the server. Open the `Protocols` folder for the SQL Server instance that you want to work with. Locate the protocol that you want to use. Right-click the entry and choose Enable from the context menu. This step is all you need to do for the Sm, Np, and Via protocols. The Tcp protocol entry has several subentries, as shown in Figure 10.3, for the Internet Protocol (Ip) part of the protocol.

The number of Ip entries you see depends on the configuration of your machine. Each default Ip entry works with one address on your machine, including the loopback (local) address. The only way to determine which Ip entry to use is to double-click the entry. You'll see the Ip Properties dialog box shown in Figure 10.4. The address you want to look at is in the IpAddress field. Figure 10.4 shows the Ip address for the loopback or local connection. Enable this Ip entry when you want to work with TCP/IP locally, but don't want to let outside clients see your machine. To enable TCP/IP connectivity, you must select Yes in the Enabled field. A TCP/IP connection requires that you enable the Tcp entry and at least one Ip entry.

NOTE Make sure you disable the server protocols when you no longer need them. Simply right-click the desired protocol and choose Disable from the context menu.

The final step is to enable the required client protocols. Select the `Client Network Configuration\ Client Protocols` folder to view the list of client protocols, as shown in Figure 10.5. Right-click a protocol and choose Enable from the context menu to enable the protocol. The Order column determines the order in which the client calls the various protocols looking for a connection to the server—the client stops when it locates an active protocol, so the order you choose is important.

FIGURE 10.2
Start the SQL Browser service to ensure clients can locate your system.

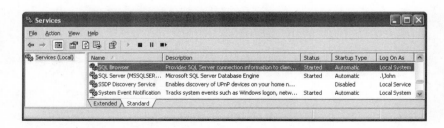

FIGURE 10.3
When working with
TCP/IP, make sure
you enable at least
one Ip entry.

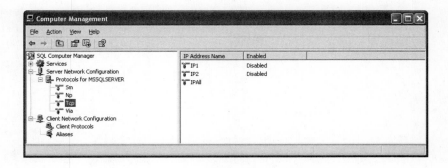

FIGURE 10.4
The IpAddress field tells
you which connection
the Ip entry affects.

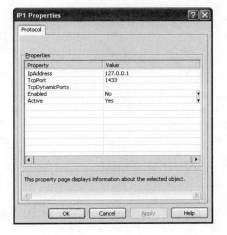

FIGURE 10.5
Both client and server
must have the same pro-
tocol enabled to create a
connection.

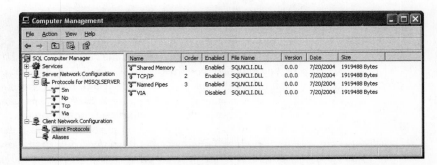

It's easy to change the order of the protocols. Right-click the Client Protocols folder and choose
Properties from the context menu. You'll see the Client Protocols Properties dialog box shown in Figure 10.6. To change the order, highlight one of the protocols and click either Move Up or Move Down
as needed. Notice that this dialog box also lets you selectively enable or disable the client protocols.

FIGURE 10.6
Use the Client Protocols
Properties dialog box to
change protocol order.

CREATING AN ALIAS

An alias provides an alternative means of creating a connection between a client and a server. Normally, when a client makes a request, it uses the default SQL Server instance. The client tries one protocol after another until it locates the server. You can use other instances, but it's time consuming. Using an alias short-circuits the process by specifying a specific SQL Server instance, a particular protocol, and a particular connection methodology.

To create an alias, right-click the `Aliases` folder and choose New Alias from the context menu. You'll see the Alias—New dialog box shown in Figure 10.7. This dialog box contains everything needed to create a custom connection to SQL Server.

Begin by typing a name in the Alias Name field. The name you choose is important because this is the value you enter in the Select or Enter a Server Name field of the Connection Properties dialog box in Visual Studio (see the "Creating a Connection to SQL Server" section of the chapter for additional information). The example uses a value of `SpecialConnect`, but you can use any value you want.

After you enter the alias name, type the name of the SQL Server instance in the Server field. If you want to use the default instance, type a `.` (period) in place of the name. Otherwise, provide the name of the SQL Server instance you want to use, not the name of the machine. When working with TCP/IP as the protocol, you can also type the IP address in place of the server name. Figure 10.5 shows the IpAddress field for the Ip1 protocol—the loopback, or local connection, in this case.

Select the protocol you want to use. An alias can use named pipes, TCP/IP, or VIA as the protocol. The shared memory protocol only applies to direct connections.

Depending on the protocol you choose, you can enter a value in the Connection String field. When working with named pipes, you must enter the named pipe of the server you want to use. You obtain this value by right-clicking the protocol entry in the `Server Network Configuration\Protocols for Instance` folder and choosing properties. The named pipe value appears in the PipeName field of the Np Properties dialog box. When working with TCP/IP, you provide the `TcpPort` value (see Figure 10.5) for the Ip protocol you want to use. When working with VIA, you provide the server port number located in the ListenInfo field of the Via Properties dialog box.

Figure 10.8 shows a completed TCP/IP alias. The connection relies on the default SQL Server instance, so the Server field contains a period. The Protocol field shows that this is a TCP/IP connection. The Connection String field shows the TCP/IP port number—the same number that appears in Figure 10.4. With all of the information shown, the machine could now access the server using this alias—all you need to do is type it as the server name when making the connection.

FIGURE 10.7

An alias represents a custom connection to the SQL Server instance you want to use.

FIGURE 10.8

The SpecialConnect alias provides a TCP/IP connection to the default SQL Server instance.

Using the SQL Server Management Studio

SQL Server Management Studio (SSMS) is the tool that you use most often when working with SQL Server 2005—at least when you perform tasks manually. This single tool replaces both Enterprise Manager and Query Analyzer. It also sports an interface that's more consistent with other Microsoft offerings such as Visual Studio .NET. In short, you end up with an easy-to-use tool that lets you do more without opening as many applications. Figure 10.9 shows a typical view of SSMS.

FIGURE 10.9
The SSMS interface
is reminiscent of
many other Microsoft
tools including Visual
Studio .NET.

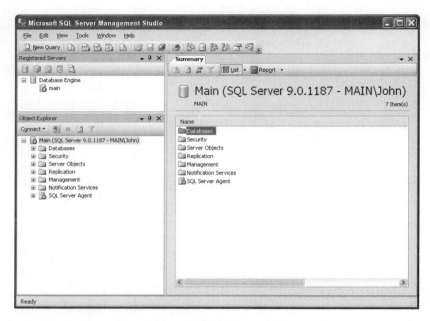

The following sections don't explore every feature of SSMS. This complex tool performs many tasks you won't need to perform for this book. Consider these sections an overview of the features you'll use most often to perform common tasks within Visual Studio for Web pages.

WORKING WITH OBJECT EXPLORER

Object Explorer helps you view the features of your SQL Server installation from one location. The Object Explorer pane appears in the lower left corner of Figure 10.9. To view an object, simply select it in the list. The Summary tab on the right side of the SSMS window displays the basic information for the selected object. You can use Object Explorer to view any of the major categories of information shown in the Object Explorer pane—the contents of which vary by the SQL Server features you have installed.

A common use of Object Explorer is to view the databases that SQL Server manages. To use this feature, simply click the plus sign next to Databases in Object Explorer. Continue to drill down into the database information until you see the information you need. Figure 10.10 shows a view of the Northwind database that you can install using the instructions in the "Obtaining the Northwind and Pubs Sample Databases" section of the chapter.

In all cases, clicking on an object in the Object Explorer pane shows its detail in the Summary tab. However, many objects provide additional information. To see the additional information, right-click the object and choose Properties from the context menu (there isn't any additional information when the Properties entry is missing from the context menu). Figure 10.11 shows a typical view of one of these Properties dialog boxes. In this case, the figure displays the specific properties for the Alphabetical List of Products view.

FIGURE 10.10
Use Object Explorer to
locate SQL Server fea-
tures such as databases.

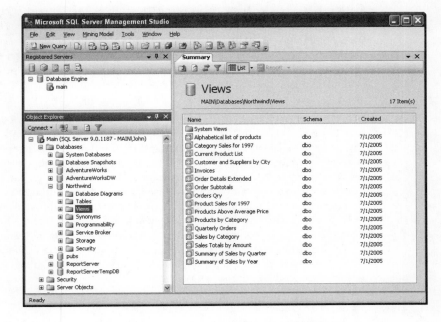

FIGURE 10.11
Many objects provide
a Properties window
where you can set object
particulars.

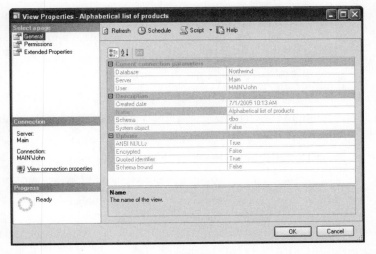

Use the Select a Page list to choose the kind of information you want to work with for the selected object. Figure 10.11 shows the General page, but this object also includes a Permissions and Extended Properties page. You can't change any entries that appear grayed out, just as you can't when working with any other Windows application.

It's important to differentiate the purpose of Object Explorer from other SSMS features. Object Explorer works with objects, not with data. You can see the properties of a view object, but you can't see the data provided by the view using Object Explorer. To work with data you create a query or you can select one of the context menu options that display the data. For example, when working with a view object, you can right-click the object and choose Open View to see the data. If you decide to modify the view script instead, simply choose Modify from the context menu. SSMS automatically opens the correct tool for the task. Consequently, while Object Explorer provides quick access to the tools you need, it isn't always the tool you need to perform a task.

CREATING QUERIES

You'll use Visual Studio to perform many tasks with SQL Server, rather than rely on SSMS. The book discusses these tasks as part of the examples that follow in this chapter and other chapters in the database section. However, it's often more convenient to create queries using SSMS because you can see the results instantly and tweak your query without working too hard at it. Once you have a working query, you can create a stored procedure for it or simply add it to your code.

To create a new query, simply click New Query on the toolbar. You'll initially see a blank query, but you can build a query quite quickly using drag and drop and a little SQL. Figure 10.12 shows an example of a query you can build very quickly using a little SQL and some drag and drop.

To create this query, open the Northwind database and the Tables object, as shown in Figure 10.12. The following steps help you complete the query. You'll find this example in the \Chapter 10 folder of the source code on the Sybex Web site.

1. Type **SELECT * FROM** as shown in the figure.

2. Drag and drop the dbo.Categories table entry from Object Explorer onto the query.

3. Type **AS C JOIN** and then drag and drop dbo.Products onto the query.

4. Type **AS P ON**. Now you need to open the Columns object for each of the tables.

5. Drag and drop the CategoryID column for each of the tables, as shown in Figure 10.12 and separate the entries with an equals sign.

6. Type **WHERE** and drag and drop the CategoryName field. You need a value at this point.

7. Right-click the Categories table entry and choose Open Table from the context menu. You'll see a list of product categories.

8. Select Beverages in the list. Right-click this entry and choose copy.

9. Select the query again, right-click the end of query, and choose Paste from the context menu.

10. Add an equals sign between the CategoryName field and Beverages.

11. Enclose Beverages within single quotes and your query will look like the one shown in Figure 10.12.

12. Click ! Execute on the toolbar. The output you see at the bottom of the display should look similar to the output in Figure 10.12. You have just listed all of the products that fall within the Beverages category in the Northwind database.

The point of this exercise is to demonstrate how effective drag and drop can be in helping you create queries of any complexity. By using drag and drop, you reduce the risk of error in typing table, column, or even data values. After you complete a query, you can copy it to the clipboard and use it in your code or use it as part of a stored procedure. The idea is that you can create error free queries very quickly using this technique.

TIP Don't worry about making the text look perfect as you type. You can use the options on the Edit ➤ Advanced menu or the SQL Editor toolbar to format the text later.

FIGURE 10.12
Create queries quickly using drag-and-drop techniques.

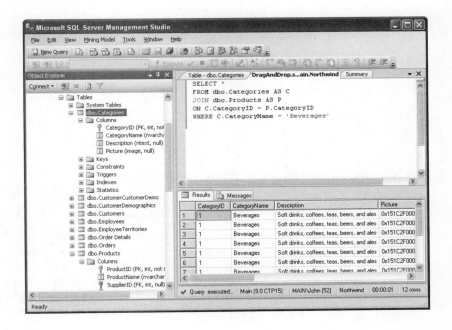

USING TEMPLATES

Not all queries are simple or easily remembered. That's where Template Explorer comes into play. This new feature provides ready-made templates for your SQL Server queries. Use the View ➤ Template Explorer command to display the Template Explorer window shown in Figure 10.13.

You'll find a template for just about every purpose in this list. Figure 10.13 shows the templates for tables, but you'll also find templates for most other relatively complex tasks (other than selecting, inserting, or deleting data). To use a template, drag and drop it from Template Explorer to a blank query. Figure 10.13 shows the default query that the Create Table template produces. As you can see, the template provides suggested values for each of the entries to give you an idea of what you need to type to complete the template. As with the query example in the "Creating Queries" section, using drag and drop for as many of the entries as possible reduces the risk of error.

Fortunately, you don't have to rely on the templates that Microsoft provides. Right-click on any folder and you can add another folder or a new template. It's a good idea to create new templates in a special folder so that you can separate them from the original Microsoft templates. To create a new folder, select New ➤ Folder from the context menu and type the name of the new folder.

FIGURE 10.13

Design complex queries quickly using a template, rather than typing it from scratch.

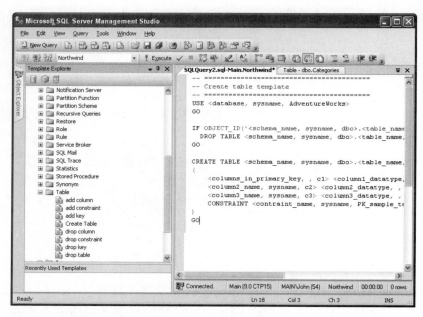

To create a new template, select New ➤ Template from the context menu. Type the name of the new template and press Enter. Right-click the new template entry and choose Edit from the context menu. You'll see a blank query where you can type the template you want to create. The convention is to use angle brackets where you want the template user to replace a value. For example, you might create a new template called Select with Join and provide the following code for it. You'll find this example in the \Chapter 10 folder of the source code on the Sybex Web site.

```
SELECT <Database_Fields>
FROM <Table_1> AS <Alias_1>
JOIN <Table_2> AS <Alias_2>
ON <Alias_1>.<Column> = <Alias_2>.<Column>
WHERE <Column> = '<Value>'
```

Using this template means that you don't have to remember how to write a select query that relies on a join. Of course, this is a simple example, but you can create templates of any complexity using this technique, which greatly simplifies the task of creating working queries for your applications as .NET code or as stored procedures.

TIP You can make any template or query part of a group project and add it to source control. To use this feature, access Visual SourceSafe using the File ➤ Source Control menu options. Chapter 14 examines team development issues in detail.

DESIGNING QUERIES

You might decide that the last thing you want to do is to write any query code by hand. Within limits, SSMS can perform the work for you using the Query Designer. To use this technique, create a new query by clicking New Query on the SQL Editor toolbar. Choose the database you want to use from the Available Databases drop-down list. Click Design Query in Editor next and you'll see an Add Table dialog box like the one shown in Figure 10.14. This figure shows the Northwind database and the example in this section will replicate the code you manually created in the "Creating Queries" section of the chapter.

To select tables for use in the query, click the first table and then Ctrl+Click the remaining tables. Click Add to add the tables to the query, and Close to get rid of the Add Table dialog box. It isn't possible to duplicate the query in the "Creating Queries" section of the chapter precisely. To add the filtering criteria found in that section, you must select the individual fields, which produces a query that isn't quite as efficient as the hand-coded alternative. Figure 10.15 shows the result in this case.

Notice the use of an entry in the Filter field for CategoryName to control the output as before. The difference in the output code is in the SELECT portion of the statement—the Query Designer lists the fields individually. It's not a fatal flaw and won't cause a noticeable performance problem, in this case, but it could cause problems with an application that manages large amounts of data. To add an alias for each table, right-click the table entry and choose Properties from the context menu. Type the alias you want to use in the Alias property and click Close.

FIGURE 10.14
Choose the tables you want to use from the list displayed for a particular database.

FIGURE 10.15
Use the graphical interface to create the query you need to extract data.

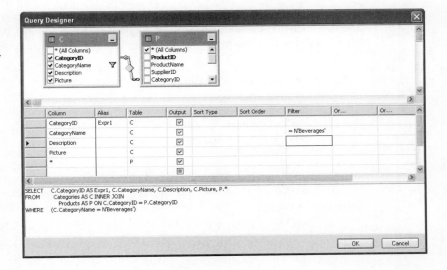

When you finish designing the query using the graphical interface, click OK. The Query Designer transfers the code to the new query you created. Click ! Execute and you'll see the same results as the code in the "Creating Queries" section. You'll find this example in the \Chapter 10 folder of the source code on the Sybex Web site.

DEFINING EFFICIENT QUERIES

You might not realize it, but SSMS can help you create efficient queries. Even simple queries are quite easy to test for efficiency. The SQL Editor toolbar contains two essential buttons to help you along. The first, Include Actual Execution Plan, provides a graphical depiction of how SQL Server interprets the query you create. The differences between two queries can be dramatic, even when the query output is the same. By viewing the execution plan, you can understand how different queries affect SQL Server and use the information to make your queries more efficient. Figure 10.16 shows a typical example of an execution plan.

Unfortunately, the execution plan only tells you how SQL Server reacts—it doesn't provide hard statistics you can use for comparison purposes. The second toolbar button, Include Client Statistics, provides the hard statistics you need to determine whether your query optimization efforts are headed in the right direction. Figure 10.17 shows a typical example of client statistics for a query.

The statistics begin by telling you how much time a query requires. The display then breaks down the statistics into discrete tasks so that you can better understand how SQL Server is spending its time answering your request. For example, look at the network statistics to determine how many round trips each request requires. By reducing the number of joins in a query, you can improve overall performance. Likewise, by modifying the number of fields you request, you can reduce the amount of data returned and improve processing type. The point is that you can try various query formats out to create a balance between the data you actually need for an application and the performance you can expect. It's impossible to perform this task from within the Visual Studio environment—you need to use SSMS to perform the task.

Using the query found in the "Creating Queries" section of the chapter as a starting point, you can easily improve performance by making a small change. Because you already know the contents of the Categories table—the fact that the CategoryName field is always going to contain Beverages, you can reduce the network load by modifying the query to send just the product information you need. In addition, you don't actually need all of the product information. Change the query, as shown here. You'll find this example in the \Chapter 10 folder of the source code on the Sybex Web site.

```
SELECT P.ProductID, P.ProductName, P.SupplierID, P.QuantityPerUnit,
       P.UnitPrice, P.UnitsInStock, P.UnitsOnOrder, P.ReorderLevel,
       P.Discontinued
FROM dbo.Products AS P
JOIN dbo.Categories AS C
ON C.CategoryID = P.CategoryID
WHERE C.CategoryName = 'Beverages'
```

This change in the query reduces the number of bytes received from 155,202 to 19,819, but increases the bytes sent from 432 to 738. Even so, the number of packets that the client and server have to process changes from 40 to 7. In short, the technique saves considerable network time and results in a significant savings in processing time. It's not enough time to notice using this small database example, but the idea is that you can still measure the difference even if you can't see it.

FIGURE 10.16
The execution plan shows how SQL Server reacts to the query you create.

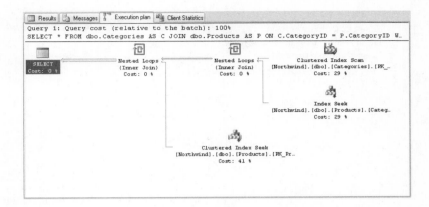

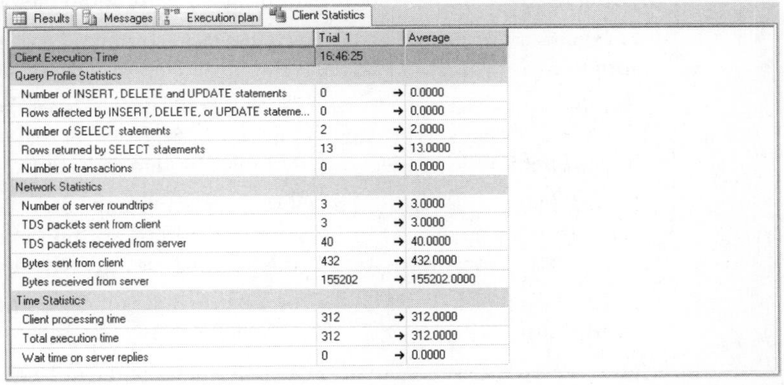

FIGURE 10.17
Review the client statistics to quantify changes due to query optimization.

Using the SQLCmd Utility

The SQLCmd (Structured Query Language Command) utility is one of the most useful features of SQL Server. You can perform a number of tasks from the command line using this utility. In fact, the utility easily lends itself to use with both scripts and batch files, so you can create a setup once and then execute it whenever needed. The following sections describe how to use to use this utility both interactively and at the command prompt. (You'll see additional usage examples as the book progresses.)

USING SQLCMD INTERACTIVELY

One of the best ways to learn how to use SQLCmd is to create an interactive connection. All you need do is type **SQLCmd** and press Enter at the command prompt to start an interactive session. It's also possible to specify any required command line switches that don't cause the program to exit. For example, the -S, -P, and -U command line switches all work fine. Once you start the interactive session, you'll see a new prompt that lets you enter commands. Figure 10.18 shows an interactive session consisting of several commands using the Northwind database.

FIGURE 10.18
Use SQLCmd interactively to discover how it works and see the best ways to create scripted sequences.

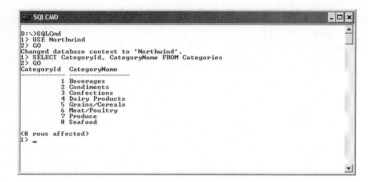

The commands in Figure 10.18 mix standard SQL statements with special commands that SQL-Cmd understands. Anyone who uses Query Analyzer regularly will recognize the GO command. The following list describes the commands that SQLCmd understands.

!! *Command*   Executes any operating system command. For example, when you want to clear the clutter on your display, you can type **!! CLS** and press Enter to clear the screen.

:Connect *ServerName*[*InstanceName*] [*Timeout*] [*Username* [*Password*]]   Creates a connection to a different server and SQL Server or SQL Server instance. You can specify the amount of time to wait for the connection to complete and include both a username and password as needed.

:Error *Filename* | **STDERR** | **STDOUT**   Redirects the error output to the specified filename, the standard error device (STDERR), or the standard output device (STDOUT). SQLCmd defaults to sending the error information to the STDERR device, which is the display.

:Help   Displays a list of all the commands that SQLCmd understands along with very brief descriptions.

:List   Prints the content of the statement cache. SQLCmd clears the statement cache after each successful transaction, so this command might not display anything, even after you work with SQL-Cmd for a while.

:ListVar   Displays the script variables you set, along with selected environmental variables including SQLCMDCOLSEP, SQLCMDCOLWIDTH, SQLCMDDBNAME, SQLCMDEDITOR, SQLCMDERRORLEVEL, SQLCMDHEADERS, SQLCMDINI, SQLCMDLOGINTIMEOUT, SQL-CMDMAXFIXEDTYPEWIDTH, SQLCMDMAXVARTYPEWIDTH, SQLCMDPACKETSIZE, SQLCMDSERVER, SQLCMDSTATTIMEOUT, SQLCMDUSER, and SQLCMDWORKSTATION.

NOTE   Some environment variables are read-only, which means you can view them, but not change them directly. These environment variables include SQLCMDDBNAME (set with the –d switch), SQLCMDPACKETSIZE (set with the –a switch), SQLCMDSERVER (set with the –S switch), SQLCM-DUSER (set with the –U switch), and SQLCMDWORKSTATION (set with the –H switch).

:On Error [EXIT | IGNORE]   Determines the action that SQLCmd performs when an error occurs. When you choose the EXIT option, SQLCmd stops execution and exits when it encounters an error. Otherwise, SQLCmd displays the error information and attempts to execute the next statement.

:Out *Filename* | **STDERR** | **STDOUT**   Redirects the standard output to the specified filename, the standard error device (STDERR), or the standard output device (STDOUT). SQLCmd defaults to sending the output to the STDOUT device, which is the display.

:Perftrace *Filename* | **STDERR** | **STDOUT**   Redirects performance information to the specified filename, the standard error device (STDERR), or the standard output device (STDOUT). SQLCmd defaults to sending performance information to the STDOUT device, which is the display.

:ServerList   Displays a list of the available servers. Note that this output isn't always correct. A server might not have the SQL Browser service running, so it won't appear on the list. The server must broadcast and the client must receive the server information for the :ServerList command to display it within SQLCmd. In addition, just because you see a server doesn't mean you can connect to it. You must have the proper rights to access the server.

:SetVar [*VariableName* [*Value*]]   Defines the value of a script or environmental variable. For example, to set the SQLCMDCOLSEP environmental variable to use an asterisk, you'd type :SetVar SQLCMDCOLSEP "*" and press Enter.

:XML ON | OFF   Determines whether SQLCmd outputs data as standard text or XML.

ED   Starts the selected text editor and places the contents of the statement cache in it for editing. When you exit the text editor, SQLCmd places the edited content on screen. The default editor is the DOS Edit.COM. You can change the editor by modifying the SQLCMDEDITOR environment variable using the :SetVar command.

EXIT [(*ExitValue*)]   Ends the interactive session. You can optionally provide an output value to any script that initiated the interactive session. The output can include a numeric value, query, or other statement. When the parentheses are empty (there's no return value), the batch file processing continues without the return value. Using EXIT by itself is equivalent to issuing a QUIT command.

GO [*Count*]   Executes the content of the statement cache as a batch job. The optional Count value defines the number of time to execute the batch.

QUIT   Ends the interactive session without any return value, batch, or scripting support provided.

R *Filename*   Loads a file containing Transact SQL statements for execution as a batch. The file can contain any legitimate commands or SQL statements, including the GO command.

RESET   Empties the statement cache. You can use this command to remove any unneeded commands from the statement cache.

USING SQLCMD AT THE COMMAND LINE

Scripts, batch files, and even you will want to rely on the SQLCmd command line interface to perform many tasks. For example, you can execute a query at the command line without ever using the interactive interface. In addition, the command line interface has certain advantages—you can use redirection to obtain specific effects that you might not ordinarily have access to, such as saving the output in a processed file. SQLCmd supports the following command line switches—all of which are optional (make sure you replace variable information with actual data).

WARNING   Case does count when working with these command line switches. For example, an uppercase U defines your username, while a lowercase u defines Unicode output. The list groups uppercase and lowercase switches when they produce similar results—they never produce the same results. The SQLCmd utility also lets you use the dash (-) or slash (/) for command line switches—even though the dash appears in the list.

-A   Creates a dedicated administrative connection (DAC) to the database. This feature works with SQL Server 2005—not earlier versions of the product. Normally, you won't need this kind of connection. However, you might want to view hidden tables, such as sys.sysallocunits, where SQL Server requires you to have a DAC. You can't bind to hidden tables unless you have a DAC connection. This connection also works when SQL Server is in an abnormal state and not responding to a SQL Server connection. The "Using a Dedicated Administrator Connection" help file topic provides additional information about this command line switch.

-a *PacketSize*   Determines the size of the individual transfers between the client and the server. In general, you don't need to worry about the packet size for smaller databases because you won't notice a performance advantage. However, as the database size increases, it pays to optimize the packet size to improve overall performance. Valid packet sizes range from 512 through 65,535.

-b   Configures SQLCmd to exit when an error occurs, rather than ignore the error and simply list it to the default error output.

-c *CommandTerminator*   Defines a command terminator for Transact SQL statements. The default setting uses the word GO, but you can use any terminator desired. Avoid using words or symbols that have special meaning. The terminator you select must still appear on the separate line—just as GO normally does.

-d *DatabaseName*   Loads a specific database when SQLCmd starts.

-e echo input   Adds any input statements to the beginning of any output. This feature is helpful when you use a file or other output other than the display because it repeats the input commands for later analysis.

-E trusted connection   Creates a connection between the client and server using a trusted connection, rather than requesting a username and password.

-f *Codepage* | i:*Codepage* [,o:*Codepage*]   Determines the language support provided by SQLCmd. The -f switch defines the codepage for both input and output. As an alternative, you can specify the input codepage using the i argument and the output using the o argument. This feature doesn't provide any translation functionality—it simply changes the language support, such as date and monetary format that SQLCmd provides.

TIP   The codepage values supported by your system will vary by the languages you have installed. You can find a list of standard Windows codepage values at http://www.microsoft.com/globaldev/reference/cphome.mspx.

-h -1 | 1   Determines whether SQLCmd displays headers as part of the query output. The default setting of 0 outputs headers at the beginning of the query output. Use a value of –1 to inhibit header display. A value of 1 displays the headers for every output row.

NOTE Whenever a command line switch accepts a negative value, such as -1, you must place the value immediately after the switch. For example, if you want to inhibit header display, you must supply the switch as -h-1. Otherwise, SQLCmd will interpret the space as the start of a new switch and display an error message.

-H *Hostname*   Defines the host used to execute commands. This command affects the work-station name that it returned by the sp_who stored procedure by modifying the content of sysprocesses.hostname. The default setting uses the current computer as the host.

-I   Sets the QUOTED_IDENTIFIER connection option on.

-i *Filename*   Loads the requested filename containing Transact SQL commands into the state-ment cache for execution within a batch. The file can contain any legitimate commands or SQL statements, including the GO command.

-k [1 | 2]   Removes (1) or replaces (2) control characters encountered during processing.

-l *Timeout*   Determines the login timeout value—the time that SQLCmd waits for login informa-tion from the user. The default value is 8 seconds.

-L[c]   Displays a list of servers accessible from the current machine. Note that this output isn't always correct. A server might not have the SQL Browser service running, so it won't appear on the list. The server must broadcast and the client must receive the server information for it to appear in the list.

-m *ErrorLevel*   Sets the error level at which SQLCmd displays error information. SQLCmd won't display any errors less than the requested level. Use a value of –1 to display all errors, including informational messages.

-o *Filename*   Redirects SQLCmd output to the requested file.

-P *Password*   Accepts the user password for access to the requested database.

-p[1]   Prints performance statistics. Adding a 1 after the command line switch tells SQLCmd to use the colon format for output.

-q *"Query"* **and -Q** *"Query"*   Queries the database for data based on the query string. The query string must appear within double quotes. The uppercase version of the switch makes the query and immediately exits from SQLCmd. The lowercase version shows the results of the query and then an interactive prompt.

-R   Sets SQLCmd to use the locale settings specified for the client machine.

-r [0 | 1]   Redirects the message output to the STDERR device (normally the screen) when you don't specify an argument or use a value of 1. Only error messages with a severity level of 11 or greater are redirected when 0 appears as the argument.

-s *Separator*   Defines the character used as a column separator. SQLCmd normally uses a space between columns. You must enclose special characters (| ; & < >) in double quotes.

-S *Server*   Defines the name of the target server. The target server determines the location of the SQL Server database.

-t *Timeout*   Defines the time that SQLCmd waits for a query before it exits. Commands don't time out if you don't specify this value.

-U *Username*   Accepts the username for purposes of identification.

-u   Outputs the data in Unicode format, even when the input file is in another format.

-V *SeverityLevel*   Defines the level of error severity required before SQLCmd outputs the error information. Any errors less severe than the requested severity level are ignored and not reported.

-v *VariableName = "Value"* ...   Defines one or more variables for use in processing commands. SQLCmd accesses the value using the variable name supplied. You must enclose the value within double quotes. A single command line switch can define multiple variables.

-W   Removes leading and trailing spaces from the output data. Most developers combine this switch with the –s switch to prepare data for use with another application.

-w screen width   Defines a screen width between 8 and 65,535 and characters. The default setting of 80 characters matches most screens. Larger values let you prepare data for output to a file as a contiguous string, rather than multiple strings. Whenever the data length exceeds the screen width, SQLCmd wraps the data to the next line.

-X[1]   Disables the ! ! and ED commands to reduce security risks. When you supply a 1, SQLCmd adds an error message stating "Error: The ED and !!<command> commands are disabled." whenever the user attempts to use the disabled commands.

-y *Width* **and -Y** *Width*   Limits the number of characters displayed on screen. The –y (lowercase) switch controls large variable types including varchar(max), nvarchar(max), varbinary(max), xml, UDT (User-defined Data Types), text, ntext, and image. The –Y (uppercase) switch controls standard variable types including char, nchar, varchar(n), nvarchar(n), and sql_variant. When working with varchar(n), n is between 1 and 8,000. When working with nvarchar(n), n is between 1 and 4,000.

-z *Password* **and -Z** *Password*   Modifies the password of the trusted user. The uppercase version of the switch changes the password and immediately exits from SQLCmd. The lowercase version changes the password and then displays an interactive prompt.

You can use the command line interface for a variety of tasks such as adding automation to your applications. Of course, you'll want to start by trying the commands manually. For example, Figure 10.19 shows the results of a query made at the command line.

FIGURE 10.19
The command line interface lets you automate tasks by using batch files or scripts.

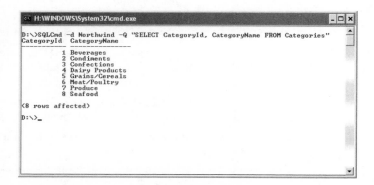

Notice that this query uses the uppercase -Q switch, so SQLCmd simply displays the results on screen. Using redirection, you could place this command in a batch file and execute it whenever necessary. Adding XML functionality by loading a command file would let you extract data from a database and place it in a folder on your Web site. The Web application you create would immediately begin using the new data. Adding this feature to the Task Scheduler would automate the task still further. Your Web application would receive constant updates and you would never have to do anything manually except change the data in the database.

Creating a Database Connection

You'll use Server Explorer (see the overview provided in Chapter 3) to create database connections when working with Visual Studio. However, this feature appears in a special area of Server Explorer because this is a special function that you might not attach to a local computer or server resource you would access for other purposes such as working with queues or services. Many companies use a separate server or even a server farm to support databases, so it makes sense to support database connectivity as a special feature. The following sections describe how you use Server Explorer to create a database connection. You'll discover more about the database management issues that Server Explorer addresses in other areas of the book, including the "Designing a Database" section of this chapter.

Creating a Connection to SQL Server

Creating a connection to SQL Server is relatively easy. All you need to know is the name of the server and the name of the database that you want to use. You can also use an alias as the server name (see the "Creating an Alias" section of the chapter for details). Figure 10.20 shows a typical database connection with the various entries that you might see for a SQL Server database.

FIGURE 10.20
Server Explorer provides great access to all of the database elements you need to manage.

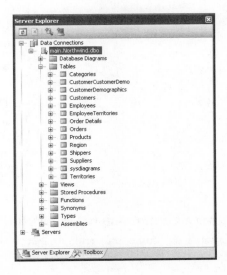

Begin the connection process by right-clicking the Data Connections entry in Server Explorer and choosing Add Connection from the context menu. You'll see the Add Connection dialog box shown in Figure 10.21. Select the server you want to access in the Server Name field. Choose a user identification technique. Finally, select the database you want to use.

You have two choices when connecting to a particular database. The first option is to choose a database already found on the local server by selecting it from the drop-down list shown in Figure 10.21. The second alternative is to select the Attach a Database File option and locate the database file on the hard drive. This second option is especially useful for databases on your Web site, such as the configuration information database, ASPNETDB.MDF, located in the \App_Data folder. Whichever option you choose, click Test Connection to verify the connection actually works and click OK.

TIP You'll find four buttons at the top of the Server Explorer window shown in Figure 10.20. The Refresh button creates a new database query and updates the information shown in Server Explorer. The Stop Refresh button helps you end long queries. Click Connect to Database when you want to create a new connection. Click Connect to Server when you want to gain access to another server on the network. Visual Studio .NET defaults to connecting to the local server, but you can connect to any server for which you have access. You don't have to have a server connection to create a database connection—the server connection appears as part of the database connection.

FIGURE 10.21
Create a database connection by defining a server and database name.

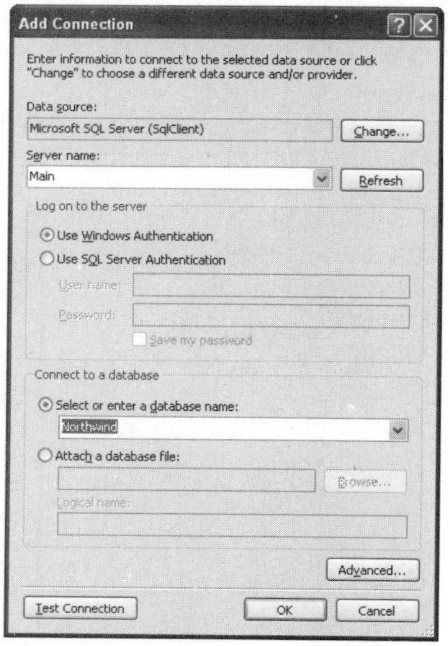

Creating a Connection to Other DBMSs

The initial Visual Studio setup assumes that you want to use SQL Server. Many developers have other kinds of connections to create and Visual Studio is up to the task of accommodating them. All you need to do is choose a different data source than the default. Display the Add Connection dialog box by clicking Connect to Database in Server Explorer. Click Change next to the Data Source field and you'll see a list of provider options, as shown in Figure 10.22.

FIGURE 10.22
Select a provider that matches a connectivity option for your database.

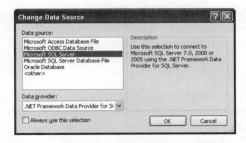

The default provider is .NET Framework Data Provider for SQL Server. This special provider includes code that enhances the performance of a SQL Server or SQL Server connection, but doesn't do much for other databases. Oracle users also have access to a specialized provider, so you should select this option when working with Oracle databases.

TIP   Notice that the list in Figure 10.22 includes a special Microsoft SQL Server Database File entry. Select this data source when you want to access a SQL Server file without adding the data to a server. For example, you might only need a temporary or local connection to the database file, so using this option makes sense. Use the Microsoft SQL Server data source as described in the "Creating a Connection to SQL Server" section of the chapter when you want to add the contents of the database file to the server.

The option with the best performance for connections to other databases is the .NET Framework Data Provider for OLE-DB provider. After you choose a data provider, select a data source. For example, when you want to work with an Access database, choose the Microsoft Access Database File data source. This special data source provides the fastest connection for Microsoft Access databases.

The list of data sources also includes the somewhat generic Microsoft ODBC Data Source option. Most databases provide ODBC support. Even open source databases such as MySQL provide ODBC support through third party add-ons. Consequently, there's little chance that you can't create a connection to your database, even if you have to use a slower ODBC setup. The "Creating a Connection to Microsoft Access Using ODBC" section of the chapter shows how to use this old and reliable connectivity method.

Creating a Connection to Microsoft Access Using ODBC

ODBC has been around for many years. You can easily find it in products that predate Windows 95. In fact, this technology has been around for so long that many developers view it as a kind of one-size-fits-all solution to database connectivity. It's hard to find a database that can't use ODBC to create a connection. Since Visual Studio provides full ODBC support, you should be able to create a connection to any database you want—at least within reason. This section describes how to use ODBC to create a connection to Microsoft Access. The amazing thing is that this process works relatively well for other databases too—most of them simply change the form required to make the connection meet specific driver needs.

NOTE   The example in this section relies on a sample Access database that you'll find in the \Chapter 10 folder of the sample code on the Sybex Web site. You can use this database to experiment with connections as needed to see how Access works with Visual Studio.

CREATING THE ODBC CONNECTION

Before you can tell Visual Studio which ODBC connection to use, you have to create the connection. You define the connection using the ODBC Data Source Administrator that you access using the Data Sources (ODBC) applet in the `Administrative Tools` folder of the Control Panel. Figure 10.23 shows what this dialog box looks like with the sample database connection entered.

NOTE   One of the problems with using ODBC is that you have to define the connection or Data Source Name (DSN) on every machine that requires it. The need to define a DSN on every machine isn't such big deal for a small organization, but imagine doing it for thousands of machines and you'll know why most network administrators want another solution.

To create the connection, click Add. You'll see the Create New Data Source dialog box where you select a connection type. Every ODBC source on your computer has a special driver—the driver has a name such as Microsoft Access Driver (`*.MDB`). Select the Access driver and click Finish. This act starts the driver and you'll see a driver-specific dialog box such as the ODBC Microsoft Access Setup dialog box shown in Figure 10.24. Note that this dialog box shows the entries required to access the database.

FIGURE 10.23
Use the ODBC Data Source Administrator to create an ODBC connection.

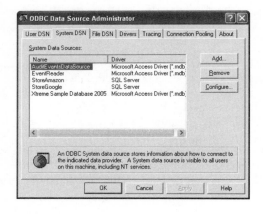

FIGURE 10.24
Fill in the information required to let the driver access the database.

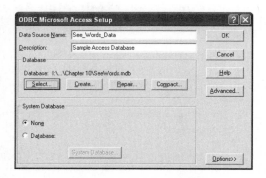

The information you provide to create an ODBC connection varies by driver. In most cases, you'll need to provide a database name and security information as a minimum, but many drivers require additional input. When working with an Access database, you need to provide the location of the database by clicking Select and choosing the database file using the Select Database dialog box. After you add the database connection, type a name for the connection in the Data Source Name field. Even though the Description field is optional, you'll likely want to provide information in it, as well, so you can identify the connection easier.

At this point, you need to decide whether to provide a default login for the connection. Most connections are more secure when you request the login information from individual users. When you decide to create a default login, click Advanced. You'll see a Set Advanced Options dialog box. Type the default authorization information in the Login Name and Password fields. Click OK to close the Set Advanced Options dialog box and a second time to close the ODBC Microsoft Access Setup dialog box.

ADDING THE CONNECTION TO VISUAL STUDIO

Once you create an ODBC connection, you can use it within Visual Studio. Begin by clicking Connection to Database in Server Explorer. Always remember that Microsoft assumes that you're going to use SQL Server, so the first thing you need to do is click Change to display the Change Data Source dialog box. Choose the Microsoft ODBC Data Source option and you'll notice that the data provider automatically changes to the .NET Framework Data Provider for ODBC option. Click OK and you'll notice that the Add Connection dialog box changes, as shown in Figure 10.25. Notice that the figure already has the DSN selected.

NOTE   Notice that the dialog box shown in Figure 10.25 has two options for selecting a DSN. Choose the first option when you create a user or system DSN using the technique described in the "Creating the ODBC Connection" section. The second option lets you use a machine or a file DSN. File DSNs can be especially handy when you need to support multiple machines because you simply include the DSN file with the application. Of course, this option assumes that every machine will have the same connection options—which isn't always safe for large organizations.

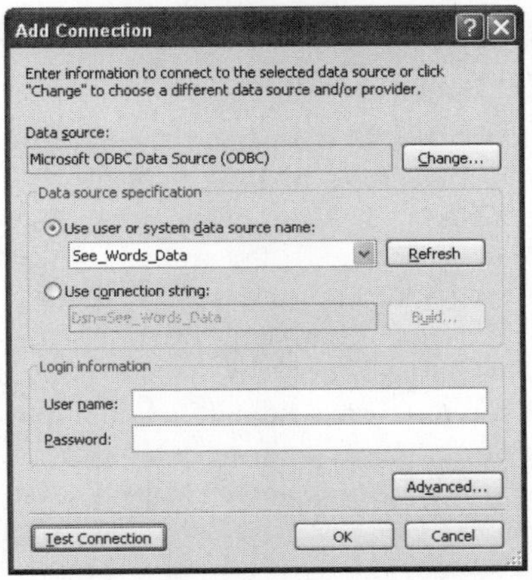

FIGURE 10.25
ODBC connections require that you supply a DSN for the connection.

Depending on how you plan to use the database, you'll need to provide a username and password. When the password is blank, you can leave the username blank as well in some cases. Make sure you check Blank Password. You'll also need to decide whether the user can save the password so they don't need to enter it again.

After you choose a DSN, click Test Connection to ensure the connection works. Click OK to complete the connection. Figure 10.26 shows how the sample database appears when you use an ODBC connection (bottom) contrasted to an OLE-DB connection (top).

The results are the same—you gain access to the same data no matter which connection you use. The difference is performance. The OLE-DB connection will outperform the ODBC connection. In addition, the OLE-DB connection doesn't require configuration on a machine-by-machine basis. Of course, ODBC is a viable solution when OLE-DB connections aren't possible.

FIGURE 10.26
OLE-DB and ODBC connections provide access to the same data, but with different performance.

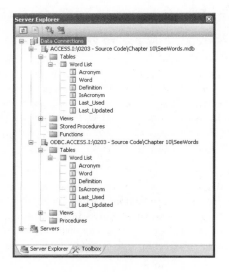

Designing a Database

When you work with data, you need to design a database to store the information for later use. In some cases, this means creating a simple XML storage container, as shown in previous chapters of the book. XML is increasingly becoming a storage medium of choice, especially for simple projects because it doesn't require any special DBMS to use—it has the advantage of being inexpensive and simple. However, complex data storage usually requires something better. Many small businesses rely on Microsoft Access, while others use third party solutions such as MySQL. Unfortunately, you can't create an Access or MySQL database within Visual Studio. You can define elements of the database, but you must create the initial database using the resources of that DBMS.

Visual Studio does provide a means for creating SQL Server databases within the IDE. In addition, when working with SQL Server, you can create databases using scripts. The following sections show how to create a new database using a simple dialog box and how to add the Northwind and Pubs databases to your existing SQL Server setup. This section part is especially important because many of the remaining database examples in the book rely on the Northwind database.

Developing a SQL Server Database Using the Wizard

Creating a new SQL Server database using Visual Studio is relatively easy. To begin, right-click the Data Connections entry in Server Explorer and choose Create New SQL Server Database from the context menu. You'll see the Create New SQL Server Database dialog box shown in Figure 10.27. This figure shows the required entries in place.

Select the server you want to use for the database from the Select or Enter Server Name field. Type a name for the database in the Enter a New Database Name field. You can optionally change the database security, but most developers now use the default Windows integrated security option, as shown in Figure 10.27. Click OK and Visual Studio will add the new database to the Server Explorer. You can now add tables and other resources as needed to the database. Chapter 11 examines this topic in detail.

NOTE The \Chapter 10 folder contains the scripts required to create the MovieGuide database and import data for it. To use these scripts, you must edit the location to match a location on your hard drive. The location you choose must contain an uncompressed folder or the scripts will fail. The failure message tells you that the script attempted to create a compressed read/write database. The CreateMovieGuide.SQL script creates the files used to store the data. The MovieGuide.SQL script creates the tables within the database. Finally, the Import Records.SQL script imports the data from the MovieGuideData.DAT file into the tables. The ImportRecords.SQL script is currently set to use the same folder as the database for the Movie GuideData.DAT file, but you can easily change this if necessary.

FIGURE 10.27
Use the Visual Studio IDE to create any new SQL Server database you need.

Obtaining the Northwind and Pubs Sample Databases

Many developers are used to working with the Northwind and Pubs database with other Microsoft products. These two databases have become so standard that many authors, including myself, rely on the presence of these databases to ensure everyone can see example code without a lot of extra effort. Unfortunately, you won't find either database installed as part of the default SQL Server installation—you won't find an option for installing them either. However, you can find scripts for creating these databases in SQL Server online at http://www.microsoft.com/downloads/details.aspx?familyid=06616212-0356-46a0-8da2-eebc53a68034&displaylang=en. The name of the file you'll receive is SQL2000SampleDb.MSI. Even though Microsoft originally created this file for SQL Server 2000, it works just fine with SQL Server.

After you download the script files, you'll need to run them. Right-click the file and choose Install from the context menu. You'll see a Welcome dialog box that tells you that this file contains the sample databases for SQL Server 2000. Click Next, read the licensing agreement, and agree to it. Keep following the prompts until you install the sample database scripts in the appropriate directory.

At this point, you have two scripts for creating the sample databases. If you used the default installation settings, these files appear in the \Program Files\Microsoft SQL Server 2000 Sample Database Scripts folder of your machine. The InstNwnd.SQL file will create the Northwind database and the InstPubs.SQL file will create the Pubs database.

To install the databases, open a command prompt. Type **OSQL -E -i InstNwnd.SQL** and press Enter. The OSQL utility will create the Northwind database for you (this process can take quite some time). When the utility completes, you'll see the command line along with what appears as nonsensical output, as shown in Figure 10.28. Once the Northwind database is complete, type **OSQL -E -i InstPubs.SQL** and press Enter. The process will repeat itself.

NOTE If you try to run the OSQL utility and find that you receive an error message at the command prompt, it means that the SQL Server installation didn't modify the path information for your system as it should have. In some cases, this makes your installation suspect and you should reinstall the product if you experience other problems. To use the installation scripts, copy them from the installation folder to the \Program Files\Microsoft SQL Server\90\Tools\binn folder. You can run the OSQL utility at the command prompt from this folder to create the two sample databases.

You'll want to test the installation to make sure it worked. Open a copy of Visual Studio and use the View ➢ Server Explorer command to display the Server Explorer. Right-click Data Connections and choose Add Connection from the context menu. Server Explorer will display the Connection Properties dialog box shown in Figure 10.29 (this one already has all of the information filled out).

Type the name of your machine in the Select or Enter a Server Name field. Click the down arrow in the Select or Enter a Database Name field. You should see both the Northwind and Pubs databases, as shown in Figure 10.29. If you don't see these entries, it means that an error occurred. Try running the scripts a second time. A second failure usually means that there's a problem with your SQL Server setup and you might need to reinstall the product.

FIGURE 10.28

The OSQL utility runs for quite a while and displays output like this as it completes.

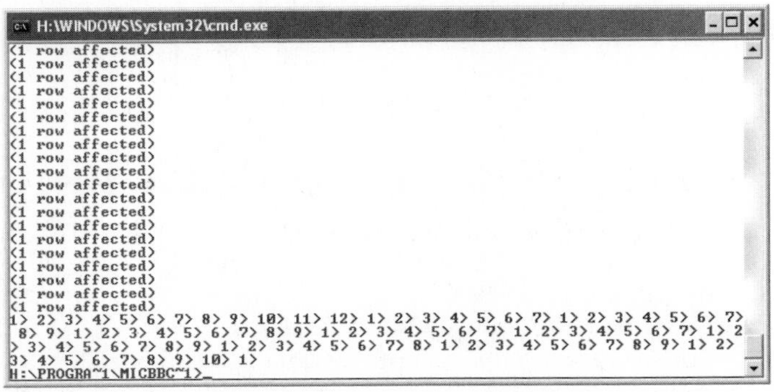

FIGURE 10.29
Use the Connection
Properties dialog box
to check for the two
databases.

You need to make sure you can actually access the database. Choose the Northwind database. Click Test Connection. When the scripts install the databases properly and you can access them, you'll see a success message. Click OK to clear the success message and Cancel to clear the Database Connection dialog box. You can close Visual Studio if desired.

NOTE   Because you're the only one using SQL Server, you don't need to worry about assigning login permissions for the test database. If you want to test any applications created in this book with the full version of SQL Server, you probably will need to assign login permissions to the test database to ensure they work as anticipated.

Relying on Code-free Data Binding

Once you create a connection to a database, the first concern is using it. The interesting thing about newer Microsoft products is that you don't have to do all of the work. In fact, when you have simple display needs, you don't have to do any of the work. One of the fastest and easiest ways to display data elements on screen is to simply drag and drop what you need onto the form—not code it. Yes, the IDE is creating code for you in the background, but the idea is that you aren't spending the time required to create the code.

In fact, you can get many of the features that developers want today without creating any code at all. Try this experiment. Drag and drop the Categories table from Server Explorer onto a new Web form. You'll find that Visual Studio automatically adds a `GridView` and a `SqlDataSource` control to the page for you. The Common Grid View SmartTag does the rest. Simply check the options you want and you'll see them added, automatically, without coding, as shown in Figure 10.30. You'll find this example in the `\Chapter 10\CodeFree` folder of the source code on the Sybex Web site.

FIGURE 10.30
The best way to create simple displays is to not code them.

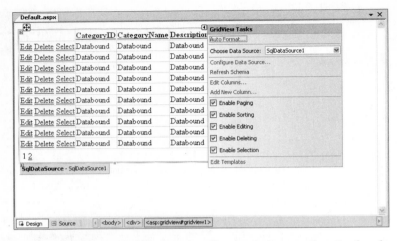

Start up the application. You'll find that all of the functionality works just as advertised and you haven't created a single line of code—at least, not personally. One of the biggest issues that developers need to consider is how much work to allow the IDE to do for them. As you can see, the IDE can do a lot of work, but it's also easy for a developer to feel that the automatic method isn't necessarily best. It isn't the best way to code complete complex applications, but simple pages really do work best when you let the IDE do the coding for you.

Defining Your Development Goals

This chapter shows you some basics of working with databases with Visual Studio. You discovered the many ways to design databases, create connections for them, access them from Visual Studio, and finally create an application using them. This chapter also describes several Visual Studio features including Server Explorer and a number of toolbars. All of these features make it easier for you to work with database applications.

Now it's time to work with the database features in more detail. You might have an existing database that you want to access from Visual Studio or simply create a new database for experimental purposes. Don't forget that Microsoft provides you with a number of sample databases you can use for experimentation, so if you want to work on coding technique, you can simply rely on one of the existing databases. The goal is to build proficiency working with Visual Studio to create database applications using the vast number of resources this product provides.

Chapter 11 takes you further on the road to working with databases efficiently in Visual Studio. You'll discover that you have access to a number of database management options that make it easier to manage your database. For example, you can create views to see the data in another way or stored procedures to perform some tasks using the DBMS, rather than writing local code. In many cases, the features described in this chapter cannot only reduce the work you have to do, but also make it easier to locate mistakes and even test the database as needed.

Chapter 11

Using SQL Server 2005 Efficiently

SQL Server comes with some interesting tools you can use to perform specialized tasks such as checking the performance of the queries you create. Chapter 10 discusses many of these tasks. However, most of the work you do with SQL Server actually occurs within the Visual Studio IDE. Yes, you can use command line utilities, such as SQLCmd, to perform some tasks, but the daily work that you perform occurs within the IDE. In fact, the IDE provides a number of resources, including Server Explorer and several toolbars that help you perform the required work.

Once you create one or more tables that you can use within Visual Studio, you'll need to create all of the add-ons that come with database programming, such as views and stored procedures. All of these resources help you define the database application and create something that works efficiently. For example, sometimes it's faster to create a view of the data, rather than construct it from scratch every time someone uses the application. Stored procedures sometimes work faster than local code because they keep all of the data on the server—the client simply receives the finished product. You need to consider where data manipulation occurs to ensure the application performs well.

A new feature in this version of SQL Server is the existence of a connection to the Common Language Runtime (CLR). Fortunately, you can work with this new feature as part of your application code in SQL Server. Although you probably won't see the full effect of CLR within SQL Server, you obtain enough information to understand how using CLR can definitely reduce the workload for the developer. Of course, all of that new functionality comes with a stiff price tag.

SQL Server also provides full support for XML. Some developers view this feature as nice to have, but not very exciting. XML is an essential feature for Visual Studio because you can do so many things with XML within your Visual Studio applications. The samples in previous chapters have shown you everything from data storage to survey results to configuration settings. All of these kinds of data manipulation work well with Visual Studio and XML. Adding this capability to SQL Server only completes the circle because your desktop applications still gain access to the full benefits of a full-fledged database. XML becomes an end location for some types of data storage—not a permanent piece of the application puzzle.

TIP This book provides a good overview of using SQL Server from a Visual Studio perspective. If you're planning to write a number of database applications, you'll want to learn more about making SQL queries using a book such as *SQL Queries for Mere Mortals* by John L. Viescas and Michael J. Hernandez (Addison Wesley, 2000). To get the most out of SQL Server, you'll also want to get a copy of *Mastering SQL Server 2005 Express Edition* by Mike Gunderloy and Susan Harkins (Sybex, 2005).

Accessing the Database from Visual Studio

Creating a database means that you have a container to store data and objects—everything from data tables to triggers used to signal an event. You could easily create new databases using the SQL Server Management Studio (SSMS), but it's easier to create databases without leaving the Visual Studio IDE. While you can't perform every task in the IDE, you can perform most common tasks and that means fewer applications to deal with and better use of your time. In addition, the easiest method of managing your database is the Visual Studio IDE. Quick changes really are fast when you use the Visual Studio IDE to perform them. The following sections introduce many of the concepts you'll use to create database applications in Visual Studio.

Using the Server Explorer

Server Explorer is the main interface between Visual Studio and SQL Server. The "Creating a Database Connection" section of Chapter 10 describes how you can create a connection to SQL Server using Server Explorer, but Server Explorer can do a lot more than create simple connections. You can use it to create every object type that the database supports, including new tables.

NOTE   Throughout the book, I'll use the technically correct term, *fields*, to refer to the smallest element that you can access within a database. Most developers know and understand this term, which is the reason I use it in this book. Microsoft has chosen to use *columns* as a replacement term for *fields*, so you'll see this term when working with Microsoft products, but not with products from other vendors. I'll also use the term, *records*, to refer to a collection of fields that defines a single entry in a table. Microsoft uses the term *rows* to refer to *records*.

RECONFIGURING A DATASOURCE

You'll eventually run into problem where you move a project from one machine to another or install a SQL Server update and your application suddenly forgets everything it ever knew about the data source. Reconfiguring the DataSource control can help in these situations. Simply follow these steps to get your data source back without having to reconfigure the entire page.

1. Select the DataSource control in Design view.

2. Choose the Configure Data Source option from the DataSource control SmartTag. You'll see the Configure Data Source wizard. The important part now is not to change anything.

3. Click Next at each wizard step. Ensure that the settings you previously used are still valid for this setup. If not, change just the settings that you must change to make the DataSource control functional.

4. Click Test Query on the final page to ensure the data source is working again. If not, click Previous to make any required changes.

5. Click Finish to complete the update. Visual Studio will display a message box asking whether you want to refresh the fields and keys for the view controls.

6. Click No each time Visual Studio asks to refresh the controls. If you click Yes, you must reconfigure the affected view control.

7. Test your application to ensure the changes work as anticipated.

DISPLAYING THE DATA

In addition to creating, deleting, and modifying objects, you can use Server Explorer to view the various objects. For example, open the Categories table in the Northwind database. Right-click the Categories entry and choose Show Table Data from the context menu. You'll see the table data, as shown in Figure 11.1. This view lets you edit the data, just as you can when working with an application. More importantly, this view lets you see the effects of tasks your application performs on the data.

To create a new object, right-click the folder that holds the object (such as Tables) and choose the Add New option for the object you want to add on the context menu. For example, to add a new table, you would select the Add New Table option. You'll normally see the new item created outright or a wizard will take you through the process of creating the new object. Other sections of this chapter discuss the details of creating specific objects such as views.

MODIFYING THE TABLE AND ASSOCIATED FIELDS

You might decide, at some point, that you need to add a new field to the table or change part of the table schema. To view the table structure, right-click the table and choose Open Table Definition from the context menu. Figure 11.2 shows what you'll see for the Categories table.

The upper half of the display contains a list of fields for this table, defines the field data type, and shows whether the field allows nulls. The display also shows the primary key using the yellow key icon. To set the primary key, select the fields you want to use to define the key (use Ctrl+Click to select multiple fields), right-click one of the highlighted fields, and choose Set Primary Key from the context menu.

FIGURE 11.1
Use Server Explorer to perform tasks such as querying the database.

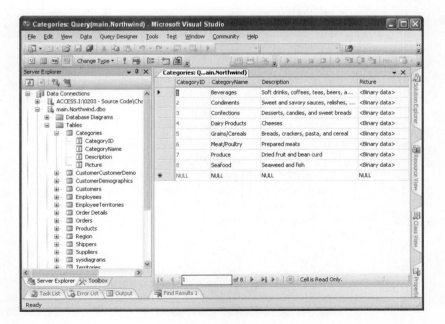

FIGURE 11.2
Define the table schema
using an interface that
looks similar to the one
in SQL Server.

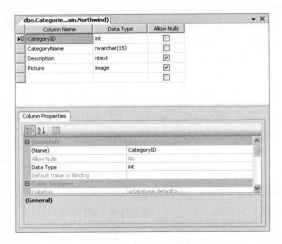

The lower half of the display contains a description of the highlighted field. You use the lower field to add information, such as a field description or data type. This is also where you add a default value for the field or define computed fields. The data includes some nonchangeable values as well, such as whether you can use the field in an index. In short, you get all of the same functionality that you'd expect from SQL Server; it's just in a different place.

Working with Indexes

The same interface shown in Figure 11.2 lets you create indexes as well. All you need to do is right-click the upper pane and choose one of the indexing options. However, you need to decide which kind of index to create. Visual Studio helps you create the following three index types.

Standard A standard index provides indexing for internal SQL Server use. Select the Indexes/ Keys context menu option to create a standard index. You order the data by specifying an index. This option also lets you create keys for use with the table—both primary and foreign. Most developers already know how to use this kind of index.

Full Text Some types of data stores require a full text index. For example, you might create a database to hold all of the Web pages on your Web site. To help users locate the information they need quickly, you'd provide a full text index. This kind of index requires that you create a full text catalog as part of the database. The full text index support is a separate installation option and it only works with specific field types. Given the special nature of this index, I don't discuss it in detail in this book. You can find a full discussion of this topic at `http://msdn.microsoft.com/ archive/en-us/dnarexnt00/html/ewn0092.asp`.

XML An XML index lets you order data so it works well as XML output. The column contains XML data that SQL Server orders for you. This is an especially important feature for Visual Studio because it's likely that you'll output data as XML at some point. To use this index, you must add a special field to the table of the XML data type. The "Creating an XML Index" section of the chapter demonstrates how to create an XML index using Visual Studio.

TIP   Visual Studio users do have options other than using a full text index in SQL Server to perform full text searches of their Web site. Third party products such as the Zoom Search Engine (http://www.wrensoft.com/zoom/index.html) from Wrensoft Web Software make creating full text searches easier.

Standard indexes work with a subset of the data types that SQL Server supports. For example, you can't create a standard index for the `ntext` data type, but you can create it for fields with a specific size such as an `int` or `timestamp`. To create a standard index, right-click any of the columns and choose Indexes/Keys from the context menu. You'll see the Indexes/Keys dialog box shown in Figure 11.3. In fact, this dialog box already has one index, `CategoryName`, and one key, `PK_Categories`, defined.

Click Add to add a new index to the list. You must define the index by clicking the ellipsis (...) in the Columns field. This entry displays the Index Columns dialog box where you can choose one or more fields to use for the index. The Index Columns dialog box only displays fields that you can index. As you add fields to the list, you'll see fewer options—you can only add a field one time to an index. Most developers also provide a new, descriptive, entry in the (`Name`) field and a `Description` field entry so that it's easier to remember the purpose for the index later.

FIGURE 11.3

Create new indexes as needed to order the data in your table.

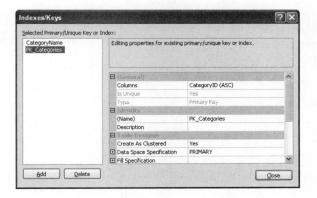

DEFINING RELATIONSHIPS

Relationships define how two or more tables interact. Many database applications provide a visual layout of these relationships with pointers showing the interactions. You can work with relationships using the Foreign Key Relationships dialog box shown in Figure 11.4. To display this dialog box, select the Table Designer ➤ Relationships command or right-click anywhere in the upper panel of the database designer and choose Relationships from the context menu.

A relationship between two tables exists when one table defines its content based on the content of another table. For example, the Products table contains a list of products, each of which belongs to a particular product category. Consequently, even a category in the Categories table can have many products listed under it. A customer may request a beverage (the category), but you can't fulfill the request until you know the specific beverage (the product).

To define a new relationship, you begin in the table that needs the data from the other table. The Products table requires a list of Categories, so you'd begin in the Products table. Open the Foreign Key Relationships dialog box by right-clicking anywhere within the table definition and choosing Relationships from the context menu. Click Add. The IDE automatically creates a new entry for you that has FK (for foreign key) and the name Products twice, `FK_Products_Products`. The first name always reflects the table that needs the information, while the second reflects the table that has the information, so, normally, you'd change the name of the new relationship to `FK_Products_Categories`, but this entry already exists. Leave the name as is for now.

Define the relationship by clicking the ellipsis (...) in the Tables and Columns Specification field. You'll see the Tables and Columns dialog box shown in Figure 11.5. This dialog box already has the relationship defined. Notice that the Categories table appears in the left pane and that it has the `CategoryID` field selected. Likewise, the Products table appears in the right pane with the `CategoryID` field selected. Generally, developers create tables with matching field names where relationships exist to avoid confusion and to make the relationships clearer. Notice that the IDE automatically renamed the relationship to reflect the naming convention—it added the 1 to the end of the name because this is the second occurrence of that relationship. Click OK to close the Tables and Columns dialog box.

Deleting a relationship is easy, but the effects can be devastating when your database relies on the relationship. Consequently, you don't want to delete the relationship without thinking about it for a long time first. To remove the relationship you just created, highlight the `FK_Products_Categories1` entry in the Foreign Key Relationships dialog box and click Delete. Click Close to close the Foreign Key Relationships dialog box.

FIGURE 11.4
Define relationships between tables as needed.

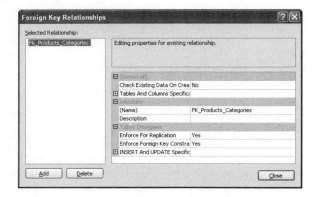

FIGURE 11.5
Always begin defining a relationship in the table that needs information.

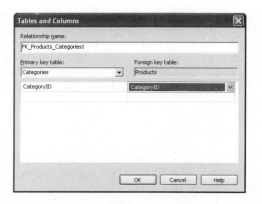

MAKING QUERIES

Queries are the basis for obtaining information from the database, so it's important to know how to work with them. Fortunately, you can experiment as much as you want with Visual Studio by creating queries with Server Explorer. To try a simple query, right-click the Categories table and choose New Query from the context menu. You'll see an Add Table dialog box, as shown in Figure 11.6. The title of this dialog box is a little misleading because you can also choose views (a type of stored query), functions (a programmatic method for obtaining data), and synonyms (an abstraction for a specific database object with special security or other settings) as a source of data.

FIGURE 11.6
Add tables, views, and functions to your queries as data sources.

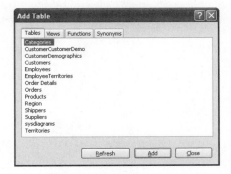

Let's say that you want to determine the number of products that each customer has purchased. You would need to use the Customers, Orders, and OrderDetails tables. You can Ctrl+Click on each table and then click Add to add them to the query. After you add the tables, click Close to close the Add Table dialog box. At this point, you can see the Query Designer window, which contains four panes. These four panes include (from top to bottom):

Diagram   Shows a graphical representation of the tables and their relationships. This display also includes special symbols to represent special table conditions and features.

Criteria   Describes how you want to use the various database elements. For example, you can set the sort order or define special methods of working with the data.

SQL   Contains the SQL that results from the tables, their relationships, and the criteria you select.

Results   Displays the output of any SQL statements you create and execute.

Once you add the data sources, select the information you need. You'll want to know the company name, so check the CompanyName field in the Customers table. Notice that CompanyName appears in the Criteria pane of the Query Designer display. You'll want to sort the output by the CompanyName field, so select Ascending in the Sort Type column of the Criteria pane. Notice that making this selection also adds a 1 to the Sort Order column and a special icon to the CompanyName field entry in the Diagram pane.

None of the tables provides a count of the products that the company has purchased. However, by typing **COUNT(ProductID)** in the next empty row in the Criteria pane, you can tell the query to count the number of products for you. Notice that Query Designer automatically adds a new Group By column to the Criteria pane and displays the word Count in it for the ProductID field. In addition, notice that Query Designer adds special symbols to the Diagram pane to show the new query criteria. Likewise, the CompanyName field now includes the word Group By in its Group By column entry and it also has a special symbol added to the Diagram view. Because counting the ProductID entries for each customer isn't the same as using the field directly, you must supply an alias—essentially a name—for the counted value. Type **[# of Products]** in the Alias column for the ProductID row in the Criteria pane.

Click Execute SQL (the exclamation mark on the toolbar) and you'll see a Query Designer display like the one shown in Figure 11.7. This view will also display any relations between multiple tables. The point is that this is where you choose the data you want to see and how you want to see it. (The figure shows the query selections and output in this case—your initial view will contain less information.) The Query Designer in Visual Studio works very much like the one in the SQL Server Management Studio (SSMS), which the "Designing Queries" section of Chapter 10 describes.

FIGURE 11.7
The IDE shows the tables, views, and functions you've selected, along with any relations between them.

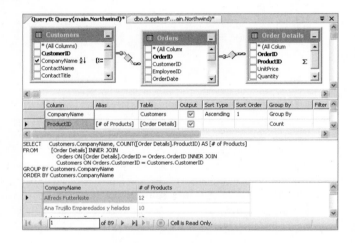

Creating Database Diagrams

Visual Studio doesn't include many of the potent entity relationship (ER) diagramming features of third party products. Consequently, large companies usually invest in high-end third party products for designing databases and applications alike. However, you don't want to ignore the features that Visual Studio provides either because they do work in many situations and you'll want to use them wherever possible to reduce your workload. Other chapters will describe some of these features, but every developer should know about the database diagrams that you can create using either Visual Studio or SSMS.

Unfortunately, the Northwind database doesn't include any diagrams, so you'll need to create one of your own. Right-click the Database Diagrams folder and choose Add New Diagram from the context menu. You'll see the Add Table dialog box shown in Figure 11.6. Unlike queries, you can only add tables to a diagram. That's because a diagram shows the relationship between tables, not the derivations of tables, such as views. In this case, choose the Suppliers, Products, and Categories tables so you can see the relationships between them. Figure 11.8 shows the output in Visual Studio—the output in SSMS is about the same.

FIGURE 11.8
Create database diagrams to show relationships between the tables in your applications.

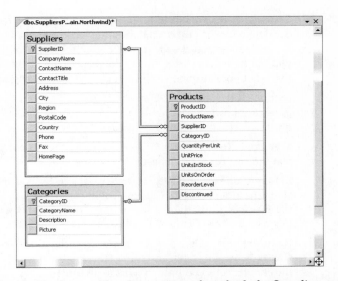

In this case, you can see that the Products table relies on input from both the Suppliers and Categories tables. The diagram shows the related fields graphically so there's no confusion about the source of information for a particular entry. What you can't see is that the diagram also allows you to work with the tables in various ways. Select the relationship lines and you can modify an existing relationship. It's also possible to create new indexes and to change the individual field definitions as required. All of this information appears in the Properties window where you can view and change it as needed. In short, using diagrams makes it considerably easier for you to work with complex database setups in your applications.

Using the Table Designer Toolbar

The Table Designer toolbar automatically appears whenever you open a table definition. This toolbar contains features that help you work with tables with greater ease. Figure 11.9 shows how this toolbar appears. The following list describes the toolbar features.

FIGURE 11.9
Use the Table Designer Toolbar to create and manage tables for your application.

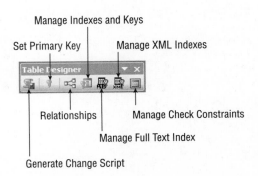

Manage Check Constraints   Displays the Check Constraints dialog box where you can add a constraint for the current database. A constraint ensures the DBMS enforces whatever database integrity rules you choose in addition to those that SQL Server normally enforces. For example, you might decide that a contact database ensures that a user have at least one, but no more than five, telephone numbers. You can also check for range errors and other kinds of integrity rules.

Manage XML Indexes   Displays the XML Indexes dialog box, which contains a list of the XML indexes for the selected table. See the "Creating an XML Index" section of the chapter for additional information about XML indexes.

Manage Full Text Index   Displays the Full text Index dialog box, which contains a list of the full text indexes for the database. You must create a full text catalog to use a full text index.

Manage Indexes and Keys   Displays the Indexes/Keys dialog box, which contains a list of the standard indexes for the database, along with any primary key definitions. See the "Working with Indexes" section of the chapter for details on working with standard indexes. You create a primary key using the Set Primary Key button on this toolbar.

Relationships   Displays the Foreign Key Relationships dialog box, which describes the relationship between this table and other tables in the database. The "Defining Relationships" section of the chapter tells you how to work with foreign keys.

Set Primary Key   Sets the primary key for the table. A primary key consists of the fields required to create a unique table entry.

Generate Change Script   Displays the Save Change Script dialog box shown in Figure 11.10. This dialog box contains all of the changes you propose making to the table. You can use a change script to move a change from one system to another. For example, you can move a change from your development machine to a production server. Change scripts are also a good way to document changes you make to the table schema.

FIGURE 11.10
Use change scripts to document changes you make to the database and move them to other systems.

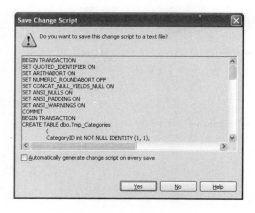

Using the Data Design Toolbar

This toolbar appears when you work with data sources or when you create a Data Component. Figure 11.11 shows how this toolbar appears. The following list describes the features it provides.

Preview Data   Displays the Data Preview Dialog box. This is the only control available for both data sources and data components. Figure 11.12 shows a typical preview. The Select an Object to Preview field contains the data object that you want to view. You'll see a hierarchical list of available objects, in most cases, with the leaf node as the selectable object. Click Preview and you'll see the data provided by a data object such as a query. The purpose of this option is to let you see the results of configuration changes you make before you begin using the object within your code.

Add New Data Source   Displays the Data Source Configuration Wizard. You use this wizard to create a connection to a data source on your system.

Generate Dataset   Creates a dataset based on a data source. Generally, the IDE automatically creates a `DataSet` control for you, so you won't need to use this option.

FIGURE 11.11
The Data Design toolbar provides quick access to indexes, keys, and change scripts.

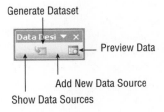

Generate Dataset

Preview Data

Add New Data Source

Show Data Sources

FIGURE 11.12
Preview the data objects you create to ensure they work as anticipated.

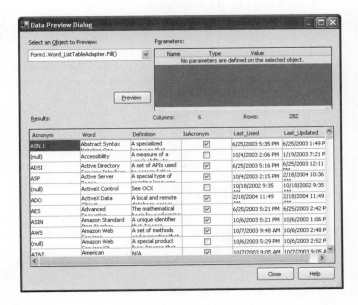

Show Data Sources   Displays the Data Sources window. This window contains a list of every data source you create. You can use it to add data to your application—either individual fields or entire tables. The window includes a special feature that lets you choose the kind of control it creates. For example, an individual date field could rely on any of these controls: `DateTimePicker`, `TextBox`, `Label`, `ComboBox`, `LinkLabel`, or `ListBox`. Figure 11.13 shows a typical view of a Data Sources window with the control selection list shown. Notice that you can choose the None option when you don't want the field to appear in the output, even when you select the table.

FIGURE 11.13
The Data Sources window helps you choose data items for your application.

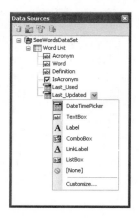

Using the Query Designer Toolbar

The Query Designer toolbar becomes active whenever you create a database query. However, the IDE doesn't always display this toolbar automatically, so you may need to activate it by right-clicking the toolbar and choosing Query Designer from the context menu. The Query Designer toolbar appears, in some cases, such as when you work with the Query Designer window shown in Figure 11.7. Figure 11.14 shows the Query Designer toolbar. The following list describes the features it provides.

Add New Derived Table   Creates a table that it derived from the other resources in the query. You use derived tables to speed queries by reducing the time required to gather information from multiple sources.

Add Table   Displays the Add Table dialog box shown in Figure 11.6. Once you select a table for the query, click Add and the IDE will add it to the Diagram pane where you can choose the fields you want to use.

FIGURE 11.14
Open and close panes, choose a query type, and perform other query tasks with this toolbar.

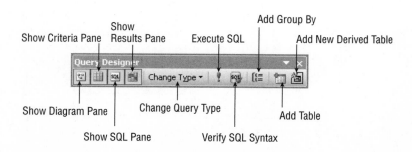

Add Group By Defines grouping criteria for a result set. Essentially, this means that the system will interpret the tables, rather than present the information directly on screen. The "Creating a Group" section of the chapter provides additional information about this particular feature.

Verify SQL Syntax Analyzes the SQL statement created by the various Diagram pane and Criteria pane selections. When the SQL statement is correct, you see a success message stating that the input will work as written. Likewise, when there's an error, the dialog box contains error information. It's a good idea to verify the SQL syntax before you try to execute it so you can receive the results faster (completely incorrect syntax won't execute anyway and partially incorrect syntax may yield erroneous results).

Execute SQL Executes the SQL statement and places the output in the Results pane. The Results pane contains a table that relies on a grid view.

Change Query Type Modifies the query type, which changes the output received from the query. For example, the output could appear as an addition to an existing table, rather than part of the Results pane. See the "Modifying the Query Output Type" section of the chapter for additional information on this feature.

Show Results Pane Displays the Results pane on screen when selected. The Results pane receives the output from a query in most cases. Keeping the Results pane hidden until you finish designing the query can save screen real estate for query design needs.

Show SQL Pane Displays the SQL pane on screen when selected. The SQL pane displays the results of selections you make in the Diagram and Criteria panes. You can also manually add SQL information (although this act isn't recommended because the IDE tends to remove any changes you make by hand).

Show Criteria Pane Displays the Criteria pane on screen when selected. The Criteria pane helps you modify the way in which the IDE reacts to database fields you choose from the list of available fields. For example, you can create field groupings, modify the sort order, and create field evaluations rather than use the actual field data. The order of the fields in the Criteria pane also affects the order of the fields in the Results pane (or other output you choose).

Show Diagram Pane Displays the Diagram pane on screen when selected. The Diagram pane contains a graphic representation of the tables you choose and the relationships between them. Use this pane to choose the fields you want to appear in the output.

Two of the Query Designer toolbar buttons perform special tasks. The following sections describe these two tasks.

MODIFYING THE QUERY OUTPUT TYPE

The Visual Studio IDE always assumes that you can create a selection query—one that selects values from one or more tables and displays the result in the Result pane. Ultimately, you can place the results anywhere, but the Result pane is the output when working in the Query Designer window. However, you have quite a few other query options, as shown in Figure 11.15. All you need to do is choose the new output type. The following list describes each of the query types.

Select Creates a standard output set using the Results pane. This is the default query option.

Insert Results Places the results in an existing table. When you choose this option, the IDE displays the Choose Target Table for Insert Results dialog box, which contains a complete list of tables for the current database. The table you choose receives the results of the query when you click Execute SQL. Since the changes this option creates are permanent and could damage entries in an existing table, you'll want to use this option with care.

Insert Values   Places the values you supply into an existing table. When you choose this option, the IDE displays the Choose Target Table for Insert Values dialog box, which contains a list of the open tables. You can't save the results into other tables that the database might contain. After you select this option, the IDE automatically closes every other open table. Type the values you want to insert in the SQL pane as part of the VALUES argument or within the New Value column of the Criteria pane. Click Execute SQL to add the new values to the selected table.

Update   Defines an update query where the SET argument contains a list of values to insert into a table. Unlike an insert values query, an update query can affect the content of existing records when you provide filter criterion. Or you could provide a filter that tells the IDE to change a value for every record that contains a CategoryID value of 1.

Delete   Defines a delete query where the IDE removes records from the selected table as defined by the WHERE argument. Because this query permanently removes data from a table, you should use it with care.

Make Table   Creates a new table in the database to hold the results of a query. The IDE displays the Make Table dialog box where you enter the name of the new table. The table appears within the database after you click Execute SQL. It has all of the same features as any other table, so you can modify it as needed to meet specific needs.

FIGURE 11.15
You have access to a number of query types using the Query Designer toolbar.

CREATING A GROUP

Groups help you derive new information from the existing data by grouping data together and by analyzing it. For example, you can group data by one field and then count how many times that field occurs in another table. The kinds of analysis you can perform depends on the data types of the data fields you choose. You don't have to limit yourself to numeric fields—you can perform analysis on text fields too. For example, it's possible to create statistical information, such as the average length of a customer remark on a survey, based on the survey entries in the database.

To see how this feature works, create a new query that includes the Products and Categories tables. Select the CategoryID and CategoryName fields of the Categories table and the CategoryID field of the Products table. Click Add Group By on the Query Designer toolbar. You'll see a new Group By column added to the Criteria pane. Change the CategoryID entry for the Products table from Group By to Count. Notice that the Diagram pane now shows a summation symbol for the CategoryID field and that the field is no long checked. Change the Alias column entry for the CategoryID field to [Number Of Products] and click Execute SQL. Your display should look like the one shown in Figure 11.16.

FIGURE 11.16

Grouping information can help you learn more about the information the database provides.

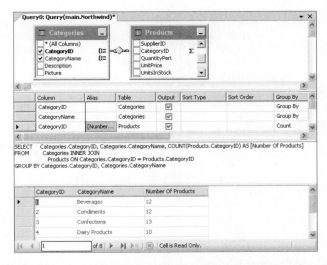

The point of this exercise is that you've created new information from the existing data. You now know how many products appear in each category. For example, the Beverages category has 12 items in it. You could output this data to another table and use it as an input to an application that tells the user how many of each kind of item to expect. Normally, this kind of data would require analysis every time you needed to do it, but now how you have a special table set aside for the purpose and a query to recreate the totals as needed, rather than every time you want to display them.

Creating a Blank Database

It's possible to use a number of techniques for storing data on a Web site and you certainly aren't limited to using SQL Server. For example, you've already discovered how to use XML databases in the "Creating a Help Request Form" section of Chapter 7 and you use an XML database for holding advertisements for a Web site. However, some applications require the robust functionality of SQL Server. The shopping cart example in Chapter 16 is an example of such a requirement. This section doesn't focus on a particular application requirement, but instead focuses on technique. The ABC Incorporated Web site requires a beneficial suggestion Web page and this section shows how to build a database to hold all of the required information.

Adding the Database

To add a new database to your project, right-click the \App_Data folder in Solution Explorer and choose Add New Item from the context menu. You'll see a modified version of the Add New Item dialog box, as shown in Figure 11.17. This is an example of how the IDE modifies the dialog boxes to make it easier to find what you need. Only the items that you can add to the \App_Data folder appear in this dialog box, even though it would normally contain a number of items that you use for general coding purposes. Select the SQL Database entry and use Suggestions.MDF as the filename. Click Add to add the database to your project. You may have to wait several seconds for the addition to complete.

WARNING Don't delete the database from your hard drive because SQL Server and Visual Studio will continue to look for it. Delete the database connection from Visual Studio first, use the SQLCmd utility (see the "Using the SQLCmd Utility" section of Chapter 10 for details) or SSMS to drop the table from the master table in SQL Server, and finally remove the database from your project using Solution Explorer.

All that you have, at this point, is a blank database. It doesn't contain anything—no tables, views, stored procedures—nothing of any consequence at all. You can use Server Explorer to create the database. However, before you can do anything, you need a connection to the database. In this case, adding the connection is simple—double-click the database entry in Solution Explorer and the IDE will create a connection to it for you in Server Explorer.

It's at this point that you could run into problems. The database in question doesn't actually exist in SQL Server. Check for yourself by opening SSMS and looking for the database in the list—you won't find it because it isn't added to SQL Server. The database only exists as a file in your project and it's only accessible from your project now. You can certainly add the database to SQL Server later, but you don't have to do so at any time. However, because the database isn't part of SQL Server, you might see the error message shown in Figure 11.18. This error message tells you that you don't have SQL Server Express installed on your machine. Visual Studio relies on SQL Server Express to interact with these special SQL Server files in your project. To work with a database, as shown in this section, you must have SQL Server Express installed on your system. To continue using the database in this manner in a production environment, the server must have SQL Server Express installed as well.

FIGURE 11.17
The Add New Item dialog box modifies its content to work with the kind of folder you select.

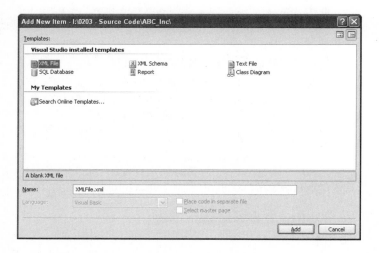

FIGURE 11.18
Watch out for error messages that result when you don't have SQL Server Express installed.

Designing the Tables

The example database includes several tables. Each of these tables will serve a different purpose as the chapter progresses and help you understand a particular database concept as it applies to SQL Server. To create a new table, right-click the Tables folder for Suggestions in Server Explorer and choose Add New Table from the context menu. The example uses the tables listed below. Tables 11.1 through 11.4 define the structure of the tables. You can find the Suggestions database in the `\ABC_Inc\App_Data` folder of the source code provided on the Sybex Web site.

Categories Defines a list of categories in which to place the various suggestions (see Table 11.1). Using a standard list of categories makes it possible to search for specific kinds of suggestions as needed.

TIP Microsoft Plans to phase the NText data type out. They recommend using the NVarChar(Max) data type instead.

UserData Provides a list of users (see Table 11.2). It's important to associate every beneficial suggestion with a particular person so that the company can request additional input later as needed. The application could also use this database as a means of verifying the identity of users making beneficial suggestions for security purposes.

Departments Defines a list of departments for the company (see Table 11.3). Special department names include None for outside users and Reviewer for reviewers of company products. The purpose of this table is to associate the user with a particular area of the company.

Suggestions Contains the beneficial suggestions (see Table 11.4). Each beneficial suggestion is associated with both a user and a category. You can display the suggestions in various ways, so it's important to create stored procedures and views for working with the data. Fortunately, you'll find the information you need to implement both stored procedures and views in other sections of the chapter.

TABLE 11.1:   Categories Table Structure

FIELD NAME	TYPE	LENGTH	ALLOW NULLS	NOTES
CategoryID	Int	N/A	No	IsIdentity is set to Yes, with a seed value of 1 and an increment of 1. This is the key field.
CategoryName	NVarChar	25	No	
Description	NVarChar	MAX	Yes	

TABLE 11.2:   UserData Table Structure

FIELD NAME	TYPE	LENGTH	ALLOW NULLS	NOTES
UserID	Int	N/A	No	IsIdentity is set to Yes, with a seed value of 1 and an increment of 1. This is the key field.
UserName	NVarChar	25	No	

TABLE 11.2: UserData Table Structure *(CONTINUED)*

FIELD NAME	TYPE	LENGTH	ALLOW NULLS	NOTES
DepartmentID	Int	N/A	No	Has a default value of 1, which equates to accounting. This field is a foreign key.
Email	NVarChar	25	Yes	
Telephone	NVarChar	10	Yes	
Approved	Bit	N/A	No	Has a default value of 'FALSE', which equates to 0 for a bit field.

TABLE 11.3: Departments Table Structure

FIELD NAME	TYPE	LENGTH	ALLOW NULLS	NOTES
DepartmentID	Int	N/A	No	IsIdentity is set to Yes, with a seed value of 1 and an increment of 1. This is the key field.
Name	NVarChar	25	No	
Manager	NVarChar	25	No	

TABLE 11.4: Suggestions Table Structure

FIELD NAME	TYPE	LENGTH	ALLOW NULLS	NOTES
SuggestionID	Int	N/A	No	IsIdentity is set to Yes, with a seed value of 1 and an increment of 1. This is the key field.
CategoryID	Int	N/A	No	This field is a foreign key.
UserID	Int	N/A	No	This field is a foreign key.
Title	NVarChar	50	No	
Description	NVarChar	MAX	No	

Assigning the Relationships

When you finish creating the tables, you'll also need to create the relationships between them. Click Relationships on the Table Designer toolbar to accomplish this task. The "Defining Relationships" section of the chapter provides additional details on how you create relationships between tables. Figure 11.19 shows the structure and relationships of the tables for this example.

FIGURE 11.19
A database diagram can be incredibly helpful in presenting the relation-ships between tables.

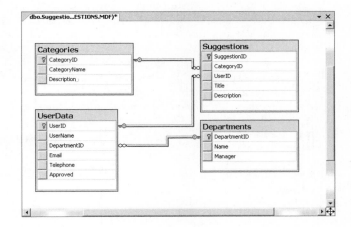

Creating and Accessing Stored Procedures

Stored procedures provide an application-like functionality to SQL Server. You write these functions as separate entities and then call on them as needed to perform tasks at the database. The advantage of using stored procedures is that you don't have to move the data across a network—it stays right at the server, which means you gain a performance advantage in processing large amounts of data. SQL Server also compiles stored procedures, so they don't incur the performance loss of interpreted SQL statements that you send to the server using other techniques. However, the performance gain for the client comes at the cost of server processing cycles. The server performs the analysis and sends just the result to the client. Consequently, you have to consider where to spend processing cycles. In many cases, stored procedures are the best option when you work with large datasets because the network performance penalty is enormous.

TIP   Many developers use stored procedures to help keep data secret. A stored procedure processes the data on the server, away from prying eyes. In addition, stored procedures help you control data access and the tasks the client can perform. The client sees only the information that you want seen, so the chances of a security breach are less. Breaches can still occur, but using the stored procedure provides one less avenue that a cracker can use for gaining access.

Working with Stored Procedures

Both the Northwind and Pubs sample databases come with a number of stored procedures you can try—they're all fully functional. You'll find the stored procedures in the Stored Procedures folder of Server Explorer, as shown in Figure 11.20. Each stored procedure appears as a separate entry in the folder. Within each stored procedure, you can find external variables that you must supply as input to the stored procedure—the input variables appear with an at (@) sign in front of them.

Seeing how these stored procedures work is relatively easy. Right-click the stored procedure entry and select Execute from the context menu to start it. Try starting the CustOrderHist stored procedure. Because this stored procedure includes an input variable, you'll see the Run Stored Procedure dialog box shown in Figure 11.21. This dialog box contains a list of all of the variables the stored procedure supports. You must provide values for any of the input variables in the list. Some stored procedure variables have a default value, but that's not the case for the CustOrderHist stored procedure. Type **ALFKI** in the Value column and click OK. The stored procedure executes, but doesn't really show you much.

To work with a stored procedure in a way that produces a result, you manually create a page that includes a data source and a grid or other means of viewing the output. Interestingly enough, you can create a perfectly acceptable view without writing any code in many cases. You'll find this example in the `\Chapter 11\StoredProcedure` folder of the source code on the Sybex Web site.

FIGURE 11.20
Server Explorer contains a complete list of stored procedures for the selected database.

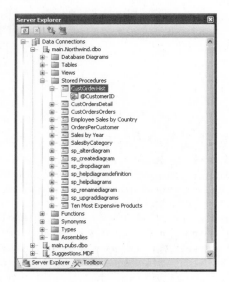

FIGURE 11.21
Whenever you execute a stored procedure, you must provide any required input values.

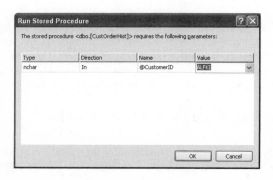

The first task is to create a data source using a `SqlDataSource` control. You could use other controls, but this one provides the best performance the SQL Server-specific features. Click Configure Data Source on the `SqlDataSource` SmartTag and you'll see the Configure Data Source wizard. Begin the process by selecting a data connection and clicking Next. This page also lets you create a new data connection, should you need one. The first page of interest appears in Figure 11.22. The default settings use a specific table for the input, but you can select stored procedures as an option, as shown in the figure.

Changing from the default setting takes you along a different path than configuring a standard data source. Click Next and you'll see the Define Custom Statements or Stored Procedures dialog box. Depending on your system, you might have to wait a minute or two to see the dialog box, but it will show up. The IDE has to query SQL Server about all of the stored procedures for the target database, so it may require a little time to complete the task. Choose the Stored Procedure option and select CustOrderHist from the list. Click Next and you'll see the Define Parameters dialog box shown in Figure 11.23. This figure shows the dialog box with the entries added.

When you click Show Advanced Properties, the IDE changes the display to show all of the information about input, which includes its data type and name. Notice that you could also provide a parameter source as input—the IDE configures the data source in a way that lets you pass the information at runtime, rather than design time.

Once you complete the parameter step, click Next and you'll see a Test Query dialog box. Click Test Query and you'll see a Parameter Values Editor where you can provide a specific input, or simply accept the test value you provided. Click OK and you'll see sample output. If the query completes as expected, click Finish—the data source is ready to use.

Now you have to decide on a means to display the data source. The `GridView` control provides the easiest and most reliable configuration. However, you can use any control that you want. All you really need to do is select the data source you created in the Choose Data Source field of the associated control's SmartTag. When using a `GridView` control, it's usually a good idea to select the Enable Paging and Enable Sorting options so you can see the data in other ways. Figure 11.24 shows the results of using a stored procedure to display information from the database.

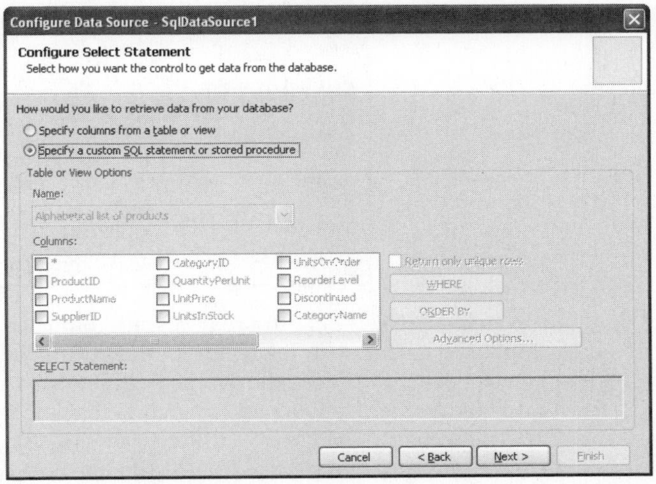

FIGURE 11.22

Choose a stored procedure as your data source, rather than a specific table.

FIGURE 11.23
Provide any required data entries for the stored procedure you choose.

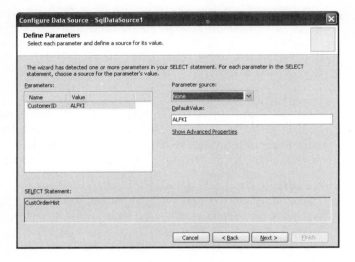

FIGURE 11.24
You don't have to write code to create simple displays with stored procedures in Visual Studio.

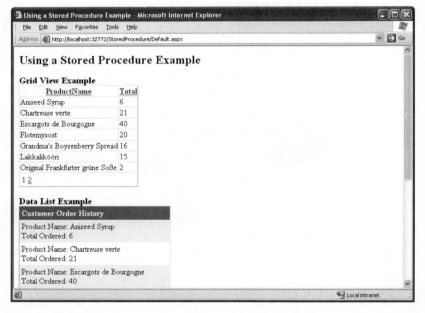

Not even the DataList control requires any coding on your part. Figure 11.24 shows this control as a comparison to the GridView control. Configuring the DataList control is a little more time consuming. You begin by defining the data source as normal. However, at this point, nothing displays on the control because you haven't told it what to display. To create the display, click Edit Templates. The SmartTag actually changes to a different mode—one designed for editing the templates.

Begin the configuration process by selecting the ItemTemplate option in the Display field. This is a general item template, but you can configure the various template elements individually as well.

For example, if you want alternating items to look different from a general item, select the Alternating ItemTemplate option. The area beneath the DataList control will change, at this point, and you can add both text and controls to the area.

Controls can have a connection to the database. You have to use the SmartTags when creating a data binding because the data binding options don't appear in the Properties window. Select Edit DataBindings from the control's SmartTag and you'll see a display similar to the one shown in Figure 11.25. (If you can't select the Field Binding option as shown, click Refresh Schema to re-create the connection with the database.) The display shows the three most common control properties to bind to a field in the database, but you can use any field that makes sense by checking Show All Properties. Once you associate a particular property with a data field, click OK and the IDE makes the appropriate changes automatically.

Template editing doesn't end with the data you want to present. You can also control headers, footers, and separators. The DataList control is extremely flexible, so you can change it any way you want. After you configure the items, header, footer, and separators as needed, click End Template Editing on the DataList control SmartTag. As soon as you end template editing, you'll notice that the appearance of the control changes to show the modifications you made.

Now comes the fun part. Select the Auto Format option on the DataList control SmartTag. You'll see an Auto Format dialog box where you can choose a theme for the control. The left pane shows the theme options, while the right shows how the theme will appear with the template options you chose. That's why it's important to create the templates first—you want to see how the theme looks with your actual design. Once you select a theme, click OK and the DataList control will reflect the new formatting. Even though using the DataList control is a lot more work to configure, it's better than writing the code to create the same display manually. The point is that you need to try the various viewing controls to discover which one saves you the most time and provides the best presentation of your data.

FIGURE 11.25
Use the DataBindings dialog box to change the connection between a control and a database.

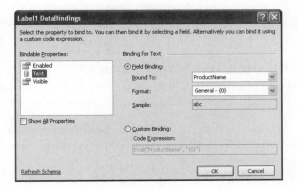

Modifying Stored Procedures

At some point, you'll want to modify the stored procedures that you create. You might need to change how they work, fix a bug in the routine, or simply see how you performed a task in the past. Whatever the reason, Visual Studio provides an editor for your stored procedures, so you don't need to leave the IDE to make changes. To begin the editing process, right-click the stored procedure that you want to modify and choose Open from the context menu. You'll see the editor shown in Figure 11.26 open with the stored procedure loaded.

FIGURE 11.26
Modify stored procedures using the local editor to avoid leaving the IDE.

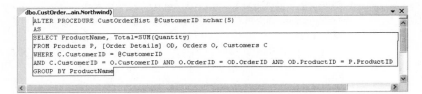

```
dbo.CustOrder...ain.Northwind)                                              ▼ × 
ALTER PROCEDURE CustOrderHist @CustomerID nchar(5)
AS
SELECT ProductName, Total=SUM(Quantity)
FROM Products P, [Order Details] OD, Orders O, Customers C
WHERE C.CustomerID = @CustomerID
AND C.CustomerID = O.CustomerID AND O.OrderID = OD.OrderID AND OD.ProductID = P.ProductID
GROUP BY ProductName
```

The display might look a bit odd at first, but think about what you're doing for a second and it makes perfect sense. This display is actually a SQL statement that asks the DBMS to alter the stored procedure named CustOrderHist that includes a single input named @CustomerID, which is a variable of type nchar with a length of 5. The code for the stored procedure appears in the box below the ALTER PROCEDURE SQL statement.

As shown in Figure 11.26, a stored procedure actually consists of T-SQL statements, just as you would create for a view or a query. Stored procedures don't include standard programming statements such as loops. You use stored procedures to encapsulate a series of T-SQL statements and provide a convenient means of providing input to them. Consequently, even though a stored procedure is more flexible and program-like than a query, it still isn't what most developers would consider a functional programming language. A stored procedure focuses on telling the DBMS what you want to do, rather than how to do it.

NOTE   SQL Server actually relies on a language called Transact-SQL (T-SQL) to perform tasks. This language is fully compatible with American National Standards Institute (ANSI) and International Standards Organization (ISO) SQL, but includes extensions that make the language more flexible. T-SQL can help you perform many programming tasks in addition to manipulating data using standard SQL statements.

After you edit the stored procedure, you save it just as you would any other file. In the background, the IDE sends the SQL request to the DBMS and asks it to make the change to the stored procedure. However, as far as you're concerned, you've simply saved a file.

Creating New Stored Procedures

Now that you have a better idea of how stored procedures work, it's time to create a stored procedure for the Suggestions database you designed in the "Creating a Blank Database" section of the chapter. The Visual Studio IDE lets you create new stored procedures using the same editor that you used to modify a stored procedure in the "Modifying Stored Procedures" section of the chapter. You need to consider several Web site tasks where you want to provide the user with a specific level of access, but not full access, to the database. The Suggestions database contains the following stored procedures.

AddSuggestion   Lets a user add a new beneficial suggestion to the database. You'll normally make this stored procedure accessible to anyone with an approved entry in the UserData table.

ShowAllSuggestions   Displays all of the current beneficial suggestions to an administrator. Only approved users will gain access to this stored procedure.

ShowSuggestionByUser   Displays all of the current beneficial suggestions for a particular user. Anyone with an approved entry in the UserData table can access this stored procedure to see their list of suggestions.

ShowSuggestionByCategory   Displays all of the current beneficial suggestions for a particular category to support staff. Only administrators and approved department staff can use this stored procedure.

RemoveSuggestion   Let's say an administrator or approved department staff removed a suggestion after someone has acted on it. Theoretically, you could replace this method of handling beneficial suggestions with one that marks the suggestion with approved or denied, but the database would eventually accumulate a number of inactive suggestions. Removing suggestions after contacting the user who makes it is a better idea.

AddUser   Lets a user request access to the beneficial suggestion system. Even though the user can add an entry, the stored procedure doesn't provide access to the Approved field. Consequently, a user won't gain access to the system until an administrator approves access by setting the Approved field to 'TRUE' (a value of 1).

ApproveUser   Works with the GetUnapprovedUser view described in the "Creating a View" section of the chapter to let the administrator approve new users. The purpose of this stored procedure is to set the Approved field for a specific use to 'TRUE'.

NOTE   You might wonder how the application handles the Departments and Categories tables. These tables don't have complex interactions with the other tables from an input perspective. Consequently, you can add new entries to either table without problem. Viewing the entries won't cause a problem either. Deleting entries could cause problems because other tables rely on these tables for input so the application won't allow you to delete entries. The forms for working with these tables appear in the \ABC_Inc\Suggestions folder of the source code on the Sybex Web site. You create them as you would the Northwind Categories table example described in the "Relying on Code-free Data Binding" section of Chapter 10.

Now that you know about the stored procedures supplied with the example, it's time to build them. The following sections describe the three common stored procedure types: select, insert, and delete.

WORKING WITH SELECT STORED PROCEDURES

To create a new stored procedure, right-click the Stored Procedures folder for the Suggestions database and choose Add New Stored Procedure from the context menu. You'll see an editing window similar to the one shown in Figure 11.26. The IDE does provide you with hints on creating your own stored procedure, so you don't start with a blank screen. However, you'll also notice differences between the window shown in Figure 11.26 and the one you use to create a new stored procedure—the most important of which is that the stored procedure begins with CREATE PROCEDURE, rather than ALTER PROCEDURE.

This first stored procedure (ShowAllSuggestions) will display all of the beneficial suggestions, so you won't need to add any input arguments. Remove the input argument section, along with the text that appears after AS. At this point, you have a blank stored procedure that you can name dbo.ShowAllSuggestions. Rather than type the code required for this query, place the cursor on the line immediately after AS. Right-click the editor window and choose Insert SQL from the context menu. You'll see the Query Builder window first, and then the Add Table dialog box. This example relies on the Suggestions table, so you'll select it. However, the Suggestions table relies on data found in the UserData and Categories tables, so you'll need to select them as well. You'll need to choose some data from each of the tables, as shown in Figure 11.27. It's also important to add the sorting criteria shown.

After you finish creating the query, click OK. Query Builder will insert the new query directly into the stored procedure, so you won't need to type anything. Click Save and Visual Studio will save the stored procedure for you. Here's the code for the resulting stored procedure.

```
CREATE PROCEDURE dbo.ShowAllSuggestions
AS
SELECT      Suggestions.Title, Categories.CategoryName,
            Suggestions.Description, UserData.UserName, UserData.Email,
            UserData.Telephone
FROM        Categories
INNER JOIN Suggestions ON Categories.CategoryID = Suggestions.CategoryID
INNER JOIN UserData ON Suggestions.UserID = UserData.UserID
ORDER BY    Categories.CategoryName, UserData.UserName,
            Suggestions.Title
RETURN
```

The ShowAllSuggestions stored procedure works well enough, but it doesn't let you limit the output. The ShowSuggestionByUser and ShowSuggestionByCategory stored procedures are two examples of how you can limit the output by providing SQL Server with additional information. The process for creating these two stored procedures is the same as the process for creating ShowAllSuggestions, with one small change. Instead of setting the filter criteria as described for ShowAllSuggestions, you set the Filter field for the user or category that you want to see. For example, here's the query for the ShowSuggestionByUser stored procedure.

```
CREATE PROCEDURE dbo.ShowSuggestionByUser
    (
        @Name nvarchar(25)
    )
AS
SELECT      Suggestions.Title, Categories.CategoryName,
            Suggestions.Description, UserData.Email, UserData.Telephone
FROM        Categories
INNER JOIN Suggestions ON Categories.CategoryID = Suggestions.CategoryID
INNER JOIN UserData ON Suggestions.UserID = UserData.UserID
WHERE       (UserData.UserName = @Name)
ORDER BY    Categories.CategoryName, UserData.UserName,
            Suggestions.Title
RETURN
```

When someone calls this stored procedure, they supply a name value for the @Name argument, which is of type nvarchar, the same as the UserName field. The number in parenthesis tells the stored procedure to limit the input length of @Name to 25 characters. Notice that the stored procedure doesn't return the username in the results because the caller would need to know this information to make the request. Reducing the number of fields that you return in a result will improve application performance, so look for reductions like this whenever possible. The ShowSuggestionByCategory stored procedure works precisely the same way, except that you set the CategoryName field filter to match the name of the category that the user wants to see.

FIGURE 11.27

Create the query for your stored procedure using Query Builder whenever possible to avoid errors.

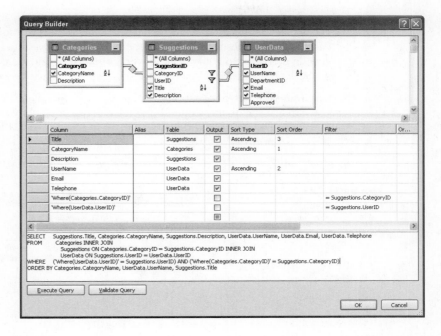

CREATING A WEB PAGE BASED ON A STORED PROCEDURE

Now that you have several shiny new stored procedures, you'll want to test them. The example in this section provides access to the ShowAllSuggestions, ShowSuggestionByCategory, and ShowSuggestion ByUser stored procedures. Except for a few small differences in configuration, all three stored procedures work essentially the same. You'll find this example in the \ABC_Inc\Suggestions folder of the source code on the Sybex Web site.

Using a stored procedure requires a little more work than working with a table directly. You begin by placing a SqlDataSource control on the form. The following steps lead you through the configuration process.

1. Select Configure Data Source from the control's SmartTag and you'll see the Configure Data Source wizard shown in Figure 11.28. Given that you've probably worked with the Suggestions database in several ways, you should already have a connection string setup for your project—the IDE creates it for you automatically. However, if you don't see a connection string for the Suggestions database, click New Connection and you'll see the Add Connection dialog box. Simply create a new connection using the technique described in the "Creating a Database Connection" section of Chapter 10.

2. Choose the database connection string and click Next. The wizard will ask you to configure the select statement. The default selection relies on a view or table in the selected database, but you need to use a stored procedure.

3. Select the Specify a Custom SQL Statement or Stored Procedure option, then click Next. The wizard will ask you to define a custom statement or select a stored procedure. You must select

the stored procedure option, as shown in Figure 11.29 and choose a stored procedure from the list. Notice that this dialog box includes one tab for every action you can perform on the database. You can choose a custom statement or stored procedure for each action if desired. However, in this case, you only need to worry about selecting data, so all you need to configure is the Select tab, as shown in the figure.

4. Configure the database actions as required and click Next. You'll see a dialog box where you can test the query. Depending on the setup you use, you might not be able to test the query—the wizard could display an error in some cases. This is generally the case with stored procedures.

5. Click Finish. The IDE creates the required connection for you.

FIGURE 11.28
Create a connection to the database or use an existing connection when one exists.

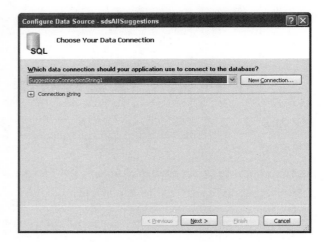

FIGURE 11.29
Configure each of the actions you want to perform using a custom statement or stored procedure.

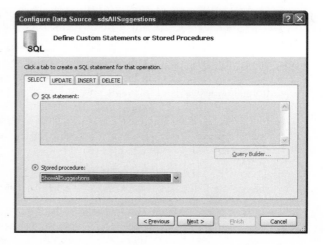

Depending on the stored procedure, you might encounter a few additional dialog boxes during the configuration process. For example, many stored procedures include input arguments and you need to define values for them, in many cases (in other cases, you assign the values programmatically—you'll discover more on this second technique as the chapter progresses). Figure 11.30 shows a typical parameters dialog box. You'll see this dialog box when configuring the ShowSuggestionBy-User stored procedure.

In this case, the stored procedure accepts a value from the Web form. One of the controls automatically provides the required value, so the data exchange takes place automatically without any coding on your part. You can also obtain values from a number of other sources including cookies, the session state, and the query string. The data source you use depends on how you configure your application.

Once you create all of the stored procedures you need, along with the required data sources, you can begin putting a form together. The example uses a `GridView` control for output. However, to make the `GridView` control work properly with multiple input sources, you need to use the `DataSource` property to hold the `SqlDataSource` control name, rather than the `DataSourceID` property, which is the only one accessible in the Properties window. Of course, using the `DataSource` property means that you have to set up the `GridView` control, gvOutput, to provide output from the outset. Add the following little piece of code to the `Page_Load()` event handler ensures you'll see data at the outset.

```
' Perform this task only the first time.
If Not Page.IsPostBack Then
   ' Set the data source.
   gvOutput.DataSource = sdsAllSuggestions
   gvOutput.DataBind()
End If
```

FIGURE 11.30
Supply values for the stored procedure input arguments as needed.

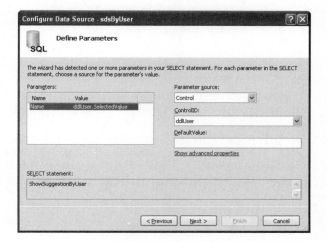

Switching between views is the responsibility of a `RadioButtonList` control, `rblViewMode`. By selecting the correct option, the user can see all of the suggestions, suggestions made by a specific user, or suggestions within a particular category. The code simply changes the output to use a different data source. Because each data source relies on a different stored procedure for input, the results reflect the requirements and output of that stored procedure. Here's the code used to select between view modes (only one selection appears in the book because all three entries use precisely the same technique).

```
Protected Sub rblViewMode_SelectedIndexChanged( _
    ByVal sender As Object, ByVal e As System.EventArgs) _
    Handles rblViewMode.SelectedIndexChanged

    ' Choose a viewing mode.
    Select Case rblViewMode.SelectedValue
        Case "All"
            ' Don't display any inputs.
            lblUser.Visible = False
            ddlUser.Visible = False
            lblCategory.Visible = False
            ddlCategory.Visible = False

            ' Choose the correct data source and update the display.
            gvOutput.DataSource = sdsAllSuggestions
            gvOutput.DataBind()
        Case "By User"
            ... Selection Statements ...
        Case "By Category"
            ... Selection Statements ...
    End Select
End Sub
```

Viewing the data by user or by category requires additional input to the stored procedure. You could ask the user to type the value, but that would lead to errors and other problems (such as crackers trying to break your security). By adding two additional data sources (for a total of five) to the application, you can supply the user with `DropDownList` controls, `ddlUser` and `ddlCategory`, which ensure that the user can only input correct values. The `sdsCategories` data source relies on the Categories table, while the `sdsUsers` data source relies on the special `GetApprovedUsers` view discussed in the "Creating a View" section of the chapter. By using this technique, you don't have to write any code to perform the actual transition. The example simply updates `gvOutput` to reflect the new selection by providing a `SelectedIndexChanged` event handler, as shown here.

```
Protected Sub ddlUser_SelectedIndexChanged( _
    ByVal sender As Object, ByVal e As System.EventArgs) _
    Handles ddlUser.SelectedIndexChanged

    ' Update the data source.
    gvOutput.DataSource = sdsByUser
    gvOutput.DataBind()
End Sub
```

The resulting application provides full access to all three stored procedures and lets you customize your view of the data. Figure 11.31 shows typical output from this application.

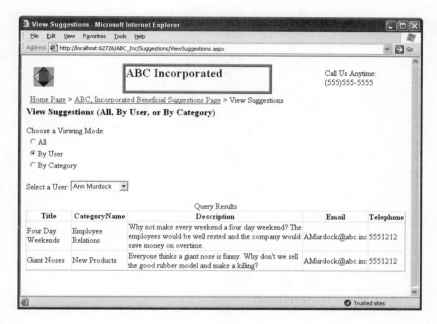

Working with Insert Stored Procedures

This section discusses the AddNewUser stored procedure because it contains all of the elements of a typical insert stored procedure. You begin building an insert stored procedure as you would any other stored procedure discussed to this point. SQL Server doesn't require any secret codes or odd programming constructs to make an insert stored procedure work. Because this stored procedure requires input to work, you'll want to define the parameters, @UserName, @DepartmentID, @Email, and @Telephone, first. Here's the code for the first part of the example.

```
CREATE PROCEDURE dbo.AddNewUser
    (
        @UserName nvarchar(25),
        @DepartmentID int = 0,
        @Email nvarchar(25),
        @Telephone nvarchar(10)
    )
AS
```

This example actually requires two queries. First, you must ensure that the user doesn't already exist in the system. Second, you must handle the input values provided by the user. The first portion of this query is a different form of the select query you have already used in other parts of the chapter. Here's the query that checks for a valid user.

```
-- Define the user checking variable.
DECLARE @UserInstance int

-- Check for the requested user and place the result in @UserInstance.
SELECT    @UserInstance = COUNT(UserName)
FROM      UserData
WHERE     (UserName = @UserName)

-- If @UserInstance is greater than 0, then the user already exists
-- and the stored procedure will raise an error.
IF @UserInstance > 0
   BEGIN
      RAISERROR('This user already exists!', 17, 1, @UserName)
      RETURN -1
   END
```

The code begins by creating a variable to hold the results of a check on the user. You can use variables as needed to make your code functional. Notice the comment preceding this code uses a double dash (--). You can also use this kind of comment for a single line. When you want to enclose multiple lines, use a starting and closing comment like this.

```
/* This is a multiple
   line comment. */
```

The SELECT statement doesn't create output for the caller in this case—it assigns the value created by counting the number of instances of UserName to @UserInstance. T-SQL supports simple IF statements that you can use to check the value @UserInstance. When this value exceeds 0, the code knows that the user already appears in the database and raises an error using the RAISERROR() function (no the lack of a second E isn't an error in the book). The arguments include a string describing the error, the severity of the error, state information (a number between 1 and 127), and a list of errant arguments. The code then returns a negative value to indicate the error. For other error handling examples, see the AddSuggestion stored procedure supplied as part of the Suggestions database.

Now you create a query to handle the input values—just as you would for a select stored procedure. However, after you select the tables you want to use (UserData in this case), you must right-click the Query Builder window and choose Change Type ➤ Insert Values from the context menu. This act changes the appearance of the Query Builder Criteria and SQL panes, as shown in Figure 11.32.

The input arguments you supply with the query use the same names as the arguments you provide as input to the stored procedure. Consequently, you make the UserName field equal to the @UserName argument. Some fields don't have entries. For example, you don't supply a value for the UserID field because SQL Server assigns this value automatically. Identity fields always supply their own value—you never assign a value to them as part of your stored procedure. The Approved field doesn't require a value because SQL Server assigns it a default value of 'FALSE' as mentioned in Table 11.2.

Now that you have an insert stored procedure to use, it's time to add it to a Web page. The "Creating a Web Page Based on a Stored Procedure" section of the chapter describes the basic process for using a stored procedure. However, you'll encounter a few minor changes to the basic SqlDataSource configuration process. The most important change is that you'll configure the settings on the Insert tab, rather than the Select tab as before. In some cases, you might actually find it easier to configure the `SqlDataSource` directly, rather than use the wizard (the wizard tends to assume that you always want to configure the data source for selection). Use these steps to use the manual configuration process.

1. Select a data connection in the `ConnectionString` property. If the connection doesn't appear in the list, select the `<New Connection>` option.

2. Choose `System.Data.SqlClient` in the `ProviderName` property.

3. Choose `StoredProcedure` in the `InsertCommandType` property. This change lets the data source know that you don't plan to use a standard SQL query to retrieve the data.

4. Click the ellipses in the `InsertQuery` property. You'll see the Command and Parameter Editor dialog box shown in Figure 11.33. You use this dialog box to configure the stored procedure and its parameters.

5. Type the name of the stored procedure you want to use.

6. Click Refresh Parameters. This act retrieves all of the parameters that you need to handle with your code. You can also create automatic connections, just as you did when using the wizard.

7. Associate each parameter that you don't want to code by hand with a control, cookie, query string value, or other data input.

8. Click OK. The data source is now ready to use.

FIGURE 11.32
An insert query uses a different Query Builder display to provide entries for the input data.

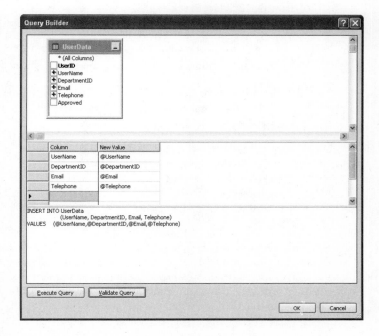

FIGURE 11.33
Enter the stored procedure information using this dialog box.

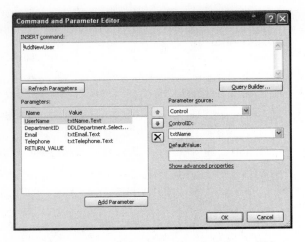

No matter how you configure the data source, inserting new records is incredibly easy once you complete the task. The example uses a simple button to perform the insertion. A user fills out the new user information and clicks the button. The `btnAdd_Click()` event handler takes care of the rest using a few simple lines of code shown here.

```
Protected Sub btnAdd_Click( _
    ByVal sender As Object, ByVal e As System.EventArgs) _
    Handles btnAdd.Click

    Try
        ' Try inserting the form information.
        txtResults.Text = SDSAddUser.Insert().ToString() + " user added."

    Catch SQLErr As System.Data.SqlClient.SqlException
        ' Display the error message when the insert fails.
        txtResults.Text = SQLErr.Message

    End Try

    ' Make the results visible.
    lblResults.Visible = True
    txtResults.Visible = True
End Sub
```

Notice that the code is wrapped in a `Try...Catch` block. Using well-defined error handling is essential if you want to display useful information to the user, rather than let the user see the usual .NET error messages. The essential bit of code is to call the `SDSAddUser.Insert()` method. That's right, you don't need anything fancy to create the new record—just insert the information on the form directly into the database when using this technique.

WORKING WITH UPDATE STORED PROCEDURES

Most of the work that users perform with a database centers on updating records in one form or another. The ApproveUser stored procedure sets the Approved field for a user record to true—at least it will when the record is valid. As with the insert stored procedure discussed in the "Working with Insert Stored Procedures" section of the chapter, you need to provide both error handling and actual update code as part of your insert stored procedure. Here's the code for the ApproveUser stored procedure.

```
ALTER PROCEDURE dbo.ApproveUser
    (
        @Name nvarchar(25),
        @Approved bit = False
    )
AS

-- Define the user checking variable.
DECLARE @UserInstance int

-- Check for the requested user and place the result in @UserInstance.
SELECT    @UserInstance = COUNT(UserName)
FROM      UserData
WHERE     (UserName = @Name)

-- If @UserInstance equals 0, then the user doesn't exist
-- and the stored procedure will raise an error.
IF @UserInstance = 0
    BEGIN
        RAISERROR('No user by this name.', 17, 1, @Name)
        RETURN -1
    END

-- Perform the approval.
UPDATE    UserData
SET       Approved = @Approved
WHERE     (UserName = @Name)
RETURN
```

As you can see, it begins by checking the username using the same approach as the AddNewUser stored procedure. However, in this case, the stored procedure checks the result against 0 to ensure the user actually exists, rather than ensuring the user doesn't exist.

Notice that the example doesn't perform any input checking on @Approved. The reason is that this parameter has a default value assigned to it. Even if the caller doesn't provide an input value, the worst that will happen is that the user will remain on the unapproved list.

Creating an update query means setting Query Builder to output the right code. Right-click anywhere in the Query Builder dialog box and choose Change Type ➢ Update from the context menu. Figure 11.34 shows a typical update query. Notice that you must set two types of entries. The first chooses the record to update, while the second provides the values to set in the record. In this case, the code selects a particular user based on the UserName field and updates the Approved field.

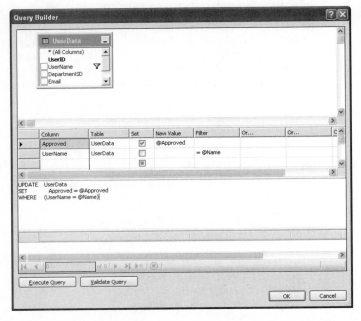

The example code that relies on this stored procedure also uses the GetUnapprovedUsers view. The code fills a `GridView` control that has the Select button enabled. When a user selects an entry and clicks Approve Selected Users, the code calls on the `btnApprove_Click()` event handler shown here.

```
Protected Sub btnApprove_Click( _
    ByVal sender As Object, ByVal e As System.EventArgs) _
    Handles btnApprove.Click

    Dim UserName As String  ' Holds the selected username.
    Dim Results As Int32     ' Number of rows updated.

    ' Determine whether the user has selected a name.
    If gvUsers.SelectedRow Is Nothing Then

        ' If not, display an error message.
        txtResults.Text = "No Row Selected"
    Else

        ' Place the user name in the @Name parameter.
        UserName = gvUsers.SelectedRow.Cells(1).Text
        SDSApprove.UpdateParameters("Name").DefaultValue = UserName

        ' Perform the update.
        Results = SDSApprove.Update()
```

```
    ' Display the results.
    txtResults.Text = Results.ToString() + " user named " + _
                      UserName + " updated."

    ' Update the grid view.
    gvUsers.DataBind()
End If


' Make the results visible.
lblResults.Visible = True
txtResults.Visible = True
End Sub
```

Notice that this example sets one of the parameters for the data source manually. The data source knows what input the ApproveUser stored procedure requires and provides named arguments that you can use. The code sets the `DefaultValue` property to reflect the name of the user that the input specifies. The code then calls the `SDSApprove.Update()` method to perform the actual update and displays the results on screen. The `gvUsers.DataBind()` call is essential. If you don't add this call, `gvUsers` will contain to display all of the users, instead of just those that haven't been approved during this session.

WORKING WITH DELETE STORED PROCEDURES

Eventually, everyone needs to remove old information from a database. Deleting an entry is almost too easy, as shown by the RemoveSuggestion stored procedure shown here.

```
CREATE PROCEDURE dbo.RemoveSuggestion
    (
        @SuggestionID int
    )
AS

DELETE FROM Suggestions
WHERE    (SuggestionID = @SuggestionID)

RETURN
```

The code accepts the one undeniably unique piece of information about suggestions in the database—the SuggestionID value. It then uses a simple query to remove a single record based on that input.

The form associated with this stored procedure borrows elements of other examples you've already seen. It uses a `GridView` control to provide a means of selecting a record similar to the one used with the ApproveUser example. Once the user selects a suggestion for deletion, clicking Delete Suggestion executes the following code.

```
Protected Sub btnSubmit_Click( _
    ByVal sender As Object, ByVal e As System.EventArgs) _
    Handles btnSubmit.Click
```

```
        Dim Results As Int32      ' Number of rows updated.

        ' Determine whether the user has selected a name.
        If gvSugs.SelectedRow Is Nothing Then

            ' If not, display an error message.
            txtResults.Text = "No Row Selected"
        Else

            ' Place the suggestion number in the @SuggestionID parameter.
            sdsRemSug.DeleteParameters("SuggestionID").DefaultValue = _
                gvSugs.SelectedRow.Cells(1).Text

            ' Perform the deletion.
            Results = sdsRemSug.Delete()

            ' Display the results.
            txtResults.Text = Results.ToString() + " suggestion removed."

            ' Update the grid view.
            gvSugs.DataBind()
        End If


        ' Make the results visible.
        lblResults.Visible = True
        txtResults.Visible = True
    End Sub
```

The example begins by checking for a selected record. If the user doesn't select a record, the code displays an error message.

When the user does select a record, the code places the value in the `SuggestedID` parameter using the `DefaultValue` property. The actual deletion takes place when the code calls `sdsRemSug` `.Delete()`. The code displays the results on screen and calls `gvSugs.DataBind()` to update the `GridView` control.

Developing Stored Procedures with .NET

As described in the "Creating New Stored Procedures" section of the chapter, a stored procedure written with T-SQL can perform simple application tasks, such as comparisons, and manipulate data. Generally, a standard stored procedure provides all the functionality you need when you want to move the processing load from the client to the server in order to avoid the performance hit of moving large amounts of data over the network.

Most developers who work with T-SQL know that it's possible to perform many tasks, but also realize that T-SQL isn't a full-fledged language—it lacks basic support for programming constructions such as array and structures such as the for each loops. You won't find strong data typing in T-SQL and there isn't any way to create a class. In short, T-SQL is quite capable for many tasks, but it won't do everything as easily as a language such as Visual Basic or C#. That's where using the CLR support built into SQL Server comes into play.

Unfortunately, you pay a price for the flexibility that CLR provides. Creating a stored procedure that relies on CLR means creating a special kind of DLL—it requires the Class Library template. The coding technique itself can become relatively complex. You can see an example of the process in the DevX article at `http://www.devx.com/dotnet/Article/21286`. Another view of the same process appears as part of the Writing and Executing Your First Yukon CLR Procedure article at `http://www.c-sharpcorner.com/Longhorn/Yukon/First-CLR-Procedure.asp`. The bottom line is that this is a relatively complex process, so you need a good reason to use it.

Most small to medium-sized businesses will never need the functionality provided by the CLR support in SQL Server—it's simply overkill for the kinds of tasks that most small business perform. In fact, many developers find that T-SQL works fine for large projects as well. The only time that you really need the extra flexibility that CLR provides is when you need to perform complex manipulation of huge datasets.

Learning More about Stored Procedures

Stored procedures could easily require a book or perhaps two for a full explanation because you can do a lot with them. This section provides specifics on working with stored procedures with Visual Studio and a few hints about stored procedures as well, but you'll probably want to know a lot more about them at some point. Try SQL Server Stored Procedure Basics at `http://www.awprofessional.com/articles/article.asp?p=25288` if you want a basic tutorial. Another great tutorial appears as SQL Server Stored Procedures 101 at `http://www.devarticles.com/c/a/SQL-Server/SQL-Server-Stored-Procedures-101/`.

A number of sites offer short articles that tell how to handle specific issues. For example, the SQL Team.com site offers a number of stored procedure–specific articles including one on error handling at `http://www.sqlteam.com/item.asp?ItemID=2463`. You can find a list of undocumented stored procedures to use at SQL-Server-Performance.com (`http://www.sql-server-performance.com/ac_sql_server_2000_undocumented_sp.asp`). The MS SQL City at site also includes undocumented stored procedures at `http://www.mssqlcity.com/Articles/Undoc/SQL2000UndocSP.htm`, along with a wealth of other information.

Should you decide to use a stored procedure with an ASP file, rather than using ASP.NET for a particular solution, you can find everything you need in the Microsoft Knowledge Base article at `http://support.microsoft.com/support/kb/articles/Q164/4/85.asp`. Of course, half the fun of working with Visual Studio is that you have access to the resources that ASP.NET can provide. Consider this article an example of all the coding you'd need to do when using older technology.

Using Views

A view is a special kind of select query. It helps you create a particular perspective of the data in the database. Like a query, a view relies on a SQL statement to obtain the information. In fact, the editing window looks precisely the same as the one shown for queries in Figure 11.16. The big difference between a view and a query is how SQL Server works with them. Views provide a data perspective, a means of seeing the data in a certain way. On the other hand, a query requests something from the database—the concepts are the same, but the uses are different. The database also stores all of the views you create—a query appears as an external DTQ file. The following sections describe how to work with views.

Using the View Designer Toolbar

You'll see the View Designer toolbar every time you open an existing view for editing or creating a new view. The View Designer toolbar looks a lot like the Query Designer toolbar described in the "Using the Query Designer Toolbar" section of the chapter. Compare Figure 11.14 with Figure 11.35 below and you'll find there are a few omissions from the Query Designer toolbar because you don't need to perform these tasks when working with views. The "Using the Query Designer Toolbar" section of the chapter provides full descriptions of all the View Designer controls.

FIGURE 11.35

Use the View Designer toolbar to modify and verify the entries in a view you create.

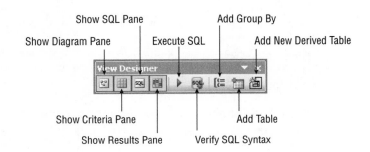

Creating a View

Views are very helpful snapshots of a particular database setup. They offer the advantage of letting you decided how the user interacts with the data and you can set them up with different security from the database itself. You can create as many views of your data as you need to understand it fully. Here are the views used for the beneficial suggestion example application.

GetUnapprovedUsers   Displays a list of users that the administrator hasn't approved yet. The output from this view helps the administrator make an approval decision. Consequently, it includes all of the essential information about the user.

GetApprovedUsers   Displays a list of users that the administrator has approved. The application uses this view to locate users who can make beneficial suggestions. The view hides all of the user information except username and identification. Consequently, this view also provides a margin of safety for the user and the application.

To create a new view, right-click the Views folder and choose Add New View from the context menu. The IDE displays the Add Table dialog box shown in Figure 11.6. Choose one or more tables, views (yes, a view can act as input to another view), or functions as needed. Once you select the input items, click Close. Now you configure the view just as you would a query.

Using XML Support

One of the more useful additions to SQL Server is XML support. As you've seen in previous chapters, good XML support can be quite valuable for any Web site. Of course, you might wonder why someone would rely on XML files when they already have a perfectly good connection to SQL Server. There are a number of good reasons for using XML in place of a dynamic connection—perhaps you don't want the Web site user to see the live data or be able to access it through nefarious means. An XML file with regularly updated information provides much of the functionality of a live connection, but without the security risks.

The XML data might represent a particular view of the data that you don't want to maintain in the database. Creating the XML file from code as needed might be less expensive from a performance perspective than maintaining the live connection to a complex manipulation.

In some cases, the XML data might actually act as an input to the rest of your application. For example, you can safely gather user input in an XML file on your Web site, scan it for potential problems, such as scripts or viruses, and then add it to your database. Whatever reason you have for working with XML files, the following sections help you discover the connection between SQL Server and XML.

Creating an XML Index

SQL Server provides a special XML data type that you can use for a field. The XML data field can contain either a full XML page or an XML fragment. No matter what kind of XML the field contains, indexing it requires special techniques. The XML index makes working with XML fields easier. For the purposes of this demonstration, you'll want to add an XML data field to one of the existing databases such as Categories temporarily. Simply type the name of the field (the example uses XML_Index) when viewing the table definition and choose xml in the Data Type column.

Now that you have a new XML field, you can index it. Begin by highlighting the XML field. Click Manage XML Indexes and you'll see the XML Indexes dialog box shown in Figure 11.36. Click Add to add the new index, as shown in the figure. You don't have to do anything special to the index—it's ready for use.

FIGURE 11.36
XML data fields require special indexing through an XML index.

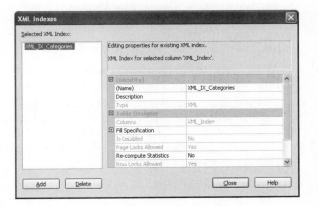

Using the XML Data Toolbar

The XML Data toolbar is accessible whenever you're working directly with XML data in the IDE. It includes features for moving between records with greater ease than if you have to scroll through the data manually. Figure 11.37 shows the controls for this toolbar. The following list describes each of the controls.

Create Schema Defines a schema based on the content and structure of the records within the XML file. A schema provides rules that maintain the integrity of the file and make it easier to important external data into a database table when both use the same schema. Generally, it's a good idea to use schemas to help enforce data input requirements when you plan to move data between XML and SQL files.

Go to New Row   Places the cursor after the last row of data so that you can add a new row.

Go to Last Row   Places the cursor at the last row of data in the file.

Go to First Row   Places the cursor at the first row of data in the file.

FIGURE 11.37
Use the XML Data
Toolbar to create,
manage, and interact
with XML data.

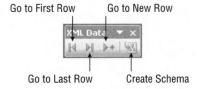

Using the XML Schema Toolbar

The XML Schema toolbar appears whenever you work with an XSD file. The XML Schema toolbar contains features that make it easier to edit the schema. Figure 11.38 shows the controls for this toolbar. The following list describes each of the controls.

Zoom   Determines the magnification factor used to present the data. A higher zoom lets you see more of the data, while a lower zoom provides a better overview of all of the elements.

Preview Dataset   Displays the Dataset Properties dialog box. This dialog box contains a hierarchical view of the data elements within the schema. However, instead of presenting a graphical view of the schema, this dialog box displays the various element properties and makes it easier for you to decide how to work with the schema.

Make Type Global   Changes the entity from a simple to a complex entry so it can have a global presence.

Edit Relation   Displays the Edit Relation dialog box. This dialog box lets you modify the relations between various tables. The first table always contains the primary key, while the second contains the foreign key. The Key field contains the name of the relationship as it appears in the schema. You can also choose whether any constraints apply to just the foreign key or to both the primary and foreign key.

Edit Key   Displays the Edit Key dialog box, which contains the name of the element and the key field. This dialog box also contains options for setting a primary key and defines whether the key is nullable.

FIGURE 11.38
Use the XML Schema
Toolbar to create and
managed XSD files.

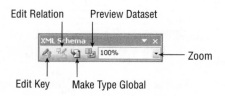

Defining an XML Schema

As your applications increase in complexity, you'll want to ensure the XML data you collect remains secure. One way to improve security and maintain data integrity is to create a schema file. The best way to perform this task is to create the SQL Server database and associated tables first when you want to maintain a connection between the XML files and SQL Server. You can then drag and drop the tables onto the schema, as shown in Figure 11.39.

The IDE won't maintain any relationships normally found in the database—you must re-create them manually. Click Edit Relation and provide entries to define the relationship between the two tables. The relation appears as a line between the two tables with a diamond in the middle, as shown in Figure 11.39. You'll find an example schema in the \Chapter 11\XMLSample folder of the source code on the Sybex Web site.

FIGURE 11.39

Create a schema by moving tables from the database to the design area.

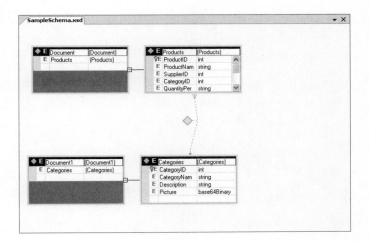

Using the XML Control

The XML control provides a convenient means of displaying XML data on screen using XSLT without resorting to script. You'll find this example in the \Chapter 11\XMLSample folder of the source code on the Sybex Web site. The control is very simple. The DocumentSource property contains the name and location of the XML file, while the TransformSource property contains the name and location of the XSLT file. You don't have to do anything else to make this control work.

Defining Your Development Goals

This chapter has demonstrated techniques you can use to work efficiently with SQL Server. The main idea is to think about where you want to process information to improve performance, reliability, and security. As your applications become more complex, you need to include the flexibility that these features provide. For example, a simple database application might not need a trigger, but you can bet that you'll want to use this feature as your database application grows. Of course, the big addition for SQL Server is the full XML support that it provides. Visual Studio users really need this support to create efficient Web applications.

Now it's time to play with the database. Try creating a new database, fill it with tables, add some views, and work with stored procedures. Database applications require that you fully understand how each of the individual features work toward a cohesive whole. Although you can build an application using nothing but stored procedures and a little glue code, the result is going to be inefficient because you aren't making best use of all the functionality the DBMS provides. Only by working with the various features can you discover how to use them with your particular application.

Chapter 12 helps you understand one of the most important features of Visual Studio .NET for many organizations—the ability to create reports. Let's face it, most organizations run in reports. When they finish creating one report, they use it as input for another report, resulting in endless reams of data. Your ability to create reports quickly and easily can improve your own performance and make it considerably easier to meet the demands of everyone in your organization.

Chapter 12

Creating an ASP.NET Crystal Reports Web Site

The computer was supposed to usher in the era of the paperless office. Here we are, many years later, still shuffling paper around. In fact, if anything, computers have made it possible for companies to churn out yet more paper. Any hopes you have of avoiding paper with your Web application will instantly disappear the first time an executive decides to look at the output. Reporting, the act of putting the data you've collected on paper, is an essential part of every application—even Web applications. Fortunately, you don't have to reinvent the wheel when using Visual Studio—you have access to a feature limited version of Crystal Reports in Visual Studio 2005, which will meet the vast majority of your needs.

This chapter provides you with a great overview and many details of Crystal Reports. You'll build an application to create reports from the beneficial suggestions database described in Chapter 11. However, you can easily use Crystal Reports with any of the databases on the ABC, Incorporated Web site. After you read this chapter, you might be amazed at just how easy it is to put reports together. Woe betides the forests in your area, but at least you'll be home on the weekends.

Creating the RPT File

The Report (RPT) file is the basis for everything you do with Crystal Reports in Visual Studio. It is the starting point for any output you want to create, whether the output is desktop or Web based. However, this chapter focuses on Web-based development for the obvious reasons. You can find the completed report file in the \ABC_Inc\Reports folder of the source code provided on the Sybex Web site.

TIP According a recent InfoWorld article (http://www.infoworld.com/article/05/08/09/HNbolinux_1.html?source=NLC-TB2005-08-09), Crystal Reports might become your best interoperability alternative. The company recently added support for Linux to their product line. This means that a report you create in .NET could possibly provide output for Linux users, as well, with the proper infrastructure.

Adding the Crystal Report

Adding a new report to your application is the same as adding any new object. Begin by right-clicking the project entry in Solution Explorer and choosing Add New Item from the context menu. You'll see the Add New Item dialog box. Choose the Crystal Report entry, type a name for the report in the Name field, and click Add. The example uses `BeneficialSuggestions.RPT` as the report name. The Beneficial Reports application on the ABC, Incorporated Web site has been a big success, so now the owner wants a report that summarizes the suggestions so someone can act on them.

NOTE   The first time you create a report, you'll see a licensing dialog box. Read the terms of the agreement carefully, select I Accept the License Agreement, and click OK to clear the dialog box.

Selecting the Database

Every Crystal Report begins with the Crystal Reports wizard. You'll use the wizard to define basic elements of the report, such as the report type. The following steps show how to use the wizard.

1. Select the Using the Report Wizard option on the initial dialog box shown in Figure 12.1. The Crystal Reports Gallery dialog box also lets you choose a report type. The version of the product that ships with Visual Studio lets you create standard page-based reports, cross-tabulated reports, and mailing labels. Each of the major report types includes a number of customization features you can use to enhance the overall appearance of the report. You'll use the Standard option for most reports. The Cross-Tab option is most useful when you want to provide a comparison, such as sales by district by quarter for last year. Sales would be the data, district would make up one axis, and quarter would make up the second axis. Including one year's worth of data would provide a time limit for the data.

TIP   If you don't want to use the wizard, simply select As a Blank Report in the initial dialog box, click OK, and Crystal Reports will take you directly to the design area. You can also use an existing report as a basis for a new report. This option opens the possibility of creating report templates that include all of the data sources and basic layout. You then use the existing report (the template) as the basis for the complete reports you want to create.

FIGURE 12.1
Select the wizard option and the report type using this dialog box.

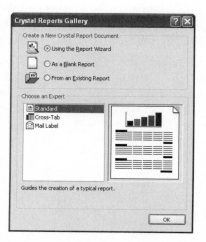

2. Choose a report type. The example uses the Standard report option. Click OK. You'll see the Standard Report Creation Wizard shown in Figure 12.2. Think of each of the folders in the wizard as a data pocket—a place that holds data for your report. Some pockets automatically contain information, such as the datasets within your current project or the connections you've created in Server Explorer. Don't get confused about some of the folder names. For example, the Current Connections folder refers to current Crystal Reports connections. Because Crystal Reports doesn't always show every connection at your disposal, this example shows how to create a new connection.

3. Select the `Create New Connection\OLE DB` folder. Selecting this option automatically displays an OLE DB (ADO) dialog box shown in Figure 12.3 when you haven't created any connections in the past. Otherwise, this action displays the list of database file connections you've created for Crystal Reports. When you see a list of connections, right-click the `OLE DB` folder, and choose Add Connection from the context menu.

FIGURE 12.2

The folders in the Standard Report Creation Wizard provide pockets for report data.

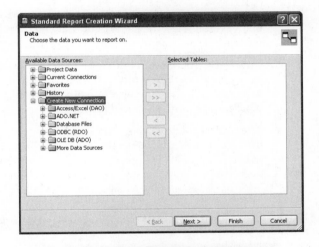

FIGURE 12.3

Select a standard data provider from the list or select a custom provider using the Data Link File option.

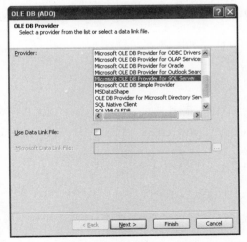

4. Choose a data provider. The example uses the Microsoft OLE DB Provider for SQL Server option. Click Next. You'll see the Connection Information dialog box shown in Figure 12.4. This dialog box is where things can get tricky because it doesn't provide you with much help.

5. Type `.\SQLEXPRESS` in the Server field. This entry provides two important pieces of information. First, it defines a local connection. The local connection always uses a period—you can substitute the actual server name. Second, the connection relies on SQL Server Express as the instance of SQL Server to use, not the default SQL Server installation. If you've given SQL Server Express a different name on your machine, you must use the name you provided in place of the standard SQLEXPRESS. Remember that SQL Server won't allow you to open a file—you must make the database part of SQL Server in order to use SQL Server as the DBMS.

6. Select the Integrated Security option. If you don't choose this option, you need to provide a valid name and password in the User ID and Password fields.

7. Type Suggestions in the Database field. You can't select the information from the drop-down list. As far as any of the automation is concerned, the Suggestions database doesn't exist. Normally, you'll select the name of the database server from the Server drop-down list and the name of the database from the Database drop-down list.

8. Click Next. You'll see the Advanced Information dialog box shown in Figure 12.5. This dialog box already has the required additional information filled out. Steps 9 through 11 tell you how to provide this information. Normally, you won't have to provide additional information, but database files require special attention.

9. Click Add Property. You'll see an Edit Property Value dialog box like the one shown in Figure 12.6. Type **AttachDbFilename** in the Property field. Type the full path location of the `Suggestions.MDF` file on your hard drive in the Value field. You must provide the full path or the connection may not work properly. Don't include double quotes around the path information because the connection will fail.

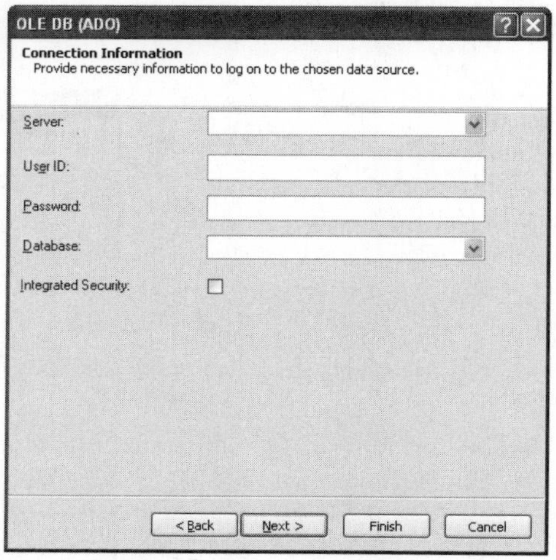

FIGURE 12.4
Create a connection to the server and database you want to use.

FIGURE 12.5
You must provide additional properties to make a file connection work.

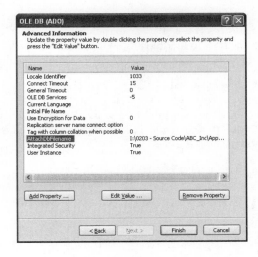

FIGURE 12.6
The Edit Property Value dialog box lets you tell the DBMS more about a connection.

10. Click OK. Add a second property. In this case, type **Integrated Security** in the Property field (the space is important) and **True** in the Value field.

11. Add a third property. Type **User Instance** in the Property field and **True** in the Value field.

12. Click Finish. After a few seconds, you'll see the Standard Report Creation Wizard again, but this time you'll see the new connection, as shown in Figure 12.7. The tables, views, and stored procedures you create will appear in the `Suggestions\dbo` folder, as shown in the figure—Crystal Reports generally shows any data by owner.

Make sure you look at some of the Web-based application-specific report sources for Crystal Reports. For example, Figure 12.8 shows the .NET Objects folder. This folder provides the means for measuring and reporting on various Web site features, such as the number of pages accesses for target pages. These folders help you understand your Web site better and provides the written reports you need to make decisions about the Web site as a group.

Choosing the Data

The data you choose depends on what you want in the report. You can use individual tables, views, or stored procedures as a data source. The example uses the Categories, Suggestions, and UserData tables from the Suggestions database shown in Figure 12.7. To add the tables to the report, highlight the entry in the left column and click the right pointing button in the middle of the display. You'll see the table entry copied to the right side—the Selected Tables list. When you've finished selecting the data sources you want to use, click Next. Because the example uses multiple tables, the report has to know how to link them up. Figure 12.9 shows the default setup, which is the setup used for the example. However, you can change the linkage information as needed to address any requirement.

TIP   The tables, views, and stored procedures you select are accessible after you complete the wizard. Consequently, choose all of the data sources you need, not just the tables that you'll need to complete the wizard. Doing so now will save time and effort later. See the "Working with Field Explorer" section of the chapter for additional information on how the information appears after the wizard is finished.

FIGURE 12.7
A successful local database file connection shows all of the objects you would expect.

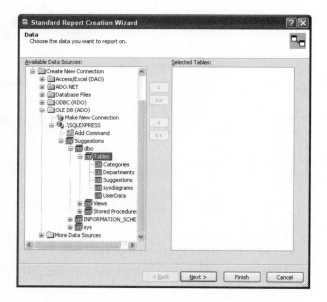

FIGURE 12.8
Web-based applications have access to a number of unexpected data sources, such as statistics.

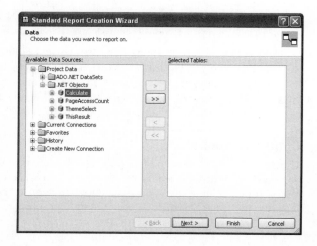

The linkage determines how the report arranges and uses the data. The next step is to select the detailed data you want to display. After you create the required linkage, click Next and you'll see the Fields dialog box shown in Figure 12.10. The figure shows the detail fields that the example uses. The report will organize the information first by category, then by user, and finally by individual user suggestions. These suggestions form the detail lines of the report. Using this approach will make it quite easy to discuss the various user ideas.

FIGURE 12.9
Select the table linkage that best meets the needs of the report you want to create.

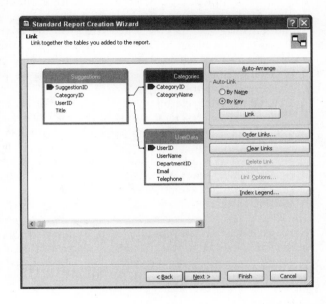

FIGURE 12.10
Define the data you want to use from the tables for the report.

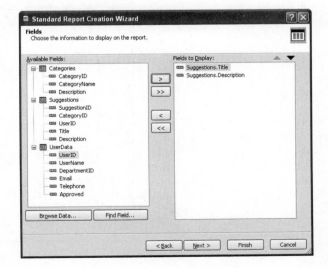

The idea of organization leads into the next dialog box. When you click next, you'll see the Grouping dialog box shown in Figure 12.11. This is where you create major grouping levels. Move the major grouping fields from the left side to the right to create a grouping, as shown in the figure. Of course, you can move elements around as needed later to create a complete group. For example, you'll want to create a group from the UserName, Email, and Telephone fields. However, in this case, the major field is the UserName—you'll add the Email and Telephone fields later. You'll see how to combine these fields later in the chapter. For now, use the grouping shown in Figure 12.11.

You can also summarize data in a report. For example, you might want to total the sales of people in your organization. Click Next after you create the report grouping and you'll see the Summaries dialog box shown in Figure 12.12. Notice that the figure already shows the one summary for this report—the count of the number of suggestion submissions for each user. To obtain this summary field, highlight the UserID field entry in the Summaries table and click the right pointing button. Choose Count from the drop-down list.

Depending on the selections you make, you'll see a number of additional setup screens for the wizard. The next dialog box for the example will ask you to choose an order for the groups. For example, you could choose the top five groups based on the number of submissions made. The example leaves these settings unchanged. You might also see filtering options that let you choose which records appear on screen. Figure 12.13 shows that the example sets the report to display only approved users—those who can make beneficial suggestions. The reports can also include a chart at the top of the display, but the example doesn't use this feature.

The final page of the Standard Report Creation Wizard asks you what kind of report presentation you want to use. These options appear in Figure 12.14. Essentially, the choice comes down to one of personal preference. The selection you make depends on company guidelines and your personal feelings about the report output. In addition, some formats work better than others do for certain kinds of data. The example uses the Standard report output. However, if this report was presenting last year's sales numbers, the Table or Executive formats might work better.

FIGURE 12.11
It's best to group the data to make the report easier to read and use.

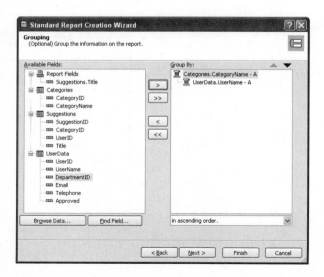

FIGURE 12.12
Summarize information as needed to provide processed output.

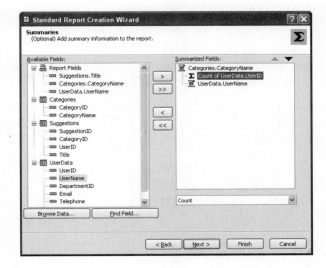

FIGURE 12.13
Use filtering to ensure you see just the data you need in the report.

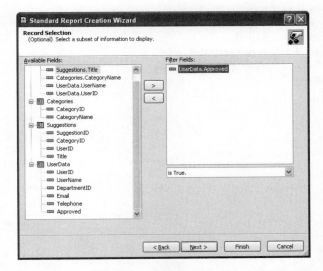

At this point, you can click Finish. What you'll end up with is a report that looks like the one in Figure 12.15. It probably won't contain all of the information you want, but the basic report will contain the correct information. All of the groupings will be correct and you'll see the right summary information. However, the headings might not be completely correct—you might need more information. Some of the detail fields will probably contain too much information. All of these problems are easy to fix—the most important issue is getting a basic report put together.

FIGURE 12.14
The report format options give your report the extra pizzazz that you need for a presentation.

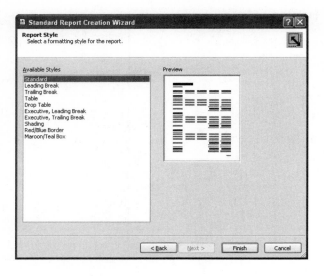

FIGURE 12.15
The wizard output probably won't be perfect, but it will provide a good basis for completing the report.

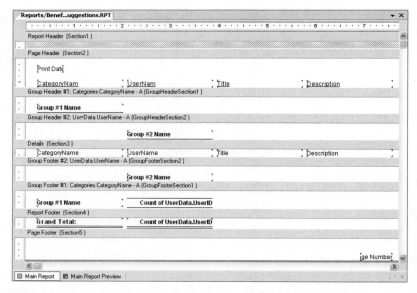

Many developers find the report view in Figure 12.15 is good for configuring the report, but not very effective for visualizing the output. The problem is that the little squares showing the extent of the data fields don't really tell you very much because they don't contain any data. Fortunately, Visual Studio has a solution for that problem. Click the Main Report Preview tab and you'll see sample report output, as shown in Figure 12.16.

Some of the flaws in this report are instantly obvious when you view it using real data. For example, the employee information isn't complete—it has only the employee name and no contact information. Of course, you already knew about that problem because the topic came up within this section. It would be nice to have a description of each category as well, but that problem is also easily fixed. The column headings aren't necessary, but if you do keep them, you'll want to use something better than the column headings shown now. The employee name also appears twice for each entry; removing the second entry will save space and make the report more readable. Finally, the detail data, as expected, contains too much information.

FIGURE 12.16
Use real data to determine how the report will appear to end users.

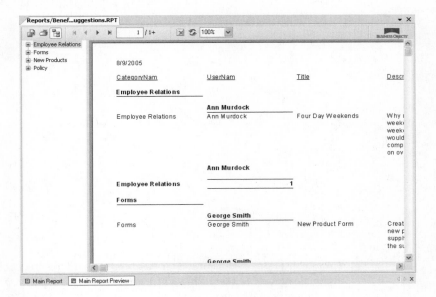

Working with Field Explorer

Once you design an initial report using the wizard, the first task is to add and remove fields as needed to provide a complete view of the data. Generally, you need to use the Field Explorer to accomplish this task. The Field Explorer shown in Figure 12.17 contains a number of field types, not just those from the database. Each folder contains a different type of information derived from a specific resource. The following list describes the various Field Explorer entries in detail.

Database Fields   The database fields appear at the top of the list, as shown in the figure. This folder contains all of the tables that you selected when you began creating the report, so you want to be sure that you choose all of the data sources you need even if you don't use them in the report creation process. If you find you didn't include all of the data sources you needed to complete the report, right-click the Database Fields folder and choose Database Expert from the context menu to change the current setup.

Formula Fields   If you need to show the output of a Crystal Reports formula on the report, you can create one using any data that the report has available, constants, or any data you wish to add. Simply right-click the folder and choose New. When creating a formula, you have the choice of using the expert or the editor. The expert provides a wizard-like interface for writing formulas. The editor lets you select data using a Query Builder–type interface. The option you choose depends on how you want to build the formula—trying both options is probably the best choice.

FIGURE 12.17
The Field Explorer lets you choose from existing fields or create your own.

Parameter Fields   The Parameter Fields entry is interesting because it lets you query the user about the dynamics of working with the report. For example, you might ask the user to select a specific category of beneficial suggestion to output. This feature generally doesn't work well with Web-based applications (although, there are exceptions), so this chapter doesn't discuss it in detail. You should probably avoid using this feature with Web-based applications you build. It does work very well with desktop applications, however, so don't avoid it completely.

Group Name Fields   Initially, this folder contains all of the groups you defined using the wizard. However, you can also use it to create new groups as needed. To add a new group, right-click the folder and choose Insert Group from the context menu. Group sorting is another feature of this folder. In this case, the sorts you have available depend on the groups that you create. You can choose to sort all or none of the entries, display the top or bottom number of entries, or display the top or bottom entries by percentage. You can change this setting by right-clicking the folder and choosing Group Sort Expert from the context menu. Although you can't see it in Figure 12.17, this folder also contains the filtering options for your report. To change the filtering criteria, right-click the folder and choose Select Expert from the context menu. You'll see the Select Expert dialog box where you can see the current selection criteria and add new filters as needed.

Running Total Fields   Reports rely on running total fields for calculated data, such the amount of widgets sold during the month of January or during the rest of year. A running total field is not the same as a summary. A summary performs a simple calculation on data, such as counting the number of items. A running total performs an evaluation on a data field or a summary; it actually manipulates the data in some way to derive new information based on existing data.

SQL Expression Fields You use the SQL expressions to manipulate database information and present it as part of the report. After right-clicking the folder and choosing New, you'll see the same Formula Workshop display you do when creating a formula manually for your report. The difference is that you can access SQL-specific functions and that you'll generally use this feature to work specifically with information from the database. This folder doesn't include an expert mode.

Special Fields Most reports require data that isn't part of your data store. In fact, this data isn't something you ask Crystal Reports to compute or derive from existing data. For example, most reports will require the current date and a page number. These items all appear in the Special Fields folder. Unlike other folders, you can't add new entries to this folder. The entries you see in Figure 12.17 are the entries that you receive for every report. Notice that the entries only describe the kind of data, not its format. You define the format of this data as you do for any other data, by using the various formatting features that Crystal Reports provides.

Unbound Fields The entries in this folder consist of data fields of a specific type that aren't bound to a data source of any kind. The entries you see in this folder are limited to the data types that Crystal Reports supports directly. You would use these entries to provide amplifying data that is outside the realm of the data source. For example, you might want to know the name of the machine that generated the report. This information requires a data field, but it isn't bound to the database in any way, so you'd use the String data type found in this folder. You can't add or delete entries from this folder.

As with Server Explorer, you simply drag and drop entries from Field Explorer onto the report form to use them. The placement you choose determines how the item will react in the report. For example, if you place an item in a group section, then you'll only see the output from that item when the report begins a new group. Likewise, entries in the details section only appear when the report outputs detail information. You'll see how the various sections work as the chapter progresses.

Formatting Report Entries

Most Visual Studio developers are used to using the Properties window to work with objects in an application. Theoretically, you can use the Properties window to work with Crystal Reports objects too, but the entries are a little difficult to understand, as shown in Figure 12.18. In fact, unless you truly understand Crystal Reports, you might find the properties nearly impossible to make out.

Fortunately, you have a better choice than to try to figure out the Properties window. Right-click any object, no matter what source, and you'll find a Format Object entry on the context menu. Select this entry and you'll see a Format Editor dialog box similar to the one shown in Figure 12.19 that lets you format the object. The unique characteristic of the Format Editor dialog box is that the contents change to meet the needs of a specific object. Figure 12.19 shows the Format Editor dialog box for a print date, which will differ from the Format Editor display for a database field. Consequently, not only is the Format Editor easier to use than the Properties window, it also helps you to concentrate on the task.

NOTE The X-2 buttons you see sprinkled throughout the Format Editor let you create a formula for a particular display option. Using this feature means that you can create complete display and usage criteria for objects that need them. For example, you might decide to display a particular object only on even pages. This feature is also helpful to display data when a particular circumstance occurs, such as a negative number on a financial report.

FIGURE 12.18
You can use the Properties window to configure Crystal Reports objects, but you won't enjoy it.

FIGURE 12.19
The Format Editor provides object-specific formatting information.

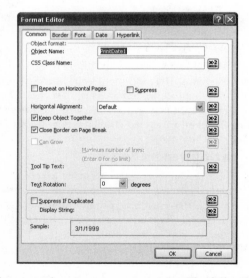

Every Format Editor dialog box does contain some common entries. The following list describes the tabs that you'll commonly see and explains how you use them.

Common   This tab contains important information about the object as a whole, such as the object name. You'll also find a wealth of formatting information and restrictions on object display.

TIP   You'll also find an interesting entry on the Common tab, the CSS Class Name. A report that you create for a Web-based application need not appear in printed format—you can present the information on a Web page as well. Consequently, providing a CSS Class Name entry means that you can provide the viewer with the means of changing the appearance of your report without actually changing anything in the report itself.

Border The default border settings depend on which of the report styles you choose (see Figure 12.14 for details). However, you can change the border for a particular object without any problem using the options on this tab. You can control the line style, the background and foreground colors, whether the object has a drop shadow, and other special features. Selecting the Tight Horizontal option trims excess white space around the object, so the border flows immediately around the object, rather than the area you designed the object to consume.

Font The Font tab contains all of the entries that you expect, including the font name, size, and special embellishments such as strikethrough. Using an equation, you can present objects in a number of colors. For example, you can present negative numbers in red and positive numbers in black.

Hyperlink You'll only use this feature for reports displayed on a Web page. The option on this tab lets you add a hyperlink to the object that will take the reader to a Web site, download a file, display another report, or send email. As with most configuration objects, you can also use a formula to change the functionality of the settings on this tab. For example, you might use the object content to determine what kind of hyperlink to present.

Setting the Report Options

You can modify options for the report as a whole by right-clicking the report and choosing any of the entries on the Report menu within the context menu shown in Figure 12.20. Many of these options are already familiar. For example, you've already learned about the Select Expert and the Formula Workshop in the "Working with Field Explorer" and "Formatting Report Entries" sections of the chapter. All of these entries work with the report as a whole, however, so you can use them to make global changes, rather than changes to individual objects or data sources.

The three items of interest in this section appear at the bottom of the menu. Select the Set the Print Date and Time option if you want to use a static date for this report in place of today's date. You might want to use a static date when the date is unchanging—perhaps you downloaded it to an XML file from the company database to reduce potential security problems. The Summary Info option displays a Document Properties dialog box that contains information such as the author name, keywords, and report description on one tab and document statistics on a second tab.

FIGURE 12.20
Make global changes as
needed using the options
on the Report menu.

The Report Options option of the Report menu displays the Report Options dialog box shown in Figure 12.21. These options can make a significant difference in the report output. Notice the null display options. Generally, Crystal Reports assumes that you want to display a blank when an object contains a null value. However, you can set the report to display a default value when the object is null. This can be very helpful when a database contains a number of fields that can accept null values that you don't want to appear blank on the form. You might want to replace the null value with N/A or other default value.

Some of the entries in the Report Options dialog box affect the performance of your report. For example, if you check the Perform Grouping on Server option, the report will have a different performance curve. On the positive side, the client machine will run the report faster and the system will have better network characteristics. However, you pay a price for this performance advantage in increased server load. Because Crystal Reports performs more of the work on the server, you'll find that the server bogs down faster and can support fewer users.

A few of the options affect both report appearance and performance. For example, if you check the Select Distinct Records option, all application elements will perform better because the report generates less data. In addition, the user will have less information to read in order to view the content of the report. However, sometimes you need the repetitive data to present the data as it really appears in the database. The Select Distinct Records option only displays distinct records, which means that the user won't see redundant data—even redundancy is a form of data so you need to consider how the user will use the report.

FIGURE 12.21
Use the Report Options to make global changes to your report features.

Inserting and Removing Fields

The data that a report presents appears within the fields or objects that you choose. Consequently, the ability to modify the fields that appear on a report is very important to the result you eventually see. Removing fields is relatively easy. Simply highlight the field you want to remove and press Delete. Of course, now the field is completely gone.

Completely removing a field works fine when you really don't need it any longer. For example, you can remove the CategoryName and UserName fields from the Details section of the example report because this information already appears as part of a category heading. You can also remove the extra Group #2 Name entry in the Group Footer #2 section because it simply repeats information found in the header.

After you make delete the unneeded fields, move the remaining Title and Description field entries in the Details section to the left. Elongate the Description field so it consumes more of the remaining page space. These changes ensure that the report uses page space efficiently. The changes also give the report a finished appearance that looks like the report was custom designed using hand-coding techniques.

TIP Notice that the Page Header section content automatically changes to match the Details section content when you remove the CategoryName and UserName fields. Crystal Reports often automates the tasks you need to perform to create a report. However, this feature can turn into a liability when Crystal Reports makes the wrong assumption. Always watch automated changes carefully for potential problems.

Sometimes you don't want to remove a field completely, however, because you need it for a calculation. A field that you don't need is still a liability, but you can reduce the effect it has on the report. Begin by right-clicking the field and choosing Format Object from the context menu. Select the Common tab and check the Suppress option. Click OK to make the change permanent. The field won't appear in the output any longer. However, it still consumes report space. Reduce the size field and move it to an unused area of the report. Make sure you keep the field in the same section so it works as anticipated.

The report wizard often doesn't provide enough flexibility for you to add all of the data you want to a heading. As a result, you'll end up inserting additional fields into a report. The example report currently has two areas that are lacking information. First, the report doesn't provide a category description. Second, the user information is incomplete. You can solve both problems by inserting fields into the required sections. Begin by dragging the Description field of the Categories database to the Group Header #1 section of the form. You can resize the section as needed to accommodate the new field. The example also uses an italic font to display the description. Perform the same task for the user data. However, this time you'll place the information in Group Header #2 immediately after the user's name and format the data as it is for the user. Figure 12.22 shows the layout for the example report.

FIGURE 12.22
Layout for the example report

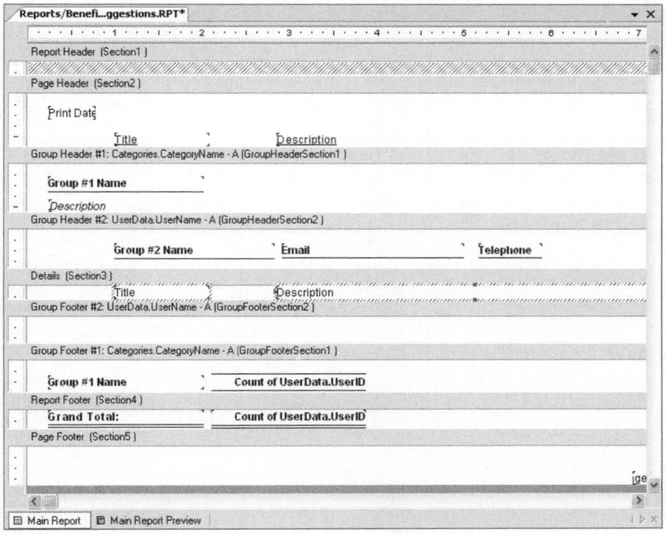

Inserting and Removing Sections

Sections define the layout of the report and determine how each section of the report works. A details section displays one element for every record—a group section displays just one element for each group in the report. Sometimes a blank section can cause problems. Not only does a blank section consume report space, but it might also have negative effects on how the report works. Notice that the example report in Figure 12.22 shows a blank section, Group Footer #2. To remove a section, right-click it and choose Delete Section from the context menu. When you choose this option, the IDE completely deletes the section and you'll have to recreate any fields the section contains if you decide to reinstate the section later.

WARNING   Always highlight the section—the gray bar—when you want to work with the section as a whole. Clicking within the section means that you're working with the data that the section contains. It's important to use the correct object when working within a report.

Unfortunately, Group Footer #2 doesn't include the Delete Section entry on the context menu. Crystal Reports automatically generates this section for you as the result of creating report. However, you do have two other options. The first is to choose Hide (Drill-Down OK). Select this option when you want to hide any data the section contains, but want to continue using the section for calculations or other needs. The second is to choose Suppress (No Drill-Down). Select this option when you don't want to use the section for any purpose. Use this second option for the Group Footer #2 section. The section doesn't contain any data and you don't want it consuming space on the report. Notice that the IDE grays out this section when you select the Suppress (No Drill-Down) option. However, the most noticeable results are on the report. Figure 12.23 shows the final report.

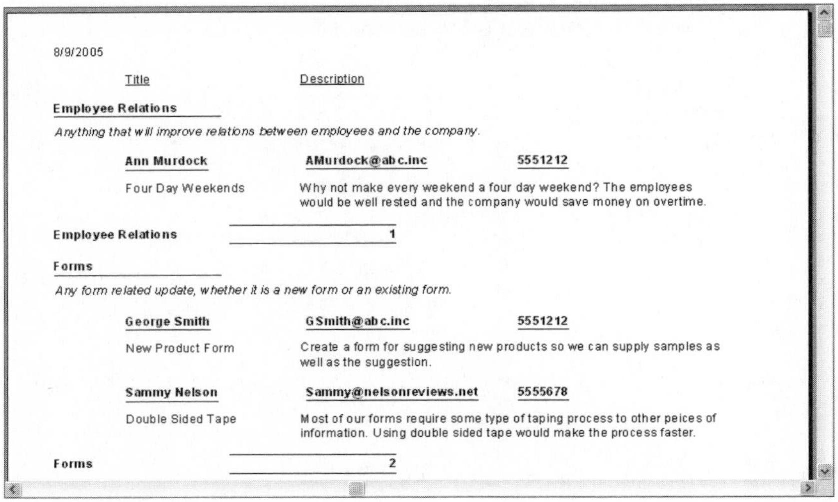

FIGURE 12.23
The final report contains all of the information needed and in a nice format.

You have multiple options that you can use to create new groups. The first is to right-click the section entry immediately before the one you want to add and choose Insert Section Below from the context menu. Crystal Reports will insert a new section that you can configure using either the Properties window or the Group Expert. The second option is to right-click any section entry and choose Section Expert from the context menu. Figure 12.24 shows the Section Expert dialog box.

The controls for using the Section Expert appear across the top of the Sections list. You can insert new sections, delete sections that you create using the Section Expert, and merge two sections together. On the right side of the dialog box are the settings for the highlighted section. You use these settings to control the appearance and functionality of the section. For example, check the Suppress (No Drill-Down) option to keep the section from displaying as part of the report. The Color tab lets you select a background color for the section—the default doesn't include any color.

When working with groups, you have a third option for adding new sections to the report. Right-click any group section entry and choose Group Expert from the context menu. The Group Expert looks and works like the grouping options in the Standard Report Creation Wizard (see Figure 12.11 for details). You can't delete group sections created using the Grouping Wizard unless you delete the group itself. Consequently, when you need to remove a section such as Group Footer #2 from a report, you must hide or suppress it, rather than try to delete it.

Developing the Output Page

Creating a report is just the first step in getting the information out to a viewer. Fortunately, Crystal Reports provides a number of controls that make creating output for a report a lot easier. The following sections describe the controls that you use to create a Web-based application. (Don't confuse them with controls that you use on the desktop—the two sets of controls are completely different.) You can find this example in the \ABC_Inc\Reports folder of the source code provided on the Sybex Web site.

FIGURE 12.24
Add new sections using
the Section Expert.

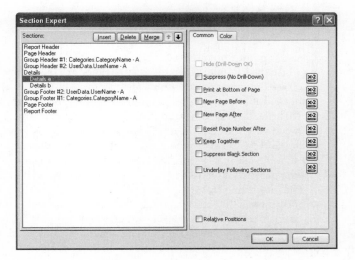

Using the *CrystalReportSource* Control

Every Crystal Reports Web page begins with a `CrystalReportSource` control. This control acts the same way as a data source does for a database application. To use this control, drag and drop it onto the form. Select the Configure Report Source option from the control's SmartTag. You'll see a Configure Report Source dialog box. The only entry in this dialog box lets you choose an existing report from the current folder, create a new report, or browse the hard drive to locate an existing report. No matter which option you choose, you'll eventually end up with a report name in the report location field. The example uses the full path to `BeneficialSuggestions.RPT`. You'll need to change the path to match your machine setup.

Once you provide a report name, click OK. After you make this change, you'll notice that the `CrystalReportSource` control adds another item to the SmartTag. Select the Edit Report option and the report editor described in the previous sections of the chapter opens so that you can make any required changes to the report.

Using the *CrystalReportViewer* Control

After you configure a `CrystalReportSource` control, you can add a `CrystalReportViewer` control to the Web page. You can use the SmartTag shown in Figure 12.25 to perform the required configuration. The most important setting is the Choose Report Source field. Select the `CrystalReportSource` control from the list of entries in the drop-down list to make the control functional.

FIGURE 12.25
Add new sections using the Section Expert.

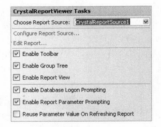

At this point, you might see a several second delay. The control will configure itself using the information in the RPT file. When the `CrystalReportViewer` control completes the configuration process, you'll see the report from within Design view. The `CrystalReportViewer` control provides a wealth of configuration settings, including one to prompt the user for any parameters you created as part of the RPT file (testing shows that this particular feature is problematic, so you want to use it with care).

When you first start the application, you'll see a logon screen. This logon screen asks the user for a name and password for the database. The logon screen also includes a Use Integrated Security check box that the user can use instead. You can disable this feature by setting the `EnableDatabaseLogon Prompt` property to false. Figure 12.26 shows the default output in Internet Explorer.

The interesting feature is that you can let the user print a local copy of this report. The local copy will appear as a PDF file by default. When the user clicks print, Adobe Acrobat actually starts and lets the user send the data to a local printer. An alternative is to use the ActiveX output. You select this option using the `PrintMode` property. Both options work well. The ActiveX option has the advantage of not needing any additional software on the user's machine, but the user must use Internet Explorer to employ this option. The PDF option has the advantage of working across multiple platforms, but the user must have Adobe Acrobat, Acrobat Reader, PDF printer software, or a compatible application installed to use it.

The default output includes a number of useful features. The group tree lets the user select a particular category first, and then a user within that category. The report includes automatic search capability and the user can choose a zoom level to overcome the problems of small print. You'll also find that the report provides several options for moving between pages including the familiar next and previous controls, along with a go to input. In short, considering you didn't write a single line of code to produce this output, Crystal Reports can produce some very impressive output.

FIGURE 12.26
A view of the report on a Web page.

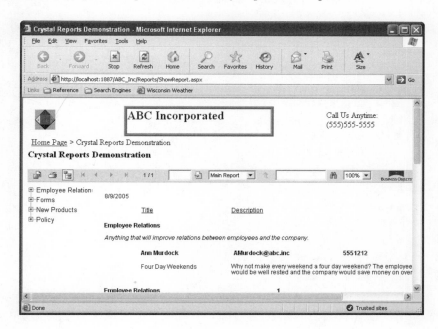

Defining Your Development Goals

This chapter has demonstrated techniques for working with Crystal Reports. Obviously, this application isn't the only reporting tool your disposal. Reports are so important to most businesses that many third parties create reporting tools with features that are only limited by the developer's imagination. The important concept to take away from this chapter is that you're going to create reports—lots of them. However, by generating good reports, the type that contain all of the information that management needs, you can save yourself a little time and a few trees in the forest as well.

Now it's time to work with Crystal Reports to generate your own reports. You'll want to spend some time with the version of the tool that comes with Visual Studio before you leap into buy the full-fledged product. Make sure you take time to design the reports, ensure they meet everyone's expectations, and look for ways to output the reports in other than printed form. When you do use a printed form, make sure you spend time looking at actual printed output—it matches what you see on your screen to a point, but the printed output usually varies a little and these little differences do matter.

Chapter 13 discusses techniques for working with multi-tier Web-based applications. Most businesses don't create single tier or even client-server applications—the applications must run on multiple systems across networks. In fact, many Web-based applications today run across vast domains with the borders of states and countries nonexistent as far as the application is concerned. Considering the implications of such applications, understanding how a multi-tier application differs is essential to both you and your business.

Chapter 13

Developing Multi-tier Applications

Many applications remain simple throughout their lifetime and don't cause their owners undo stress. Whenever possible, keep your applications simple—don't add gizmos that you really can't use. Sometimes, however, you do need some extra flexibility, not only to make the application run better but to also keep the data safe and ensure that both the user and application follow all the rules. Complex applications that have multiple layers of support and business logic are multi-tier. Contrast this with single tier applications (a simple Web page) or client/server applications (those where the Web page communicates directly with a backend application such as a database).

Developers create multi-tier applications for a number of reasons. Some applications are large enough that they require support from multiple servers—breaking the workload into smaller pieces helps create an environment where multiple servers can work well together. In some cases, multiple applications require the same component parts. For example, a database access routine might work well for more than one application, so there isn't a good reason to write the same code multiple times—breaking the code into tiers lets all applications access the common code. Sometimes breaking a complex application design into multiple pieces can reduce complexity—making it easier to code each piece rather than focus on the application as a whole. No matter what reason you have for creating a multi-tier application, the user interface, middle tier, and backend components must work well together to produce a cohesive whole.

Adding to the complexity of applications today is the need to support multiple device types. Most users now want to use the applications you develop on their desktop, laptop, Personal Digital Assistant (PDA), and cellular telephone. In addition, some companies use other device formats such as the digital notepad (see the Web site at `http://micro-wiz.com/warda/crosspadxp.html` for an example) and Tablet PC (see the Hewlett-Packard site at `http://www.hp.com/hpinfo/newsroom/feature_stories/2002/tablepc02.html` for an example). Some users expect computers to accept both keyed and handwritten input. Workers delivering goods might need a computer setup that looks and acts like a pad of paper. The point is that your need for a multi-tier application might revolve more around your need to support multiple devices than an actual application design requirement.

Binding with Middle Tier Objects

Most books on design divide the application environment for multi-tier applications into three areas. The user interface is the part of the application that the user sees. Actually, if you're used to the old client/server terminology—the user interface is the client—fat (normally a desktop application) or thin (normally a Web application), it doesn't matter. The middle tier contains all of the business logic, most of the security, all of the server interface, and even the server-side applications (such as data and event loggers). The backend normally includes the DBMS and any special software required to interact with it. You'll also find the backup systems here. Some large systems are now calling it a data store because they rely on exotic storage technologies to perform the task of managing data.

You already know that you can create a direct connection to the backend when necessary, but how about the middle tier components that you might need to access? Fortunately, Visual Studio is also quite adept at creating these middle tier connections. The following sections discuss the middle tier and demonstrate several middle tier scenarios.

Understanding the Middle Tier

The middle tier is where you provide server-side resources that the client will use in connection with an application. The idea is to keep your data safe by hiding it behind the middle tier. When someone wants to access data on the server, they must run the gauntlet of server-side components guarding that data before obtaining access to it. However, it's important to think about the entire middle tier as a means of data hiding of various sorts. Most developers call the software used to create the middle tier, middleware. Generally, middleware is a series of components, rather than an actual application. Here are some of the tasks that the middle tier performs.

Security Ensures the user has the required access. In addition, with .NET, you can determine whether the code has the required rights as well. Determining whether you have the right user accessing your site with the correct application is a significant way to improve security.

Calculations Provides feedback for calculated items. However, don't limit calculations to math— a calculation could be a date, time, or anything you want. The idea is that the middleware receives input from the client and uses that input to provide some kind of result. The reason that most companies perform this task in middleware, rather than at the backend, is to reduce the performance hit of returning the calculation. In addition, the middleware can restrict calculations to those who need them and accomplish the calculation based on the current application requirements.

Database Access Creates secured and restricted access to the database. A direct connection to the database could mean that the user gains more access than a particular situation warrants. You might want to give the user full access to a table from a desktop application, but restrict that access from a Web application. You might go so far as to restrict access based on the user's current role. Middleware monitors that access to the database and frees up processing cycles on the database server so it can do what it does best—serving up data.

Data, Error, Security, Performance, and Other Logging Monitors the system for unusual conditions, requests, or events. Many developers are afraid that users will see monitoring as a big brother complex. However, monitoring has many legitimate and necessary uses. Checking data flow can help a developer create a better system setup—one more in tune with user requests. Logging errors tells a developer about problems with the application. Some forms of error logging can help the developer find and squash application bugs. Every Web application should include security monitoring—you never know when the bad guys will find a way in. It's also important to use performance logging as a means for checking system health—a good performance checking system can mean the difference between bringing an additional server online to save the day or watch the system crash due to an unexpectedly heavy load.

Redirection Sends users to appropriate components to match specific needs or application loads. The browser a user has installed on their system can make a big difference in the way they interact with your server—sometimes this means sending browser users to a component that can meet their specific needs. In some cases, you'll want to redirect user requests from a busy server to one that's less busy to improve application performance. Finally, you can use redirection for simple data hiding. The application loses track of the source of the information and doesn't really care as long as it continues to receive the data it needs.

Background Processing   Creates a long-term processing session to let higher priority short-term tasks proceed. Sometimes a request requires many system resources to process and placing the request at the head of the list means that users with short requests have needless waits. Placing a request that requires a lot of system resources on the back burner means the short requests get processed in the timely manner, but that the long-term request is eventually fulfilled as well.

Creating Direct Connections

Many developers still consider the direct connection the best type to provide for the middle tier. Direct connection technologies such as Distributed Component Object Model (DCOM) and Component Object Model Plus (COM+) provide a stable communication medium with well-known features and functionality. Even though .NET component technology is newer, it offers the advantages of DCOM and COM+, with a few additional security features, such as code access checks added in for good measure. In addition, direct connections often provide enhanced security and use features such as an encrypted data stream to keep prying eyes at bay. Many developers also point out that direct connections usually provide higher performance than other connections, such as Web services, because they rely on various forms of data compression (Web services use XML, which is admittedly not very compact).

To create a direct connection to a local component, right-click the project entry in Solution Explorer and choose Add Reference from the context menu. You'll see the Add Reference dialog box shown in Figure 13.1. The .NET tab contains a list of components that appear in the Global Assembly Cache (GAC) on the local machine. Generally, you'll use this tab to access existing .NET Framework assemblies or assemblies used for multiple applications within your company. The COM tab contains native code components registered on the local machine. Remember that you must register COM+ components locally by exporting the COM+ application and installing the stub on the local machine. The Projects tab contains a list of references you can create to other projects in the current solution. The Browse tab lets you locate components that exist on the local machine or even on a networked drive but that aren't registered. You'll normally use this technique to access custom assemblies that you design for use with one or two applications. The Recent tab contains a list of components that you have recently accessed no matter what their source. You can see how a direct connection works by viewing the example in the \Chapter 13\DirectConnect folder of the source code provided on the Sybex Web site.

CREATING GLOBAL .NET CONNECTIONS

When you want to use a global assembly, highlight its entry on the .NET tab of the Add Reference dialog box. You can highlight multiple entries by Ctrl+Clicking on them. Click OK. For example, highlight the System.Data.SqlXml assembly and click OK. Visual Studio will automatically create a Web.CONFIG file for you, when your project doesn't have one already, and add the System.Data.SqlXml assembly reference shown here.

```
<assemblies>
    <add assembly="System.Data.SqlXml,
        Version=2.0.3600.0,
        Culture=neutral,
        PublicKeyToken=B77A5C561934E089"/>
</assemblies>
```

FIGURE 13.1
Use the Add Reference
dialog box to add new
references to your
project.

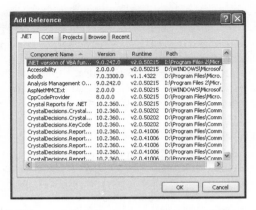

All of your referenced assemblies will appear within the <assemblies> element. The assembly reference includes the assembly name, version, culture (locale), and a public key token for security. The PublicKeyToken attribute is especially important because it identifies assemblies with a strong name—a prerequisite for inclusion in the GAC. (A strong name is a digital signature you add to the component—see the "Adding a Strong Name to the Component" section for details.)

CREATING COM, COM+, AND DCOM CONNECTIONS

Creating a reference using COM, COM+, or DCOM relies on the COM tab of the Add Reference dialog box. From a Visual Studio perspective, all three kinds of connections look the same. However, they're very different in reality. COM components exist on the local machine, while COM+ and DCOM components exist on a remote machine. COM+ relies on an installed stub for communication and actually relies on DCOM at a low level for direct communication, while DCOM relies on a configured setup.

To begin, you need to create the local registry entries for whatever communication technology you want to use. When working with COM+, the application you export provides all of the required information (see the "Creating the COM+ Application" section of the chapter for details). When working with either COM or DCOM components, you'll use the RegSvr32 utility to register the component. Simply type **RegSvr32 MyComponent.DLL** at the command prompt (where MyComponent.DLL is the name of your component and could have an EXE or OCX, OLE Custom eXtension, extension as well) and press Enter. You'll see a success message.

DCOM components require special configuration. Open the Component Manager console located in the Administrative Tools folder of the Control Panel and select the Component Services\Computers\ My Computer\DCOM Config folder shown in Figure 13.2. This folder contains a list of all of the components registered on the local machine—not all of these component execute on a remote machine (in fact, the majority of the components execute locally).

NOTE Older versions of Windows rely on the DCOMCnfg (Distributed COM Configuration) utility to configure DCOM for use. This utility works the same as the Component Manager console—just the appearance of the windows differs. To open this utility, select Start\Run, type **DCOMCnfg** in the Open field, and click OK. You'll see a list of components on the Applications tab that you can highlight. Click Properties to display a dialog box similar to the one shown in Figure 13.3.

Configure a component for use with DCOM by right-clicking the component entry and choosing Properties from the context menu. The example uses the Windows Media Player, but you can work with any component. You'll see the component Properties dialog box show in Figure 13.3. The Location tab is the most important for configuring the component because it determines where the component will execute. In this case, the Windows Media Player executes on a remote machine named WINSERVER. As far as .NET is concerned, the component is still executing locally—only this configuration change lets you use the remote component.

FIGURE 13.2
DCOM components require special configuration using the Component Manager console.

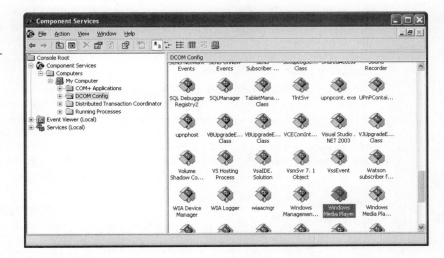

FIGURE 13.3
Choose the location where you want a DCOM component to execute.

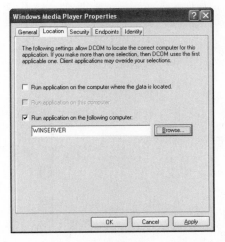

Make sure you check out the other tabs on the component Properties dialog box as well. The General tab contains the authentication level required to access the component. For example, if you're extremely paranoid about network communications, you can set the authentication level to Packet to ensure every packet provides authentication information. The Security tab lets you set access, launch, and configuration permissions for the component. Use the option on the Identity tab to determine which credentials to use for authentication (interactive user, launching user, a particular user, or the system account). Finally, the Endpoints tab lets you determine how the DCOM communication takes place—which protocols are used.

After you register and configure the component as needed, you can create a reference to it in .NET. Right-click the project entry in Solution Explorer and choose Add Reference from the context menu. This time you'll select the COM tab. Highlight the component you want to use and click OK. Visual Studio can't work with native code directly—it must use an interoperability layer to access the native code. Consequently, you won't see an entry for a COM, COM+, or DCOM component in Web.CONFIG—instead, the IDE creates a \Bin folder and places the interoperability module in there, as shown in Figure 13.4.

CREATING LOCAL CONNECTIONS

You can create local connections for either .NET or COM components. Local components aren't global—they might not be located on the local machine, but you haven't registered them for global use. To create this kind of connection, right-click the project entry in Solution Explorer and choose Add Reference. Select the Browse tab of the Add Reference dialog box shown in Figure 13.5. Notice that this dialog box accepts a variety of input types including DLL, EXE, and OCX files, as well as Type Libraries (TLB) and Object Libraries (OLB). You can see how a local connection works by viewing the example in the \Chapter 13\DirectConnect folder of the source code provided on the Sybex Web site.

FIGURE 13.4
COM, COM+, and DCOM connections require use of an interoperability module.

FIGURE 13.5
Use the Browse tab to locate local, unregistered components.

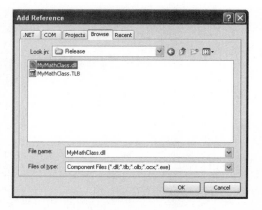

Unlike global assemblies, all local components appear in the \Bin folder—it doesn't matter whether the component relies on .NET or COM. The only difference is that the IDE copies the actual component into the \Bin folder for a .NET component, but relies on an interoperability assembly for COM components.

Developing Web Service Connections

Web service connections have a distinct advantage over direct connections. A direct connection requires that the client know about the server, know where the server physically resides, and knows enough about the server to make the connection. When you make a connection with a Web service, all you need is an URL. In both cases, you need to know about server security and you have to have an API to use, but Web services comes out ahead again here because using Web Services Description Language (WSDL), you can download the essentials of the API from the Web site. In short, Web services provide an enhanced environment for creating middle tier connections.

WARNING The example in this section relies on advanced programming techniques that you can skip if you want. This technique is extremely useful, especially when you need to create components that work in a variety of environments. Using this technique, you can create one component that works with both local and remote applications. However, you don't have to master this technique immediately to use Visual Studio. In fact, you may find that you never have to use a technique quite this exotic to provide interoperability in your application.

You have many options for creating Web services using .NET alone, but you also have options for creating Web services using standard components. In fact, sometimes you don't have to create the Web service at all. The example in the "Using Google to Create a Site Search" section of Chapter 8 is really a kind of middle tier Web service connection to a database—one that you didn't create, but can access nonetheless. In short, you have many opportunities to use Web services as a means of connecting to the middle tier.

NOTE This application only works on systems that have access to COM+ 1.5 or above, which means it won't work on Windows 2000 systems. It will work on newer versions of Windows such as Windows XP and Windows Server 2003. (If you're using Windows Vista, it should work there, as well, but I haven't actually tested it in that environment.) In addition, unlike other examples in this book, you must have Internet Information Server (IIS) installed to use this example because COM+ relies on IIS to create the Web service.

The example in this section provides a useful technique that works for more than one kind of connection. Your organization might have a number of older COM or COM+ components. In addition, you might want to gain the advantages of using .NET to create components that will work with both desktop applications and those that you create with Visual Studio. The technique shown here shows how to develop such a component, turn it into a Web service, and then access it from Visual Studio.

DESIGNING THE INTERFACE

Let's begin with the interface. You must create an interface for the class because COM and COM+ might not see the methods you expose otherwise. The interface must include two attributes: [Guid], which contains the Globally Unique Identifier (GUID) for the interface, and [ComVisible], which makes the interface visible to COM and COM+. You'll find that .NET automatically provides a GUID for you if you fail to include the [Guid] attribute, but you'll quickly find that this approach can leave your registry with tons of orphaned entries. Adding the [Guid] attribute is quick and easy, so it makes sense to use it to save time. Listing 13.1 shows the interface for this example. You'll find this example in the \Chapter 13\MyMathClass folder of the source code on the Sybex Web site.

The interface simply lists the methods that it supports. You implement this interface to build the component. The act of creating the interface provides a well-defined access method for the component that COM and .NET users understand equally well.

You might wonder where the mystery number for the [Guid] attribute comes from. Select the Tools ➢ Create GUID command and you'll see the Create GUID utility shown in Figure 13.6. (If you don't find this option on the Tools menu, you can also open the program at \Program Files\ Microsoft Visual Studio 8\Common7\Tools\GUIDGen.EXE.) Select option 4, as shown, and click Copy to place the new GUID on the clipboard. Paste the result into your code and remove the curly braces, {}, from either end of the GUID.

LISTING 13.1: Designing an Interface

```
[Guid("2D0B6B56-8572-4f25-8B13-E5CF81783E77")]
[ComVisible(true)]
public interface ISimpleMath
{
    Int32 DoAdd(Int32 Input1, Int32 Input2);
    Int32 DoSub(Int32 Input1, Int32 Input2);
    Int32 DoMul(Int32 Input1, Int32 Input2);
    Int32 DoDiv(Int32 Input1, Int32 Input2);
}
```

FIGURE 13.6
Define a GUID for your component using the Create GUID utility.

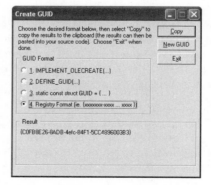

CREATING THE COMPONENT

The class comes next. You must implement the interface in your class to create the required linkage. Like the interface, the class uses the [Guid] attribute, but not the [ComVisible] attribute since the interface makes the methods public. The GUID you use for the class must be different from the one you used for the interface. The [ClassInterface] attribute contains one of the ClassInterfaceType enumeration values. Always use `AutoDual` unless you have a good reason for using one of the other options (such as making the component available to only VB6 or only VC++ developers). Listing 13.2 shows the component code. You'll find this example in the `\Chapter 13\MyMathClass` folder of the source code on the Sybex Web site.

Notice that this class inherits from the `ServicedComponent` class. This entry isn't too important when you want to use the component for COM or COM+ work, but Web services require it. What will happen if you don't include this entry is that COM+ will export the basic interface information, but won't create the required method declarations, so COM+ will appear to create the Web service and even IIS will seem to show that the Web service will work, but you won't be able to access the methods in the Web service. You'll find the `ServicedComponent` class in the `System.EnterpriseServices` namespace. Theoretically, you can also inherit from the Component class, which results in a less complex implementation, but can also introduce problems in using the Web service in some cases (the export isn't as precise as it could be).

LISTING 13.2: Define the Component Code Based on the Interface

```
[Guid("33933BDB-794D-4d3e-963A-D6FBCEE068E4")]
[ClassInterface(ClassInterfaceType.AutoDual)]
public class SimpleMath : ServicedComponent, ISimpleMath
{
    public SimpleMath()
    {
    }

    public Int32 DoAdd(Int32 Input1, Int32 Input2)
    {
        return Input1 + Input2;
    }

    public Int32 DoSub(Int32 Input1, Int32 Input2)
    {
        return Input1 - Input2;
    }

    public Int32 DoMul(Int32 Input1, Int32 Input2)
    {
        return Input1 * Input2;
    }

    public Int32 DoDiv(Int32 Input1, Int32 Input2)
    {
        return Input1 / Input2;
    }
}
```

The code for this example is purposely simple so that you can concentrate on the technique of creating the middleware connection, rather than the intricacies of the code itself. Any code you normally use for a .NET class will work in most cases. However, there are special situations where you have to use the `InteropServices` namespace members such as the `Marshal` class to create a bridge between .NET and the Win32 environment. For example, when you want to pass a complex custom object, you need to marshal it because CLR won't know what to do with it.

ADDING A STRONG NAME TO THE COMPONENT

Creating the code is a good start, but you must perform one additional task—give the component a strong name. To do that, open a command prompt and use the:

```
SN -k MyKey
```

command to create a key pair. This key pair signs the component to ensure no one can tamper with it. You add the strong name to the top of the component (after the Using directives or Imports statements) file using code like this:

```
[assembly: AssemblyKeyFile(@"..\..\MyKey")]
```

Adding the `[assembly]` attribute directly to the code is the older method of performing the task. Most developers prefer it because the attribute is easily accessible and distinctly visible in the code. However, Visual Studio .NET 2005 also supports adding the key to the project properties. This is the method that Microsoft prefers, so you'll see a warning message when you use the old method (the code still compiles and the component works fine, so you don't have to worry about using the old technique).

To add the key to the project properties, right-click the project entry in Solution Explorer and choose Properties from the context menu. Select the Signing tab shown in Figure 13.7. Check the Sign the Assembly option, choose <Browse> from the drop-down list, and select your key file.

FIGURE 13.7
Add your strong name key to the project properties dialog box when using the new signing technique.

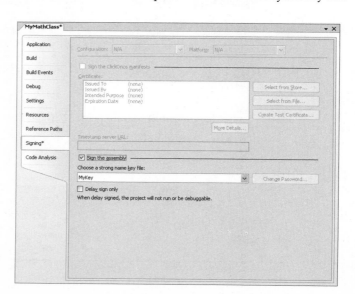

TIP   You don't have to use the SN utility any longer with Visual Studio .NET 2005 unless you want to create a single key file for all of your projects. Simply select the <New> option in the drop-down list on the Signing tab of the project properties dialog box. The IDE will display a Create Strong Name Key dialog box where you enter the name of the key file and (optionally) a password to protect it. This technique doesn't offer all of the features of using the SN utility, but it's fast and suitable for testing purposes.

Now you can compile the component. It's ready for use as either a COM or COM+ application.

REGISTERING THE COMPONENT

Unlike .NET applications, you must register COM and COM+ components for use because the COM environment looks for component entries in the registry. However, you don't use the normal RegSvr32 utility to perform this task with .NET components; you use the RegAsm utility instead. The RegAsm utility has more than a few command line switches, but you won't normally use most of them—they're for special purposes. The example component creates MyMathClass.DLL. To register this class in such a way that COM+ can use it, you'd type **RegASM MyMathClass.DLL /tlb:MyMathClass.TLB** at the command prompt and press Enter. RegAsm will create all of the required registry entries to use MyMathClass. In addition, it creates a type library that you must have to add the component to COM+.

Before you make any changes to the code or recompile the component, make sure you unregister the component from the registry. Again, you use the RegAsm utility to perform this task. In this case, you type **RegASM MyMathClass.dll /unregister** at the command prompt and press Enter.

Using RegAsm is good enough when you want to use COM+ alone. However, in this example, you also want to access the component as a Web service. To make the component usable at this level, you must also register it in the Global Assembly Cache (GAC) using the GACUtil utility. Like RegAsm, GACUtil includes a number of interesting switches you won't normally use. To register the example component, simply type **GACUtil -i MyMathClass.DLL** at the command prompt and press Enter. Figure 13.8 shows the results of using the RegASM and GACUtil commands to register the sample component.

Notice that the output from the RegAsm utility tells you that it registered the component types and that it exported these types to a type library file. If you don't see both entries, then the component registration won't work. Likewise, make sure that the GACUtil tells you that it successfully added the assembly to the cache. The most common problem in adding an assembly to the cache is that the assembly lacks a strong name (see the "Adding a Strong Name to the Component" section for details).

FIGURE 13.8
Register the component you want to use for a Web service and add it to the GAC.

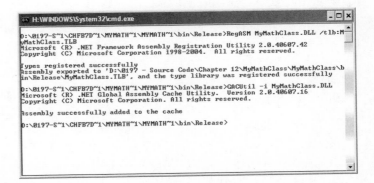

Removing the assembly from the GAC is equally easy. Simply type `GACUtil -u MyMathClass` at the command prompt and press Enter (notice that the DLL extension is omitted). Note that you must remove the component from the GAC before you unregister it, so the unregistration process follows the reverse order of registration.

CREATING THE COM+ APPLICATION

Now that you have a component to test with COM+, it's time to create the COM+ application. This is a two-step process. First, you create the COM+ application and then you add the component to it. However, when working with .NET components, you need to exercise a little extra care because sometimes the component will appear to register without problem, but you can't access the methods due to any of a number of errors.

To start the process, open the Component Services console found in the Administrative Tools folder. Right-click the folder and choose New ➢ Application from the context menu to create a COM+ application—you'll see the Welcome to the COM+ Application Install Wizard dialog box. Skip past the welcome screen and you'll see the Install or Create a New Application dialog box. Click Create an Empty Application and you'll see the Create Empty Application dialog box shown in Figure 13.9.

Because we want to expose this application as a Web service, you have to make it a server application. Type an application name (the example uses COMPlusTest) and define an application type (it must be Server Application). Follow the rest of the prompts using the default options.

You're now the proud owner of a new COM+ application. However, this application doesn't have any components in it, so it won't do anything. Open the application and right-click the Components folder. Select the New ➢ Component option from the context menu. You'll see the COM+ Component Install Wizard.

The COM+ Component Install Wizard lets you add components to an existing application. Skip past the welcome dialog box and you'll see the Import or Install a Component dialog box where you have several options for adding a component. Click Install New Component. You'll see a Select Files to Install dialog box. Highlight the TLB file created by RegAsm and click Open. (The example uses the TLB file located in the `\Chapter 13\MyMathClass\MyMathClass\bin\Release` folder of the Sybex Web site.) At this point, you'll see the Install New Components dialog box. Notice that it contains the name of the component and the component status, as shown in Figure 13.10.

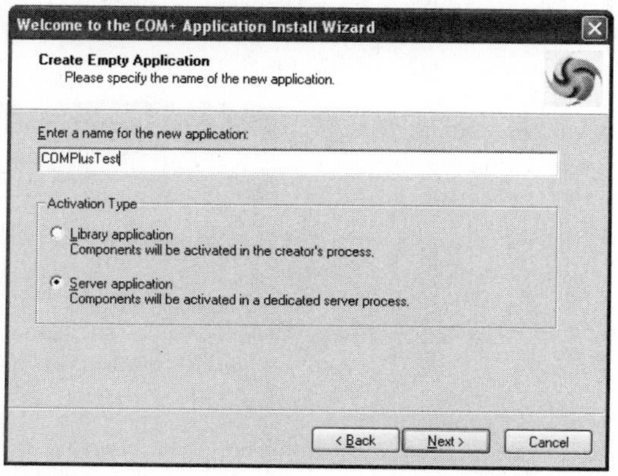

FIGURE 13.9

Create a new COM+ application to hold the .NET component.

It's important to check out this dialog box carefully because it can tell you whether the .NET component installed successfully. Make sure you check the component name to ensure it's correct. Also, check whether COM+ found the interfaces. Errors in this dialog box usually indicate that RegAsm didn't work correctly (you had the wrong switches) or the component is missing one or more [ComVisible(true)] entries. Once you verify the entries, follow the rest of the prompts to add the component.

Now you can verify the COM+ application setup. Open the Interfaces, look for the ISimpleMath interface, and check out the methods. Your application should match the one shown in Figure 13.11. When any of the interfaces or methods is missing, it usually indicates some type of error in your code, such as missing [ComVisible(true)] entries or an invalid [ClassInterface(ClassInterfaceType .AutoDual)] entry.

FIGURE 13.10
Check the component name and status to ensure it installed correctly.

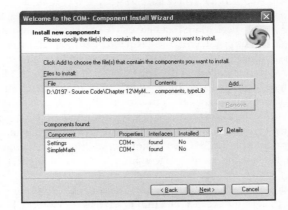

FIGURE 13.11
Verify the application setup is correct.

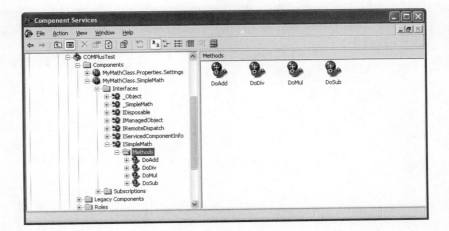

DEFINING THE WEB SERVICE

At this point, you could use the component using standard COM or COM+ techniques. That's great when you have a local connection, but what if you want to make this component available to someone who relies on an Internet connection. Microsoft has made it possible for users of COM+ 1.5 and above to expose a COM+ application as a Web service by making a few small changes to the application setup.

To begin the process, right-click the COM+ application entry in the Component Services console—COMPlusTest in this case—and choose Properties from the context menu. Select the Activation tab and you'll see an entry for SOAP like the one shown in Figure 13.12 when you have COM+ 1.5 or above installed on your system.

To create a Web service, check the Uses SOAP option, as shown in Figure 13.12. Type a name for the Web service. Make sure this name will make sense to anyone accessing the Web application because COM+ uses this name to create the required Internet Information Services (IIS) entry. The example uses MathTest because it's a simple descriptive name. Click OK.

At this point, you could run into a number of errors. The most common error is that you didn't register the component in the GAC. The second most common problem is that you don't have ASP.NET support installed on IIS. The `\WINDOWS\Microsoft.NET\Framework\v2.0.40607` folder on your system contains the `ASPNet_RegIIS.EXE` utility that you can use to add ASP.NET support to IIS. This utility runs for several minutes, so don't become concerned about the registration time. Make sure you restart IIS when you finish installing ASP.NET support. Another common problem is that IIS isn't running. It sounds odd, but IIS isn't always running on some development machines and you might not notice if you're not working on a Web project at the moment.

When the setup is successful, you can go to a special Web page for the application. For the example, it's `http://localhost/MathTest/Default.aspx`. This page displays a single link that takes you to the Web Services Description Language (WSDL) for the Web service. For this example, the WSDL appears at `http://localhost/MathTest/MyMathClass.SimpleMath.soap?WSDL`. Keep track of this WSDL URL because you need it to create a connection from outside applications to your COM+ application disguised as a Web service. This is also the time to check whether COM+ created a good WSDL file. Make sure you look for methods, as shown in Figure 13.13.

FIGURE 13.12
Only COM 1.5 and above users will have the SOAP entry available.

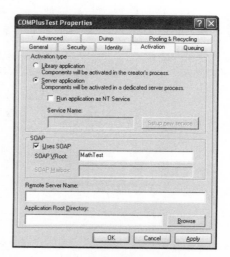

FIGURE 13.13

The WSDL COM+ creates should show the methods you exported.

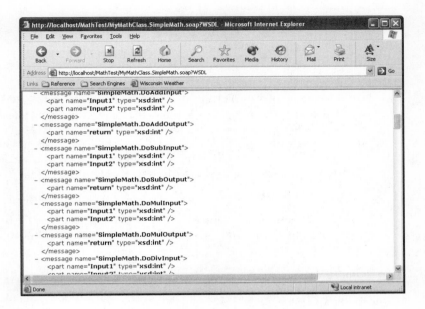

USING THE WEB SERVICES FROM VISUAL STUDIO

The Web service created by COM+ is accessible from any outside source that has the proper permissions. Visual Studio is included in the list of sources. In fact, you can use this same Web service from the full version of Visual Studio .NET, or other language products such as Java or PHP. Web services provide great access to your code no matter what the other party is using.

To access the Web service, you need to create a Web reference. Right-click the project entry in Solution Explorer and select Add Web Reference from the context menu. You'll see an Add Web Reference dialog box. Type the WSDL URL for the Web service in the URL field and click Go. The Add Web Reference dialog box should access the Web service and display information about it similar to that shown in Figure 13.14. You can see how the connection works by viewing the example in the \Chapter 13\WebServiceConnect folder of the source code on the Sybex Web site.

Click Add Reference to add the Web service to your application. Unlike local references, the IDE creates a WebReferences folder for a Web service, as shown in Figure 13.15.

Notice that each server has a separate folder and included within that folder is the Web service entry, which includes a WSDL and a Discovery Map (DISCOMAP) file. The WSDL file looks precisely the same as the information shown in Figure 13.14. The DISCOMAP file contains a simple reference to the WSDL file so that Visual Studio can locate it again later, as shown here:

```xml
<?xml version="1.0" encoding="utf-8"?>
<DiscoveryClientResultsFile
    xmlns:xsi="http://www.w3.org/2001/XMLSchema-instance"
    xmlns:xsd="http://www.w3.org/2001/XMLSchema">
  <Results>
    <DiscoveryClientResult
        referenceType="System.Web.Services.Discovery.ContractReference"
```

```
            url="http://localhost/MathTest/MyMathClass.SimpleMath.soap?WSDL"
            filename="SimpleMath.wsdl" />
    </Results>
  </DiscoveryClientResultsFile>
```

The DISCOMAP file is yet another form of XML used with Visual Studio. In this case, the `<DiscoveryClientResult>` tells the kind of reference the DISCOMAP file contains and describes where to find it. The `url` attribute defines the remote location, while the `filename` attribute contains the local filename. Because Visual Studio creates the DISCOMAP file for you automatically, you should never edit it, but it's helpful to know that the file exists and how the IDE uses it.

Now you can create a Web form, add buttons and code to it, and test it. Before you can access the Web service though, you need to add a reference for it. Here's the Visual Basic version.

```
    Imports localhost
```

Listing 13.3 shows some code you can use for testing purposes (the full example implements all four math functions). You'll find this example in the `\Chapter 13\MyMathClass` folder of the source code on the Sybex Web site.

FIGURE 13.14
The final confirmation that the COM+ application is accessible is the information the Web service displays.

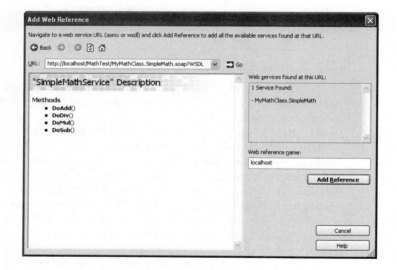

FIGURE 13.15
Visual Studio creates special entries for each Web reference that relies on a folder structure.

All you need to do is create an object based on the Web services class, SimpleMathService. This class includes all of the functionality required to interact with the Web service, including any custom methods such as DoAdd().

The next step is to use one of the methods to update the current application. In this case, the application retrieves two text values from the form, converts them to Int32 values, and passes them to the DoAdd() method. The DoAdd() method adds the values together and passes them back as an Int32 value, which the code converts to the string and displays on the form. Figure 13.16 shows typical output from this application.

LISTING 13.3:   Using the COM+ Application as a Web Service

```
Sub btnAdd_Click(ByVal sender As Object, ByVal e As System.EventArgs)
    ' Create the new Web service reference.
    Dim SMS As New SimpleMathService

    ' Obtain the output from the DoAdd() method call.
    txtOutput.Text = _
        SMS.DoAdd(Int32.Parse(txtInput1.Text), _
                  Int32.Parse(txtInput2.Text)).ToString()
End Sub
```

FIGURE 13.16
The output of this application relies on middleware—a COM+ component on the server.

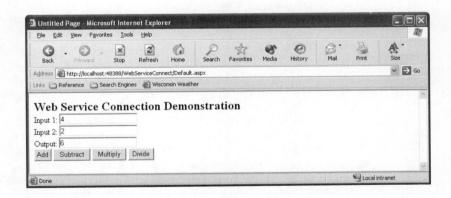

Working with Multiple Device Types

Most developers have to face the prospect today of working with multiple device types. Users want to access their Web data using desktop, laptops, notebooks, PDAs, and cellular telephones. You can't even count on the kind of devices remaining constant—users frequently turn in their cellular telephones and PDAs to get the latest model. In short, you need a method of allowing access to the Web application that doesn't depend on a particular kind of device. The Web application should automatically accommodate whatever device the user attempts to use. The following sections describe this process in detail.

Understanding WAP/WML, XHTML Mobile, and cHTML

As a mobile device developer, you'll run into a wealth of new acronyms for specifications that you might not know about. This is especially true when working with cellular telephones because they represent one of the newest areas of application development. Sometimes it's tough to know which languages to pursue and even less where to find information about them.

One of the most popular languages today is eXtensible HypterText Markup Language (XHTML). The reason this language is so popular is that it seeks to combine all of the previous mobile device presentation languages so that you only have to consider one, standards-based, language for your mobile device development. Unfortunately, the reality is that you must often support both older and newer technologies when working with mobile devices because some users will buy less expensive older models and attempt to access Web your application with them. You can learn more about this particular language at `http://www.w3.org/TR/xhtml1/` and `http://www.w3.org/TR/xhtml2/`.

Visual Studio provides support for XTHML 1.1. The use of this standard means that Visual Studio applications support most new devices and some older devices, but not all of the devices that could access your Web site. You can verify the use of the XHTML standard by creating a project with a `ContentPager` control and viewing the resulting `<DOCTYPE>` tag by right-clicking the Web page and choosing View Source from the context menu. Generally, you'll see a `<DOCTYPE>` tag such as this one:

```
<!DOCTYPE html PUBLIC "-//W3C//DTD XHTML 1.1//EN"
                      "http://www.w3.org/TR/xhtml11/DTD/xhtml11.dtd">
```

You can create applications that support other standards using Visual Studio, but that means hand coding the pages. Whether the additional coding is worth the effort depends on the project. When most of the people accessing your Web site use these older standards, you need to consider their needs. (Public Web sites should either check the client information of people accessing their Web site or rely on surveys to determine the kind and version of the browser that a visitor uses.) The rest of this section provides helpful tips you can use in gaining information about other mobile devices standards.

Two of the most important languages for developers are Wireless Markup Language (WML) (introduced by Nokia and Openwave) (`http://www.oasis-open.org/cover/wap-wml.html`) and Compact HyperText Markup Language (cHTML) (used as a source for i-Mode by NTT DoCoMo). These two languages describe the technique used to communicate with a mobile device such as a PDA or cellular telephone and therefore describe what you'll use to write applications for them. More importantly, these technologies present the starting point for mobile communications, and newer technologies tend to incorporate at least parts of these older specifications (not that the older specifications are out of use—new models come out that support them all the time). Fortunately, companies such as NTT DoCoMo, Nokia, Ericsson, and Openwave, part of the Open Mobile Alliance (OMA), do support XHTML, so these older specifications will become obsolete with time.

NOTE The world of online development is in a constant state of flux. Most developers feel that XHTML will replace both WML and cHTML—articles such as the one titled, "NTT DoCoMo Proposes XHTML as New WAP Standard" at `http://asia.internet.com/news/article.php/668041` tend to confirm that older technologies are on their way out. Other developers dispute this viewpoint, but you still need to consider your development options carefully. Make sure you consider eXtensible Hypertext Markup Language (XHTML) for complex applications with many elements. It helps you to display your application in segments with relative ease.

Many vendors use the Handheld Device Markup Language (HDML) (`http://www.w3.org/TR/NOTE-Submission-HDML-spec.html`) or WML because they're easy to understand. Both of these technologies use the concept of cards and decks to break up information into easily managed pieces. Of course, the mobile device you use has to provide support for these standards (most older devices do) before you can use the tags within a document. Unfortunately, using any of these solutions normally prevents your Web application from appearing properly on a desktop machine.

You can obtain a wealth of specification information for WML (and other mobile technologies) at `http://www.wapforum.org/what/technical.htm`. It's surprising to see just how many WML specifications are already available online—make sure you select the most current version of the specification when you do download it. The Wireless Developer Network has a tutorial on using WML at `http://www.wirelessdevnet.com/channels/wap/training/wml.html`.

One of the first places to look for cHTML information is the World Wide Web Consortium (W3C) site at `http://www.w3.org/TR/1998/NOTE-compactHTML-19980209/`. This discussion document helps explain some of the issues in using cHTML. A good introduction to i-Mode and cHTML appears at `http://www.devx.com/wireless/articles/i-Mode/i-ModeIntro.asp`. You can find an interesting article that explains how cHTML works, including example code, at `http://www.ddj.com/documents/nam1012432089/`.

Using the *ContentPager* Control

Creating an XHTML-compliant Web page will allow most devices to access it, but there's a problem to consider. Most mobile devices have small screens and limited display options. Trying to stuff a page that fits well on a desktop machine display onto a cellular telephone display isn't going to work. Consequently, you need some means for dividing the page into smaller pieces for mobile devices, while continuing to use the full capability of a desktop machine. Unfortunately, when working with Visual Studio, this means creating two sets of pages—one for the desktop and another for the mobile device. However, you can use a single Web page for all mobile devices, so the problem only involves a duplication of work at one level.

When working with a mobile device, the `ContentPager` control helps you create smaller pages with a minimum of effort. All you need to do is divide the page content into small segments and use the `ContentPager` control to move between them. Every mobile device will receive the same amount of text, so you need to balance the needs of very small devices with those that have larger displays.

To begin creating paged content, decide which elements will appear on every page and which elements you plan to display in sections. For example, a Web site header should appear on every page, but a section of content will only appear on one page. You also need to split content that appears in side areas from the main content and provide a link to it. Once you make these decisions, place the content that you plan to display in section in a container control, such as a `Panel`. Finally, place a `ContentPager` control at the bottom of the page. Figure 13.17 shows an example layout.

You also need to configure the `ContentPager` control. As a minimum, you must define the `ControlToPaginate` and the `ItemsPerPage` properties. The `ControlToPaginate` property contains the name of the control that contains the material to section—`pnlContent` in this case. The `ItemsPerPage` property contains the number of items to display per page. The number of items is always one greater than the actual number of items because the `ContentPager` control adds a blank line at the bottom of the display. In this example, you need to include one line for the header and two lines for each of the sections, so the `ItemsPerPage` property contains a value of 4.

To see how this example works, you'll need an emulator. This section relies on the Openwave emulator (see the "Working with Emulators" section for details on downloading this emulator). Once you get Openwave installed and have restarted your machine, you'll want to test this product. If you installed the 6.2.2 version, all you get is the emulator. To start the emulator, select the Start ➤ Programs ➤ Openwave SDK 6.2.2 ➤ Openwave SDK 6.2.2 HTTP option. You'll see the emulator start. The emulator automatically goes to the Openwave test site on first use, but you can change that location by opening the SDK Configuration dialog box using the Tools ➤ Options menu. Select the Browse tab and change the Homepage field.

Unfortunately, Visual Studio doesn't know about the emulator. Start the application and you'll see the usual Internet Explorer display. Copy the address in the Address field to the clipboard and paste it into the Go field of the emulator. After a few seconds, you'll see how the page looks in the emulator. It should look like the display in Figure 13.18.

FIGURE 13.17
Section the output to make it easier to display on small devices.

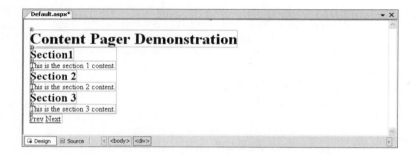

FIGURE 13.18
Use an emulator to display the mobile device page so you can ensure it actually works. Image courtesy Openwave Systems Inc.

Working with Emulators

One of the problems that developers must solve when working with mobile devices is testing for multiple models. Because of this requirement, most developers turn to emulation software (a feature that Visual Studio doesn't have) to help test their applications. An emulator provides the equivalent environment of the mobile device that it's supposed to model. I stress the word *equivalent*, because most of these emulators don't provide a complete picture of the mobile device environment. You can rely on an emulator to tell you whether the application fits within the screen area that the mobile device provides, but you can't rely on it to tell you about memory issues or whether a particular device has a piece of support software you need. These other issues require testing on an actual device—something you should do for at least a subset of the mobile devices you want to support.

TIP   Keep apprised of the latest Microsoft mobility and embedded system developments at `http://msdn.microsoft.com/mobility/`. This Web site includes many of the links you'll need to download the latest Microsoft products to make your Web Services mobile application development easier.

I chose the emulators used to test the application in the sections that follow because they provide a broad range of support, and you can download evaluation units. I also tested each of these emulators with Visual Studio—however, your experience might vary from mine based on your system configuration. Here are the download locations so that you can get your copies of the products before you begin this section. The following sections assume that you've downloaded the software required for the installation.

◆ Microsoft eMbedded Visual Tools 3.0 (2002 edition): `http://www.microsoft.com/downloads/details.aspx?FamilyId=F663BF48-31EE-4CBE-AAC5-0AFFD5FB27DD` (full development package) or `http://www.microsoft.com/downloads/details.aspx?FamilyId=25F4DE97-AE80-477A-9DF1-496B85B3D3E3` (emulators only) or `http://www.microsoft.com/downloads/details.aspx?FamilyID=2dbee84a-bd94-4167-b817-2b2e548b2e92` (older full development version)

TIP   Because it's such a large download (205 MB), Microsoft provides eMbedded Visual Tools 3.0 (2002 edition) on a CD. You can order the CD to avoid the download time. In addition, even though Windows XP isn't listed as one of the supported platforms, developers find the product installs just fine on Windows XP. Make sure you copy the CD key at the bottom of the download page when you do download your copy of eMbedded Visual Tools 3.0 from the Internet.

◆ Openwave SDK: `http://developer.openwave.com/dvl/tools_and_sdk/openwave_mobile_sdk/phone_simulator/`

◆ Microsoft Smartphone 2003: `http://www.microsoft.com/downloads/details.aspx?familyid=8fe677fa-3a6a-4265-b8eb-61a628ecd462` (requires eMbedded Visual C++ 4.0) or Microsoft Pocket PC 2003 emulator for eMbedded Visual C++ 4.0 at `http://www.microsoft.com/downloads/details.aspx?FamilyId=9996B314-0364-4623-9EDE-0B5FBB133652`

Defining Your Development Goals

This chapter has provided you with some ideas for working with multi-tier applications, especially that all-important middle tier. Creating great applications often means dividing the applications into smaller parts to optimize the various code components. However, you must balance that requirement with the need to keep things simple—not to make the application any more complex than necessary. Increasing the complexity for most developers today is the requirement to not only create applications that work in a number of environments but also on a number of devices. This chapter helps you balance all of that complexity while meeting the needs of everyone using the application.

Now it's time to put everything presented in the last three chapters to use. You now know that Visual Studio can create relatively complex applications and support a number of devices. It's possible to access any number of data sources and use the tools that Visual Studio provides to manage those data sources. Only you can determine how the various Visual Studio features can help you create robust applications that users can rely on. It's time to brainstorm some ideas, spend some time experimenting, and look at how Visual Studio can interact with the resources you have from other products to create a complete solution.

Once you have a complete application designed and partially developed, it's time to consider fit-and-finish issues. No one wants a drab application and Chapter 14 demonstrates some techniques for adding pizzazz to your next application. Yes, this chapter tells you how to use some of those processing cycles and other resources you saved by creating an efficient application to improve the user experience. An improved user experience usually equates to another kind of performance gain. Making the user more efficient usually nets better throughput than the best-tuned application can provide—of course, there's that matter of balance to maintain and Chapter 14 shows you how.

Part 5

Developing Full-blown Web Applications

In this part:

Chapter 14

Designing Dynamic Pages with Pizzazz

Most people like a Web site that has a little pizzazz—that something extra that dresses up the Web site and makes it fun to use. Pizzazz doesn't have to be an eye-popping array of snappy special effects that make the site unusable to anyone with any kind of special viewing need. Sometimes the subtle effects are better because they add a little surprise—one that the user can appreciate. For example, a mouse-over effect might not seem very exciting, but it's something small that the user will see and appreciate every time they use your Web site.

For many people, the concept of pizzazz goes hand in hand with what it does for them—something glitzy that makes your Web site stand out attracts attention, but perhaps not the right kind of attention. However, a fully customizable site has a lot of pizzazz and it also does something for the user—it attracts the right kind of attention. Unfortunately, a one-size-fits-all approach won't work in this case. Some developers use hosted sites, others have setups that won't tolerate a lot of server-side processing, and still others need a level of customization that older technologies don't address. Consequently, this chapter provides several ideas on providing customization for your Web site, including both traditional client- and server-side scripting, along with some additional WebPart techniques you can use. (All of these techniques require some kind of coding, unfortunately, but you still have quite a few choices.)

Depending on how you construct your Web site and the audience you're targeting, you might want to add various kinds of media to your Web site. Visual media presentations are the most common because they work even in a cubicle. Audio media is also popular, but it can cause problems in situations where quiet is the rule. In some cases, you'll want to combine both video and audio media to provide a movie-like experience for users. Of course, this technology also has some serious uses. For example, many tutorials benefit from the use of media, and you can use alternative media for other purposes as well. One of the least used forms of media is physical interaction. A good example of this form of media is a training site where the user provides input and the site reacts to that input. It's not quite the same as filling out a form because the reaction isn't the same every time.

Dynamic presentations are also important ways to add pizzazz to your Web site. Unfortunately, most dynamic presentations available today are cheesy advertisements for products of dubious quality. However, you could just as easily use these technologies to provide a tip of the day on your Web site or tidbits of interesting information. The idea is that dynamic presentations need not present just one kind of information—you can use the technology for many useful kinds of presentations.

NOTE Even though the ABC Incorporated Web site demonstrates all of the pizzazz described in this chapter, you would never use all of these forms of pizzazz on a single Web site. Adding too much pizzazz is distracting and overusing it could cause the viewer to miss the entire point of the pizzazz in the first place. Use pizzazz in a focused way by following the guidelines in the "Avoiding Pizzazz Overkill" section of the chapter.

Combining Themes, Scripts, and Other Techniques

Sometimes all the pizzazz you need for a Web site exists in technologies that you already know— combining these technologies in new ways can create the effects that you want. Chapter 4 describes how to use technologies such as master pages and themes. These two technologies can give your Web site a specific look. Chapter 5 tells you how to create a level of interactivity with the user. Sure, the interaction relies on form technology, but that might be all you need in many cases. Finally, Chapter 6 describes how to use scripts to accomplish a number of tasks. For example, using the `<Object>` tag might be all you need to display specialized content using a control that already exists on the user's machine. The sections that follow describe how you can combine these three essential techniques, along with other techniques described in previous chapters, to define a page with pizzazz.

Avoiding Pizzazz Overkill

One of the problems with learning a new technology is that you want to use it everywhere, even places where it doesn't make sense. A page with pizzazz often combines several technologies in subtle ways to produce a particular effect. For example, you might create a simple layout with an icon in the upper left corner, a banner, a sidebar with a list of favorite URLs, and a main content area—it's a simple layout, yet it divides the information you want to present effectively. Add to the layout scripts that automatically change content based on user preferences and color based on a theme, and you have a page with pizzazz that the user will like.

Pizzazz overkill can occur in other ways. For example, you need to consider whether everyone can use the Web page that you design. A Web page that includes a lot of glitz or understated colors can cause more than a few problems. You need to ask whether a user that has scripting support turned off can see the page as you intended (even if some of the special features don't work). It's also important to determine whether the page is accessible (see Chapter 21 for details). Users with special sight, hearing, or cognitive needs will probably want to view your Web site as well, but a Web site with too much glitz could hinder their efforts.

Performance is another concern when you add pizzazz to a Web site. Every bit of pizzazz you add uses resources—consumes memory, hard drive space, processing cycles, and network bandwidth. The resources have a real world value, and you need to consider how much the pizzazz will cost. In addition, pizzazz has less tangible costs associated with it. For example, pizzazz increases the number of things that can break on the Web page, which reduces reliability. Pizzazz can also raise security concerns because it increases the number of potential holes that crackers can use to attack your site. In short, you have to moderate your desire to create a great looking page with the costs of creating it.

Using Layout, Themes, and Code Behind Effectively

Pages with a combination of layout, theme, and code behind support can provide a great visual presentation. You can create visual effects (see the "Creating Special Effects" section of the chapter), add automatically updated materials (see the "Creating a Dynamic Presentation" section of the chapter), or provide some type of media presentation (see the "Working with Media" section of the chapter)—all with just these three technologies. The example in this section shows how you can incorporate some types of code behind in a manner that won't affect the presentation for users who don't have scripting enabled. Remember that many ASP.NET features automatically generate scripts behind the scene, so script support is a concern in some cases. You'll find this example in the \ABC_Inc folder of the source code on the Sybex Web site.

UNDERSTANDING THE PROBLEM

The majority of the ABC Incorporated Web pages rely on one of two master pages: `Default.MASTER` or `InfoPage.MASTER`. Unfortunately, you can't assign a theme to a master page. The master page will adopt a theme when the content page relies on one or you can assign a theme to all pages on a Web site by adding a <pages> element to the `Web.CONFIG` file, as shown here.

```
<pages theme="MyTheme"></pages>
```

Because of the `<pages>` element, both of these master pages rely on the same theme—the MyTheme entry found in the `\ABC_Inc\Themes` folder. However, you can decide to give the user a choice of which theme to use. The example in this section adds two additional themes, Sunny and Cloudy. The "Designing Your Own Themes" section of Chapter 4 describes how to construct a theme.

The example assumes the developer doesn't want to waste page space allowing the user to change the theme setting on every page—just the main (default) page. However, the change has to show up on every page. Consequently, the example must add code to several locations in order to implement a theme change. The `Default.ASPX` page requires code to implement the change, while the remaining Web site pages need some means to recognize and display the current theme. The most efficient method of performing this task is to add the selection specific code to `Default.ASPX` code behind file and the theme recognition and configuration code to a class file.

You might wonder why the example doesn't add the common code to the master page code behind file. The problem is that a theme selection occurs during the pre-initialization phase. In fact, you must make this change as part of the `Page.PreInit()` event handler. The pre-initialization phase is the same time frame in which the master page selection occurs. Consequently, the master page doesn't exist at the time you want to assign a theme to the content page—the change must occur within the page. Of course, you don't want to repeat the code on every page either, so using a separate class is the best way to handle this particular problem.

ADDING THE USER CONFIGURATION CODE

One of the essentials of understanding this example is to know how various Web page features affect the event cycle. Changing a theme means adding a user control for the purpose to a Web page and monitoring the user's activity with that control. To add a feature like this to your Web page, you need to add a `DropDownList` control to the Web page. Configure this control with the options the user can change. You also need to set the `AutoPostBack` property to `True` so that the user sees any changes instantly. The example has two icons that the user can choose for the upper right corner. Changing the display is relatively easy, as shown here.

```
<asp:Label ID="lblSelectTheme" Runat="server"
           Text="Select Theme"
           Font-Bold="True" Font-Size="Medium">
</asp:Label><br />
<asp:DropDownList ID="ddlSelectTheme" Runat="server"
                  ToolTip="Themes change the display appearance."
                  AutoPostBack="True">
   <asp:ListItem Selected="True">Default</asp:ListItem>
   <asp:ListItem>Sunny</asp:ListItem>
   <asp:ListItem>Cloudy</asp:ListItem>
   <asp:ListItem>None</asp:ListItem>
</asp:DropDownList>
```

Changing a theme requires more work than most other display or physical Web page features because the theme is set before the system initializes the Web page. This part of the example gives the user a choice—the ability to use one of the themes or no theme at all. You'll need to add a DropDownList control to the Web page and configure it with the themes the user can select. As before, you need to set the AutoPostBack property to True so that the user sees any changes instantly.

NOTE Physical changes, such as allowing the user to choose a different icon, are relatively simple. The user makes a choice that you record as a personal setting. When the page loads, the code locates the personal setting and makes changes to the display accordingly. The code relies on a simple case statement to make the change. It simply changes the icon filename. Because the automatic post-back also refreshes the display, the user sees the icon change immediately. You still need to decide whether to make the change global by implementing the code as part of a master page or local to a single Web page by changing the individual page's code.

The first task is to provide a means for the user to select a theme. Space considerations won't normally allow you to add this selection to every page and it isn't always a good idea to do so even when you have the space. Leave these settings on a central page so that the user can find them quickly, but the settings won't clutter the screen either. The ABC Incorporated Web site places the settings on the Default.ASPX page. Listing 14.1 shows how to implement a page that has a theme change.

LISTING 14.1:   Working with Theme Changes

```
Protected Sub Page_Load(ByVal sender As Object, _
                        ByVal e As System.EventArgs) Handles Me.Load

   Dim ThemeName As String = ""   ' Holds the theme name.

   ' Don't process the theme information on a postback.
   If Page.IsPostBack Then
      Return
```

```vb
        End If

        ' Get the cookies for the page.
        If Not Request.Cookies("ddlSelectTheme") Is Nothing Then
            ThemeName = Request.Cookies("ddlSelectTheme").Value
        End If

            ' If the query string doesn't contain a theme name, exit.
        If ThemeName Is Nothing Then
            Return
        End If

        ' Choose a theme setting based on the user request.
        Select Case ThemeName
            Case "Default"
                ddlSelectTheme.SelectedIndex = 0
            Case "Sunny"
                ddlSelectTheme.SelectedIndex = 1
            Case "Cloudy"
                ddlSelectTheme.SelectedIndex = 2
            Case "None"
                ddlSelectTheme.SelectedIndex = 3
        End Select
    End Sub

    Protected Sub ddlSelectTheme_SelectedIndexChanged( _
        ByVal sender As Object, ByVal e As System.EventArgs)

        ' Create a theme cookie.
        Dim ThemeCookie As New HttpCookie("ddlSelectTheme")

        ' Set the cookie.
        ThemeCookie.Value = ddlSelectTheme.SelectedValue
        ThemeCookie.Expires = DateTime.Now.AddMonths(1)
        If Response.Cookies("ddlSelectTheme") Is Nothing Then
            Response.Cookies.Add(ThemeCookie)
        Else
            Response.Cookies.Remove("ddlSelectTheme")
            Response.Cookies.Add(ThemeCookie)
        End If

        ' Redirect the response so that it includes the
        ' required theme information.
        Response.Redirect("Default.aspx")
    End Sub
```

As you can see, changing a theme isn't nearly as simple as changing an icon, even though they both require the same amount of effort during design time. The best place to begin this example is in the `ddlSelectTheme_SelectedIndexChanged()` method. The code calls this event handler when a user selects a different theme. Remember that the theme change can only occur in the `Page_PreInit()` method, but ASP.NET doesn't call this method except when the page loads. Consequently, the `ddlSelectTheme_SelectedIndexChanged()` method uses the `Response.Redirect()` method to create a new Web page that just happens to be the same as the one the user is currently viewing. Because this one change affects all of the pages on the ABC Incorporated Web site, you don't want to use any fragile means of storing the data such as using hidden controls. The code overcomes this problem by creating a cookie containing the current control status information.

TIP The example code in Listing 14.1 shows the code using a combination of the `Response.Cookies.Remove()` and then the `Response.Cookies.Add()` method to change an existing cookie value. This seemingly convoluted approach overcomes an error that can occur with the `Response.Cookies.Set()` method not changing the cookie value. Microsoft will eventually fix this error and you'll be able to use the `Response.Cookies.Set()` method to change the cookie value.

The `Page_Load()` method begins by checking the `Page.IsPostBack` property. Processing the theme information during a postback can cause problems because the setup will often change the `ddlSelectTheme.SelectedIndex` property back to its original value, rather than use the new value the user selected.

The theme is set, but ASP.NET can't initialize the controls properly. The act of redirecting the page destroys this information. Consequently, when the page calls the `Page_Load()` method, it reconstructs the control settings from the cookie saved earlier using the `Request.Cookies` collection. However, you don't want to spend a lot of time performing an initialization if this isn't a new page, so the code first checks whether ThemeName has any data—if so, it completes the initialization. All you need to do is change the `SelectedIndex` property value as needed.

CREATING THE THEME RECOGNITION AND CONFIGURATION CLASS

The user isn't going to want to make this change for just one page. Since you can't initialize the theme as part of the master page, you'll need to add code to the individual pages. However, you don't want to add fragile code that is easy to break either. Adding the code to the pages makes updates hard. The example uses the following simple code in the `Page_PreInit()` method to provide theme support for every Web page that can support it.

```
Protected Sub Page_PreInit( _
    ByVal sender As Object, _
    ByVal e As System.EventArgs) Handles Me.PreInit

    ' Set the current theme.
    ThemeSelect.SetTheme(Me.Page)
End Sub
```

As you can see, the `Page_PreInit()` method simply calls the `ThemeSelect.SetTheme()` method in the class file. The class file defines this method as `Shared` so you don't even have to create an instance of the `ThemeSelect` class.

NOTE   Adding a new class to your ASP.NET application is the same as any other item that you might want to add. However, when you select a Class from the Add New Item dialog box, the IDE will display a dialog box telling you that the class should appear within a special \Code folder. Always tell the IDE that you want to create this folder to ensure the Web pages can access the class as needed.

The ThemeSelect class includes just one method, but obviously, you can create as many methods as required to handle various initialization tasks. Listing 14.2 shows the code you'll need to create the ThemeSelect class.

The code begins by obtaining a copy of the cookie saved earlier. When this cookie doesn't exist, the code doesn't perform any changes. Because this is a class with global implications, the method accepts the current page, whatever that page might be, as input. It then uses the ThisPage.Page .Theme property to make the actual theme change. Unfortunately, when a developer calls this method anywhere but the Page.PreInit() event handler, changing the theme raises an error. You'll want to provide error-handling code to avoid potential Web site problems. Figure 14.1 shows typical output from this application.

LISTING 14.2:   Creating a Class for Initialization Tasks

```vb
Public Shared Sub SetTheme(ByVal ThisPage As Page)

    Dim ThemeName As String = ""   ' Holds the theme name.

    ' Get the cookies for the page.
    If Not ThisPage.Request.Cookies("ddlSelectTheme") Is Nothing Then
        ThemeName = ThisPage.Request.Cookies("ddlSelectTheme").Value
    End If

    ' If the query string doesn't contain a theme name, exit.
    If ThemeName Is Nothing Then
        Return
    End If

    ' Choose a theme based on the user request.
    Select Case ThemeName
        Case "Default"
            ThisPage.Page.Theme = "MyTheme"
        Case "Sunny"
            ThisPage.Page.Theme = "Sunny"
        Case "Cloudy"
            ThisPage.Page.Theme = "Cloudy"
        Case "None"
            ThisPage.Page.Theme = ""
    End Select

End Sub
```

FIGURE 14.1
Creating Web pages with configuration options, such as the ones shown here, add pizzazz and also complexity.

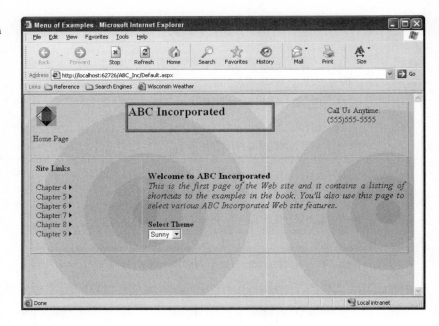

Creating Special Effects

Many Web sites use special effects. They can add pizzazz to a Web site, while accommodating users that don't have scripting enabled in many cases. For example, if a user who doesn't have scripting enabled visits a Web site that has the mouseover special effect enabled, the only thing that will happen is that the user won't see the special effect. The information is still available, but with a little less pizzazz.

Mouseover with Internet Explorer and Older Browsers

The mouseover effect is one of the most common special effects that you'll find on Web sites. Whenever the user passes the mouse over a control or other page feature that has the appropriate code attached, the mouseover effect takes place. To create this effect, you actually need to track two events: `onmouseover` and `onmouseleave` as shown in Listing 14.3. You'll find this example in the `\ABC_Inc\ MouseOver` folder of the source code on the Sybex Web site.

LISTING 14.3:   Creating a Mouseover Effect

```
<!DOCTYPE html PUBLIC "-//W3C//DTD XHTML 1.1//EN"
                      "http://www.w3.org/TR/xhtml11/DTD/xhtml11.dtd">
<html xmlns="http://www.w3.org/1999/xhtml" >
<head>
    <title>Special Effects Demonstration</title>
    <script type="text/javascript">
```

```html
<!--
    function HighlightControl(Control)
    {
        // Save the old settings.
        OldBackground.value = Control.style.backgroundColor;
        OldFontColor.value = Control.style.color;

        // Highlight the control so the user can see which
        // one is selected.
        Control.style.backgroundColor = "Blue";
        Control.style.color = "White";
    }

    function RemoveHighlight(Control)
    {
        // Return the control color to normal.
        Control.style.backgroundColor = OldBackground.value;
        Control.style.color = OldFontColor.value;
    }
-->
</script>
</head>
<body>
    <!-- These two hidden controls are used for the mouseover
         scripts. -->
    <input type="hidden" id="OldBackground" />
    <input type="hidden" id="OldFontColor" />

    <!-- These controls actually appear on screen. -->
    <h1>Special Effects Demonstration</h1>
    <p>
        <label id="lblInput" for="txtInput">Input: </label>
        <input type="text" id="txtInput" accesskey="I"
               onmouseleave="RemoveHighlight(this)"
               onmouseover="HighlightControl(this)" />
    </p>
    <p>
        <input type="submit" id="btnSubmit" value="Submit"
               accesskey="S"
               onmouseleave="RemoveHighlight(this)"
               onmouseover="HighlightControl(this)" />
    </p>

</body>
</html>
```

The code begins when a user passes the mouse over a control that has the `onmouseover` event defined such as `txtInput`. You generally won't use the mouseover effect for inactive controls such as `lblInput`—the effect shows the control that has mouse focus. In some respects, it actually helps make your page more accessible for those with low-vision needs, but generally, it's just a bit of pizzazz. The event fires and calls the `HighlightControl()` function. Notice that the code calls the function with the special `this` keyword, which refers to the current control. In effect, you're passing a reference from the current control to the function, which allows you to create generic functions that work for a number of controls.

The `HighlightControl()` function begins by saving the current control settings to hidden controls. You could also use a global variable to perform this task. The point is that you must save the data in some way because not every control has the same color scheme. For example, even if you use the standard colors, a pushbutton has a different background color than a text box. Notice that the control reference appears in `Control`. Unfortunately, using this technique means that you won't get any support from IntelliSense—you must know the various properties and methods that the control supports. The function ends by assigning a new color to the control background and text using the `backgroundColor` and `style.color` properties.

When the mouse leaves the current control, the control fires the `onmouseleave` event, which calls the `RemoveHighlight()` function. Like the `HighlightControl()` function, the `RemoveHighlight()` function receives a reference to the current control through the `this` keyword. The `RemoveHighlight()` function simply restores the original color settings to the control. Because the mouse can only highlight one control at a time and there isn't any chance that the mouse cursor can move from one control to another without firing the `onmouseleave` event, there's never a chance that you'll corrupt the control data by using a single pair of global variables to hold the old data. Figure 14.2 shows a typical example of a mouseover effect.

The example uses a simple color change to demonstrate the effect of the mouseover. However, you aren't limited to color changes. You could use special icons, make sounds, or do just about anything else that makes sense for the browser environment. The basic principle is always the same. You handle the `onmouseover` and `onmouseleave` events so that the page can display the special feature and then remove it as soon as the user moves the mouse cursor away from the control.

FIGURE 14.2
Mouseover effects can be subtle, but you can use any pizzazz technique desired.

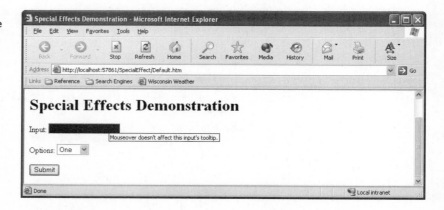

USING MOUSEOVER WITH ASP.NET

You might have noticed that none of the ASP.NET controls sports an `OnMouseover` event, which would seem to preclude using ASP.NET controls with this interesting feature. The fact is that you can't create a mouseover effect directly with the control, but you can use a little HTML to make the effect happen. Simply surround the ASP.NET control with a `<span>` tag, as shown here. (You'll find this example in the `\ABC_Inc\MouseOver` folder of the source code on the Sybex Web site.)

```
<span id="txtHighlight"
    onmouseout="RemoveHighlight(this)"
    onmouseover="HighlightControl(this)">
    <asp:TextBox ID="txtInput" BackColor="white" runat="server" ForeColor="Black">
        Hello World
    </asp:TextBox>
</span><br />
```

The `<span>` tag provides the necessary package to hold the ASP.NET control and allow it to use the `onmouseover` and `onmouseout` events, just as you would with any HTML control. The script does require a small change, however, to make it work as intended. Remember that you're wrapping one control within another, so you can't interact with the control directly. Here's an example of the ASP.NET version of the script for saving the background color described in the "Mouseover with Newer Browsers" section of the chapter.

```
theOldBackground.value = Control.childNodes[0].style.backgroundColor;
```

Notice that you must reference the child node of the `<span>` tag using `Control.childNodes[0]`. Otherwise, the control works precisely as it would in any other Web page. The user gets a special mouseover effect and you still get all of the benefits of using ASP.NET.

Mouseover with Newer Browsers

The only problem with the code shown in Listing 14.3 is that it won't work with some newer browsers such as Firefox. Yes, it works fine with older browsers and Internet Explorer (all versions), but you won't see the mouseover effect in Firefox. Of course, this begs the question of why you can't simply use a script that works with Firefox. Unfortunately, older browsers don't understand the newer Java-Script coding techniques. Consequently, you're stuck building pages that pursue multiple standards, telling people with older browsers that the scripts won't work, targeting the older browsers, or focusing on one or two browsers and hoping for the best. It's not a very pretty picture and you shouldn't expect it to change in the near future.

To make a mouseover effect work with newer browsers, you need to enclose all of the HTML code within a `<form>` tag—controls don't exist without a form, even though you can see them in the various debugging screens. The newer browsers also don't understand the `onmouseleave` event used in Listing 14.3—you must use the `onmouseout` event instead (unfortunately, older browsers don't understand the `onmouseout` event, so you must include the `onmouseleave` event for them). Finally, you'll need to make some changes to the script—it's only a little more complex, as shown in Listing 14.4, but definitely more complicated than the simpler script shown in Listing 14.3. You'll find this example in the `\ABC_Inc\MouseOver` folder of the source code on the Sybex Web site.

LISTING 14.4:   Using the Updated Mouseover Effect

```
function HighlightControl(Control)
{
    // Get the controls.
    var theOldBackground = document.getElementById("OldBackground");
    var theOldFont = document.getElementById("OldFontColor");

    // Save the old settings.
    theOldBackground.value = Control.style.backgroundColor;
    theOldFont.value = Control.style.color;

    // Highlight the control so the user can see which
    // one is selected.
    Control.style.backgroundColor = "Blue";
    Control.style.color = "White";
}

function RemoveHighlight(Control)
{
    // Get the controls.
    var theOldBackground = document.getElementById("OldBackground");
    var theOldFont = document.getElementById("OldFontColor");

    // Return the control color to normal.
    Control.style.backgroundColor = theOldBackground.value;
    Control.style.color = theOldFontColor.value;
}
```

Modern writers of JavaScript code can't get anywhere without going somewhere else first. Both of the scripts start by obtaining references to the controls that the script in Listing 14.2 accesses directly. You must use the `document.getElementById()` method or Firefox and other modern browsers will complain. The older technique of using the `document.all()` method should work, but the browser will complain about it nonetheless. Once you can access the control, you can manipulate it much as you would any control—there isn't much difference between Listing 14.2 and Listing 14.3 in this area.

Presentation

Beauty is in the eye of the beholder, and nowhere is this truer than Web sites. In many cases, the artwork a Web site provides can mean the difference between boring and exciting—the information is the same, the presentation is different. However, unlike works of art you see in a museum, beauty on a Web site is more of the architectural sort where form follows function. That's the point of the example in this section—a marquee provides important information to the viewer and a bit of pizzazz for the Web page. It's a functional architectural detail that you probably shouldn't skip.

TIP   You don't have to build all of the software required to provide a special effect on your Web site. Many third party vendors provide common special effects in easy-to-use packages. For example, you'll find a list of these products on the Advanced Presentation Tools Collection Web site at `http://www.jpowered.com/catalogue/specialeffects/`.

Many people are familiar with banner advertisements, which are essentially graphics with some intelligence added. The `<marquee>` tag is simpler to implement, yet you can dress it up in a number of ways. Fortunately, this tag seems to work with most browsers in use today. Of course, you might want a purely ASP.NET solution for a corporate Web site, so you might want to use the `AdRotator` control described in the "Using the AdRotator Control" section of the chapter instead of this solution. Here's a typical example of a `<marquee>` tag (the one used in the example).

```
<marquee id="ScrollTip"
         behavior="slide"
         direction="right"
         loop="infinite"
         scrollamount="5"
         scrolldelay="100"
         width="80%"
         bgcolor="yellow">
    This is the first message.
</marquee>
```

As you can see, the `<marquee>` tag provides a lot of room for customization. It actually has a number of other changes you can make. For example, you can attach style information to the `<marquee>` tag to change the appearance of the information it provides. The following list describes the special `<marquee>` tag features that you'll want to use to add pizzazz to your Web page.

behavior   Defines how the `<marquee>` tag presents the text. The slide option scrolls the text in one direction and stops when the text reaches the end. The alternate option scrolls the text between sides—when the text reaches one end, it reverses and moves toward the other side. The scroll option continuously scrolls the text in one direction—the text appears to scroll off one end of the display and reappears on the other end.

direction   Determines the direction of scroll, either right or left.

loop   Determines the number of times the text scrolls. A value of infinite means the text continues to scroll forever.

scrollamount   Defines the number of pixels that the text moves per update.

scrolldelay   Defines the amount of time in milliseconds between updates.

bgcolor   Modifies the background color of the marquee. Using a contrasting or coordinating color can greatly add to the effect of the tag.

One of the complaints by some developers about the `<marquee>` tag is that it doesn't really change. Yes, the viewer sees the text you want to provide, but it doesn't provide a resource for changing that text or any of the special effects. Fortunately, you can write a script that not only changes the text, but modifies the behavior of the display as well. To make matters even better, all of these modifications happen on the client machine automatically. Listing 14.5 shows a sample of what you can do. You'll find this example in the \ABC_Inc\MouseOver folder of the source code on the Sybex Web site.

LISTING 14.5:   Designing a Marquee

```
function SetMarqueeFeatures()
{
    var SelType;    // Holds a random number.

    // Choose a behavior.
    SelType = Math.round(Math.random() * 2);
    switch (SelType)
    {
        case 0:
            ScrollTip.behavior = "scroll";
            break;
        case 1:
            ScrollTip.behavior = "slide";
            break;
        case 2:
            ScrollTip.behavior = "alternate";
            break;
    }

    // Select a direction.
    SelType = Math.round(Math.random());
    if (SelType = 0)
        ScrollTip.direction = "right";
    else
        ScrollTip.direction = "left";

    // Set the scrolling.
    ScrollTip.scrollAmount = Math.round(Math.random() * 10) + 5;
    ScrollTip.scrollDelay = Math.round(Math.random() * 200) + 100;

    // Set the message.
    SelType = Math.round(Math.random() * 4);
    switch (SelType)
    {
        case 0:
            ScrollTip.innerText = "This is the first message.";
            break;
        case 1:
            ScrollTip.innerText = "Second message.";
            break;
        case 2:
            ScrollTip.innerText = "A third message.";
            break;
        case 3:
            ScrollTip.innerText = "The fourth message.";
            break;
        case 4:
```

```
          ScrollTip.innerText = "Showing the last message.";
          break;
   }

   // Set the timeout value for changes in appearance.
   self.setTimeout("SetMarqueeFeatures()", 10000);
}
```

The page calls the `SetMarqueeFeatures()` function when the page loads using the `onload` event of the `<body>` tag. The code begins by creating a random number between 0 and 2 using `Math.round(Math.random() * 2)`. The first call to `Math.random()` produces a random number between 0 and 1. Multiplying this value by 2 creates a random number between 0 and 2, but it's a real number (one with a decimal) and not an integer (a whole number). The `Math.round()` function rounds the number as needed to produce an integer. The code uses the resulting random number to choose between one of the three `<marquee>` tag behaviors. The code uses this same technique to choose between a right and left scrolling direction.

The `scrollAmount` and `scrollDelay` property values are important because the user is going to see a change in the scrolling rate immediately. This particular change, more than most of the others you can make, will grab the user's attention every time the message changes, which ensures that the user is at least aware of the messages that you want to provide.

The next task is to display a message, which relies on the same random number technique as before. The example hard codes several messages, which might not fulfill your needs if you have many pages with marquees and want to change the messages regularly. You could store the messages in an XML file or a database. The idea is to know how many messages there are and choose from them randomly as needed.

The final bit of code might look a little confusing at first, but it serves an important purpose. You use the `self.setTimeout()` function to time an event that occurs at a specific time interval. The event only happens once, so the example calls this function every time the marquee changes. The first argument is an expression—a call to the `SetMarqueeFeatures()` function in this case. The second argument contains the delay in milliseconds before the event occurs, so this example changes the marquee every 10 seconds. Figure 14.3 shows a typical example of a marquee that appears at the top of a page.

FIGURE 14.3

The *<marquee>* tag provides one of many presentation aids for Web developers.

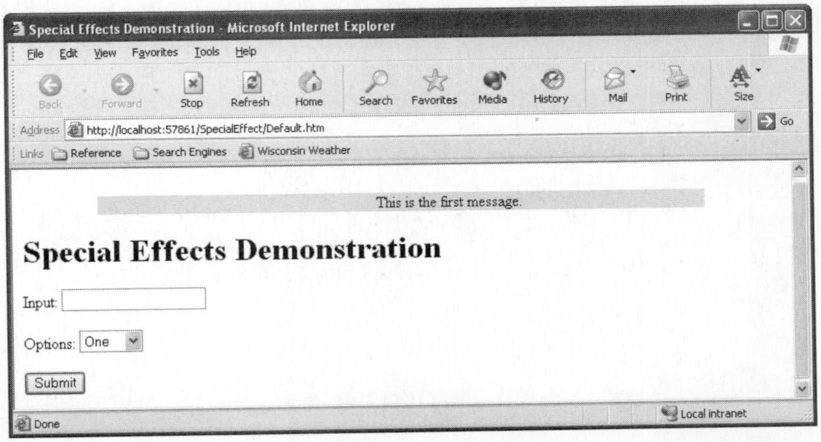

Selection Using Scripts

One of the more interesting special effects that you can add to a Web page is also one of the more useful features. Any time you can provide the user with a suggestion about what to enter in a form, you'll find that you greatly reduce errors and improve the input you receive. Creating a form so that it automatically selects certain options based on previous user input represents one way to provide a suggestion. However, you don't want the form constantly changing its appearance either, so it's important to make the automatic selection timely. The best way to accomplish this task is to attach the selection code to the `onfocus` event, as shown here.

```
<label id="lblOption" for="selOption">Options: </label>
<select id="selOption" accesskey="O"
        onfocus="ShowPreference()"
        onmouseleave="RemoveHighlight(this)"
        onmouseover="HighlightControl(this)">
    <option>One</option>
    <option>Two</option>
    <option>Three</option>
</select>
```

The example in this section relies on input from the `txtInput` control. Type a number such as one, two, or three, into the text box and the contents of this drop-down list changes automatically when the user selects `selOption`. The input and output of this example is simple, but you can create any level of complexity necessary. For example, you could even parse the input to locate specific bits of information that the code can use to make a decision on helping the user.

This special effect provides a lot of value, but it's not very hard to implement. Listing 14.6 provides an example of the code you'd need to include on your Web page to implement this special effect. You'll find this example in the \ABC_Inc\MouseOver folder of the source code on the Sybex Web site.

The code relies on a simple `switch` statement to choose between valid options. When working with a fixed number of choices, the `switch` statement is the best way to approach the problem. However, you'll need to choose a technique that best suits the result you want to achieve—in some cases, you might have to provide an equation or rely on data manipulation.

It's not possible to know how the user will type in the data you want to check. The best way to overcome this problem is to convert text to uppercase using the `toUpperCase()` function. Unfortunately, IntelliSense won't tell you that this particular function exists—it stops with the `value` property. In this case, you'd need to look at a JavaScript reference such as the one found at the W3Schools site at `http://www.w3schools.com/js/js_obj_string.asp`. This Web site provides a wealth of reference information that you can use when IntelliSense doesn't include everything you need.

A final bit of code shows how to implement the `default` case. Whenever you create a script like this, you should include a `default` case to ensure the code chooses something. Otherwise, you could find that the code behaves strangely in some environments. Figure 14.4 shows how this particular feature works. Typing **Three** in txtInput and then pressing Tab to move to `selOption` automatically chooses Three as the value in `selOption` as well.

LISTING 14.6:   Modifying an Input to Show the Preferred Response Based on Previous Input

```
function ShowPreference()
{
    // Convert the input to uppercase and then
    // choose an option.
    switch (txtInput.value.toUpperCase())
    {
        case 'ONE':
            selOption.selectedIndex = 0;
            break;
        case 'TWO':
            selOption.selectedIndex = 1;
            break;
        case 'THREE':
            selOption.selectedIndex = 2;
            break;

        // The default option occurs when the
        // user doesn't provide input.
        default:
            selOption.selectedIndex = 0;
            break;
    }
}
```

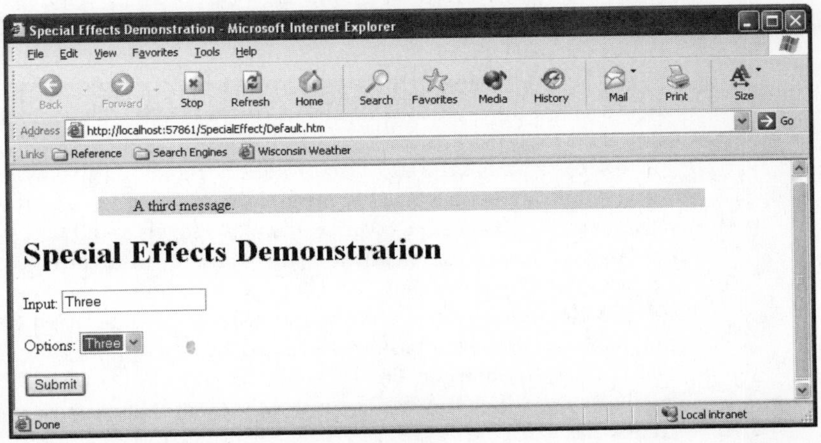

FIGURE 14.4
Automatic changes based on user input reduce the risk of user input errors.

Progressive Input Using Scripts

Anything you can do to make the user's life easier normally reduces support costs and rework time for your code. Keeping forms simple and easy to understand is necessary when you don't know the experience level of the user. Consequently, creating a form that hides complex details unless the user actually needs them can garner a number of useful results. Not only will the user spend less time filling out the form, but you'll also spend less time answering questions.

This example relies on two techniques. First, you must hide the controls so that the user can't see them (or even select them). You can perform this task by using a simple set of style changes for the tags you want to hide. Second, you must provide a means for displaying the controls, but only when the user actually needs them. In most cases, you'll have to provide some kind of mechanism to perform this task. The following code shows how to structure the `style` attribute of tags to hide them completely.

```
<p>
    <label id="lblSecondOpt" for="selSecondOpt"
           style="visibility: hidden; display: none;">
        Second Option:
    </label>
    <select id="selSecondOpt" accesskey="2"
            style="visibility: hidden; display: none;"
            onmouseleave="RemoveHighlight(this)"
            onmouseover="HighlightControl(this)">
        <option>A</option>
        <option>B</option>
        <option>C</option>
    </select>
</p>
```

Setting both the `visibility` and the `display` styles ensures that the user can't select the control or see it on screen. It's important to remember that the user can still see the tabs by viewing the source code for the page, but the tags won't appear on screen until the trigger event for displaying them occurs. You'll find these styles on the Layout tab of the Style Builder dialog box, as shown in Figure 14.5. You can access the Style Builder dialog box by clicking the ellipses in the `Style` property for any control in the Properties window.

The second part of the task is to provide a trigger for displaying the optional input. Although this example only shows one level of progressive input, you can provide as many levels as needed to answer a particular need. Of course, too many levels aren't necessarily good either—at some level of complexity, the user becomes confused. Listing 14.7 shows the selection script for this example. You'll find this example in the \ABC_Inc\MouseOver folder of the source code on the Sybex Web site.

The code begins by determining the value the user selected from `selOption`. Always remember that JavaScript uses zero-based indexes, so the first option, One, actually has a `selectedIndex` value of 0. When the user selects Two, the code sets the `style.display` property for each of the controls to a blank string, which means the control uses the default value of displaying the control. The code actually has to set the `style.visibility` property of each control to visible to ensure the control displays as anticipated. When the user selects any other value in `selOption`, the code sets the two optional controls so they remain invisible.

FIGURE 14.5
Use the layout options to hide the less needed controls on a page.

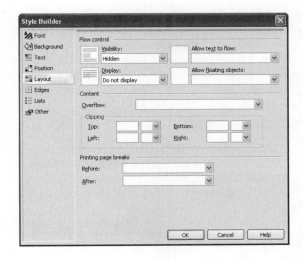

LISTING 14.7: Displaying Optional Controls Based on User Input

```
function ShowSecondOpt()
{
    // Determine whether the user has selected Two.
    if (selOption.selectedIndex == 1)
    {
        // Display the second option.
        lblSecondOpt.style.display = "";
        lblSecondOpt.style.visibility = "visible";
        selSecondOpt.style.display = "";
        selSecondOpt.style.visibility = "visible";
    }
    else
    {
        // Otherwise, hide the second option.
        lblSecondOpt.style.display = "none";
        lblSecondOpt.style.visibility = "hidden";
        selSecondOpt.style.display = "none";
        selSecondOpt.style.visibility = "hidden";
    }
}
```

Before this code activates, you need to add another event to selOption. The onchange event fires whenever the user changes the selection. This act calls the ShowSecondOpt(), as shown here.

```
onchange="ShowSecondOpt()"
```

One of the elements you have to consider when working with code that modifies the presentation is interactions. Listing 14.6 shows a technique for modifying the `selOption` selection by changing the `selectedIndex` property value based on text that the user types into `txtInput`. That listing also has a potential for interaction. Changing the `selectedIndex` property value won't trigger the `selOption` `onchange` event. Consequently, you won't see the expected change. The easiest way to correct this problem is to add another call to the end of the `ShowPreference()` method, as shown here.

```
// Handle any change to the second option as well.
ShowSecondOpt();
```

Once you create the basic triggering mechanism and overcome any potential interactions, you can test the resulting progressive form. The big issue is to ensure the progression is more help than hindrance, which means testing by users followed by a survey. Figure 14.6 shows how the optional selection looks when triggered by the `selOption` change.

FIGURE 14.6
Selective input is a helpful bit of pizzazz that reduces the complexity of forms.

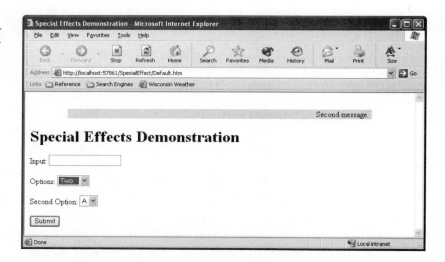

Selection and Progressive Input with ASP.NET

The principle of providing a selection order and hiding choices that the user need not know about applies no matter which technique you use to build a Web page. The problem is getting the desired effect using the programming strategy approved by the IT department in your company. Every company has different requirements, so it's important to have several solutions available so that you can create an application with the required strategy in mind. Fortunately, the ASP.NET developer has at least three good strategies available for implementing both selection and progressive input for any Web application as listed here.

◆ Scripts

◆ Code behind

◆ Client callback

The "Selection Using Scripts" and "Progressive Input Using Scripts" sections show a purely scripted solution. Using this solution offers the advantage of relying on the client for computing power, which reduces the server power needed to implement a solution. The client also gains the advantage of a fast response time. However, this solution requires that you either use HTML controls, as shown in Listing 14.6 or a control container as described in the "Using Mouseover with ASP.NET" sidebar. In addition, you lose some control over the solution because the code executes on the client. Technically, you can mix ASP.NET and HTML controls to achieve specific goals, but you'll find that the goals often collide or won't work at all when a single control requires both client and server processing.

One obvious ASP.NET solution is to set a control's `AutoPostBack` property to `True`. Whenever a user makes a change, the page posts back to the server for processing. You can make options visible or invisible depending on the choices the user makes. This option offers the maximum benefit in control. You can examine every input and verify that the application is working as anticipated. Using this solution increases both reliability and security. However, this solution incurs a large cost in performance. Every change the user makes causes a postback to the server. Network traffic increases to the point that the user may very well give up trying to fill out the form.

A middle ground solution is to rely on client callback. This solution uses a combination of local scripting and code behind. Only the control information posts back to the server—not the entire page. Consequently, this solution incurs a far smaller performance penalty and gives you nearly the same level of control over the form progression. From an application perspective, client callback represents a nearly perfect solution. However, from a developer perspective, the solution is error prone and difficult to implement in complex environments. You need to perform more than the usual level of testing to ensure the connection works as anticipated. The "Scripting with Client Callback" section of Chapter 6 describes this technique in detail.

Understanding the Ever Changing Browser Playing Field

Different browsers see pages differently, even when the page relies on ASP.NET. For example, start the WebParts project in Chapter 6. Copy the address from the Address field in Internet Explorer and paste it to the Address field in Firefox (as an example). Figure 14.7 shows that the display is different, as are the requirements for using the page. For example, Internet Explorer displays a drop-down list with a mouseover effect and automatic postback for changing the layout, while Firefox uses a drop-down list and a separate command button.

FIGURE 14.7
Firefox and other browsers see ASP.NET pages differently than Internet Explorer.

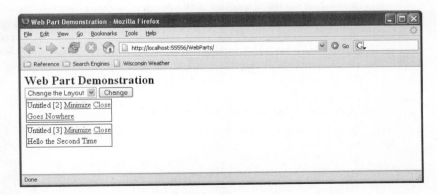

The problem with this display is that it represents extra work. You couldn't write a single procedure for using even this simple page because elements like the catalog won't display the same way, or using the same steps in Firefox as when you use Internet Explorer. Because ASP.NET generates the code for you automatically, you also don't have any way of fixing the presentation. In short, you're stuck writing multiple operating procedures for the page—one for each browser that the users choose.

Pizzazz only works well when everyone has a level playing field—one in which the user can have certain expectations fulfilled for the browsers you've chosen to target for the application. When the only browser you support is Internet Explorer, it's relatively easy to create a user customization experience based exclusively on WebParts. Unfortunately, not everyone is thrilled with Internet Explorer and the potential security risks it possesses. As an example, InfoWorld recently ran an opinion piece on the topic at `http://www.infoworld.com/article/04/12/03/49enterwin_1.html`.

Microsoft still owns the browser market, but their grip is loosening a little. According to a ComputerWorld article at `http://www.computerworld.com/developmenttopics/websitemgmt/story/0,10801,97754,00.html?source=NLT_AM&nid=97754`, 4.7 million people downloaded Firefox in its first month. The Mozilla Suite and Netscape both increased their market share as well. In fact, 1 out of every 10 visitors to your Web site is probably using something other than Internet Explorer and there's good reason to expect that number to increase. However, this fact doesn't mean that developers will return to the unmanaged chaos of the browser wars era of computing. Browser developers are working harder to create standards-based products that work on the majority of Web sites.

The problem with using too much Microsoft gizmo technology on a public Web site is that you run into problems that you can't solve easily because you allow Microsoft to generate the underlying code for you. That's why you need to test your applications with several browsers and in multiple environments to ensure they work well everywhere. You might be surprised to see how well the Microsoft code works as long as you don't test the boundaries too much of what it can do. In some cases, however, you'll still need to rely on direct coding techniques, such as using JavaScript, to ensure the pages you create work for everyone.

Creating a Dynamic Presentation

Most Web pages contain a lot of static (unchanging) content. Even when the content changes from day to day, the content stays consistent during the entire viewing period. Dynamic content can keep users viewing the information on your site longer when used appropriately (and can just as easily drive them away when you make the Web site too dynamic). You create dynamic content by enforcing automatic changes to the appearance of the display. For example, the tip area could change periodically to show a new tip, even if the user hasn't changed Web pages. The following sections describe several types of low-cost dynamic content—the kind that doesn't require hours of programming and an investment in innovative technologies.

Using the Substitution Control

Imagine, for a moment, the cost of moving entire pages back and forth between the server to provide truly dynamic content. If you don't want to imagine that amount of wear and tear on your server, not to mention the resulting performance drop, then you'll want to discover the Substitution control. This control lets you designate a specific area of a Web page as non-cached (or dynamic). The rest of the Web page remains untouched during the session, but ASP.NET refreshes this one area to provide dynamic content the user can see. The thing that sets this technique apart from other automatic refresh techniques presented in the chapter is that it doesn't rely on a client-side script—it relies on server-side processing, so you gain the advantages that server-side processing can provide, such as updates to database information.

The Substitution control provides only text output. Therefore, you can't use it to create an entire data form. However, you can use as many Substitution controls as needed to refresh just the text portions of a data form. You can also include tags as part of the output, so you could conceptually build whatever you want from standard HTML tags and create the output you want.

Before you begin working with the Substitution control, you need to set the Web page to use caching. The default setup assumes that you want to refresh all of the content every time the user requests a refresh. Generally, you want to refresh the content every time when working on the code for the project, but refreshing it every time on a production system wastes resources. Adding the OutputCache directive shown here solves the problem.

```
<%@ OutputCache Duration="120" VaryByParam="None" %>
```

The Duration attribute of the OutputCache directive defines how many seconds the system waits between refreshes of static data. In this case, the system waits 2 minutes between refreshes. The VaryByParam attribute tells which parameters to use to vary the output cache—the value of None is standard. You must provide both attributes.

LOOKING FOR NEW WEB APPLICATION TECHNOLOGIES

There's always a new technology on the horizon and the smart developer checks them out to see which technologies can address specific application development problems. You've already seen a number of methods for working with JavaScript in this book, including the script injection technique shown in the "Handling *<body onload="PageLoad()">* Scripts" section of Chapter 9. Embedding ASP.NET controls within HTML tags can also make your applications script friendly. The point is that there are many ways to achieve a particular goal today.

Developers have created a new programming paradigm called Asynchronous JavaScript And XML (AJAX) that can give Web applications a desktop application feel across programming platforms. The technology works with existing browsers, but you do need an AJAX engine to use it. You can get an overview of this new technology at http://www.infoworld.com/article/05/05/23/21FEwebapp_2.html and http://www.infoworld.com/article/05/05/23/21FEwebapppush_1.html?source=NLC-WS2005-05-25. You'll find a complete description of this technology at http://www.adaptivepath.com/publications/essays/archives/000385.php. The amazing feature of this technology is that it reduces network traffic by making requests only as needed. An application can replace part of a page, rather than request the entire page from the server. In addition, requests occur asynchronously, which means both client and server can handle information as time permits, rather than immediately.

Generally, AJAX technology only works well with corporate applications now because of differences in the way different browsers work with the technologies involved. AJAX isn't a new technology, merely a new use of existing technology combined with an AJAX engine. The same problems you have with JavaScript today also occur when you use AJAX. Likewise, a browser display problem that occurs with XML today will also appear when you display data using AJAX. Only the way in which the technologies work together differs. However, the coupling of these technologies can greatly change the way your Web applications work.

Creating the function used to provide dynamic output to the Substitution control comes next. The example provides a static time output for comparison purposes as part of the Page_Load() event handler. This event handler only outputs the time for comparison purposes. Listing 14.8 shows both methods. You'll find this example in the \ABC_Inc\Dynamic folder of the source code on the Sybex Web site.

LISTING 14.8:   Defining Substituted Output

```
Shared Function GetCurrentTime(ByVal Context As HttpContext) As String
    Dim Output As New StringBuilder()    'Output Data

    ' Get the User Name supplied as part of the context.
    Output.Append("User Name: " + _
                Context.User.Identity.Name + "<br />")

    ' Get the session time from the context.
    Output.Append("Session Time: " + _
                Context.Timestamp.ToLongTimeString() + "<br />")

    ' Get the current server time.
    Output.Append("Current Time: " + _
                DateTime.Now.ToLongTimeString() + "<br />")

    ' Return the entire string.
    Return Output.ToString()
End Function

Private Sub Page_Load(ByVal sender As Object, _
                        ByVal e As System.EventArgs) Handles Me.Load
    ' Display the static load time for the page.
    lblStartTime.Text = DateTime.Now.ToLongTimeString()
End Sub
```

The GetCurrentTime() method declaration is important. You must create this function as Shared as shown, and it must include the HttpContext input argument. The function must return a String value since that is the only kind of output that the Substitution control accepts. The IDE tends to produce unhelpful error messages at times when you forget any of these design requirements. For example, if you create the GetCurrentTime() method as Public, rather than Shared, the IDE will tell you there's an access error, but won't really help you fix the problem.

The Context object is extremely helpful—it includes a wealth of information you can use for creating the Substitution control output. For example, the Context object includes both Request and Response objects so that you can discover specifics about the client as needed. The code shows the User.Identity.Name property, which contains the username when the user logs into the Web page, and the Timestamp property, which contains the time at the user machine.

Notice the inclusion of the <br /> tag between lines of information. You can include any tags that you want in the output. If you want to create a table to display database information—there isn't any problem with you doing just that. However, you must create all output as HTML—don't use any ASP.NET tags because the system won't interpret them for you.

The code ends by obtaining the current server time and including it in the output. Figure 14.8 shows the output from this application. The static time—the time when the page is first opened—is a full minute behind the dynamic time. In addition, the Substitution control output appears on three lines because of the addition of the <br /> tags.

FIGURE 14.8

Use the *Substitution* and *AdRotator* controls to provide dynamic content.

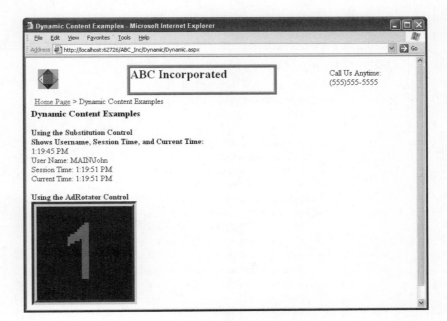

Using the *AdRotator* Control

Many developers view the AdRotator control as a means for creating click-through advertisements. It's true that you can use this control for that purpose. However, you could just as easily use it for other purposes. For example, you could use this control to display a tip of the day and point people to places to learn more information about the tip. An AdRotator control also provides an excellent method for making people aware of less used content on your Web site or providing entertaining content (think joke of the day). Any rotating content works well with this control, so don't limit your choices.

You'll use a special tag to add an AdRotator control to your Web site. This control has only one essential attribute, AdvertisementFile, as shown here.

```
<asp:AdRotator ID="arAds"
               Runat="server"
               AdvertisementFile="Data/Ads.xml"
               BorderStyle="Groove"
               BorderWidth="10"
               BorderColor="#ffccff"
               Width="25%" />
```

The `AdvertisementFile` attribute tells the control where to find the content you want to display. This content must appear in a specially formatted XML file described later in this section. It usually pays to set off the `AdRotator` control in some way—the example uses a grooved border and special coloration. Make sure you set at least the `Width` attribute as well so the controls take up the same amount of room across the display.

The special XML file is really just another kind of database. It includes one entry for every content item you want to display, as shown in Listing 14.9. You'll find this example in the `\ABC_Inc\Dynamic` folder of the source code on the Sybex Web site.

LISTING 14.9: Creating a List of Display Entries

```xml
<?xml version="1.0" encoding="utf-8" ?>
<Advertisements>
    <Ad>
        <ImageUrl>../Images/One.GIF</ImageUrl>
        <NavigateUrl>~/Default.ASPX</NavigateUrl>
        <AlternateText>Back to this Site</AlternateText>
        <Impressions>80</Impressions>
        <Keyword>ImageOne</Keyword>
    </Ad>
    <Ad>
        <ImageUrl>../Images/Two.GIF</ImageUrl>
        <NavigateUrl>~/Default.ASPX</NavigateUrl>
        <AlternateText>Back to this Site</AlternateText>
        <Impressions>80</Impressions>
        <Keyword>ImageTwo</Keyword>
    </Ad>
</Advertisements>
```

As you can see, the example uses two entries that differ by the Graphics Interchange Format (GIF) file displayed. The root node for this file is `<Advertisements>`, which contains individual `<Ad>` elements. Each `<Ad>` element is an individual content entry, so you need to create one of them for each piece of content you want to display. An `<Ad>` element must contain the following entries.

<ImageUrl>   Defines the location of the image that the `AdRotator` control displays. You can use any common Internet display format including GIF, Joint Photographic Experts Group (JPEG), and Portable Network Graphic (PNG). The image can be any size, but you should strive for standard sizes to make the `AdRotator` output work better on the page. You don't have any limitations on the information the image contains.

<NavigateUrl>   Points to the redirection location. The user goes to this location after clicking on the `AdRotator` control.

<AlternateText>   Contains the text to display when the image is unavailable. This text should describe the image so that people can understand the content you want to provide. Anyone using a screen reader also requires this content in order to hear a description of the image you provided.

<Impressions> Determines the weighting of this image for display. The `AdRotator` uses a weighted random selection for images. Images with the same `<Impressions>` value have an equal chance of getting selected for display, while images with a lower value have less of a chance.

<Keyword> Contains a keyword for this image so that you can track click-through events. The click information appears in the `aspnet_SiteCounters` table of the ASPNetDB database located in the `\Data` folder—setting `CountViews` to `True` tracks the number of times that the content appears on screen, while setting `CountClicks` to `True` tracks the number of times that a user actually clicks on the content.

The default setup displays the `AdRotator` as a banner. However, you can change the `AdType` property to create a pop-up or pop-under window as well. Given the number of browsers that now include filters for both pop-up and pop-under windows, you'll probably want to use the default banner approach whenever possible. Figure 14.8 shows the banner content for this example.

Working with WebParts

Microsoft definitely designed some WebParts for users. The "Using WebParts to Automate User Customizations" section of Chapter 6 describes these WebParts. You might not want to provide access to this powerful feature for novice users, but power users can definitely benefit from the functionality they provide. The WebParts described in the sections that follow are more powerful—you wouldn't want to grant even power user access to them in some cases. Microsoft designed these controls to meet the needs of administrators and developers better.

Dressing Up the WebParts

At some point, you'll want to dress up the appearance of the editors you create for the user. The style information appears as separate tags within the various zones, as shown in Listing 14.10. Each style entry affects a different part of the display. You'll find this example in the `\ABC_Inc\WebParts\Advanced` folder of the source code on the Sybex Web site.

LISTING 14.10: Developing Configurable Web Pages Using WebParts

```
<asp:EditorZone ID="EditorZone1"
                Runat="server"
                HeaderText="My Editor Zone">
    <ErrorStyle BackColor="#FFFFCC"></ErrorStyle>
    <HeaderStyle BorderColor="#00008b"
                BackColor="#ffffcc"></HeaderStyle>
    <FooterStyle BorderColor="#00008b"
                BackColor="#ffffcc"></FooterStyle>
    <PartTitleStyle ForeColor="#00008b"
                BackColor="#ffffcc"></PartTitleStyle>
    <PartChromeStyle Font-Bold="True"
                BorderColor="#00008b"
                BackColor="#ffffcc"
                ForeColor="#cc0066"></PartChromeStyle>
```

```
            <PartStyle BorderWidth="5px"
                       BorderStyle="Groove"
                       BackColor="#ffffcc"
                       BorderColor="#cc0066"></PartStyle>
        <ZoneTemplate>
            <asp:AppearanceEditorPart Runat="server"
                                      ID="AppearanceEditorPart1" />
            <asp:LayoutEditorPart Runat="server" ID="LayoutEditorPart1" />
            <asp:BehaviorEditorPart Runat="server"
                                    ID="BehaviorEditorPart1" />
            <asp:PropertyGridEditorPart Runat="server"
                                        ID="PropertyGridEditorPart1" />
        </ZoneTemplate>
    </asp:EditorZone>
```

You don't have to provide style information for every part of the zone, but it does help create a cohesive look when you do so. All of the part styles begin with the word *Part*, as shown. When you edit the <PartStyle> tag, you're changing the appearance of the part itself. The only odd entry in the list is the <PartChromeStyle> tag, which affects the outer area of the part entry. Think about the chrome on a car, it dresses up the outer boundaries. That's what the chrome does for your application as well. Figure 14.9 shows an example of how chrome affects the editor display.

TIP Many developers find it easier to work with the various zone settings from Source view once they create an initial design. Rather than opening each style entry separately in the Properties window, you can make all of the settings changes at once by copying the information from an existing zone and pasting it into a new zone.

FIGURE 14.9
Dress up the editors you provide for the user once you finish configuring them.

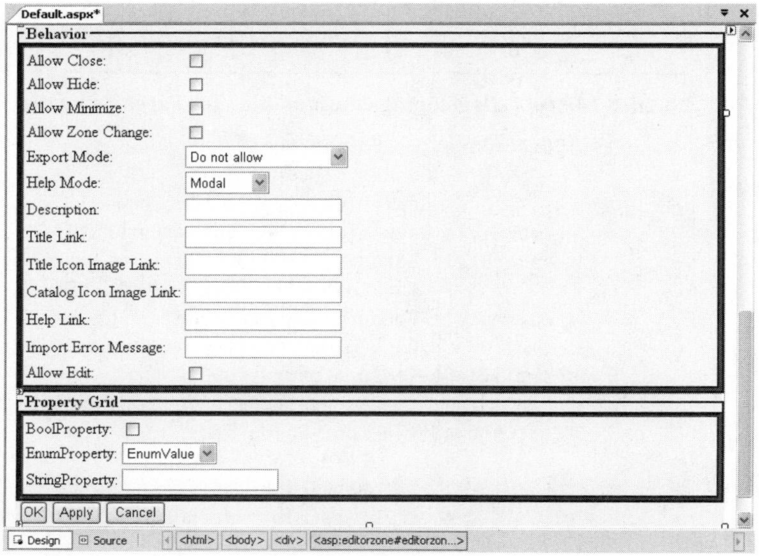

Using the *BehaviorEditorPart* Control

The BehaviorEditorPart control helps you adjust a Web page for everyone's needs. This control lets you choose how a Web page acts in shared mode—the mode where everyone is affected. To use this control, you begin by adding it to an EditorZone, <ZoneTemplate> section, as shown here:

```
<asp:BehaviorEditorPart Runat="server" ID="BehaviorEditorPart1" />
```

Listing 14.10 shows how the control looks in context with an EditorZone.

Of course, this is a powerful control, so you don't want to give just anyone access to it. You must adjust the security settings for WebParts in the Web.CONFIG file for the application by adding the code shown in Listing 14.11 to the <system.web> section of the file. You'll find this example in the \ABC_Inc\WebParts\Advanced folder of the source code on the Sybex Web site.

LISTING 14.11:   Authorizing Use of the *BehaviorEditPart* Control

```
<webParts>
    <personalization>
        <authorization>
            <allow users="MAIN\John"
                roles="admin"
                verbs="enterSharedScope"/>
        </authorization>
    </personalization>
</webParts>
```

Each user has a separate <allow> tag entry within the <authorization> section. To make this example work, you must change my information to match your information on your server. Once you make the change, you can run the example and you'll see a new BehaviorEditPart control, as shown in Figure 14.10. To see this display, you must first select Shared in the Personalization Scope, choose Edit in Display Mode, and finally choose Edit from the drop-down list for a particular control.

As you can see, this control lets you change usage settings. All of these settings are WebPart properties. Here's a list of the properties that they change (the actual property name appears in parenthesis when it differs from the name the control uses on screen).

Description   Provides a short description of the WebPart. The Web page automatically uses this information in tooltips, catalogs, and to meet other user needs.

Title Link (TitleUrl)   Provides a location for additional information about the WebPart. For example, you could explain the content of the WebPart and how to use it.

Title Icon Image Link (TitleIconImageUrl)   Contains an URL for an image used to represent the WebPart in the control's title bar.

Catalog Icon Image Link (CatalogIconImageUrl)   Contains an URL for an image used to represent the WebPart in the catalog of controls.

Help Link (HelpUrl)   Contains a link to the help file for the WebPart.

FIGURE 14.10
Use the *BehaviorEditPart* control to modify the Web page properties for everyone.

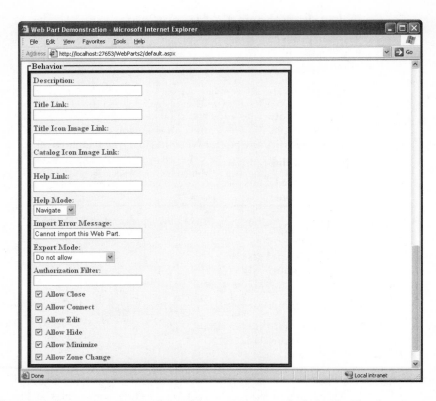

Help Mode (HelpMode)   Determines the mode used for navigating to the help file. The three common modes are modal, modeless, and navigate. When using the modal mode, the help opens in a separate window and the user must close the window before working anymore with the application. When using the modeless mode, the help opens in a separate window, but the user doesn't have to close the window before working with the application again. When using the navigate mode, the help file opens in the current window and the user navigates back to the application window.

Import Error Message (ImportErrorMessage)   Contains the error message that the application displays when an error occurs during a Web part import.

Export Mode (ExportMode)   Determines whether the user can export all, some, or none of the content of a WebPart. When you set a WebPart to allow export of nonsensitive or all of the data, you must also change the <webParts> element in the Web.CONFIG file to allow export by adding the enableExport attribute like this: <webParts enableExport="True">. When you export the WebPart, the application creates a file with the WEBPART file extension. You can then import the WebPart into any other Web page that supports imports using the ImportCatalogPart control.

Authorization Filter (AuthorizationFilter)   Determines whether a user can add a WebPart to a page. Normally, this entry is blank so a user can add any WebPart as long as the user has proper permission and the Web page has the correct features enabled. However, you can set this value so the `WebPartManager` will check the WebPart for the specified string before it imports the WebPart. In short, this filter lets you control which WebParts a user can add to a Web page without disabling the feature.

Allow Close (`AllowClose`)   Determines whether a user can close a WebPart.

Allow Connect (`AllowConnect`)   Determines whether the WebPart will allow other controls to form a connection with it for data exchange or other programmatic needs.

Allow Edit (`AllowEdit`)   Determines whether the user can edit the content of the WebPart.

Allow Hide (`AllowHide`)   Determines whether the user can hide the WebPart from view.

Allow Minimize (`AllowMinimize`)   Determines whether the user can minimize the WebPart.

Allow Zone Change (`AllowZoneChange`)   Determines whether the user can move a WebPart between zones.

Using the *DeclarativeCatalogPart* and *ImportCatalogPart* Controls

The `DeclarativeCatalogPart` and `ImportCatalogPart` controls represent two alternative methods of letting a user add content to a Web page. When working with the `DeclarativeCatalogPart` control, you create a list of useful, but optional controls to display on screen. The `ImportCatalogPart` control lets the user import a new WebPart and place it on screen. In both cases, the WebPart isn't part of the standard page and won't appear as part of a `PageCatalogPart` control as described in the "Adding New Items with the *CatalogZone*" section of Chapter 6.

Adding the `ImportCatalogPart` control is easiest. All you need to do is add the control to the page like this:

```
<asp:ImportCatalogPart ID="ImportCatalogPart1" runat="server" />
```

When the user opens the Web page and requests a catalog addition, they'll see an Imported WebPart Catalog section like the one shown in Figure 14.11. The user clicks Browse to display a Choose File dialog box and locate a file with a WEBPART extension. Once the user selects the file, they'll see one or more WebParts listed in the Imported WebPart list, as shown in Figure 14.11. The user selects the WebPart and adds it to the display as normal.

FIGURE 14.11
Importing WebParts lets a user create a truly customized Web page.

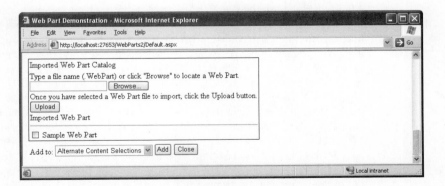

The `DeclarativeCatalogPart` control requires a little more work. You must define the optional controls as part of the Web page. Listing 14.12 shows a typical example of the entries for a `DeclarativeCatalogPart` control. You'll find this example in the `\ABC_Inc\WebParts\Advanced` folder of the source code on the Sybex Web site.

LISTING 14.12:   Adding a *DeclarativeCatalogPart* Control to a Web Page

```
<asp:DeclarativeCatalogPart ID="DeclarativeCatalogPart1"
                            runat="server">
    <WebPartsTemplate>
        <asp:HyperLink ID="lnkSpecial"
                       Title="Special Hyperlink"
                       runat="server">
            The Special Link
        </asp:HyperLink><br />
        <asp:Label ID="lblSpecial"
                   Title="Special Label"
                   runat="server"
                   Text="The Special Label">
        </asp:Label>
    </WebPartsTemplate>
</asp:DeclarativeCatalogPart>
```

You can add any kind of control to this WebPart that you can add to a `PageCatalogPart` control. In addition, the user chooses the WebPart and adds it to the Web page as with the `PageCatalogPart` control. The main difference between the two controls is how the `WebPartManager` controls them. The `DeclarativeCatalogPart` control supplies what amounts to optional controls that you might not want every user to access.

Understanding How Much Customization to Provide

After working with the WebParts examples in Chapter 6 and the additional examples in this chapter, you might think that users could spend all of their time rearranging page elements and not getting much work done. You could be correct. In fact, some users play around with the controls so much that their Web page becomes pretty much useless and you'll find that you spend too much time getting their Web page back into a usable state. In short, it's easy to provide too many customization features when using WebParts, so you have to plan the page carefully.

The first concept to include in your plan is that you don't have to let the user customize everything—even if they ask for that right. Every Web page contains some material that the user will need no matter what they want to do with it. If the Web page is devoid of such content, you might want to ask whether you really need it. Consequently, make sure you identify any content that the user must have to use the page and exempt it from customization (or at least removal from the screen).

You also need to consider the experience level of the user. It's important to keep powerful controls out of the hands of novices who will have no idea of how to use them. In fact, you should consider whether some power users need all of the features that WebParts could provide. To ensure everyone gets the features they need, you either need to create separate pages (hard to maintain) or program the access based on the login user (difficult to write for bulletproof access). Generally, you should probably provide a user page and an administrator page to separate the two levels of controls at least.

Working with Media

Users once frowned on media because of the cheesy presentations assaulted them from their browser window—usually at the worst possible time. As developers become better at incorporating media in a workplace-sensitive manner and the need to present information, such as training sessions, that doesn't quite meet the text presentation that most Web sites use increases, so is the use of media. It's possible to create all kinds of different media—everything from static graphic animations to live presentations. This section discusses a few of the common media types that you can use to add pizzazz to your Web site.

NOTE The available graphic formats for Web pages increases almost daily as developers discover new ways to present them. For example, Scalable Vector Graphics (SVG) rely on XML to store the data required to construction three-dimensional (3D) images on screen based on equations. The graphics have infinite resolution because they're based on vectors, rather than pixels. Of course, it also requires more time to process such an image because the browser has to recreate it for every request. Engineering and other graphics-intensive Web sites use SVG because standard graphics simply can't meet their needs. You can learn more about this technology at http://www.w3.org/ Graphics/SVG/. Some companies, such as Adobe (http://www.adobe.com/svg/main.html) are also heavily involved in SVG research.

Media Uses

Media has many uses on the Internet. What was once a toy has become a tool as developers begin adding media for use in marketing products and as a means for making training more effective. In addition, major news stations now include video and sound on their Web sites to get the news across to a broader audience. Many corporations are also making use of media, as witnessed by the many media presentations that Microsoft is making available to developers. Good media can enhance content and make a boring Web site a joy to use. Generally, the best media enhances the user experience in some way. It helps the user understand a topic better than pure text can do. Here are some ways that you can use media to create a more effective Web site.

Training Using video, sound, and static pictures can create a more effective training Web site. Users can see and hear the techniques they're supposed to learn, making the training better (people learn better when they experience a topic in more ways). In addition, the training takes on a human appearance. Instead of interacting with a computer, the person interacts with a trainer who just happens to appear on the computer.

Entertainment Media can provide entertainment. For example, you could provide access to the video that you took of your vacation last year. Quite a few Web sites offer animated GIFs—those little graphics that provide a bit of a sparkle for any Web site. One of the more interesting places to find animated GIFs is the Webdeveloper.com Web site at http://www.webdeveloper .com/animations/. Another interesting place to look is Animation Factory at http://www .animationfactory.com/animations/. However, don't limit yourself because there are literally thousands of Web sites that offer free graphics.

Nonverbal Information　Some topics don't lend themselves to easy description in text. For example, trying to explain precisely how a particular bird sounds is going to be hard when the user doesn't have the same frame of reference that you do. You'd both have to have the same understanding of the sounds that birds make and even then, it would be hard. However, a simple audio file can say everything that the words can't.

Presentations　It doesn't matter what kind of presentation you want to make, most presentations work better when you include various kinds of media. Even a simple slideshow containing charts, graphs, and other information that backs up any claims you make can be very helpful. One place that can provide an interesting perspective of presentations used as advertisements is AdCritic at `http://www.adcritic.com/`. If nothing else, you'll discover what other people have done incorrectly so you can avoid making the same mistake.

Sometimes media can also cause problems. For example, imagine that you're sitting in a cubicle at work and everything is relatively quiet. Suddenly, you stumble on a Web site that plays marching music. The Web site has not only embarrassed you, but also disturbed everyone else in the office. The Web site developer could have avoided this problem by making the media optional—something the user had to activate manually as a matter of choice. Generally, you want to make a Web site media optional unless you know that the user is expecting media of some type.

One rule of thumb to remember is that the more media you include on your Web site, the more platform specific it becomes. Making a Web site platform specific isn't a big problem when you know which browsers users will have installed on their system, but it's nearly impossible to determine this kind of information for a public Web site. Less platform specific is better because more people can visit and enjoy your Web site. Most media makes Web sites platform specific in one or more of the following ways.

Browser Variances　Every browser has specific features that it supports, but not every browser supports every feature. Consequently, you might use a media tag that works well on one browser, but not on another. In addition, even when two browsers provide the same feature support, they'll likely support it in different ways, which means the media might not look as expected on every system.

Plug-in Problems　Some types of media require use of plug-ins—extra bits of code that you ask the user to add to a browser. For example, when you use RealAudio, you need a plug-in to hear the sounds that the data stream obtains for you. Not every add-in supports every browser. Consequently, you might lock some browser users out by simply choosing the wrong plug-in to implement the media you want to provide.

Client-side Scripting　In some cases, you can implement media use through a client-side script. The script might support an add-in or object, or it might provide standalone functionality. In either case, the fact that many browsers don't provide full scripting support means that users of these browsers won't be able to enjoy the media you provide. This problem is especially worrisome when using Java applets since Internet Explorer 6 users have to download a Java runtime in order to use Java. Considering the Internet Explorer 6 share of the market, you could end up locking out many people.

Animated GIFs

The animated GIF file is the oldest form of animation on the Internet. You've probably seen the animated GIF on more than one Web site because it's very common. The little cartoon characters, twirling banners, and exploding stars that you see on various Web sites are probably animated GIFs.

TIP It often helps to look at other people's animated GIFs as you create your own for ideas they might have used. To verify an image on a Web page is an animated GIF from Internet Explorer, right-click the image and choose Properties from the context menu. You'll see the location and name of the image on the host system—any image that has a file extension of GIF and has an animated effect is an animated GIF. To save the image to your hard drive for better viewing, right-click the image and choose Save Picture As from the context menu. When you see the Save Picture dialog box, choose a location to save image and click Save. Some developers use a no right-click code to thwart you from saving the image. In these cases, you can usually find the animated GIF in the browser cache and retrieve it from there.

An animated GIF contains a series of still images that the browser plays back at the speed determined by the developer. You can add a number of special effects to GIFs and optimize them for size and playing speed. Most browsers do support this form of animation. The tools for creating an animated GIF are readily available and you can get some tools for little to no cost. Consequently, most developers experiment with this form of animation first.

Visual Web Developer supports animated GIF files, but it doesn't provide the tools required to create an animated GIF. To create an animated GIF, you need a drawing program to create the individual frames of the animation program and a program to put them together into a single file. One of the better products available on the market for creating animated GIF files is the GIF Construction Set from Alchemy Mindworks (http://www.mindworkshop.com/alchemy/gifcon.html). This product is shareware, so you can try it before you buy it. Figure 14.12 shows a typical editing session with this product. You'll find this example in the \ABC_Inc\Images\AnimatedGIF folder of the source code on the Sybex Web site. (Newer versions of Corel's Paint Shop Pro, http://www.jasc.com, also have an animated GIF creation feature that you might want to try.)

On the left side of the display is a series of frames. The browser displays these frames one after the other. You add frames using the Edit ➤ Insert Block ➤ Image command. Double-click an image and you see the Edit Image dialog box on the right side of Figure 14.12. Notice the Control Block field is checked and that the Delay field is set to 1. This is how you control the display time for each frame in your animation.

Placing an animated GIF on a Web page is relatively easy. All you need to do is add an `<asp:Image>` tag to your application and set the `ImageUrl` property to point to the image you want to display. Make sure you set the `Width` and `Height` properties to maintain the proper image size. Finally, set the `AlternativeText` property, as shown here, so viewers with vision problems can still enjoy your art. (You'll find this example in the \ABC_Inc\Media folder of the source code on the Sybex Web site.) Figure 14.13 shows the output from this example.

```
<asp:Image ID="imgAnimatedGIF" runat="server"
           Width="90" Height="90"
           ImageUrl="~/Images/AnimatedTime.gif"
           AlternateText="This is an animated GIF of a clock where the
                          minute hand moves. The clock has a red back
                          with yellow hands and a yellow background." />
```

TIP As an alternative to the <asp:Image> tag, you can always use the <img> tag to reduce application complexity and server load. The use of an <img> tag points to the success of the animated GIF. Even when a browser doesn't provide the required support, which is rare, the use of this standard tag lets the user see the first frame of the animated GIF, so the Web page doesn't look bare. Consequently, always make the first frame of your animated GIF something that can stand alone so the user sees something useful even when the animation isn't available. The <img> tag has one advantage over the <asp:Image> tag. Sometimes you don't want the animated GIF to run continuously. You can add the loop attribute to the <img> tag to let the image animate for a set number of times and then stop.

FIGURE 14.12
Create a series of frames and tell the browser how to display them.

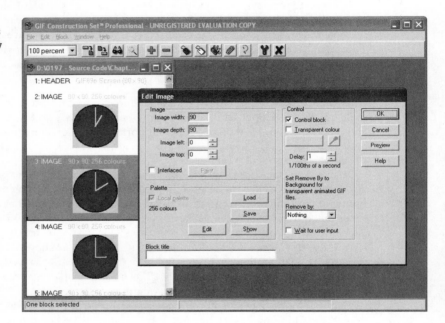

FIGURE 14.13
The output application appears as an animated image that stops when finished.

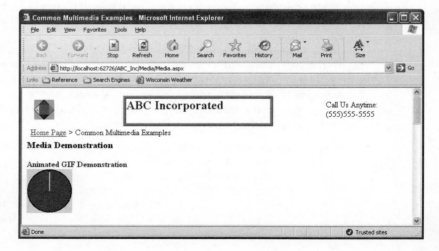

Audio

The next most popular media addition to Web sites (after animated GIFs) is audio. Some people actually play whole symphonies in the background, but that's the exception rather than the rule. In this case, you have three tags to choose from for adding audio to your Web page, and you could possibly add other techniques. Listing 14.13 shows the various techniques. You'll find this example in the \ABC_Inc\Media folder of the source code on the Sybex Web site.

The <embed> tag is the first technique you can use. You define the audio file as part of the src attribute and can use the loop attribute to keep the sound file from playing continuously. It plays the audio immediately after the Web page loads. Most developers use this tag to provide background music for the Web site. It's popular on some product sites where the developer wants to extend the shopping experience to include the elevator music that the buyer would hear in the store. Generally, you should avoid using this approach unless you know that the user is expecting the sounds and won't open it up in an office environment. The <embed> tag creates a sound control, as shown in Figure 14.14, so the user can start or stop the sound, as well as set its volume.

TIP   You can also use the <bgsound> tag to create background sounds. The <bgsound> tag is most compatible with Internet Explorer, while the <embed> tag is most compatible with other browsers. For the greatest compatibility with all browsers, always use the <embed> tag. When you want to be sure that Internet Explorer users will get maximum functionality from the background sound, use the <bgsound> tag.

The <a> tag is the second technique. Using this technique, you define the audio file you want to play as part of the href attribute. The sound only plays one time, so there isn't any need for the loop attribute. You should use the title attribute, in this case, to describe the sound to the user (avoiding any unpleasant surprises).

LISTING 14.13:   Adding Audio to a Web Page

```
<asp:Label ID="lblAudio" runat="server"
            Font-Bold="true" Font-Size="Medium"
            Text="Audio Playback Demonstration" /><br /><br />
<asp:Label ID="lblEmbedAudio" runat="server"
            Text="Using an Embed Tag" /><br />
<embed id="embedAudio" src="../Images/tada.wav" loop="1"
      title="This sound file makes the Tada sound, which is often
              associated with the completion of a task." /><br /><br />
<asp:Label ID="lblHlAudio" runat="server"
            Text="Using a Hyperlink" /><br />
<asp:HyperLink ID="hlAudio" runat="server"
                NavigateUrl="~/Images/tada.wav"
                ToolTip="This sound file makes the Tada sound, which is
                        often associated with the completion of a
                        task.">
    Play a Sound
</asp:HyperLink>
```

FIGURE 14.14
The sound control lets the user choose when to play the sound and controls volume.

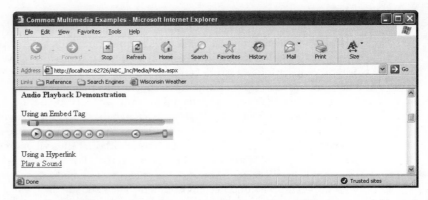

Another way to play sound files is to use the `<object>` tag. You can find a description of this technique in the "Developing with the *<Object>* Tag" section of Chapter 6. Using this technique, you can choose whether to play the sound immediately or wait for user input. In addition, the user gains access to the various controls that the Windows Media Player provides, so the user can play the file more than one time if desired or even pause the sound. This particular approach works great when you want to include sound within a training site so the user can pause the presentation as needed.

Video

Video is still somewhat rare on most Web sites. Yes, you'll find it in the expected locations such as news Web sites and online music stores, but most developers don't include video yet on the average Web site. As with audio, you have a number of options for playing video, as shown in Listing 14.14. You'll find this example in the `\ABC_Inc\Media` folder of the source code on the Sybex Web site.

LISTING 14.14:   Adding Video to a Web Page

```
<asp:Label ID="lblMovie" runat="server"
          Font-Bold="true" Font-Size="Medium"
          Text="Movie Playback Demonstration" /><br /><br />
<asp:Label ID="lblMouseHover" runat="server"
          Text="Runs When Mouse Hovers: " /><br />
<img id="imgMouseHover"
    border="1"
    dynsrc="../Images/TimeFlies.wmv"
    start="mouseover"
    loop="1"><br /><br />
<asp:Label ID="lblPageLoad" runat="server"
          Text="Runs When Page Loaded: " /><br />
<img id="imgPageLoad"
     border="1"
     dynsrc="../Images/TimeFlies.wmv"
```

```
        start="fileopen"
        loop="1"><br /><br />
<asp:Label ID="lblWMP" runat="server"
           Text="Using an Object Tag" /><br />
<object width="200" height="275"
        classid="CLSID:05589FA1-C356-11CE-BF01-00AA0055595A"
        type="application/oleobject"
        id="WMP">
    <param name="filename" value="../Images/TimeFlies.avi">
    <param name="Appearance" value="0">
    <param name="AutoStart" value="0">
    <param name="AllowChangeDisplayMode" value="-1">
    <param name="AllowHideDisplay" value="0">
    <param name="AllowHideControls" value="-1">
    <param name="AutoRewind" value="-1">
    <param name="Balance" value="0">
    <param name="CurrentPosition" value="0">
    <param name="DisplayBackColor" value="0">
    <param name="DisplayForeColor" value="16777215">
    <param name="DisplayMode" value="0">
    <param name="Enabled" value="-1">
    <param name="EnableContextMenu" value="-1">
    <param name="EnablePositionControls" value="-1">
    <param name="EnableSelectionControls" value="0">
    <param name="EnableTracker" value="-1">
    <param name="FullScreenMode" value="0">
    <param name="MovieWindowSize" value="0">
    <param name="PlayCount" value="1">
    <param name="Rate" value="1">
    <param name="SelectionStart" value="-1">
    <param name="SelectionEnd" value="-1">
    <param name="ShowControls" value="-1">
    <param name="ShowDisplay" value="-1">
    <param name="ShowPositionControls" value="0">
    <param name="ShowTracker" value="-1">
    <param name="Volume" value="0">
</object><br /><br />
<asp:Label ID="lblVideo" runat="server"
           Text="Using a Link"
           AssociatedControlID="hlVideo" /><br />
<asp:HyperLink ID="hlVideo" runat="server"
               NavigateUrl="../Images/TimeFlies.avi"
               ToolTip="This video file shows a time countdown.">
    Play Video
</asp:HyperLink>
```

The first two techniques are similar—they both rely on the `<img>` tag. This is one situation where you must use the `<img>` tag because the `<asp:Image>` tag lacks the required functionality. However, you should notice a few differences between an `<img>` tag used to display a graphic and one used to display a movie.

1. Define the video source using the `dynsrc` (dynamic source) attribute. Using the `dynsrc` attribute lets the browser download the file and start playing it as pieces become available. (You can get an overview of the nonstandard attributes for the `<img>` tag at `http://www .redbrick.dcu.ie/help/reference/html-tags/TAG_IMG.html`.)

2. Use the `loop` attribute in this case—video tends to replay itself in some browsers even though it shouldn't.

3. Define the `start` attribute because it defines when the video plays. In the first case, the user must pass the mouse over the video to play it and in the second, the video plays immediately when the page loads.

This example points out the need to keep your HTML coding techniques handy because ASP.NET doesn't answer every client-side coding need. Figure 14.15 shows how these two entries appear on the Web page.

A second approach is using the `<object>` tag. It's important to define a precise size for the video, in this case, using the `width` and `height` attributes (otherwise, the Windows Media Player tends to choose odd sizes that won't work with your video). You should also provide type information so that the `<object>` tag knows how to interact with the video. The code shows the most common type information.

FIGURE 14.15

Using the *<img>* tag lets the user see the presentation as part of the display.

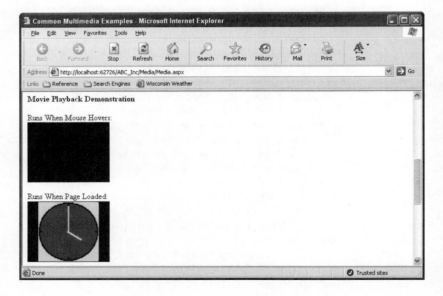

TIP   One other issue with this approach is that you have to use Audio Video Interleaved (AVI) files, not Windows Media Video (WMV) files. Unfortunately, current versions of Microsoft's products don't produce anything but WMV files, so you need a converter such as Fx Video Converter to create the AVI file. You can download this product at `http://www.brothersoft.com/Multimedia_ Graphics_Video_Conversion_Fx_Video_Converter_20561.html`. The vendor markets this product as shareware, which means you can try it before you buy it.

As with audio, you must define a number of `<param>` tags to go with the `<object>` tag. The code shows the common video settings, but you should experiment to see what works best with your video. You must provide a filename for the video, and experimentation shows that the filename works better when you don't need to include path information. In short, make sure the video appears in the same folder as the Web page used to display it. Figure 14.16 shows a typical Windows Media Player display for the example video using the settings shown.

The third technique is to use a simple `<a>` tag. All you need to do is assign a filename to the `href` attribute. Providing a description of the video as part of the title tag is also helpful, but might not be necessary given the way that most developers use video. You should make sure that your video includes captioning for people who can't turn up the audio (for example, due to workplace restrictions). The link method works differently for video, in most cases, than it does for audio (although the precise reaction depends on the browser). The user will normally see a copy of the Windows Media Player start, as shown in Figure 14.17 to play the video. The browser downloads a temporary copy of the video first and then plays the video, so this technique can take longer to start the video than other methods might.

FIGURE 14.16
The *<object>* tag technique provides the user with access to controls.

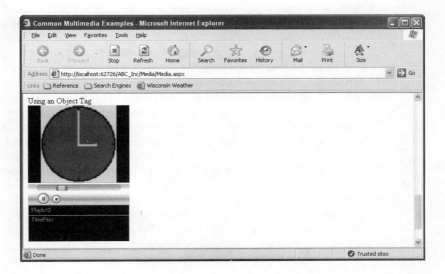

FIGURE 14.17
A link downloads the image locally and then loads it into a local copy of Windows Media Player.

Interactive

Interactivity comes in a number of forms today—some of which you can use right now and other forms that are only in the testing phase. The most basic type of interactivity is the form. When a user fills out a form and your server receives it, a two-way communication takes place. The user is interactive, but in a static kind of way. Chapter 7 describes how to use forms.

The next level of interactivity is a form that mutates to meet specific needs. The "Selection Using Scripts," "Progressive Input Using Scripts," and "Selection and Progressive Input with ASP.NET" sections of the chapter describe this kind of interactivity. The form isn't static anymore, but it isn't dynamic. However, the improvements described in these two sections let companies create training programs where the user can learn something quickly. By combining video, audio, and special form effects, a user can feel as if the computer is interacting with them in a new way. Although the Web site is a continuous advertisement, the interactive tutorial on Web pages at `http://www.davesite.com/webstation/html/` is a good place to see what you can accomplish with only a little work (some interactive tutorials are absolutely gorgeous, but you also have to pay to see them).

One of the better examples of interactive media is also free. If you've been following the latest in space technology, you know that the Mars rovers have made more than a little splash. They've lasted well over the time that NASA expected them to and have delivered some amazing pictures of Mars. Anyone who has ever wondered what it would be like to drive the Mars rover can do so at `http://robotics.jpl.nasa.gov/tasks/scirover/operator/wits/homepage.htm`. This Web site is an excellent example of an interactive media taken about as far as anyone can go today.

Many people are also discovering the wonders of interactive television. Given that some television stations are experimenting with online feeds to computer systems, it might not be long before you'll see an interactive video where you can become part of the show. Unfortunately, the technology isn't quite there yet and it's going to be quite a while before you can incorporate such technologies on your own Web site (perhaps as part of a video). To learn more about interactive television and discover how it might be coming to a computer near you, check out the Interactive Television Alliance at `http://www.itvalliance.org/`. Yahoo provides a list of businesses that are currently involved with interactive television at `http://dir.yahoo.com/Business_and_Economy/Business_to_Business/Entertainment_and_Media_Production/Television/Interactive/`.

Defining Your Development Goals

This chapter has demonstrated many levels of pizzazz you can add to your Web site. Choosing the right level is a matter of planning the Web site, understanding what message you to present to users, and discovering user needs that fit in with that message. Overall, the best strategy is the one that keeps the page simple, caters to user requirements, and still gives your Web site that something extra it needs to compete on the Internet.

Now it's time for you to consider the pizzazz factor for your Web site. It's important to think about these issues during the initial design phase, but to allow room for change as you create the critical components of your Web site as well. If you have an existing Web site, you might want to poll Web site users to determine what they would like to see changed on the current Web site. Make sure you consider functionality over glitz. Always ask what the user will get out of this feature, rather than simply assume that the user will love the eye candy you provide. Take time to create a plan that works and you'll find that the pizzazz you add is going to make a real difference in Web site statistics.

Chapter 15 discusses techniques for creating downloadable applications—the kind used for Web sites such as Windows Update. Many Web sites now use specialized applications to create an interactive environment. For example, you'll find specialized Web applications used for collaboration. The special application downloads over the Internet and creates a secure connection that two or more people use to discuss an important issue. Of course, someone with less than honorable intentions could misuse the environment the special application creates, so Chapter 15 also discusses techniques for easing user concerns and ensuring the special application really is as secure as you tell the user it is.

Chapter 15

Working with Client-side Controls

Most Web applications get along just fine without the added complication of a custom control download. Creating a custom control can be time consuming, and users usually aren't willing to download them without good reason. However, you'll eventually run into an application requirement that needs a custom control. For example, a lot of conferencing software relies on custom controls to speed communication and to reduce the risks of someone's overhearing. Financial applications sometimes rely on custom controls for security reasons. You'll also find custom controls used for update applications. The most common example of a custom control used for this purpose is Windows Update.

Custom controls used over the Internet have to address a number of concerns, not the least of which is building the trust of the user. Besides quality control issues, you should sign a custom control used over the Internet. Signing ensures that no one has tampered with the control. The digital certificate that you use for signing the control comes from a reliable third party—one that everyone trusts. The digital certificate certifies that you really are who you say you are.

Once you overcome the basic issues of building, testing, and signing the control, you need to provide a means of downloading it from the Internet. Depending on the kind of control you build, the user usually needs to download the control to the local machine. In most cases, installation is automatic—the user doesn't do anything more than indicate it's OK to install the control.

At this point, you have a control sitting on the user's machine. Now you have to build your Web pages to use the control. Of course, there's still plenty of room for problems. For example, a poorly designed control could cause memory problems on the user's machine. Controls also invite a number of security problems, so you need to ensure the control works flawlessly (hopefully, but be prepared to fix bugs anyway).

Understanding User Concerns about Controls

Custom controls give the developer an immense amount of power and responsibility for the client system. Unlike scripts and other technologies, controls have direct access to the system resources and you don't even need to do anything of a cracking nature to gain that access. Greater trust brings with it greater responsibility. As a control developer, you have a greater responsibility to the user because of the trust that the user places in you.

A poorly constructed control can wreak havoc on a user system without even trying too hard. It's not just a matter of erasing data files or even causing the browser session to crash—controls are a lot more powerful than that. With a poorly constructed control, a developer can crash a system or cause so much damage that the user must format the hard drive and start over from scratch. No wonder many users are quite leery of working with controls. The point is that you must develop a rapport with the user and build trust. The controls you create must be free of bugs, reliable, secure, fast, and should not compromise the user's system. The second you lose the user's trust, you can be sure that you'll also lose any access that the control could provide.

Even after you gain the user's trust, you must consider other potential problems. For example, even a user who trusts you to provide a great control will have privacy concerns. A control can drain a computer system of every piece of private information and not leave much in the way of crumbs afterward. You can be sure that any breach of privacy is going to meet with a very negative response. Sometimes, a privacy breach is completely innocuous and your company might not even create the problem directly. If you can access your control, so can someone else. Consequently, you must have policies in place to ensure any code you create meets strict privacy criteria and then perform testing to ensure the code actually meets the criteria. This could mean hiring a hacker to test your control for breaches. Make sure you perform destructive outside testing on a test machine to ensure the integrity of your control.

Interception is another potential problem that users worry about when working with controls. You must consider interception at several levels. At the very least, a cracker could discover enough about the participants in a conversation over the Internet to engage in wrongful activity such as identity theft. Without proper safeguards, your conversation is completely open and the cracker won't have any problem listening to it. A more harmful type of interception occurs when a cracker actually begins to participate in the conversation. The man-in-the-middle attack is well known, but it still happens when a control relies on sloppy coding techniques. Make sure you use proper data encryption and rely on strong security measures to avoid tampering by outside parties. Again, make sure you have this part of your code tested by an outside party that specializes in this form of security. The extra time really gives you a better sense of security.

You might run into situations where the user isn't going to trust you no matter how diligently you test your control. Written policies and a great security record only go so far in building user trust. When the user is part of your company, you can force the issue of course, but other situations require more care. It always pays to have an alternative in mind when you work out a communication strategy. Some users will always trust the telephone over the computer, even though the telephone is theoretically more open to security breaches because it doesn't provide the encryption your application can provide.

Creating a Control

Objects—controls or components—can provide you with a great deal more flexibility in creating your Web application. You need to create a stand-alone object that the user can download. This limitation means that you have to create an object that can execute by itself using only the resources that the user machine is likely to possess, such as a copy of the .NET Framework. (You can create a software package to make up for gaps in the user's installation, but this approach is laden with pitfalls and quickly becomes messy because you can't assume anything about the user's machine.) Make sure you test the download technology to ensure it works on a broad range of machines (one of the constant problems that many users complain about on some well-known Web sites, including Microsoft Windows Update).

NOTE Even though you can create controls and components as part of a Visual Web Developer projects—they aren't stand-alone. You use them as part of the project. Chapter 20 describes these component (see the "Creating Standard Components" section) and control (see the "Creating Standard Controls" section) templates in detail. You must use the built-in Visual Studio language features to create a stand-alone component or control.

It's also important to give any components or controls you create a strong name—signing it to ensure that no one can tamper with it. The "Adding a Strong Name to the Component" section of Chapter 13 describes how to perform this process. All of the components and controls in this chapter have a strong name, even though the chapter doesn't describe the process again as part of creating the component or control. The following sections show how to create a control to use as a Web application extension.

NOTE The examples in the following sections appear as separate projects, rather than as part of the ABC, Incorporated Web site. The main reason for this change in course is that you would normally develop components and controls as separate projects in the real world environment. You don't want to tie your components and controls to a Web project, but rather make them part of a separate project. This approach lets you use the component or control in a number of environments and make changes to the code independently of the applications that use the component or control.

Understanding the Difference between Controls and Components

Many developers are unaware of the differences between controls and components. Both provide a modular method of adding functionality to an application and both rely on classes (essentially object blueprints). Instantiated classes create objects made up of code and data that expose functionality through properties, methods, and events. In short, they both have many similarities that lead to confusion with some developers. The only problem is that controls and components serve distinctly different purposes.

The main difference between a control and a component is that a control provides an interface—something the user can see. The user interacts with controls directly and uses them to perform work. Consequently, controls are usually task oriented. Components hide in the background and the user is often unaware of their existence. Consequently, components are usually service or process oriented. Even though the underlying technology for controls and components is the same, the results (or output) are different.

Designing a Control

The example in this section uses an augmented label to download content directly from a secret location on the Web server. A user clicks a link or button on the Web page and sees the content—the example uses a button. It's also possible to automate the download—you could use the page load event to perform the task for example. You can use this technique for a number of tasks, such as displaying generalized help on screen. Multiple applications can share the same help stored in a central location to reduce costs. This example isn't quite that complex—it downloads some special text and displays it on screen. The use of a special label lets you either hard code the target or provide it as properties. The whole purpose of this example is to demonstrate that you can create custom controls for direct communication and rely on a user event to activate the control.

TIP Don't assume that you're limited to .NET controls or that you even have to support the controls you want to use on your Web site. Microsoft provides a number of controls that you can access directly from a Web site at http://activex.microsoft.com/. The Web site documentation tells you how to use the controls within a Web page as well.

Listing 15.1 shows the code you'll use to create the example in this section. Notice that the example actually inherits from a Windows form control, rather than a Web control. You'll find this example in the \Chapter 15\SampleControl folder of the source code on the Sybex Web site.

LISTING 15.1:   Creating a Simple Control

```
[Guid("80299918-7D92-499e-B55B-5514649E759F")]
public class SpecialMessage : Label
{
    // Private global variables.
    Uri     _ResourceURL;   // Resource URL

    public SpecialMessage()
    {
    }

    public String ResourceURL
    {
        get
        {
            // Return the string that the user provided as input or
            // nothing when the URL is invalid.
            if (_ResourceURL == null)
                return "";
            else
                return _ResourceURL.AbsoluteUri;
        }
        set
        {
            // Use a try...catch block in case the user passes
            // something other than a valid URI.
            try
            {
                _ResourceURL = new Uri(value);
            }
            catch
            {
                // Display an error message.
                this.Text =
                    "Invalid URL: Use http://myserver/resource.htm";
            }
        }
    }

    public String ResourcePort
    {
        get
```

```csharp
    {
        // Return the current port string or a value or 0
        // when the URL is invalid.
        if (_ResourceURL == null)
            return "0";
        else
            return _ResourceURL.Port.ToString();
    }
}

public Boolean IsValidURL
{
    get
    {
        // Verify that the resource URL is valid. The _ResourceURL
        // variable is null when the URL is invalid.
        if (_ResourceURL == null)
            return false;
        else
            return true;
    }
}


public String GetResource()
{
    HttpWebRequest   Request;      // Web resource request.
    HttpWebResponse  Response;     // Response from server.
    Stream           DataOut;      // Output data stream.
    StreamReader     ReadMe;       // Data from server.
    String           TheData;      // Contains the actual data.

    // If the URL isn't valid, then return.
    if (_ResourceURL == null)
        return "";

    // When the URL is valid, try to retrieve the data.
    this.Text = "Creating the Request";
    Request = (HttpWebRequest)WebRequest.Create(_ResourceURL);

    // Place the response code within a try...catch in case
    // the request is invalid.
    try
    {
        // Get the response.
        this.Text = "Getting the Response";
        Response = (HttpWebResponse)Request.GetResponse();
```

```
                // Obtain the data stream.
                this.Text = "Obtaining a Data Stream";
                DataOut = Response.GetResponseStream();

                // Build a link to the data.
                this.Text = "Creating the Data Link";
                ReadMe = new StreamReader(DataOut);

                // Retrieve the data.
                this.Text = "Retrieving the Data";
                TheData = ReadMe.ReadToEnd();

                // Clean up.
                this.Text = "Cleaning Up";
                ReadMe.Close();
                DataOut.Close();
                Response.Close();

                // Return the data.
                this.Text = TheData;
                return TheData;
            }
            catch (WebException WE)
            {
                // Return the exception information.
                return WE.Response + "\r\n" +
                       WE.Status + "\r\n" + WE.Message;
            }
        }
    }
```

The example begins by declaring the `SpecialMessage` class. Notice that the class inherits from the `Label` class (the basis for the control of the same name). You should also define the `Guid` attribute with an appropriate GUID for the control. The "Designing the Interface" section of Chapter 13 describes how to perform this task. The class also contains one private global variable, `_ResourceURL`, of type `Uri` that contains the location of the secret resource. As with all well-designed controls, this control doesn't provide direct access to `_ResourceURL`; it relies on properties that provide error checking to do the job.

The `ResourceURL` property lets the developer using the control request a specific resource from the Web server. The example only verifies that the property receives a properly formatted Uniform Resource Identifier (URI)—it doesn't check to ensure the resource is of the correct type, such as a text file. When the control receives an invalid URI, the code throws an exception and the `catch` statement displays an error message, rather than change the property value. The `get` part of the property returns either a null string (when the control hasn't received a URI) or the complete URI contained within `_ResourceURL`.

NOTE The term *URI* defines any resource on the Internet, including various kinds of objects. A Uniform Resource Locator (URL) is a specific kind of URI. Microsoft chose to use the generic URI for the .NET Framework so that a single class could access any resource. You can use various properties and methods to ensure the URI that someone supplies is correct. For example, you can verify that the URI points to a file by checking the IsFile property.

The developer using the control will need methods for checking the control status. The example provides two methods. First, the developer can check the ResourcePort property, which contains the port number contained within _ResourceURL. In many cases, Web sites hide resources using a different port than the standard port 80. The second property, IsValidURL, is more direct. When the control receives an invalid URI, it ignores it, which means _ResourceURL remains null. A simple check of this variable provides an output value as to the validity of the URI.

The main part of the control is the GetResource() method. When the control has a valid URI, the code uses the URI to access the resource. Remember that this is a label control, so you can display status messages using the Text property. Generally, you don't need to perform this task when working with a label, but a user working with a slower connection to a large resource might want to see the status messages to ensure the control is working as anticipated.

The first step is to create a connection between the client and the server using the WebRequest .Create() method. Unfortunately, you can't use the resulting WebRequest object directly—you must coerce it into a usable form, such as the HttpWebRequest object shown in the code.

Now that the code has a connection to the server, it can obtain the response to the request it made using the Request.GetResponse() method. Again, the resulting WebResponse object isn't very useful—you must coerce it into a usable object such as the HttpWebResponse object shown in the code. You might wonder why this call appears in a try...catch block when the original request doesn't. The request never fails because it's a request—the code doesn't receive the error information until it retrieves the response. Consequently, you must always place the response code in a try...catch block.

Once the code has access to the response, it creates a data stream to retrieve the response data using the Response.GetResponseStream() method. To read the response data, the code creates a new StreamReader, ReadMe. The code now relies on standard stream reading methods to obtain the data by using the ReadMe.ReadToEnd() method. The result ends up in TheData, which the code outputs to both the label and as a String to the caller. Notice that the code cleans up after itself by closing all of the open processing elements. The main error to watch for during the entire processing cycle is the WebException, which the code outputs to the caller as a String in the catch statement.

NOTE You'll find a simple example of how to use this control in the \Chapter 15\TestControl folder of the source code on the Sybex Web site. A description of how to use controls and components within the enterprise environment appears in the "Deploying a Component or Control to the Client" section of the chapter.

Designing a Component

Components generally provide a nonvisual service. The example in this section calculates the tax on a product. Although this isn't a complex component, it does demonstrate many useful component features. Listing 15.2 shows the code for this example. You'll find this example in the \Chapter 15\ SampleComponent folder of the source code on the Sybex Web site.

LISTING 15.2: Creating a Simple Component

```
[Guid("CF8FE83E-5FFC-4bc0-82BE-8426F8BFE823")]
public class ComputeTax
{
    // Global variables used for calculation.
    Single  _Rate;              // Contains the tax rate.
    Decimal _TaxableSale;       // Contains the sale plus tax.
    Decimal _TaxOnly;           // Contains just the tax.

    public ComputeTax()
    {

    }

    public ComputeTax(Single Rate)
    {
        // Verify that the tax rate is within the acceptable range.
        if ((Rate > .01) && (Rate < 1.00))
            _Rate = Rate;
        else
            throw new ArgumentOutOfRangeException(
                "Rate", Rate, "Rate must be between .01 and 1.00.");
    }

    public Single TaxRate
    {
        get
        {
            // Return the current tax rate.
            return _Rate;
        }
        set
        {
            // Verify that the tax rate is within the acceptable range.
            if ((value > .01) && (value < 1.00))
                _Rate = value;
            else
                throw new ArgumentOutOfRangeException(
                    "Rate",
                    value,
                    "Rate must be between .01 and 1.00.");
        }
    }

    public Decimal TaxableSale
    {
```

```
        get
        {
            return _TaxableSale;
        }
    }

    public Decimal TaxOnly
    {
        get
        {
            return _TaxOnly;
        }
    }

    public Decimal AddTax(Decimal SaleValue)
    {
        // Verify the user has provided a correct sales value.
        if (SaleValue < 0)
            throw new ArgumentOutOfRangeException(
                "SaleValue",
                SaleValue,
                "Sale value must be a positive number.");

        // Verify the user has defined a tax rate.
        if ((_Rate == 0) || (_Rate == null))
            throw new ArgumentNullException(
                "Rate",
                "You must define a tax rate before making this call.");

        // Calculate the sale amount with tax.
        _TaxableSale = SaleValue * (1 + Convert.ToDecimal(_Rate));
        _TaxOnly = SaleValue * Convert.ToDecimal(_Rate);

        // Return the computed tax amount.
        return _TaxableSale;
    }
}
```

The example begins with the class declaration. In this case, the class is stand-alone and doesn't inherit from any other classes. Always make sure that you include the Guid attribute with the class declaration in case the developer wants to use the GUID reference method. The GUID reference method relies on a GUID in the <Object> tag like this.

```
<object classid="clsid:80299918-7D92-499e-B55B-5514649E759F"
        height="50"
        width="100"
        id="lblTest2">
```

```
<param name="Name" value="lblTest" />
<param name="Text" value="Empty Space">
<param name="ResourceURL"
    value="http://localhost:5892/TestControl/SpecialMessage.TXT">
</object><br />
```

By referencing a specific GUID, the developer ensures that the `<Object>` tag has access to a specific version of the control. Of course, one side effect of this decision is that the code could conceivably fail more often because the reference is so specific.

The class uses three private variables to store information about the tax computation. As with controls, you never provide direct access to internal component variables. Instead, always rely on properties to change the variable value. You can also use other techniques, such as allowing the developer to set the variable value with the constructor or as part of a method call.

This example shows how to use an overloaded constructor. Always provide a constructor that doesn't accept any input values when writing components for the Internet. You can't provide an input value to the constructor from the `<Object>` tag. However, including the overloaded constructors is a good idea when you expect the developer to use the component in more than one environment or in multiple ways. For example, you could access this component from the code behind and use the overloaded constructor that way.

It's essential to check your inputs no matter where they come from. In this case, the second constructor checks `Rate` to ensure it falls within the proper value range. When the input fails to meet expectations, the code retains the current `Rate` value and throws an `ArgumentOutOfRangeException` exception. Make sure you use the correct exception or create a special exception. Don't throw a generic exception unless that's the most appropriate course of action—it seldom (if ever) is the correct selection. In addition, notice that the code provides complete information. The `ArgumentOutOfRangeException` exception supports several overloaded constructors that allow only partial information input, which isn't the best way to help the developer using your component to understand the situation.

You might wonder why the code uses exceptions, rather than handling the error within the component. Always use exceptions within components to allow the developer to handle the error within the application code. In this case, however, the component works within a scripted environment using the `<Object>` tag. There's little chance of catching any errors. Figure 15.1 shows the result of an error in this environment. In this case, the developer forgot to define the tax rate before requesting the taxable sales amount. The well-defined exception information tells the developer precisely what went wrong and which variable requires change. Consequently, this error is easy to repair.

The class includes several properties. The `TaxRate` property lets the developer set the tax rate in any environment, including a scripted environment. Notice that this property provides the same error handling as the overloaded constructor. The `TaxableSale` and `TaxOnly` properties provide outputs to the developer. It doesn't make sense to let the developer change them because the developer is requesting this information from the component. The `TaxableSale` property outputs the sales price of an item with tax included, while the `TaxOnly` property outputs just the sales tax for the item.

The `AddTax()` method determines the taxes for an item and returns the sales price with tax included. Notice that this method uses the `Decimal` data type. Always use the `Decimal` data type for financial calculations to avoid rounding errors. Converting numbers from human readable base 10 numbers to computer readable base 2 numbers normally results in some type of rounding error. When working with large numbers or even many iterations of small numbers, these rounding errors accumulate and present inaccurate results. The down side to the `Decimal` data type is that it requires more resources and incurs a performance penalty.

FIGURE 15.1
Providing well-defined exceptions means easier debugging in a scripted environment.

The AddTax() method begins by checking the inputs and throwing the correct exceptions when the input is incorrect. Notice that the code checks every input, which is a good component design feature. Never assume that someone else got their code right—always assume that the input data could have errors and you'll run into fewer reliability and security problems. The trade-off for these checks is a slight performance hit, but the performance hit is worthwhile in today's development environment.

After the code checks the inputs, it performs the required calculations and stores the information locally. The AddTax() method ends by returning the item price with tax included to the caller.

NOTE You'll find a simple example of how to use this component in the \Chapter 15\TestComponent folder of the source code on the Sybex Web site. A description of how to use controls and components within the enterprise environment appears in the "Deploying a Component or Control to the Client" section of the chapter.

Deploying a Component or Control to the Client

Getting your control or component onto the client machine is an essential part of working with client-side controls. You can accomplish this task in a number of ways, not all of which are obvious from working with the Microsoft documentation and examples. The following sections describe one technique that you can use.

Working with native code (non-.NET code) has one big advantage when using the <Object> tag—the tools that Microsoft created work perfectly with native code. When you create an <Object> tag for a native code COM DLL, you can provide a Codebase attribute that will show where to get the DLL when the user doesn't have it installed. The system automatically downloads, installs, and registers the control or component based on the entries you provide. This technique absolutely will not work with .NET controls and components for one very good reason—the .NET control or component requires a different set of utilities for registration. Consequently, Microsoft recommends an awkward reference method that doesn't provide you with the full functionality that the <Object> tag can provide. The sections that follow provide a unique solution that relies on generally unused <Object> tag behaviors and the Microsoft Installer.

WARNING As you begin working with more complex examples and think about moving your .NET Framework 1.0 and 1.1 code to run on systems using the .NET Framework 2.0, you need to consider compatibility issues. Microsoft has made some decisions in design the .NET Framework 2.0 that cause older applications to behave differently or sometimes not at all. The compiler will normally let you know about the issue and sometimes provides a solution for the problem. You can learn more about this issue on the MSDN Web site at http://msdn.microsoft.com/library/default.asp?url=/library/en-us/dnnetdep/html/netfxcompat.asp.

Working with the ActiveX Control Test Container

Visual Studio provides a number of tools that you can use to verify the operation of the controls you create. The ActiveX Control Test Container (TSTCON32.EXE) is an older utility, but it still does a great job of testing your controls. In fact, this particular tool can point out flaws in your .NET control that you would never find using any other technique because the ActiveX Control Test Container is expecting a native code executable. In other words, if there is any chance that your .NET control will cause a problem on the client's machine, this utility is very likely to point it out—even when debugging and experimentation on your development machine say the control is working fine. This utility helps you to test the features of your ActiveX control in a special environment designed to help you locate flaws quickly. Figure 15.2 shows what the ActiveX Control Test Container looks like with the `SampleControl` control example loaded.

Before you begin working with this utility, use the `RegisterControl.BAT` batch file located in the `\Chapter 15\SampleControl\SampleControl\bin\Release` folder to register the control. Use the following steps to load your .NET control into the ActiveX Control Test Container.

1. Select the Edit ➢ Insert New Control command to load an ActiveX control in the test container. You'll see an Insert Control dialog box that lists all of the registered native code controls on the local machine. The dialog box won't list any .NET controls.

2. Click Implemented Categories. You'll see the Implemented Categories dialog box.

3. Check the .NET Category option and clear the Controls option. Click OK. The ActiveX Control Test Container will display a new list of controls in the Insert control dialog box. This list contains only .NET controls—not native controls.

4. Highlight the control you want to test. Click OK. You'll see the control within the ActiveX Control Test Container. If you don't see the control, then you probably didn't expose a required interface or register the control correctly.

NOTE   The ActiveX Control Test Container is quite flexible. You can also insert an ActiveX control into the current test container from a stream or from storage using the appropriate Edit menu command.

FIGURE 15.2
The ActiveX Control Test Container allows you to check the operation of controls that you create.

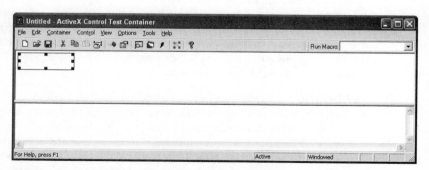

The following sections explore a few of the more important tasks you can perform with ActiveX Control Test Container. You'll likely need to perform one or more of these tasks as the book progresses. For example, when using an ActiveX control in a multi-language environment, you'll normally want to test it using this utility. As a minimum, you'll want to check to see that you can access the methods and properties that the control provides.

WARNING Even though you can create controls using a number of interface types, the ActiveX Control Test Container only works with C/C++ type interfaces. Consequently, you must add the `[ClassInterface(ClassInterfaceType.AutoDual)]` attribute to any control you want to test using this utility. However, from a broader perspective, it's usually best if you add this interface to ensure your control provides maximum compatibility.

CHECKING PROPERTIES AND METHODS

It's important to check all of the properties you define for a control to ensure the control will behave as anticipated. The .NET environment makes it possible for you to create a property that should work, but doesn't actually work as needed. For example, you might need to marshal a value from the Win32 API environment to the managed environment. Unfortunately, unless you can isolate the control and test it in an independent test environment such as the ActiveX Control Test Container, you'll have trouble figuring out precisely where the problem lies.

ActiveX Control Text Container checks the availability of both methods and properties. In addition, you can change these features of your ActiveX control to see whether they work as intended. The normal method used to change the properties is through a property page. Simply click on the Properties button (or use the Edit ➤ Properties command) to display control's Property dialog. Figure 15.3 shows what the Property dialog for the `Windows Media Player` control looks like.

Unfortunately, Microsoft doesn't provide an easy method for implementing property pages in .NET. You have to resort to all kinds of odd tricks to accomplish the tasks. Consequently, all you'll normally see is a nearly blank Properties dialog box with the Name property. Fortunately, even if the properties for a control you design don't appear in their entirety on property pages, you can still access them by looking through the list of methods supported by your control. You'll find that ActiveX Control Test Container creates a get and set method for every property your control supports. However, it's still easier to access properties (at least those created for design time use) through a property page for the most part.

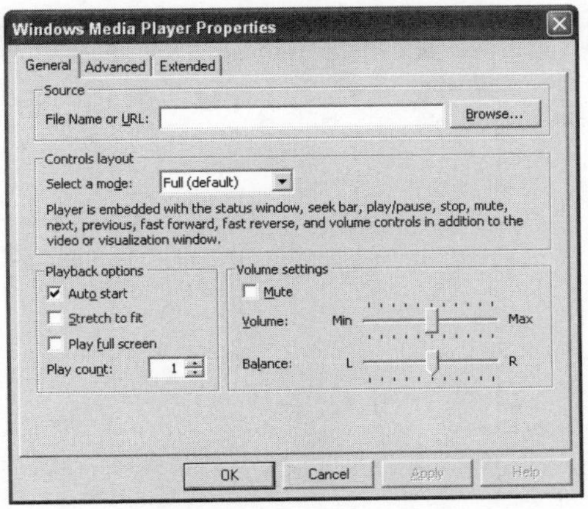

FIGURE 15.3

Edit properties using the Properties dialog box when the control provides the required support.

TIP   Even though Microsoft doesn't provide the tools required to create a property page directly, you can still provide this functionality for your controls using low level programming techniques, including PInvoke. For an in depth discussion of Win32 API programming techniques that rely on PInvoke, see my book, *.NET Framework Solutions: In Search of the Lost Win32 API* (Sybex, 2002). You can find a discussion of the required technique on the Code Guru Web site at `http://www.codeguru.com/Cpp/COM-Tech/activex/general/article.php/c8545/`. The Code Project Web site at `http://www.thecodeproject.com/cs/miscctrl/HadiPropertySheet.asp` also provides a wealth of valuable information in overcoming the lack of property pages support in the .NET Framework.

Methods are usually less error prone than working with properties, but you still need to check them for problems. All you need to do to interact with the methods your control supports is use the Control ➢ Invoke Methods command (you can also click the Invoke Methods button on the toolbar). In addition to the get and set methods for various properties, you'll find all of the other methods that your control supports in the Invoke Methods dialog box shown in Figure 15.4.

To use a particular method, such as ResourceURL (PropPut), you select its entry in the Method Name list. To set a property, you always use the PropPut option—to read it you use the PropGet option. Setting and checking a property requires several steps.

1. Select the PropPut method of property you want to modify. When a property lacks a PropPut method, it means that the property is read-only and you can't change it.

2. Type the new property value in the Parameter Value field. For example, if you want to change the `ResourceURL` property of the `SampleControl` control, you might type **`http://localhost/SpecialMessage.TXT`**.

3. Choose a value type in the Parameter Type field. All of these types are COM specific. Consequently, when you type a string, you select the VT_BSTR entry.

4. Click Set Value. It's important to note that clicking Set Value only sets the property value within the ActiveX Control Test Container, not within the object. You'll see the new value in the Value column of the Parameters list.

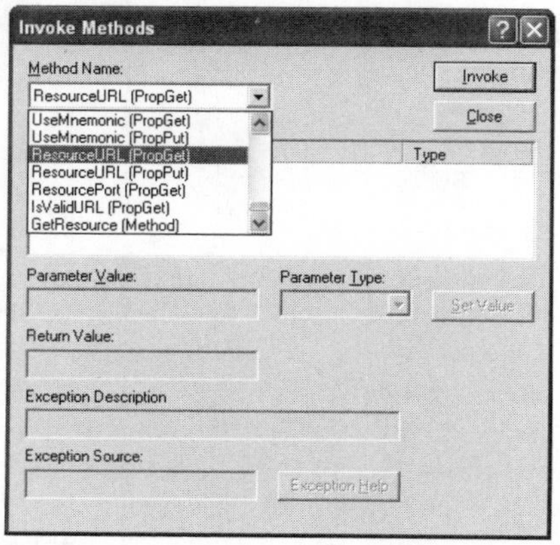

FIGURE 15.4
Verify that each method provides the result you intended as output.

5. Click Invoke. This step sets the value within the object. You'll see a return value (if any) in the Return Value field. When the property doesn't return a value, you'll see VT_EMPTY as the return value as shown in Figure 15.5.

6. Select the PropGet method of the property you want to check. Write-only properties won't provide a PropGet method.

7. Click Invoke. You'll see the current value of the property in the Return Value field. If the property works as anticipated, the return value should match the value you provided as input.

Methods characteristically work the same as properties. You'll set any required property values, click Invoke, and verify the return value. Using these techniques provides you with a COM eye view of your .NET control. You'll see how COM views the control, rather than looking at the control from the .NET perspective—the only perspective that the Visual Studio IDE supports.

TIP The ActiveX Control Test Container doesn't always fully unload from memory, which might prevent you from updating the type library (TLB file) during a registration. When this problem occurs, right-click the Taskbar and choose Task Manager from the context menu. Select the Processes tab and highlight the TstCon32.EXE entry. Click End Process, and then click Yes at the warning dialog box to release the instance of the type library so you can update it.

FIGURE 15.5

Properties behave in a very specific way when you change their values.

TRACKING EVENTS

Events are the basis of many ActiveX control activities. ActiveX Control Test Container has two windows. The upper window displays the controls you've loaded for test, while the bottom window displays any output from the control. Output, in this case, occurs (at least, in most cases) because some event has fired. The control derives some events from custom programming; other events occur as part of normal control operation (as part of the base class). For example, you'll normally see a Click event generated when the user clicks a button.

ActiveX Control Test Container provides two levels of event logging. The first level is at the container level. To set these logging options, use the Options ➤ Logging command to display the Logging Options dialog box. The Logging Options dialog box lets you to choose where the logging output appears. As mentioned earlier, the default setting sends any log entries to the Output window. You can also choose to stop logging all events from all controls that you currently have loaded or to place the log entries in a file. The Log to Debugger Window option is supposed to send the log entries to the debug window of your favorite programming language product, but support for this feature is flaky at best. (The Log to Debugger Window option doesn't work with Visual Studio .NET.)

The second level of logging is at the control level. Normally, ActiveX Control Test Container logs all control events, but that can lead to developer overload and make the detection of a specific event more difficult. It's important to select a specific set of events to monitor, in most cases, if you want to get optimal results. You must select the control that you want to work with before using the Control ➢ Logging command to display the Control Logging Options dialog box.

The Control Logging Options dialog box has three tabs. Each tab controls a major event logging type.

Events   Contains a list of all of the events that your control can fire. For example, when a user clicks the control, it normally fires an event.

Property Changes   Contains a list of all the standard property changes, but not necessarily all of the properties that the control provides. The control fires logging events only if an actual change takes place, not if the client requests the current value or the ability to change the property.

Property Edit Requests   Contains a list of property edit requests. The control fires a request event whenever the client requests the ability to edit the property, which generates the logging event. In other words, a request event log entry appears even if no actual change takes place.

The Property Edit Requests tab lets you to do something that the other logging options don't. The Always, Prompt, and Never options change how the ActiveX Control Test Container reacts to edit requests. In most cases, you'll want to allow the control to accept changes as normal. However, in some situations you may want the control to prompt you before it grants permission or to deny permission so that the property value remains constant during testing. Whichever option you choose, the ActiveX Control Test Container utility still logs the edit request event so that you can maintain a record of control activity.

TIP   You can load more than one ActiveX control at a time to see how two or more controls interact. For example, you might have a visible control that relies on input from an invisible control like a timer. This feature is especially important when working with data-related controls like those used to set the database and table source.

TESTING PERSISTENCE

Persistence is the ability of a control to retain its values from one session to the next. In most cases, you want your control to retain any property values that the user sets. Read-only properties, on the other hand, may change from session to session and therefore don't require persistence. It doesn't matter whether a property is persistent or not, you still have to ensure that it reacts as intended.

ActiveX Control Test Container provides three levels of persistence testing: Property bag, stream, and storage. Generally, it's a good idea to test your control in all three environments to make sure that the persistence it provides actually works. Two of the testing methods, stream and storage, require you to save the control to disk, then read it back into the test container. The third method, property bag, provides instant feedback.

Creating the *<Object>* Tag

You can't use the standard CAB when working with .NET components and controls because the technology is limited. The lack of support for .NET means that you can't use the `Codebase` attribute for the `<Object>` tag either. However, you do have an alternative—one that you don't see used very often. You can place a message between the opening and closing `<Object>` tag that contains the information required to download a control, as shown in Listing 15.3. You'll find this example in the `\ABC_Inc\Downloadable\FileDownload` folder of the source code on the Sybex Web site.

LISTING 15.3:   Defining a Special *<Object>* Tag for .NET

```
<object classid="clsid:80299918-7D92-499e-B55B-5514649E759F"
        height="50"
        width="150"
        id="lblTest">
    <param name="Name" value="lblTest" />
    <param name="Text" value="Empty Space">
    <param name="ResourceURL"
        value="http://localhost:36868/FileDownload/SpecialMessage.TXT">
    The required control is missing.
    <a href="Downloads/InstallControl.msi">Install?</a><br />
    Press Refresh when the installation completes to see the control.
</object><br />
```

This `<Object>` tag contains all of the same elements as any other `<Object>` tag. However, notice the text between the opening and closing tags. The text includes a link for a Microsoft Installer (MSI) file. The text only appears when the object referenced by the GUID isn't present on the local machine. Consequently, the user will only see the message shown in Figure 15.6 when they need to install the component or control. Unfortunately, this particular feature is underused right now.

When the user clicks the Install? link shown in Figure 15.6, the browser asks whether it should open or save the file. Make sure you instruct the user to click Open. At this point, the browser downloads the MSI file and starts the installation process. The installation looks like any other installation, and you can remove the component or control using the Add or Remove Programs applet in the Control Panel. Interestingly enough, this technique makes it easier to work with downloaded components and controls than using the standard method of creating a CAB file. Not only is it easier to remove the component or control when you're finished using it, but you can also determine the download location for the component or control.

Working with the Microsoft Installer

You have several choices for working with the Microsoft Installer (also called the Windows Installer). The two most practical choices are to use the Setup Project template in Visual Studio .NET or to rely on the Microsoft Installer SDK that's part of the Platform SDK, which you can download at `http://www.microsoft.com/msdownload/platformsdk/sdkupdate/`. However, if you want to save a lot of time and effort, use the batch file download found on the Desktop Engineer's Junk Drawer site at `http://desktopengineer.com/article.php?story=20041001112453379`.

FIGURE 15.6
Adding text between the opening and closing *<Object>* tag lets you provide additional information.

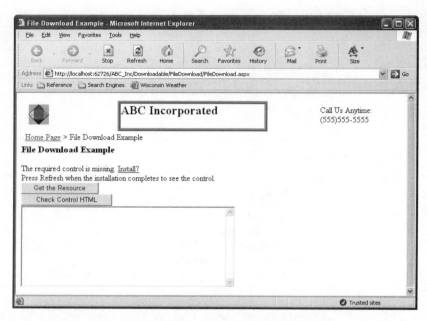

This section relies on the easiest to use of the options, the Visual Studio .NET Setup Project template. To begin using this technique, you must create a new Setup Project. The Setup Project outputs an MSI file. All you need to do is provide a few configuration settings to create the MSI file. You'll find this example in the \Chapter 14\InstallControl folder of the source code on the Sybex Web site.

TIP If you prefer working with XML, rather than creating a project in Visual Studio .NET or using the Microsoft Installer SDK, you can create the required MSI file using the XML2MSI utility found at http://msi2xml.sourceforge.net/. In fact, this Web site also includes a utility for converting your MSI file to XML so that you can document its content. You can see an example of the output from this utility in the InstallControl.XML file found in the \Chapter 14\InstallControl\ Debug folder as part of the source code on the Sybex Web site.

The MSI file for this example has to perform two tasks and an optional third task. The two required tasks are to download and install the component or control. After the component or control is in its installed folder, the MSI file must provide some means of registering the component or control so that the Web page can use it. These two required tasks are the same tasks that the Codebase attribute of the <Object> tag normally performs. The MSI file can also perform the optional task of uninstalling the component or control when the user finished using it.

TIP The Microsoft Installer is a relatively complex piece of software. It pays to know where you can find good documentation on it. Microsoft provides a complete list of the standard documentation at http://msdn.microsoft.com/library/en-us/msi/setup/roadmap_to_windows_ installer_documentation.asp. You should also consider checking sites such as the Desktop Engineer's Junk Drawer at http://desktopengineer.com/index.php?topic=0070MSI.

Installing the component or control isn't much of a problem. You could perform that part of the task using the `Codebase` attribute. All you really need to do is tell the MSI file which application files it should contain. The File System tab of the project opens automatically after you create it. To add a file, right-click the folder where you want the file to appear and choose Add ➤ File from the context menu. Figure 15.7 shows the files for this example—they all appear in the Application Folder, as shown. The `RegAssembly.EXE` file is a special application for registering the component or control. The `RegisterControl.BAT` file contains instructions for registering the component or control. The `SampleControl.DLL` file is the special control used for this example, but you can include any component or control you want. Finally, the `UnregisterControl.BAT` file contains the instructions for removing the component or control.

The MSI file won't know any more about registering the components or controls than the CAB file does, but it does include a special feature for performing custom actions. To see the custom actions, right-click the project entry in Solution Explorer and choose View ➤ Custom Actions from the context menu. Add Install and Uninstall actions to the project, as shown in Figure 15.8, by right-clicking the selected action and choosing Add Custom Action from the context menu. You'll see a Select Item in Project dialog box where you can choose the action to perform. This dialog box only accepts certain kinds of files—it specifically excludes the batch files that could perform the task, so you need to create a custom application to work with the batch files (see the "Registering the Component or Control" section of the chapter for details).

FIGURE 15.7
Add the list of files that you want to install as part of the component or control.

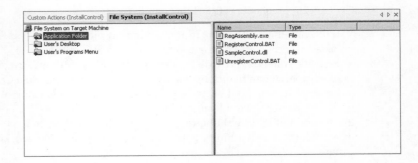

FIGURE 15.8
Include any custom actions required to install the component or control.

Each custom action is an executable and you can include all of the normal executable information in the Properties dialog box for each entry. The example only requires one change. You must include a /R argument for the `Uninstall/RegAssembly.EXE` entry to ensure the special application removes the component or control registration. At this point, you can define any specific application information by clicking the project entry in Solution Explorer and changing the entries in the Properties window. Afterward, compile the installation program. Place all five resulting files (including the MSI file) in the download directory for your Web site. The example in the `\ABC_Inc\Downloadable\` `FileDownload` folder on the Sybex Web site shows how to perform this task.

Signing the MSI File

After you set up the installation program, you'll need to decide whether to sign the MSI file. Signing the MSI file has a number of advantages, not the least of which is ensuring that no one can tamper with the file without raising flags. To begin this process, display the project Property Pages dialog box shown in Figure 15.9 using the Project ➢ Project Properties command. Check the Authenticode Signature option at the bottom of the dialog box.

You must provide three inputs. First, you need a certificate. You can obtain certificates in a number of ways. The "Using the MakeCert Utility" section of the chapter describes one technique; the "Using the Certification Authority Utility" describes another. It's important to convert the certificate from the X.509 CER format to the Software Publisher Certificate (SPC) format using the Cert2SPC utility like this:

```
Cert2SPC JohnCert.CER JohnCert.SPC
```

You provide the name of the input and output files as arguments. The Certificate File field of the project Property Pages dialog box only accepts SPC entries.

Second, you must provide the Private Key (PVK) filename used to create the certificate. This file requires special command line switches when you use the MakeCert utility. You should receive it automatically or at least have the option to export it when using other certificate techniques.

Third, you can provide an optional Timestamp Server URL entry. If you leave this field blank, the system will ignore the setting. Only use this setting when working with a certificate from a trusted Certificate Authority (CA). Don't use this field when working with a test certificate that you generate.

FIGURE 15.9

Sign your MSI file to prevent tampering and to identify yourself to the user.

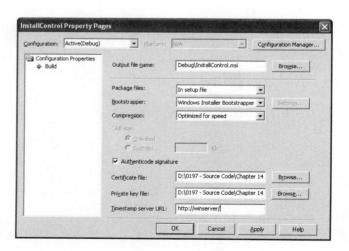

Adding the Authenticode information creates a few changes in the development environment. First, you must supply the private key password every time you build the project, so you won't want to add the signature until you have debugged your download application. Second, the user will see the Authenticode signature information when downloading the application. The Authenticode signature is requirement for many systems—the browser won't even offer to download the MSI file without it in some cases.

TIP Authenticode is an essential security technology for Web applications of all types. You can learn more about Authenticode technology at `http://www.microsoft.com/technet/archive/security/topics/secaps/authcode.mspx`. Unfortunately, not even Authenticode technology is completely bulletproof. Read about one issue that has occurred with VeriSign issued certificates at `http://www.verisign.com/support/advisories/authenticodefraud.html`. Fortunately, such occurrences are incredibly rare, so Authenticode enjoys a good reputation in the user community.

StrongName versus *Publisher* Evidence

You have two major choices when signing a control or component using Visual Studio .NET. You use either the `StrongName` or `Publisher` evidence classes. The choice you make depends on how you want to use the control or component.

A strong name consists of a public/private key pair that a developer can generate on the local machine using the SN utility. The developer applies the certificate using the `[assembly: AssemblyKeyFile("")]` entry in the `AssemblyInfo` file. This kind of security relies on your ability to determine the public key in advance. A trusted source would need to send the public key to you or you could use a key pair generated for your own use. A strong name doesn't provide verification, nor can you determine who owns a key based on the information in the assembly alone. The `StrongName` evidence type is useful for personal or shared projects, but it isn't something you could trust for projects with someone you don't know.

On the other hand, `Publisher` evidence relies on an X.509 certificate (digital signature). A CA verifies the identity of an application independently of the development environment by identifying the developer directly. This technique ensures that you can trust the identity information because you trust the CA. You'd normally use this technique to validate code received from a third party that you don't know.

Certificates come from a number of sources. Third party certificates come from a Certificate Authority (CA) such as VeriSign (`http://www.verisign.com`), Entrust (`http://www.entrust.com`), or Thawte (`http://www.thawte.com`). These three companies create the certificates commonly used in public venues. You can also create a CA using the Certificate Services feature of Windows Server 2000 or 2003 (this feature doesn't come with workstation version of Windows, such as Windows XP). Microsoft also provides the MakeCert (Make X.509 Certificate) and Cert2SPC (X.509 Certificate to Software Publisher Certificate) utilities to create temporary, test certificates. The certificate generated by these utilities is only good for testing purposes because it doesn't contain the CA information. No matter what certificate source you use, you apply the certificate to an assembly using the SignCode utility.

You may read some texts that appear to say that one or the other form of evidence is better (usually with a strong emphasis on the `Publisher` evidence). Both forms of evidence have specific uses and you should use the form of evidence that best meets your needs. The important consideration is keeping the certificate or key file in a secure location to ensure that no one can sign code that you create. Neither form of evidence is worth anything once a third party has access to your key file.

Registering the Component or Control

As noted in the "Working with the Microsoft Installer" section of the chapter, you can't provide direct access to a batch file within an MSI file, even if that's all you really need. The application presented in this section could fulfill any operating system (shell) access functionality required. However, in this case, the application specifically helps you create an environment for executing one of the two registration batch files (the first registers the component or control, while the second unregisters it). Listing 15.4 shows the code you need for this portion of the example. You'll find this example in the \Chapter 15\RegAssembly folder of the source code on the Sybex Web site.

LISTING 15.4:   Shell Access to Batch Files

```
// Track the progress of the registration or removal.
Process ControlProc;

private void frmMain_Load(object sender, EventArgs e)
{
    // Get the Windows directory.
    String WinPath = Environment.GetEnvironmentVariable("WinDir");

    // Get the current path.
    String PathInfo = Environment.GetEnvironmentVariable("Path");

    // Set the current directory to point to the installation
    // directory.
    String AppDir = Application.ExecutablePath.Substring(
        0, Application.ExecutablePath.IndexOf("RegAssembly") - 1);
    Directory.SetCurrentDirectory(AppDir);

    // Make sure the .NET Framework is installed.
    if (!File.Exists(
        WinPath + @"\Microsoft.NET\Framework\v1.1.4322\RegAsm.EXE"))
    {
        MessageBox.Show(".NET Framework not installed!");
        return;
    }

    // Verify the .NET path is in place.
    if (PathInfo.IndexOf(
        WinPath + @"\Microsoft.NET\Framework\v1.1.4322\") == -1)

        // Set the .NET path.
        Environment.SetEnvironmentVariable(
            "Path", PathInfo + ";" +
            WinPath + @"\Microsoft.NET\Framework\v1.1.4322\");

    // Determine the action to take.
```

```
        if ((Environment.CommandLine.IndexOf("/R") != -1) ||
            (Environment.CommandLine.IndexOf("/r") != -1))

            // Remove the assembly.
            ControlProc = Process.Start("UnregisterControl");

        else

            // Register the assembly.
            ControlProc = Process.Start("RegisterControl");

        // Wait until the process is complete.
        ControlProc.EnableRaisingEvents = true;
        ControlProc.Exited += new EventHandler(ControlProc_Exited);

        // Return the path to its original state.
        Environment.SetEnvironmentVariable("Path", PathInfo);
    }

    private void btnClose_Click(object sender, EventArgs e)
    {
        // Close the form.
        Close();
    }

    void ControlProc_Exited(object sender, EventArgs e)
    {
        // Enable the Close button so the program can end.
        btnClose.Enabled = true;
    }
```

The code begins by declaring a very important variable, `ControlProc`. This variable tracks the activity of the shell process so that the application knows when the batch file is complete. Otherwise, the application could end prematurely with the registration or unregistration status of the component or control unsure.

The `frmMain_Load()` method executes immediately when the form loads, so the user doesn't have to do anything special and you can call this application from an MSI file without worrying about automation requirements. The code begins by obtaining the current Windows path and the path information provided by the user environment. The application requires this information to locate the .NET Framework, verify that it's installed, and provide access to the RegAsm and GACUtil utilities.

The next step is to point the application to the application directory using the `Directory` `.SetCurrentDirectory()` method. The current directory is the `\Windows\System32` folder because that's where the Microsoft Installer works. Of course, before the code can perform the redirection, it must determine the application folder using the `Application.ExecutablePath` property. An issue when using this property is that it includes the executable name, which the code must remove using string manipulation, as shown in the listing.

The code also needs to know the status of the .NET Framework. The example relies on a specific version, but you can check any version. All versions of the .NET Framework include the required RegAsm and GACUtil utilities—all work equally well in installing your control or component. Consequently, you might simply want to look for any version of the .NET Framework that will work with your control or component. In this case, the code looks for the RegAsm.EXE file using the File.Exists() method. If this file doesn't exist, then it's safe to assume the user doesn't have the .NET Framework installed either.

This example works by opening a command prompt and executing a batch file. The batch file contains the RegAsm and GACUtil commands discussed in the "Working with the Microsoft Installer" section of the chapter. Consequently, the environment must contain a reference to the .NET Framework path or the commands will fail. The code looks for the .NET Framework reference in the path. If it doesn't exist, then the code adds it using the Environment.SetEnvironmentVariable() method. Note that you must separate the various paths with a semicolon, as shown in the code.

At this point, the code can perform one of two tasks. When the user provides the /R command line switch, the code will remove the control or component by unregistering it using the UnregisterControl.BAT file. Otherwise, the code calls on the RegisterControl.BAT file to register the component or control. Notice how the code keeps the control or component specifics external to the application. All you need to do to use this application with other controls or components is change the batch file—no code changes needed. In both cases, the Process.Start() method executes the batch file.

Once the code has created the process, it needs some way to track its progress and provide a report back to the application. To set up this state, the code relies on ControlProc, which contains a reference to the process. The code begins by enabling process events (they are disabled by default) using the ControlProc.EnableRaisingEvents property. It then points the Exited event to the ControlProc_Exited() event handler. When the batch file ends, the code calls ControlProc_Exited(), which enables the Close button. At this point, the user can click Close to close the application form. You could automate this process even further by having the ControlProc_Exited() event handler close the form.

Setting .NET Security

Even after you create a great download application, sign everything as needed, and add all of the code required to ensure a secure environment, you can run into problems getting the component to work on the client machine. In all cases, the problem will derive from changes made to the .NET environment to make it more secure. The default .NET environment (one without any changes) always runs controls and components created using the precautions mentioned so far in the chapter.

To create an environment where the control or component will run, you need to make one change to the code itself and the control or component user will need to make a configuration change to the .NET environment. The coding change is a simple attribute that you add to the beginning of the component or control namespace as follows:

```
[assembly: AllowPartiallyTrustedCallers]
```

The AllowPartiallyTrustedCallers attribute lets partially trusted code, such as that found in a Web browser, to call a strong named component or control. You can still control access to component or control functionality using other security attributes and tests within the code.

TIP A single chapter can't discuss all of the security features that .NET provides. You can find a complete treatment of the subject in my book, *.NET Development Security Solutions* (Sybex, 2003).

After you make the attribute change to the code, the user must also make a change to the .NET configuration using the Microsoft .NET Framework 2.0 Configuration console found in the Administrative Tools folder of the Control Panel. The user must create a special code group for your component or control and assign permissions to it (generally, you provide full trust, but you could possibly use limited trust levels as well). The following steps describe how to set up the required trust entry.

1. Open the .NET Framework 2.0 Configuration\My Computer\Runtime Security Policy\Machine\Code Groups\All_Code entry shown in Figure 15.10. The code group entries define how a system reacts to code from various environments. A local control or component will have higher privileges than code you download from the Internet.

2. Right-click the All_Code folder and choose New from the context menu. You'll see a Create Code Group dialog box.

3. Type a name for the security settings in the Name field and a description in the Description field. Proper setting identification can reduce the number of errant and duplicate settings on your machine. In addition, proper identification makes it easy to remove settings you no longer need—making it easier to maintain a secure environment.

FIGURE 15.10

Create a new security policy for your component or control.

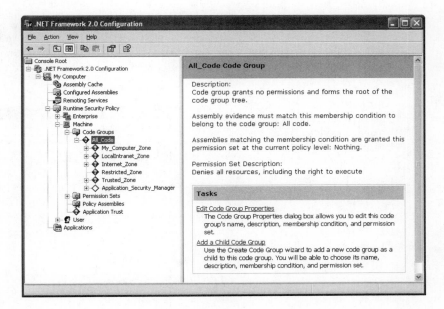

4. Click Next. You'll see the Choose a Condition Type dialog box. The condition type determines how the system identifies the code you want to work with. It's important to set this feature correctly because you don't want just anyone to have a given level of access to the system.

5. Select Strong Name from the Choose the Condition Type for this Code Group field. Using a Strong Name condition type ensures that only code signed with your digital signature receives the added permissions. Other code lacks the required Strong Name and therefore won't run with increased permissions.

6. Click Import. Locate the DLL containing the signature you want to use. Click Open. The Choose a Condition Type dialog box now has a signature in it, as shown in Figure 15.11. Notice that you can set additional limitations on the strong name by checking the Name and Version options (don't change the text in these fields). You can choose to allow any control or component signed with your digital signature to run by keeping the options cleared, choose a particular component or control by checking the Name option, and a specific component or control implementation by checking the Version option.

7. Click Next. You'll see the Assign a Permission Set to the Code Group dialog box. This is where you determine what rights the code has to execute. It's important to assign just the rights that the code needs, rather than take the easy way out and assign it rights to do anything. The goal is to let your code execute, not to give full trust to any code that might decide to piggyback onto your code. However, for testing purpose on a secure machine—one that isn't connected to the Internet, you can use the FullTrust setting.

8. Assign an existing set of rights to the code or create a new permission set, and then click Next. Click Finish. The Microsoft .NET Framework 2.0 Configuration console will add the new permission. Your code will execute with the rights you assigned to it at this point.

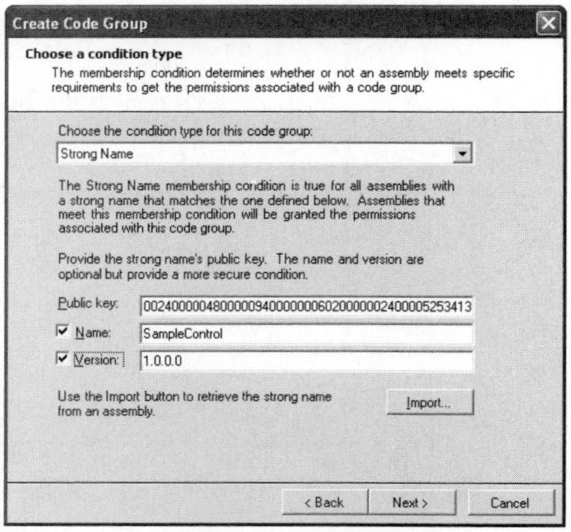

FIGURE 15.11
Set the level of strong name support required to maintain a secure environment.

DISCOVERING THE VISUAL WEB DEVELOPER PORT

Working with components and controls often means knowing which port Visual Web Developer will use for the Web server. This number is random. However, it remains the same for a particular project during each invocation. Consequently, you can perform testing against a specific port for a particular project.

The port number appears as part of the Solution (SLN) file that Visual Web Developer creates for you. After you create the project, build and start it one time (even if the project doesn't contain any information). The act of starting the Web server generates the random port number.

You'll find the SLN file in the `\Documents and Settings\User Name\My Documents\Visual Studio\ Projects\Project Name` folder of your hard drive (where *User Name* is your name and *Project Name* is the name of the project you want to examine). Open the SLN file using a text editor such as Notepad and you'll find the `ProjectSection` entry shown here.

```
ProjectSection(WebsiteProperties) = preProject
    VWDPort = 5892
EndProjectSection
```

The `VWDPort` entry contains the port number for this project (but not any other project). When necessary, you can access the Web site directly by adding the port number to the URL like this:

```
http://localhost:5892/
```

Considering the Security Issues of Using Controls

Security is an essential part of working with controls. You must maintain a secure environment to retain the user's trust. It's important to realize that security is problematic—that you can't rely on security to remain stable or even constant. Someone is going to find a way through your security measures, so you must couple good programming techniques with constant vigilance.

One way to improve your chances of creating a secure environment is to employ digital certificates on your Web site and in all your code. A digital certificate is a series of numbers forming an identity that acts as a key to lock and unlock files, identify a particular individual or company, and perform other cryptographic tasks. It's more secure than the public/private key combination generated by the Strong Name utility (SN.EXE). The "*StrongName* versus *Publisher* Evidence" sidebar provides an overview of digital certificate issues.

The following sections describe some significant security issues for control developers. Creating a secure environment for downloadable application elements means using Secure Sockets Layer (SSL) for communication, encrypting any data you send between machines, and verifying the user. Make sure you also read about the general security issues described in Chapter 18.

Using the MakeCert Utility

The MakeCert utility has a number of purposes, but the most important purpose for developers is creating test certificates. These certificates don't have a verifiable source, so you can't use them to sign a control, component, or installation program that you want to send to someone. However, they do allow you to set up and test your application realistically with all security measures in place. Here's the best command line to use when creating a certificate for testing.

```
MakeCert -sv JohnCert.PVK -n "CN=John Mueller" -m 24 -len 1024 -nscp JohnCert.CER
```

The -sv switch generates a private key file. You must have a private key file to sign anything with Visual Studio .NET. Always follow this switch with a filename that includes the PVK file extension.

The -n switch isn't mandatory, but you'll find that it's less confusing to use the certificate if you include it. Provide a name for your certificate using the CN (context name) entry as a minimum.

Always set a time limit for the certificate—even test certificates. The -m switch provides a convenient means to perform this task. Simply specify the number of months that you want to use the certificate for testing. Because this is a test certificate that could end up somewhere else, make the time interval short.

Use the -len switch to define the size of the key. Always use the same length for testing that you use for your actual certificate (the one used in the production environment) to ensure you see accurate results.

You only need the -nscp (Netscape Client Authentication Extension) switch for the Web environment, and you might not even need it there if you can guarantee everyone will use Internet Explorer. Even so, including this switch doesn't materially affect the certificate, so it's better to include it whenever possible.

Finally, you provide the name of the certificate you want to create. It's normally a good idea to use the same name for the certificate as you use for the private key file so that you can relate the two. In addition, the filename must end with the CER extension.

Using the Certification Authority Utility

A Certificate Authority (CA) is an organization that can verify who you are and provides a reputation that other people trust. Many organizations make use of third party CAs to obtain digital certificates for signing their code. This is always the best approach if you intend to make your code available to third parties that don't know you or your organization. For example, this is the approach you should use when developing shrink-wrap software.

NOTE   The CA setup for this section is a Windows 2000 server with all the latest patches and an enterprise CA installed. Your browser views will vary from the ones shown if you use a nonpatched version of Windows 2000 or a stand-alone CA. Some of the options mentioned in the following sections aren't available to systems that lack Active Directory support or if you perform the setup using a server that isn't a domain controller. However, even with these differences, the basic concepts are the same. You still need to obtain a code-signing certificate using the server options that you do have available.

Using a certificate generated by a third party isn't necessarily cost effective for an organization that plans to send its software to a few trusted partners who know the developer well. In this case, using the CA built into server operating systems such as Windows 2000 Server or the newer Windows 2003 Server is a less expensive alternative. Even a locally generated certificate store (a place for storing your certificate) identifies the issuing authority, making it a lot more difficult for someone to forge a key. The easiest way to obtain a certificate is to use your browser. The following steps show how.

1. Open your browser and access the certificate server using an URL similar to `http://YourServerName/CertSrv/Default.asp`. (The URL you type very likely points to your company's intranet site, rather than a location on the Internet.) Make sure your browser has scripting and cookies enabled (it probably will). You'll see the initial Microsoft Certificate Services Web site.

2. Select the Request a Certificate option, and click Next. You'll see a Choose Request Type screen. This is where knowledge of the various policies in the Policy Settings folder of the Certificate Authority console is helpful. Notice that the only entry is a User certificate. Double-click the User entry in the Policy Settings folder and you'll see a User Properties dialog box similar to the one shown in Figure 15.12. Notice that the User certificate doesn't include code signing. Consequently, this certificate would be useless for a developer.

3. Choose the Advanced Request option and click Next. You'll see an Advanced Certificate Requests screen. Because you probably don't have a smart card or an existing certificate, you'll need to choose the first (default) option of filling out a form.

4. Click Next. The Web server will tell you that it's downloading an ActiveX Control to your system. Be patient, the download can take a considerable amount of time even on a high-speed network. After some time, you'll see the form shown in Figure 15.13. This is where you fill in the requirements for your certificate.

5. Select the Code Signing option in the Certificate Template field.

6. Select a Cryptographic Service Provider (CSP) from the list in the CSP field. One of the best choices is the Microsoft Strong Cryptographic Provider, but even the Microsoft Base Cryptographic Provider 1.0 works well. The various CSPs feature different options such as key length. A longer key makes the key harder to break, but can also increase some factors such as code size.

7. Set the Key Usage option to Both so that you can use the Code Signing key for both needs.

FIGURE 15.12
Selecting the User certificate is useless for a developer.

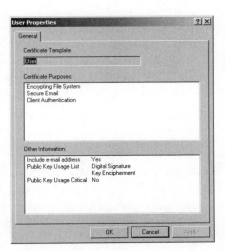

FIGURE 15.13
Wait for the ActiveX Control to download so you can see this form.

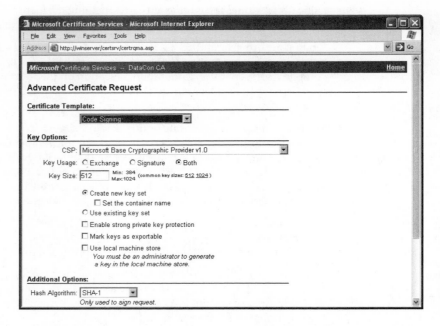

8. Set the Key Size. A larger key is more secure, while is a smaller key is more efficient. The minimum key size you should consider for code is 1,024, but some CSPs offer keys up to 16,384 bits in length. If your security needs are exceptional, you should also check the Enable Strong Private Key Protection option.

9. Check the Mark Keys as Exportable option. This check enables the Export Keys to File option. Check this option as well and type the name of a file in the File Name field. This step is essential because it gives you a physical key you can use as input to Visual Studio.

10. Select a Hash Algorithm option. Pay careful attention to this step. You must select one of the options that Visual Studio supports such as Secure Hashing Algorithm 1 (SHA-1) or Message Digest 5 (MD5). Don't select options such as MD2 or MD4 because you'll run into problems getting them to work right.

11. Click Submit. Internet Explorer will display a Generating Request message for a moment, and then you'll see a Create Private Key Password dialog box.

12. Type a password in the Password field, and again in the Confirm Password field. Click OK. Internet Explorer will display a success message.

Defining Your Development Goals

This chapter has demonstrated some of the techniques you can use to add downloadable code to your Web site. It's important to remember that downloadable code answers special needs—it's the option of last choice, rather than first choice. However, a well-designed control can make a significant difference in many applications. Not only do they affect the performance and security of the

Web application you create, but you'll find that they make the user experience better and reduce support costs in some cases (in other cases, a custom control can become a real support nightmare). The bottom line is that custom controls really do answer special needs.

Now it's time to determine whether a custom control does have a part in your Web application. The first thing you should do is list any Web needs that a custom control could answer and determine whether you can do without them—that's right, it's better not to use a custom control unless you really need one. After you determine that you do need a better solution than the one that you have now, make sure you exhaust other alternatives first. For example, you might find that a combination of server- and client-side scripting and fulfill the requirement. It's also important to look for third party vendors that might meet the need. Once you exhaust all of the possibilities, begin designing your custom control. Make sure you think about all of the pitfalls before you put one line of code down because Web applications are a lot more demanding than the desktop in this area.

Chapter 16 moves beyond application components to a full application. This chapter helps you build a shopping cart application from start to finish. When you finish, you'll understand how Visual Web Developer can help you build real world applications—at least within reason. More importantly, this chapter puts all of the pieces together from previous chapters. It helps you make sense of the information you've received from previous chapters—including this one. After you finish this chapter, you should have a much better idea of what ASP.NET 2.0 brings to your development environment and how well Visual Web Developer uses those capabilities.

Chapter 16

Creating a Shopping Cart Application

As more and more companies create online stores where they can sell their goods, the need for shopping cart applications—a means for tracking those purchases—becomes more important. You can build a shopping cart application using Visual Web Developer, but creating the complex application that most companies require will prove time consuming because you must consider issues such as online security and privacy from the outset of the project. Even though the shopping cart application in this chapter will handle modest requests, a large corporate site will require additions to the concepts presented. You should consider the example in this chapter as a great starting point for your own shopping cart application.

The importance of this chapter goes beyond the shopping cart application itself—this chapter shows how to combine many of the technologies discussed in the previous 15 chapters. Web pages are very simple in concept but can become quite complex in implementation. This chapter helps you understand how to combine the various features effectively.

Building a shopping cart application means a lot more than just settling on the products you want to sell and the price you expect to receive for them. Shopping cart applications require great database support, and you have to make them as bulletproof as possible. Privacy and security are big concerns as well. Anyone who's suffered a break-in of essential customer information will tell you that sales drop significantly once word gets out (and it generally will). You must also consider how the user will interact with the shopping cart and how to handle error conditions. For example, you must consider what to do when the user decides to abandon a shopping cart. As with real shopping carts, you can't simply leave all the abandoned shopping carts lying around—someone must restock the shelves with the products they contain and put the shopping carts away.

Before you can make your shopping cart accessible, you also have to perform stringent testing. Most developers know that they have to test the ability of the application to store orders correctly and perform the required math. It's even possible to include testing for credit card handling (you must determine whether the card number is even good). However, you also have to test the unusual. For example, many developers now test their code to see what happens when they place virus code in any of the input fields because some users will perform that act. Testing with multiple browsers is also necessary if you want to gain maximum benefit from your shopping cart application.

Understanding the Alternatives to a Custom Application

This section isn't about discouraging you from creating your own shopping cart application. Actually, creating a shopping cart application is a great idea even if you decide to use an off-the-shelf solution because you'll at least have a better idea of what you want after you go through a few iterations of the test cycle on your own application. Creating a shopping application also helps you understand how the various Visual Web Developer features work, so there are all kinds of good reasons to create a custom application. However, after you work with the application for a while, you might discover that it's too much work or that you simply can't get what you want from Visual Web Developer—at least, not everything you want. The reason to look for alternatives to a custom application has nothing to do with learning—it has everything to do with saving time and money. The following sections describe some of the alternatives to the custom application that you should consider before, during, and after you create your own shopping cart application.

Alternative Uses of Shopping Cart Applications

Don't get the idea that shopping cart applications only solve shopping needs. Yes, most shopping cart applications do appear as part of an online store, but that's not the only use for them. For example, you can create an information site where the user collects the information needed, and then downloads that information all at one time. Otherwise, the user has to download the information one piece at a time and that detracts from the information gathering experience.

The Windows Update Catalog at `http://v4.windowsupdate.microsoft.com/catalog/en/default.asp` provides an excellent example of an alternative strategy for working with shopping cart applications. This Web site uses the concept of a download basket, as shown in Figure 16.1. The benefit of this approach is that the user can collect everything in one place before downloading the required updates.

You could use the shopping cart scenario for any kind of object collection. A Web site might offer a collection of links for specific purposes. You could let the user gather these links into a shopping cart and add them to their browser all at one time. Even if you aren't making a permanent change, you could let the user download the various pages all at one time. In short, you need to think outside the traditional shopping cart uses to gain a full appreciation of just how beneficial this kind of software can be.

FIGURE 16.1
Use shopping cart applications any time you want to let the user collect objects of any kind.

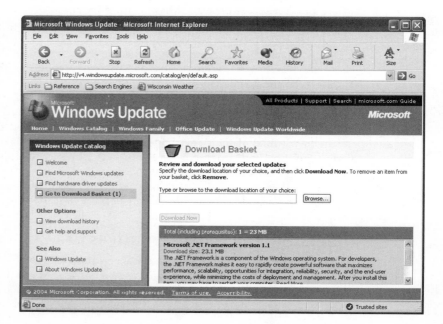

Sidestepping the Pitfalls

No one will ever do things precisely the way that you do them, and this fact is the number one reason to consider creating a custom shopping cart application. You can search every corner of the Internet looking for the perfect application—the elusive one that has every feature that you ever envisioned—and you'll never find it. The perfect application is an illusion—even the application you build yourself won't perform every task as expected, but it'll be the closest match you can find. When you look for a complete solution or at least pieces you can incorporate into your own application, you need to look for something that you can live with—the application or component that does almost everything you want, but not quite. Remember that the goal of searching for an off-the-shelf solution is to save time and money, so you're exchanging a little functionality that you want for the time and money you need.

Another misconception is that an off-the-shelf solution won't require the extra work of testing. Whenever you install any software on your system, you have to test it fully—if for no other reason than to ensure it really does work as advertised. However, because you expect a shopping cart application to handle sensitive data, such as the user's credit card information, you need to spend extra time ensuring the off-the-shelf application you get is also safe. Users expect that your application will handle their data safely, no matter where you obtained it. You can avoid some problems by performing the proper research. Ask questions such as whether a third party organization tested the application for security problems. If possible, talk with other companies that have used the product. Always get a full demonstration of all product features whenever you can. Read online reviews about your shopping cart software of choice to get other viewpoints on potential problems.

A major part of the cost of implementing any software solution is training—a hidden cost that you might not initially think about. Even if you're a one-person business, you still need training on software when you buy it off the shelf. One of the issues to consider is whether the vendor offers training. On-site training can be very effective, but expensive and not repeatable. Training tapes, followed by hands-on training, can offer a better solution when you have a motivated staff. The point is that when you build your own software, you must come up with a training solution yourself (which might not be any training at all if you both create and use the software). Third party software always requires some type of training, so custom software actually has a slight edge in this area at times.

Getting a Complete Solution

Sometimes the best solution is to get a premade shopping cart application that includes all of the required support such as training and access to the required online accounts. Try to get a product with a merchant account or built-in online payment support. Common online payment programs include Authorize Net, Worldpay, Nochex, and PayPal. Some of the companies that offer complete shopping cart solutions appear in the following list (note that I haven't listed a lot of the more interesting solutions, such as <cf_ezcart> ColdFusion Shopping Cart Application, `http://www.cf-ezcart.com/`, because they don't support standard HTML, ASP, or ASP.NET).

Online Shopping Cart Software for E-commerce `http://www.online-store.co.uk/`

ShopJS `http://www.anweb.com/shopjs/`

3DCart `http://www.3dcart.com/`

.netCart Shopping Cart `http://www.411asp.net/home/webapps/shopping`

Sometimes an ISP or Web hosting vendor can be a great source of information about shopping cart applications. For example, the Globalnet GNP Web Hosting site at `http://www.globalnetpromotions` `.com/free-commerce-shopping-cart-hosting-review.htm` contains a list of shopping cart applications of every description. You might also want to look at the list of solutions on Google at `http://directory.google.com/Top/Computers/Software/Business/E-Commerce/Shopping_Carts/`. Don't forget the Microsoft ASP.NET starter kits available at `http://asp.net/Default.aspx?tabindex=8&tabid=47`. One of these kits contains a shopping cart, and you'll find other components that you might want to add to the application. However, no matter where you obtain information about a complete solution, make sure you ask many questions and test the product features to ensure you're getting what you need.

Obtaining Application Components

Getting a full-fledged shopping cart application might seem attractive until you look at the requirements for using it. At some point, you might decide that you'd prefer to build a solution of your own, but not the entire solution. Working with components that someone else has built provides some of the time and money savings that a full solution provides, but also lets you customize the application and ensure it works almost as well for your specific needs as a custom application would.

TIP Besides the one found in this chapter, you'll find a number of shopping cart development tutorials on the Internet. In many cases, these tutorials rely on other languages, but it's good to look through them anyway because you can pick up some good ideas or procedures. For example, Macromedia provides an in-depth article that focuses on technical issues such as Secure Socket Layer (SSL) support at `http://www.macromedia.com/devnet/mx/dreamweaver/articles/build_shopping_cart.html`. In addition, this particular article includes a link to a hosted example of the shopping cart.

Generally, you'll need to look through Web sites that cater to developers to find the components you need. For example, you'll find a full-fledged shopping cart application on the CodeToad site at `http://www.codetoad.com/asp/` and `http://www.codetoad.com/asp.net/`. You can download this code and customize it to meet specific needs. It's also possible to add component pieces from other examples on this site to your application.

Sometimes it's better to buy known good code from a third party vendor such as The ASP.NET Resource Index. This site contains a credit card charge program, .netCharge CC Processing, at `http://www.411asp.net/home/webapps/shopping/creditca`. By adding this component to your application, you can avoid many of the problems with creating the credit card charging software on your own. The idea is to reduce the time and money to create a shopping cart application, without losing the actual hands-on experience.

Developing a Merchandizing Plan

Before you begin designing your application, you need a merchandizing plan. This plan defines a number of shopping cart application elements including:

◆ Defining the layout of your store

◆ Determining how to present the products

◆ Creating a flow of product data from page to page

◆ Refining the user data you want to track

◆ Obtaining a merchant account for product payment

All of these elements define how you design your shopping cart application. For example, you need to consider whether the user has to log into the Web site before or after shopping. The following sections discuss these issues.

Creating a Web Site Layout

Some people think that you can build a Web site with a good generic layout and that users will flock to it. The problem is that the generic Web site doesn't work. You must add a certain level of pizzazz to attract people's attention. In addition, you need to consider how everything will fit together. For example, you need to offer products at a good price, focus attention on the products you want to sell, and provide the user with enough information to make up for the lack of a physical buying experience. You have to do all of this work without the usual physical media that you might have relied on in the past.

Unfortunately, some online stores stop with the basics. However, have you ever noticed that real stores move their products around and change the path the shopper takes to encourage new sales? Every store does it—you walk in one day to find everyone hurriedly moving products around so that you have to memorize the new product locations—it seems like a cruel joke. However, there's a good reason for the changes—they force the shopper to see new products and perhaps spend a little more time in the store shopping. Likewise, you have to consider ways to move things around on your Web site without making the changes cumbersome for the user—remember that the next Web site is always a click away.

Presenting the Product

The way you present the product for sale can affect the shopping cart application and the results you get from it. For example, you need to consider whether you'll accept coupons that take a percentage off the sales price of the item. It's also important to consider how to handle sales and what to do about people who buy large quantities, rather than single items.

The display you create also affects ease of use. For example, you need to consider the checkout icon—the place the user clicks to purchase the items in their basket. Some Web sites include a Remove Item from Shopping Cart button directly on the product page; others place this functionality in the shopping cart application. You need to decide where this functionality will reside before you begin the design phase. An important issue to remember while making these decisions is consistency. Users are less confused when you offer consistent features, even when those features might not follow the latest trends in user design.

Product presentation also affects the page layout. For example, Figure 16.2 shows a typical view from Amazon.com. Notice that the layout includes a picture of the product and an offer to show a larger version of the image. The user can search inside the book and see other readers' reviews. Notice that the Add to Shopping Cart button appears in a different color in the upper right corner—the buyer can't miss it. However, if you can't buy it today, Amazon offers to store it as a wish for someone else to buy. In short, the application accommodates future as well as present sales. To create a truly robust shopping cart application, you need to consider all of these features (and others that you brainstorm).

FIGURE 16.2
Page layout affects sales
as well as the construc-
tion of your shopping
cart application.

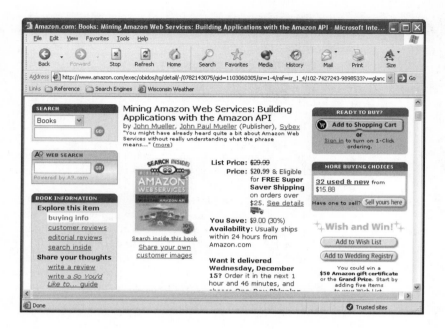

Developing the Product Data Flow

Once you decide the user interface issues, you need to consider how the data will flow within the application. For example, when you request that the user log in as part of the initial application screen, you need to track the user information in some way—usually through a database. A simple customer identification number might be all that you need to track the shopping cart as it moves through the sale and eventually to the checkout. The bottom line is that you need a user database of some sort to include shipping information and other important facts about the user.

No matter when the user logs in, you need to present the user with a list of products to buy. You could create an individual Web page for every product, but that probably wouldn't be very efficient. Most Web sites use a database to store the unique product information and then modify a single Web page with the required information. This feature works very much like the master pages described in the "Designing Master Pages" section of Chapter 4. All you do is fill in the blanks with product information that comes from the database.

A third piece of data flow is the shopping cart and the order it creates. You could simply store the shopping cart in memory and move it from page to page as the user shops. This technique depends on keeping every user separate and ensuring there aren't any glitches on your system. Because you'll eventually need to generate an order within a database at some point, it's usually better to store the shopping cart on the server in a database during the entire process. Of course, you need some way to handle abandoned shopping carts when you use this technique. It's a choice of the complex database solution over the less reliable memory solution.

These three databases: user, product, and orders are essential for any shopping cart application. You don't actually have to create three databases—you could store all three kinds of data in a single database using well-defined tables. The point is that the user data will likely include more than one table, as will the order information.

The product information could reside in a single table, but it's more likely that you'll need multiple tables to ensure you can define the products fully. For example, you might want to include a list of items that other people buy, as shown in Figure 16.3. You could generate this list in several ways—some Web sites simply use their search engine to locate suitable products. The application then displays those products that are selling best. You could also hand tune the list and include those that you either want to get rid of or that you want to sell along with the product as a special deal. The point is that you can create complex databases of information for your products, but the only thing you have to have is a list that includes a product name, description, and selling price.

FIGURE 16.3
Make the product listings robust to ensure buyers can find what they want.

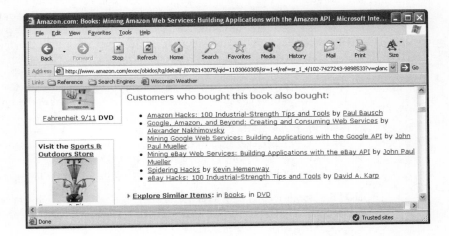

Tracking User Data

You have to track the user data at some point. The amount of user data you track depends on your system requirements. Requesting that the user log on before beginning the shopping experience is usually easier on the shopping cart developer because you can associate products with a specific user identifier. It's possible to track the user with this number during the entire transaction. Remember that Web servers have no concept of state, so you must have a method in place to track the user.

It's also a good idea to determine how to track the user data. Many shopping cart applications rely on cookies, which is a great technique to use until you want to interact with a user who has cookies turned off. Some shopping carts retain user information in a database on the server and use an identifier such as the Session ID to track the user. The advantage of this method is that the user doesn't require any special browser support to use it. Unfortunately, using this approach means that the header contains identifying information (such as the Session ID) that the server won't remember from session to session. A few shopping cart applications rely on a mix of both client- and server-side tracking, which makes the code very complex, but also benefits from the advantages of both environments.

Getting the Payment

You must open a merchant account with a local bank to handle the credit card transactions for your Web site. The bank exchanges the credit card information you provide for cash in an account, so you need to create this communication channel as part of creating your shopping cart application. It's best to find a bank that has a lot of experience working with the Internet and has a strong Internet presence. If possible, try to find a bank that uses a Web service to perform the transactions because a Web service is going to be a lot easier to use with Visual Web Developer. Avoid getting an account with a bank that uses a custom portal—such interfaces are difficult to write in Visual Web Developer, don't hide changes very well (so you'll spend lots of time rewriting the code), and don't lend themselves to use with third party products. It's also important to consider the rates the bank charges for a merchant account—they vary a lot.

If you decide that none of your local banks can meet your needs, you can always rely on an online service such as PayPal. Even though most people associate PayPal with eBay, PayPal Web Services are completely separate from eBay Web Services. However, eBay developed both Web services.

PayPal is a system for taking care of all the financial details for purchases. For example, you can use PayPal on eBay to buy new products. However, eBay isn't the only place you can use PayPal. It's also possible to use PayPal to buy products on Amazon. PayPal isn't just a solution for big stores either; you'll also find PayPal on other Web sites such as Barefoot Productions shown in Figure 16.4. In short, PayPal is another form of payment service akin to a credit card, but without the potential security problems of credit cards because your information resides on a single secure site (at least you know where to go when your information is compromised).

You'd use PayPal Web Services if you wanted to add a simple payment mechanism to your own Web site. The purchases need not be for eBay or Amazon or any other particular online site—they can be for your own merchandise. Before you can use PayPal, you need to obtain new credentials from PayPal Developer Central at `https://developer.paypal.com/`.

NOTE   Some of you might already use eBay Web Services to market products online. You can't use the eBay Web Services credentials to access PayPal—you need PayPal-specific credentials.

FIGURE 16.4
PayPal is one solution for businesses that don't have a local bank that offers online credit card services.

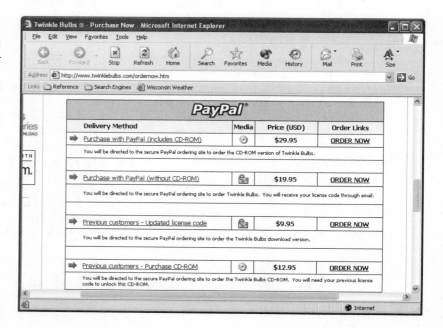

Once you obtain PayPal credentials, you'll notice that PayPal is willing to work with you to ensure that your application works flawlessly before you make it publicly available. This is a big advantage for anyone creating a custom application because you get a third party check as part of the development process—something that's only available to larger companies in most cases.

Amazingly, Visual Web Developer is set up to use PayPal with a minimum of coding on your part. PayPal uses a Simple Object Access Protocol (SOAP) interface to access the Web service. All you need to do is add a Web reference and then access PayPal as you would any local class from within Visual Web Developer. The "Using Google to Create a Site Search" section of Chapter 8 and the "Developing Web Service Connections" section of Chapter 13 both discuss using Web services.

Creating the Required Databases

As previously mentioned, you must create three databases at a minimum for your shopping cart application. (The application actually places all of the related tables into one database file, but the tables do represent three types of individual data.) The first contains a product listing—the items that you want to sell. The second includes a list of customers registered to buy products from your Web site. The third contains a list of orders—items that you have sold to the customer. The following sections describe each of these databases in more detail. To make things easy, the application relies on a local SQL Server database that appears in the `\ABC_Inc\ShoppingCart\Data` folder. You can learn how to create a local database in the "Creating a Blank Database" section of Chapter 11.

Product Listing

The first piece of information that your shopping cart application requires is a list of products to sell. Someone can input this information using a management application that you create or you can simply use an existing database of items. The point is that you need to provide some information about the products you want to sell to the potential buyer. These listings can become extremely complex, especially when you begin including specialized information such as buyer comments. The example uses the simpler configuration shown in Figure 16.5 for demonstration purposes.

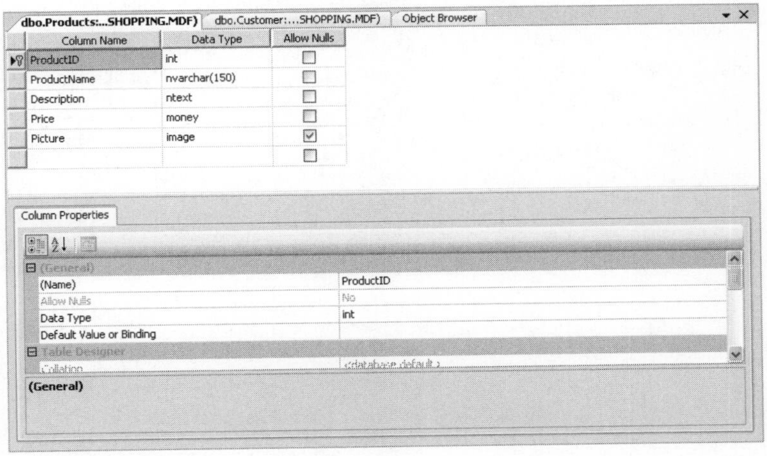

FIGURE 16.5
The product listing database contains a single table, but you could include more.

Notice that the database includes a `ProductID` field. You must include some unique method for identifying the product—one that's impossible to repeat. Otherwise, the shopping cart application is going to fail. The example relies on an `int` field type that it will need to manage using code. Theoretically, you could also use the `uniqueidentifier` field type because it automatically updates to the next value. However, you can run into problems using this field type when you need to create relationships between the various tables. A child necessarily has multiple copies of the unique value, making it impossible to create a relationship with a `uniqueidentifier` field.

TIP   Try to choose a numeric value, rather than a string, when creating the unique product identifier. You'll find that you get better performance when using a number, and data entry errors are less likely to cause unusable keys.

The other entries in the table describe the product. They include the product name, price, and description. You can't create a shopping cart table with any less information—more is better. The optional Picture field shows what the item looks like. This particular feature is so important that venues such as eBay often provide multiple pictures for each item—people want to know what they're buying.

The example application doesn't consider at least one feature that you'll probably want to include in a complete shopping cart application—the current inventory quantity. You don't want to attempt to sell something you no longer have. Some Web sites get around this issue by saying they'll put the item on back order or by offering used items (or sometimes both).

Customers

The customers database can become quite complex as well. A customer might have personal preferences, a wish list, shipping and billing addresses, multiple telephone numbers, and multiple credit cards. Each of these entries requires a separate table linked by the customer identifier. The example combines many of these features into a single table, as shown in Figure 16.6.

Notice that the `CustomerID` field uses the `int` field type, so the code needs to ensure that each entry is indeed unique; otherwise, the shopping cart application will fail. Generally, you'll want to make this a number that reflects any other sales sources, such as catalog sales so that every customer has just one identifier.

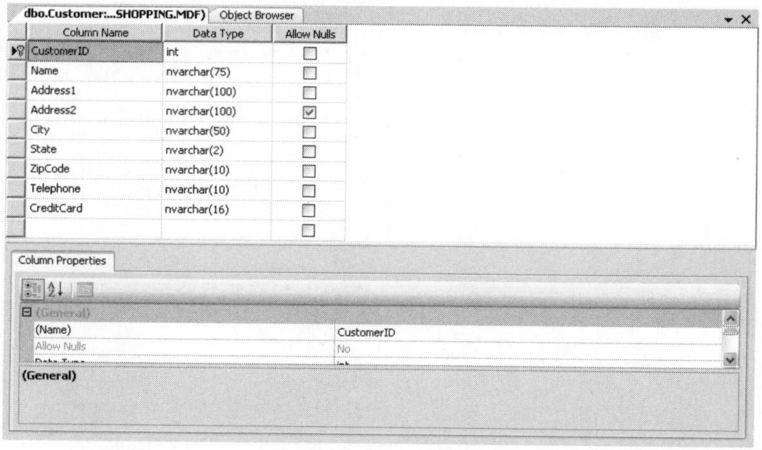

FIGURE 16.6
The customer database normally includes several tables linked with an identifier.

Orders

The orders database always requires at least two tables. The first contains the main order information, such as the customer identifier and the date. The second contains a list of items that the customer purchased for a particular order. Because these tables rely on other tables for input, you also have to create the required foreign keys. Figure 16.7 shows the structure for the orders table—the one that holds the order-specific information.

This table contains the identifying information for the order as a whole. The example includes a unique order identifier and customer identifier, the order date, and a flag that shows whether the order is completed. Some applications include more status information. However, as you add more status information, users have a better chance of entering incorrect data. An order could end up with conflicting status indicators. Normally, it's best to keep the order database as simple as possible to enhance data integrity. Of course, you could always include a date that you shipped the product, rather than the simple status flag shown. Good application additions include tracking who filled the order and how you shipped it. Make sure you include a tracking number with the order if you track the shipping method. Nothing is more frustrating for the customer than to know that the order shipped, but not the details.

The Foreign Key Relationships dialog box includes two entries in this case. The orders table has a relationship with the customers table—you need the customer information to know where to send the product. The orders table must also supply its identifier to the order items table. Otherwise, you won't know which item entries belong to the order.

The order items table also requires input from other tables. Figure 16.8 shows the structure of this table and the associated relationships.

The order items table includes a pointer to the order identifier and the product that the customer ordered. The table defines the number of items ordered, but doesn't include a total price because an application can easily calculate this value as needed. You have to consider whether you'll reference the data later. The price of each product will fluctuate. If you think you'll need the total (based on today's prices) later, then you'll want to include a total field.

FIGURE 16.7
Use this table to track individual orders.

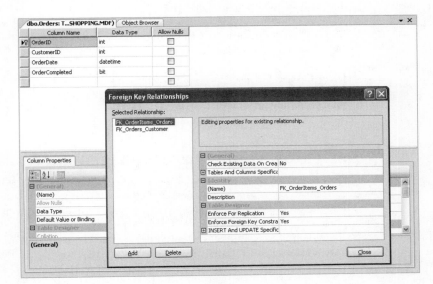

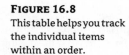

FIGURE 16.8
This table helps you track the individual items within an order.

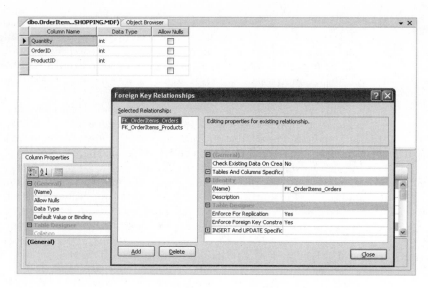

Defining Table Relationships

You can easily get lost in all of the various tables, their contents, and relationships during the initial design process. For this reason, you'll want to create a physical representation of the various tables to ensure you can see any problems. Unfortunately, both SQL Server Express and Visual Web Developer lack a graphic design tool, such as the Diagrams folder found in full version of SQL Server, for seeing the database.

The best way to overcome the problem of physical representation is to create a Data Component using the Add New Item dialog box (right-click the project entry in Solution Explorer and choose Add New Item from the context menu). Add data components for each of the tables and you can see the relationships between them, as shown in Figure 16.9. This technique provides an easy method for tracking your database design as you work with Visual Web Developer.

TIP Make sure you choose the * (All Columns) option in QueryBuilder when creating the Data Component. After you make changes, right-click the table with the changes and choose Configure from the context menu. When you see the Data Component Configuration Wizard dialog box, click Finish to update the table entries automatically.

Designing Appropriate Management Applications

Once you design enough of your application, you'll also want to start building management applications for it. For example, you need a method for changing the product entries and a technique for seeing the orders. You'll also want to make it convenient for administrators to learn more about the application status and upload files when necessary. You'll need to decide how to provide the management features. A number of companies now have an all-Web application interface, even for the people working within the company, but using a desktop application is just as viable.

FIGURE 16.9
Make sure you understand the table relationships before you begin coding.

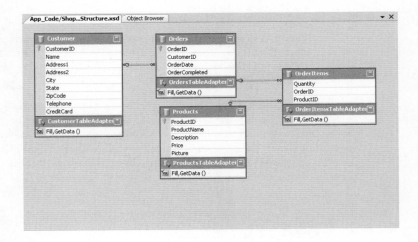

NOTE You might wonder why I'm discussing management applications before the actual application. It helps to create at least some basic management applications before you begin writing code so that you can interact with the databases in comfort. After all, being a developer should mean creating the tools you need to work efficiently. Consequently, you'll find that developing the tools you need before you write the application can help point out pitfalls in your design and make it easier to meet deadlines.

Many companies are turning to Web applications for management tasks because a Web page offers a level of mobility that a desktop application can't. You can access the Web page from anywhere needed to check the status of orders, make sure the Web site is functioning as anticipated, modify (add, remove, or update) customers, and make required database changes.

Choosing Management Tasks

One of the first things you'll want to create is a centralized access point for your tools, which means creating a method for accessing a particular tool. Although you can use any number of techniques for performing this task, this example shows a new control to try with ASP.NET 2.0. In this case, it uses the RadioButtonList to present a list of management options. These management options automatically change the appearance of the Web page based on code behind because the control provides automatic postback and calls the rblMgntOption_SelectedIndexChanged() method when a selection changes, as shown here.

```
<asp:RadioButtonList
        ID="rblMgntOption" Runat="server"
        AutoPostBack="True" BorderStyle="Outset"
        BorderWidth="5px"
        OnSelectedIndexChanged="rblMgntOption_SelectedIndexChanged">
    <asp:ListItem Value="DoNothing" Selected="True">
        Do Nothing
    </asp:ListItem>
    <asp:ListItem Value="UpdateCustomers">
```

```
        Update Customers
    </asp:ListItem>
    <asp:ListItem Value="ChangeProducts">Change Products</asp:ListItem>
    <asp:ListItem Value="ReviewOrders">Review Orders</asp:ListItem>
    <asp:ListItem Value="GoHome">Return to the Main Page</asp:ListItem>
</asp:RadioButtonList>
```

Notice that the `RadioButtonList` control includes a series of `ListItem` entries, just as you would see for any list control. Each of these `ListItem` entries is a single option. The first option sets the `Selected` attribute to true so the page displays with one option selected. Using this control means you don't have to worry about groups or placement of individual controls within a group. All you need to do is select Edit Items from the Common RadioButtonList Tasks SmartTag to display the ListItem Collection Editor Dialog box shown in Figure 16.10. You can use this dialog box to change the option order, add new options, and remove options you no longer need, as well as configure the various options.

The `RadioButtonList` control requires some type of code behind support to function. Because the example application works with databases, the actual functionality resides in a central display method (explained in the "Displaying the Data" section of the chapter). However, you still need to define a task for the Return to the Main Page option, as shown here.

```
Sub rblMgntOption_SelectedIndexChanged(ByVal sender As Object, _
                                ByVal e As System.EventArgs)
    ' Provide a means to go to the main page.
    If rblMgntOption.SelectedIndex = 4 Then
        Response.Redirect("GoShopping.aspx")
    End If

    ' Refresh the data.
    DataRefresh()
End Sub
```

FIGURE 16.10
Use the ListItem Collection Editor to add new options to a Radio-ButtonList control.

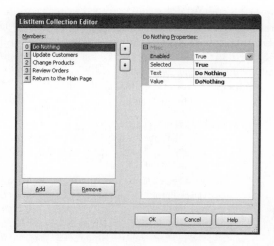

This code checks the `SelectedIndex` property. Remember that this property is zero based, so the number is always one less than the actual selection. The `Response.Redirect()` method appears a lot in this chapter because it provides a very handy method for moving the customer from place to place in the store. The goal is to let the customer spend as much time as needed in the aisles, but to make the trip to the checkout stand as easy as possible.

Displaying the Data

Writing one flexible method for displaying data is often easier than writing three methods to perform the task. This example shows one technique you can use to reduce the amount of code you need to write. A single method can display any of the databases that you'll edit while working with the application. In fact, you'll find that the code for displaying each database isn't unique—only a few lines change depending on the database you want to work with, as shown in Listing 16.1. You'll find this example in the `\ABC_Inc\ShoppingCart` folder of the source code on the Sybex Web site as part of the `CartManage.ASPX.VB` file.

LISTING 16.1:   Displaying the Data on Screen

```
Private Sub DataRefresh(Optional ByVal RecNum As Int32 = -1)
    ... Variable Declarations ...

    ' Determine whether the user has selected the Do Nothing option.
    If rblMgntOption.SelectedIndex = 0 Then
        ' Hide the data editing features.
        lblDataEdit.Visible = False
        dvDataEdit.Visible = False
        Return
    End If

    ' Make the data editing features visible.
    lblDataEdit.Visible = True
    dvDataEdit.Visible = True

    ' Determine the path for this application.
    ThisPath = Page.MapPath(Page.AppRelativeVirtualPath)
    ThisPath = ThisPath.Replace("\CartManage.aspx", "\")

    ' Create the database connection.
    Conn = New SqlConnection( _
        "Server=Main;" + _
        "Integrated Security=True;" + _
        "Database=ShoppingCartData;" + _
        "AttachDBFilename=" + _
            ThisPath + "Data\Shopping.mdf")

    ' Create a data adapter based on the request. Set the unique
    ' details view features to ensure the user can only select the
```

```
        ' functional options.
        Select Case rblMgntOption.SelectedIndex
            Case 1
                Adapt = New SqlDataAdapter("SELECT * FROM Customer", Conn)
                dvDataEdit.AutoGenerateDeleteButton = True
                dvDataEdit.AutoGenerateInsertButton = True
            Case 2
                Adapt = New SqlDataAdapter("SELECT * FROM Products", Conn)
                dvDataEdit.AutoGenerateDeleteButton = True
                dvDataEdit.AutoGenerateInsertButton = True
            Case 3
                Adapt = New SqlDataAdapter( _
                    "SELECT dbo.Orders.*, dbo.OrderItems.ProductID, " + _
                    "dbo.OrderItems.Quantity FROM dbo.OrderItems " + _
                    "INNER JOIN dbo.Orders ON " + _
                    "dbo.OrderItems.OrderID = dbo.Orders.OrderID", Conn)
                dvDataEdit.AutoGenerateDeleteButton = False
                dvDataEdit.AutoGenerateInsertButton = False
        End Select

        ' Fill a dataset with the required information.
        DS = New DataSet("ShoppingData")
        Adapt.Fill(DS)

        ' Set up the details view.
        dvDataEdit.DataSource = DS
        dvDataEdit.AllowPaging = True
        dvDataEdit.AutoGenerateEditButton = True

        ' Select the record number.
        If RecNum > -1 Then
            dvDataEdit.PageIndex = RecNum
        End If

        ' Display the data.
        dvDataEdit.DataBind()
    End Sub
```

The code begins by checking the rblMgntOption.SelectedIndex property. When the user chooses to do nothing, the code doesn't display the database. This is a nice option to add to your applications because it lets the user hide any sensitive information from other people during visits. When the user has selected one of the database options, the code makes a Label and a DetailsView control visible. The DetailsView control isn't configured—you use the same control for all of the databases.

TIP   Notice the use of the ThisPath variable in Listing 16.1. You don't know where your application will finally reside, so making the paths as resistant to awkward problems as possible will reduce your workload later. In this case, the Page.MapPath() method maps a relative URI to a path on the local machine. Unfortunately, this path contains the name of the current file. Consequently, the code uses the ThisPath.Replace() method to remove the filename. Now the code has a path to use that isn't based on something you hardwired, but rather the actual location of the file on disk.

The database connection requires three components in this case. However, the example also shows how to use other connection types. The code begins by opening a connection to the database using a SqlConnection object. It then defines the information the application will retrieve from the database using a SqlDataAdapter object. Finally, the code retrieves the data from the database and stores it in a DataSet. The DetailsView binds to the DataSet to display the information on screen.

Notice that the code uses the same connection, Conn, for all three displays because the tables all appear in the same database file. The connection uses a string to define the name of the server, determines whether you want to use integrated (Windows XP) security, defines the name of the database, and tells where the database is located. The Server argument is always the name of the machine that holds the database file, while the AttachDBFilename is the physical location of the database on the machine (which means you can put it anywhere).

The code creates a unique data adapter for each of the displays, so the code relies on the rblMgntOption.SelectedIndex value to determine which view to create. The SqlDataAdapter constructor accepts the T-SQL select statement as input, so the code can create Adapt in a single step. This section of code also determines the functionality of the DetailsView control, dvDataEdit. The user will have to create new records and delete old ones when working with the customers and products, but shouldn't perform these tasks with orders, so the code configures dvDataEdit differently in this case.

The next step is to create the DataSet, DS. The first step creates the object, while the second fills it with data using the Adapt.Fill(DS) method call. At this point, the code can display the data on screen. To perform this task, the code begins by setting the dvDataEdit.DataSource property to point to the data source. It also sets display properties used by all three information presentations.

The next piece of code checks the content of an optional argument for this method. The optional declaration appears as part of the method declaration, Optional ByVal RecNum As Int32 = -1. All optional arguments must appear last. In addition, you must still define a type for the optional argument, along with a default value. Notice how the code tests this default value to determine whether it should set the record number for the example. Using this technique extends the functionality of DataRefresh() so it can display the initial data or the results of a change with equal ease.

The final step binds the dataset to the data view using the dvDataEdit.DataBind() method. You must perform this binding operation every time the dataset changes or the display won't change. Figure 16.11 shows a typical initial view (remember, there are three for this example). To change views, the user merely selects another database from the list.

Changing Pages

It's unfortunate, but all of the automation you saw in Chapter 11 simply disappears whenever you want to do anything other than what Microsoft originally envisioned for you. For example, when working with the example in the "Creating a View" section of Chapter 11, you received paging support automatically. Figure 16.11 shows that this application also provides paging support—it must or the user would always see the first record. This example shows that adding any customization at all to the standard `DetailsView` control means that you have to provide the paging support. Fortunately, adding paging support isn't hard, as shown here.

```
Private Sub dvDataEdit_PageIndexChanging( _
    ByVal sender As Object, _
    ByVal e As System.Web.UI.WebControls.DetailsViewPageEventArgs) _
    Handles dvDataEdit.PageIndexChanging

    ' Display the requested page.
    DataRefresh(e.NewPageIndex)
End Sub
```

This example shows the flexibility that adding the optional argument to `DataRefresh()` (see Listing 16.1) provides. The `DetailsViewPageEventArgs` object, `e`, provides a special `NewPageIndex` property with the page number that the user selected. All you need to do is refresh the data with the selected page number in mind.

FIGURE 16.11
A single method can display any of the data you need when you use flexible programming methods.

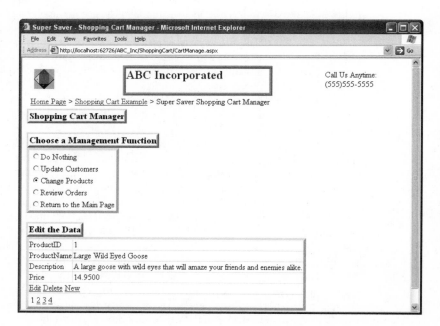

Changing Modes

The `DetailsView` control shown in Figure 16.11 also provides various modes of operation. Again, the automation you saw in Chapter 11 disappears when you perform any form of customization. This example provides edit, delete, and insert modes, besides the standard select mode shown in Figure 16.11.

You implement mode changes in two ways. First, you must create a generic mode changing mechanism that handles all mode-changing events. Second, you must create specific mode-handling code for the event. This section discusses the generic mode-changing mechanism provided by the event handler shown in Listing 16.2. You'll find this example in the `\ABC_Inc\ShoppingCart` folder of the source code on the Sybex Web site as part of the `CartManage.ASPX.VB` file.

LISTING 16.2:   Providing Generic Mode Changes for *DetailsView*

```vb
Private Sub dvDataEdit_ModeChanging( _
    ByVal sender As Object, _
    ByVal e As System.Web.UI.WebControls.DetailsViewModeEventArgs) _
    Handles dvDataEdit.ModeChanging

    If e.NewMode = DetailsViewMode.Edit Or e.NewMode = DetailsViewMode.Insert Then
        ' Hide the managment options from view while editing.
        lblMgntOption.Visible = False
        rblMgntOption.Visible = False

        ' Disallow page changes again.
        dvDataEdit.AllowPaging = False
    Else
        ' Display the managment options from view while editing.
        lblMgntOption.Visible = True
        rblMgntOption.Visible = True

        ' Allow page changes again.
        dvDataEdit.AllowPaging = True
    End If

    ' Change the display mode.
    dvDataEdit.ChangeMode(e.NewMode)

    ' Refresh the data.
    DataRefresh()
End Sub
```

Look again at Figure 16.11, and you'll notice that the program lets the user select other databases when working in select mode. This action would prove disastrous when in edit or insert mode. The user could accidentally change mode in the middle of an edit or new record creation and lose data. The code changes the appearance of the display for each mode based on the `e.NewMode` passed as part of the `DetailsViewModeEventArgs` argument. However, these visual changes don't change the appearance of the control.

The code uses the `dvDataEdit.ChangeMode(e.NewMode)` method to change the control's appearance. Of course, this change doesn't affect the on-screen appearance of the data. To make the on-screen change, the code also calls `DataRefresh()` without the optional argument. Interestingly enough, the code automatically retains the current record so the user sees a mode change, not a record change. Figure 16.12 shows a typical mode change to the edit mode.

FIGURE 16.12

The edit mode lets the user change the content of a database.

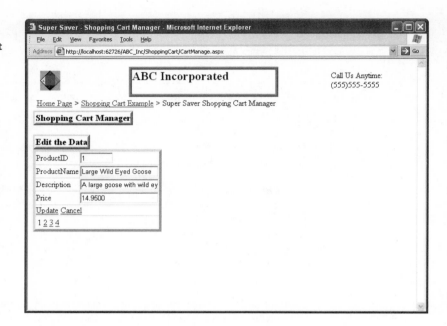

Creating New Records

Clicking the New link shown in Figure 16.11 fires the `ItemInserting` event (pre-processing), followed by the `ItemInserted` event (post-processing). The application insists that you create an `ItemInserting` event handler, but the `ItemInserted` event handler is optional. In fact, unless you plan to provide some type of data massaging after the fact, it's better not to implement the `ItemInserted` event handler. Listing 16.3 shows the essential parts of the `ItemInserting` event handler. Note that the code in the listing isn't complete. You'll find the complete version of this example in the \ABC_Inc\ShoppingCart folder of the source code on the Sybex Web site as part of the `CartManage.ASPX.VB` file.

LISTING 16.3:   Inserting Records

```
Private Sub dvDataEdit_ItemInserting( _
    ByVal sender As Object, _
    ByVal e As System.Web.UI.WebControls.DetailsViewInsertEventArgs) _
    Handles dvDataEdit.ItemInserting

    ... Variable Declarations ...

    ' Determine the path for this application.
    ThisPath = Page.MapPath(Page.AppRelativeVirtualPath)
    ThisPath = ThisPath.Replace("\CartManage.aspx", "\")
```

```
' Open the connection.
Conn = New SqlConnection( _
    "Server=Main;" + _
    "Integrated Security=True;" + _
    "Database=ShoppingCartData;" + _
    "AttachDBFilename=" + _
        ThisPath + "Data\Shopping.mdf")
Conn.Open()

' Initialize DoInsert.
DoInsert = New SqlCommand()

Select Case rblMgntOption.SelectedIndex
    Case 1
        ' Create the SQL command.
        DoInsert = New SqlCommand( _
            "INSERT INTO [Customer] ([CustomerID], [Name], " + _
            "[Address1], [Address2], [City], [State], " + _
            "[ZipCode], [Telephone], [CreditCard]) VALUES " + _
            "(@CustomerID, @Name, @Address1, @Address2, " + _
            "@City, @State, @ZipCode, @Telephone, @CreditCard)", _
            Conn)

        ' Get the current CustomerID.
        CurrData = CType(dvDataEdit.Rows(0).Cells(1).Controls(0), _
                        TextBox)

        ' Create a parameter based on this value.
        Parm = DoInsert.CreateParameter()
        Parm.ParameterName = "CustomerID"
        Parm.DbType = DbType.Int32
        Parm.Value = Int32.Parse(CurrData.Text)
        DoInsert.Parameters.Add(Parm)

        ... Lots of Other Parameters ...

    Case 2
        ... Database specific SQL Command ...

        ... Lots of Parameters ...

End Select

' Execute the query.
Try
    DoInsert.ExecuteNonQuery()
    Conn.Close()
Catch ex As Exception
```

```
        End Try

        ' Display the managment options from view while editing.
        lblMgntOption.Visible = True
        rblMgntOption.Visible = True

        ' Allow page changes again.
        dvDataEdit.AllowPaging = True

        ' Change the display mode.
        dvDataEdit.ChangeMode(DetailsViewMode.ReadOnly)

        ' Refresh the data.
        DataRefresh()
    End Sub
```

The first task the code performs is creating a database connection. You always need to provide the same arguments for the connection including the server, security, database, and filename entries. This section shows how to use a command, rather than an adapter, to interact with the database. Consequently, you must open the connection because the command won't do it for you (the adapter does perform this task).

WARNING   One error that some developers make when working with databases in Web applications is to assume the Web application has a state. They try to save resources by creating a global connection that will remain open for the entire session. The only problem is that Web applications have no state. Consequently, the connection always closes after the request even when you use a global variable. It's always better to use a local variable and to open and close the database connection for each request.

The next step is to create a command. The content of the command depends on the database you want to work with. All of the commands include the name of the database, the fields affected by the data insertion, and a series of values to insert into those fields. The information you provide is in standard T-SQL syntax. Of course, you must provide information to place in the data fields using the SqlParameter object, Parm. You can obtain this information from two sources. The first is the DetailsViewInsertEventArgs object, e, that the system passes to your event handler. The code retrieves the information from the Values property. Unfortunately, e isn't a reliable source of input data because of a bug in the .NET Framework.

A better source of information is dvDataEdit. Look again at Figure 16.12, and you'll notice that the data fields are actually TextBox controls. The code accesses these controls directly and retrieves the required information from them. Each DetailsView control consists of multiple rows of two columns—the name of the data field and the data within that field. Consequently, when you want to access the ProductID value in Figure 16.12, you would retrieve the value of the textbox (control 0) in row 0, cell 1 by placing dvDataEdit.Rows(0).Cells(1).Controls(0) in a local TextBox control, CurrData, and viewing the CurrData.Text property. The code can't access the textbox directly because the control could be anything (such as a check box) and the field could even contain multiple controls. Notice how the code uses CType() to convert the object to a specific control.

To create `Parm`, the code defines the parameter name, the data type, and a value. The parameter name must match the value name in the T-SQL statement without the @ (at) sign. The `DbType` value must come from the `DbType` enumeration, as shown in the code. The parameter doesn't become permanent until the code assigns it to `DoInsert` using the `Parameters.Add()` method.

After the code creates the required command and its associated parameters, it performs the data insertion using the `DoInsert.ExecuteNonQuery()` method. After the insertion completes, the code closes the connection. Whenever you explicitly open the connection, you must also close it manually. Notice that the code executes the command within a `Try...Catch` structure. Even a perfectly formed command can fail for a number of reasons, so using a `Try...Catch` structure is essential. You can provide any level of error handling that you feel is appropriate. In many cases, you won't want to inform the user of the error, but you'll want to create an event log entry for the network administrator.

NOTE   The example doesn't provide any error handling to make the code easier to understand. A complete shopping cart application will provide full error handling. Chapters 16 and 17 provide information on various kinds of error handling and error trapping you can provide for applications.

The code ends by restoring the data editing view so the user can select another database if desired. Notice that the code also changes the mode using `dvDataEdit.ChangeMode(DetailsViewMode.ReadOnly)` to the selected or read-only mode. Figure 16.13 shows a typical view of the application in insert mode (using the customer database in this case).

Note that the display contains two options. When the user clicks New, the system calls the `dvDataEdit_ItemInserting()` event handler. Clicking Cancel doesn't call the inserting event handler, but it does call the `dvDataEdit_ModeChanging()` event handler, so you have to make sure the application works in both instances.

FIGURE 16.13
Use insert mode to add new records to a database.

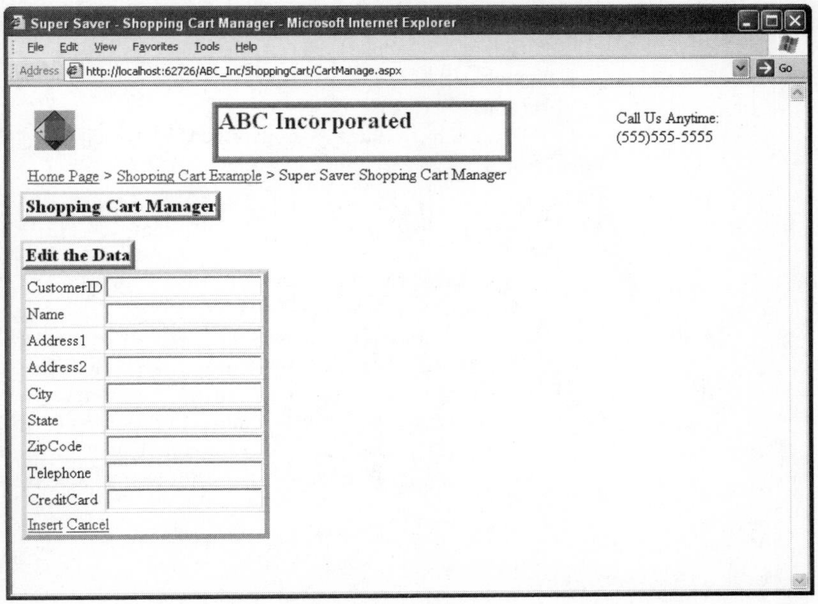

Updating Records

All of the databases require edit mode support. In many respects, this process differs only by the SQL command and the way you prepare the parameters. However, the orders database introduces special problems because you need to provide a means for updating both the Orders and the OrderItems tables. You could do this as part of a complex SQL command, but it's easier to handle the two tables separately. Listing 16.4 shows the essential code you need for this part of the example. Note that the code in the listing isn't complete. You'll find the complete version of this example in the \ABC_Inc\ ShoppingCart folder of the source code on the Sybex Web site as part of the CartManage.ASPX .VB file.

LISTING 16.4:   Editing Records

```
Private Sub dvDataEdit_ItemUpdating( _
    ByVal sender As Object, _
    ByVal e As System.Web.UI.WebControls.DetailsViewUpdateEventArgs)

    ... Variable Declarations ...

    ' Determine the path for this application.
    ThisPath = Page.MapPath(Page.AppRelativeVirtualPath)
    ThisPath = ThisPath.Replace("\CartManage.aspx", "\")

    ' Open the connection.
    Conn = New SqlConnection( _
        "Server=Main;" + _
        "Integrated Security=True;" + _
        "Database=ShoppingCartData;" + _
        "AttachDBFilename=" + _
            ThisPath + "Data\Shopping.mdf")
    Conn.Open()

    Select Case rblMgntOption.SelectedIndex
        Case 1
            ' Create the SQL command.
            DoUpdate = New SqlCommand( _
                "UPDATE [Customer] SET [Name] = @Name, " + _
                "[Address1] = @Address1, [Address2] = @Address2, " + _
                "[City] = @City, [State] = @State, " + _
                "[ZipCode] = @ZipCode, [Telephone] = @Telephone, " + _
                "[CreditCard] = @CreditCard " + _
                "WHERE [CustomerID] = @original_CustomerID", Conn)

            ' Get the current CustomerID.
            CurrData = CType(dvDataEdit.Rows(0).Cells(1).Controls(0), _
                        TextBox)
```

```
        ' Set the original CustomerID.
        Parm = DoUpdate.CreateParameter()
        Parm.ParameterName = "original_CustomerID"
        Parm.DbType = DbType.Int32
        Parm.Value = Int32.Parse(CurrData.Text)
        DoUpdate.Parameters.Add(Parm)

        ' Create a paramter based on this value.
        Parm = DoUpdate.CreateParameter()
        Parm.ParameterName = "CustomerID"
        Parm.DbType = DbType.Int32
        Parm.Value = Int32.Parse(CurrData.Text)
        DoUpdate.Parameters.Add(Parm)

        ... Lots of Other Parameters ...

Case 2
        ... Database specific SQL Command ...

        ... Lots of Parameters ...

Case 3
    Dim Completed As CheckBox    ' Special for order completed.

        ' Create the SQL command for the Orders table update first.
        DoUpdate = New SqlCommand( _
            "UPDATE [Orders] SET [OrderDate] = @OrderDate, " + _
            "[OrderCompleted] = @OrderCompleted " + _
            "WHERE [OrderID] = @original_OrderID", Conn)

        ... Lots of Parameters ...

        ' Get the current OrderCompleted.
        Completed = CType(dvDataEdit.Rows(3).Cells(1).Controls(0), _
                        CheckBox)

        ' Create a paramter based on this value.
        Parm = DoUpdate.CreateParameter()
        Parm.ParameterName = "OrderCompleted"
        Parm.DbType = DbType.Boolean
        Parm.Value = Completed.Checked
        DoUpdate.Parameters.Add(Parm)

        ' Complete the Orders table update before moving on to
        ' OrderItems
        Try
            DoUpdate.ExecuteNonQuery()
        Catch ex As Exception
```

```
                    End Try

                    ... Database specific SQL Command ...

                    ... Lots of Parameters ...

            End Select

            ' Execute the query.
            Try
                DoUpdate.ExecuteNonQuery()
                Conn.Close()
            Catch ex As Exception

            End Try

            ' Display the managment options from view while editing.
            lblMgntOption.Visible = True
            rblMgntOption.Visible = True

            ' Allow page changes again.
            dvDataEdit.AllowPaging = True

            ' Change the display mode.
            dvDataEdit.ChangeMode(DetailsViewMode.ReadOnly)

            ' Refresh the data.
            DataRefresh()
    End Sub
```

The code begins with the standard connection code. It then creates the Sql Command object, DoUpdate. The T-SQL statement is a standard update command. It includes the name of the table and instructions on setting each of the fields. The T-SQL statement limits the update to a single statement using the WHERE clause. Notice that the current T-SQL statement doesn't include an entry for the CustomerID field. (The same holds true for the ProductID and OrderID fields.) The reason for this omission is that you never change the key field of a table. Consequently, with proper application design, the user should not be able to change the key field entries at all. In short, the current CustomerID field value will always match the original_CustomerID field value for the selected record.

Unfortunately, errors do happen and it would be nice to know that you have the correct values. The DetailsViewUpdateEventArgs object, e, includes both OldValues and NewValues properties. The OldValues property contains the original value of the field before the user changes it. Use this property, whenever possible, to obtain the original_CustomerID field value. The most reliable method of retrieving the original_CustomerID value is using the same method you use to obtain all of the other field values using the CType(dvDataEdit.Rows(0).Cells(1).Controls(0), TextBox) method. Once you have the required values, you create the Parm values. The products database works much like the customers database, so there's no need to explain it separately.

The orders database requires special handling, as previously mentioned. You need to work with the tables individually. Always update the parent table first and then the child table, or the database will complain about referential integrity issues. The code begins by creating a `SqlCommand` that works with the individual table, rather than both tables together, as the code does for the `DataRefresh()` method.

The `Orders` table also includes a special feature. Figure 16.14 shows that this table includes a Boolean value that the system creates as a `CheckBox`. Consequently, you need to change the code for retrieving the value, as shown in the listing. The `Completed.Checked` property defines whether the order is complete.

Once the code creates the proper command and parameters for the `Orders` table, it uses the `DoUpdate.ExecuteNonQuery()` method to perform the change. The code then proceeds to create a command and parameters for the `OrderItems` table. The code doesn't execute this command immediately—it uses the standard code used by all of the other databases. This code performs the same tasks as inserting a new record. The code begins by executing the query. It then resets the display properties and sets the mode to `DetailsViewMode.ReadOnly`. The final step calls `DataRefresh()` to present the changes on screen.

Deleting Records

Removing records from the database turns out to be the easiest task of all (perhaps a reflection of the saying that it's easier to destroy than to create). Only the customers and products databases allow this action—you don't want to remove orders from the system by accident. Listing 16.5 shows the essential code you need to perform this task. Note that the code in the listing isn't complete. You'll find the complete version of this example in the `\ABC_Inc\ShoppingCart` folder of the source code on the Sybex Web site as part of the `CartManage.ASPX.VB` file.

FIGURE 16.14

Make sure you use the appropriate controls when working directly with the DetailsView.

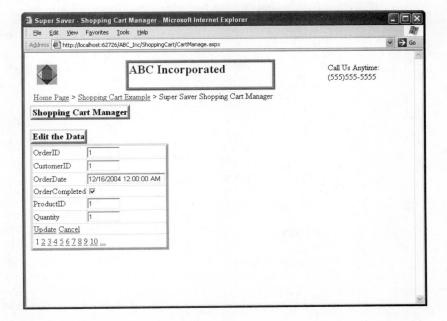

LISTING 16.5:   Deleting Records

```
Private Sub dvDataEdit_ItemDeleting( _
    ByVal sender As Object, _
    ByVal e As System.Web.UI.WebControls.DetailsViewDeleteEventArgs) _
    Handles dvDataEdit.ItemDeleting

    ... Variable Declarations ...

    ' Determine the path for this application.
    ThisPath = Page.MapPath(Page.AppRelativeVirtualPath)
    ThisPath = ThisPath.Replace("\CartManage.aspx", "\")

    ' Open the connection.
    Conn = New SqlConnection( _
        "Server=Main;" + _
        "Integrated Security=True;" + _
        "Database=ShoppingCartData;" + _
        "AttachDBFilename=" + _
            ThisPath + "Data\Shopping.mdf")
    Conn.Open()

    Select Case rblMgntOption.SelectedIndex
        Case 1
            ' Create the SQL command.
            DoInsert = New SqlCommand( _
                "DELETE FROM [Customer] WHERE " + _
                "[CustomerID] = @original_CustomerID", Conn)

            ' Create a parameter based on the CustomerID.
            Parm = DoInsert.CreateParameter()
            Parm.ParameterName = "original_CustomerID"
            Parm.DbType = DbType.Int32
            Parm.Value = Int32.Parse(dvDataEdit.Rows(0).Cells(1).Text)
            DoInsert.Parameters.Add(Parm)

        Case 2
            ... Database specific SQL Command ...

            ... Lots of Parameters ...

    End Select

    ' Execute the query.
    Try
        DoInsert.ExecuteNonQuery()
        Conn.Close()
```

```
        Catch ex As Exception

        End Try

        ' Refresh the data.
        DataRefresh()
    End Sub
```

The code begins by creating the usual database connection. It then creates a SQL command that reflects the particular database in use. Notice that you only need the database name and the WHERE clause containing the specific record to delete.

As with other event handlers described in this section, you can use the e.Values property to obtain the value of the record to delete. However, you obtain better results by using the dvDataEdit .Rows(0).Cells(1).Text property. Notice that the code doesn't access any controls in the cell in this case—there aren't any. The controls only exist when you perform some type of edit. When the cell doesn't contain a control, the Text property contains the value of the cell.

Because the delete process never displays an editor, you also don't have to worry about returning the display to its pre-edit state or modifying the condition of dvDataEdit. The only tasks that this event handler must perform to complete the action is to call DoInsert.ExecuteNonQuery() to remove the record, close the database connection, and then call DataRefresh() to display the changes on screen.

Creating the Front End Pages

The example shows two techniques for handling online applications. The first technique is modifying a single form to handle every need that the user might have. This technique appears in the "Designing Appropriate Management Applications" section of the chapter. The second technique combines several forms with blank areas to create specialized content. This section explores this second technique. The user moves from form to form and each of these forms modifies itself prior to presentation to display custom information for that user. The following sections lead you through the buying process for the shopping cart application.

Viewing a List of Products

Before someone visiting your Web site can buy anything, they need to see a list of potential purchases. Some Web sites have handled this problem by creating page after page of custom content in the past. Unfortunately, this approach is extremely time consuming and it isn't even very accurate. It's better to generate the display from the contents of the product database. That way, the information the user sees is accurate as of the moment that the browser makes the request—you can't get timelier than that. The example uses the PlaceHolder control to accomplish this task. The PlaceHolder control represents content that you plan to add later and it appears like this:

```
<asp:PlaceHolder ID="phProducts" Runat="server"></asp:PlaceHolder>
```

When you display this page without the appropriate code behind, all you see is a blank because the PlaceHolder control doesn't have any content. Listing 16.6 shows the code required to build content on the Web page using the PlaceHolder control. You'll find this example in the \ABC_Inc\ShoppingCart folder of the source code on the Sybex Web site as part of the GoShopping.ASPX.VB file.

LISTING 16.6: Creating Content on the Fly

```
Private Sub Page_Load(ByVal sender As Object, _
                        ByVal e As System.EventArgs) Handles Me.Load

    ... Variable Declarations ...

    ' Determine the path for this application.
    ThisPath = Page.MapPath(Page.AppRelativeVirtualPath)
    ThisPath = ThisPath.Replace("\GoShopping.aspx", "\")

    ' Create the database connection.
    Conn = New SqlConnection( _
        "Server=Main;" + _
        "Integrated Security=True;" + _
        "Database=ShoppingCartData;" + _
        "AttachDBFilename=" + _
            ThisPage + "Data\Shopping.mdf")

    ' Create the data adapter with the required select statement.
    Adapt = New SqlDataAdapter("SELECT * FROM Products", Conn)

    ' Fill a dataset with the required information.
    DS = New DataSet("ShoppingData")
    Adapt.Fill(DS)

    ' Define the Table.
    ProdTbl = New Table()

    ' Create content for the Web page.
    For Each DR In DS.Tables(0).Rows
        ' Create a new table row.
        ProdRow = New TableRow()

        ' Create a cell within the row.
        ProdCell = New TableCell()

        ' Define content for the cell.
        ThisLink = New HyperLink()
        ThisLink.NavigateUrl = "Products.aspx?ProdID=" + _
                            DR("ProductID").ToString()
        ThisLink.Text = DR("ProductName").ToString()
        ThisLink.ID = DR("ProductID").ToString()

        ' Add the content to the cell and the cell to the row. Place
        ' the row in the table.
        ProdCell.Controls.Add(ThisLink)
        ProdRow.Controls.Add(ProdCell)
```

```
        ProdTbl.Controls.Add(ProdRow)
    Next

    ' Add the table to the placeholder.
    phProducts.Controls.Add(ProdTbl)
End Sub
```

The example code begins by creating a connection to the database. It then uses a data adapter to obtain the list of products from the Products table. Finally, it creates and fills a dataset. Now the code can display the data. However, it must display the data as links.

The code creates a `Table` object, `ProdTbl`, next. The `ProdTbl` output is a standard HTML table. The example uses this table to organize the product links.

At this point, the code begins a loop where it processes every product entry in `DS.Tables(0)`. The code uses a `DataRow`, `DR`, to hold a single product entry. The loop begins by creating a row for the table and a single cell to place within that row. The cell will hold a single product link.

`ThisLink` is a `HyperLink` control that the code creates to hold a single product link. The product name appears in the `Text` property, the URL for the product appears in the `NavigateUrl` property, and the product identifier appears in the ID property. Notice the technique used to create the URL. The same page processes all products, even though the page will appear differently to the user depending on the product displayed. The query string holds the `ProdID` argument that contains a unique value, the product identifier from the database. Consequently, the `Products.aspx` page can identify which product to display based on its identifier.

Now that the code has all of the required objects, it builds a nested series of objects that result in a new table row. All of these controls create a standard HTML table, one tag at a time. The order in which you nest the various elements is important because the nesting affects the appearance of the table on screen. When the table is complete, the code places the resulting table into the `PlaceHolder` control, `phProducts`. The user sees a series of product links similar to the ones shown in Figure 16.15.

FIGURE 16.15
Creating page content on the fly lets you provide up-to-date information.

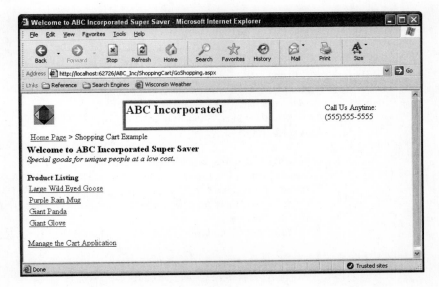

Displaying Product Specifics

Once the user selects an interesting item, you'll want to display specifics about it and encourage the user to place the item in the shopping cart. Trying to create a separate Web page for each product isn't the most efficient way to perform the task unless the individual products are extremely different. Consequently, the next step is to display information about the product based on its entry in the products database using a single generic Web page. Listing 16.7 shows how to perform this task using just the product identifier as a source of information. You'll find this example in the \ABC_Inc\ShoppingCart folder of the source code on the Sybex Web site as part of the Products.ASPX.VB file.

LISTING 16.7:   Showing Product Specifics

```vb
Private Sub Page_Load(ByVal sender As Object, _
                      ByVal e As System.EventArgs) Handles Me.Load

    ... Variable Declarations ...

    ' Determine the path for this application.
    ThisPath = Page.MapPath(Page.AppRelativeVirtualPath)
    ThisPath = ThisPath.Replace("\Products.aspx", "\")

    ' Create the database connection.
    Conn = New SqlConnection( _
        "Server=Main;" + _
        "Integrated Security=True;" + _
        "Database=ShoppingCartData;" + _
        "AttachDBFilename=" + _
            ThisPage + "Data\Shopping.mdf")

    ' Create the data adapter with the required select statement.
    Adapt = New SqlDataAdapter( _
        "SELECT * FROM Products WHERE ProductID=" + _
        Request.QueryString.GetValues("ProdID").GetValue(0).ToString(), _
        Conn)

    ' Fill the dataset.
    DS = New DataSet("ShoppingData")
    Adapt.Fill(DS)

    ' Display the data on screen.
    lblName.Text = DS.Tables(0).Rows(0).Item("ProductName").ToString()
    lblDescription.Text = _
        DS.Tables(0).Rows(0).Item("Description").ToString()
    lblPrice.Text = _
        "Your price today: " + _
```

```
        Format(Convert.ToDecimal( _
            DS.Tables(0).Rows(0).Item("Price")), "$#,##0.00")


        ' Store the product ID for later.
        hidProductID.Value = _
            DS.Tables(0).Rows(0).Item("ProductID").ToString()
    End Sub
```

The code begins by creating a database connection. It then creates a data adapter to access the product data. However, this request obtains just one product by including the WHERE clause. The query string, `Request.QueryString.GetValues("ProdID")`, contains the product identifier used to select the single record. Consequently, the code uses the `GetValue(0).ToString()` method to obtain this value in string form. Finally, the code creates a `DataSet`, DS, to hold the single record.

The display code shows how to implement a form view without using the `FormView` control. In this case, three `Labels` hold all of the information required for the buyer to make a decision. Notice that `lblPrice` requires special formatting. A raw `Decimal` value appears with four numbers after the decimal point and without a dollar (or other currency) sign. The `Format()` method accepts the `Decimal` value as input and outputs a formatted string, as shown in Figure 16.16.

Figure 16.16 includes a Buy This Item push button. When the user clicks Buy This Button, the application must make a decision. The user must log into the system to make a purchase. If the user isn't logged in, the `btnBuy_Click()` event handler calls a login page to accept the buyer's login information. Otherwise, it calls a Web page that places the item in the buyer's shopping cart, as shown in Listing 16.8. You'll find this example in the `\ABC_Inc\ShoppingCart` folder of the source code on the Sybex Web site as part of the `Products.ASPX.VB` file.

FIGURE 16.16
Display as many specifics as needed to make the sale.

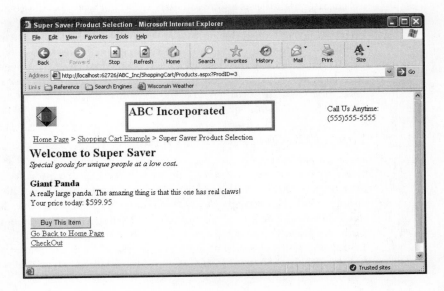

LISTING 16.8:   Adding Products to the Cart

```
Sub btnBuy_Click(ByVal sender As Object, ByVal e As System.EventArgs)
    ' Determine whether the user is logged in.
    If (Request.Cookies.Count = 0) Or _
        (Request.Cookies("UserID") Is Nothing) Then

        ' Get the user logged in.
        Response.Redirect( _
            "Login.ASPX?ProdID=" + _
        Request.QueryString.GetValues("ProdID").GetValue(0).ToString())

    Else
        ' Go directly to the shopping cart.
        Response.Redirect( _
            "ShoppingCart.ASPX?ProdID=" + _
        Request.QueryString.GetValues("ProdID").GetValue(0).ToString())

    End If
End Sub
```

Notice that the code uses the query string again to transfer information to the next page. In many cases, the query string represents the best method to use to transfer information because you can track what the user is doing with greater ease. Using a query string can reduce support costs.

The user identifier is another matter. You don't want this information displayed publicly. In fact, you don't even want this information transferred directly from page to page, so the application relies on a cookie to perform the job. However, the user might not have logged in yet, so the `Request` `.Cookies.Count` is 0, or the user might have stray cookies (odd, but it happens), so you also need to check for the user identifier using `Request.Cookies("UserID")`. When either of these conditions are true, the code redirects the buyer to the login page using the `Response.Redirect()` method. Otherwise, the code redirects the buyer to the shopping cart page. In both cases, the code passes the product identifier as part of the query string.

Logging the User into the System

It's important to create a secure environment for logging into the system. In fact, you might want to use Secure Sockets Layer (SSL) for everything in this chapter. For the sake of clarity, the example avoids some of the security you would normally use, including the user password. The example simply asks for a username. Type the wrong username—one that doesn't appear in the customer database—and you'll see an error Web page. Otherwise, the system redirects the buyer to the shopping cart page. The system creates a cookie to store the user identifier after a successful login. Listing 16.9 shows how all of these events take place in the example. You'll find this example in the `\ABC_Inc\ShoppingCart` folder of the source code on the Sybex Web site as part of the `Login.ASPX.VB` file.

LISTING 16.9:   Defining a User Login

```
Sub btnSubmit_Click(ByVal sender As Object, _
                    ByVal e As System.EventArgs)

    ... Variable Declarations ...

    ' Determine the path for this application.
    ThisPath = Page.MapPath(Page.AppRelativeVirtualPath)
    ThisPath = ThisPath.Replace("\Login.aspx", "\")

    ' Create the database connection.
    Conn = New SqlConnection( _
        "Server=Main;" + _
        "Integrated Security=True;" + _
        "Database=ShoppingCartData;" + _
        "AttachDBFilename=" + _
            ThisPage + "Data\Shopping.mdf")

    ' Create a request using the username.
    Adapt = New SqlDataAdapter( _
        "SELECT * FROM Customer WHERE Name='" + txtUserName.Text + "'", _
        Conn)

    ' Attempt to get the customer record.
    DS = New DataSet("CustomerData")
    Adapt.Fill(DS)

    ' Check for the CustomerID.
    If DS.Tables(0).Rows.Count = 0 Then

        ' Tell the user the account doesn't exist.
        Response.Redirect("LoginError.ASPX")

    Else

        ' Otherwise, place the CustomerID in a cookie and redirect the
        ' user to the shopping cart page.
        Response.Cookies.Add(New HttpCookie("UserID", _
                DS.Tables(0).Rows(0).Item("CustomerID").ToString()))
        Response.Redirect( _
            "ShoppingCart.ASPX?ProdID=" + _
        Request.QueryString.GetValues("ProdID").GetValue(0).ToString())
    End If

End Sub
```

The code begins by creating a connection to the database. It then creates a data adapter that queries the customer database for the username entered on the Web page in `txtUserName.Text`. The code creates a `DataSet`, DS, and fills it with the customer record. DS always contains a record when the customer exists, so checking `DS.Tables(0).Rows.Count` tells the code whether the customer is valid or not.

When the customer name is valid, the code creates a cookie to hold the user identifier using the `Response.Cookies.Add()` method. Because this cookie lacks an expiration date, the browser deletes it immediately after the session ends. After the code creates the cookie, it uses the `Response.Redirect()` method to send the buyer to the shopping cart. Notice that the code passes the same product identifier that the user chose on the products Web page shown in Figure 16.16.

Displaying the Shopping Basket

Eventually, the user will want to see a list of items in the shopping basket. Some Web sites force the user to go to a special location to perform this task. The example simply displays the shopping cart after the user selects each item—much as you would look into a shopping cart at the store after selecting an item from the shelf. The example doesn't use a very complex shopping cart display because other parts of the example have already shown how to display product information (see the "Displaying the Data" section of the chapter). Listing 16.10 shows how to create a simple shopping cart display Web page. You'll find this example in the \ABC_Inc\ShoppingCart folder of the source code on the Sybex Web site as part of the ShoppingCart.ASPX.VB file.

LISTING 16.10: Showing the Products

```
Private Sub Page_Load(ByVal sender As Object, _
                      ByVal e As System.EventArgs) Handles Me.Load

    ... Variable Declarations ...

    ' Don't perform any extra processing for a postback.
    If Page.IsPostBack Then
        Return
    End If

    If Not Request.QueryString.Item("ProdID") Is Nothing Then
        If Request.Cookies.Get("Products") Is Nothing Then
            ' Create an item list for just the current item.
            ItemList = Request.QueryString.Item("ProdID") + "=1"

            ' Create a cookie to include the new item.
            Response.Cookies.Add(New HttpCookie("Products", ItemList))
        Else
            ' Get the current items and combine with the new item.
```

```vbnet
            ItemList = Request.Cookies.Get("Products").Value + "&" + _
                    Request.QueryString.Item("ProdID") + "=1"

            ' Update the cookie to include the new item.
            Response.Cookies.Set(New HttpCookie("Products", ItemList))
        End If
    End If

    ' If there isn't anything to do, exit.
    If ItemList Is Nothing Then
        Return
    End If

    ' Create the dataset.
    DS = New DataSet("OrderedItems")
    DS.Tables.Add(New DataTable("Orders"))
    DS.Tables("Orders").Columns.Add("ProductID", GetType(Int32))
    DS.Tables("Orders").Columns.Add("Quantity", GetType(Int32))

    ' Split the string into a list of items.
    Items = ItemList.Split(Convert.ToChar("&"))
    lblItemNoteB.Text = Items.Length.ToString()

    ' Process each of the items.
    For Each Item In Items

        ' Split the ProductID from the Quantity.
        ItemSplit = Item.Split(Convert.ToChar("="))

        ' Create a new table entry.
        DR = DS.Tables("Orders").NewRow()

        ' Add the data.
        DR("ProductID") = Int32.Parse(ItemSplit(0))
        DR("Quantity") = Int32.Parse(ItemSplit(1))

        ' Place the data in the table.
        DS.Tables("Orders").Rows.Add(DR)
    Next

    ' Display the items on screen.
    gvItems.DataSource = DS
    gvItems.DataBind()
End Sub
```

It's important to remember that Web pages have no state information. Consequently, if you provide a shopping cart update function as part of the Page_Load() event handler, you must provide some means of detecting when a page load is part of a postback versus a product addition. The Page.IsPostBack property provides this information. When this value is true, the page loads as the result of a user click on a postback control on the Web page, rather than as a redirection from another Web page for a product addition. The code simply returns when this happens so that the buyer doesn't end up with extra items in their shopping cart.

When another Web page calls the shopping cart page, the shopping cart page expects a product identifier as part of the query string. However, a user might decide to call the page directly without the product identifier, so you must include code to detect this condition. If someone calls the page without a product identifier, then the ItemList is going to contain nothing and the code returns. You should probably add error-handling code, at this point, but the choice is up to you. The important factor is that the code doesn't add an item to the shopping cart.

The shopping cart list appears in a single cookie. The cookie uses a special encoding technique to hold the list of items in an amazingly small space. All you really need is the product identifier and the number of items the user wants (the example is hard wired for one item, but you can easily add code to allow other quantities). Therefore, a single item appears as a product number, followed by an equals sign, followed by the quantity, such as 2=1 for one of product number 2. The buyer hopefully purchases more than one item, so the code separates each item pair by an ampersand (&). Two items might appear as 2=1&3=1 for one of product number 2 and one of product number 3. Using this technique, an entire shopping cart can appear in just a few bytes on the user's hard drive.

You must also differentiate between the first product the buyer selects and those that follow. When the buyer adds the first item, Request.Cookies.Get("Products") won't have a value. The code creates a new string value with the single item. It then uses the Response.Cookies.Add() method to add the single item to the list of cookies. However, after the first product, the code must obtain the other items first, and then add the new item to ItemList. The code then uses the Response.Cookies .Set() method (notice the difference in method names) to change the existing cookie.

The Web page now has access to a list of shopping cart items in a string, which isn't very useful. The code creates a DataSet, DS, next to hold the shopping list for display purposes. Because there isn't a database to construct the table within DS, the code creates the table manually. Notice that the code creates the table first, and then adds the columns to the table.

Now it's time to break the data into pieces and store the information in DS. The ItemList.Split() method splits the string into an array of product strings (product identifier and quantity pair). It places the number of items into lblItemNoteB.Text so the buyer can see how many items appear in the shopping cart.

A For Each...Next loop processes the array items and splits them into value pairs using the Item.Split() method. Now that the code has the values split into individual pieces, it can create a new DataRow, DR, to hold the single row of data. The code places the individual data elements into DR, and then adds DR to DS using the DS.Tables("Orders").Rows.Add() method. The loop continues until it processes all of the shopping cart items.

Eventually, the code creates a dataset that contains all of the shopping cart items. It sets the gvItems.DataSource property to DS and displays the result using the gvItems.DataBind() method. Figure 16.17 shows a typical shopping cart display.

FIGURE 16.17

Display the content of the user's shopping basket before making the sale.

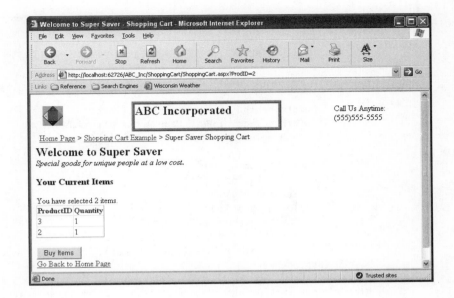

Making the Sale

The buyer eventually adds all of the required items to the shopping cart and wants to check out. The Buy Items pushbutton shown in Figure 16.17 lets the buyer place an order. Obviously, this act can lead to a wealth of additional pages where the buyer selects a credit card and performs other tasks. The example takes a shortcut and stores the credit card locally. Eventually, the application must store the order, which is the important part of making a purchase for the seller. Listing 16.11 shows the required code to store an order. You'll find this example in the \ABC_Inc\ShoppingCart folder of the source code on the Sybex Web site as part of the ShoppingCart.ASPX.VB file.

You can use a number of techniques for obtaining an order number or even set the database to provide it for you automatically. The example begins by creating a connection to the database, setting up an adapter to retrieve the current orders, and then looking at the last order in the list to determine the next order number in line. This technique works fine for simple Web sites, but you'll want to set up something better for a Web site with high volume. The last order number ends up in LastOrder.

Now that the code knows which order number to use, it creates an entry in the Orders table. All the code needs is the order number in LastOrder, the client identifier that appears in the UserID cookie, the current date, and a value of False for the OrderCompleted field.

After the code adds the new record to Orders (which tends to prevent another buyer from using the order number), it requests the list of products from Request.Cookies.Get("Products").Value. The code splits the values using the same method described in the "Displaying the Shopping Basket" section of the chapter. Although this might seem like unnecessary extra work, always remember that Web pages have no state. Consequently, the page doesn't know about the dataset created earlier in the Page_Load() event handler.

LISTING 16.11: Entering the Order

```
Sub btnBuy_Click(ByVal sender As Object, ByVal e As System.EventArgs)

    ... Variable Declarations ...

    ' Determine the path for this application.
    ThisPath = Page.MapPath(Page.AppRelativeVirtualPath)
    ThisPath = ThisPath.Replace("\ShoppingCart.aspx", "\")

    ' Open the connection.
    Conn = New SqlConnection( _
        "Server=Main;" + _
        "Integrated Security=True;" + _
        "Database=ShoppingCartData;" + _
        "AttachDBFilename=" + _
            ThisPath + "Data\Shopping.mdf")
    Conn.Open()

    ' Get the current records to determine the next available OrderID.
    Adapt = New SqlDataAdapter("SELECT * FROM Orders", Conn)

    ' Fill a dataset with the required information.
    DS = New DataSet("OrderData")
    Adapt.Fill(DS)

    LastOrder = _
        Convert.ToInt32( _
            DS.Tables(0).Rows(DS.Tables(0).Rows.Count - 1).Item(0))

    ' Create the order entry first.
    DoInsert = New SqlCommand( _
        "INSERT INTO [Orders] ([OrderID], [CustomerID], " + _
        "[OrderDate], [OrderCompleted]) VALUES (@OrderID, " + _
        "@CustomerID, @OrderDate, @OrderCompleted)", Conn)

    ' Create the OrderID parameter.
    Parm = DoInsert.CreateParameter()
    Parm.ParameterName = "OrderID"
    Parm.DbType = DbType.Int32
    Parm.Value = LastOrder + 1
    DoInsert.Parameters.Add(Parm)

    ... Lots of Parameters ...

    ' Perform the query.
```

```
Try
    DoInsert.ExecuteNonQuery()
Catch ex As Exception

End Try

' Get the list of items to process.
ItemList = Request.Cookies.Get("Products").Value

' Split the string into a list of items.
Items = ItemList.Split(Convert.ToChar("&"))

' Create one OrderItem entry for each product.
For Each Item In Items

    ' Split the ProductID from the Quantity.
    ItemSplit = Item.Split(Convert.ToChar("="))

    ... Database specific SQL Command ...

    ... Lots of Parameters ...

    ' Perform the query
    Try
        DoInsert.ExecuteNonQuery()
    Catch ex As Exception

    End Try

Next

' Close the connection when complete.
Conn.Close()

' Clear the Products cookie.
Response.Cookies.Remove("Products")

' Thank the buyer for the order.
Response.Redirect("Thanks.ASPX")
End Sub
```

Instead of creating a dataset to hold the data, the btnBuy_Click() method begins creating records in the OrderItems table—one for each shopping cart item in the list. The loop eventually ends and the code closes the connection to the database.

The next step is essential. The code removes the product list from the cookies so that the shopping cart is empty again using the Response.Cookies.Remove() method. If you fail to perform this task, the shopping cart will remain full until the buyer closes the browser and the browser deletes the cookie for you. Consequently, if the buyer visits your Web site again to get a missed item, the shopping cart will remain intact and you'll lose a sale (or experience the woes of an irate buyer who received two of everything). The code ends by redirecting the buyer to a thank you Web page.

Defining Your Development Goals

The shopping cart application in this chapter is basic, but it provides a good basis on which to build the online shopping experience of your dreams. You've discovered the benefits of creating the application as simply as possible—adding all of the constraints required to make sure the application works as you envisioned. No one wants a virus lurking around on their system after a cracker crashes the application, steals all the credit card information, and loses any sales visitors requested during the day. Online applications can become a nightmare, but you can manage it with careful planning. You really can make this shopping cart application work.

Of course, the first task you must perform is to determine whether someone has already done all of the required work. Yes, there's a nice feeling when you create something on your own, but most businesses don't have time to reinvent the wheel. If you can't find an application that does everything you need, you can look for third party add-on products to make your programming journey a little easier. The bottom line is that you should have fun with this application and make it as useful as you like, but make sure you spare yourself a little pain whenever possible too. At the very least, you should try this application out so you can put everything discussed in Chapters 1 through 15 together into a cohesive picture.

Chapter 17 starts a new topic—putting the finishing touches on your application. The least loved, but most needed, changes include debugging your application completely. Chapter 17 helps you discover that debugging isn't just a painful way to experience your application—you really do gain something by debugging the application fully. In many cases, the best gain is the knowledge you acquire about your application. Most applications are so complex that developers don't realize how hard they are to understand until they try to debug them. The resulting experience builds knowledge and helps the developer understand coding in a way that a well working application could never demonstrate.

Part 6

The Finishing Touches: Debug, Secure, and Distribute Your Application

In this part:

Chapter 17

Debugging Your Applications

Many developers view debugging as a task that "real programmers" don't need to perform. Unfortunately, debugging (the act of looking for errors in code) is something that everyone has to perform because no one writes perfect code. The programmers who do write nearly perfect code are the same programmers who rely on debugging, just as an author relies on good editors to help proof a manuscript.

Somewhere, hidden in a remote location you didn't think to check, is a bug (a coding error) that someone's going to encounter. The moment that the user encounters the bug, an error occurs and your application could crash and, in a worst-case scenario, take the rest of the system with it. Of course, bugs figure into other potential problems—just as bugs in Microsoft applications receive constant attention as crackers use them to gain access to the user's system. In short, debugging is an essential task to perform even if you do write the mythical perfect code.

Fortunately, Visual Web Developer provides a wealth of debugging aids for you. In many cases, you don't have to do anything special to make these aids work. The IDE simply provides them for you. Interpreting the various windows and debugging features can take a little time, so this chapter not only tells you that they exist but how to interpret them as well.

Visual Web Developer also provides two ranges of debugging. Localized debugging helps you find bugs on your system as you create the application. Remote debugging helps you locate bugs that only show up when someone accesses the application from another location. It's important to perform both ranges of checking to ensure your application runs as intended in all situations.

Understanding Why Debugging Is Important

Debugging is the only effective means you have for fully testing your application and preventing outside entities from using your application for nefarious reasons. Good testing methodologies rely on both expected and unanticipated input to expose bugs that you explore using debugging techniques. Users look at bugs as nonentities devoid of any characteristics. All a user knows is that a bug causes the program to crash and lose data. You can't afford to have that perspective. Bugs have personalities, in that they vary by:

- Type
- Cause
- Effect
- Severity
- Other factors that you include in your personal classification system

Smart developers rely on the bug personalities to define the presence and the cure for the bug. Debugging is the act of defining, detecting, categorizing, and fixing the bug. All newly developed applications have bugs—some of them are quite difficult to locate because they exist within the coding logic, some are simply a matter of not adding a required feature, and some exist as part of the development environment. For example, your application could experience an error because there's a bug in the .NET Framework—an error you must report if you have any hope of ever getting it fixed by Microsoft.

Bug classification determines when and where you'll detect the bug. It also defines how difficult the bug is to locate and the amount of help you can anticipate receiving from the IDE. You can classify bugs into the following four types:

◆ Syntax

◆ Compile

◆ Runtime

◆ Semantic

The following sections describe the four bug classifications and help you understand how each of them affects your debugging efforts. More importantly, these classifications provide you with a better idea of just why debugging is so important.

TIP   The best way to find bugs is to know your coding style. Keeping notes helps you understand patterns in your programming so that you can correct techniques that lead to bugs. More importantly, understanding your personal style helps you develop techniques for finding bugs based on past mistakes. Knowing what you did in the past can help you locate and squash bugs today.

Considering Syntax Errors

Syntax errors are the easiest errors to avoid but are also some of the hardest errors to find. A syntax error can include a spelling mistake, misuse of punctuation, or a misuse of a language element. When you forget to include an `End If` for an `If...Then` statement in Visual Basic, it's a syntax error. Likewise, C# developers encounter syntax errors if they fail to provide a closing curly brace. Syntax errors even occur in HTML. Forgetting a closing tag can cause a syntax error in many cases. The idea is that syntax errors occur when the code is misspelled, ill formed (lacking a required element), or used incorrectly in other ways.

Typos are a common syntax error. They're especially hard to find when you make them in variable names. For example, all programming languages view `MySpecialVariable` and `MySpecialVaraible` as two different variables, but you might miss the typing error. You can rely on Visual Web Developer to find most variable typos for you as you write your code.

NOTE   Visual Basic developers will remember the `Option Explicit` declaration from previous versions. This declaration still exists, but the IDE now adds it by default. You'd have to tell the IDE not to add this declaration to the code. One reason the IDE adds this feature automatically is to reduce the probability of a typo existing within the code.

You can easily miss some of the subtle aids to locating syntax errors if you don't view tasks that the IDE performs carefully enough. The balloon help shown in Figure 17.1 for the `Request.MapPath()` function provides a cue that you could miss. The IDE displays the balloon help shown in the figure only when it recognizes the function name that you type. When you don't see the balloon help, it's a cue that the IDE doesn't recognize the function name, and you need to look at your code. You might find that you haven't included a reference or a required statement, but you can also use this method to detect typos and other syntax errors.

TIP No matter what you do, a few syntax errors can slip by and cause bugs in your program. You can look at the errors for hours and not actually see them because you've worked with the code for so long. Asking someone else to look at your code often helps because that person isn't familiar with the code. Make sure that you ask someone with the same or better programming skills than you have to ensure that they understand your code. It's also essential that you comment your code heavily to help the other person understand what it's supposed to do.

Syntax errors also include errors in logic (the construction of expressions in your program). You can create a loop that processes the loop structure statements once too often or not often enough. An If statement can use an expression that works most of the time but isn't quite right, so it doesn't produce the correct result all of the time. Code with logic errors runs because the IDE and compiler don't know that the expression is incorrect. The only way to find this kind of syntax error is to debug the program. See the "Using the Visual Web Developer 2005 Debugging Features" section of the chapter for details.

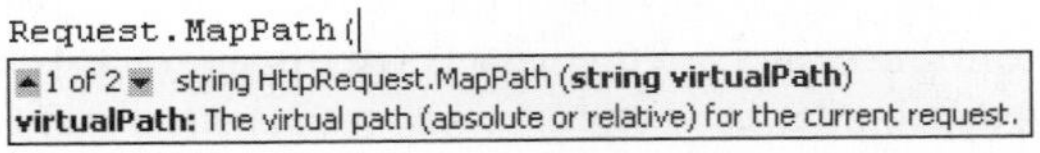

FIGURE 17.1

Balloon help assists you in locating syntax errors in your code.

```
Request.MapPath (
  ◢ 1 of 2 ◣   string HttpRequest.MapPath (string virtualPath)
  virtualPath: The virtual path (absolute or relative) for the current request.
```

Considering Compile Errors

The .NET language compiler contains a syntax checker, among other features. The IDE uses the compiler to look for errors that prevent the program from running properly. For example, when working with Visual Basic, you might create an If...Then statement and not include the corresponding End If statement. The syntax-checking portion of the compiler runs constantly, so the IDE finds some mistakes almost immediately after you make them.

The IDE uses the compiler to find many of the syntax errors that you make and displays an error indication similar to the one shown in Figure 17.2. When you create a syntax error, the IDE displays the location with a squiggly underline, normally in red. Hover the mouse over the error to see what it is, as shown in Figure 17.2.

NOTE The Visual Web Developer IDE uses different colors to display various error conditions. For example, the default compiler error uses a blue squiggly underline. The color of the underline provides another clue as to the kind of error that you made and helps you fix it more quickly. It's also important to know that you can modify the colors that the IDE uses to highlight errors. Choose the Tools ➢ Options command to display the Options dialog box. The Environment\Fonts and Colors folder contains the color options for errors. Select the error type that you want to change in the Display Items list and modify the presentation as needed.

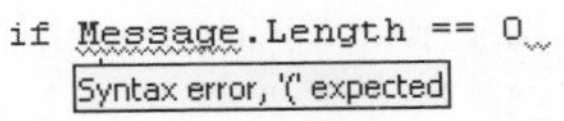

FIGURE 17.2

The IDE displays some syntax errors.

```
if Message.Length == 0
  Syntax error, '(' expected
```

Missing elements are another syntax error that the IDE finds with relative ease. For example, when working with Visual Basic, if you fail to include an `End If` for an `If...Then` statement, the IDE always finds it and displays an error presentation similar to the one shown in Figure 17.2. However, in some cases, the IDE won't find syntax errors until you try to run the program. In addition, the IDE might not always find the precise error location—sometimes it highlights another area of the block where a syntax error occurs. Fortunately, these situations are rare, so you'll generally get great help from the IDE when it comes to syntax errors.

The compiler also finds many of the punctuation errors that you can make in your code. When a line of Visual Basic code becomes too long, and you try to move to the next line without adding a continuation character, the compiler notices the error and tells you about it. On the other hand, since C# doesn't require the use of continuation characters, you won't see this kind of error when working with the C# language. The assistance you get is language specific based on the errors that the syntax-checking feature of the compiler is designed to recognize. The complier also notes missing periods between elements of a statement or missing parentheses from function calls.

Considering Runtime Errors

Some errors aren't the result of poor coding practices. Runtime errors happen when something outside your application is incorrect. A disk access request can fail, or the user can type the wrong information. In both cases, the application environment causes the problem. Your application code is correct, but the program still fails because of this external error.

Runtime errors are the reason why many large companies such as Microsoft run beta programs. (A beta program is a vendor-sponsored method of getting a program before the developers have finished it for the purpose of testing and evaluation.) A large base of users can help you find runtime errors that depend on a particular machine configuration or a specific kind of user entry technique.

NOTE   Don't confuse runtime errors with errors that occur at runtime. You can observe a syntax error at runtime. The fact that the syntax error occurs when the application is running doesn't mean that the error suddenly changes into a runtime error. Most errors can occur while the application is running (at runtime), but runtime errors (as a category) always occur when the application is running.

Unlike other kinds of errors, the IDE never provides help with runtime errors and it's not even very easy to anticipate them. Code that you know will work well can still fail in the runtime environment because this environment is so uncertain. You can trap runtime errors or change the program flow to ensure that they don't happen, but the fact remains that you won't see a runtime error until you run your application on enough machines to expose it. Unfortunately, you'll find that while runtime errors are hard for you to find, crackers are drawn to them as bugs are to light. Coding defensively—anticipating whatever can go wrong will—is the only way to overcome this particular kind of error. For example, consider this code.

```
void btnTest_Click(object sender, EventArgs e)
{
    TextReader  OpenFile;   // References the Open File.

    // Open the file for reading.
    OpenFile = new StreamReader("DoesNotExist");
```

```
        // Display the contents on screen.
        txtOutput.Text = OpenFile.ReadToEnd();

        // Close the file after reading it.
        OpenFile.Close();
    }
```

You won't find anything wrong with this code. It should work as presented as long as the requested file exists. However, because the file doesn't exist, the application displays the error shown in Figure 17.3 when the user clicks btnTest.

The error isn't in the code—it's in the environment. Because the file DoesNotExist is missing, the application experiences an error. You can trap such an error using the technique shown here.

```
void btnTest_Click(object sender, EventArgs e)
{
    TextReader  OpenFile;    // References the Open File.

    try
    {
        // Open the file for reading.
        OpenFile = new StreamReader("DoesNotExist");

        // Display the contents on screen.
        txtOutput.Text = OpenFile.ReadToEnd();

        // Close the file after reading it.
        OpenFile.Close();
    }
    catch (FileNotFoundException FNFE)
    {
        txtOutput.Text = "The file wasn't found.";
    }
    catch (Exception ex)
    {
        txtOutput.Text = "Unexpected Exception: " +
            ex.Message;
    }
}
```

The difference, in this case, is that the code traps the error. The try...catch statement tells the compiler that you expect one or more errors to occur. Each error is an exception that the catch portion of the statement handles. The FileNotFoundException exception handles the specific case where a file is missing. However, you don't know that this is the only exception that will occur. You could rely on the .NET Framework documentation to tell you about every error, test every possible error condition, pass the error on to the next level, or simply provide a generic exception handler for the Exception class, as shown in the listing. The point is that when you run the code this time, the user will see a nice error message, rather than the output shown in Figure 17.3. More importantly, the application won't crash—it recovers from the runtime error.

FIGURE 17.3
Runtime errors occur because the environment is incorrect.

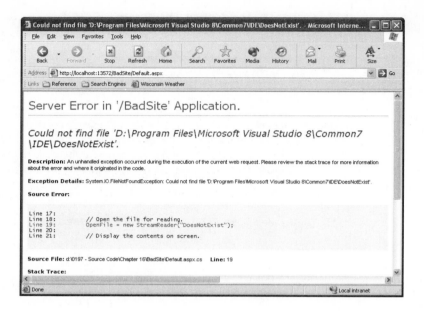

Considering Semantic Errors

A particularly difficult error to find and understand is the semantic error, which is an error that happens when the application code and logic are correct, but the meaning behind the code isn't what you intended. For example, you could use a Do...Until loop in place of a Do...While loop when writing Visual Basic code. Even if the code is correct and you use the correct logic, the code won't produce the result that you expected because the meaning of a Do...Until loop is different from a Do...While loop.

The meaning that you assign to your code has to match the words that you use to write the code. Just as a good book uses precise terms, a good program relies on precise statements to ensure that compiler understands what you want to do.

Introducing semantic errors in subtle ways is easy. Writing an equation the wrong way can result in output errors. When you use the wrong equation to determine the next step in a loop, the problem becomes worse because the error looks like a syntax or runtime error. The steps between loops or the expression used to make a decision are very important. The most common error is leaving the parentheses out of an equation. The application interprets $1 + 2 * 3$ as 7, but $(1 + 2) * 3$ as 9. The missing parentheses are easy to miss when you frantically search for an error.

In many cases, you won't even receive a notification such as the one shown in Figure 17.3 when a semantic error occurs. The application appears to work fine, but the output is incorrect. Unless you specifically test for incorrect output, the application could enter the production environment flawed. One method of testing for semantic errors is to include Debug.Assert() method calls within your code, as shown here:

```
void btnTest2_Click(object sender, EventArgs e)
{
    Int32 Test = 1 + 2 * 3;
    Debug.Assert(Test == 9, "Test Should Equal 9!");
}
```

This method appears in the `System.Diagnostics` namespace, so you'll need to add the additional reference to your code. When the runtime environment encounters the `Assert()`, it determines whether the test condition is true. When the condition is false, you'll see an error dialog box similar to the one shown in Figure 17.4. The dialog box tells you about the error and asks whether you want to proceed. The point is that the error is no longer hidden—you can find it based on your expectations for the code.

FIGURE 17.4

Use the *Assert()* method to locate semantic errors in your code.

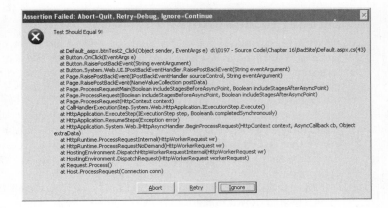

Using the Error Lookup Utility

Corporate applications tend toward the complex. You probably won't create many pure .NET applications at the outset—most corporations have far too much invested in Win32 code to rewrite applications completely, so it's important to consider some of the complications you'll encounter. Generally, you won't need the Error Lookup utility unless you're working with the Win32 API using PInvoke. However, it pays to know about this utility because there are times when you receive an odd error and suspect the underlying cause is something happening with Windows itself. You'll find the Error Lookup utility in the `\Program Files\Microsoft Visual Studio 8\Common7\Tools` folder as `ErrLook.EXE`. Figure 17.5 shows what this utility looks like.

To use this utility, type the error number in the Value field and click Look Up. You'll see the error in human readable form in the Error Message field. Whether the error makes sense depends on whether it originated from Windows or .NET. When you see a message that doesn't make sense for Windows, then you'll want to trace it down to a .NET cause.

FIGURE 17.5

Use the Error Lookup utility to learn more about some of those mysterious Windows errors.

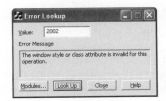

One of the Error Lookup utility features that many developers fail to use is adding other modules. Any module that provides error information using the standard Win32 format is searchable by this utility. Of course, the assumption is that your error actually resides in the module and that the developer who created it didn't take any shortcuts. To add a new module, click Modules. Type the name of the module in the Module Name field of the Additional Modules for Error Searching dialog box, such as AdvAPI32.DLL, and click Add. When you type an error number, you'll see any entries in the additional modules.

Locating Hidden Errors

It's entirely possible for your application to contain a hidden error—one that no one will ever see and you might not even notice. The ABC Incorporated Web site contains one such error as part of the indexing page located in the \ABC_Inc\Searches\CustomSearch folder. When you run this application normally, you'll see a list of pages that won't load. The Web site includes only one such entry—the ProductQuery.ASPX Web page located in the \ABC_Inc\Feedback\HiddenFields folder. If the application didn't include the list of failed pages, you would never notice the problem at all—Visual Studio doesn't generate an error during compilation and the application runs without displaying an error either. In fact, you can search the code and not find any error in it either. The issue is one of how the indexing application loads the Web pages. Figure 17.6 shows the Exception Helper pop-up that appears only when you run the example using the debugger.

Notice that links provided on this pop-up. Click View Detail and you'll see a complete description of the error as shown in Figure 17.7. Click Enable Editing and the Exception Helper pop-up disappears. The IDE highlights the line of code that caused the problem and you can edit it as needed. You can display the Exception Helper pop-up again by selecting its entry from the SmartTag that appears when you hover the mouse over the highlighted code. Finally, you can copy the exception to the clipboard so you can place it in a log or document the error using some other technique.

Theoretically, the bug isn't a real error; at least not the in the common use of the term. The error occurs because the Web page is expecting input that a Web page would normally provide, but the indexing application doesn't. Here's the problem code.

```
' Verify the information was sent.
If strProdName.Length = 0 Then

    'Raise an error.
    Throw New ArgumentNullException("hidProductName")
End If
```

This is actually error trapping code that normally serves a useful purpose. It alerts the caller to a problem in the input. However, it gets in the way when you load the Web page for indexing. This is an example of a hidden bug—one that you might not ever see, but could cause a problem for your Web site. In this case, the Web page isn't indexed, so no one can find it using the custom search application.

You need a two-part solution to fix this problem. The indexing routine isn't concerned about any of the data on the Web page—just the three <meta> tags that the Web page must contain to appear within the index. Consequently, you can add code that includes the <meta> tags, but stops processing immediately afterward for pages that require specialized input to display that information. Begin by adding request header code to the `GetWebPage()` method of the `IndexPages.ASPX.VB` file located in the `\ABC_Inc\Searches\CustomSearch` folder of the source code as shown here.

```
' Add a session variable so that the Web page knows this
' is an index.
PgRequest.Headers.Add("Indexing:True")
```

Because this request header isn't included for any other request than indexing, it's unique and you can check for it in the Web page. All you need to do now is add this little snippet of code to Web pages, such as the `ProductQuery.ASPX` Web page, to bypass the normal processing so the indexing routine sees the `<meta>` tags, but nothing else.

```
' Verify that we aren't indexing the page.
If Not Request.Headers("Indexing") Is Nothing Then
    Return
End If
```

In this case, the code checks for the presence of the unique header. When the header exists, the code simply returns without creating the page content. However, you need to make sure that this code appears after any `<meta>` tag code because the Web page still has to produce the `<meta>` tags for indexing purposes.

FIGURE 17.6
Visual Studio provides a pop-up that automatically appears when unhandled exceptions occur.

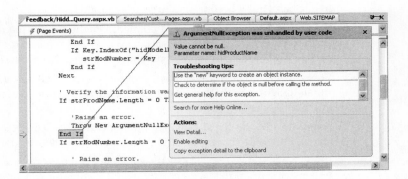

FIGURE 17.7
Discover the complete details of any unhandled exception that occurs using this dialog box.

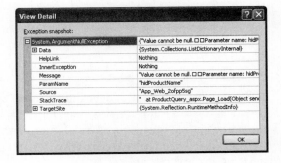

Using the Visual Web Developer 2005 Debugging Features

You don't have to rely on code alone to find the bugs in your code. Once you know that a bug exists, you can use various resources that the IDE provides to locate the bug. However, locating the bug doesn't always mean a lot. After all, you might see the bug without really knowing how to fix it. The IDE also provides the resources you need to test alternative code or change values. The following sections describe the resources that the IDE provides for testing your code in the form of visual aids.

Using the Debug Toolbar

The Debug toolbar, as seen in Figure 17.8, automatically appears every time you start an application for debugging. However, many developers display it all the time so they can start the application for debugging without using the menu. This toolbar contains all of the features needed to step through code one statement at a time. The following list describes the toolbar features.

Windows   Displays a list of debugging windows. This isn't a complete list of windows—only the currently available debugging windows. For example, when you're not in debugging mode, you'll only see the Immediate window—the Locals, Watch, and Call Stack window entries only appear while in debug mode.

Hexadecimal Display   Changes the numbers in the various debugging windows from decimal to hexadecimal. The change in base lets you switch between numbers that most humans understand very well to those that the computer understands. Sometimes you can't easily see an error in one base, but it becomes quite clear in another.

Step Out   Moves the statement pointer from the current method to the next statement in the method that called it. The application executes all of the statements between the current position and the end of the current method without forcing you to step through the individual steps.

Step Over   Moves the statement pointer over a called method. The application executes all of the statements within the called method, but you don't have to step through them one statement at a time.

Step Into   Moves the statement pointer into the called method and places the pointer on the first statement within that method. This feature lets you see the details of a called method.

Show Next Statement   Places the statement pointer on the next statement that the application will execute or on the current statement if it contains executable code. Use this feature to see where the statement pointer will go next when you see a series of structure or variable declarations statements.

Restart   Restarts the current application. The debugger resets all variables to their pre-execution state. Use this option when you want to start the application over without executing the remaining statements.

Stop Debugging   Stops the debugger. Use this option to return the IDE to editing mode.

Break All   Places the IDE in debug mode for all of the currently attached applications. In most cases, you use this feature when debugging multithreaded applications.

Start or Continue   Starts the application. The IDE is still in debug mode and it will stop application execution when you next click Break All or the IDE encounters a breakpoint (a special stop indicator) in the code.

FIGURE 17.8
The Debug toolbar contains a number of features to make runtime debugging easier.

Stop Debugging
Step Over
Start or Continue
Show Next Statement
Hexadecimal Display
Debug
Hex
Break All
Step Into
Windows
Restart
Step Out

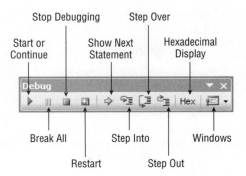

Using the Immediate Window

The Immediate window is one of the most useful debugging features that Visual Web Developer has to offer. You can use this feature to test the validity of statements or check the value of variables. It also lets you change the value of variables or the properties of objects while debugging. Consequently, you can use this feature to perform "what if" analysis of your code while looking for an answer to coding problems. Figure 17.9 shows a typical view of the Immediate window with a query in place.

TIP You can execute single commands to the IDE using the Immediate window. Simply type the > (greater than) symbol and start typing the command you want to issue. For example, if you want to open a file, you could type **`>File.OpenFile`** and press Enter. When you type `File` without the > symbol, IntelliSense displays the members of the File class, not the File menu. However, if you want to issue a number of commands, you should use the Command window instead.

The Immediate window provides full IntelliSense support. Whenever you type a `.` (period), IntelliSense shows the members of the object that you're working with. This means that you can continue to work with objects even while debugging the application and perform additional tests to see what works best.

Changing the values of variables is one of the tasks you'll perform most often. To change a variable or property value, simply type the variable or property name and set it equal to a value. For example, if you wanted to change the `txtOutput.Text` property value to Hello, you'd type **`txtOutput.Text = "Hello"`** and press Enter. The Intermediate window displays the new property value on the line after the entry you make.

FIGURE 17.9
Use the Immediate window to test alternative values and code.

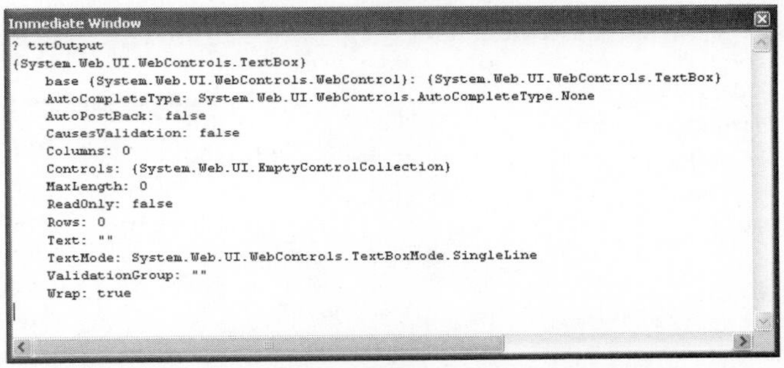

Immediate Window
? txtOutput
{System.Web.UI.WebControls.TextBox}
base {System.Web.UI.WebControls.WebControl}: {System.Web.UI.WebControls.TextBox}
AutoCompleteType: System.Web.UI.WebControls.AutoCompleteType.None
AutoPostBack: false
CausesValidation: false
Columns: 0
Controls: {System.Web.UI.EmptyControlCollection}
MaxLength: 0
ReadOnly: false
Rows: 0
Text: ""
TextMode: System.Web.UI.WebControls.TextBoxMode.SingleLine
ValidationGroup: ""
Wrap: true

It's also possible to evaluate any expression within the Immediate window. For example, you could type **? txtOutput.Text == "Hello"** and press Enter to determine whether the txtOutput.Text property contains the value Hello. Notice the addition of the ? to the entry. The ? tells the IDE that you want to perform a query, rather than work directly with the variable. The expression must appear in the correct form, as well, for the language you're using. For example, C# requires a == (double equals sign) for Boolean expressions.

The ? is actually shorthand for the Debug.Print() method. You can use any of the Debug class methods within the Immediate window without adding the > symbol. However, if you want to issue a debug command, then you must add the > symbol.

The Immediate window also supports the use of Mark mode. You use this mode to work with any previously issued command. For example, if you didn't type quite what you wanted to type for a previous command, simply highlight the incorrect part of the command and start typing the correction. The Immediate window automatically copies the old command as you type the changes—reducing the amount of typing you must perform to issue any command.

Eventually, you'll end up with many entries in the Immediate window. To remove old entries, right-click the window and choose Clear All from the context menu. You'll also notice that this menu contains options for cutting, copying, and pasting entries in the Immediate window.

Using the Command Window

The Command window has a lot in common with the Immediate window. For example, you can evaluate variables and display their values (see the "Using the Immediate Window" section for details). However, the main purpose for using the Command window is to issue commands. For example, type the word File and you'll see a list of associated File menu commands, as shown in Figure 17.10. Notice that the Command window always provides a > symbol on every line that you use to type commands.

Sometimes it's inconvenient to move your hands from the keyboard to display another window. You can switch windows by using a command. For example, if you want to move from the Command window to the Immediate window, type **immed** and press Enter. Here's a list of shortcuts for moving between windows.

- callstack (Call Stack window)
- cmd (Command window)
- immed (Immediate window)
- locals (Locals window)
- View.Output (Output window)
- watch (Watch window)

FIGURE 17.10
Output commands to the IDE using the Command window.

Using the Output Window

The Output window performs a number of important tasks. You'll actually see two versions of this window. The first is the Build output shown in Figure 17.11. The second, Debug, contains the output from various startup and debugging tasks. Use the Show Output From drop-down list to change the views.

Figure 17.11 shows a successful build. You'll also find any errors that the application encounters during the build process in this view. Double-clicking on any error in the list takes you to the location of the errant code. Consequently, you can build the application and then visit each error the compiler finds in turn.

The Debug view of the Output window always contains startup messages when you start the application. Figure 17.12 shows a typical example of the messages that Visual Web Developer generates for a simple application. Looking through the list of loaded entries can help you determine the source of startup failures or other problems later during application execution. By following the list of startup entries, you can determine errors such as loading the wrong version of a referenced DLL.

The Output window also displays debugging messages that you produce using a number of Debug class methods. You place these entries in your code and they execute only when you debug your application. Figure 17.13 displays some entries produced using the essential Debug class methods.

FIGURE 17.11

Verify the results of a build operation using the Output window.

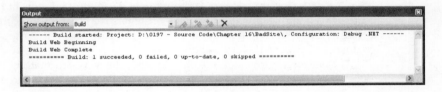

FIGURE 17.12

See debugging statements as your code executes to determine how events take place.

FIGURE 17.13

Add debugging statements to your code to see events and code flow.

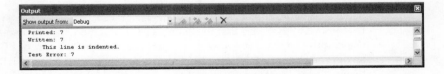

To produce these entries, you need to include special code in your application. Here are the entries used to produce the output in Figure 17.10.

```
// Display the value of the variable.
Debug.Print("Printed: " + Test.ToString());
Debug.WriteLine("Written: " + Test.ToString());

// Display an indented line.
Debug.Indent();
Debug.Print("This line is indented.");
Debug.Unindent();

// Display a line only when a specific condition exists.
Debug.WriteLineIf(Test <= 9, Test, "Test Error");
```

The `Debug.Print()` and `Debug.WriteLine()` methods work about the same from an Output window perspective. The difference comes in the flexibility that each method offers. When using `Debug.Print()`, you can provide a list of values as an array in the second argument. On the other hand, the `Debug.WriteLine()` method lets you specify an error category as the second argument. Neither of the second arguments shows up in the Output window but do affect any listeners you create for your application (writing debug listeners is a complex topic that won't appear in this book). Note that there's also a `Debug.Write()` method you can use to write several entries on the same line, rather than placing them on separate lines.

The Output window doesn't allow much in the way of formatting, but you can indent text to make the various levels easier to see. For example, you might want to indent each layer of calls in your application. Use the `Debug.Indent()` and `Debug.Unindent()` methods to add and remove levels from the output. You can use the `Debug.IndentLevel` property to determine the current indent level of your code. The `Debug.IndentSize` property lets you set the number of spaces between each indent level.

Sometimes you don't want to display a debug statement every time in the Output window. You can control debug statement output using the `Debug.WriteLineIf()` method. The first argument is an expression that controls the display of the debug statement. Whenever the statement is true, the debug statement appears in the Output window. Note that you also have access to the `Debug.WriteIf()` method when you want to display the output on the same line.

The "Considering Semantic Errors" section of the chapter discusses the use of the `Debug.Assert()` method. You can also create a condition where the assertion always occurs using the `Debug.Fail()` method, as shown here.

```
// Display a failure.
Debug.Fail("It Failed", "This is a failure message.")
```

It's important to realize that the `Debug.Fail()` method always displays an assertion, so you can't use it in the regular code flow. However, you can use it as part of a `Catch` statement or as part of an optional code flow. Figure 17.14 shows typical output from both the `Debug.Assert()` and `Debug.Fail()` methods. Notice that this content looks very much like the information in the dialog box shown in Figure 17.4, so the Output window provides the means for you to preserve the assertion information.

FIGURE 17.14
Assertions and failures also appear in the Output window.

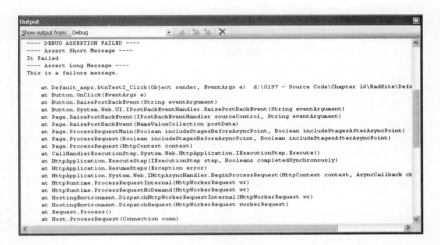

Using the Error List Window

Visual Web Developer provides a number of methods for managing application errors. The Error List window presents a list of the problems in your code. The window separates the entries into errors, warnings, and messages, as shown in Figure 17.15. Notice that the window shows the number of each entry type at the top of the window. In addition, you can set the window to display any combination of errors, warnings, and messages by clicking on the appropriate entry at the top.

The Error List window is always active when you're writing your code. Whenever you make a mistake that the system catches as you type, it appears in the Error List window. In addition, the IDE adds any errors that it finds when it compiles your code to the list. Consequently, you can simply go down the list to locate the current problems in your code. Double-click on any entry and the IDE takes you to that error in the code.

It's easy to reconfigure the Error List window to meet your specific needs. All of the configuration options appear on the context menu that appears when you right-click the window. Beside the options that you expect to see on the list such as Copy and Delete, you'll also find the Sort By and Show Columns submenus. These submenus define how the window orders any error entries and what information it displays about them. You can sort the entries by priority, category, default order, description, file, line, column, and project. The displayable columns include category, default order, description, file, line, column, and project (the IDE always displays the error priority).

FIGURE 17.15
Determine which errors the IDE has detected using the Error List window.

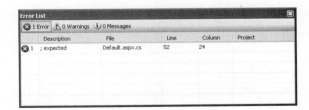

Using the Locals Window

The Locals window helps you see the active state of local application variables. This window contains a list of all the variables associated with the current method or property. It doesn't show variables outside the current scope. For example, if you have a global variable, it won't appear in this window even if the current method or property performs some task with the variable. You'll see the values of any arguments used to call the method. The Locals window shows the variable name, value, and type, as shown in Figure 17.16.

The entries show the local variables for the btnTest2_Click() method shown in Listing 17.1. The sender and e variables are part of the arguments for the method, while Test appears within the method. Click the plus sign next to any variable and you'll see the properties and objects it contains (if any). You'll find this example in the \Chapter 17\BadSite folder of the source code on the Sybex Web site.

Notice that some of the variables listed in Figure 17.16 contain magnifying glass icons in the Value column. When you click this icon, you'll see a list of Visualizers, including the text, XML, and HTML Visualizers shown in the figure. Select any of the Visualizers from the list and you'll see the value displayed in that format. Using Visualizers helps you see the data in a specific format. This technology is especially helpful when working with Visual Web Developer because you often run into XML data embedded within an object.

LISTING 17.1:   Exploring the Locals Window

```
void btnTest2_Click(object sender, EventArgs e)
{
    // Create a variable based on a math expression.
    Int32 Test = 1 + 2 * 3;

    // Display the value of the variable.
    Debug.Print("Printed: " + Test.ToString());
    Debug.WriteLine("Written: " + Test.ToString());

    // Display an indented line.
    Debug.Indent();
    Debug.Print("This line is indented.");
    Debug.Unindent();

    // Display a line only when a specific condition exists.
    Debug.WriteLineIf(Test <= 9, Test, "Test Error");

    // Display a failure.
    Debug.Fail("It Failed", "This is a failure message.");

    // Ensure the value is correct.
    Debug.Assert(Test == 9, "Test Should Equal 9!");
}
```

Depending on how you set up a method, you might see some interesting calling arguments. In this case, `sender` is a `Button` control—the one handled by this event handler. This means you have access to a global variable, `btnTest2`, at a local level.

Figure 17.16 shows one local variable that isn't declared anywhere—`this`. Every method and property has access to the `this` object, which refers to the local application. The `this` object contains a reference to the application as a whole and everything that the application contains, as shown in Figure 17.17. Consequently, even though the Locals window legitimately accesses only local variables, the `this` object provides a view of the application as a whole.

The best way to use the Locals window is to view just local variables and occasionally glimpse the application. When you need to view specific variables, especially those at the global level, then you really need to use the Watch window described in the "Using the Watch Window" section of the chapter. The Watch window not only lets you reduce the number of items you have to track but also lets you organize the variables so that you can perform debugging with greater ease.

FIGURE 17.16

All of the local variables appear in the Locals window.

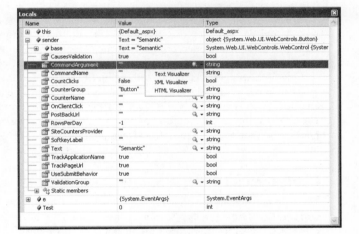

FIGURE 17.17

Every local method has access to the *this* object, which contains access to some global elements.

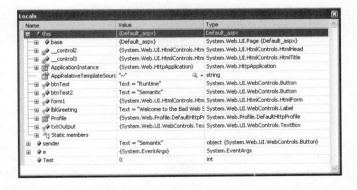

Using the Watch Window

The Watch window provides a custom view of variables, expressions, and objects within your application. You'll place variables, expressions, and objects that you want to watch in this window. The easiest way to do this is to highlight the code in question and drag it to the window. The Watch window also allows you to type variables and functions by hand. You can create multiple Watch windows for a given debugging session. The Watch window shows the variable name, value, and type, just like the Locals window, so the two windows operate similarly. Figure 17.18 shows a typical view of the Watch window.

In this case, you see a local variable, an object on a form, a class with static properties, and an expression. The local variable is also available in the Locals window, but these other entries help you understand why the Watch window is so useful. For example, when working with objects, you don't need to drill down to find it in the `this` object. In fact, you can go further than shown in Figure 17.18. When you want to view just one property in the object, you can use dot syntax within the Watch window to see it directly—you could see the `txtOutput.Text` property directly, rather than have to find it in a list of properties.

The ability to create expressions in the Watch window is also important. You can look for important changes as you step through the application. For example, you could use this method to determine precisely when one variable becomes greater than another variable in the code. The changes signify the point where an error occurs in the execution of your application.

One of the biggest problems with using the Watch window is that you can develop tunnel vision. You can become so focused on the variables that you choose to watch that you miss clues to resolving an application error. That's why the Locals window is so important. This window shows you all of the variables for the current method or property. When you begin feeling that you're missing something—it's usually time to move from the Watch window to the Locals window long enough to see if anything is happening within the application that you need to know about.

Using the Call Stack Window

The Call Stack window answers the question of how the application got to the current point of execution. Every time the application makes a call, CLR adds the call to the call stack. When the call returns, CLR removes it from the call stack. In short, the Call Stack window shows you a list of pending calls, which tells you how the application accessed the current function, as shown in Figure 17.19.

The call at the top of the stack is the current call. As you progress down the list, you get closer to the original calling point. In this case, the original caller is the `btnVisit_Click()` event handler. However, that entry contains a lot more useful information, as shown here (the entry normally appears on one line, but is split due to space requirements).

```
hpvr_og5.dll!Default_aspx.btnVisit_Click(object sender = Text = "Call Methods",
➡System.EventArgs e = {System.EventArgs}) Line 66 + 0x8 bytes
```

The entry begins by telling you the name of the DLL, `hpvr_og5.dll`. You won't recognize the name of this DLL because Visual Web Developer generates it for you when you compile the application. The `Default_aspx` Web page appears within the DLL, which contains the `btnVisit_Click()` method. This method requires two input arguments. Notice that the call stack tells you the input argument type, name, and default value. For example, `sender` is an `object` type that has a default `Text` property value of Call Methods. The entry ends with the location of the `btnVisit_Click()` method within the source file and the number of bytes that this method requires.

Sometimes it's not enough to look at the Call Stack window. Fortunately, double-clicking an entry takes you to that method within the source code. Viewing the code doesn't alter the call stack, nor does it change the order of execution, but it does help you understand the program flow better.

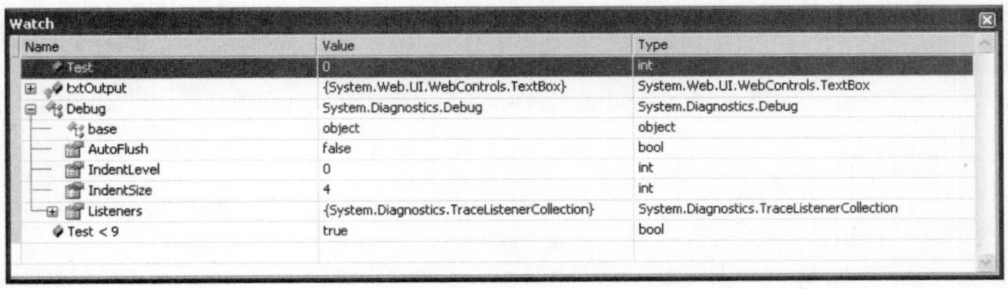

FIGURE 17.18
Watching the values and objects in your application can help track tricky bugs.

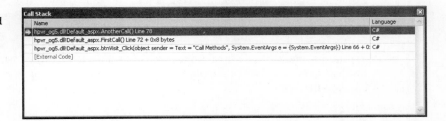

FIGURE 17.19
Determine the path used to reach a method using the Call Stack window.

Managing Breakpoints

Knowing how to use the windows isn't helpful until you know how to stop the application at precise points of execution. One way to stop application execution is to click Break All on the Debug toolbar shown in Figure 17.8. However, this method isn't very precise. Breakpoints address the need for precision. Whenever your application is running in debug mode and it encounters a breakpoint, the debugger stops the application so you can examine the values and single step through the order of execution. Only when the application stops precisely do the various debugging windows become helpful.

Working with breakpoints is very easy. To add a breakpoint to a line of code, right-click the line of code and choose Breakpoint ➢ Insert Breakpoint from the context menu. The IDE highlights the line of code in red (as a default) and places a circle in the left margin of the IDE, as shown in Figure 17.20.

In this case, the code stops at the line that verifies the value of `Response.Cookies`. You can't place breakpoints on lines of code that simply declare a variable—the code doesn't allow you to see an action, so there really isn't a good reason to stop there. The breakpoint indicates the start of a command. In other words, the application won't actually assign a value to `Test` until you step past this line of code using any of the step commands on the Debug toolbar such as Step Over (you can also use the options on the Debug menu if you wish).

Removing a breakpoint is just as easy as adding one. To remove the breakpoint, right-click the line of code containing the breakpoint and choose Breakpoint ➢ Remove Breakpoint from the context menu. Sometimes, however, you don't actually want to remove the breakpoint—you simply want to disable it for a while. In this case, choose the Breakpoint ➢ Disable Breakpoint command instead. The line remains highlighted as before, but the IDE displays a hollow circle. The breakpoint remains in place, but the IDE won't stop at it during the debugging process.

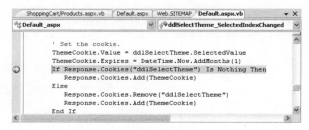

At some point, you'll want to use the disabled breakpoint again. Use the Breakpoint ➤ Enable Breakpoint command to enable the breakpoint again.

Visual Web Developer also provides a number of global breakpoint commands that you'll find on the Debug menu. For example, you can enable all of the breakpoints in an application using the Debug ➤ Enable All Breakpoints command. Note that many of these global commands only appear when you need them. For example, you won't see the Enable All Breakpoints entry on the Debug menu when none of the breakpoints are disabled.

When you run your application in debug mode, the breakpoints become active. As soon as the application encounters a breakpoint, execution stops in that thread and you can begin stepping through the code. The IDE highlights the breakpoint line in yellow and you'll see an arrow in the breakpoint circle.

Defining Your Development Goals

This chapter has helped you understand the levels and ranges of debugging that Visual Web Developer provides. You've seen the debugging tools that Visual Web Developer provides in action. Debugging is an essential task—one that every developer must understand completely or the current situation with faulty applications will never resolve itself. From some perspectives, this is the most important chapter in the book because many developers don't really understand debugging well. It doesn't matter whether you write a "Hello World" application or the next must-have tool for users, every application requires debugging.

Now it's time to develop your debugging skills. One way to do this is to create code with errors purposely to see how the system reacts. Interestingly enough, you won't find much help in this area, even though working with broken code is a very good way to develop debugging skills. Try exchanging a broken application with a friend so that you don't know what to expect. It's only by seeing simple cases of errors that you can begin to see patterns in complex applications. Simple studies help you understand the problems that certain classes of bugs can create so that you can spot them faster in real applications.

Chapter 18 describes another important area of application development—security. Most developers know that users expect secure applications and every developer wants to avoid becoming the next one mentioned in a trade press magazine as leaving a huge gaping hole in an application that crackers exploited. Security is an important issue because crackers have become quite adept at finding and using security holes in applications for their own purposes. Chapter 18 helps you understand the risks and overcome them without devoting your life to tracking down every potential problem, real or not.

Chapter 18

Designing Secure Applications

Enterprise applications come under constant attack from internal and external threats. Everyone from the disgruntled employee to a slighted customer to someone who simply wants to damage your Web site for bragging purposes is targeting your security. Given that most enterprises have a wealth of information to protect, security should be a major application consideration. In fact, security can't be an afterthought for your Web site—you need to include it as part of the basic application design and follow through with security reviews as your application begins to take shape.

Previous chapters have already discussed security issues. For example, the "Considering the Security Issues of Using Controls" section of Chapter 15 describes how to generate certificates and shows how to use them in Secure Sockets Layer (SSL) communications. All of these security topics are important. Explore any newspaper or magazine today, and you'll find that security is a topic of discussion in many venues, even those outside the developer community. This chapter discusses security in earnest. It won't discuss the topics that appeared in other chapters, but will provide a general discussion of security for your applications. For example, you'll find sections that discuss general security issues and that consider the need to create a security plan for both your organization and the applications you create.

This chapter also discusses specialized controls you can use to verify data that a user provides. The techniques extend to gaining information about the data methods received from other parts of the application and helping you understand how to build a cohesive security picture for your application. Only when your application provides the required level of security at all failure points can you feel reasonably sure that application security is as good as you can make it.

WARNING   Security isn't an issue that you visit once or twice during the life of your application—you visit this issue constantly. In fact, it's better to assume that a cracker is going to break through your security and maintain vigilance based on that assumption. Yes, good barriers will keep honest people honest and even deter some less skilled individuals, but a determined cracker will always find a way to break down your security precautions.

Understanding the Common Security Issues

It's important to understand the general security issues of the .NET environment. More importantly, it's important to understand how .NET interacts with the online environment supported by Visual Web Developer. One of the most secure computer environments is one in which the computer has no outside access at all. Using a computer means exposing it to some level of risk from security intrusions. The more public and connected the computer, the less secure it becomes. In fact, think for a moment about software such as a firewall, virus protection, or spyware detectors. All of this software has one thing in common—it reduces the connectivity that the computer provides in some way, making the computer less accessible. Accessibility—the ability of the computer to communicate—represents a security risk. The following sections describe how .NET helps and how it doesn't help your security efforts.

NOTE   This chapter doesn't consider a number of security techniques that enterprise computer systems commonly employ such as keeping the intranet and associated Web server disconnected from the outside world. You must provide these other forms of security, as well, to ensure you provide the greatest possible deterrent to outside intrusion.

Considering the Security Issues That .NET Resolves

When Microsoft started designing .NET, the world of computing was moving from the local area network (LAN) and wide area network (WAN) to the Internet. The individual user and group approach Windows used didn't necessarily reflect the best way to pursue security in a distributed environment. In addition, the current environment was too open to potential attacks from outside.

To overcome the security problems inherent in Windows, Microsoft enhanced the role-based security approach originally found in COM+ to work as a general programming methodology. In addition, the managed environment maintains better control over resources that tend to create problems in the unmanaged Windows environment. These two security changes, along with the object-oriented programming strategy of the .NET Framework, summarize what you'll find as security enhancements in the .NET Framework. Here's a list of the critical security enhancements for the .NET Framework.

Evidence-based Security   This feature determines what rights to grant to code based on information gathered about it. The Common Language Runtime (CLR) (pronounced clear) examines the information it knows about an assembly and determines what rights to grant that code based on the evidence. CLR matches the evidence against a security policy, which is a series of settings that define how the administrator wants to secure a system. Web applications generally have fewer rights than desktop applications, but as demonstrated in the "Setting .NET Security" section of Chapter 15, you can change the security policy to meet specific needs.

Code Access Security   CLR uses this feature to determine whether all of the assemblies in a calling chain (stack) have rights to use a particular resource or perform a particular task. All of the code in the calling chain must have the required rights. Otherwise, CLR generates a security error that you can use to detect security breaches. The purpose of this check is to ensure that a cracker's code can't intercept rights that it doesn't deserve. Only .NET provides the unique ability to validate code security, as well as user security (the older Windows system concentrated all efforts on the user). A piece of code that can execute locally might not execute over the Internet because of this feature.

Defined Verification Process   Before the Just-in-Time (JIT) compiler accepts the Microsoft Intermediate Language (MSIL) assembly, it checks the code the assembly contains for type safety and other errors. This verification process ensures that the code doesn't include any fatal flaws that would keep it from running. The checks also determine whether an external force has modified strongly named code. After JIT performs these checks, it compiles the MSIL into native code. CLR can run a verified assembly in isolation so that it doesn't affect any other assembly (and, more important, other assemblies can't affect it).

Role-based Security   If you know how role-based security works in COM+, you have a good idea of how it works in .NET. Instead of assigning security to individuals or groups, you assign it based on the task that an individual or group will perform. The Windows security identifier (SID) security is limited in that you can control entire files, but not parts of those files. Role-based security still relies on identifying the user through a logon or other means. The main advantage is that you can ask the security system about the user's role and allow access to program features based on that role. An administrator will likely have access to all of the features of a program, but individual users may only have access to a subset of the features. Role-based security is an essential strategy for the enterprise environment because users aren't always working in a secure environment. Using role-based security, you can provide a user on the road with fewer rights than they would have in the office based on their environment.

Cryptography   The advantages of cryptography are many. The concept is simple—you make data unreadable by using an algorithm, coupled with a key, to mix up the information. When the originator supplies the correct key to another algorithm, the system returns the original data. Over the years, the power of computers has increased, making old cryptography techniques suspect. The .NET Framework supports the latest cryptographic techniques, which ensures your data remains safe. Some enterprises are still relying on the Data Encryption Standard (DES) for encryption. Considering a cracker can break this encryption in just a few hours now, you should consider this encryption technique obsolete and move to the Advanced Encryption Standard (AES). You can read about the differences between these two standards on the SecureAge Technology Web site (`http://www.secureage.com/webpages/enews1.shtml`).

Separate Application Domains   You can write .NET code in such a way that some of the pieces run in a separate domain. It's a COM-type concept where the code is isolated from the other code in your program. Many developers use this feature to load special code, run it, and then unload that code without stopping the program. For example, a browser could use this technique to load and unload plug-ins. This feature also works well for security. It helps you run code at different security levels in separate domains to ensure true isolation.

Determining Where .NET Can't Help

Security is a problem precisely because it's a system designed by one person to thwart access to resources by another person. What one person can create, another can just as easily destroy. In fact, it's always easier to destroy than to create—so crackers have a significant advantage over those of us trying to create a secure environment. Consequently, security is an ongoing process. You need to know the threats your system faces so that you can monitor and protect against them. Security requires good communication in an enterprise environment because no one has the entire security picture—most individuals have pieces that they can contribute to the view of security as a whole.

Most developers focus on writing bulletproof code and adding as many security precautions to the code as possible without slowing application performance to a crawl. Although the .NET Framework provides a good basis for building applications with robust security, it can't protect you from other sources of security problems. The sections that follow detail these security problems. They provide suggestions on how you can use .NET along with other strategies to reduce problems to a minimum.

NOTE It is important to consider the full range of threats to your Web site. For example, one new technique that crackers use is called cross site scripting (XSS). An XSS attack can take a number of forms, but the two most common forms are through postings on the Web site or by adding script to input fields on a form. Products such as Open Web Application Security Project's WebGoat can help reduce the risk of XSS attacks. You can learn more about this product at `http://techrepublic` `.com.com/5138-3513-5733744.html?tag=nl.e101`.

BALANCED CODING REQUIREMENTS

One of the biggest security problems you'll face is the balanced coding requirement. Everyone wants a secure application, but they aren't willing to pay the price to get it. Secure code necessarily uses more resources and runs more slowly (all other things being equal) than nonsecure code. Secure code also introduces reliability problems (the code would rather fail than provide access to an intruder) and is less flexible (it's less tolerant of hostile environments). It doesn't matter whether the code fails gracefully when a security problem occurs—all the user sees is that the code has failed. When enough users complain that the secure code you wrote doesn't allow them to be completely lazy, management will likely request that you relax the rules. Management will also ask you to rewrite the code when it works too slowly on antiquated equipment or requires too many resources. At some point, all of the competing requirements balance and you have an application that everyone can live with. The result is likely less secure than it should be.

The .NET Framework helps you create code that's amazingly secure, but generally, that code won't meet the balance that you need. The question becomes one of how secure you actually need the code to be. For example, you could put your collection of interesting pens from the office in Fort Knox and be assured that the collection is perfectly safe. However, does a pen collection really need that much security? You must answer the level of security question. It's important to make this decision as part of the design process before you begin writing code. Security only works well when you design the application to use it, rather than bolt it on later.

However, the decision you make can have unanticipated and unwelcome consequences. Consider the scenario where a hole in your security—one that you decided not to fill because filling it caused too much of a performance hit—acts as a conduit for cracker activity on your system. The cracker manages to gain access to the system through the application you built. It's not a big deal for the current application because it doesn't store any critical data, but the cracker has also inadvertently gained access to the database containing customer credit card information. The design decision probably seemed acceptable for this one application, but not when viewed from a whole system perspective. In short, you must make your design decisions—discover the point of balance—based on the needs of the entire system and not just one application or group of people.

STUPID USER TRICKS

You've likely heard all of the jokes and stories, and seen some of user-related problems yourself. The most horrid story I've read appears in an InfoWorld article titled "Stupid User Tricks." One is about a traveler who had taped both the dial-in phone number for his server and his password to the outside of his laptop carrying case (`http://www.infoworld.com/article/03/01/24/030127Security_1` `.html`). Finding plenty of horror stories is never a problem—solving the security issues users create is another story.

After 18 years of consulting, one of the first security scans I perform at a client site is to check the area surrounding desks for pieces of paper with passwords on them. Invariably, I usually find at least one piece of paper with not just one, but several passwords on it. The passwords aren't even hard to figure out. It almost seems that the user is determined to make it easy for the janitor to make off with all of the company passwords.

TIP   One of the reasons that users write down passwords is that network administrators insist on using interesting passwords such as jk$LL12Z# to make life harder for crackers. Unfortunately, these passwords are nearly impossible for users to remember and with the continuing advances in computer technology, even these difficult passwords won't remain viable for so long. A better approach is to use a pass-phrase. A pass-phrase relies on an easily remembered phrase that's difficult to guess because of its length. For example, you could use a phrase such as "I love listening to Pink Floyd at 8:00." This phrase is 39 characters long, includes both uppercase and lowercase letters, and has numbers and special characters, including spaces, which most cracking tools don't consider today. You can read more about this technique at http://www.pcmag.com/article2/ 0,1759,1736152,00.asp.

To an extent, the .NET security features can help overcome problems users create. No, it won't automatically detect Post-it notes placed on the monitor, but it does ensure that the user doesn't gain rights to resources by using code incorrectly. Code access security helps in this regard. For example, when a user requests access to a file, the user's rights are checked and the rights of the code are checked. If either check fails, then access to the file fails.

Training, well-written *policies* (instructions for handling various security situations), and *rules* (requirements that everyone must meet) with some teeth in them can also help with user security problems. However, this is one area where you'll continually have problems because people will normally find a way around rules that are inconvenient. The .NET Framework can help here as well. You can write code such that the network administrator controls security policies, not the user. This technique makes it possible for the network administrator to monitor problems and ensure the program has a reasonable chance of maintaining a secure environment.

SOME EXTERNAL FORCES

Most people associate external forces that threaten security with crackers. This group does receive a lot of attention from the media, which is why they're the group that many programmers consider first (and perhaps last). While crackers do cause a great many problems, they aren't the only external force to consider.

Employees on the road or recently let go from the company can cause a great deal of harm to your applications. The problem is twofold:

◆ Using the old Windows security system, an application might execute at the same privilege level whether the employee accesses it from a desktop or from a remote location. The .NET Framework considers this issue by adjusting the rights of an application based on the zone in which it executes.

◆ An employee is much more familiar with the security setup and organization of your system than any cracker. Unfortunately, this is a problem that .NET can't help you solve. Someone determined to break into your system is almost certainly going to do it. The only way to overcome this problem is to monitor the system constantly.

Other programs can also affect your application—at least if it's a Web-based application. In a day when distributed applications can rely on services that your program can provide, it's possible that some other programmer you've never met will cause a security problem on your system and not even realize it. The .NET Framework helps you solve this problem by adhering to standards-based security. New standards such as WS-Security and WS-Inspection make it easier to write programs that work across platforms and provide a secure environment. You can learn more about these standards at Web Services Specifications site (`http://msdn.microsoft.com/library/en-us/dnglobspec/html/wsspecsover.asp`).

Inept network management can also cause serious problems. A network administrator could restore old policies to a server or overwrite the recently patched files for your application. Newer versions of Windows have some protection for both of these issues. For example, Windows File Protection can help ensure only the latest version of your files remain on disk. The .NET Framework also helps by making version checks before it loads files and executes them. An overwritten file would have the wrong version number and .NET would display an error indicating this fact. This fix may not make the user very happy, but at least you'll know the cause of the problem.

Another source of external problems is the connections you create with other businesses. Distributed applications are becoming more common as companies invest more in Web services. The problems with distributed applications are many, and you can't expect the .NET Framework to solve them all. Many of the strategies for overcoming this problem hinge on standards-based application development such as using the WS-Security standard for your application.

Wireless devices present one of the most prevalent and least understood security problems for developers today. Some wireless networks aren't secure. Anyone with the proper equipment can come along and access the network from outside the company. Some people are using this technique to spread illicit email using company Internet connections without anyone knowing. The .NET Framework can't do anything about this kind of security problem—you must overcome it by securing the wireless network.

Something's always attacking your data, even nature. Fortunately, keeping your data safe, or at least knowing when someone has tampered with it, is relatively easy because this is an area where security professionals have spent a lot of time. First the bad news—if you have any kind of data transfer at all (even on a LAN), be prepared for situations when that data is compromised. The good news is that the .NET Framework uses the latest technologies, such a cryptography to secure your information.

POORLY PATCHED SYSTEMS

Patches are problematic no matter how you look at them. First, there's the problem that the existence of a patch tells many users that the vendor didn't test the program well. Second, there's the issue of compatibility. Some patches actually cause more problems than they fix by creating compatibility problems or introducing new problems into a system.

Enterprise environments also introduce a number of odd problems. For example, an enterprise might not apply patches immediately due to compatibility concerns. A patch might begin by running on several test systems, move to a test group, and finally to the enterprise as a whole. Consequently, your application might actually have to work in several distinct environments without failure.

Although these issues are probably not going away any time soon, you still need to patch your system to ensure it has the latest security features and that any security holes are fixed. Developers must test their code using the same patches and updates the user will have because some patches introduce application environment or execution issues. (When working with public applications, always assume the user has the current patches installed and make this policy public on your Web site.) For example, many applications stopped working when users applied Windows XP Service Pack 2 (SP2) because the developers didn't consider all of the security issues that Microsoft addressed as part of the patch. You need to think about the results of not patching your system and consider how the lack of patches affect any programs you produce on the system. With this in mind, you'll want to use three tools to check your system for problems before you begin developing a new program.

Windows Update   Always check Windows Update to verify the status of any patches for your system. Windows Update works automatically. All you need to do is select the updates you want to download. The one mistake that some developers make is not reading the information about a patch (or any other update for that matter) before they install it. This may lead to problems on a development machine. You can find Windows Update at `http://www.windowsupdate.com/`. It also pays to check the Windows Update Catalog at `http://v5.windowsupdate.microsoft.com/catalog/en/default.asp` (the precise version number for Windows Update will vary by the version of Windows you use—the URL supplied in the chapter is for Windows XP).

Microsoft System Update Services (SUS)   Microsoft SUS can reduce the burden of updating multiple machines for a business. This system helps you download and distribute updates in a safe environment. Learn more about this product at `http://www.microsoft.com/windows2000/windowsupdate/sus`. (Microsoft is changing the name of SUS to Windows Update Services or WUS.)

Microsoft Baseline Security Analyzer (BSA)   Windows setups can become quite complex. It's easy to miss an update when you have multiple pieces of software to consider. Add to this problem the issue of individual driver updates, and security can become a considerable problem. The Microsoft BSA won't solve all of your problems, but it can help by providing a comprehensive list of problems within a system. Learn more about this product at `http://www.microsoft.com/technet/security/tools/mbsahome.mspx`.

NOTE   Some people report problems downloading and using the updated drivers that Microsoft provides as part of Windows Update and other update services it supports. Generally, it's a better idea to obtain driver updates directly from the vendor to ensure it will work with your system. In addition, never update a driver unless you experience the issue the driver addresses or the driver contains a security update that you must install to maintain your system.

INEPT ENTERPRISE POLICIES

I actually knew of a moderately sized business that lacked a real network administrator and had a policy in place that made every network user an administrator. The person who was supposed to administer the network was simply too lazy to set up the required features and didn't want to hear user complaints about not being able to access a particular file or feature. Imagine what would happen if a cracker decided to attack the company's Web application. The network would transmit administrator commands from every infected machine and eventually crash under the weight of infection.

Setting enterprise policies is one case when the .NET Framework might actually increase the number of security problems your application will have to face. Microsoft assumes that every network administrator is faithful, loyal, hardworking, conscientious, and knowledgeable. The .NET Framework is set up to ensure the network administrator has maximum access to security features. Unfortunately, some network administrators just aren't up to the task and you'll have to find ways to overcome this problem.

Training is one way to help network administrators fulfill their new role with the applications you create. Many will find it quite surprising that they can control who uses a particular function within their components and specific features in an application. However, the best strategy is to use imperative and declarative security effectively in your applications to ensure they maintain some level of security even if the network administrator doesn't do anything at all.

Distributed applications are notorious for opening security holes because these applications make hidden resources visible to users through an Internet connection. It's amazing that some companies don't have security policies in place to protect from these problems. What's even more amazing is that a few companies actually end up opening new holes in their firewall and other security features to enable an application to work. For example, some companies still rely on Distributed Component Object Model (DCOM) applications to create distributed applications. The .NET Framework isn't the only solution at your disposal, but by using modern Web services techniques, you can greatly reduce the risks distributed applications impose. Fortunately, Visual Web Developer can help you create robust Web applications that keep security holes to a minimum using Web services.

One of the most interesting security problems is one in which a company follows all other best practices, but then fails to lock up the computer so that no one can access it physically. If someone can gain physical access to a server, they can control the server in a relatively short time. A worst-case scenario occurs when the company not only leaves the computer in the open, but also thoughtfully provides a monitor and keyboard so that anyone entering the room can modify the server setup. Although the best policy is to lock up the computer, there are alternatives if you must keep the computer in plain view. For example, you can add physical locking to the system. SecurityWare (`http://www.securityware.com/`) provides a number of specialized computer-locking mechanisms that make physical access a lot more difficult.

WINDOWS FILE PROTECTION VULNERABILITIES

Windows File Protection is thought to be a safe way to install executable files on a system because those files are supposedly signed. Unfortunately, there's a well-known method to create files that Windows File Protection will trust even if they aren't signed by an appropriate digital certificate. You can read the detailed version of the problem on the Bugtraq site at `http://archives.neohapsis.com/archives/ntbugtraq/2002-q4/0122.html`. A Microsoft security bulletin on the topic appears at `http://www.microsoft.com/technet/security/bulletin/MS00-072.asp`.

The interesting thing about the .NET Framework is that it doesn't rely on this security mechanism. When you sign a control, component, or application, CLR verifies the signature. The signature uses a hash mechanism that exists outside the Windows File Protection environment, so CLR ensures the security of the file. You can always check the token used to secure a file with a strong name that's contained within the Global Assembly Cache by viewing the content of the `\WINDOWS\assembly` folder. Figure 18.1 shows a typical example of the content of this folder.

Creating a Security Plan

Crackers depend on a certain level of disorganization within a company in order to employ their trade. The social engineering attacks that most crackers use rely on the user not knowing whom to contact regarding company policy or even knowing that the company has a security policy. That's why it's important to create a security strategy for your organization before you even begin coding the application. The strategy should spell out how you plan to approach certain issues, such as a password inadvertently lost or a breach of the database.

FIGURE 18.1
Managed files use a
unique signature
system that ensures
their integrity.

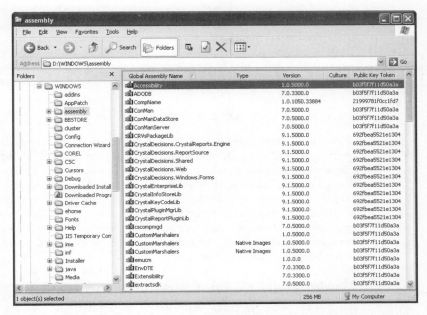

Security plans are great, but you need to translate that plan into code. New programming features in Visual Studio .NET rely on your ability to define the application user. For example, you can't develop a role-based security strategy for an application until you know which roles the users could fulfill as they use the application. Make sure you include roles based on environment as well as actual tasks. Always use the policy of least access to ensure a user has the minimum rights required to perform a task.

WARNING   Avoid a common security problem in enterprises—creative developer fixes. Some developers brainstorm roles they think an organization will need, but this approach leaves holes from unused roles in the application implementation and makes the application more complicated to configure. Only create roles that your organization actually requires.

The developer also needs to decide how to implement security. You can configure security at the client, the server, or both. Security can appear as an internal programmed function, something the administrator can configure using an MMC snap-in or other tool, a user-controlled application feature, or an add-on implemented as needed for distributed requirements. In many cases, an application requires several levels of security and uses more than one method for implementing it. The application design should specify what type of security to implement and qualify how to implement it. Never hardwire the security into a Web application—always implement the main security features at the server.

Another consideration is the type of security you want to implement. You have a choice of traditional Windows security, newer role-based security, or third party implementations. Third party implementations are important because Windows doesn't fill every gap in the modern application. For example, if you choose to use the SOAP or some other XML-derivative to transfer data, you'll need a third party product to secure the information in most cases (using a secure server connection does help).

Most developers find that role-based security works best at the server. It enables the developer or network administrator to create a security policy based on the tasks the user must perform, rather than focusing on the user's job title or other personal information. Role-based security is extremely flexible because you can employ it programmatically or rely on the network administrator to configure it. A developer also has the option of enforcing a minimum-security level and allowing the network administrator to enforce more stringent security measures as needed.

Configuring ASP.NET

Visual Web Developer works with ASP.NET to provide a specific level of security for your applications. Generally, you add special attributes to your code, in addition to actual security checks, to implement application security. Control and component security generally relies on a combination of attributes and coded security checks too, but always requires some level of configuration, as demonstrated in the "Setting .NET Security" section of Chapter 15. Applications can also require configuration, but this configuration information appears as part of the Web.CONFIG file. ASP.NET itself also requires some level of configuration in the form of local and server policies. The following sections describe the generic issues you need to consider—look for specific issues in application, control, or component sections of the book.

Working with the Configuration Web Site

The System.Web.Security namespace is the one that you'll use for the majority of your Web security needs—no matter what type of application you want to create. For example, this namespace contains the PassportIdentity class. The following sections describe essential security that you can provide using a combination of the Web.CONFIG file and classes such as the FileAuthorizationModule class.

TIP   Microsoft has scaled back their goals for Passport according to a ComputerWorld article at http://www.computerworld.com/managementtopics/outsourcing/itservices/story/0,10801,96838,00.html. Passport is still a solid technology, and you'll find it useful for some types of security needs, such as when you host a number of satellite companies or groups from partner companies. This chapter won't include a Passport example due to space concerns. However, you can find such an example in my book, *.NET Development Security Solutions* (Sybex, 2003).

DEFINING FILE SECURITY USING THE *FILEAUTHORIZATIONMODULE* CLASS

The FileAuthorizationModule class doesn't look like very much from the description in the help files. However, this class is exceptionally important because it's one of the few distinct links between Windows security and the security employed by the .NET Framework. Whenever a caller requests a resource such as a file, the FileAuthorizationModule class authenticates the caller against the Windows Access Control List (ACL). This isn't the role-based or code access security that a .NET application normally relies on to authenticate a caller.

TIP   Web security takes a number of forms. While the classes in the System.Web.Security namespace can help you keep your data safe to a certain extent, most applications still require additional security measures such as the WS-Security standard (http://www-106.ibm.com/developerworks/webservices/library/ws-secure/). You can read about a number of products on the market today to help developers make the most of the potential of WS-Security in the InfoWorld article at http://www.infoworld.com/article/03/04/15/15appnews_1.html.

The tie-in with older Windows technology is important. For example, without this link, ASP.NET impersonation (the use of a default account in place of the standard user account to access a resource) wouldn't work. This class also provides a way for you to restrict access to certain resources such as a file to specific callers using standard security measures. This means that someone who accesses the site using a PDA will have the same rights to that file as if they were accessing it from their desktop—a good feature when used to deny or grant access to a resource based on credentials, rather than other factors.

An alternative to using the FileAuthorizationModule class is to rely on the UrlAuthorization Module class. Although this option might seem more in line with the .NET way of working with security, you must manually enter the information used for authorizations purposes in the Web.CONFIG file. Here's an example of an authorization entry:

```
<authorization>
    <allow users="John"/>
    <allow roles="Administrators"/>
    <deny users="Guest"/>
    <deny roles="Guests"/>
</authorization>
```

In this case, the user named John and anyone in the Administrators role would gain access to the resource, but CLR would deny the user named Guest and anyone in the Guests role access. The problem with this technique is that it doesn't necessarily work well with all callers (including wireless devices where the username or role is ambiguous at times) and it keeps the authorization information in plain text form on the Web server. In short, using the FileAuthorizationModule class method is the more secure choice in this case. CLR uses the FileAuthorizationModule class automatically when you fail to include an <authorization> section in the Web.CONFIG file.

You can learn more about the various roles of these two classes in security in Microsoft Knowledge Base article 306590 at http://support.microsoft.com/default.aspx?scid=kb;[LN];306590. Note that using the FileAuthorizationModule class can result in errors due to a bug in the .NET Framework implementation. See Knowledge Base article 317955 at http://support.microsoft.com/default.aspx?scid=kb;[LN];317955 for details.

DEFINING FORM SECURITY USING THE *FORMSAUTHENTICATION* CLASS

The FormsAuthentication class can help you overcome some of the issues with authenticating clients who can't use the more secure Windows login. For one thing, it helps you create an environment in which ASP.NET authenticates the caller, but it doesn't matter quite as much who the caller is, where the caller is located, or what device the caller is using. This form of authentication relies on special server configuration, application configuration, and a few programming tricks. Listing 18.1 shows the first part of this application. You'll find this example in the \ABC_Inc\Security\ FormAuthenticate folder of the source code found on the Sybex Web site.

This example begins by calling one of the secure pages on the Web site. Because Default.ASPX is the only available Web page, the example calls it. However, the user never sees the Web page because the server automatically redirects the user to the Login.ASPX page shown in Figure 18.2. Notice the ReturnUrl argument in the query string—the server automatically adds it for you so that you can create code that knows where the user started. All of these tasks happen without any code on your part, but you need to know that they occur.

> **NOTE** Figure 18.2 shows one of the problems of using master pages and themes with a login page. The text information appears, but any other resources can become unavailable. Consequently, logos, background images, and other items that normally dress up your Web site won't appear on the login page. The user can still work with the resulting Web page, but it won't have as much pizzazz as the other Web pages on the site.

LISTING 18.1: Defining the Login Page

```
private void btnLogin_Click(object sender, System.EventArgs e)
{
    HttpCookie  AuthCookie; // Authorization cookie.

    // Verify the user has proper access.
    if (!FormsAuthentication.Authenticate(txtName.Text,
                                          txtPassword.Text))
        throw new SecurityException(txtName.Text +
                                    " is not authorized!");

    // If the user is authenticated, generate a cookie.
    AuthCookie = FormsAuthentication.GetAuthCookie(txtName.Text, true);

    // Place the cookie in the response.
    Response.Cookies.Add(AuthCookie);

    // Redirect to the default page.
    Response.Redirect(Request.QueryString.Item("ReturnUrl"));
}
```

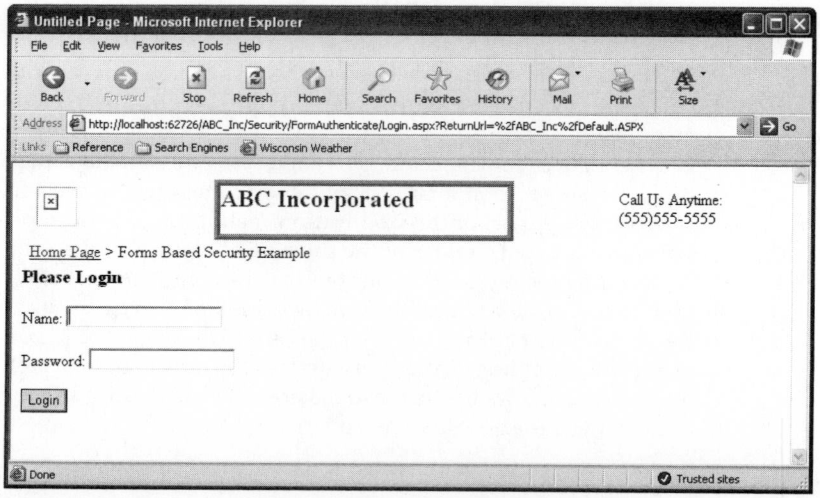

FIGURE 18.2
The login page appears automatically when the user requests a secure page.

At this point, the login page waits for the user to type a username and password, and then click Login. When the user provides the required information, the code calls on the `FormsAuthentication` `.Authenticate()` method to authenticate the user against the data stored in the `Web.CONFIG` file. This method of authentication doesn't rely on the standard Windows names and passwords—a caller must appear in a separate credential database to access the page.

NOTE The application is currently set to accept `John` as the username and `hello` as the user password. You can create a hash for any password you wish by modifying the `Forms` `Authentication.HashPasswordForStoringInConfigFile("hello", "SHA1")` line of code shown in Listing 18.3.

At this point, ASP.NET has authenticated the user or the application has generated a `Security` `Exception` and the caller hasn't gained access to anything. The code stores the authentication information in a cookie and redirects the caller to the target page.

You can't ask for forms authentication and not provide any data to support it. The `Web.CONFIG` file requires additional entries to make this type of authentication work. Listing 18.2 shows the changes you'll need to make.

LISTING 18.2:   Modifying the *Web.CONFIG* File

```
<!-- Use the Login.ASPX form for authentication. -->
<!-- <authentication mode="Forms">
  <forms loginUrl="Login.ASPX" requireSSL="true"> -->

<!-- Use this line for testing with Visual Web Developer. -->
 <authentication mode="Forms">
  <forms loginUrl="Login.ASPX">

    <!-- Create a list of credentials. -->
    <credentials passwordFormat="SHA1">
       <user name="John"
             password="AAF4C61DDCC5E8A2DABEDE0F3B482CD9AEA9434D" />
    </credentials>

  </forms>
</authentication>

<!-- Deny access to users who aren't authenticated. -->
<authorization>
    <deny users="?" />
</authorization>
```

You need to pay careful attention to several features of this configuration file. First, notice the `requireSSL="true"` attribute. It's extremely dangerous not to include this entry because the user's name and password appear in plain text otherwise. You should also set the server to use SSL by changing the Secure Communications entry on the Directory Security tab of the application Properties dialog in the Internet Information Services console. (You could also change just the entry for the particular file, but securing the entire application is better.)

WARNING   The built-in Web server doesn't support SSL. To test this example with the built-in Web server, you must use the second <forms> element—the one that doesn't require SSL. Use the first <forms> element when you move the application from your local machine to a production server.

Second, notice the passwordFormat="SHA1" attribute. All of the passwords in the credentials list are hashed using the SHA1 encryption standard. Listing 18.3 shows one technique you can use to obtain the required information. Because the cracker could access the configuration file, you want to keep all sensitive data encrypted.

Third, notice the <authorization> element now contains a <deny> child. This entry specifically denies access to any unauthenticated callers.

Once ASP.NET authenticates the user, the application redirects them to the FormAuth.ASPX page. In this case, the page shows several of the other FormsAuthentication object features. Listing 18.3 shows the code for this portion of the example.

LISTING 18.3:   Generating Forms Authentication Statistics

```
private void Page_Load(object sender, System.EventArgs e)
{
   // Get the information for the current user and display it.
   lblOutput.Text = "Forms Cookie Name: " +
      FormsAuthentication.FormsCookieName +
      "<BR/>Forms Cookie Path: " +
      FormsAuthentication.FormsCookiePath +
      "<BR/>Is SSL Required? " +
      FormsAuthentication.RequireSSL;

   // Hash a password for storage in the configuration file.
   lblHashPwd.Text = "Hashed Password for hello:<BR/>" +
      FormsAuthentication.HashPasswordForStoringInConfigFile(
         "hello", "SHA1");
}
```

The code begins by listing a few statistics for the page. Notice that you can determine the SSL status of the page before you do anything. Always check the FormsAuthentication.RequireSSL property to ensure the application uses SSL. The code uses the FormsAuthentication.HashPasswordFor StoringInConfigFile() method to generate a hash for the password for user John using the SHA1 standard. Figure 18.3 shows typical output from this application.

FIGURE 18.3
The default page shows the hash value for "hello" along with status information.

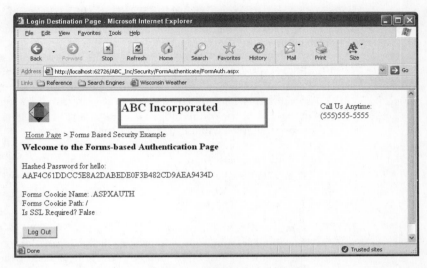

It's important to provide a means of logging out of the Web site. The example adds a separate Log Out button, as shown in Figure 18.3. Here's the simple code you need to implement this feature.

```
Protected Sub btnLogout_Click( _
    ByVal sender As Object, ByVal e As System.EventArgs) _
    Handles btnLogout.Click

    ' Sign out.
    FormsAuthentication.SignOut()
End Sub
```

Using the Login Controls

Many Web sites today provide a login system that anyone can use. For example, you might sign up to use a list server or gain access to the latest information on a news server. You might also want to make this system part of a shopping cart application (see Chapter 16). The point is that you want to know who these people are, but you don't necessarily want to limit their access to the Web site. Generally, the user signs up for access and you send them an email granting access to the Web site after checking their credentials. The following sections describe a list of controls that make setting up this kind of login system a lot easier. In fact, you'll find that you don't have to do much work at all to make it operational. You'll find this example in the \ABC_Inc\Security\Login folder of the source code on the Sybex Web site.

NOTE   This example has two roles already provided: visitor and administrator. Each role has a sample user assigned to it. The visitor role has George with a password of 456&hello. The administrator role has JohnM with a password of 123&hello. Microsoft has set ASP.NET 2.0 authentication to require passwords that contain a combination of numbers, special characters, and letters. Using a combination of characters reduces the chance that a cracker will guess a password, but can increase the chance the user will forget the password or write it down as well.

USING THE ASP.NET WEB SITE ADMINISTRATION TOOL FOR SECURITY

Many of the login controls, such as the actual Login control, contain a special Administrate Website option on the associated SmartTag. You won't see this particular link anywhere else. Choose this option and you'll see the ASP.NET Web Site Administration Tool shown in Figure 18.4.

This utility helps you create a secure environment for your application. It works at the Web site level, not at the global server level. The settings it creates appear in the AspNetDB.MDF file in various tables. For example, when you create roles, they appear in the aspnet_Roles table. The user data appears in two locations. You'll find the user entries in the aspnet_Membership table and the roles these users occupy in the aspnet_UsersInRoles. The general per user security profile information appears in the aspnet_Profile table. Because you can protect the database, creating a security setup using this technique is safer than using the Web.CONFIG file discussed earlier in the chapter. However, you can't make changes as quickly and this method isn't as compatible as the Web.CONFIG file—it only works with ASP.NET 2.0. In short, you must choose the kind of security you want to create based partly on the needs of the system.

NOTE   Some security settings still reside within the Web.CONFIG file—the ASP.NET Web Site Administration Tool simply makes managing the settings easier. For example, allowing or denying access still requires use of the <authorization> element with <allow> and <deny> child elements. Each folder of your Web site can have different settings so you can control security at the folder level and also programmatically within individual files. View the Web.CONFIG files in the \ABC_Inc\Security\Login folder of the source code on the Sybex Web site for details.

When you initially set up a Web site, the first link you'll want to click is Security. The Security page, shown in Figure 18.5, lets you set the kind of authentication the Web site uses and defines whether the application relies on role-based security. Always use role-based security for pure ASP.NET applications because it provides the highest level of security and requires the least amount of programming.

FIGURE 18.4

Use the ASP.NET Web Site Administration Tool to create users and roles, and set Web site security.

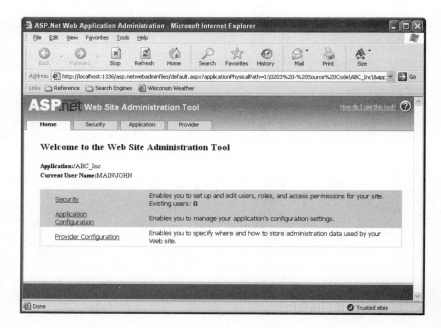

The tool lists two choices when you choose the Select Authentication Type option. You can choose local security, where the application relies on integrated Windows authentication based on the server entries and Internet security, where the user must log in using a form. The settings are a little misleading. You should use local security whenever you create a private Web site—one where you know the users in advance. Use the Internet setting when you plan to allow unknown users to create an account and receive access after you approve them. To gain maximum benefit from the examples in this chapter, you should select the Internet option. Otherwise, the various security forms have less effect on the actual functioning of the Web site. When you select the Internet option, the form shown in Figure 18.5 changes to let you add new users to the Web site. (See the "Creating New Users" section of the chapter for additional information.)

After you add the initial users to the Web site, you'll need to determine whether you want to enable roles for them. It's important to create roles that the users will actually fill, not roles that you think you might need at some point. Excess roles create security gaps that you won't want in your application. When you click the Enable Roles option shown in Figure 18.5, the system enables the Create Roles and Manage Roles options. You use these links to work with roles for this application—the roles don't affect the Web server as a whole. Click Create or Manage Roles and the ASP.NET Web Site Administration Tool will display a text box where you add a role name. Enter all of the roles you want to create first, and then click the Manage link for each role. Add users to each role based on that user's needs.

The directory structure you create makes a big difference when you begin setting up the access rules using this tool. You can't choose individual files, so you must arrange the individual Web pages in folders where you can apply the same access rule to the entire folder. For example, you'll want to make the login folder accessible to everyone, including anonymous users, but the data folders available only to logged-in users. An administrative folder might only provide access to the administrators group and you might have statistical folders available to power users. Figure 18.6 shows settings for the Administrative folder for this example. In this case, the settings would deny access to anonymous users.

FIGURE 18.5

Modify the security settings before you perform any other tasks.

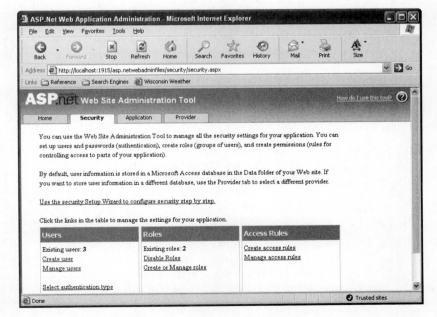

FIGURE 18.6
Make user settings changes as needed to provide a secure application environment.

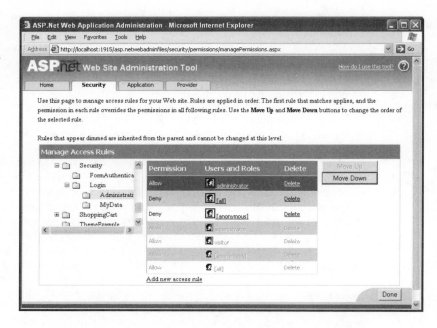

TIP Don't assume that you can't fine-tune your security setup. The settings you create with the ASP.NET Web Site Administration Tool only provide a starting point. You can also make changes by adding code to your application. For example, you can display content based on whether the user is in a specific role. Consequently, you have very fine control over the security of your application, but you must mix settings and coding techniques to obtain this control.

Every time you create a new user setting for a folder, the IDE actually creates a new Web.CONFIG file for that folder. In fact, you can change settings for a folder by changing the content of the Web.CONFIG file. Here are the settings you'll find for the folder shown in Figure 18.6.

```
<configuration
    xmlns="http://schemas.microsoft.com/.NetConfiguration/v2.0">
    <appSettings/>
    <connectionStrings/>
    <system.web>
        <authorization>
            <allow roles="administrator" />
            <deny users="*" />
            <deny users="?" />
        </authorization>
    </system.web>
</configuration>
```

As you can see, the <authorization> element contains a list of <allow> and <deny> entries that define user access to the contents of the folder. In either case, you can allow or deny access using roles or users. Use roles whenever possible to reduce the work required to maintain the Web site.

Logging Existing Users In

The Login control is the most essential for creating a secure Web site using the techniques described in this section. It's the only control that you must include somewhere in the Web site. Otherwise, no one can log in and, therefore, no one can see the data you want to provide. However, enterprise Web sites often include a combination of public and private data, so the placement of this control is important. The ABC Incorporated Web site provides an example of this sort. You can access the vast majority of the Web site without any security at all—it's public. However, to gain access to the `~/Security/Login/MyData/DataPage.aspx` page, the user must provide a username and password.

Configuring this control is a little odd. You can simply dump the control on the page and not do anything with it, or you can set it to perform certain tasks automatically. In general, the only feature you really need to define is where to go after the user logs into the Web site using the `Destination PageUrl` attribute. Here's a typical Login control setup.

```
<asp:Login ID="liMain" Runat="server" AccessKey="L"
           CreateUserUrl="~/NewUser.aspx"
           CreateUserText="Create New User Account"
           DestinationPageUrl="~/MyData/DataPage.aspx"
           InstructionText="Type your name and password."
           BorderPadding="5" BorderStyle="Ridge"
           PasswordRecoveryText="I Forgot My Password"
           PasswordRecoveryUrl="~/RecoverPassword.aspx"
           HelpPageText="Get Password Help"
           HelpPageUrl="~/HelpOnPasswords.aspx">
    <InstructionTextStyle BorderStyle="Ridge" BorderWidth="4px"
                          BackColor="Black" ForeColor="White">
    </InstructionTextStyle>
    <FailureTextStyle Font-Bold="True" ForeColor="Red"
                      Font-Size="Large" >
    </FailureTextStyle>
</asp:Login>
```

The entries you choose to use depend on what login features you want to provide. For example, you only need to provide the `CreateUserUrl` and `CreateUserText` attributes when you want to allow outsiders to create a new user. Of course, the user changes don't actually take effect until the administrator approves them (unless you allow unfettered user creation on your Web site). You can see any new users by clicking Manage Users on the Security tab of the Web Site Administrator Tool. The new users will appear in the list, as shown in Figure 18.7. Notice that the Active checkbox for Sam is clear, which means that Sam has signed up for an account, but doesn't have access to the Web site.

WARNING The login page won't work correctly if you don't name it Login.ASPX. The system automatically redirects all user requests to Login.ASPX when the user isn't logged in unless you set the LogoutAction="Redirect" property for the LogoutStatus control. Fortunately, you don't have to implement any special logic to return the user to the page they requested. The Login control automatically handles the ReturnUrl query string variable for you. All the user has to do is log in and the redirection occurs automatically.

The `InstructionText` is optional, but it provides the user with helpful information, especially when you are working with less experienced users. Make sure you include a distinctive <Instruction TextStyle> element to focus the user's attention on this additional information. You might also want to define the `HelpPageText` and `HelpPageUrl` when you're working with many novice users. The help page should provide clear instructions on how to use each of the options. In addition, you might want to provide the email address of the support center for your company.

Users are going to forget their passwords. It doesn't matter what kind of user you work with, there's a very good chance that even advanced users will forget their password from time to time. Consequently, you should always define the optional `PasswordRecoveryText` and `Password RecoveryUrl` entries to help the user regain access to the Web site. As part of this addition, you'll also want to define a `<FailureTextStyle>` element to ensure the user actually notices when an error has occurred. Notice that this control performs all these tasks without any code—all you need to provide is the proper settings changes.

FIGURE 18.7
The administrator must activate new users before they gain access to the Web site.

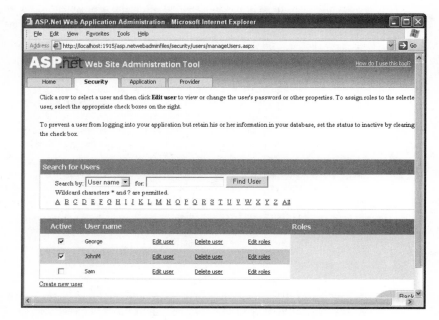

DEFINING A LOGIN VIEW

As part of the login page, you should also show the user their current login status. You provide this information as part of the `LoginView` control. As a minimum, you'll want to provide both a logged in message and a logged out message. However, you can also provide messages based on the user's role. For example, you might want to include special information for administrators. Here's a typical example of the `LoginView` control at work.

```
<asp:LoginView ID="LoginView1" Runat="server">
    <RoleGroups>
        <asp:RoleGroup Roles="Administrator">
        <ContentTemplate>
            Welcome Administrator<br />
            <asp:HyperLink ID="hlSeeData1" Runat="server"
                        NavigateUrl="MyData/DataPage.aspx">
```

```
            See the Data
        </asp:HyperLink><br />
        <asp:HyperLink ID="hlAdminister" Runat="server"
                        NavigateUrl="Administrative/AdminPage.aspx">
            Manage the Web Site
        </asp:HyperLink>
    </ContentTemplate>
    </asp:RoleGroup>
</RoleGroups>
<LoggedInTemplate>
    You are currently logged in.<br />
    <asp:HyperLink ID="hlSeeData2" Runat="server"
                    NavigateUrl="MyData/DataPage.aspx">
        See the Data
    </asp:HyperLink>
</LoggedInTemplate>
<AnonymousTemplate>
    You are currently not logged in.
</AnonymousTemplate>
</asp:LoginView>
```

The `<LoggedInTemplate>` element provides the information for logged in users. The system doesn't limit you to using text—you can include any required controls as well. The example includes a link for the logged in user to return to the main data page. The `<AnonymousTemplate>` element provides a simple message for anyone visiting the Web site. This is the message that anyone visiting the Web site sees when they first visit because everyone is anonymous at the outset.

The `<RoleGroups>` element begins a series of entries that defines specific messages for users in specific roles. The example provides a special message for the Administrator group. You create a `RoleGroup` control by selecting the Edit `RoleGroups` option on the `LoginView` control SmartTag. Provide the names of the roles you want to support and then define the special messages for each group. You can perform this task using Design view, but sometimes this task is easier using Code view because you can copy message elements from other templates. Figure 18.8 shows typical output from this application. This figure shows a logged-in administrator.

LOGGING USERS OUT

It's important to offer the user an opportunity to log out of the system on every protected Web page. Otherwise, some users will simply remain logged in, even after they leave your Web site to visit other locations. Although the system will eventually timeout and force a logoff, your Web site will remain more secure and perform better when you let the user log out of the system. The `LoginStatus` control lets you add login and logout functionality to your Web pages. All you need to define is the logout URL, as shown here (notice that the control includes the `LogoutAction` argument, which allows you to redirect the user anywhere you want after logging out).

```
<asp:Label ID="lblLogout" Runat="server" Text="Login Status: ">
</asp:Label>
<asp:LoginStatus ID="lsLogout" Runat="server"
                LogoutPageUrl="~/Security/Login/Login.aspx"
                AccessKey="L" LogoutAction="Redirect" />
```

FIGURE 18.8
Design whatever style of login you need with a few simple settings changes.

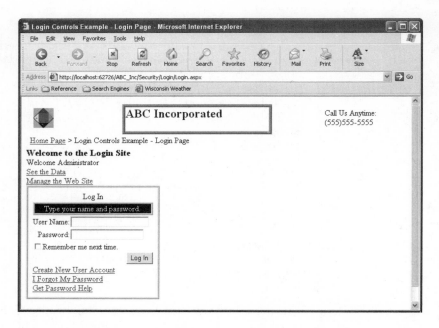

CREATING NEW USERS

Whether you allow anyone to create new users on your Web site depends on the kind of Web site you own. A Web site that provides access to news stories or other reading material might simply want to track which users are reading what material, which means that security isn't the focus of logging in and you can provide free access to the feature. On the other hand, you might want to provide a means for letting administrators quickly add users to a Web site. You use the same `CreateUserWizard` control, but the control appears on an administrator page instead of on an easily accessible part of the Web site. The `CreateUserWizard` control also offers an incredible amount of customization potential. You can define your own processing steps and even include specialized functionality.

The actions that the `CreateUserWizard` control performs when someone creates a new user depends on the level of customization you incorporate. A basic setup creates a new user who doesn't belong to any role. Consequently, a user could request access to the Web site, but not actually gain any access to it until you assign the user to a group when you set up the Web site security correctly. The example uses this approach. You can create a new user, but the user only gains access to the Web site after the administrator adds the user to a role. Here's a basic `CreateUserWizard` control setup.

```
<asp:CreateUserWizard ID="CreateUserWizard1" Runat="server"
                      CancelDestinationPageUrl="~/Login.aspx"
                      ContinueDestinationPageUrl="~/Login.aspx"
                      CompleteSuccessText="Successfully created"
                      DisableCreatedUser="True"
                      DisplayCancelButton="True">
```

```
<WizardSteps>
    <asp:CreateUserWizardStep Runat="server"
                            Title="Sign Up for Your New Account">
    </asp:CreateUserWizardStep>
    <asp:CompleteWizardStep Runat="server" Title="Complete">
    </asp:CompleteWizardStep>
</WizardSteps>
</asp:CreateUserWizard>
```

To make even the basic control functional, you must provide a `ContinueDestinationPageUrl` argument property. Because this control doesn't provide a means of escape (getting back to previous page) by default, you should set the `DisplayCancelButton` argument to True and provide a `CancelDestinationPageUrl` argument value. The `CompleteSuccessText` argument shows what the user will see for a successful addition.

This control works by creating a series of steps for the user to follow to sign up for your Web site. A default control includes just two steps. The first displays the sign-up page shown in Figure 18.9. You can change this page as needed. The second displays a completion page.

The `<WizardSteps>` element contains a list of steps the user must complete to create a new account. You can add any number of intermediate steps or change the default steps as needed. This flexibility lets you create a new account creation process of any complexity. You add additional steps using the `WizardSteps` property in Design view. Click the ellipsis and you'll see the Wizard Steps Collection Editor dialog box where you can add and remove steps as needed.

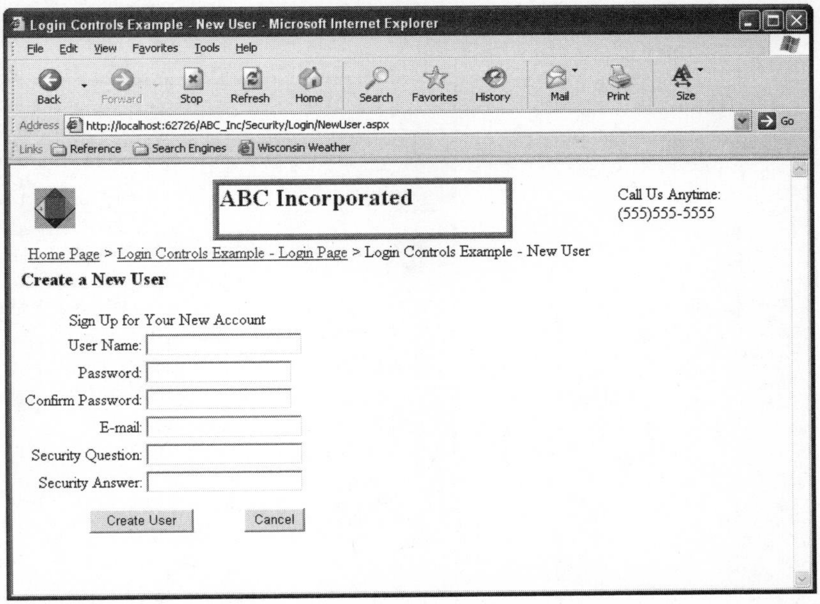

FIGURE 18.9
The default page requests a minimum of user information to create an account.

CHANGING PASSWORDS

Many Web sites make it easy to create an initial account, but nearly impossible to change your password later. Given the security breaches that Web sites suffer today, allowing the user to change their password whenever necessary is important. The ChangePassword control makes adding this feature extremely easy. Here's a typical example of this control.

```
<asp:ChangePassword ID="cpPassword" Runat="server"
                    CancelDestinationPageUrl="~/MyData/DataPage.aspx"
                    ContinueDestinationPageUrl="~/MyData/DataPage.aspx">
</asp:ChangePassword>
```

The control only needs two essential arguments. The CancelDestinationPageUrl argument tells the control where to send the user after clicking Cancel. Likewise, the ContinueDestinationPageUrl argument defines where to redirect the user for a successful change. Generally, you'll set both destinations the same. Figure 18.10 shows a typical view of the ChangePassword control in action.

RECOVERING A PASSWORD

Nothing saps customer support resources like sending users lost passwords. The PasswordRecovery control automates the process. This is an extremely simple control to use, as shown here.

```
<asp:PasswordRecovery ID="PasswordRecovery1" Runat="server"
                      SuccessPageUrl="~/Login.aspx">
</asp:PasswordRecovery>
```

FIGURE 18.10
Use the *ChangePassword* control to reduce the complexity of user password changes.

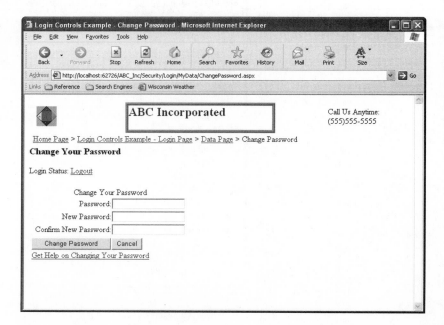

All you need to provide is the `SuccessPageUrl` attribute so the control knows where to send the user after a successful recovery. The actual recovery is a three-step process. The user begins by proving a name and clicking Submit. The next step, shown in Figure 18.11, requests the user's special question. In this case, it's the user's name, but normally you'd choose something such as the name of the user's cat. When the user answers the question successfully, the system sends their password to the email account that the user supplied. The combination of the special question and the email destination makes this process reasonably safe.

NOTE   You must configure an email server on the Application tab of the ASP.NET Web Application Administration Tool to use the `PasswordRecovery` control. Simply click the Configure SMTP E-mail Settings link, and you'll see settings you can use to update the email information for your server.

Checking All Incoming Data

One of the most common exploits for any Web application that relies on forms is to trick the form into doing something the originator didn't envision. Unfortunately, Web applications often prove difficult to monitor for these kinds of errors. The reasons include the use of text for all entries, the lack of strong data typing, and the problems of forcing scripts to perform tasks normally associated with full-fledged programming languages. Fortunately, ASP.NET provides validators to make it easier to maintain security by ensuring the user can only input values that you want to use.

FIGURE 18.11
Reduce user support costs by automating password recovery.

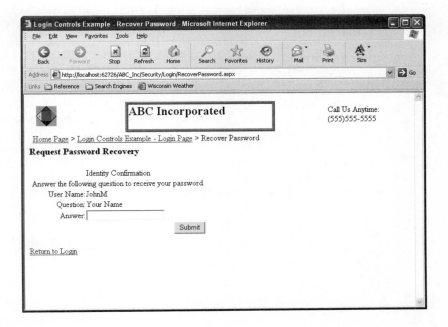

An Overview of the Validators

Validating Web applications can become quite complex, so Microsoft provides validators. A validator is a special control that ensures the user enters the right type of data and in the proper range. Each kind of validator performs a specific check, so you might use several validators together to provide full data entry coverage for your application.

Although validators vary in functionality, all validators require an error message found in the Text property that the user sees and uses to correct the error on the Web page. For example, when a user types a value that's outside the correct range, the RangeValidator displays the error message in the Text property. In addition, all validators provide a ControlToValidate property that you use to associate the control with the validator. (Some validators might require two controls as input.) Visual Web Developer supports several validator types, but here are the types you'll commonly use for applications.

CompareValidator The CompareValidator accepts two controls as input and then compares the value of each control. If the two controls don't match the condition you specify, the Compare Validator displays an error message. The name of the second control appears in the Control ToCompare property. The Operator property defines the comparison between the two controls. For example, if you choose the GreaterThan option, the value of the control listed in the Control ToValidate property must be greater than the value of the control listed in the ControlToCompare property. A Type property ensures the second control contains data of the correct type, but this is almost superfluous because the two controls won't compare if their types don't match.

RangeValidator The RangeValidator ensures the input in a control falls within a range of values. The MinimumValue and MaximumValue properties contain the limit of values the user can input. You'll use the Type property to determine what type of data the control will accept. The RangeValidator accepts common types including string, integer, double, date, and currency. If the input doesn't fall within the selected range of values or is of the wrong type, the control will display an error message.

RegularExpressionValidator The RegularExpressionValidator uses an expression consisting of a specially formatted string that defines the kind of input required to validate the content or format of the input. For example, you could use an expression that evaluates input for all numeric entries or all character entries. You'll find that the Microsoft help topics tend to focus on the format of the expression, as do the built-in expressions. However, the example in this section will show you how to build an expression that defines the content of the expression. The expression used for comparison with the input of the target control appears in the ValidationExpression property. Click the ellipsis in this property to display the Regular Expression Editor dialog box shown in Figure 18.12.

FIGURE 18.12
The Regular Expression Editor helps you choose a predefined expression or create one of your own.

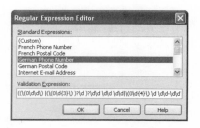

RequiredFieldValidator   This is the easiest of validators to understand. If the target control is blank, the validator displays an error message. Some developers use an asterisk in place of the error message and simply display one error message for all required fields. However, the use of a custom error message for each control means that you can provide example input for each field.

ValidationSummary   Most of the validation controls display errors immediately after the control loses focus. Some users can find this behavior distracting or frustrating. Use the `Validation Summary` to display a list of page errors at one time and in one place. Set the `Display` property of the validator control to `None` in order to suppress the standard display and make it appear in the summary instead. Figure 18.13 shows a typical Web page with a `ValidationSummary` control.

Notice that I haven't mentioned any need for application code. All of the validators perform their job without any coding on your part. The only work you need to perform is configuring the validator as described in the list. The validator performs the rest of the work for you at that point.

All of the validators provide client-side support. This feature forces the client to fix any errors in the form before the browser will send it to the server. Using a validator means your server will have to react to fewer poorly formatted messages and will work more efficiently. Of course, validators can only check for specific problems.

You can use multiple validators on one field to ensure the application detects as many problems as possible. In addition, the `CustomValidator` enables you to create special validators that can react to some unique conditions. Unfortunately, the `CustomValidator` requires you create code to make it functional, which makes a `CustomValidator` the custom programming solution for special situations.

FIGURE 18.13
Use a Validation Summary to consolidate form error messages.

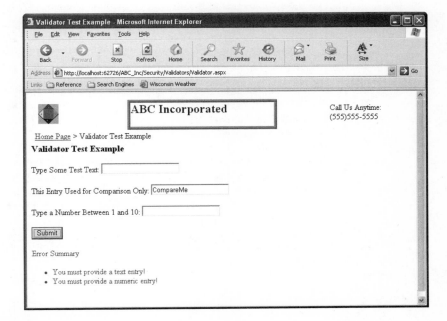

WARNING   Visual Web Developer still includes and supports the CustomValidator control, but you should avoid using it. Microsoft has marked this control as obsolete. You might not see this control in the next update of ASP.NET. Even so, the CustomValidator control can be quite useful in special situations.

Using Validators in an Application

Validators only require that you provide any required settings for use. The example in this section shows all of the essential validators so you can see how they work with a form. Listing 18.4 shows the test code for this example. You'll find this example in the \ABC_Inc\Security\Validators folder of the source code on the Sybex Web site.

LISTING 18.4:   Using Validators to Check Data Input

```
<form id="frmValidatorTest" runat="server">
<div id="Heading">
    <asp:Label ID="lblGreeting" Runat="server"
               Text="Validator Test Example"
               Font-Bold="True" Font-Size="X-Large"></asp:Label>
</div>
<div id="TestArea">
    <p>
        <asp:Label ID="lblTestEntry" Runat="server"
                   Text="Type Some Test Text: "
                   AssociatedControlID="txtTestEntry"></asp:Label>
        <asp:TextBox ID="txtTestEntry" Runat="server"></asp:TextBox>
        <asp:RequiredFieldValidator
            ID="rfvTestEntry" Runat="server"
            ErrorMessage="You must provide a text entry!"
            ControlToValidate="txtTestEntry" Display="None" >
        </asp:RequiredFieldValidator>
        <asp:RegularExpressionValidator
            ID="revTestEntry" Runat="server"
            ErrorMessage="Type 2 to 15 Characters Only!"
            ControlToValidate="txtTestEntry" Display="None"
            ValidationExpression=
            "[ABCDEFGHIJKLMNOPQRSTUVWXYZabcdefghijklmnopqrstuvwxyz]{2,15}">
        </asp:RegularExpressionValidator>
        <asp:CompareValidator
            ID="cvTestEntry" Runat="server"
            ErrorMessage=
                "txtTestEntry Doesn't Compare with txtCompare!"
            ControlToValidate="txtTestEntry"
            ControlToCompare="txtCompare" Display="None">
        </asp:CompareValidator>
    </p>
    <p>
```

```
        <asp:Label ID="lblCompare" Runat="server"
                    Text="This Entry Used for Comparison Only: "
                    AssociatedControlID="txtCompare"></asp:Label>
        <asp:TextBox ID="txtCompare" Runat="server">
            CompareMe
        </asp:TextBox>
    </p>
    <p>
        <asp:Label ID="lblNumeric" Runat="server"
                    Text="Type a Number Between 1 and 10: "
                    AssociatedControlID="txtNumeric"></asp:Label>
        <asp:TextBox ID="txtNumeric" Runat="server"></asp:TextBox>
        <asp:RequiredFieldValidator
            ID="rfNumeric" Runat="server"
            ErrorMessage="You must provide a numeric entry!"
            ControlToValidate="txtNumeric" Display="None">
        </asp:RequiredFieldValidator>
        <asp:RangeValidator
            ID="rvNumeric" Runat="server"
            ErrorMessage="Type a value between 1 and 10!"
            ControlToValidate="txtNumeric" Display="None"
            MinimumValue="0" MaximumValue="10" >
        </asp:RangeValidator>
    </p>
    <p>
        <asp:Button ID="btnSubmit" Runat="server"
                    Text="Submit"
                    AccessKey="S" PostBackUrl="Default.aspx" />
    </p>
</div>
<div id="SummaryArea">
    <p>
        <asp:ValidationSummary ID="Summary" Runat="server"
                                HeaderText="Error Summary" />
    </p>
</div>
</form>
```

The kinds of validators you use will depend on the kind of input you expect from a control. The example uses three controls, as shown in Figure 18.13. The first contains text input and relies on the `RequiredFieldValidator`, `RegularExpressionValidator`, and `CompareValidator` controls to ensure validity. The `RequiredFieldValidator` control doesn't require any special configuration.

The `RegularExpressionValidator` control requires some means of determining correct output. Although you can rely on the Microsoft supplied templates, in some cases, they won't fulfill most needs. Generally, you'll have to provide a template. The template for this example looks like this.

```
[ABCDEFGHIJKLMNOPQRSTUVWXYZabcdefghijklmnopqrstuvwxyz]{2,15}
```

The information within brackets tells the `RegularExpressionValidator` control which characters are acceptable. A cracker can't send a virus script to your server using the characters shown. The numbers within curly brackets define the acceptable character limits. A user can provide any input that relies on text between 2 and 15 characters long. This comparison could introduce problems in some cases. Notice that the list of acceptable characters doesn't include a period or spaces. You could conceivably set up a situation where the user can't provide the required input.

The `CompareValidator` control also requires special input. In this case, `txtTestEntry` must compare with `txtCompare`. This control can provide you with help when the user provides a value that doesn't match a value you expected. Generally, you won't need to use it, but it's nice to know the control is available when you do. Because of the three controls provided in this example, the only text that the user could type that would pass the tests is `CompareMe`.

Numeric input requires different handling from text input. When working with numbers, you're normally looking for a value between two ranges. Consequently, the numeric input relies on the `RequiredFieldValidator` and `RangeValidator` controls. Like the text input, the `RequiredField Validator` control only ensures that the user provides some kind of input—it doesn't require specific input.

The `RangeValidator` control requires that you provide the `MinimumValue` and `MaximumValue` attributes. These two attribute ensure that the input is a number that falls between the required minimum and maximum value. The user can't provide a script and have it pass the test. For that matter, typing three, in place of 3, won't pass the test either. The user must provide numeric input for this validator to accept the input. Figure 18.14 shows output from the various checks performed by this example.

FIGURE 18.14
Validation reduces the chances of someone sending you data you don't want.

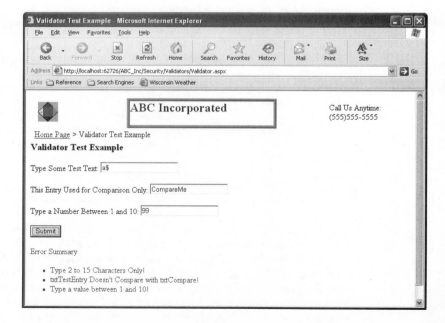

CHOOSING BETWEEN CODE AND AUTOMATION

All of the validators listed in this section perform their tasks well. In fact, you can improve Web site security greatly by using just these controls. However, it's important to know that you can accomplish the same tasks using code. For example, the following code will check input for length and verify that it contains the correct kind of data.

```
private void btnTest_Click(object sender,
                           System.EventArgs e)
{
    Regex   CheckChar = new Regex(@"\w{5}");

    // Verify the string isn't too long.
    if (txtInput.Text.Length > 5)
        throw new ArgumentException(
            "The Input string is too long!");

    // Verfiy the content of the string.
    if (!CheckChar.IsMatch(txtInput.Text))
        throw new ArgumentOutOfRangeException(
            "Incorrect data in the input string!");

    // Show the text in txtOutput.
    txtOutput.Text = txtInput.Text;

    // Make the component visible.
    txtOutput.Visible = true;
}
```

This code guarantees that no one can enter any special characters in the data entry field. In addition, the input must contain five or less characters. You can assure a safe Web page either way, but using the coded approach can guarantee better flexibility and better control over the security check. Using controls is faster and less error prone. The choice of code or controls comes down to one of determining what you want to do. Generally, you'll use controls because you won't need the special functionality that coding can provide, but it's good to remember that you have a choice.

Hardening Your Applications against Outside Intrusion

As important as security and validation are, you still need to do more to protect your application from hostile influences. Of course, your first line of defense is constant vigilance—make sure you check your application for damage, look for unwanted (or unexpected) files on your system, and verify that your database is intact whenever possible. A check here or there can make a significant difference in your system's security. The following sections describe some other tactics you can use to keep crackers at bay.

Preventing Data Leaks

Your Web site has a data leak. It doesn't matter how well you secure the site or whether the people using it are trustworthy, the data leak is there. Many developers discount the problem of data leaks because they think they have followed every security procedure. However, data leaks occur not because of a programming problem, but because of an implementation problem. Displaying any information at all on a Web site causes an information leak for your organization. Of course, since the purpose of a Web site is to provide information to viewers, your application wouldn't be worth very much without at least a small information leak. In addition, some kinds of information leaks are actually good for your organization, such as when you announce a new product.

Part of your responsibility as a developer is ensuring your design doesn't leak data that's better left private. For example, make sure your templates, databases, and Web pages contain only the information that they need to contain. Of course, these data sources still have to provide functionality, so you can't leave them blank. Make sure that you don't confuse protected company information with essential user information. You still have to make the Web page accessible and it still requires good help to avoid confusing the user.

Data leak protection can take other forms. For example, your organization might rely on a database to supply information for Web pages. At some point, your program will need to access the required database record, extract the data, apply it to a page, and output the result. This setup provides a perfect opportunity to scan for forbidden words, such as the name of a new secret project, during the extraction phase using regular expression parsing. Obviously, this form of data leak protection won't fulfill every need—a smart user that's determined to leak information will find some other words to do it. This limitation is the same reason that spam filters are only partially successful.

Many people complain that digital rights management is a bad thing and it can be a bad thing when used for the wrong purposes. This book doesn't discuss matters that are legal, philosophical, or ethical, except when it comes to working with code. Information leaks occur when someone passes data from your Web site to a second person that shouldn't view it. The data transfer can occur as part of covert information sharing or as an accidental data release as part of an email. If you want to maintain the secrecy of proprietary company information that you must make available on the Internet, make sure you use digital rights management. Even if someone obtains a copy of the file, it's useless without the password required to open it for viewing. After you decide to protect the file using some type of encryption (such as password protection for Adobe Acrobat files), you should also use data encryption to transfer the data. Ensuring no one can access your data without permission and then guarding the data through encryption doesn't accomplish much if you don't protect the means for obtaining it. Make sure that your security measures really do keep unwanted people out of the system.

Encrypting Your Data

Data encryption is an essential data protection technique today and you really can employ it on Web sites. You have a number of choices to make, such as the use of symmetric or asymmetric encryption. Remember that the asymmetric technique found in the `System.Security.Cryptography` `.AsymmetricAlgorithm` class relies on a public/private key pair, making it the logical choice for Web communications because you can trust others with the public key, while keeping the private key safe on your system. The use of two keys makes it possible to work with others in a secure manner without exposing yourself to needless risk.

Encryption also relies on an encryption technique and a specific hash algorithm. When working with Web-based algorithms, you need to consider the likes, dislikes, and requirements of the other participants in a data exchange. The most common encryption technique in use today is Rivest, Shamir, and Adleman (RSA). You can find this algorithm in the RSA class and the implementation in the `RSACryptoServiceProvider` class.

Some developers see data encryption as an all-or-nothing undertaking. The facts are less clear. You actually have multiple encryption choices and strategies to choose from when working with Web applications. However, you can group these approaches into whole message or individual element categories. When you use SSL to create an application, the system encrypts the entire message. Encryption and decryption time is one reason why SSL communication takes so much time. Likewise, you can implement channel sinks to perform the task if you don't want to rely on a pure SSL approach. A channel sink lets you maintain control over the communication.

Encryption always increases the size of the message, consumes additional processing time, and generally slows everything down. Consequently, the smart developer uses enough encryption to ensure sensitive data remains safe, but not so much encryption that the system slows to an unacceptable speed. Desktop applications have faster communication channels, so full message encryption isn't quite as much a burden as with Web applications. Partial message encryption is much faster and resource efficient when working with Web applications.

Defining Your Development Goals

This chapter has explored general security issues—those that affect your application and your company as a whole. You can't ignore security issues in today's environment. Too many crackers are waiting to probe your application, locate the hole they want to use, and compromise your system for you to ignore security in even the smallest application. This chapter provides tools you need to combine with the security topics in other chapters in this book to create a good security setup for your application.

It's time to begin setting up your security strategy. In fact, you should have security polices in place before you write even one line of code. Make security part of the foundation of your application and include it at every level of the design and implementation process. Make sure you schedule security testing and revise your security strategy as needed. Planning is an essential part of creating a robust security environment for both your application and your organization.

Chapter 19 discusses an incredibly important issue for large applications—optimization. It's important to ensure your application makes good use of valuable resources and still delivers data to the user in a timely manner. In some cases, you'll find that speed of delivery will run counter to efficient resource use, so you'll need to make a choice on which is more important. Optimization can also affect the security and reliability of your application—nothing is free, you always have to consider the gains and losses of a particular decision. Chapter 19 helps you make sense of the difficult task of optimizing your application. Although this chapter can't provide a specific solution for your application, it helps you understand your choices better and provides you with techniques you can use to make a great optimization decision.

Chapter 19

Optimizing Your Applications

At some point, you'll have enough of your application built that you'll want to begin optimizing it. Depending on the development model you use, this process (along with testing) can be ongoing, can occur as different modules become ready, or it can happen in one big lump at the end of the development process. No matter when you optimize your application, it can be an error prone and frustrating experience. The question isn't necessarily one of coding skills, but of defining what you want to optimize and how to optimize it. For example, you can optimize an application to provide superior security or reliability at the cost of the user experience or application speed. Consequently, you must have a good idea of what you want to do before you even begin the optimization process.

TIP   This book doesn't discuss software engineering goals in detail. For example, it doesn't tell you about the various methods of designing an application, which can affect how you optimize it. To obtain a better perspective of how software engineering plays a role in making the optimization experience better, get *Coder to Developer* by Mike Gunderloy (Sybex, 2004). Likewise, to understand how user habits affect the optimization process, review *Developer to Designer* by Mike Gunderloy (Sybex, 2005).

Once you know what you want to optimize and how you want to optimize it, you need some way to measure performance. Developers rely on performance counters for this task. However, it's important to realize that a performance counter isn't a measure of performance, any more than a ruler is a measure of length. A performance counter provides a count of something that you must then interpret. Consequently, using the right performance counter and interpreting it correctly partially determines the success of the optimization process. This chapter reviews four performance counter types:

◆ Those provided as part of applications (including Windows)

◆ Those that appear as part of the .NET Framework

◆ Custom counters that you create when none of these other options work

Finally, the chapter discusses two optimization tools that you can use to make the optimization process easier. You can find many other tools on the market and the tool you use depends on your specific needs. The two tools found in this chapter simply show some of the features that you can expect from an optimization tool. Considering that you get Analysis Server free with some versions of Visual Studio, this is a great place to start to build knowledge about the optimization process.

Working with Performance Counters

As previously mentioned, a performance counter is a measuring tool that's open to interpretation by the person using it. As you'll see in the "Defining the Custom Performance Counter" section of the chapter, the technique used to measure something is also up to the developer. A performance counter doesn't simply count something—it counts it in a particular way. Consequently, you can count the number of times an error occurs as a total, as an incremental count during a time interval, as a percentage of some other measure, and myriad other ways. The following sections discuss how to work with performance counters to achieve your optimization goals. The "Testing Your Application" section of the chapter describes how to monitor performance counters separately and as part of a custom application.

Understanding Performance Counters

Anyone who understands performance counters knows that they stretch the term *performance*, in most cases, and that counting can include many forms of numeric analysis. Some developers automatically assume that performance equates to speed, but it doesn't. In some respects, the term *performance* is a bit of a misnomer because you can use performance counters to count anything. Think of performance counters as statistics generators. In fact, here are some interesting uses that you can apply to performance counters.

Resource Usage   Performance could relate to resource usage—an application could detect when it's using resources inefficiently or too quickly and adjust its operation, potentially preventing a system crash.

General Event Monitoring   Performance counters can measure how much or how many of a particular event has occurred, usually within a given time. Tracking network packet usage falls into this category. However, you can track any event—even user clicks on a form's Submit button.

Detecting External Attacks   When used as a statistics generator, you can use performance counters to monitor your system for unexpected events such as a Distributed Denial of Service (DDOS) attacks. For example, you might have so many requests of a certain type on a given day and know that these events occur within a predictable range. Suddenly, your Web site receives three or four times the number of requests. Even though everything might look normal otherwise, an indicator like this can signal the beginning of a DDOS attack

Training   Companies are always looking for ways to improve efficiency, but the question is where. You can also use performance counters to monitor user events. For example, you can answer questions such as how often users make an error when using a particular Web page. When you notice a negative usage trend, you can detect it and providing training in that area. Ultimately, troubleshooting both code and user habits results in overall efficiency improvements without invoking a painful process that everyone will dislike. Users with proper training in the right areas are less frustrated. Developers who know precisely where to look for coding problems also reduce their workload.

Using Standard Performance Counters

You'll find standard performance counters in a number of places. How you use these standard performance counters depends on your application and the capabilities of the application that provides them. Here are a few performance counters to consider for your application.

Windows Windows comes with standard performance counters that let you check everything from the amount of memory available for applications to the number of processing cycles that a particular process is using. You can use these counters to monitor the environment to ensure your application has enough resources to run efficiently. It's also possible to use these counters to monitor user activity and to check the overall health of an application. The Windows counters are general in nature, however, so you can't count on them to tell you about specific application issues.

Installable Servers Many installable servers include performance counters. For example, you can use the Internet Information Services (IIS) counters to tell you about the current state of IIS. You can determine the cache hit level, for example, to tune IIS performance. In fact, it's possible to use this information to modify your Web pages programmatically to provide a dynamic performance tune for your IIS application (within limits). SQL Server also provides counters that you can use to optimize your backend application performance. In fact, you'll find that most installable servers provide at least a few performance counters.

Visual Studio .NET Add-ins Many Visual Studio .NET add-in products provide performance counters so that you can monitor them from within your application. For example, the full version of Crystal Reports provides performance counters that you can use to manage your application better. You might decide to make some reports temporarily unavailable or forgo processing them immediately when the server load exceeds a certain value or you notice that the add-in is working slowly.

Applications Many third party applications provide performance counters. Depending on how you use these applications, you change your application behavior to meet certain needs. For example, when an instance of the application on one server becomes slow or lacks resources, you can move requests to another server with better performance characteristics. In short, it's all about finding what you need, when you need it.

Using .NET Specific Performance Counters

Your applications run using the services of the .NET Framework within the Command Language Runtime (CLR). Consequently, even if the server has every resource needed and is running quite fast; your application will run incredibly slow when CLR isn't in good health. In fact, these counters provide the first level of defense for your application—they help you to understand when the optimization problem is within Windows, CLR, or your application. In some cases, you might be surprised to find that you have to tweak Windows or CLR, not your application, to achieve a desired result.

The number of .NET performance counters that Microsoft provides is relatively impressive. In fact, you might find that you can avoid creating a custom counter through judicious use of a .NET performance counter. The following list provides a quick overview of the various .NET performance counters you can access.

.NET CLR Data You'll use these counters to obtain access to data connection information. For example, you can discover the number of times that a connection failed or a command didn't execute. By monitoring these numbers, you can look for patterns in data usage—everything from cracker activity (signaled by an inordinate number of failed connections) to a misconfigured application (perhaps the commands aren't executing).

.NET CLR Exceptions   Use these performance counters to discover the number of exceptions for CLR as a whole or as the result of individual applications. Often, these counters signal unresolved error conditions that you need to check for your application. You can also use these numbers to detect configuration, resource, timing, cracker, and other issues.

.NET CLR Interop   These counters are exceptionally important when your application depends on non-.NET resources. Most companies today have applications that rely partly on .NET and partly on COM or Windows. You can use these counters to ensure the two environments are working efficiently with each other.

.NET CLR Jit   The main use for these performance counters is to verify that the Just-in-Time (JIT) compilation process works as expected. If you suddenly see a lot of JIT activity and know you haven't made any changes to your application code, you have to wonder what changed. Often unexpected activity with these performance counters signals configuration changes or unexpected (perhaps unwanted) changes occurring in the background.

.NET CLR Loading   These counters help you determine how fast application elements load. You can also check the class loader state. For example, you can determine how many bytes the class loader has loaded into memory. One essential performance counter measures the number of load failures—a value that should always appear at 0 (or at least very low) on a healthy system.

.NET CLR LocksAndThreads   Use this performance counter to check the number of threads that an application loads. In addition, you can use it to check resource lock status. For example, you can detect the number of lock contentions that have occurred. In some cases, you might have to optimize the locking code to reduce the number of lock contentions to obtain good application performance.

.NET CLR Memory   Use these counters to detect global and application-specific memory usage. In some cases, complex applications require memory monitoring to ensure that the application runs efficiently. Sometimes you'll find that releasing resources manually, rather than waiting for garbage collection, helps overall system performance and the performance of the individual application. This technique works especially well when an application uses a number of objects that require large memory allocations.

.NET CLR Network   These counters show .NET-specific network statistics, which may differ from the Windows network statistics. Generally, you'll want to use these counters for applications that require large amounts of remote resources.

.NET CLR Remoting   Don't confuse these counters with those used for networking—these counters measure application interaction with remote objects. For example, you can check how many proxy objects your application requires.

.NET CLR Security   You'll use these counters to verify the performance of the security system, not check system security. For example, you can detect the number of runtime security checks that your application makes. These counters are important for optimization because they can point out the cost of security to your application. Higher security usage levels reduce resources and processing cycles available for actual application work.

You might also find special .NET performance counters in the list. For example, you might find a provider counter for Oracle or SQL Server in the list. These other performance counters help you monitor the activities of these special Visual Studio .NET add-ins.

Creating Custom Performance Counters

Sometimes you need a custom performance counter to achieve a specific result. In any situation where you need specifics about internal application performance, you generally need a custom performance counter. Of course, you should always verify that none of the standard performance counters provides the same information (see the "Working with Performance Counters" section of the chapter for details). The following sections describe how to create a custom performance counter, add it to your application, and then monitor it using a number of techniques. In addition, you'll see how to use the performance data to your advantage in optimizing your application and how to avoid some of the problems that developers encounter when using performance counters incorrectly.

DECIDING HOW TO PACKAGE YOUR PERFORMANCE COUNTER

It's relatively easy to decide how to package a performance counter for a desktop application. In many cases, you'll place the performance counter directly within the application. As long as the application is running, so is the performance counter. Given that you don't care about application performance when the application isn't running, this methodology works just fine. However, you might also decide to place the performance counter in a Web service. You can use this approach when you need to track performance in several application modules.

Web applications don't have any state, they don't run continuously, and multiple users access the same Web pages. Consequently, it's much harder to place the performance counter within the Web application. When you do place it within the Web application, you have to be concerned about other instances of the performance counter, and things can get quite messy very quickly. In short, you can't use the application as a packaging method for Web-based performance counters in many instances. Adding the performance counter directly to the application works best when you have a very specific element to watch (such as a specific error that users encounter) and you don't expect to see this counter in use often.

Of course, you can use the other desktop solution—a Windows service. Adding special code to your application lets you attach to the Windows service and tell it to provide any required performance counter updates. This method has the advantage of letting you use a single performance counter for any application that requires it. Unfortunately, it's not automatic—there's that special code requirement. Because Windows services can also prove complex to write, many developers shy away from them. (Happily, writing a Windows service using .NET is a lot easier than any method Microsoft provides.) A Windows service works best when you need to use the same performance counter across multiple applications.

Long-time developers will remember that IIS relies on Internet Server Application Programming Interface (ISAPI) filters to perform many tasks. In fact, ASP.NET relies on an ISAPI filter to redirect ASPX requests to ASP.NET from IIS. An ISAPI filter is extremely flexible and it can work with any file extension—it doesn't even have to be a standard file extension, you can invent your own. The only problem with using the ISAPI filter approach is that you have to write the code using Visual C++, which means it's not a good solution for many companies. This is the method to use when you require extreme flexibility.

The technique that many developers end up using is to write an HttpModule. In fact, that's the technique used in this chapter. Using an HttpModule lets you intercept any ASP.NET event and respond to it. (Consequently, you can't use an HttpModule to work with standard HTML pages or anything that isn't ASP.NET related.) For example, when a user requests a particular Web page, you can intercept the request, make any updates to the performance counter, and pass the request along to the next HttpModule in line. This approach works best when you need to provide performance monitoring for a number of Web pages in a single application based on a specific event and the ASP.NET limitation isn't a concern.

Defining the Custom Performance Counter

The ABC Incorporated Web site wants to monitor specific Web pages for activity to ensure that people are accessing them as needed. Because Web page access is a specific kind of event, it's possible to use an `HttpModule` to perform the task. (See the "Deciding How to Package Your Performance Counter" sidebar to discover the best packaging to use for particular Web page activities.) In fact, you can intercept as many of these 17 standard events as you wish (listed in the order that ASP.NET executes them).

- ◆ `BeginRequest`
- ◆ `AuthenticateRequest`
- ◆ `PostAuthenticateRequest`
- ◆ `AuthorizeRequest`
- ◆ `PostAuthorizeRequest`
- ◆ `ResolveRequestCache`
- ◆ `PostResolveRequestCache`
- ◆ `PostMapRequestHandler`
- ◆ `AcquireRequestState`
- ◆ `PostAcquireRequestState`
- ◆ `PreRequestHandlerExecute`
- ◆ `PostRequestHandlerExecute`
- ◆ `ReleaseRequestState`
- ◆ `PostReleaseRequestState`
- ◆ `UpdateRequestCache`
- ◆ `PostUpdateRequestCache`
- ◆ `EndRequest`

For this example, all that the code really needs to consider is the `BeginRequest` event. This event occurs immediately after IIS responds to a request—it's the first event in the HTTP event chain. The example begins by adding a new class to the application. Listing 19.1 shows the code you'll add to creating the performance counter. You'll find this example in the `PageAccessCount.vb` file located in the `\ABC_Inc\App_Code` folder of the source code found on the Sybex Web site.

LISTING 19.1:   Creating a Performance Counter for Web Pages

```
Public Class PageAccessCount
    Implements IHttpModule

    ' Contains all of the counters.
```

```vb
Private CounterCollect As CounterCreationDataCollection

' Information used to create the counter.
Private CounterData As CounterCreationData

' Performance counters for this application.
Private WebPageVisits As PerformanceCounter

' Time tracking object.
Private SampleTime As DateTime

' Tracks the number of page visits.
Private Visits As Int32

Public Sub Dispose() Implements System.Web.IHttpModule.Dispose
    ' Make sure you clean up the counters.
    WebPageVisits.RemoveInstance()
    PerformanceCounterCategory.Delete("ABC Incorporated")
End Sub

Public Sub Init(ByVal context As System.Web.HttpApplication) _
    Implements System.Web.IHttpModule.Init

    ' Initialize the date/time value.
    SampleTime = DateTime.Now

    ' Set the initial number of visits.
    Visits = 0

    ' Add the beginning and ending event handlers.
    context.AddOnBeginRequestAsync( _
        New BeginEventHandler(AddressOf UpdateCount), _
        New EndEventHandler(AddressOf EndProcess))

    ' Initialize the performance counter collection.
    CounterCollect = New CounterCreationDataCollection()

    ' Create a counter.
    CounterData = New CounterCreationData( _
        "User_Web_Visits", _
        "Shows the number of visits to a particular Web page.", _
        PerformanceCounterType.NumberOfItems32)

    ' Add the counter to the collection.
    CounterCollect.Add(CounterData)

    ' Add this counter collection to the list of performance
    ' counters.
```

```vb
    If Not PerformanceCounterCategory.Exists("ABC Incorporated") Then
        PerformanceCounterCategory.Create( _
            "ABC Incorporated", _
            "Shows the number of visits to a particular Web page.", _
            PerformanceCounterCategoryType.MultiInstance, _
            CounterCollect)
    End If

    ' Define the actual Web page counter.
    WebPageVisits = New PerformanceCounter( _
        "ABC Incorporated", _
        "User_Web_Visits", _
        "Sample_Page", _
        False)

    ' Set the initial instance value.
    WebPageVisits.RawValue = 0
End Sub

Public Function UpdateCount(ByVal Sender As Object, _
                           ByVal e As EventArgs, _
                           ByVal cb As AsyncCallback, _
                           ByVal extraData As Object) _
                           As IAsyncResult

    Dim Result As New ThisResult()    ' Shows the current result.
    Dim ThisPath As String            ' Shows the requested path.

    ' Determine whether the sample interval of 1 second has
    ' expired.
    If SampleTime.AddSeconds(1) < DateTime.Now Then

        ' Set the new number of visits.
        WebPageVisits.RawValue = Visits

        ' Reset the visits counter.
        Visits = 0

        ' Reset the sample interval.
        SampleTime = DateTime.Now
    End If

    ' Get the requested path.
    ThisPath = My.Request.Path

    ' Determine whether the request is for the sample page.
    If ThisPath = "/ABC_Inc/Performance/CustomCounter/PageCount.aspx" Then
```

```
        ' Update the counter.
        Visits += 1
    End If

    ' Return the result.
    Return Result
End Function

Public Sub EndProcess(ByVal ar As IAsyncResult)

End Sub
End Class
```

The code begins with `Init()`, which accepts an application context as input. The first two lines set the current sample time and the number of visits to the sample Web page. As part of setting up the event handler, the code uses `context.AddOnBeginRequestAsync()` to define the beginning event handler, `UpdateCount()`, and the ending event handler, `EndProcess()`. You must perform this step for every event that you want your performance counter to handle. It's the same concept as connecting a button to the code behind that supports it.

The code then creates the performance counter. To begin, the code defines a `CounterCreation DataCollection` object, which contains all of the counters that you want to add to the operating system environment. This object eventually defines the Performance Object field entry in the Add Counters dialog box of the System Monitor snap-in for the Performance console located in the Administrative Tools folder of the Control panel as shown in Figure 19.1.

FIGURE 19.1
Every performance counter object has a physical presence in the System Monitor snap-in.

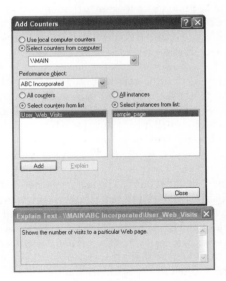

The next step is to create a counter using a `CounterCreationData` object. A counter collection can contain as many counters as needed to perform a given task. A counter typically defines a particular task, such as counting the number of visits to a Web page, but isn't specific—you wouldn't create a counter for a specific Web page. Counters come in a number of types. For example, you can tell Windows to create a counter that presents an average or counts the number of items per second. In this case, the example uses `PerformanceCounterType.NumberOfItems32`, which simply counts the number of items. Notice the other two arguments for `CounterCreationData()`. The first contains the counter name, which appears in the Select Counters from List field in Figure 19.1. The second argument contains a help string, which appears in the Explain Text dialog box when the user clicks Explain, as shown in Figure 19.1. Once the code defines the counter, it adds it to the collection using `CounterCollect.Add()`. At this point, you would create any additional counters you needed and add them to the collection.

Before the code can do anything else, it must create the performance counter. However, you must always verify that the performance counter doesn't exist before you create it using `Performance CounterCategory.Exists()` or the .NET Framework could generate an error. When the performance counter doesn't exist, the code creates it using `PerformanceCounterCategory.Create()`. The first argument supplied with this call contains the name of the performance counter as a whole as it appears in the Performance Object field shown in Figure 19.1. The second argument provides a help string. This help string doesn't appear anywhere in System Monitor, but it does come in handy when you access the performance counter using the Visual Studio .NET IDE. The third argument defines the instance data for this counter. Because you might want to count hits on multiple Web pages, which would require multiple instances, the code uses the `PerformanceCounterCategory Type.MultiInstance` constant.

At this point, the counter is available, but not usable. To make the counter usable, the code adds a `PerformanceCounter` object. This object appears in the Select Instances from List field in Figure 19.1. The four arguments for the `PerformanceCounter()` constructor include the name of the performance counter container, the name of the performance counter, the name of this instance (which cannot contain any spaces), and a Boolean value describing the read/write status of this performance counter. Always set this last value to `False`. The code also initializes the instance by setting its `RawValue` property to 0.

Assuming that the administrator installs the `HttpModule` (see the "Adding the Performance Counter to Your Application" section for details), the `UpdateCount()` event handler waits for a user to request a Web page. ASP.NET sends every Web page request for the host Web site to the `HttpModule`, which means `UpdateCount()` must perform some filtering. Actually, `UpdateCount()` must perform three tasks. First, it creates a result value to send to the `EndProcess()` event handler when it finishes its work. You'll discover more about this process in the "Creating an IAsyncResult Class" section.

Second, `UpdateCount()` determines whether the sample time has expired. The example uses 1 second as a sample time, but you could use any value you want. In fact, if you add an XML settings file, you can read it in and change this value without making any changes to the code. You'll find many examples of XML file use in the book, such as the search site example in Chapter 8. When the sample period ends, the code adds the number of visits to the `WebPageVisits.RawValue` property, which makes this value available to any application monitoring application performance. The code resets both the number of visits and the sample time for another series of samples.

Third, `UpdateCount()` updates the number of visits. The current request always appears within the `My.Request.Path` property. The code places this value in `ThisPath` and compares it to the sample page path. Again, you could easily place the page you want to monitor in an XML configuration file to make this process completely configurable without changing any code. The code updates Visits with the latest visit when the user requests the sample page.

You'll noticed that EndProcess() doesn't contain any code. The reason is that the performance counter process is so short that you can complete it synchronously. The EndProcess() event handler only comes into play when you need to perform asynchronous processing for a longer coding requirement. The idea is to let the other HttpModule entries proceed while you continue to perform processing in the background.

The application calls Dispose() before it ends. The performance counter for this application is unimportant when the application isn't running. Rather than cause confusion for any system administrator using System Monitor to check out the system, it's better to remove the counters before the application exits. The WebPageVisits.RemoveInstance() and PerformanceCounterCategory .Delete() methods perform this task—the counter will disappear from the Performance Object list of the Add Counters dialog box. You must close and reopen the Add Counters dialog box to see this change.

Creating an *IAsyncResult* Class

Older versions of ASP.NET provided event overrides for synchronous operation, but the latest version provides only the asynchronous entries. However, you can still perform synchronous tasks. When creating the beginning event handler for an HttpModule, you must provide a class that implements the IAsyncResult interface as a return value. Listing 19.2 shows a typical implementation for synchronous operations. You'll find this example in the PageAccessCount.vb file located in the \ABC_Inc\App_Code folder of the source code found on the Sybex Web site.

This example shows a minimal implementation. When you perform asynchronous operations (a bad idea for performance reasons with a performance counter), you need to add code to handle multithreading. Every implementation of IAsyncResult includes the four properties shown. You can add other properties and methods as needed to accomplish a given task.

In this case, the code only needs to override the constructor, New(). Notice how the constructor sets the four fields used to feed the properties. The _AsyncState field doesn't matter, in this case, because you aren't doing anything in EndProcess(). The ending event handler relies on state information to know how to handle the result of an asynchronous operation. The _AsyncWaitHandle field contains a reset handle—indicating that the process is finished. The code creates this handle using the AutoResetEvent() method and setting it to True. Most applications use an asynchronous wait to improve system performance and negate the requirement to monitor the IsCompleted property. The _CompletedSynchronously field indicates that the UpdateCount() event handler accomplished the task completely in a synchronous fashion. Finally, _IsCompleted shows that the task is complete.

LISTING 19.2:   Defining a Class that Implements *IAsyncResult*

```
Public Class ThisResult
    Implements IAsyncResult

    ' The four property values.
    Private _AsyncState As Object
    Private _AsyncWaitHandle As WaitHandle
```

```vb
        Private _CompletedSynchronously As Boolean
        Private _IsCompleted As Boolean

        Public Sub New()
            ' Initialize the four values.
            _AsyncState = 0
            _AsyncWaitHandle = New AutoResetEvent(True)
            _CompletedSynchronously = True
            _IsCompleted = True
        End Sub

        Public ReadOnly Property AsyncState() As Object _
            Implements System.IAsyncResult.AsyncState

            Get
                Return _AsyncState
            End Get
        End Property

        Public ReadOnly Property AsyncWaitHandle() _
            As System.Threading.WaitHandle _
            Implements System.IAsyncResult.AsyncWaitHandle

            Get
                Return _AsyncWaitHandle
            End Get
        End Property

        Public ReadOnly Property CompletedSynchronously() As Boolean _
            Implements System.IAsyncResult.CompletedSynchronously

            Get
                Return _CompletedSynchronously
            End Get
        End Property

        Public ReadOnly Property IsCompleted() As Boolean _
            Implements System.IAsyncResult.IsCompleted

            Get
                Return _IsCompleted
            End Get
        End Property
    End Class
```

Adding the Performance Counter to Your Application

Creating an `HttpModule` doesn't mean that the application will use it. You must install the `HttpModule` by making an entry in `Web.CONFIG`. In fact, it's great that you must perform this task because it means that you can turn performance monitoring on or off without having to compile the code again. Here's the simple code you'll use to add the performance counter to the application. You'll find this example in the `\ABC_Inc` folder of the source code found on the Sybex Web site.

```
<httpModules>
    <add type="PageAccessCount" name="ABC_Inc"/>
</httpModules>
```

Yes, it really is that easy. The `<add>` element contains two attributes. The `type` attribute defines the name of the class containing the performance counter. You can optionally add the namespace when necessary. The `name` attribute defines the name of the assembly that contains the performance counter. Because this performance counter appears as part of the application, it has the same assembly name as the application, but you can just as easily place performance counters in an external assembly.

Testing Your Application

Having a performance counter to check the optimization of your application and see how it reacts to users opens all kinds of possibilities for testing. Of course, the easiest method for working with a performance counter is to rely on the features provided by the Performance console located in the Administrative Tools folder of the Control Panel. However, you can also rely on any third party application that uses performance counters to generate reports or create a monitoring application of your own. You don't have many limits in how you can access the information the performance counter provides. It really comes down to how you interpret the performance counter output.

This section assumes that you want to use the System Monitor snap-in of the Performance console to work with the performance counter. Start the ABC Incorporated application, at this point, so you can test it. Remember that the performance counter isn't active until you run the application. Use the following procedure to view the output of this application:

1. Open the Performance console located in the Administrative Tools folder of the Control Panel. You'll see the Performance console consisting of the System Monitor and Performance Logs and Alerts snap-ins.

2. Select the System Monitor snap-in. The right pane now contains a graphic display of some type.

3. Remove any existing performance counters by clicking Delete (the button with an X on it) until any existing counters are gone.

4. Add a new counter to the display by clicking the Add button (looks like a plus sign). Select the application name, ABC Incorporated, in the Performance Object field, and `User_Web_Visits` from the Select Counters from List field.

5. Click Add, and then Close.

6. Go to the following URL: `http://localhost:62726/ABC_Inc/Performance/CustomCounter/PageCount.aspx` and click Refresh multiple times. You'll see System Monitor output that equates to the clicks you provide. Figure 19.2 shows a typical example.

7. Go to the Home Page (`http://localhost:62726/ABC_Inc/Default.ASPX`) and begin choosing pages at random. You'll notice that the System Monitor doesn't record any events unless you select the monitored page.

FIGURE 19.2

Use a performance counter to detect user activity on the Web site.

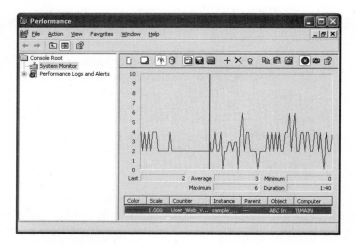

Avoiding Performance Counter Woes

Unfortunately, some developers learn about performance counters and run amuck with them. A reality of using performance counters is that they affect the performance of the very applications they're supposed to monitor. The performance counter uses some amount of resources including both memory and CPU time to run. Consequently, the measurement isn't precise and it's very hard to compensate for the performance drop in a complex application. Fortunately, the measurement error is extremely small, in most cases, but it's still there. Every counter you add to the application adds to the problem.

A custom application can mitigate the problem of performance counter drag by making them a configurable option—allowing the administrator to turn the counters on or off as needed. This option still incurs an infinitesimal penalty because the code still needs to check whether the counter is on or off, but the penalty is so small with a modern computer that it doesn't really matter. In general, make all of your counters configurable so the application runs at the fastest possible speed. A problem with many of those high-end applications is that the counters are on all the time, making it impossible to determine how much drag the monitoring system is placing on the application.

TIP It's possible to make a good guess as to how much your performance counter loads the system by placing two copies of the same counter in the code, taking a measurement, and then removing one of the counters to see the effect. The performance difference is the drag placed on the application by that particular counter. This technique isn't foolproof and you do need to monitor the counters individually to obtain an accurate result, but it does work well enough that you can make some determinations on how to advise an administrator who wants to use the counters.

Another issue to consider is whether a particular statistic is a good candidate for a performance counter. For example, many applications include one or more memory performance counters. In at least one case, I saw an application where the output of the counter was a straight line—no change at all. The problem is that the application never created any dynamic structures, so its memory footprint didn't change. Developers, administrators, and power users alike know about the memory the application requires, so a performance counter is a waste of time. Using performance counters to measure variable data of consequence is essential.

Analyzing Your Application

Microsoft provides a number of built-in tools that you can use to analyze your application. These analysis tools help you optimize your application by looking for common flaws or placing a load on the application so you can see how it performs. Some of these tools only work in a team development scenario so you'll learn about them in Chapter 23. The following sections describe the tools that you can use in any scenario to optimize your code.

TIP   Besides the tools that Microsoft provides with Visual Studio, you'll want to locate third party tools to help you analyze your code and make it better. One such product is Refactor! for Visual Basic 2005 (`http://www.devexpress.com/vbrefactor/`). The goal of this tool is to help you simplify your code wherever possible—making it both easier to read and improving speed. You can read a short InfoWorld review of this product at `http://www.infoworld.com/article/05/05/10/HNrefactor_1.html?source=NLC-AD2005-05-12`.

Using Code Analysis

Visual Studio contains a code analysis feature. Essentially, this feature verifies that your code meets minimum standards for good coding practice. You can check everything from the naming of your variables to security to how you design certain application elements. Microsoft turns this feature off by default. Select Website ➢ Code Analysis Configuration to work with this feature. You'll see the Code Analysis Configuration dialog box shown in Figure 19.3.

FIGURE 19.3
Code analysis can help you locate potential performance problems with your application.

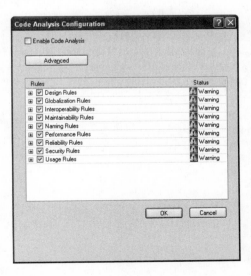

Each of the entries in the Rules field is a major rule category. Click the plus sign next to any rule category to see the individual rules. You can choose to ignore any rules that fall outside your normal company policy by clearing the check next to it. Give a rule a higher priority by clicking the Warning icon and changing it to an Error icon.

Check Enable Code Analysis and click OK to enable this feature. Whenever you build your application from this point on, the IDE will present you with a list of code analysis warnings and errors that you can use to improve your code. These messages appear in the Error List just as any other application error does.

Using the Performance Wizard

The Performance Wizard helps you check how your application runs. Select the Tools ➢ Performance Tools ➢ Performance Wizard command to begin using this tool. You'll immediately see the Performance Wizard dialog box. The following steps get you started.

1. Select the target you want to profile. The default setting profiles the current application. However, you can also profile external files including DLLs, EXEs, and other ASP.NET applications. This section assumes that you're going to check the local application.

2. Click Next. You'll see the Specify Profiling Method dialog box. You have two options: check the entire application (Sampling) or check a specific set of Web pages (Instrumentation). Use the Sampling option when you begin the optimization process. Once you get most of the Web pages optimized, look for trouble areas by selecting the Instrumentation option. This section assumes that you're checking the entire Web site.

3. Select Sampling and click Next. You'll see a summary dialog box that tells you which configuration options you chose.

4. Click Finish. At this point, you'll see the Output and the Performance Explorer windows displayed. The Wizard has created a performance session in the Performance Explorer as shown in Figure 19.4.

5. Right-click the ABC_Inc entry in Performance Explorer and choose Properties from the context menu. You'll see an Object Property Pages dialog box.

6. Select Events. You'll see a list of events that you can choose to monitor. The example monitors the ASP.NET Events. However, you can choose any combination of events desired, but you must choose at least one event to obtain a useful report.

7. Click OK. Visual Studio makes the performance monitoring changes.

FIGURE 19.4
Performance Explorer displays the performance sessions you create and resulting reports.

8. Click Launch at the top of the Performance Explorer dialog box and Visual Studio will start your application.

9. Check various Web pages and perform tasks with the sample application.

10. Close the browser window. You'll see Visual Studio performing the analysis of the session. Eventually, you'll see a Performance Report Summary similar to the one shown in Figure 19.5. The various tabs on this report tell you about the performance of your application from different perspectives. The screenshot shows the list of function calls and how many times the application called them during the test period. Interestingly enough, the list shows the Windows DLL calls as well as those to managed DLLs so you can see how .NET and Windows interact.

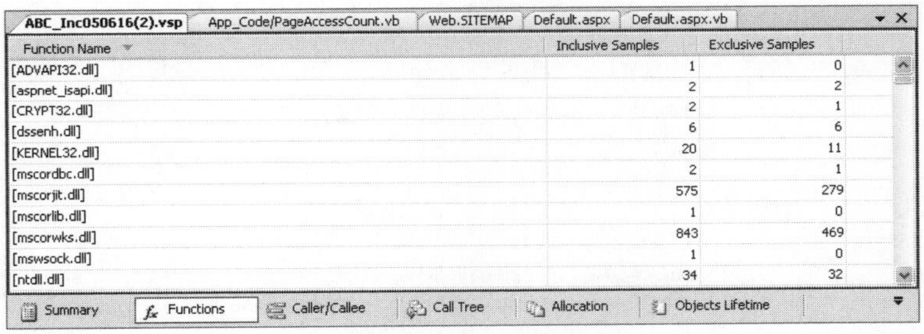

FIGURE 19.5
View the results of tests you made on your application using the supplied reports.

Defining Your Development Goals

This chapter has demonstrated how to optimize your application using both performance counters and optimization tools. Both techniques work extremely well, but at different times and in different ways. You can use performance counters at any time, but should provide a means of turning them off when the developer or administrator doesn't need them so they don't use additional processing cycles. Optimization tools provide developer-specific help during various development phases and the post-development process. Although you don't use optimization tools for the entire application life cycle, relying on them during the development process greatly reduces the optimization task.

Now it's time to consider the optimization needs for your application. Make a plan that begins with optimization goals. Move on to how you plan to quantify optimization needs, including security, reliability, speed, and user needs. Consider the requirement to build custom performance counters so you can monitor and assess items that don't fall within the normal sphere of optimization. Finally, define precisely how you'll implement the optimization requirements and determine what defines success. Once you have all of these pieces in place, you're ready to begin your application optimization.

Chapter 20 helps you discover downloadable applications. Generally, you use downloadable applications when a control or component won't perform the task fully. In some cases, the user will have to install the application to make it functional. A downloadable application provides functionality needed between business partners or as part of a solution for a work-at-home scenario. Downloadable applications are well-defined methods of providing interaction between trusted entities. In short, this chapter visits an area that's equally viable in the future as it is available today.

Chapter 20

Creating Downloadable Applications

Downloadable applications are a special kind of software where the user can work with the application from a Web page, rather than having it stored on the local desktop. A downloadable application differs from controls and components that the user can download because they're self-contained and perform a specific task. One way to view downloadable applications is as a variant of the helper application that browsers have always relied on to display some types of data. For example, when you click a PDF link online, the browser will more than likely open a copy of Adobe Acrobat Reader to view the information (provided you have the Adobe Acrobat Reader software installed).

The Internet, trade press, and just about every other source you can imagine have discussed downloadable applications for years. For example, Microsoft has considered creating downloadable forms of its Office products. However, you'll notice that they haven't done it and part of the reason is that creating large downloadable applications isn't practical without the required resources such as network bandwidth. It's possible to create small or even medium-sized downloadable applications. For example, you could probably create a calculator program and offer it as a downloadable application on your Web site.

Needless to say, anytime you create an application that the user downloads and executes from the Internet, there's going to be security concerns. You need to address user fears about downloading and using the application. Obviously, a downloadable application requires a higher level of trust than components or controls discussed in previous chapters (see Chapter 15 for details about controls and components in general). As part of allaying fears about your downloadable application, you also need to address setup and configuration issues.

This chapter addresses downloadable applications in several forms (both component and control) and considers how you can access them as you would any helper application. The Visual Web Developer environment comes with several examples of downloadable applications that you can use as examples and as a basis for ideas for your own applications.

The final section of the chapter considers the alternatives to downloadable applications. Leaping onto an interesting technology is only natural for a developer, but it might not be the best solution for the user. Sometimes you can achieve just as much using standard technologies as you can a downloadable application. This section discusses the various possibilities. Once you've looked at the other alternatives, you can determine whether downloadable applications are the best solution for your needs.

Considering Potential Security Problems

Companies have two audiences to consider when creating a downloadable application. The first group works within the company. Internal users don't have much to worry about when working with your application—after all; you're responsible for the application, their machine, and the data they manage. The security concern, here, is ensuring the application will actually work as intended under load in the corporate environment. In addition, you need a corporate policy—one that the user actually knows about—that considers the requirements for working with downloadable company applications. Even so, the pressure is on the IT staff to provide a safe application environment for everyone. Self-inflicted security wounds are a major cause of concern for companies today, especially with all of the unwanted media attention these attacks tend to garner.

The second group includes visitors to your Web site. Most outside users view the Internet as a comfortably anonymous place where they don't have to volunteer any information or expose their identities in any way unless they really want to. Consequently, you have people running around pretending to be all kinds of things they aren't. Scripts expose some of the privacy of individuals, controls and components expose a little more, and there's little chance of hiding much with a downloadable application. Consequently, downloadable applications make people feel uncomfortable—people view them as a personal assault on privacy and, as a result, on security as well (the two go hand in hand for most people, even though they really are separate issues). The "Developing a Privacy Policy" section of Chapter 5 discusses privacy policies—make sure your privacy policy addresses any use of personal information that a downloadable application might require.

Any time you download content to the client machine without really knowing what effect that content will have, you risk damaging the user's system. The End User Licensing Agreement (EULA) found with most software packages is evidence that software companies understand this issue far too well. However, well-informed users understand there's still a commitment from shrink-wrap companies to resolve any difficulties an installation might create that they might not get as part of an application download. A downloadable application has the highest probability of creating problems of any content the user might get, so naturally the user is leery of accepting such content.

It's also unlikely that you'll post a precise analysis along with accompanying source code of your downloadable application. Users tend to suspect the hidden nature of the downloadable application you create. Because a downloadable application will likely execute at the same privilege level as the user, you could gain access to financial records and the like without the user's knowledge. In short, the user has to have considerable trust that your company won't steal sensitive information.

An issue that you might not consider is the security risks for your company when you create a downloadable application. Crackers often depend on obtaining code that they can analyze and check for holes. Your company could open a gaping hole in its security defenses by creating a downloadable application. A downloadable application could have a buffer overflow or other problem that a cracker exploits to gain access to the server. Because of the nature of these errors, a security breach might go unnoticed for days or even weeks. Every moment that the cracker has access to your system is another moment that the cracker can challenge your system integrity and you might lose data (or even control of the system). Generally, by creating a downloadable application, you have more to lose from a security perspective than the user—even though the user will fail to notice this problem.

Security breaches need not occur at either the client or server end of the conversation. The fact that the conversation for external applications occurs over the open Internet also creates potential problems. A cracker could listen to the conversations and hope to break the encryption you use to secure it. For example, anyone relying on the Data Encryption Standard (DES) might as well forgo encrypting their data because this encryption technology has become relatively easy to crack as computers have become more powerful. Fortunately, .NET developers have access to the Advanced Encryption Standard (AES), which is the only form of encryption that you can rely on to remain secure—for the moment at least.

NOTE Breaking the DES encryption was big news at one time (1998, in fact), but now it's old information. Unfortunately, many downloadable applications still use it. Even the U.S. government has moved away from DES and is moving away from Triple-DES because it's unlikely to remain secure for very long (see the NetworkWorldFusion article at `http://www.nwfusion.com/research/2001/0730feat2.html` for details). You can find archived stories about the DES security problem in places such as Hasten Down the Wire (`http://www.michaelfraase.com/index.php/hasten/des_cracked_again/`) and the Cryptography Mailing List (`http://www.privacy.nb.ca/cryptography/archives/cryptography/html/1999-01/0120.html`). Look at the dates and you'll see that DES has been unusable since 1998. Now, consider the fact that many online stores still rely on DES for transactions and you'll begin to understand why well-informed users balk at using many types of online communication. Any system that relies on DES or even Triple-DES is suspect—make sure you give users a good reason to trust you by using AES.

Considering Client-side Setup and Configuration Issues

Many developers are under the assumption that application installations must follow a prescribed regimen of setting up the Windows Installer and creating complex application destinations. Microsoft was the originator of this philosophy, and it worked well during the days when the desktop was the only source of applications that Windows users had. However, many applications, such as the downloadable applications described in this chapter, now arrive from other sources. A complex installation scenario no longer works because the user can't even be sure that the application elements reside on the local hard drive (rather than on your Web server). Consequently, Microsoft changed course, as it so often does, and went back to the installation technique from the days of DOS XCopy.

NOTE For those of you who don't know what the Disk Operating System (DOS) is, it's the original operating system for the PC. The character mode DOS allowed a user to work with one application at a time. The user didn't see fancy graphics and wasn't able to multitask. The system was quite simple and many people still think DOS is worth keeping around for specific tasks. XCopy is a utility that originated with DOS. It lets someone copy an entire application, including data, from one location to another without any fancy installation or other requirements. Everything the application needs resides in a single main folder (sometimes with subfolders). XCopy can copy everything, including the subfolders, using a single command.

Of course, you might think I've gone quite mad in introducing an old technology as a means for getting your downloadable application onto the user's machine, but the technique really does work. Microsoft has fought an uphill battle on the subject, so you'll find articles such as "Determining When to Use Windows Installer Versus XCopy" (`http://msdn.microsoft.com/library/en-us/dndotnet/html/xcopywininst.asp`) on the Microsoft Developer Network (MSDN) Web site.

The problem is that XCopy isn't the right solution for every application. For example, it can actually cause problems when working with Internet Information Server (IIS) as described in the "Troubleshooting Deployment" article at `http://msdn.microsoft.com/library/en-us/vsintro7/html/vxtbstroubleshootingdeployment.asp` (see the "Web applications deployed using the Xcopy command cannot be debugged" heading for details). Note that this article prescribes using the Copy Project utility and provides a link to another article that describes how to use it. However, Microsoft is heading toward more use of XCopy by incorporating product features that make using it easier. For example, check out the new emphasis on XCopy support for SQL Server Express at `http://msdn.microsoft.com/library/en-us/dnsse/html/sseoverview.asp`. You may also want to watch the more generic deployment video called, "XCOPY Deployment" at `http://msdn.microsoft.com/vstudio/se/sevideos/`.

To use the XCopy command, you type **XCopy *SourceFile*** at the command prompt (where `SourceFile` is the name of the file you want to copy) and press Enter. The source file argument can rely on DOS wildcard characters where * is any number of characters and ? is a single character. For example, `*.DOC` would copy files with any filename and the DOC file extension. The following list contains optional arguments you can use with the XCopy command.

Destination   Specifies the location of the new files—replace Destination with the new file location. You may optionally use Destination to change the name of the copied file as well, but this feature only works well when you copy a single file.

/A   Copies only files with the archive attribute set, doesn't change the attribute.

/C   Continues copying even when errors occur.

/D:*Month-Day-Year*   Copies files changed on or after the specified date. If no date is given, it copies only those files whose source time is newer than the destination time.

/E   Copies directories and subdirectories, including empty ones. Same as /S /E. May be used to modify /T.

/EXCLUDE:*File1*[+*File2*]...   Specifies a list of files containing strings. Each string should be in a separate line in the files. When any of the strings match any part of the absolute path of the file to be copied, that file will be excluded from being copied. For example, specifying a string like `\obj\` or `.obj` will exclude all files underneath the directory obj or all files with the obj extension respectively.

/F   Displays full source and destination filenames while copying.

/G   Allows the copying of encrypted files to destination that doesn't support encryption.

/H   Copies hidden and system files also.

/I   If destination doesn't exist and copying more than one file, assumes that destination must be a directory.

/K   Copies attributes. Normal XCopy will reset read-only attributes.

/L   Displays files that would be copied.

/M   Copies only files with the archive attribute set; turns off the archive attribute.

/N   Copies using the generated short names.

/O   Copies file ownership and ACL information.

/P   Prompts you before creating each destination file.

/Q   Doesn't display filenames while copying.

/R   Overwrites read-only files.

/S   Copies directories and subdirectories except empty ones.

/T   Creates directory structure, but doesn't copy files. Doesn't include empty directories or subdirectories. /T /E includes empty directories and subdirectories.

/U   Copies only files that already exist in destination.

/V   Verifies each new file.

/W   Prompts you to press a key before copying.

/X   Copies file audit settings (implies /0).

/Y   Suppresses prompting to confirm you want to overwrite an existing destination file.

/-Y   Prompting to confirm you want to overwrite an existing destination file.

/Z   Copies networked files in restartable mode.

NOTE   You can substitute a folder (directory) for the file when using XCopy. Supplying a folder name lets you copy the entire folder to another location. Add the /S switch and you can copy the folder and any subfolders it contains.

Using the Class Diagram (CD) File

Visual Studio .NET includes the Class Diagram (CD) file—a new kind of file that you can use as an application design aid. To add a CD file to your application, right-click the \App_Code folder and choose Add New Item from the context menu. Highlight the Class Diagram entry in the Add New Item dialog box, type a name in the Name field, and click Add. You can find an example of a file of this type in the \ABC_Inc\App_Code folder of the source code found on the Sybex Web site.

It's possible to use this file in two ways. First, you can drag and drop any of the entries in Solution Explorer or the Class View onto the page. Figure 20.1 shows an example of how well this feature works. In this case, the example shows the results of dragging and dropping the two class files in the \App_Code folder onto the form.

FIGURE 20.1
View the classes you've created from a graphical perspective using a CD file.

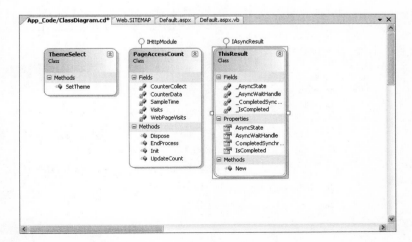

When you select one of the objects shown in Figure 20.1, you can see details about it in the Class Details window that normally appears at the bottom of the IDE by default. As you can see from Figure 20.2, the Class Details window lets you hide class items from view, create new class items, or delete items you no longer need. In short, the Class Details window helps you manage your existing classes using a graphical interface.

The second method of using the CD file is to create new classes with it. Look in the Toolbox and you'll find new tools you can use to create classes, enumerations, interfaces, abstract classes, structures, delegates, and modules. You can show an association between classes and define inheritance as needed. The Toolbox even includes a special comment tool for adding comments to your classes.

The items in the toolbox behave a little differently from the standard tools. When you drag and drop an item onto the CD file, you'll see a configuration dialog box like the one shown in Figure 20.3 for the enumeration. In this case, you provide an enumeration name, scope, and location. You can add new items to an existing class file or provide a new file for them.

Don't get the idea that this is only a graphical design tool. As you define elements of the element you add, the IDE is writing code for you in the background. In fact, when you finish working with the new item, you can right-click it and choose View Code from the context menu. Figure 20.4 shows an example of an enumeration added to the `ProcessAccessCount.VB` file from Chapter 19.

FIGURE 20.2
Manage your classes using the Class Details window.

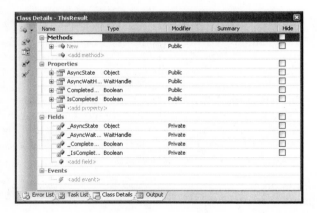

FIGURE 20.3
Use the configuration dialog boxes to provide initial information for a new item.

FIGURE 20.4
Automatically add code
to your classes by using
the class designer.

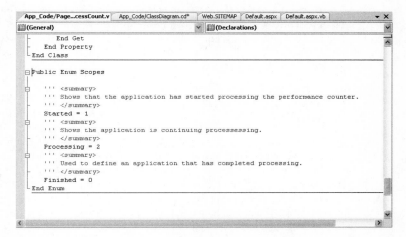

Everything you see for the enumeration in Figure 20.4 is output as part of the design process. Of course, enumerations are relatively simple to put together using this technique—this one's ready to go. Classes will still require a great deal more work, but the idea is that this tool can save you considerable time and effort, especially on large projects. The fact that you can simply drag and drop items from solution explorer means that older projects you move from earlier versions of Visual Studio work just as well as those created in Visual Studio .NET 2005.

Creating Standard Components

This section of the chapter shows how to use the built-in class template to create a component for your downloadable application. The component isn't stand-alone—you use it with other applications. However, the build process directly incorporates the component into your application—you don't have to worry about providing a means for the user to download the component. For a comparison with external components, see the component-specific sections of Chapter 15. The following sections describe how to work with a built-in component.

Designing the Component

The first step in this example is to add a component to the project. To add a built-in component to your application, select the Class template in the Add New Item dialog box (right-click the project entry in Solution Explorer and choose Add New Item from the context menu). Type a name for the class and click Add. If this is the first class you've added, the IDE will ask whether you want to create the class in the Code folder so you can use it anywhere within the Web site. Click Yes. The IDE creates the Code folder and places the class within it.

A component normally provides some type of background processing. In this case, the component makes a comparison and returns a color value based on an input. You might use such a component to provide a visual indicator based on numeric input. Listing 20.1 shows the code you'll need for this example. You'll find this example in the \ABC_Inc\App_Code folder of the source code on the Sybex Web site.

LISTING 20.1: Creating a Built-in Component

```
' Create an enumerated range of results.
Public Enum Colors
    Red = -65536
    Yellow = -256
    Green = -16744448
End Enum

' Define the private variables used to hold property values.
Dim _CompareValue As Int32

Public Sub New()
    ' Initialize the properties.
    _CompareValue = 0
End Sub

Public Sub New(ByVal InitValue As Int32)
    ' Initialize the properties.
    If (InitValue >= 0) And (InitValue <= 100) Then
        _CompareValue = InitValue
    Else
        Throw New ArgumentOutOfRangeException( _
            "InitValue", InitValue, _
            "InitValue must be between 0 and 100")
    End If
End Sub

Public Property CompareValue() As Int32
    Get
        Return _CompareValue
    End Get
    Set(ByVal value As Int32)
        ' Make sure the comparison value is in the correct
        ' range.
        If (value >= 0) And (value <= 100) Then
            _CompareValue = value
        Else
            ' Throw an error for an incorrect value.
            Throw New ArgumentOutOfRangeException( _
                "CompareValue", value, _
                "CompareValue must be between 0 and 100")
        End If
    End Set
End Property
```

```
Public Function CalcColor() As Colors
    ' Return a color based on the current value of _CompareValue.
    If (_CompareValue >= 0) And (_CompareValue <= 33) Then
        Return Colors.Red
    ElseIf (_CompareValue > 33) And (_CompareValue < 67) Then
        Return Colors.Yellow
    Else
        Return Colors.Green
    End If
End Function
```

The example begins with an enumeration. Using enumerations makes your code easier to understand and reduces the complexity of working with your component. In this case, the enumerated values translate to an Alpha Red Green Blue (ARGB) color value (where alpha is the measure of the transparency of the color). The combination of the four values produces a specific color indication on screen. In this case, the three numbers equate to the ARGB for red, yellow, and green. The enumeration shows that you can create enumerations with specific values—an important consideration, in this case, because the code uses the value to reproduce the color on screen.

The class has two constructors. Always create a constructor that doesn't require any input values to ensure someone can use the component on a Web page. The second constructor accepts the value you want to use for comparison purposes. Notice that the second constructor ensures that the input value is within the correct range. When the value is outside the correct range, the code throws an ArgumentOutOfRangeException exception, rather than handle the error within the component code.

The class includes the CompareValue property so that the developer using the control has access to the comparison value as needed. The Get portion of the property returns the _CompareValue value. The Set portion of the property uses the same technique as the second constructor to change the _CompareValue value. Always check every input to reduce the risk of getting a bad input value.

The CalcColor() method doesn't accept any input value. You could certainly create an override that would accept the comparison value as input. The method performs a numeric comparison and returns an enumerated color value based on the input. Using the technique shown reduces the risk of misinterpreting the method output.

Adding the Component to a Web Page

Now that you have a new component to use, it's time to add it to a Web page. The example Web page relies on a text box for input of the comparison value, a pushbutton to provide a means of performing the comparison, and a label for output. Because this is an ASP.NET application, all of the processing occurs as part of the code behind. Listing 20.2 shows the code you'll need for this example. You'll find this example in the \ABC_Inc\Downloadable\Component folder of the source code on the Sybex Web site.

The first thing you'll notice when using a built-in component is that you don't have to provide a reference to it—the IDE provides access to the component without the addition of a reference. Consequently, the code begins by instantiating an object based on the class. The code uses the second constructor to supply an input value directly, rather than as a second step.

LISTING 20.2: Using the Built-in Component

```vb
Sub btnCheck_Click(ByVal sender As Object, ByVal e As System.EventArgs)
    Try
        ' Create the value checking component.
        Dim CheckValue As New Calculate(Int32.Parse(txtInput.Text))

        ' Change the output background color.
        lblOutput.BackColor = _
            Drawing.Color.FromArgb(CheckValue.CalcColor())

        ' Change the foreground color so the user can see the text.
        If (CheckValue.CalcColor() = Calculate.Colors.Yellow) Then
            lblOutput.ForeColor = Drawing.Color.Black
        Else
            lblOutput.ForeColor = Drawing.Color.White
        End If

        ' Create an output string.
        lblOutput.Text = _
            txtInput.Text + " is a " + _
            CheckValue.CalcColor().ToString() + " number."

    Catch AOR As ArgumentOutOfRangeException
        ' Display the problem on screen.
        lblOutput.Text = "Input Error: " + AOR.Message

    Catch ex As Exception
        ' Display a generic message.
        lblOutput.Text = "Unknown Error: " + ex.Message

    End Try
End Sub
```

You can use the CalcColor() method to provide output in several ways. The first method uses the color value to change the lblOutput.BackColor property using the Drawing.Color.FromArgb() method. Assigning an ARGB color to the enumeration, rather than allowing the compiler to assign a value, lets you assign the color directly.

The second use of the CalcColor() method compares the output color to one of the enumerated values. The example outputs black text when working with a yellow background and white text when working with either a red or green background. The idea is to improve the readability of the display.

The third use of the CalcColor() method displays the color name as part of the application text output. When you use the output in this way, the code automatically translates the output to a color name, rather than a numeric value, as shown in Figure 20.5.

FIGURE 20.5
This example shows three kinds of output from a single method call.

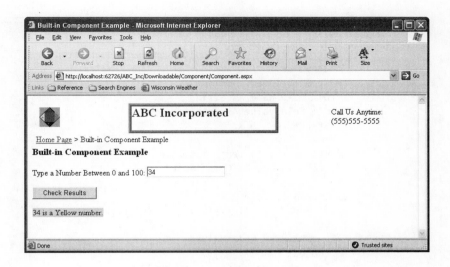

The example provides two levels of error trapping. The first level is the ArgumentOutOfRange Exception specific exception output by the component. It's better to check for specific errors when you can to ensure you can provide the best help possible to the user. The second level is a generic exception. Even though this second level keeps the application from failing completely, the output message is less helpful because the application isn't trapping a specific error.

Creating Standard Controls

Sometimes you need a special control for an application. You won't use the control in other projects— just this project. That's where a built-in control can come in handy. You add the control directly to the current project. For a comparison with external controls, see the control-specific sections of Chapter 15. The following sections describe how to work with a built-in control.

Designing the Control

The first step in this example is to add a control to the project. To add a built-in control to your application, select the Web User Control template in the Add New Item dialog box (right-click the project entry in Solution Explorer and choose Add New Item from the context menu). Type a name for the control and click Add.

Creating a built-in control isn't precisely the same as working with stand-alone controls because they rely on Web technology. You create what amounts to a specialized kind of Web page fragment and use it within the application. Consequently, this example on a RadioButtonList (rblColorSelect) and a Label (lblOutput) as a starting point. Listing 20.3 shows the code you'll need for this example. You'll find this example in the \ABC_Inc\Downloadable\Control folder of the source code on the Sybex Web site.

LISTING 20.3: Creating a Built-in Control

```
' A structure to hold a color name and associated
' ARGB value.
Public Structure ColorType
    Dim ColorName As String
    Dim ColorValue As Int32
End Structure

' Contains the current list of colors.
Dim _ColorValues As ColorType()

<Browsable(False)> _
Public Property ColorValues() As ColorType()
    Get
        Return _ColorValues
    End Get
    Set(ByVal value As ColorType())
        ' Verify that there is an input value.
        If (value Is Nothing) Or (value.Length = 0) Then
            Throw New ArgumentNullException( _
                "InitColors", "You must provide a list of colors.")
            Return
        End If

        ' Assign the values to _ColorValues
        ReDim _ColorValues(value.Length)
        _ColorValues = value

        ' Fill the color list with names.
        rblColorSelect.Items.Clear()
        For Each Entry As ColorType In _ColorValues
            rblColorSelect.Items.Add(Entry.ColorName)
        Next

        ' Set the default option.
        rblColorSelect.SelectedIndex = 0

        ' Set the label up for use.
        lblOutput.Text = _
            _ColorValues(0).ColorName
        lblOutput.BackColor = _
            Drawing.Color.FromArgb(_ColorValues(0).ColorValue)

        ' Save the data as a cookie.
        Response.Cookies.Add( _
            New HttpCookie("SavedColorValues", _
```

```
                         CreateColorString(_ColorValues)))
        End Set
End Property

Public ReadOnly Property CurrentColorName() As String
    Get
        ' Return just the color name.
        Return _ColorValues(rblColorSelect.SelectedIndex).ColorName
    End Get
End Property

Public ReadOnly Property CurrentColorValue() As Int32
    Get
        ' Return just the color value.
        Return _ColorValues(rblColorSelect.SelectedIndex).ColorValue
    End Get
End Property

Private Function CreateColorString(ByVal Input As ColorType()) _
    As String

    Dim Counter As Int32     ' Loop counter variable.

    ' Define the output string.
    Dim Output As New StringBuilder()

    ' Process each of the input elements.
    For Counter = 0 To Input.Length - 1

        ' Create a string from the individual color values.
        Output.Append(Input(Counter).ColorName + "=" + _
                    Input(Counter).ColorValue.ToString())

        ' Add a semicolon separator only when this isn't the
        ' last entry.
        If Counter < Input.Length - 1 Then
            Output.Append("&")
        End If
    Next

    ' Return the completed string.
    Return Output.ToString()
End Function

Private Function CreateColorArray(ByVal Input As String) As ColorType()
    Dim Elements As String()     ' Holds name/value strings array.
    Dim Output As ColorType()    ' Contains the output data.
    Dim Counter As Int32         ' Loop counter variable.
```

```
        Dim NameValue As String()    ' A name/value pair.

        ' Divide the string into name/value pairs.
        Elements = Input.Split(Convert.ToChar("&"))

        ' Now that we know how many name/value pairs there are, define the
        ' array size.
        ReDim Output(Elements.Length)

        ' Place one name value pair in each Output element.
        For Counter = 0 To Elements.Length - 1

            ' Split the name/value pair.
            NameValue = Elements(Counter).Split(Convert.ToChar("="))

            ' Place the values in the output.
            Output(Counter).ColorName = NameValue(0)
            Output(Counter).ColorValue = Int32.Parse(NameValue(1))
        Next

        ' Return the result.
        Return Output
    End Function

Sub rblColorSelect_SelectedIndexChanged(ByVal sender As Object, _
                                        ByVal e As System.EventArgs)
        ' Set the output to display the newly selected color.
        lblOutput.Text = _
            _ColorValues(rblColorSelect.SelectedIndex).ColorName
        lblOutput.BackColor = _
            Drawing.Color.FromArgb( _
                _ColorValues(rblColorSelect.SelectedIndex).ColorValue)
End Sub

Private Sub Page_Init(ByVal sender As Object, _
                      ByVal e As System.EventArgs) Handles Me.Init
        If (Request.Cookies("SavedColorValues") Is Nothing) Then

            ' Set the colors to their default values.
            ReDim _ColorValues(2)
            _ColorValues(0).ColorName = Drawing.Color.Red.Name
            _ColorValues(0).ColorValue = Drawing.Color.Red.ToArgb()
            ... Two Other Default Color Entries ...

        Else
            ' Retrieve the stored colors and use them to create the array.
            _ColorValues = _
                CreateColorArray(Request.Cookies("SavedColorValues").Value)
```

```
        End If

        ' Fill the color list with names.
        rblColorSelect.Items.Clear()
        For Each Entry As ColorType In _ColorValues
            rblColorSelect.Items.Add(Entry.ColorName)
        Next

        ' Set the default option.
        rblColorSelect.SelectedIndex = 0

        ' Set the label up for use.
        lblOutput.Text = _
            _ColorValues(0).ColorName
        lblOutput.BackColor = _
            Drawing.Color.FromArgb(_ColorValues(0).ColorValue)
    End Sub

    Public Sub ChangeColorSelection(ByVal NewColor As Int32)
        ' Verify the value is in range.
        If (Not NewColor < _ColorValues.Length - 1) Then
            Throw New ArgumentOutOfRangeException( _
                "NewColor", NewColor, _
                "Value is not within the range of colors listed.")
        End If

        ' Change the selection.
        rblColorSelect.SelectedIndex = NewColor

        ' Set the label up for use.
        lblOutput.Text = _
            _ColorValues(rblColorSelect.SelectedIndex).ColorName
        lblOutput.BackColor = _
            Drawing.Color.FromArgb( _
                _ColorValues(rblColorSelect.SelectedIndex).ColorValue)
    End Sub

    Public Function GetColorSelection() As Int32
        ' Return the selected index value.
        Return rblColorSelect.SelectedIndex
    End Function

    Public Sub UseDefaultColors()
        Dim Values(2) As ColorType   ' Contains the default values.

        If (Not Request.Cookies("SavedColorValues") Is Nothing) Then

            ' Set the colors to their default values.
```

```
            Values(0).ColorName = Drawing.Color.Red.Name
            Values(0).ColorValue = Drawing.Color.Red.ToArgb()
            ... Two Other Default Color Entries ...

            ' Change the color values.
            Me.ColorValues = Values
        End If
    End Sub
```

This example begins by defining a data structure to store color values. In this case, the structure includes the color name as well as the ARGB for that color. Each color requires a single entry, so the private variable, _ColorValues is an array of ColorType. The ColorValues property exposes this value to the developer using the control. Notice that the example sets the <Browsable> attribute to False to ensure the developer doesn't attempt to modify this property from the Properties window in design view. You could expose the property by creating a custom property page for it, but that task is beyond the capability of Visual Web Developer Express—you really need the full version of Visual Studio .NET to perform this task.

Setting _ColorValues requires more than the usual amount of work because this is a user control, rather than a stand-alone control. The code begins by verifying the developer has provided a valid array as input. When the developer fails to provide a valid array, the code throws an Argument NullException exception. The next step is to assign the new array to _ColorValues. Notice that the code must redimension _ColorValues to ensure it has just enough entries to contain the new array. The next three steps set up the visual components to display the new color values—the control doesn't perform this task for you automatically. Finally, there's an odd step where the code creates a cookie containing the new values using the Response.Cookies.Add() method. The reason you must perform this step is that Web pages have no state. The only way to preserve the new color choices is to create a cookie (or other storage medium) to hold them. The code uses the CreateColorString() method to convert the _ColorValues array to a string.

Sometimes an outside process might need to know the current color or color value. The CurrentColorName and CurrentColorValue perform this task. Both properties work the same—they simply return different structural elements.

The example includes two methods for converting a ColorType array to a string and back again: CreateColorString() and CreateColorArray(). Cookies only work for string values, so you must convert everything else to a string. In many cases, the task is simple, but complex data types, such as a ColorType array, require special handling.

The CreateColorString() method begins by creating a StringBuilder, Output, to hold the results of the conversion. The actual conversion process begins by combining the two ColorType fields, ColorName and ColorValue, into a name/value pair that's separated by an equals sign. The separator you choose is important—it can't appear in the data that you're trying to separate. Many developers use the equals sign because it's uncommon in actual data, but be prepared to use other characters such as the circumflex (^). The code then checks whether this is the last element in the array. If it isn't, the code adds an ampersand to the end of the string. The ampersand separates name/value pairs—making it easier to convert the data back later. Again, make sure you choose a unique character.

WARNING Choose separator characters carefully. Remember that you're working with HTML, which means that you must escape some characters, such as the semicolon (;) and space. Using un-escaped characters can produce odd results. For example, using the semicolon truncates the string after the first name/value pair. The code creates the complete string, but the cookie only accepts information up to the first semicolon. Generally, it's best to use the equals sign and ampersand when you can—these characters are always safe to use within a cookie.

The CreateColorArray() method begins by using the Split() method to create an array of name/value pairs. The next step is to process each name/value pair within the array and place the appropriate information into a ColorType array. Notice that the code again uses the Split() method to perform this task. The double use of the Split() method is the reason why you should use different separator characters for the name and value, and for the name/value pairs.

The rblColorSelect_SelectedIndexChanged() event handler is private to the control. It only changes the text and background color of lblOutput to match the current user selection. The reason you want to keep this event handler private is to circumvent outside efforts to corrupt the internal functionality of the control. The ChangeColorSelection() method makes this functionality public. However, notice that this method checks the input values before it allows a change and ensures the system updates the display properly. The GetColorSelection() method retrieves the currently selected color. You could easily use a property to perform the same task—it's a matter of personal preference in this case.

The Page_Init() method is probably the most important part of the control because it sets up the visual elements for each postback. The method begins by viewing two possible kinds of display. The first occurs when the user provides a cookie containing the name/value pairs created by the CreateColorString() method. The second occurs when the page relies on the default colors. In both cases, the code creates a _ColorValues array. The next step is to create the list of colors in rblColorSelect, so the user sees the correct color names. The code also selects the first color. The final step is to set lblOutput to display the correct color name and highlighting.

The final method, UseDefaultColors(), lets the developer set the control back to its default setting. Theoretically, you could simply delete the cookie that holds the current user colors. After experimenting for a while, however, it becomes obvious that retaining the cookie can have performance benefits if you expect the user to change the colors again. Consequently, the UseDefaultColors() method sets the cookie to the default colors, rather than deleting the cookie. Notice how the code uses the control's ColorValues property to perform this task. Using the property saves a little coding, but you could also place the code within the UseDefaultColors() method.

Adding the Control to a Web Page

Adding the built-in control to the Web page is a bit different from using a stand-alone control. Instead of selecting the control in the Toolbox, you drag and drop it where you want from Solution Explorer. This action produces a different result from using a stand-alone control as well. The IDE begins by registering the ASCX files with the Web page using a special tag, as shown here.

```
<%@ Register TagPrefix="uc1"
            TagName="SpecialSelect"
            Src="SpecialSelect.ascx" %>
```

The registration contains three attributes. The `TagPrefix` defines the prefix that the IDE will use for the control within the Web page. The `TagName` contains the class name for the control. The `Src` points to the location of the file on disk. After the IDE registers the control, it places a tag for it on the Web page, as shown here.

```
<uc1:SpecialSelect id="selTest" runat="server">
</uc1:SpecialSelect>
```

Notice that the tag includes the prefix, `uc1`, and the name of the control, `SpecialSelect`. The Web page uses the control as it would any other control and you can access any properties you define for the control on the Web page. Listing 20.4 shows the code you'll need for this example. You'll find this example in the `\ABC_Inc\Downloadable\Control` folder of the source code on the Sybex Web site.

All of the code in this part of the example is event handler related—it all helps you understand how the control works. The `btnCheck_Click()` method displays statistical information about the control. It displays the current color name and color value, along with the current selection number. Figure 20.6 shows a typical example of the output from this event handler.

The `btnChange_Click()` method creates a `ColorType` array. It fills the array with a list of colors. The final step is to assign the new colors to the control using the `ColorValues` property. Figure 20.6 shows the alternative color list.

The `btnDefaultColors_Click()` method returns the colors to their default setting. It relies on the control's `UseDefaultColors()` method to perform this task. You should always provide a means of returning the control to a default state when the setup could require more than a few lines of code.

FIGURE 20.6

Built-in controls can combine functionality and make creating pages faster.

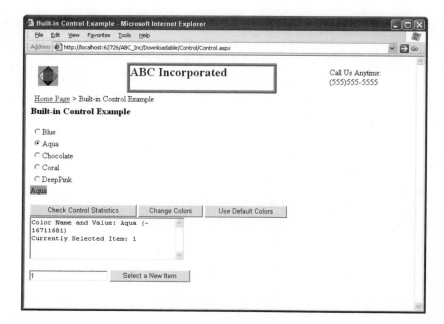

LISTING 20.4: Using the Built-in Control

```
Sub btnCheck_Click(ByVal sender As Object, ByVal e As System.EventArgs)
    ' Display statistics about the current control settings.
    txtOutput.Text = "Color Name and Value: " + _
                    selTest.CurrentColorName + " (" + _
                    selTest.CurrentColorValue.ToString() + ")" + _
                    vbCrLf + "Currently Selected Item: " + _
                    selTest.GetColorSelection().ToString()
End Sub

Sub btnChange_Click(ByVal sender As Object, _
                    ByVal e As System.EventArgs)
    Dim Colors(4) As SpecialSelect_ascx.ColorType

    ' Define the colors.
    Colors(0).ColorName = Drawing.Color.Blue.Name
    Colors(0).ColorValue = Drawing.Color.Blue.ToArgb()
    ... Four Other Colors ...

    ' Change the colors.
    selTest.ColorValues = Colors
End Sub

Sub btnDefaultColors_Click(ByVal sender As Object, _
                           ByVal e As System.EventArgs)
    ' Use the default color scheme.
    selTest.UseDefaultColors()
End Sub

Sub btnSelect_Click(ByVal sender As Object, _
                    ByVal e As System.EventArgs)
    Try
        ' Choose a new item from the list.
        selTest.ChangeColorSelection(Int32.Parse(txtItem.Text))
    Catch AOR As ArgumentOutOfRangeException
        ' Display an error if the input is incorrect.
        lblError.Text = AOR.Message
        lblError.Visible = True
    End Try
End Sub

Private Sub Page_Load(ByVal sender As Object, _
                      ByVal e As System.EventArgs) Handles Me.Load
    ' Turn off error messages.
    lblError.Visible = False
End Sub
```

The `btnSelect_Click()` method lets the user change the selection programmatically using the `ChangeColorSelection()` method. The `ChangeColorSelection()` method throws an exception for incorrect input, so you should provide some type of error display when using this technique in your own controls. The example uses a hidden label to display the information by making it visible and filling the label with the error information. Figure 20.7 shows typical error output. The `Page_Load()` event handler resets the error message as needed by making the label invisible.

FIGURE 20.7
Provide error output as needed to make the control user friendlier.

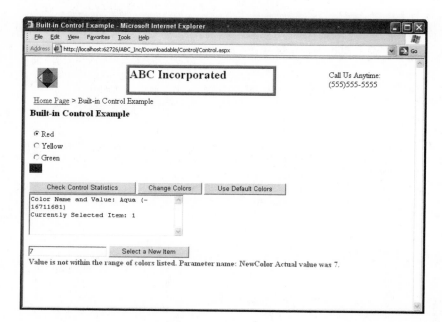

Using the *FileUpload* Control

You can do a lot with forms on a Web site. Adding user controls and interacting with the client in other ways extends your ability to gather information. However, at some point, you might need more information than these sources can provide. For example, you might need access to an application log that the user has compiled. The `FileUpload` control can help with these additional information needs. It displays a text box and browse button on screen that lets the user specify a file for upload. You must provide a separate upload button whose event handler contains code to upload the file.

The amount of checking you perform on the file depends on the application requirements. You can use the `PostedFile` property to check the information the user plans to upload. In all cases, you should quarantine the file in a special folder so that you can virus scan it and check for other problems. Listing 20.5 shows the code you'll need for this example. You'll find this example in the `\ABC_Inc\Downloadable\FileUpload` folder of the source code on the Sybex Web site.

LISTING 20.5:   Uploading Files from the Client

```
Sub btnUpload_Click(ByVal sender As Object, _
                    ByVal e As System.EventArgs)
    Dim UploadPath As String    ' Server side upload path.
    Dim UniqueStr As String     ' Date/Time stamp.
    Dim Contents As TextReader  ' File content.

    ' Create a unique DateTime string.
    UniqueStr = Request.LogonUserIdentity.Name + "_" + _
                DateTime.Now.ToShortDateString + "_" + _
                DateTime.Now.ToLongTimeString()
    UniqueStr = UniqueStr.Replace("/", ".")
    UniqueStr = UniqueStr.Replace("\", ".")
    UniqueStr = UniqueStr.Replace(":", ".")

    ' Determine the file status.
    If fuUpload.HasFile Then

        ' Create the upload path.
        UploadPath = _
            "C:\Uploads\" + UniqueStr + "_" + fuUpload.FileName

        ' Upload the file.
        fuUpload.SaveAs(UploadPath)

        ' Display the status message.
        lblStatus.Text = _
            "File saved as " + UniqueStr + "_" + fuUpload.FileName
        lblStatus.ForeColor = Drawing.Color.Black
        lblStatus.Visible = True

        ' Get all of the information from the PostedFile property.
        With fuUpload.PostedFile

            ' Display file statistics.
            lblStats.Text = _
                "Content Length: " + .ContentLength.ToString() + _
                "<br />Content Type: " + .ContentType + _
                "<br />Filename: " + .FileName

            ' When the file contains text, display the text as well.
            If .ContentType.ToUpper = "TEXT/PLAIN" Then
                Contents = New StreamReader(.InputStream)
                lblStats.Text = lblStats.Text + _
                    "<br />Contents: " + Contents.ReadToEnd()
            End If
        End With
```

```
      Else
              ' Display an error message.
              lblStatus.Text = "You must provide a filename!"
              lblStatus.ForeColor = Drawing.Color.Red
              lblStatus.Visible = True
      End If
End Sub
```

The code begins by creating a unique file string. You must create a unique file string because multiple users could attempt to upload files with the same name at the same time. In addition, a user might determine an initial upload is incorrect and attempt to upload a new version of the same file later. The newest file always overwrites older files of the same name. The example uses a combination of the username, the date, and the time. Unfortunately, all three values contain characters that you can't use in a filename. The example solves this problem by using the `Replace()` method to change the character to an acceptable value.

Determining the status of the `FileUpload` control, `fuUpload`, comes next. The `HasFile` tells whether the user has supplied a filename. If not, the code displays an error message. Otherwise, the code begins processing the file by obtaining the value in the `FileName` property. The code uses the `SaveAs()` method to upload the data from the client machine. Afterward, the code displays a successful upload message for the user that includes the augmented filename.

The example also displays statistics that you can obtain from the `PostedFile` property. All files allow you to display the content length, the Multipurpose Internet Mail Extensions (MIME) content type, and the filename supplied by the user. When the example detects a MIME type of TEXT/ PLAIN, it processes the file and displays the content as well. Figure 20.8 shows typical output from this example. Notice that the `FileUpload` control automatically clears the filename after the user uploads it.

TIP Most vendors have begun using MIME types for more than browsers—you'll find them in many applications today. The biggest reason is that you'll find standard MIME types across platforms. You can see a list of MIME standards at `http://www.mhonarc.org/~ehood/MIME/MIME.html`. Another good source of information about MIME is at `http://www.hunnysoft.com/mime/`.

Designing Custom SmartTags

You may have seen SmartTags used as part of many Office products. The developer or environment attaches SmartTags to various controls so that the user can perform tasks faster. It's also possible to attach SmartTags to Web pages. These mini-applications detect specific content and let the user interact with it in new ways.

The SmartTags are already on the user's system in many cases. Some of them come with Microsoft Office and other applications, for example, or you can provide a download for custom SmartTags on your Web site. In addition, many third party vendors provide SmartTags. All of these applications run within a host environment—similar to the way that the Microsoft Management Console (MMC) hosts various snap-in applications, such as Component Services. The host for the examples in this section is a browser, but you'll see other hosts in use.

FIGURE 20.8
Let users upload files as
needed to your Web site
to augment other kinds
of information.

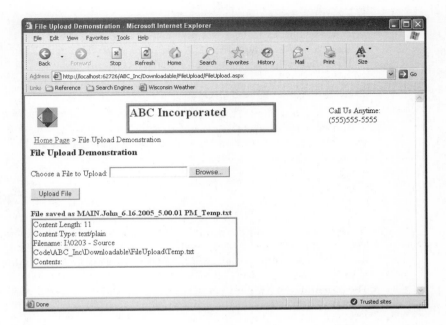

The following sections describe two SmartTag scenarios. The first is using the SmartTags that come with Microsoft Office. Because Microsoft Office appears on so many desktops, you can count on having access to these SmartTags when the majority of your Web site visitors work within the enterprise environments using Windows desktops. Of course, you should be ready to accommodate other users on a public Web site or explain this requirement to users on a private Web site. The second is using third party SmartTags that you can either download from the Internet or purchase for special needs within your company. For example, you can find special SmartTags for use within legal firms that make Web content easier to work with.

Adding Standard SmartTags to a Web Page

You already have at your disposal a wealth of SmartTags that perform common tasks such as creating an address or properly formatting a date. The problem is that working with these SmartTags isn't necessarily common knowledge—you don't find them used a lot online because many developers don't realize just how common they really are. Microsoft Office installs all of the SmartTags in the following sections—at least all of the versions of Microsoft Office that support SmartTags (they won't work with users who are still clinging to Office 97 and older). When you think about how many people have Microsoft Office installed, you begin to realize just how easy it would be to add these SmartTags to a Web page and be reasonably sure that anyone visiting the Web site will benefit. Of course, public Web sites should provide alternatives for users who don't have the proper SmartTags installed. You'll find this example in the \ABC_Inc\Downloadable\SmartTag folder of the source code on the Sybex Web site.

NOTE The following examples won't work if you didn't install SmartTag support with Microsoft Office in most cases. One exception is the Address and Places SmartTag, which you get as part of most Windows installations. Discover more about this SmartTag in the "Using the Address and Places SmartTag Plug-In" section of the chapter.

CREATING THE WEB PAGE ENTRIES

Using any type of SmartTag requires special entries on your Web page. Most of the entries appear within the <head> tag, rather than the <body> tag, which is why you can't really see them in Design view. The first set of attributes actually appears in the <head> tag like this (other <head> tag attributes removed for the sake of clarity).

```
<html xmlns:o="urn:schemas-microsoft-com:office:office"
      xmlns:st1="urn:schemas-microsoft-com:office:smarttags"
      xmlns:st2="urn:schemas:contacts">
```

These entries define three namespaces. Namespaces are identifiers for a resource you want to use. The first is the Microsoft Office namespace. The second is a general namespace for SmartTags. The third namespace is a special entry for contact information. The Uniform Resource Name (URN) (pronounced "earn") portion of the namespace tells the browser that this is identification information. The remainder of the namespace is a declaration of the identifier, which are schemas, or organized listings of data in this case. A schema defines the data construction.

NOTE An URN is not an URL. The URNs used with SmartTags exist on the client machine—not at a location on the Internet. Consequently, when the user doesn't have the required support installed on the local machine, the browser ignores the URN. The page still displays, but not with the intended functionality that the SmartTag will add.

The next step is to describe the SmartTags you want to use. Every SmartTag requires at least one entry. These descriptions tell the browser how to react to the SmartTag entry. Listing 20.6 shows all of the descriptions for the SmartTags that Microsoft Office supports natively.

Each entry in the list includes three items. The first item tells the browser that this is an entry for a SmartTag, which appears as part of the Microsoft Office namespace. The o: preceding each entry ties it to the Microsoft Office declaration in the <head> tag. The second item is the location of the definition for this SmartTag. This entry uses an URN, just as the entries in the <head> tag do. The third item is the human readable name for the SmartTag.

The vendor provides the information you use as a basis for the <SmartTagType> tags as part of an XML file where the SmartTag file is stored, or on a registry entry. All the Microsoft Office SmartTag files appear in the \Program Files\Common Files\Microsoft Shared\SmartTag folder of your machine. The registry entries appear in the HKEY_CURRENT_USER\Software\Microsoft\Office\Common\SmartTag\Recognizers key.

A special object processes all this information for Internet Explorer. You must add the following <Object> tag to activate SmartTag processing on a Web Page. (See the "Using the <Object> Tag" section of Chapter 6 for additional information about the <Object> tag.)

```
<Object classid="clsid:38481807-CA0E-42D2-BF39-B33AF135CC4D"
        id=IETag></object>
```

LISTING 20.6:   Adding SmartTag Descriptions to a Web Page

```
<o:SmartTagType
    namespaceuri="urn:schemas-microsoft-com:office:smarttags"
    name="stockticker"/>
<o:SmartTagType
    namespaceuri="urn:schemas-microsoft-com:office:smarttags"
    name="PersonName"/>
<o:SmartTagType
    namespaceuri="urn:schemas:contacts" name="Sn"/>
<o:SmartTagType
    namespaceuri="urn:schemas:contacts" name="GivenName"/>
<o:SmartTagType
    namespaceuri="urn:schemas-microsoft-com:office:smarttags"
    name="Street"/>
<o:SmartTagType
    namespaceuri="urn:schemas-microsoft-com:office:smarttags"
    name="address"/>
<o:SmartTagType
    namespaceuri="urn:schemas-microsoft-com:office:smarttags"
    name="place"/>
<o:SmartTagType
    namespaceuri="urn:schemas-microsoft-com:office:smarttags"
    name="City"/>
<o:SmartTagType
    namespaceuri="urn:schemas-microsoft-com:office:smarttags"
    name="State"/>
<o:SmartTagType
    namespaceuri="urn:schemas-microsoft-com:office:smarttags"
    name="PostalCode"/>
<o:SmartTagType
    namespaceuri="urn:schemas-microsoft-com:office:smarttags"
    name="time"/>
<o:SmartTagType
    namespaceuri="urn:schemas-microsoft-com:office:smarttags"
    name="date"/>
<o:SmartTagType
    namespaceuri="urn:schemas-microsoft-com:office:smarttags"
    name="phone"/>
```

Notice the `<Object>` tag doesn't include any parameters or arguments. You can't interact with this object in any way. The `id` value you assign is important because you use it to identify the object to the browser.

The final generic step is to add styles to identify the actual content for the SmartTags to the browser. This is one situation where embedded styles are essential. In addition, unlike most styles, this style doesn't affect the appearance of the content—the style affects the behavior of the content. Here are the two styles you need to work with SmartTags.

```
<style>
    st1\:*{behavior:url(#IETag) }
    st2\:*{behavior:url(#IETag) }
</style>
```

Notice the two styles point to a behavior URL that has the same identifier as the object. The style behavior URL and the object identifier must match or the Web Page won't work.

Don't expect a SmartTag you use on a Web page to have the full functionality that it has in a Microsoft Office document. The SmartTag knows that you're using it in a Web environment and limits the context menu choices to those that are appropriate for a Web venue. Even so, SmartTags can reduce the work a user needs to perform to accomplish tasks, so they serve an important purpose.

USING THE STOCKS AND FUNDS SMARTTAG PLUG-IN

The Stocks and Funds SmartTag detects a stock symbol and provides the user with access about that symbol. Beside all the generic entries needed to support SmartTags, you supply the special tag shown here.

```
<st1:stockticker w:st="on">MSFT</st1:stockticker>
```

The stock symbol, MSFT, placed in the `<stockticker>` tag acts as input for the SmartTag. When you hover the mouse over the purple line that appears under the stock symbol, you see an i within a circle and a square, as shown in Figure 20.9. Click on the i and you see a context menu.

This example shows some of the power of SmartTags on your Web page. The entry appears as text and yet the user can do three things with it: get a stock quote, obtain a company report, or get the latest news about the company in question.

FIGURE 20.9
Use SmartTags to provide the user with data manipulation options.

Using the Name SmartTag Plug-In

The Microsoft Office options you have installed affect the functionality of the Name SmartTag, so you'll want to test this SmartTag with the same Office features that you expect your users to have installed. The Name SmartTag can do everything from help you set up an appointment with the person to creating email or addressing an envelope. Here's the code you need to add to create a Name SmartTag entry.

```
<st1:PersonName w:st="on">
   <st2:GivenName w:st="on">George</st2:GivenName>
   <st2:Sn w:st="on">Smith</st2:Sn>
</st1:PersonName>
```

After you install the proper support, the Name SmartTag becomes exceptionally useful. Figure 20.10 shows the common options you'll see for a standard Office installation. Because each Office product adds features to this particular SmartTag, the options you see will vary depending on what you have installed on your system.

TIP   Sometimes less is better when it comes to SmartTags. You could easily replace the Name Smart-Tag with a simple link that sends an email to the person you want to contact. Just how easily you can replace this SmartTag depends on which features you need to use.

FIGURE 20.10
Decide in advance how much SmartTag functionality the user receives.

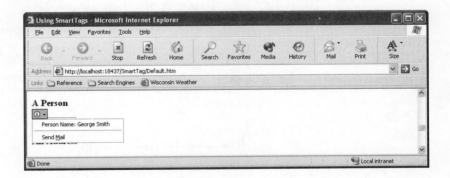

Using the Address and Places SmartTag Plug-In

The Address and Places SmartTag provides driving instructions and a map as the user needs them, as shown in Figure 20.11. The interesting part about this SmartTag is that you get at least this minimal support without having any major Microsoft Office features installed (you generally need at least one product installed to use this SmartTag).

The code for creating an Address and Places SmartTag is a little more complex. Here's the code you normally need.

```
<h3>An Address</h3>
<p>
   <st1:Street w:st="on">
      <st1:address w:st="on">
```

```
              1313 Mockingbird Lane
       </st1:address>
    </st1:Street>
</p>
<h3>A Place</h3>
<p>
    <st1:place w:st="on">
       <st1:City w:st="on">Indianapolis</st1:City>,
       <st1:State w:st="on">IN</st1:State>
       <st1:PostalCode w:st="on">46290</st1:PostalCode>
    </st1:place>
</p>
```

Notice that you need both a `<Street>` and an `<address>` tag to create an address. Likewise, to describe a place, you need a number of tags including the `<place>` tag. The remaining elements describe a particular city, state, and postal zone. The reason for these dual tags is that you can create lists. A `<Street>` tag can contain multiple `<address>` tags so you could describe a list of related entries.

FIGURE 20.11
Some SmartTags are useful even without Microsoft Office support.

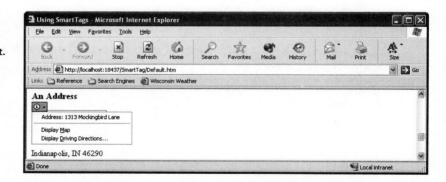

USING THE TIME AND DATE SMARTTAG PLUG-IN

The Time and Date SmartTags won't work unless you have the correct Microsoft Office features installed, most notably, Schedule Plus. The tags let you set up meetings or perform other tasks based on the time or date you enter. Here's the code you need to create a Time SmartTag.

```
<st1:time Hour="12" Minute="22" w:st="on">12:22 pm</st1:time>
```

Notice that this tag includes special attributes: `Hour` and `Minute`. Because time display formats can vary from place to place, you need to provide an easily recognizable time value for the SmartTag. The Date SmartTag works about the same as the Time SmartTag, as shown here.

```
<st1:date Month="4" Day="29" Year="2004" w:st="on">
   29 April 2004
</st1:date>
```

As with the Time SmartTag, you must provide an absolute date using the Month, Day, and Year attributes. The actual order of the attributes is unimportant as long as you provide all three entries.

USING THE TELEPHONE SMARTTAG PLUG-IN

The Telephone SmartTag is another SmartTag that won't work unless you have certain Microsoft Office features installed. Generally, installing Schedule Plus is enough to activate this tag. There aren't any special requirements for this tag, as shown here.

```
<st1:phone w:st="on">(317)572-3201</st1:phone>
```

DISABLING SMARTTAGS ON YOUR SITE

Some people don't like SmartTags because they see them as a means of gaining more information than is required. They don't want their site content to appear as part of a SmartTag and have no desire to share their information using SmartTag technology. It's true that SmartTags have a lot to offer, but developers can also abuse them and the Web sites from which they receive data. Fortunately, it's relatively easy to prevent someone from using the content on your site as part of a SmartTag solution. All you need to do is include the following `<meta>` tag at the beginning of every Web page.

```
<meta name="MSSmartTagsPreventParsing" content="TRUE">
```

The name attribute defines the kind of information this `<meta>` tag contains—a request that SmartTags not parse the page. The content attribute defines all content as off limits. Adding this `<meta>` tag doesn't have any effect on any SmartTags that you add to your Web page.

The purpose of this tag is to disable any SmartTag support added to a browser. A browser with SmartTag support could visit your site and automatically add SmartTags to keywords. The addition wouldn't affect your site, but it would affect how the user sees the site and that's what concerns many people.

Getting Pre-built SmartTags

A number of third party vendors provide additional SmartTags. You can view and sometimes download these SmartTags at `http://office.microsoft.com/en-us/marketplace/EY010504821033 .aspx`. Microsoft also produces some special SmartTags such as the Euro conversion SmartTag that you find at `http://www.microsoft.com/downloads/details.aspx?FamilyID=5879FD92-6119-4B59-9A62-A7164AC67F40&displaylang=EN`. Here are some additional SmartTag sources you should consider exploring.

ActiveDocs (`http://www.activedocs.com/?from=msomp`) Helps you create your own custom SmartTags for classes of information you need to track. This means you could create additional SmartTags that you can add to a Web page as needed to provide support to the end user.

DataPortal (`http://www.nereosoft.com/dataportal20.htm`) Helps you create SmartTags for managing your database applications. For example, you could create a SmartTag where the only thing the user needs to do to interact with a database is to type the database name. The keyword triggers a response that helps the user create database connectivity without really knowing anything about the connection itself. The emphasis is on the data.

LexisNexis (`http://support.lexisnexis.com/lndownload/`) Provides a SmartTag for developers who work with the legal community. For example, the Case Name SmartTag can search for a case name, legal reviews, and verdict information based on a case keyword typed by the user.

ProWrite (`http://www.nereosoft.com/prowrite.htm`) Lets you print Avery labels from contact information. You could use this feature to let someone print a label for your company from a Web page when mail contact is required for a transaction. For that matter, you could use the same technique to create labels for items you want to deliver to a customer based on Web site form data.

WestCiteLink (`http://www.westlaw.com/citelink`) Provides a SmartTag for developers who work with the legal community. This SmartTag specializes in finding and working with citations.

WorldLingo (`http://www.worldlingo.com/microsoft/smart_tag.html`) Provides SmartTags that translate text. You can also obtain quotes for translating large documents, uncovering business practices in other countries, and getting country-specific data.

These are just a few of the SmartTags you can obtain. News sites such as MSNBC and travel sites such as Expedia also provide SmartTags that help you perform tasks with their service. The idea is to provide the SmartTags that users of your Web site can use best.

Developing Downloadable Application Alternatives

You might think, at this point in the chapter, that downloadable applications are the greatest technology to come along. However, you also know that they come with a list of potential problems that you might not overcome—at least not easily. The problem with any powerful technology is that it comes with equally powerful issues that you have to overcome. Sometimes, the best technology is the one that provides just what you need in the smallest package and with the least amount of work. In short, downloadable applications aren't the answer to every problem. You should look for alternatives before you begin creating the downloadable application.

One of the best methods of replacing a downloadable application is to use a series of self-altering Web pages. You can see an example of this kind of technology in the shopping cart example described in detail in Chapter 16. The various pages in this application appear to perform tasks that are similar to those in desktop applications, yet the application relies on a combination of client- and server-side processing to perform the task in a standard way. In other words, even though the user has to trust you enough to enable scripting, the application doesn't require anything exotic—certainly not as exotic as a downloadable application.

In some cases, the best solution is to create a desktop application with an Internet interface. Network administrators find it easier to test desktop applications on their systems and verify their functionality, than depending on a Web application they can't control. The Web application could change and cause problems that the network administrator hadn't considered at the outset. The result is often the same, only the method you use differs. The user sees a desktop application, but underneath the desktop application is a Web application that interacts with online data sources.

You could rely on a combination of scripting and standard components or controls to accomplish tasks. Chapter 6 shows how to use this technique in a number of ways, most importantly, the `<Object>` tag. Any object that you can create with a desktop application, you can also create using a script on the client machine. The only prerequisite is that the user trusts you enough to let you work with these objects. Since many of these objects already appear on the user's machine and the user understands them, you'll likely run into fewer objections than trying to get the user to accept a downloadable application. Of course, you must fit your application requirements within the confines of what the typical user has installed.

Sometimes an acceptable third party product is the best approach. For example, most people accept Adobe Acrobat Reader as a reasonably safe product. You can embed PDF files in your Web site along with a `FileUpload` control (see the "Using the *FileUpload* Control" section of the chapter for details). A user could download the PDF, fill out any required forms, and upload it to your site. The PDF could include any form of interaction that the file format supports. For example, you'll find a list of Adobe Acrobat Reader add-ins at the FreeDownloads Center (`http://www.freedownloads center.com/Search/adobe_acrobat_reader.html`).

Defining Your Development Goals

This chapter has demonstrated how to create, implement, and use downloadable applications in a number of ways. One favorite technique on private Web sites is to use a specialized SmartTag. In fact, it might be the best way to introduce users to the idea that Web pages can do more than present static displays or even dynamic information. A well-designed Web page can do many of the same tasks that desktop applications can perform—the only difference is the Web connection. Of course, that Internet connection makes a lot of difference, so this chapter has also helped you understand user concerns that you have to address.

The problem that you must consider is whether a downloadable application is the best way to provide the functionality that a user requires. In some cases, you might want to use other approaches or even rely on a desktop application that provides a Web interface. Applications that users won't touch don't accomplish anything, so you must consider your company culture as much as you consider the usefulness of this technology.

Chapter 21 addresses an important issue, no matter what kind of Web project you create. Creating accessible Web sites is an important part of the work you perform as a developer. Accessibility means making the Web page friendly for those who have special needs of any kind. For example, a Web page that uses certain color combinations can be invisible to someone with color blindness. Likewise, adding multimedia to a Web site is great for pizzazz, but not such a great means of providing a single source of information—someone who can't hear or see won't be able to use the content on such a Web site. Even small things can affect the accessibility of a Web site. For example, you might see well enough to make out 6-point type on the screen, but most people can't read text that small. Consequently, using small type might cost you visitors. Chapter 21 addresses the full range of accessibility issues so you can create great Web sites that everyone can use.

Creating Accessible Pages

One of the most important user elements of any Web page you design is the accessibility it provides. Accessibility, in this case, is a measure of how well the user can interact with the page. It doesn't matter how well you design a Web page if someone can't see it. Not seeing a page comes in many forms—everything from not being able to decipher page elements due to color blindness to not being able to distinguish the minute text used to provide content. Accessibility covers a broad spectrum of other interface issues that appear in this chapter as well.

Fortunately, making a Web page accessible is easier now than ever before. You simply need to add a few items that you might not have added in the past. In many cases, all you need to do is define properties that make it easier for accessibility aids (such as screen readers) to understand the content of your page and relay it to the user. Of course, you may also need to verify that the resources you want to use will actually work and provide a little additional content to help those who can interact with the Web page in a certain way. For example, you can provide a description of a picture or other informational graphics for those who can't see or have limited vision.

You don't even have to perform this task completely on your own. Visual Studio provides a number of tools to make the task easier for you. In addition, you'll find a wealth of tools on the Internet for checking the accessibility of your Web page. Making a Web page accessible doesn't necessary mean spending hours slaving away at code that you don't think anyone will actually use. Sometimes, accessibility is a matter of presenting the page in a way that you hadn't considered in the past.

NOTE   This chapter relies on several small examples to show basic accessibility principles. Because the ABC Incorporated Web site has so many pages, the smaller examples will demonstrate the principles in a clearer way. The chapter then moves to the ABC Incorporated Web site for testing purposes. You'll discover how the tools described in this chapter respond to a somewhat complex environment.

Reasons to Design with Accessibility in Mind

Many developers are under the misconception that accessibility refers to code that they add to an application in order to make it usable by people with special needs, such as blindness. By adding special attributes to HTML tags, a person using a screen reader can visualize the page content and interact with it. While this is certainly one definition of accessibility, it's also the least productive and most narrow-minded interpretation. Unfortunately, it's the most prevalent view of accessibility used by government and industry today because it's the viewpoint that enjoys legal status. A broader definition helps everyone because most people have some type of special need—it might simply be the need to enlarge text when their eyes are tired, but the need is still real and Web sites that cater to this need have a distinct advantage.

NOTE   Most countries in the world today have some type of legal requirement for accessibility in place. In general, these legal requirements define how you must set up both hardware and software for someone who has a special need. Businesses are often exempt from these requirements unless they have a relationship with the government—any participation in the accessibility program is purely optional for individuals. To learn more about the accessibility requirements for the United Sates, see the Section 508 requirements at `http://www.section508.gov/`. Many countries rely on a standard based on the Web Content Accessibility Guidelines, which are stricter than the U.S. standards. Learn more about these guidelines at `http://www.w3.org/TR/WAI-WEBCONTENT/`. You may also want to look at my accessibility book, *Accessibility for Everybody: Understanding the Second 508 Accessibility Requirements* (Apress, 2003) which contains an extensive review of both programming techniques and Windows resources you have at your disposal for implementation and testing.

The best way to view accessibility is as a means of making people comfortable, not as an extra expense that the business or individual must bear. A business that pursues accessibility as a means for attracting and keeping new clients is certainly going to see a profit from their efforts. In addition, the company's employees benefit from better health, which in turn pays dividends in reduced sick time for the company. An application, whether desktop or Web-based, that's accessible is easier to use than one that lacks accessibility features. You might even find that adding accessibility features pays for itself by reducing application support costs.

The whole concept of accessibility is an important one that the developer needs to make a part of the design process. Unfortunately, most developers ignore it until the last second and only pay attention to it as part of a legal requirement. Yet something as simple as making an application or Web site screen reader accessible can net large gains for anyone who chooses to use a screen reader. Some developers would say that this statement proves their point because only those with vision deficiencies would rely on a screen reader.

Although I have good vision, I use the screen reader provided with Windows on any Web site with a lot of content (if the Web site will allow such use). The reason is simple. Using a screen reader helps me to concentrate on the content offered by the Web site. I get more out of the information I hear because I'm not constantly distracted by other Web site features, ads, or other embellishments. In addition, if the content is easy enough to understand, I can perform other tasks while my computer reads to me. Many people choose to multitask today in order to get their work completed—using a screen reader allows multitasking. The user can listen to the Web site content while performing some other task. This little tip is a real time saver when you read (listen to) as many trade journals as I do.

Including Alt attribute and bubble help (tooltips) in an application may seem like something that no one would use—especially with graphics—because the developer assumes that the user can see the image on screen. The fact is that some applications and Web sites alike present many images in such a way that deciphering them is difficult. The Alt attribute and bubble help provide clues for those with good vision, as well as those who might require a little additional help. The pop-up explanation becomes a source of additional information that everyone can use. In addition, it's quite possible that the browser won't download the image due to security concerns—the description acts as a replacement in this environment.

TIP   Lest you get the idea that accessibility affects only application use and that developers are only engaged in creating applications, there are many other areas of involvement, such as training. You can find an excellent piece written by David M. Peter and entitled, "Usability and Accessibility—Everyone Learning" on the effects of accessibility on training at http://www.david-peter.com/papers/dec2002/dec2002_paper.htm. This white paper helps you understand how accessibility can affect training goals and requirements. It also shines a light on the issue of accessibility as a methodology that affects everyone.

Carpal tunnel syndrome is the scourge of our society. One of the main causes of carpal tunnel syndrome for office workers is the keyboard and mouse. The accessibility requirements designed to ease access for those who lack good coordination also helps those who have normal use of their arms by reducing the effort required to input information. A business could easily write off the cost of improving the accessibility of their software by reducing the number of cases of carpal tunnel syndrome. In fact, because of the high cost of medical assistance, even one case of carpal tunnel syndrome prevented could pay for the required upgrades and anything after that would be money saved.

TIP   Carpal tunnel syndrome is a lot more serious and widespread than most people think. You can obtain a good overview of the topic at the National Institute of Neurological Disorders and Stroke (NINDS) Carpal Tunnel Syndrome Information Page (http://www.ninds.nih.gov/disorders/carpal_tunnel/carpal_tunnel.htm). There's a lot of good information for computer users at the MSU–Computer Science and Engineering Web site (http://web.cps.msu.edu/facility/avoid-ct.php).

Even the colors used to present information on screen can affect the productivity of those who use the application. For example, many of the same color combinations that cause problems for those with color blindness also cause eyestrain for those with normal vision. Meeting accessibility requirements for color composition can also net surprising results in reduced headaches and time off spent recovering from symptoms such as dry eyes.

TIP   If you want to obtain a quick overview of color blindness, check out the article titled, "Can Color-Blind Users See Your Site?" at http://msdn.microsoft.com/library/en-us/dnhess/html/hess10092000.asp. You might also want to visit the Color Perception Issues Web site at http://www.firelily.com/opinions/color.html.

The benefits from programming with accessibility in mind are more numerous than I've already listed in this section, and we'll explore them as the chapter progresses. The bottom line is that programming with accessibility in mind helps everyone. It benefits all users by making the computer easier to use. Businesses benefit with better sales, increased employee productivity, reduced costs, and improved customer relations. In short, you should embrace this technology with open arms because it has something for everyone.

Making Controls Accessible

Depending on the accessibility goals you set for your Web site, you can perform various levels of changes to its design. As a minimum, you should make the standard controls that you use accessible. In some cases, you can add additional information to improve the accessibility of existing controls. Visual Web Developer natively supports many of these attributes—you'll have to add other attributes by hand in Source view, but the effort is well worth the results. The following sections describe how you can make controls more accessible.

Adding Accessibility Attributes to Standard Controls

You don't need to sweat a lot to improve the accessibility of your Web site greatly. In fact, all you really need is a few simple attributes that you can add using the Properties window. In short, you don't even have to remember the names of these properties—all you need to do is remember to provide content for them. The following list of attributes can help you create accessible Web pages. The ASPX name of the property appears first, the HTML name second (that's right, the same properties work for both page types).

AccessKey/AccessKey   This attribute enables a user to access a screen element, such as a text box or a pushbutton, quickly. You can use this attribute with most of the ASP.NET controls. In addition, you can use it with the <A>, <AREA>, <BUTTON>, <INPUT>, <LABEL>, <LEGEND>, and <TEXTAREA> HTML tags.

AssociatedControlID/For   This attribute associates one element with another element. For example, you could use it to associate a label specifically with its associated text box. The value of this attribute must match the ID attribute value of the target element.

TabIndex/TabIndex   This attribute defines the element's position in the tabbing order for a form. It helps the developer control the flow of the page. Defining a tabbing order makes the page easier to understand and use.

ToolTip/Title   This attribute provides ancillary information about the associated element. The ancillary information describes the purpose and content of the element in most cases. In some cases, a developer can also use this attribute to provide basic help information for the element.

Using these attributes is relatively easy. All you need to do is think about how the user will employ the control when making accessibility choices. For example, you only need to associate a label with another control when the label actually references that control. On the other hand, all controls should have a tab index to ensure the user sees the correct page flow when pressing Tab. Listing 21.1 shows the code you'll need for this example. You'll find this example in the \Chapter 21\Accessible Control folder of the source code on the Sybex Web site.

All of this content appears within the <body> tag of the example. I chose the HTML version because it's easier to understand. In addition, when you run the ASPX version and view the source code it produces, you'll notice that it's amazingly close to the code shown here—the server simply converts the ASPX page into this HTML equivalent.

The first thing you should notice is that lblGreeting doesn't appear to have any of the accessibility tags mentioned in the list. Sometimes your Web pages will have one or two controls that lack attributes, too, so don't worry about it when you can't come up with attributes you should use to make the page accessible. In this case, lblGreeting isn't associated with any other control, it doesn't require a tooltip or speed key because the user won't actually interact with it, and the tab index is 0, which is the default. However, this control is the exception, rather than the rule.

The lblOutput control includes attributes that are common for labels. It uses the for attribute to create a connection between it and txtOutput. Although the naming convention makes the connection apparent to developers, the for attribute makes the connection apparent to many accessibility aids such as screen readers, which makes it easier for the user to interpret the display. The tabindex attribute is important because the user can actually tab to the label, unlike desktop applications where tabbing tends to skip nonfunctional display elements such as labels.

The `txtOutput` control is one that the user will interact with, so it requires different attributes. The `AccessKey` attribute makes it easier for users who can't use the mouse to select the control quickly. All the user needs to do is press Alt+C to access the control. Unfortunately, the accessibility aid won't tell the user about this key combination in most cases. The best solution is to use the first character of the associated label as a quick selection key. However, you can also format the label text to include underlines so the user knows which key to use. The `title` attribute provides balloon help. In addition, most accessibility aids will make use of this text. For example, a screen reader will read the text to the user to help in visualizing the display.

LISTING 21.1:   Using Basic Accessibility Attributes

```
<p>
    <label id="lblGreeting">Accessible Control Demonstration</label>
</p>
<p>
    <label id="lblOutput"
           for="txtOutput"
           tabindex="1">
       Check the Application:
    </label><br />
    <input id="txtOutput"
           type="text"
           accesskey="C"
           title="Holds the application output."
           tabindex="2" />
</p>
<p>
    <input id="btnTest"
           type="button"
           value="Test"
           accesskey="T"
           title="Creates application output that appears in the textbox."
           tabindex="3" />
</p>
<p>
    <a id="hlASXP"
       title="Displays a page that shows the same attributes in HTML form."
       accesskey="A"
       tabindex="4"
       href="ASPXVersion.ASPX">
        See the ASXP Version
    </a>
</p>
```

TIP It's easy to get stuck in a rut when typing the title attribute information in an application. Some developers will start every title attribute entry with the word *click*, even when the user obviously knows that a click is required. Imagine waiting several minutes for a page to finish because of long title entries and hearing the word *click* repeatedly. Using short and descriptive title entries works much better and increases the user's ability to understand the Web page content.

The example code also includes typical entries for buttons and hyperlinks. In all cases where a user will interact with the control directly, rather than using it as a visual aid (such as when working with a label), you should include the title attribute and provide an AccessKey attribute as well. Some controls do have other special entries you can make—many of which appear in the remainder of the chapter.

Using Alternative Attributes to Improve Accessibility

The common attributes described in the "Adding Accessibility Attributes to Standard Controls" section of the chapter always work, even with some of the older browsers on the market. However, sometimes you want to provide more information than these common attributes can provide. This section describes alternative attributes that you can use on your Web page.

Many alternative attributes also work with every modern browser on the market, but you can't count on them to work quite as often with older browsers. The issue isn't one of standardization. The problem with many attributes today is that developers don't know they exist, don't understand how to use them, or don't know which attributes are actually standardized. As with accessibility tags, you can find a list of accessibility attributes in the "Index of HTML elements and attributes" section of the HTML Techniques for Web Content Accessibility Guidelines 1.0 specification (http://www.w3.org/TR/WCAG10-HTML-TECHS/). The following list provides a quick overview of these attributes and tells how they're used.

Abbr This attribute contains an abbreviated form of the data found in a table cell. A screen reader could use this information to output a short form of a long repetitive table entry.

Axis This attribute places the cell of a table within a conceptual category. The Axis acts as a single dimension within an *n*-dimensional space. The user can request the browser organize the data using a particular category as a basis.

Class This attribute assigns a class name to the element. Browsers often use this feature to select characteristics for the element from a Cascading Style Sheet (CSS) file. More than one element on a Web page can share the same Class attribute value.

Dir This attribute defines the direction of the text on screen when Unicode doesn't define the direction. The acceptable values include ltr (left-to-right) and rtl (right-to-left).

HREFLang This attribute defines the language used by a resource pointed at by an HREF attribute. Developers commonly use this attribute with the <LINK> and <A> tags.

ID This attribute assigns an identifier to the element. Browsers can use this feature to select characteristics for the element from a CSS file. However, the most common use of this attribute is as a means to identify a particular element within a script or other means of page processing.

Label This attribute assigns a value to the element. The current specification only uses this attribute with the <OPTION> and <OPTGROUP> tags.

Lang This attribute defines the language used by or associated with a particular element. Developers can use this attribute to help speech and search engines to interact more successfully with Web page elements. In addition, this attribute can help the browser provide correct language-specific interaction, such as the use of punctuation.

Rel This attribute describes the relationship between the current document and the target URL. For example, you can use this attribute with the `<LINK>` and `<A>` tags to describe where the link goes. Acceptable values include `alternate`, `designates`, `stylesheet`, `start`, `next`, `prev`, `contents`, `index`, `glossary`, `copyright`, `chapter`, `section`, `subsection`, `appendix`, `help`, and `bookmark`. This attribute is important in telling the viewer what to expect from the link. For example, when a link points to a help page, you'd use the `rel` attribute with the `help` value.

Rev This attribute describes the relationship between the target URL and the current document. In other words, it tells the viewer what to expect when clicking the Back button on the browser. The acceptable values and uses for this attribute are the same as for the `rel` attribute.

Style This attribute assigns the inline style for an element. For example, the developer could use it to assign font characteristics to a `<Label>` tag. In general, you'll want to avoid using this attribute and assign a style to tags using an external CSS file. Using an external file enables users to substitute the styles they want to use to view a particular page.

UseMap This attribute associates an image map with the element. The `UseMap` value must match the value of the Name attribute of the `<MAP>` tag used to define the image map. Developers can use this attribute with the `<IMG>`, `<INPUT>`, and `<OBJECT>` tags.

Many of the attributes provided as part of the specification perform special tasks. For example, the `Abbr`, `Axis`, `Headers`, and `Scope` attributes only appear with the `<TD>` and `<TH>` tags used with tables. If you're using a product such as Visual Web Developer to create your Web applications, the IDE will generally provide you with a list of acceptable attributes for a particular tag. The problem with relying too heavily on the input provided by an IDE is that the IDE will often supply vendor-specific, as well as standardized, attributes. In sum, you need to exercise care to ensure your Web page uses only standardized attributes to ensure maximum flexibility.

Using Alternative Tags to Improve Accessibility

You also have access to a number of specialized tags that aid in accessibility. In most cases, these tags also serve other purposes, so using them provides a double benefit. Here are a few of the tags you should try.

Abbr This tag lets you define the meaning behind abbreviations on a Web page. An abbreviation is a shortened form of a word that may not form a word in and of itself as an acronym will. For example, people often use WI, Wis, and Wisc as abbreviations for Wisconsin.

Acronym This tag lets you define acronyms on first use in a Web page. Defining the acronym helps those who don't know what it means, yet lets you to use the acronym for those who expect to see it. An acronym is a word formed from the initial letters of the words of a compound term. For example, Rapid Application Development (RAD) qualifies as an acronym because it's composed of the initial letters of several words and produces a pronounceable result.

Code   This tag defines an area of the Web page containing example computer code. You always use this tag for complete listings. Use the <samp> tag for code snippets and other code samples, and the <var> tag for code variables. The reason you want to add these tags to computer code is to avoid confusing the screen reader when it comes to the odd combinations of letters used for computer code. Don't use this tag for actual computer code, such as scripts, within the Web page.

Dfn   This tag lets you define terms that the viewer might not understand the first time they appear on the Web page. Not everyone understands the technical jargon used for every trade, so defining the terms on first use makes the Web page easier to use, yet lets experienced viewers skip the material.

Kbd   This tag defines keyboard text on the Web page. Use this tag whenever you want the viewer to perform a task using the keyboard. The tag provides both visual and aural cues that let the viewer know that you want them to perform an action. You might use this tag within a procedure for setting up an application the viewer has downloaded.

Samp   This tag defines an area of sample computer code—not a full listing, but a code snippet used for explanation purposes. As with the <code> tag, don't use this tag for actual computer code, such as scripts, within the Web page.

Var   This tag defines a variable used as part of a code explanation within a Web page. As with the <code> tag, don't use this tag for actual computer code, such as scripts, within the Web page.

Organizing the Web Page

You can organize Web pages using a number of techniques. In fact, there's a wealth of such techniques throughout the book. However, from an accessibility perspective, you can see the vast majority of the organizational techniques you need to use with forms and tables. The following sections discuss both accessible forms and tables.

Working with Forms

Web forms present a few accessibility challenges. For example, it's very easy to add speed keys to a desktop application by adding an ampersand (&) in front of the letter you want to use as a speed key. Not only does this addition add the speed key, but it also underlines the letter so the user knows which key to press along with the Alt key. Web pages have no such resource—you need to perform extra coding to make the speed keys work correctly.

WARNING   Avoid assuming too much about the capabilities of the browser and other software that the user will employ to access your Web site. For example, some screen readers aren't compatible with the AccessKey attribute associated with the on-screen elements. Normally, the user can press Alt, followed by the AccessKey value to access a specific screen element. Read more about this problem in the Q306448 Knowledge Base article entitled, "INFO: Some Screen Readers Are Not Fully Compatible with Access Keys" at http://support.microsoft.com/default.aspx?scid=kb; en-us;306448.

Figure 21.1 shows a data entry form. This form isn't functional—its only function is to show some accessibility features. You'll find this example in the `\Chapter 21\AccessibleForm` folder of the source code on the Sybex Web site.

You should notice a few features about this page. First, each of the labels preceding a field has an underlined letter. This letter doesn't add any functionality as it would for a Windows application. All that the underlining does is provide a visual cue for the viewer. To add the keyboard shortcut, you must include the `AccessKey` attribute as part of the `<input>` tag for the text box. Consequently, the keyboard shortcut is associated with the actual text box, rather than the label preceding it. (You can also follow the Microsoft conventions where the label is the focus of the shortcut—read about it at `http://msdn.microsoft.com/workshop/author/dhtml/reference/properties/accesskey.asp`.)

Unfortunately, you have to use the underlined characters carefully. The `AccessKey` attribute accepts a single letter as input. Every shortcut is an Alt key combination. In short, if you have more than 36 fields (letters A through Z and numbers 0 through 9) on a form, then you'll run out of `AccessKey` attribute combinations. (Theoretically, you can use a single key more than once, but this often confuses the viewer more than helping them.)

This page also provides balloon help for every field. Like the table example discussed earlier, you'll use the title attribute to create the balloon help. It becomes obvious, in this case, that the balloon help only appears when hovering the mouse over the field. Selecting the field with the keyboard doesn't display the balloon help. Fortunately, the screen readers I tested all say the title attribute text even if it doesn't appear on screen.

Interestingly enough, the special effects demonstrated on this page are more the result of careful programming than special effects. Listing 21.2 shows the code for this example. Notice that the Web page in Figure 21.1 looks formatted, even though there's little or no formatting for the controls in this example.

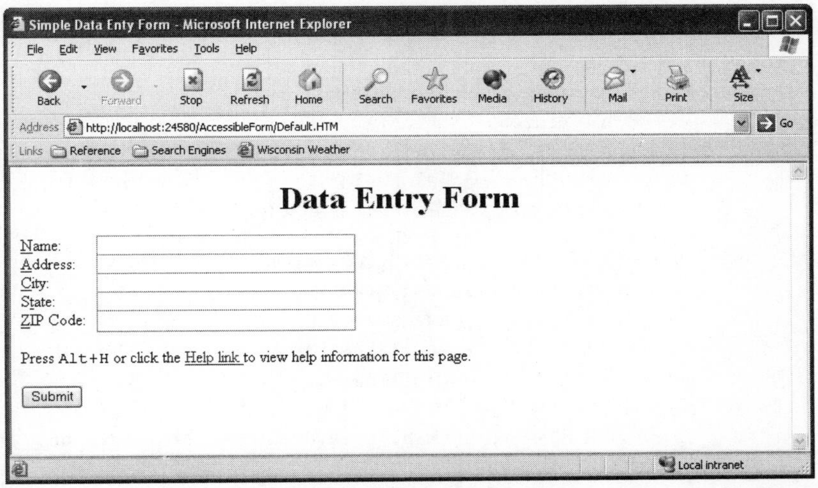

FIGURE 21.1

Using this simple data entry form will demonstrate the use of both tooltips and keyboard shortcuts.

LISTING 21.2:   Adding Accessibility Features to a Form

```
<!DOCTYPE html PUBLIC "-//W3C//DTD XHTML 1.1//EN"
                      "http://www.w3.org/TR/xhtml11/DTD/xhtml11.dtd">
<html xmlns="http://www.w3.org/1999/xhtml" >
<head>
    <title>Simple Data Enty Form</title>
    <link rel="stylesheet" type="text/css" href="SampleStyle.CSS">
</head>
<body>
    <form id="frmDataEntry"
          title="This form demonstrates data entry principles."
          name="frmDataEntry">

        <h1>Data Entry Form</h1>
        <div>
            <label id="lblName" for="txtName">
                <span class="underline">N</span>ame:
            </label>
            <input id="txtName"
                   class="data_entry"
                   title="Full name of the person."
                   accessKey="N"
                   type="text"
                   name="txtName">
        </div>

        ... Other Form Entries ...

        <div> </div>
        <div>
            Press <kbd>Alt+H</kbd> or click the
            <A id="lnkHelp"
               title="Obtain help on this page."
               accessKey="H"
               href="Help.htm"
               rev="Start"
               rel="Help"
               name="lnkHelp">
                Help link
            </A>
            to view help information for this page.
        </div>
        <div> </div>
        <div>
            <input id="btnSend"
```

```
                          title="Send the data."
                          accessKey="S"
                          type="submit"
                          value="Submit"
                          name="btnSend">
            </div>
        </form>
    </body>
</html>
```

Many of the coding elements, such as the use of the `for`, `title`, and `AccessKey` attributes, appear in the "Adding Accessibility Attributes to Standard Controls" section of the chapter. However, notice the use of the `<span>` tag to underline the speed key in `lblName`. The `<span>` tag doesn't add any actual formatting and you could override its effect by using a different CSS page for the Web site. However, the effect, in this case, is to underline the first character in the label.

The help link at the bottom of the page also uses some special formatting. For example, the `<kbd>` tag surrounds the Alt+H text because you want the user to perform this act. The actual link, `lnkHelp`, contains the usual accessibility attributes, along with the `rev` and `rel` attributes. The `rel` attribute tells the user about the information on the linked page—a help page in this case. The `rev` attribute tells the user what kind of page will appear when clicking the Back button after viewing the linked page. The combination of these two links helps the user to navigate your Web site with greater ease by providing positional cues.

The CSS for this Web page adds quite a bit to the output you see. For example, many Web sites would use tables to align the text entry fields on the page. However, this example uses a simple CSS file entry, as shown here.

```
.data_entry
{
    left: 11%;
    width: 250px;
    position: absolute;
}
```

Notice that the bottom of the page in Figure 21.1 shows a help link. All of your data entry forms should include some type of help. Figure 21.2 shows the sample help for this example. It also includes a link at the bottom of the page to return to the data entry form. Like the data entry fields, both of these links include a keyboard shortcut that makes them easy to access. The text associated with the link tells the reader what key combination to press in order to access the link quickly.

Working with Tables

Look anywhere on the Internet and you'll find a wealth of tables. Unfortunately, most of those tables will prove confusing to viewers with special needs because the page uses them as an organizational aid, rather than for their intended purpose. Accessibility friendly tables store information, rather than layouts. However, accessible tables contain a few other elements than just information. This section of the chapter provides an overview of the two table types commonly used on Web sites that are easiest to read using a screen reader.

FIGURE 21.2
Your data entry forms
should include some
type of help dialog.

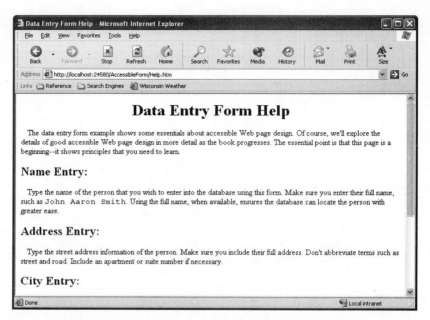

FIGURE 21.2
Your data entry forms
should include some
type of help dialog.

Before you begin working with tables, however, it's important to know about some special attributes you can use with them. The following list describes some table-specific attributes that you can use with tables to make them easier for the viewer to understand.

Headers   This attribute contains a space-delimited list of cells that form the header for a table. Using this attribute helps users of screen readers because the screen reader will announce that the cells are part of a header. Developers also use this attribute with style sheets.

Scope   This attribute often appears in place of the Headers attribute for simple tables. It defines the set of data cells that are associated with a header cell. Acceptable values include row, col, rowgroup, and colgroup. The rowgroup and colgroup values associate the header cell with a group of data cells.

Summary   This attribute defines the purpose and content of a table. Providing a summary means that someone using an accessibility aid can determine whether they want to listen through the entire table. The summary attribute also helps focus the viewer's attention on the table as a whole before hearing about the specific elements.

Tables come in a variety of sizes, content, arrangements, and formatting, so it's not possible to discuss every possible table type in a section of one chapter. The examples shown in Listing 21.3 consider two typical table types and their accessibility features. You'll find this example in the \Chapter 21\ AccessibleTables folder of the source code on the Sybex Web site.

You should notice a few construction details about these tables. First, notice that each table has a title attribute. The title attribute describes what the table contains (demonstration information). In addition to the title attribute, the tables also include the summary attribute. Many accessibility aids treat the two attributes differently, so you should include both in your tables.

LISTING 21.3:   Adding Accessibility Features to Tables

```
<!DOCTYPE html PUBLIC "-//W3C//DTD XHTML 1.1//EN"
                    "http://www.w3.org/TR/xhtml11/DTD/xhtml11.dtd">
<html xmlns="http://www.w3.org/1999/xhtml" >
<head>
    <title>Accessible table Demonstration</title>
    <link rel="stylesheet" type="text/css" href="SampleStyle.CSS">
</head>
<body>
    <h1 id="lblTitle">Table Demonstration</h1>
    <h2 id="lblTableType1">Table Type 1</h2>
    <p>
        <table id="tblType1"
              title="Shows some features every table should have."
              summary="This is a demonstration table.">
        <tr>
            <th title="This column stores the first column of data."
                id="Column1">
                Column 1 Heading</th>
            <th title="This column stores the second column of data."
                id="Column2">
                Colunn 2 Heading</th>
            <th title="This column stores the third column of data."
                id="Column3">
                Column 3 Heading</th>
        </tr>
        <tr>
            <td headers="Column1">Column 1 Row 1</td>
            <td headers="Column2">Column 2 Row 1</td>
            <td headers="Column3">Column 3 Row 1</td>
        </tr>

        ... Other Rows ...

        <tr>
            <td colspan="3"
                headers="Column1 Column2 Column3">
                Columns 1 through 3 Row 3
            </td>
        </tr>
        </table>
    </p>
    <h2 id="lblTableType2">Table Type 2</h2>
    <p>
        <table id="tblType2"
              title="Shows some features every table should have."
```

```
               summary="This is another demonstration table.">
    <tr>
        <th title="This square purposely left blank.">
        </th>
        <th title="This column stores the first column of data."
            scope="col">
            Column 1 Heading</th>
        <th title="This column stores the second column of data."
            scope="col">
            Column 2 Heading</th>
        <th title="This column stores the third column of data."
            scope="col">
            Column 3 Heading</th>
    </tr>
    <tr>
        <th title="This is the first row of data."
            scope="row">
            Row Heading 1</th>
        <td>Column 1 Row 1</td>
        <td>Column 2 Row 1</td>
        <td>Column 3 Row 1</td>
    </tr>

    ... Other Rows ...

    </table>
    </p>
</body>
</html>
```

Second, the column headings rely on the <TH> tag pair, not the <TD> tag pair. If you use the <TD> tag pair for the column headings, the accessibility aid won't know it's a heading and will read it as data. The same holds true for row headings. If you include a row heading, such as the one shown in Table Type 2, then make sure you use the <TH> tag pair for just the heading (not the data). Data should always appear within the <TD> tag pair.

Third, each of the headings also produce balloon help containing additional information using the `title` attribute—the `summary` attribute is unnecessary (and unsupported) for headings. The screen real estate for Web applications is often limited, which means that developers use short headings whenever possible. The addition of balloon help makes it possible for the user to receive additional information. To use this feature, add a title attribute to each of the headings. When users hover the mouse over the heading, they'll receive additional information about that heading.

The two table types demonstrate different accessibility support features. Table Type 1 demonstrates use of the `headers` attribute, while Table Type 2 demonstrates use of the `scope` attribute. In both cases, the purpose is to provide header information to text-only browsers and certain types of accessibility aids. Both attributes work equally well.

The choice of which one to use depends on the kind of table you want to create. In the first case, the deciding factor is that the last row of the table uses the `colspan` attribute, so it spans three columns. Using the `headers` attribute lets you associate each cell with the specific headers that support it. Notice that the last row has three headings associated with it. Make sure you separate the header identifiers with spaces, not with commas or other separator characters. Table Type 2 has both column and row headers, so using the `scope` attribute is easier. Otherwise, you'd have to type complex entries for each cell. Figure 21.3 shows the output from this example.

Figure 21.3 shows that a table can contain a lot of formatting information that doesn't necessarily appear in the Web page. This is another demonstration of the power of CSS. All of the formatting you see appears in the sample CSS file, as shown here.

```
Table
{
    padding-right: 1px;
    padding-left: 1px;
    padding-bottom: 1px;
    padding-top: 1px;
    width: 80%;
    border-right: silver thick ridge;
    border-top: silver thick ridge;
    border-left: silver thick ridge;
    border-bottom: silver thick ridge;
    margin: 1px;
}


TH
{
    border-right: blue outset;
    border-top: blue outset;
    border-left: blue outset;
    border-bottom: blue outset;
}


TD
{
    border-right: green thin solid;
    border-top: green thin solid;
    border-left: green thin solid;
    border-bottom: green thin solid;
}
```

Because this code affects all of the table entries, you only have to make one change to adjust the appearance of the table. Make sure you include entries for the table, the headers, and the data, or the table won't contain all of the formatting that it could. Especially important are the border settings because they provide separation between table cells. You can also use CSS to adjust the colors, fonts, and other table features.

FIGURE 21.3
An example of the two types of tables commonly used on Web sites.

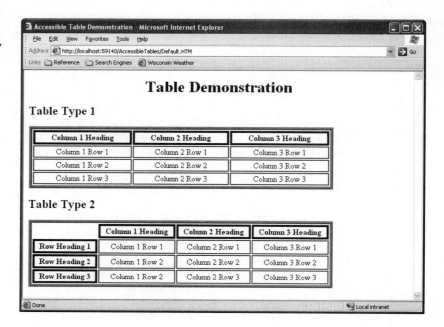

Working with Graphics

Graphics by their very nature are visual. Depending on the graphic and the equipment the viewer uses, it might require perfect vision to see a graphic. You might find yourself asking whether that's a picture of a van or a sports utility vehicle (SUV) depending on the skill of the photographer. In short, graphics can be a very confusing means of communication despite the fact that they dress up a Web site and give it real pizzazz. That's why this section is so important. You can use graphics to good effect on a Web site and offer help to people who can't make quite make them out at the same time by using the attributes in the following list.

Alt   This attribute provides a short description of a graphic element on screen. In many cases, you'll combine it with the LongDesc attribute to ensure the user receives a complete description of the graphic element.

LongDesc   This attribute provides a reference to a Web page or other resource that contains a long description of a complex graphic element. For example, the developer would use this attribute with a chart or a graph. The referenced page would provide a text description of the content of the chart or graph so users who rely on screen readers can understand the information conveyed by the graphic image. This attribute often appears with the Alt attribute.

Of these two attributes, the Alt attribute sees the most common use because more developers know about it. An Alt attribute provides a short description of a Web site element. When the user hovers the mouse over the element or selects the element in some other way (such as using a screen reader), a browser that supports the Alt attribute will provide descriptive information about the screen element. In many cases, the help is in the form of an audio description or the appearance of balloon help. However, the rendering of the `Alt` attribute depends on the browser you use.

TIP It's often helpful to have a number of tools to test your Web site. Of course, buying these tools can become quite expensive, so getting free or low-cost solutions is always helpful. The Sayz Me text-to-speech reader (`http://sayzme.sourceforge.net/`) is one such solution. It provides basic text reading capability that helps you hear what your page will sound like to someone who can't see it.

Some pictures literally are worth a thousand words. The problem with placing all the thousand words in an `Alt` attribute is that they'd be hard to read and not every user will want to hear them. Imagine waiting for a screen reader to finish saying all this information before moving on to the next element on the Web page. The `longdesc` attribute provides a link to another page with a complete text description of complex graphics. In general, the description should talk about every element of the graphic. You want to create a word picture that matches the graphic element. Listing 21.4 shows how to use these two attributes. You'll find this example in the `\Chapter 21\AccessibleGraphics` folder of the source code on the Sybex Web site.

LISTING 21.4:   Using the *Alt* and *LongDesc* Attributes on a Web Page

```
<!DOCTYPE html PUBLIC "-//W3C//DTD XHTML 1.1//EN"
                      "http://www.w3.org/TR/xhtml11/DTD/xhtml11.dtd">
<html xmlns="http://www.w3.org/1999/xhtml" >
<head>
    <title>Sample of ALT and LONGDESC Attributes</title>
</head>
<body>
    <h1 align=center>Using the ALT and LONGDESC Attributes</h1>

    <p>Simple graphics only require use of the ALT attribute.</p>
    <img align=middle
        alt="A green diamond shape that contains the word New in red."
        src="new.GIF">

    <p>Complex graphics require both the ALT and the LONGDESC
        attributes</p>
    <img align=middle
        alt="A picture of John"
        src="JohnPic.JPG"
        height=200
        width=150
        longdesc="JohnDesc.HTM">
    <a href="JohnDesc.HTM"
        title="A text description of John's picture.">[D]</a>
</body>
</html>
```

Figure 21.4 shows the output from this example. As you can see, the first image is simple, so it doesn't require the use of the `longdesc` attribute. However, as you can see from Listing 21.4, the example still uses the `Alt` attribute. Although this first image is simple, notice that describing it still presents problems. Drawing a word picture of any graphic element is going to take time, but it's an essential task.

The second image is more complex than the first. In this case, I used my picture, but any complex graphic qualifies as something that you'll want to describe in more detail than an `Alt` attribute will allow. As you can see from Listing 21.4, the second image uses the `longdesc` attribute in addition to the `Alt` attribute.

Unfortunately, if you click on the second picture shown in Figure 21.4 when using Internet Explorer, nothing will happen. Even the 6.0 version of Internet Explorer lacks support for the `LongDesc` attribute. This means that you wasted your effort unless you can come up with another solution to the problem. You'll notice that Listing 21.4 contains a strange looking [D] link in it that takes you to the same URL as the `LongDesc` attribute. The [D] link is the W3C solution to the problem, and you should always include it with your Web page so that everyone can access the long description for a graphic element.

The `JohnDesc.HTM` file that contains the long description for my picture is relatively simple text. You can see the text shown in Figure 21.5 by clicking the [D] link shown in Figure 21.4.

You should know about a special feature in this file. To format the text, I included the following tag.

```
<p align=justify style="LEFT: 15%; WIDTH: 70%; POSITION: relative">
```

FIGURE 21.4
Make sure you use the right set of tags to describe graphic elements based on their complexity.

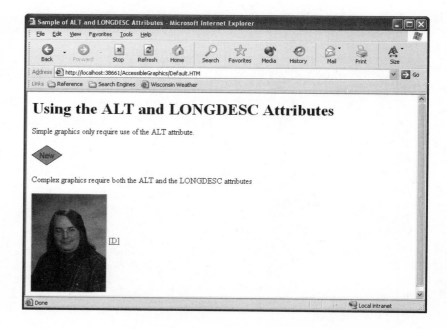

FIGURE 21.5
Create word pictures that describe complex graphics you use on your Web site.

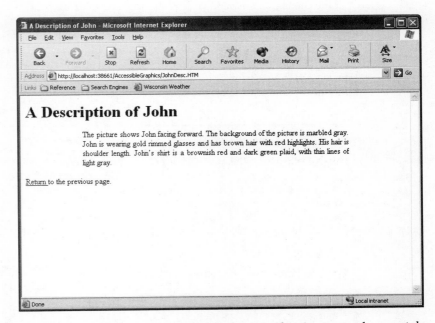

Normally, you won't format your text using this technique because the viewer may have a style sheet that works better for their particular needs. However, in this case, I chose to include the formatting information. Notice that the tag doesn't include any mention of font size and that all layouts do rely on percentages. This tag will work for most users, even those who need to use large text displays, because the formatting is flexible. It's still better to use an external CSS file, whenever possible, but you can use this approach for simple formatting on simple pages.

Using the *<NoScript>* Tag

Not everyone allows scripts to run when they browse the Internet, so you should prepare for a non-scripting scenario. To overcome this problem, you can add the <NoScript> tag to any Web page that includes a client-side script. The purpose of the <NoScript> tag is to provide output for users who don't have a browser that supports scripting or who have turned off scripting. Even though this information appears in the accessibility chapter of the book because you'll run into more people with scripting turned on when addressing accessibility needs, this particular feature helps everyone who visits your Web site.

TIP   Many ASP.NET 2.0 features rely heavily on scripting. Never assume that simply because you didn't use any scripts on a page that the output is script free. Always check the output page for scripts generated by ASP.NET. When you see these scripts, you can add a <NoScript> tag to the Web page that explains how the script is used and what features the page will lack because of scripting support loss.

If the client-side script on your Web site performs a simple task that you can easily explain in text, you can provide a description of the task within the <NoScript> tag. For example, if the client-side script creates a cookie on the user's system that holds user settings between sessions, you can explain this fact in the <NoScript> tag. The loss of the cookie won't affect the content presented by the Web site—it's a convenience for the user. Listing 21.5 shows how to use the <NoScript> tag to convey information about scripting on your Web site. You'll find this example in the \Chapter 21\NoScript folder of the source code on the Sybex Web site.

LISTING 21.5: Using the *<NoScript>* Tag to Convey Information

```
<!DOCTYPE html PUBLIC "-//W3C//DTD XHTML 1.1//EN"
                "http://www.w3.org/TR/xhtml11/DTD/xhtml11.dtd">
<html xmlns="http://www.w3.org/1999/xhtml" >
<head>
    <title>&lt;NoScript&gt; Test Web Page</title>
    <link href="MyStyle.css" type="text/css" rel="StyleSheet">
    <script type="text/JavaScript">
    <!--
        function btnTest_OnClick()
        {
            txtOutput.value = "Hello World";
        }
    -->
    </script>
</head>
<body>
    <h1>Welcome to the &lt;NoScript&gt; Test Web Page</h1>
    <noscript>
        Your browser doesn't support scripts. The only task the scripts
        on this page perform is to display Hello World in the output
        textbox when the user clicks Click Me or remove the text when
        the user clicks Reset.
    </noscript>
    <p
        <label><span class="underline">O</span>utput Textbox</label>
        <input id="txtOutput"
                tabindex="1"
                title="This is the output text box."
                accesskey="O"
                type="text"
                value="Page Output" /><br />
        <input onkeypress="btnTest_OnClick()"
                id="btnTest"
                title="See a change in the text box."
                accesskey="C"
                onclick="btnTest_OnClick()"
                tabindex="2"
```

```
                    type="button"
                    value="Click Me" />

        ... Reset Button ...

    </p>
</body>
</html>
```

The example uses standard HTML in this case. The script appears within the header area. When the user clicks Click Me, the button calls `btnTest_OnClick()`. This script sets the value of `txtOutput` to a new value. Of course, the code only works when the user has scripting enabled. When scripting isn't available, the content of the `<NoScript>` tag appears, as shown in Figure 21.6. Browsers that do have scripting enabled won't display this information.

WARNING   The `<NoScript>` tag can't fix many problems that many people have seen on Web sites. For example, it can't fix the malfunctioning banner ad that wants to store user information locally so that it can detect a hit rate for that user. In addition, the `<NoScript>` tag won't fix gadgets such as using objects. Using the `<NoScript>` tag won't make animations and special sound effects work because there isn't any text equivalent for these features. In general, if you can represent a non-scripting fix for a client-side scripting problem as a combination of standard HTML tags and text, then the `<NoScript>` tag will probably work.

One innovative use of the `<NoScript>` tag involves adding a special link to the text within the `<NoScript>` tag. Selecting this link will post the page back to the server. The server can then perform any data calculations using a server-side script. This approach allows you to use a single page for everyone. The example shown in Listing 21.6 performs the simple task of adding two numbers together, but does so in such a way that the users with scripting support use client-side scripting and those that don't use server-side scripting. You'll find this example in the `\Chapter 21\NoScript` folder of the source code on the Sybex Web site.

FIGURE 21.6
The *<NoScript>* information only appears when the browser lacks scripting.

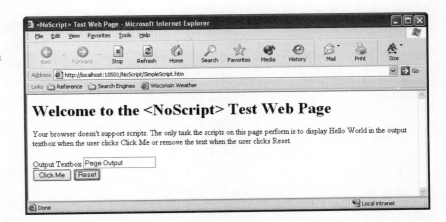

LISTING 21.6:   Accessible Friendly Scripting Code

```
<%@ Page Language="VB" %>

<!DOCTYPE html PUBLIC "-//W3C//DTD XHTML 1.1//EN" "http://www.w3.org/TR/xhtml11/DTD/
xhtml11.dtd">

<html xmlns="http://www.w3.org/1999/xhtml" >
<head id="Head1" runat="server">
    <title>Accessible Friendly Script Demonstration</title>
   <script language=javascript>
<!--
    function DoAdd()
    {
       var Value1 = parseInt(TheForm.InValue1.value);
       var Value2 = parseInt(TheForm.InValue2.value);
       TheForm.Output.value = Value1 + Value2;
    }
-->
</script>
<script runat="server">
    Sub GetValue(ByVal Name As String)
        If (Request.QueryString(Name) Is Nothing) Then
            Response.Write("0")
        Else
            Response.Write(Request.QueryString(Name))
        End If
    End Sub
    Sub DoAdd()
        Dim Value1 As Int32 ' Holds the first value.
        Dim Value2 As Int32 ' Holds the second value.

        ' Verify there is data to process.
        If ((Request.QueryString("Input1") Is Nothing) Or _
            (Request.QueryString("Input2") Is Nothing)) Then
            Response.Write("0")
        Else
            ' Try to convert the data to numbers.
            Try
                Value1 = Int32.Parse(Request.QueryString("Input1"))
                Value2 = Int32.Parse(Request.QueryString("Input2"))
            Catch FE As FormatException
                ' Output 0 when the user doesn't supply valid
                ' information.
                Response.Write("0")
                Return
            End Try
```

```
                       ' Output the calculation result.
                       Response.Write(Convert.ToString(Value1 + Value2))
                End If
            End Sub
        </script>
    </head>
    <body>
        <form id="TheForm" runat="server" method=get>
            <h1 align="center">Math Demonstration</h1>
            <div>
                <input type=text
                       id="InValue1"
                       accesskey=1
                       title="This is the first input value."
                       tabindex=1
                       name=Input1
                       value=<%GetValue("Input1")%> />
                <label> Input Value 1</label>
            </div>

            ... Another Input and Output Textbox ...
            <div>
                <button onclick=DoAdd()
                        title="Click this button to add the numbers."
                        tabindex=4
                        id=AddNumbers
                        accesskey=A>
                    Add
                </button>
            </div>
            <div>
                <noscript>
                    <div>
                        Your browser doesn't support scripts.
                        Use this button instead.
                    </div>
                    <button type=submit
                            title="Click this button to add the numbers."
                            id=NoScriptAdd
                            accesskey=N
                            tabindex=5>
                        No Script Add
                    </button>
                </noscript>
            </div>
        </form>
    </body>
</html>
```

This example doesn't use code behind—it includes the ASP.NET code directly in the header of the Web page to make the explanation clearer. You can perform the same task using code behind. Notice that the example has two script sections. The first script section runs on the client, so it doesn't include the `runat` attribute. The second script section runs on the server. You'll notice that both sections contain a `DoAdd()` function and that this function adds two numbers together. The two functions don't conflict because one function runs only on the client and the other runs only on the server.

The `GetValue()` function is important when working with server-side scripting because the two inputs will lose their values otherwise. This function simply accepts the value from the `QueryString` and outputs it again using `Response.Write()`. If there isn't a value to output, then the function outputs a 0.

These functions work in various ways, depending on whether the client has scripting enabled. The server-side scripting begins with the `<input>` tags used for the two input and one output text boxes. Notice the `value` attribute is set equal to `<%GetValue("Input1")%>` for the two input text boxes. The output text box `value` attribute equals `<%DoAdd()%>`. In all three cases, the server-side script executes when the user posts data to the server.

The example includes two `<button>` tags. The first `<button>` tag always appears on screen. Users with scripting enabled will only see this first button. Clicking the button calls the client-side `DoAdd()` function. The output of this function overrides any value provided by the server-side `DoAdd()` function when the page loaded, but only when scripting is active. Users who don't have scripting enabled see both buttons, as shown in Figure 21.7. Clicking the first button won't do anything, but clicking the second button posts the page back to the server. The server processes the two inputs, refreshes their content, and provides an output to the output text box.

Testing Your Page for Accessibility Errors

At some point, you need to test your Web page for conformance to both the HTML standards and accessibility requirements. Visual Studio provides accessibility testing as part of the IDE. Generally, you should consider this testing a preliminary check because the built-in tester doesn't fully verify your code against all of the required accessibility standards. However, the built-in tester is a fast and efficient way to get your Web site marginally accessible while you write the application code, which is the best time to make required changes.

FIGURE 21.7
This figure shows what the page will look like if the client doesn't provide scripting support.

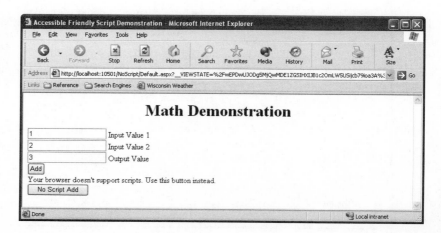

If you want full accessibility verification, you'll need a third party solution. Most of the available HTML check utilities that you purchase test an entire Web site. You'll receive a report on the compliance level of all your pages at one time. It's sort of the same as using a compiler to check for errors in your code. Shareware and freeware checkers will often let you check one page at a time. Don't discount these options because they work very well for smaller Web sites and can help you spot-check even a large corporate Web site. The following list describes some of the accessibility and HTML testers that you should consider for testing your Web pages.

Bobby This utility provides a quick check that you can use for any existing Web site. Simply feed the online version of Bobby an URL and you'll receive a report about it. Using the online version is free. The vendor also provides a full version of Bobby that will check an entire Web site without entering the individual pages for a price. Although Bobby does a great job of accessibility checking, the vendor doesn't guarantee that the product will locate every problem. You can learn more about this product at `http://bobby.watchfire.com/bobby/html/en/index.jsp`. See the "Using Bobby to Test Accessibility" section for a demonstration of this product.

Lynx This is a text-only browser that comes in versions for the Macintosh and Windows. It helps you check your Web site by displaying it in text only. This check helps you see your Web site as a screen reader will see it—making it possible to detect and correct problems with greater ease. Learn more about this product at `http://lynx.browser.org/`. You can also use the online version found at `http://www.delorie.com/web/lynxview.html`.

NIST Webmetrics Tool Suite This group of tools from the National Institute of Standards and Technology (NIST) helps you test the usability and accessibility of a Web site. For example, Web Static Analyzer Tool (WebSAT) ensures your Web page meets specific usability goals. The Web Variable Instrumenter Program (WebVIP) helps track user interaction so you know how well users are finding Web site features. There are more tools on this Web site and NIST updates them regularly. You can learn more at `http://zing.ncsl.nist.gov/webmet/`.

Opera Like Lynx, this browser enables you to see your Web site as a screen reader will see it. However, unlike Lynx, this product also helps you turn certain features on and off as needed for comparison. For example, you can toggle images off so you can see how Alt attribute will look. Opera is available for a number of platforms including Windows, Macintosh, and Linux. You can learn more about it at `http://www.opera.com/`.

W3C HTML Validation Service This Web site checks the HTML on your Web page for conformance to World Wide Web Consortium (W3C) recommendations and standards. An error on this Web site means that the coding for your Web page is incorrect, even if most browsers will read it, so this tester goes beyond usability and accessibility requirements. Don't get the idea that passing the test on this Web site automatically makes your Web site accessible. Passing the test on this Web site means that your code is correct. However, making sure you code is correct is a good first step to ensuring you can add accessibility features. Learn more about this utility at `http://validator.w3.org/`.

Web Design Group HTML Validator This Web site checks the HTML on your Web page or, as an alternative, on your computer. It also provides an option to validate a single page or the entire site. I also found that this site is a little less picky than the W3C HTML Validation Service about which pages it will check. This Web site seems to output about the same information as the W3C Web site, but it may not provide complete validation of your Web site. You can learn more about this tool at `http://www.htmlhelp.com/tools/validator/`.

The following sections walk you through the process of using the built-in accessibility checker and two of the freeware utilities to verify your Web site's code and accessibility. The reason I chose these particular utilities is that they're thorough, free for the asking, and not dependent on a particular platform.

Using the Visual Studio Built-in Checks

You can set up Visual Studio .NET so that it performs an accessibility check every time you compile your application. In fact, the IDE performs three levels of checking that include Web Content Accessibility Guidelines (WCAG) Priority 1 (`http://www.w3.org/TR/WAI-WEBCONTENT/`), WCAG Priority 2, and Section 508 Accessibility requirement checks (`http://www.section508.gov/`). Theoretically, making these checks helps you create an accessible Web site. However, testing shows that the accessibility checks in the IDE are incomplete and don't catch every error in areas that it does support. However, you should still use the IDE as a first level check. Anything you can do to make your Web pages more accessible today is a change you won't have to make tomorrow.

To verify you have accessibility checking turned on, right-click the project entry in Solution Explorer and select Properties from the context menu. Highlight the Accessibility folder and you'll see the list of accessibility checks for this project, as shown in Figure 21.8. Notice that you can turn off all of the accessibility checks, but it's a better idea to turn everything on, as shown in the figure.

Setting the accessibility options isn't enough to begin the checks. Highlight the Build folder in the Property Pages dialog box and you'll see two accessibility options, as shown in Figure 21.9. Check both options, as shown in the figure, to ensure Visual Studio verifies the accessibility features of your Web site during a build or analysis.

After you make this settings change, close the Property Pages dialog box by clicking OK. Select the Build ➤ Rebuild Solution command. Visual Studio will check your Web site for potential problems. After it checks the Web pages, you'll see a list of major accessibility problems (errors) and minor issues (warnings) in the Error List window, as shown in Figure 21.10. This list will also appear after each build.

FIGURE 21.8
Request that the IDE help you locate accessibility problems by checking the options in this dialog box.

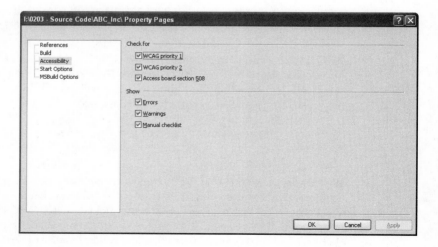

FIGURE 21.9
Add build checks for accessibility to both Web pages and the Web site as a whole.

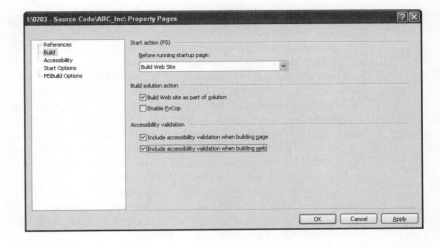

FIGURE 21.10
Look for accessibility issues to appear as errors and warnings after a build.

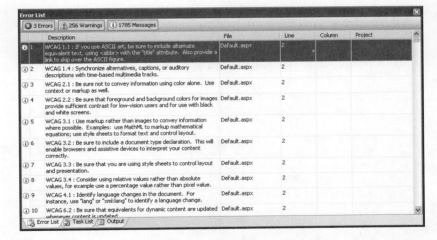

The list is going to be incomplete—no matter how often you analyze your Web site. However, you can use the generated list as a guide to fixing common errors in other parts of your Web site. For example, if you notice that the output contains a lot of errors relating to missing Alt attribute entries for graphics, you will probably want to add a check for this problem to all Web pages to ensure all of the graphics include an Alt attribute entry. Likewise, a missing ToolTip attribute in one location tells you that you need to check other areas as well. In short, the IDE can provide you with considerable help in making your Web site accessible when you use it correctly.

Figure 21.8 shows the settings for the ABC Incorporated project. Run the Web site analysis and you'll see a number of accessibility problems for this project that I purposely left in place. Fix the few errors that you see using the techniques listed throughout the chapter and run the analysis again. You should find that the Web site is completely clean by the end of the second check—at least as far as Visual Studio is concerned.

W3C HTML Validation

Corporate Web sites can benefit greatly from strict W3C compliance. A Web site that provides full compliance is less likely to experience compatibility problems. You'll perform two levels of checks on a Web page syntax and accessibility feature use.

The first level of Web site checks will ensure your code is correct. Syntactically correct code doesn't necessarily work, but it does follow all of the rules provided by the World Wide Web Consortium (W3C). The reason I emphasize syntactically correct code is that some developers don't check their code for accuracy, while others don't check their code for bugs. You must make sure that your code works and that it's syntactically correct before you perform an accessibility check. To make a syntax check, go to the W3C HTML Validation Service at `http://validator.w3.org/`. As you can see from Figure 21.11, you begin by entering the Web site URL or uploading a local file, selecting any display options, and then clicking Validate this Page.

The only problem with all of this testing technology for the ABC Incorporated Web site is that you're using the built-in Web server, so the page isn't accessible from the Internet. Lack of Internet accessibility means you can't use the URL checking method. Unfortunately, the source code files on your system aren't much use either. Uploading an ASPX file isn't going to work, especially considering the content pages lack any of the standard tags that the validator is expecting. The way around this problem is to use the File ➤ Save As command to save the Web page you want to test to the hard drive. You can now upload the page that the user will see to the W3C Web site for testing.

Sometimes the Web page won't validate correctly because it lacks a `<!DOCTYPE>` tag or character set entry. You can override these problems by selecting a value from the Character Encoding or Document Type fields. However, these selections will skew the results you obtain and you should add the proper tags to your Web page as soon as possible. (When you create a Web page using the IDE, the IDE automatically adds the required tags for you.) After you override the selections, try to validate the page again. If it still won't validate, your Web page has serious problems that you should fix immediately.

FIGURE 21.11

Use the W3C HTML Validation Service to ensure the code on your Web page is correct.

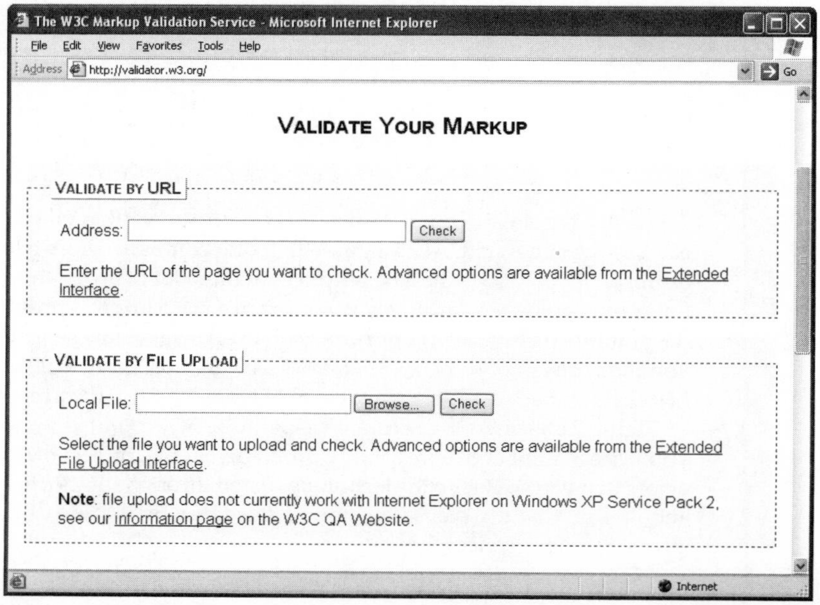

Validating a page doesn't mean it's error free—it simply means that you've fixed enough problems for the tool to tell you about the remaining errors. Figure 21.12 shows typical output from the W3C HTML Validation Service. This figure concentrates on the errors—you can also view an outline of your Web page, numbered source listing, and a parse tree of the data.

Notice that the output shown in Figure 21.12 shows the precise location of the error as the parser sees it. The output page also includes a brief message on the error and optionally provides some information on how to fix it. Generally, you'll find that this setup works well for simple errors, but doesn't provide enough information to fix complex errors.

Using Bobby to Test Accessibility

One of the oldest and most relied on methods for checking Web sites for accessibility is Bobby. The fact that Bobby is free only makes it more popular. Bobby will check a single page of a Web site for free and provide a seal of approval should the Web site pass. The Bobby check relies mainly on the honor system, so you should make sure your Web site actually passes the tests before you request use of the seal.

You can check out this valuable resource (shown in Figure 21.10) at `http://webxact.watchfire`
`.com/`. As you can see from Figure 21.13, the Web site performs both Web Content Accessibility Guideline 1.0 and Section 508 (U.S. government approved) checks on a Web site of your choosing. You'll notice almost immediately that the Web Content Accessibility Guideline check is more intense than the Section 508 check, but performing both checks can point out errors on your Web site.

All you need to do is enter a Web site URL, select the test you want to run, and then click Submit. Bobby retrieves the Web site, checks it for errors, and prints a report for you. I thought that my pure text Web site would pass on the first try, but, as shown in Figure 21.14, my Web site at `http://www`
`.mwt.net/~jmueller/` still had five glitches to fix. I've since corrected the problems with my Web site and posted an updated version.

FIGURE 21.12
The W3C HTML Validation Service provides complete information on the errors on your Web page.

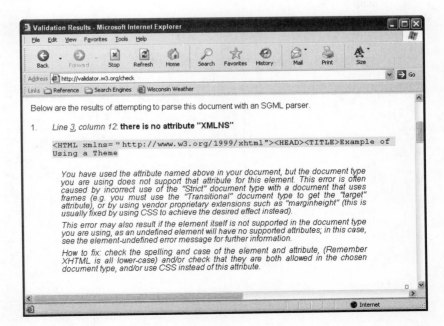

FIGURE 21.13
Bobby ensures that
your Web site meets
the required accessi-
bility requirements.

FIGURE 21.13
Bobby ensures that
your Web site meets
the required accessi-
bility requirements.

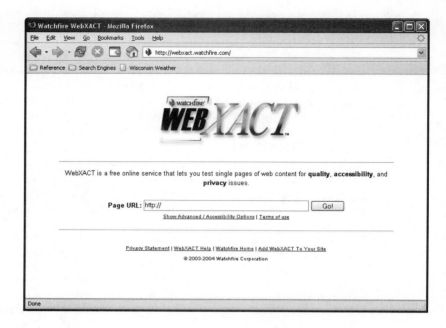

FIGURE 21.14
Even pure text Web sites
can experience accessi-
bility problems.

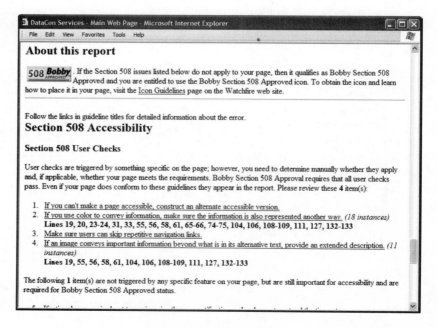

Notice that all of these errors are "user checks." A user check error is one that you have to check manually and determine whether your site is in compliance. In many cases, Bobby will raise a question that you can answer by saying that your site is in compliance. You can determine the error locations by looking for question marks on the Web page displayed above the report. Every question mark represents an issue that you need to consider, and some locations will contain more than one question mark because they break more than one rule.

Every user check in the report also contains a link you can use to obtain additional information. Generally, the additional information tells you what you need to do in order to correct the error and the rationale behind the rule. In some cases, the help also shows short code snippets with generic implementation information. The point is that you can find out the specifics of the problem using your own Web page as a source of the information.

Defining Your Development Goals

This chapter has presented an overview of accessibility issues you need to consider for your Web site. Accessibility is extremely important because many people need the functionality to interact with your Web site. The few additional minutes you spend defining properties on a Web page can mean the difference between someone who uses the content you provide and someone who clicks the next link. In the end, that's what accessibility is all about—making sure that everyone can interact with your Web site. A lack of interaction means a lack of interest in what you have to provide.

Now it's time for you to get involved. If you haven't already built your Web site, make sure you include accessibility as one of the design items. Including accessibility as part of your design saves time later and makes the addition almost invisible. Anyone who's already built a Web site should consider testing it thoroughly for accessibility needs. You might be losing visitors at this very moment because they can't use the content you have provided. Businesses should be especially aware of accessibility issues because a lack of accessibility can cost sales.

Chapter 22 considers a new area of development for many programmers—using multiple languages on multiple platforms. Company mergers, IT shifts, and differences in philosophy between managers all conspire to make the development environment more complex. Chapter 22 helps by exploring a specific scenario—one in which the developers from two different platforms must work together to create a single cohesive product. Although the target Visual Studio .NET add-on explored in this chapter doesn't answer every possible question, it does make the joint effort a lot easier. In this case, the example shows how to combine Java and Visual Studio .NET to produce a single application.

Part 7

Application Development Within the Corporate Environment

In this part:

Chapter 22

Developing Interoperable Applications

Most developers working for large corporations will face the sometimes unpleasant and challenging experience of having to integrate code from several applications as the result of an acquisition, merger, or simply an off-the-shelf software purchase. You might have to perform these tasks to integrate new applications with older software that your company owns. Sometimes you won't even be aware of the need to perform the task until you finish your latest coding project. Unfortunately, for most developers, the combinations of platforms and application languages can prove daunting because most companies don't want to write these other applications from scratch. This chapter discusses a particular scenario—one in which .NET and Java developers must work together on a single application—and uses it as a basis for describing interoperability scenarios in general.

The first task in overcoming the problems of developing interoperable applications is defining the problem domain—considering the issues that you must overcome to achieve a particular goal. This chapter only provides a brief overview of the topic of how to break an interoperability solution into smaller pieces and create a design based on the resulting problem definition.

What you'll find in this chapter is a look at three techniques you can use to implement an interoperable solution. The most common technique in use today is Web services. Using a Web service makes it unnecessary for the various pieces of the application to know much about each other—only the data exchange rules matter. Another solution is to use bridging products. A bridging product is a special piece of software that sits between the various applications components and provides data translation functionality. Finally, you can use cross-compilation technology. A special add-on translates the .NET code that you write into another language, such as Java. Each of these solutions has advantages and disadvantages.

Understanding the .NET/Java Development Scenario

Most .NET developers have never worked with Java and probably have no desire to work with Java in the future. Creating an interoperable application is all about letting everyone work with the tools that they know and still create a whole application where the components work together as anticipated. Consequently, this chapter isn't about making .NET developers into Java aficionados. In general, you won't have to know much more about Java than you know right now—the only difference is that you'll understand better how to interact with Java applications. In short, this chapter is about building bridges between application components.

The following sections provide a very brief overview of some of the design decisions you need to consider as you put your interoperable application together. For example, you have to decide which application components will rely on a particular technology. In many cases, someone else has already made this decision in some areas, but any new code you create requires careful consideration. You also have to consider which technologies work best for implementing a particular solution.

An Overview of the Corporate Mixed Language Environment

Most companies today have applications created in multiple languages. In many cases, these applications don't talk to each other because the original developers never considered the need to communicate outside the application. When ABC Incorporated acquired XYZ Company, it also inherited the Java application backend used to access the XYZ Company data. They also gained access to the XYZ Company developers and some of the IT staff. In short, ABC Incorporated now has two of every important application running. Unfortunately, running two of every application isn't very efficient and translating all of the XYZ Company data to run on your system isn't an option, so you have to find a way to make the two applications transparently run as one. This scenario is the one that many corporate developers face today.

TIP One of the basic problems that most companies have to overcome is learning the capabilities of the developers it has hired. Many managers literally don't know that they have someone on staff that has both .NET and Java experience. Make sure you perform a skills survey before you begin designing an interoperability solution so that you make maximum use of the skills that each developer on your team can offer.

Making the problem worse is the issue of ideology. The Java and .NET developers may not get along very well and may feel threatened by the combined application environment. The goal, therefore, is to let the two groups perform the tasks they do best in a less threatening environment. You achieve this goal by creating bridges between the various applications. The company policy might be to use .NET for all application front ends, but you still have to access the information that a Java backend can provide.

The problem becomes more pronounced as more languages and platforms come into play. An environment where you have a mix of .NET, Java, and PHP is certainly more complicated than one with just two languages. The issue comes down to one of simplification without loss of functionality. The ABC Incorporated users need access to the combined data that an acquisition provides. Whether you make that data available using a .NET front end or a Web-based application doesn't matter. What does matter is that all of the data appears as if it comes from one source, which means that you'll have to combine some functionality, use glue code to access multiple sources, and rely on new strategies when a data source doesn't provide a simple means of external communication.

Developing Reliable Mixed Language Solutions

You might be surprised to learn that there are many solutions available for communicating with other platforms. Some of these solutions are so unique that most developers will never encounter them. Other solutions aren't well supported by the .NET platform, so even though other developers use them regularly, you probably won't ever see them. However, you'll encounter three interoperable application strategies often enough that you'll want to think about them as your first line solutions to this problem. Table 22.1 shows the advantages and disadvantages of each solution.

TABLE 22.1:   Common Interoperable Application Solutions

STRATEGY	ADVANTAGES	DISADVANTAGES
Web Services	Web services enjoy a level of popularity that few other technologies enjoy. They are firewall friendly, easily extensible, and standards based. For example, standards such as Web Services Interoperability (WS-I) (http://www.ws-i.org/) make creating Web services relatively easy. A Web service is also language and platform independent—the client and server don't need to know anything about each other to exchange data.	Web services rely on XML, which necessarily means that the data is bulky and time consuming to transmit. In addition, the underlying transport (such as HTTP) often adds processing overhead. Because Web services generally use plain text data transfer, they can cause security breaches or other security problems. Representing some types of complex data can become problematic in Web services.
Bridging	Bridging solutions offer tightly coupled communication between application components that relies on efficient binary communication. A bridging solution is usually much faster and more secure than a corresponding Web service, but not quite as fast as cross-compilation strategies. Bridging solutions also preserve the remoting functionality that .NET provides and offers the best level of transparency for the developer. In addition, bridging solutions generally offer pass by reference so the developer works with an actual object, rather than an object copy. Most bridging solutions offer two-way connectivity (between both supported languages).	Bridging solutions can add protocol overhead that's especially pronounced when marshaling complex objects. It's also possible that the bridging engine will introduce platform scalability limitations not present in the application components, which means that the bridging engine can become an application choke point. For database requirements, bridging solutions generally don't support distributed transactions, which means data integrity could be at risk. From a security perspective, bridging solutions may not support distributed security, which means that each application component must handle security separately and that there's a risk of introducing security holes. Bridging solutions aren't standards based, so the implementation varies greatly between vendors.
Cross-Compilation	Cross-compilation solutions offer the best performance available because the application is actually running as a single entity, even though the developers see he separate elements. In addition, cross-compilation offers a highly secure environment. Developers work with full objects, no matter what the source of those objects might be. A remote object generally looks like a local resource to the developer.	Cross-compilation solutions generally work best in private application scenarios due to the tight coupling and direct resource access they require. A cross-compiled solution can become quite complex and requires more resources than other solutions. Consequently, the cost of a cross-compiled solution can become a problem for some companies. Most cross-compilation solutions are tightly coupled to the development environment and aren't standards based. Cross-compiled applications generally support one-way transformation, such as conversion of a .NET application to Java.

Although Table 22.1 shows three good solutions, you'll run into other solutions that might work in specific instances. For example, MONO (`http://www.mono-project.com/Main_Page`) is a project originally started by Novell for running .NET code on other platforms. The only problem with this solution is that you require a special development environment to use it. In addition, MONO doesn't provide good support for enterprise development. For example, it doesn't include the concept of team development. Consequently, this solution only works well for applications written by a single developer who is willing to learn how to use the special tools required. Some third party developers have created tools and even Visual Studio add-in products based on MONO, but this chapter doesn't consider those products.

Another possible solution is the Common Object Request Broker Architecture (CORBA) Remote Method Invocation (RMI) Internet Inter-ORB Protocol (IIOP). In this case, the .NET developer has to become aware of what is going on behind the scenes to use the technology. However, the resulting connection is completely transparent to any backend application. One of the better solutions in this category is Janeva (`http://www.borland.de/janeva/`), which actually integrates into the Visual Studio .NET IDE. The big thing to remember about a solution such as this one is that it can introduce scalability and security problems. Because you're relying on a foreign protocol, you can't ensure that the security features that .NET understands will translate to the other environment—generally, you have to have a solution that marshals these requirements for you or build this functionality in as part of your custom solution.

Using the Web Services Solution

One of the best solutions for many cross-language and cross-platform applications is the use of the Simple Object Access Protocol (SOAP) coupled with Web Services Description Language (WSDL). This combination makes the underlying technology almost invisible to the application developer. Using these two technologies, it doesn't matter whether you need to access IBM WebSphere, Tomcat, or Internet Information Server (IIS). In fact, the backend server becomes almost inconsequential except for the services it provides. All the Visual Studio developer needs is an URL for the Web site providing the service. You can see this strategy in action by using any of the increasing number of public Web services.

Web services provide a high level of flexibility in communicating between platforms. In addition, the client and server don't need to know much about each other because they rely on XML as a medium of exchange. The server offers the data it provides through a system of SOAP method calls. As long as the client offers the request in the desired format, the server can respond with the required information. The client obtains access to the method request format and the data schema through any of several means, but WSDL is the most widely used.

For the .NET developer, Web services have a few advantages that none of the other interoperability solutions can provide. The advantages make using Web services appealing for most developers. The biggest advantage is that Web services are free in the Visual Studio .NET environment. The IDE provides everything you need to implement a Web service solution and consume Web services as a client. Consequently, this solution always wins from a price perspective. However, it's important to consider the less obvious advantages too. For example, Web service interoperability provides full IntelliSense support, so you don't need to guess about remote methods or do anything strange to work with them.

TIP   Working with public Web services is a very good way to gain experience for creating your own Web service. The "Using Google to Create a Site Search" section of Chapter 8 provides an overview of how to use Google Web Services. You can learn about the three largest public Web services through my books, *Mining Amazon Web Services*, *Mining Google Web Services*, and *Mining eBay Web Services*. Each Web service has its own quirks, and learning about the various implementation methods can help you create the kind of Web service you really want.

When you want to use a Web services solution, you need two components. The first is the Web service. You can see an example of building a Web service in the "Developing Web Service Connections" section of Chapter 13. No matter what Web service you use, you'll also need a client component to access it. The language you use for the Web service need not match the language the client application uses—in fact, it often doesn't. When working with a Web service, you can build equally viable clients using Visual Studio (any language), Java, PHP, or even JavaScript. In fact, given the right Web service setup, you might not even have to write any code—you might simply provide the correct URL with included parameters and an online XML file. The Amazon Web Service provides this particular feature and the access technique is well worth studying.

Microsoft's documentation has a definite bias toward automatic discovery of services using Universal Description, Discovery, and Integration (UDDI). This service normally relies on the developer providing a discovery (DISCO) file. While the Visual Studio IDE does create the required discovering information for you automatically, it's an exception to the rule. Most Web services that you rely on for interoperability purposes will require a precise reference URL. To add a manual reference, right-click the project entry in Solution Explorer and choose Add Web Reference from the context menu. You'll see the Add Web Reference dialog box shown in Figure 22.1. Notice that this dialog box already contains an URL in the URL field. You'll get the URL you need for an interoperable Web service solution from the Web service developer.

FIGURE 22.1
Interoperable Web service solutions generally require that you provide an URL for a reference.

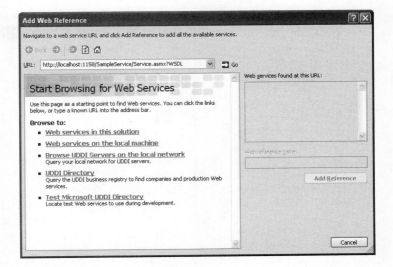

At this point, you click Go to see the methods that the Web service provides. Figure 22.2 shows a simple example that this section relies on for discussion. It's important to remember that there isn't any magic involved—the display you see in Figure 22.2 is the result of the IDE reading and interpreting the WSDL file. Because the WSDL file from any source (no matter which platform or language the developer uses for the Web service) are the same, you'll always see this display of information for any Web service you access. Even when you access a Web service using UDDI, this display is still the result of a WSDL file—all that UDDI does is make it easier to find the Web service in the first place.

When you click Add Reference, the Visual Studio IDE adds several files to your application. You'll see them in a new `\App_WebReferences` folder in your application's root folder. The files appear in a hierarchy based on the location of the WSDL file. For example, when you access Amazon Web Services, you'll see the new files in the `\App_WebReferences\com\amazon\soap` folder. Any local Web services appear in the `\App_WebReferences\localhost` folder. The first file has a `DISCOMAP` extension and contains the location of the Web service online, along with the name of the file that contains the information needed to access the Web service. The second file has a `WSDL` extension. This file contains a complete description of Web service access, including all of the method names, the names of any arguments, and their data types. Generally, you don't need to worry about the contents of WSDL file when working with Visual Studio .NET because the IDE interprets it for you.

The WSDL file is especially important because it contains the information that the IDE uses to help you use the Web service. When you see IntelliSense entries for a Web service method, you aren't seeing anything that comes from actual code. What you're seeing is the interpretation of the WSDL file. The only problem with this approach for .NET developers is that the WSDL file begins to age the moment you create the Web reference. One of the interoperability problems that .NET developers encounter is old Web service information. You can combat this problem by right-clicking the `App_WebReferences` entry in Solution Explorer and choosing Update Web References from the context menu. The IDE won't display a success message after it performs the update, but you'll see any errors in the Error List window.

FIGURE 22.2
The WSDL file provides the interoperability information the client application requires.

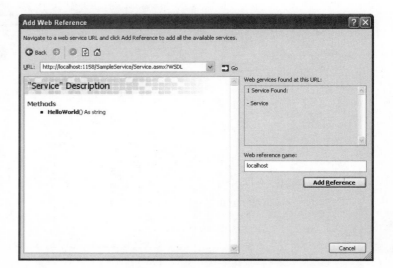

One of the errors that you'll encounter with an interoperable solution is that the Visual Studio IDE doesn't preserve the case of the URL you provide. Consequently, when you attempt to update case-sensitive Web servers, you'll receive a not found error message from the Web server. A not found error message can occur for a number of reasons, such as the Web server being offline, but always verify the case of the Web service URL in the DISCOMAP file when you suspect that the remote server might require case-sensitive input. In some cases, you might have to remove the old Web reference and create a new one to perform an update.

Using the Bridging Solution

Bridging solutions rely on glue code to create a connection between two languages. The bridging solution marshals data between the two languages using low-level code that acts and works much like PInvoke within .NET. Using binary data transfers eliminates many of the problems that you'll encounter using text-based strategies such as Web services. However, anyone who has used bridging technologies before, such as the database connectivity provided with ODBC, knows that you pay a price for the bridging in the form of overhead and complexity. Because bridging solutions add complexity, you'll find that they aren't as popular as cross-compiler or Web service solutions. However, you'll find bridging solutions work very well on company intranets and in situations where you know precisely how the remote code is going to work because you gain some significant benefits in connectivity. The following sections rely on JNBridge (`http://www.jnbridge.com/`) for discussion purposes.

An Overview of JNBridge

JNBridge offers maximum flexibility in that you can create Java to .NET connectivity and .NET to Java connectivity as needed. This particular solution offers the standard binary support as a minimum, but you can also implement the underlying connectivity using SOAP by installing a Java API for XML Processing (JAXP)–compliant XML package (you can get the Sun JAXP package at `http://java.sun.com/xml/jaxp/index.html`). Of course, if you're going to use SOAP, you really don't need a bridging solution in most cases—use a Web service instead because it's much simpler. The only time you need the Web service connectivity is when you're going to use bridging solutions in more than one scenario—such as a local connection and an Internet connection. In fact, JNBridge supports several interoperability scenarios including.

- Runing code in the same process
- Accessing code on the same machine, but in different processes
- Connecting to different machines on your LAN
- Remoting to different machines across the Internet

As previously mentioned, bridging is binary transfer oriented and it works directly with the application binaries. When a .NET developer wants to access Java classes, the JNBridge IDE only requires access to the Java binaries—not the actual source code. Consequently, you can use third party Java solutions in your .NET applications by employing this technique. Interoperability takes on an entirely different meaning when all you need are binaries to make it work. This technique relies on generating proxies (similar to what happens when using COM objects) to create the glue code between the Java and .NET binaries.

Because of the way the bridging technology works, you'll normally have to set up a bridge application on each machine where you want to access code. For example, a .NET developer that wants to access Java code on another machine will need to setup the Java portion of JNBridge on the remote machine. Otherwise, the remote machine won't have a listener for transferring data about the Java classes that the developer wants to access from .NET.

TIP One of the interesting features of JNBridge is that you can use it to create J# compatible binaries. This feature lets you bridge solutions from native Java to J#, which could improve J# functionality considerably.

Installing JNBridge

Installing JNBridge is incredibly easy. You can download a 15-day evaluation copy of the product at http://www.jnbridge.com/downloadtrial.htm. After you fill out the required form, you'll receive a response in your email. Click the link in the email you receive, and you'll download the product. Double-click the MSI file and follow the instructions to complete the installation.

JNBridge works externally to your development product. Consequently, you don't have any IDE add-on problems to consider. This is especially important for .NET developers who often have to work through add-on product problems before they gain any benefit from the add-on product. To understand the benefits and limitations of add-on interoperability solutions better, read the "Using the Cross-Compiler Solution" section of the chapter. Generally, most developers will find the external solution easier to use, but more time consuming and less friendly because it exists outside the IDE.

Creating a Bridged Application

Bridging relies on creating proxies from your existing binaries. To create a proxy, you use the JNBProxy Proxy Generation Tool found in the Start ➤ Programs ➤ JNBridgePro v2.2 menu. The first time you start this tool, you provide basic Java information. Figure 22.3 shows typical options that JNBridge supplies as a default when it can locate the required files. Theoretically, you don't have to have Java installed on your development machine—all you really need is a source for the Java binaries. However, in reality, it's better to have Java installed locally so that you can create any required proxies efficiently.

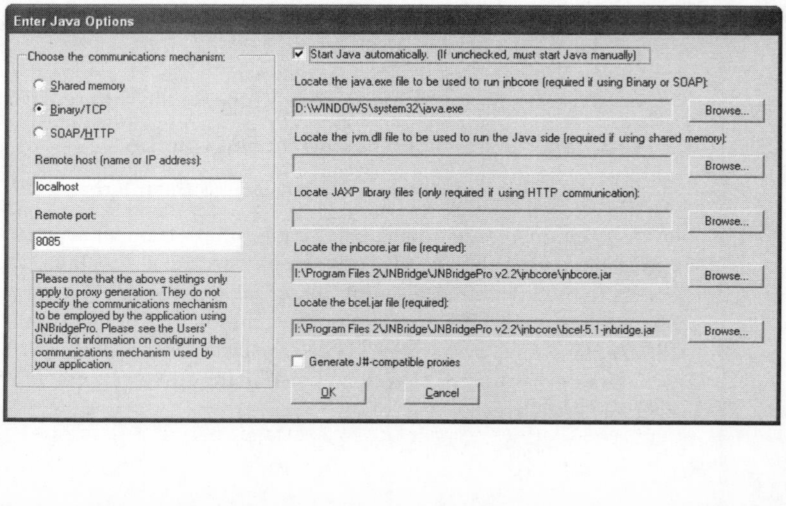

FIGURE 22.3

Set up any required Java options for your system before you create proxies the first time.

When you begin a new project, you'll see the Launch JNBProxy dialog box shown in Figure 22.4. You can create a project for making .NET code accessible to Java developers, Java code accessible to .NET developers, a recent project from your development machine, or a project you want to access on someone else's machine.

Building a proxy is about the same whether you're moving from .NET to Java or from Java to .NET. This section explores a .NET to Java move, so I've used the Java -> .NET option, which seems a little counterintuitive, but the focus is on the language that will access the code in another language. To start working with the new project, you click Edit Assembly List on the toolbar and add at least one assembly to the list. After you add an assembly, you click either Add Classes from Assembly File or Add Classes from Assembly List. In either case, you'll end up with a list of classes like the ones shown in Figure 22.4.

Check any classes you want to make accessible to Java developers and then click Add. The classes will appear in the Exposed Proxies list. Check the precise classes you want to make available. Click Build to create the proxy. JNBridge will output a JAR file that a Java developer can incorporate into their application to access the functionality provided by your .NET application. Make sure you check the results in the Output window carefully. JNBridge doesn't convert some calls very well, and the Output window tells you when this problem occurs. For example, you'll find that some `ArrayList` elements don't transfer well. You should never have a problem with standard code constructs, however, because JNBridge handles them all with aplomb.

What the developer of the other language sees depends on the development product they use. The Java files that JNBridge translated to .NET assemblies look just like standard .NET classes. You have to create a reference to the assembly before you can use it. However, there isn't anything odd to consider in accessing the class—you use the proxy just as you do any .NET class. None of the JAR files tested produced any problems with IntelliSense, but they didn't always produce accurate results in Object Browser. Likewise, the Java developer will see the standard classes supported by the JAR. However, because you're missing the source code in Java format, the help features of many Java products don't work well. Consequently, the Java developer requires good documentation to use the .NET assemblies with ease.

FIGURE 22.4
Select the classes you want to export to Java from the list provided by the assembly.

Using the Cross-Compiler Solution

A cross-compiler provides ultimate connectivity, in most cases, because the add-on actually converts the client code into the target language. Cross-compilers aren't anything new—they've been around as long as computers have been around. However, modern cross-compilers seek to improve connectivity and reduce complexity by hiding details that developers of old had to consider. Most modern cross-compilers make it appear that the developer is still using the original language, while outputting the compiled code as something else. Many cross-compilers also make resources in the other language available in a form that the developer working with the other language can use. The solution, in this case Visual MainWin, converts .NET code to Java output. However, you can literally find a cross-compiler to meet any need.

An Overview of Visual MainWin

Visual MainWin provides the developer with a lot of functionality in a small package. You can create applications using standard .NET code that ends up as Java. It's even possible to debug the result directly from the Visual Studio .NET IDE. One of the most impressive features is the ability to use enterprise beans from servers such as the J2EE Application Server and IBM WebSphere as if they're .NET classes. Overall, what you receive is indeed impressive when you consider that the Java developers on your team will never know that you used .NET to create the output they see—it's all very transparent, which makes mixed team projects that were impossible yesterday, quite possible today.

As with most add-ins that you get for Visual Studio .NET, you need to consider a few caveats when using Visual MainWin. The biggest issue is that you can only create console and Web applications—no desktop application support. Considering that many developers are neck deep in Web application projects now and the number of desktop applications has reportedly decreased, this limitation probably isn't going to affect many developers. The fact that you can work on the Web applications you need to create without worrying about the skill levels of other developers is a big help in enterprises looking to cut development costs.

You use special Visual MainWin templates to create the Java applications. This issue isn't a big deal if you normally use unmodified versions of the Visual Studio .NET templates because Visual MainSoft has done an admirable job of making the templates compatible. Generally, you won't find many differences between the Visual MainWin templates and the standard Visual Studio .NET templates. However, anyone who has customized their templates will run into problems because you have to customize the Visual MainWin templates to get the same results. This isn't an easy task because the MainSoft templates hide a lot of ugly transitional code.

Installing Visual MainWin

Before you can begin using Visual MainWin, you'll have to install it. This isn't a standard Visual Studio add-on, however, and you need to install a few additional items with it. Make certain that you read the `VMW4J2EEGettingStarted.PDF` file before you begin working with the product or you'll find that things won't work as expected. Make sure you have all of the required Visual Studio .NET functionality installed—many developers don't install Visual J#, but you need it with this product.

Installing Visual MainWin comes next. The `VMW4J2EEGettingStarted.PDF` file gets right into the installation process and does a good job of telling you how to start the tasks you need to perform when you have the CD. If you download the product from the Internet site at `http://www.mainsoft.com/vmwj2ee/register.php`, you'll need to start the setup by double-clicking the `vmw4j2ee_150.EXE` file, rather than the `Setup.EXE` file described in the PDF. The setup documents also fail to mention a license file you need to make the product work. Make sure you have the license file before you begin—the vendor sends this file to you in an email after you download the product. The email also includes instructions for installing the license. Other than these two little differences, the instructions in the PDF work precisely as stated.

The Visual MainWin installation program offers to download and install the Microsoft SQL Java DataBase Connectivity-Open Database Connectivity (JDBC-ODBC) bridge driver at some point. This procedure generally works, but you might want to have a copy of the driver handy just in case. Unfortunately, the setup instructions don't mention this requirement until you're halfway through the installation. Downloading the driver from the Microsoft Web site at `http://www.microsoft.com/downloads/details.aspx?FamilyID=9f1874b6-f8e1-4bd6-947c-0fc5bf05bf71&DisplayLang=en` before you begin is a better idea. Visual MainWin is also supposed to work with other versions of the JDBC-ODBC bridge, such as the one provided with the Sun Java SDK, but the product instructions don't include any information on accomplishing this task.

The proof that the installation succeeded is in Visual Studio .NET. As shown in Figure 22.5, you should see two new project folders: Visual MainWin VB for J2EE Projects and Visual MainWin C# for J2EE Projects. Notice that these projects look very familiar—and that's the point. These projects create Java code, but as far as you're concerned, they could just as easily be .NET applications. Of course, some of the project titles are different. You won't find any Windows form applications in the list, but you'll find the J2EE Class Library template shown in the list.

Visual MainWin is a complex product, so make sure you understand how things work before you use it. For example, I ran into a problem with Tomcat the first few times I used the product. I have IIS set to start automatically when my development machine boots. Unfortunately, this act starts a special Tomcat Web site entry. To use Visual MainWin, you must stop this Web site. It's a kind of intermediate location for the project files and it has the same TCP port setting as the Tomcat server. When you start Tomcat, you see quite a few messages scroll by in the console window, and it's very easy to miss the message that says there's a TCP port conflict. However, you won't miss the somewhat unclear message that Tomcat isn't listening when you try to create a project. I usually ended up closing Visual Studio .NET, stopping Tomcat, stopping the IIS Tomcat Web site, restarting Tomcat, and finally reopening Visual Studio .NET to fix the problem.

TIP   Make sure you run the demonstration applications that come with Visual MainWin. These demonstrations go a long way toward helping you understand how the product works. You'll find four demonstrations included with the application and another, larger, demonstration on the MainSoft Web site. The best way to use the four standard demonstrations is to open their entry in the help file and use the help file to guide you to setting things up. You'll find that the instructions work well and you'll be able to run the demonstrations with only a little effort.

FIGURE 22.5

A successful installation means you have access to the Java templates that Visual MainWin provides.

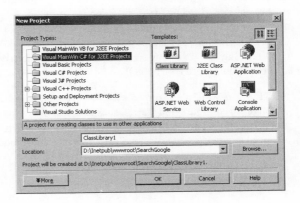

A WORD ABOUT INTEGRATED ADD-ONS

Visual MainWin integrates directly into the Visual Studio .NET IDE. The integration provides a number of benefits. For example, you don't have to leave the IDE every time you want to output code. In addition, you obtain specific benefits when debugging your application—the integration tends to make debugging a lot more seamless than some other solutions. However, you'll also encounter a number of issues when working with an integrated add-on.

In the case of Visual MainWin, one of the first problems you'll notice is that the application server configuration is static. You can view the configuration in the Visual MainWin folder of the Options dialog box (use the Tools ➤ Options command), but you can't change the settings. When you create the settings for a new Java application, all of the settings are set in stone, which can make it difficult to move the application later. Anyone who works with multiple projects on more than one server will experience problems when add-ins work like this. One method around this problem is to create hierarchies of subfolders to hold the data, but this isn't the best way to do things because you still have everything running on one drive. Admittedly, given the way that Visual MainWin currently configures IIS to act as an intermediary, it would be very hard to make this setting easy to change. Interestingly, you can change the username, password, and debug port values.

Add-ins can also cause subtle problems with the way the IDE works. For example, when working with Visual MainWin, you'll likely notice that some control features are missing. When creating accessible Web pages—those that work well with accessibility aids such as screen readers—you need to define the `AssociatedControlID` property for any labels you add to the form manually. It appears that Visual MainWin doesn't support this feature, even though it's available in the Properties window. When you attempt to compile the application, the compiler states that the property is invalid.

Adding IBM WebSphere Support to Visual Studio

If you plan to use Enterprise Java Beans (EJB) in your applications, you must have an application server such as IBM WebSphere. In many cases, you'll run both the default Tomcat server and WebSphere on the same machine to achieve your goals. Of course, adding WebSphere to your server does increase the complexity another level, so there's always a chance that you'll run into problems.

When working with something other than the default Tomcat application server, you must register the server with Visual MainWin. Otherwise, it won't recognize the server—even if you do get the port number right. The error message is vague—it tells you that you have to register the server, but not what registration means or how to do it. To perform this task, you need to choose the Tools ➤ Options command to display the Options dialog box. You'll find the new Visual MainWin folder shown in Figure 22.6. This figure shows Visual MainWin configured with both Tomcat (port 8080) and the WebSphere (port 9080).

NOTE The WebSphere projects worked every bit as well as those on Tomcat, but seemed to take a lot longer to configure and start. Debugging was also a lot slower. For this reason, you might want to begin a project on Tomcat and then move it to WebSphere later. The code itself ran about the same speed and that's what counts most when you think about it.

The big event for WebSphere is working with EJB. To create an EJB reference, you need to locate the appropriate JAR file. The example in this section relies on the `BasicCalculatorEJB.JAR` file located in the `\Program Files\WebSphere\AppServer\samples\lib\TechnologySamples` folder. Right-click the References folder and choose Add EJB Reference from the context menu. You'll need to add the JAR name to the Java Archive field and then click Fetch From Server. Figure 22.7 shows a completed addition. Click OK and you'll see the reference added to the project. The amazing thing is that you're using EJB inside Visual Studio .NET and it looks just like a standard .NET class.

Creating the Cross-Compiled Application

If you haven't noticed yet, cross-compiled applications require that you know something about the other system. For example, when working with Java, you need to have some idea of what an EJB is and might even have to set up your own server. Depending on your company, these differences could spell trouble. However, once you get past these obstacles, you open the New Project window as you have always done and select a project. Generally speaking, the setup is hard, but afterward, nothing has really changed for you as a developer.

FIGURE 22.6
Make sure you register any application server you want to use.

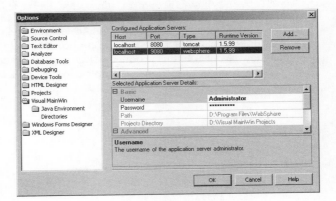

FIGURE 22.7
Visual MainWin lets you use EJB directly in your Visual Studio .NET application.

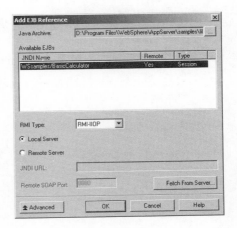

One of the first differences that you'll notice when creating a project isn't the code you write (the code is amazingly close to what you'd write for any ASP.NET application)—it's the way you add references. A .NET application lets you choose from a variety of local references including COM and .NET components, as well as the global references found in the GAC using the Project ➢ Add Reference command.

When working with Visual MainWin, you'll choose from local references—those local to the project, Web references (using Web services is precisely the same as working with .NET applications), Java references, and EJB references. To add a new assembly to your application, such as System. Drawing, you actually choose the Add Java Reference command. Note that this same dialog box gives you access to Java-specific features that you might need to include within the project; however, you don't have access to COM objects. This feature makes sense because you're creating a Java application. Developers will need to adjust to this difference. Unfortunately, you can't use the EJB reference option when working with the supplied Tomcat server—you need a third party product such as IBM WebSphere. This isn't a limitation with Visual MainWin—it's simply a function of the application server.

Now that you have a fun new tool to try out, it's time to create a project. A cross-compiler is complex, so you'll want to try a simple project first. When using a project such as Visual MainWin, it's best to try a console application first because you can compile and run it directly from the command line. This simple test tells you that everything installed correct in Visual Studio and that the technology actually does work. In fact, the console application really is a good place to start because it lets you see just how seamlessly this product works without spending a lot of time trying to figure out the Web application support. Here's a simple console application to try.

```
using System;

namespace ConsoleApplication1
{
   /// <summary>
   /// Summary description for Class1.
   /// </summary>
   class Class1
   {
      /// <summary>
      /// The main entry point for the application.
      /// </summary>
      static void Main(string[] args)
      {
         Console.WriteLine("Press Enter To Close...");
         Console.ReadLine();
      }
   }
}
```

You'll see three files after you compile the application. The first file is a standard managed executable. The second is a standard JAR file that contains all of the Java code. The third is an XML file that contains instructions for running the Java version of the application. Running the EXE file is like running any .NET application that you created in the past. To run the Java application, you need to have Java support installed on the system. The default Visual MainWin installation comes with support in the `\Program Files\Mainsoft\Visual MainWin for J2EE\j2sdk1.4\` folder. To run an application, create a path to the `\Program Files\Mainsoft\Visual MainWin for J2EE\j2sdk1.4\bin\` folder and type **`java -classpath ConsoleApplication1.jar;\PROGRA~1\Mainsoft\VISUAL~1\ jgac\VMW4J2~1\mscorlib.jar ConsoleApplication1.Class1`** at the command prompt. Press Enter and you'll see the expected output—text telling you to press Enter to close and the application waiting until you press Enter.

The command line isn't too hard to figure out. The `Java.EXE` file lets you execute command line Java applications. The `-classpath` switch tells where to find the classes used for this example. The first JAR (a compressed file similar to a ZIP) file contains the code for the sample application. The second JAR contains the Java equivalent of the `MSCorLib.DLL` file. You must include a JAR for every reference you add to your code. The final entry tells `Java.EXE` what to execute. You include both the namespace and the class name. You might think there's an easier way to test a console application, but the current product doesn't provide one when you want to run the application at the command prompt. The `RunTarget.BAT` file located in the `\Program Files\Mainsoft\Visual MainWin for J2EE\bin` folder provides functionality for Web applications—not for console applications.

Defining Your Development Goals

Most developers would prefer to avoid interoperable applications because they present challenges that require unique solutions. A developer can't simply put the pieces together and hope they work—an interoperable solution requires a special level of engineering to ensure the solution works as intended. This chapter provides an overview of the engineering principles you need to consider, but focuses on the implementation techniques you can use with Visual Studio. Fortunately, you have three basic options to choose from, rather than rely on the one-size-fits-all approach that's all too common in software development.

Now that you have some idea of what's involved in creating your next interoperable solution, you have a lot of work to do. Working with interoperable application isn't simply a matter of creating glue code or creating the right package. You must engineer the solution first, and then work on the implementation of those goals. The three implementation techniques described in this chapter help you understand a little better of just how Visual Studio can help you in this particular task.

Chapter 23 moves on to another large development issue—team development. Visual Studio 2005 provides a number of tools that make your next team development project easier. You'll find that the tools presented in Chapter 23 help you create better applications with fewer integration issues. Even a single development can benefit from using these tools. The idea is to take the chaos factor out of development and create an environment where everyone knows project status.

Chapter 23

Using the Team Development Tools

Many of the applications designed for use in the corporate environment aren't the work of one person. Complex applications require too much time and effort to develop alone. The team can also collaborate on an application, which means that there are more ideas available for solving application problems. In short, teams have a significant contribution to make in the application development strategy for companies of any size and complexity.

However, any time you have two or more people working on a project, you also have to consider communication. A team that doesn't communicate won't produce acceptable output. Team members could potentially overwrite each other's code changes and experience other problems as well without the required coordination. Working in a team environment means that you must use tools that coordinate both communication and coding efforts. In addition, your team must have a means of seeing the complete application design and focus on changes to that design as needed to meet specific application goals.

This chapter provides an overview of the various tools that Microsoft provides as Visual Studio 2005 to encourage team development. You'll discover built-in tools, such as the various diagramming tools that Visual Studio 2005 provides, as well as external tools, such as Visio. These tools can meet just about every need a small to medium-sized team will require for modestly complex projects. You'll likely need additional tools when working on complex projects or in large team scenarios. However, even in these large application development scenarios, you can view the tools described in this chapter as a good starting point.

NOTE   This chapter doesn't discuss third party tools or extreme programming scenarios. You'll need other books to answer the questions posed by these environments. Consider getting *Developer to Designer* by Mike Gunderloy (Sybex, 2005) to answer your application interface design questions. Get *Coder to Developer* by Mike Gunderloy (Sybex, 2004) to answer your application design questions. Once you begin coding your application, consider getting *Effective Software Test Automation* and *Effective GUI Test Automation* both by Kanglin Li and Mengqi Wu (Sybex, 2004). All of these books answer the complex and sometimes daunting questions posed by large team development that you'll need to answer.

Understanding the Visual Studio 2005 Team Features

Visual Studio 2005 comes with a wealth of team development features. Not all of these features are new—some are part of a long-standing array of Visual Studio features. For example, anyone who used previous versions of Visual Studio already knows about Visual SourceSafe (VSS) and Visio. (You can discover more about Visio in the "Designing Your Application Using Visio" section of Chapter 2.) However, many of the features are new. For example, the Team Foundation Server is a new product for managing your applications and team development efforts as a whole.

NOTE Visual Studio comes with VSS because it's a great choice for most developers working with small to medium-sized projects. In fact, most single developers would do well to rely on VSS to help them over development hurdles. Microsoft designed Team Foundation Server for the large team. Because the developers using this system are expecting so much from it, the product has an exceptionally high operating system and hardware installation requirement. A minimal setup includes a Windows 2003 Server with Active Directory installed. A minimal system includes 1 GB of RAM, 20 GB hard drive space (just for the basic installation), and a 2.6 GHz processor. However, to get good performance, you actually need three such servers. Obviously, a single developer or even a moderately sized team won't have the resources to use this product. Consequently, this chapter only provides a rough overview of Team Foundation Server and focuses instead on the product that most developers will use, VSS.

The centerpiece of large team development in Visual Studio 2005 is the Team Foundation Server. You install this product on one, two, or three servers depending on the size of your team and the application requirements. The Team Foundation Server relies on the standard three-tier architecture with separate components for the client, application, and data tiers. The components can all appear on the same server or you can install the components for each tier on a separate server. This chapter doesn't include the Team Foundation Server installation because it can become quite complex. Make sure you obtain and read the current Team Foundation Server installation guide before you begin the installation (or prepare to waste a lot of time getting the installation right). Here are some Team Foundation Server resources you should consider reviewing.

- Ask Burton FAQ Blog (http://lab.msdn.microsoft.com/vs2005/teamsystem/askburton)

- Current Team Foundation Server Installation Manual (http://www.microsoft.com/downloads/details.aspx?FamilyId=E54BF6FF-026B-43A4-ADE4-A690388F310E&displaylang=en)

- Microsoft Forums (http://forums.microsoft.com)

- Online Known Issues for Team Foundation Server (http://lab.msdn.microsoft.com/teamsystem/tfsknownissues.aspx)

- Online Readme for Team Foundation Server (http://lab.msdn.microsoft.com/teamsystem/tfsreadme.aspx)

- Visual Studio Team System FAQ (http://lab.msdn.microsoft.com/vs2005/teamsystem/burtonfaq.aspx)

- Visual Studio Team System Getting Started (http://lab.msdn.microsoft.com/teamsystem/gettingstarted/default.aspx)

TIP   Some developers will miss a new feature in Visual Studio 2005—the team development project. A team development project offers all of the features of a standard project, but it also includes all of the team development features that Visual Studio can provide. To create a team development project, select the File ➢ New ➢ Team Project option, rather than the standard project. To use this option, you must have a Team Foundation Server installed and configured. Don't use this option when you want to create a project that relies on VSS.

Another team development component of Visual Studio is the Visual Studio Team System (VSTS). As with Team Foundation Server, this product feature focuses on the needs of large development teams—one where the organization really does require one or more individuals whose sole role is testing user interfaces. This feature helps developers on a team focus their attention by defining specific roles for each developer. The roles not only help developers understand their responsibilities but also keep the team members from stepping on each others toes as they vie for resources and code access during the development process. In short, this portion of the product is essentially an organizational aid that the team members can use to ensure everyone understands what is going on with the project. Lest you think that you don't need such an organization aid, communication (or the lack thereof) is often cited as a major cause of large project failures. Organization aids are essential to your success as a development team.

The team development tools also include a number of design aids. You can use many of these design aids for individual development as well, but Microsoft included them in Visual Studio 2005 with team development in mind. This chapter discusses a number of these design aids including the Application Connection Diagram, System Diagram, and Logical Datacenter Diagram. All of these design aids help you create better applications because there's less confusion between the team members.

TIP   Microsoft is constantly adding new functionality to their products and providing documentation updates. One of the best ways to keep current with the changes is to visit the Visual Studio 2005 Team System Home (`http://lab.msdn.microsoft.com/teamsystem/default.aspx`) periodically. This Web site provides you with articles, updates, workshops, presentations, forums, and other information about the team development features of Visual Studio 2005.

Depending on the version of Visual Studio 2005 you purchase, you might not find any team features at all. None of the Express editions include these features and you'll find very limited support for only a few of the team features in the Standard Edition. In fact, to obtain all of the features described in this chapter, you need the Visual Studio 2005 Team Suite edition. Fortunately, you can obtain some team development features without buying them as part of Visual Studio. For example, you can obtain a copy of Visual SourceSafe (`http://msdn.microsoft.com/vstudio/previous/ssafe/`) separately. It's also possible to obtain Visio (`http://office.microsoft.com/en-us/FX010857981033.aspx`) separately.

NOTE   You might need more information than the resources in this section provide. The LearnVisualStudio.NET Web site at `http://www.learnvisualstudio.net/` provides videos you can use to learn all aspects of Visual Studio development, including team development.

Working with Visual SourceSafe (VSS)

Most developers are familiar with VSS. This tool has appeared in many versions of Visual Studio, as a stand-alone product, and with other Microsoft products. The essence of VSS is that it's a vault for your code—you store your code in VSS to ensure that you can restore it later. However, VSS does more than simply guard your code. The purpose of any source control product is to help you overcome some of the natural problems with development. For example, you had a working copy of your application last night, but some unknown change today is causing the code to fail in a big way. When you don't use a source control product, your only choice at this point is to retrace your steps. However, by using VSS you can restore that working version without retracing your steps. In fact, a source control product will perform some basic tasks for everyone including:

◆ Keeping the code safe

◆ Allowing multiple developers work on the same project without overwriting anyone else's changes

◆ Providing a safe environment for reversing changes

◆ Tracking application versions

◆ Tracking changes to individual application versions

◆ Defining a safe point for compiling application versions

◆ Providing application status information to the lead developer

◆ Maintaining application development environment security

Even though most developers view source control as something that groups use, source control really is for everyone. Even a single developer working on a homegrown project can benefit from source control. Anything that helps you maintain a better coding environment is an aid that you shouldn't ignore. The following sections describe how to work with VSS in just about any environment. You'll also see some basics of setting up and maintaining a project using this product.

Administering VSS

Before you can do anything with VSS, you need to configure it. Use the Visual SourceSafe Administrator application that you access using the Start ➢ Programs ➢ Microsoft Visual Studio 2005 ➢ Microsoft Visual SourceSafe ➢ Microsoft Visual SourceSafe Administration command. To begin working with VSS, select the File ➢ New Database command to start a new database or the File ➢ Open SourceSafe Database command to use an existing database. Simply follow the prompts to create or open the database as needed.

TIP Use a separate database for each major Visual Studio solution. This technique ensures that you can set the options for each solution separately and reduces the risk of application data contamination. A separate database also allows you to set security as needed for that solution, rather than include everyone on every solution.

When you create a new database, VSS automatically adds entries for the administrator, guest, and any local users. None of these entries have passwords, so you need to add passwords to any entries you want to keep. Make sure you delete any entries that you don't want to have access to the project. For example, most development teams won't require the Guest entry unless they rely on outside consultants (even then, you should probably provide separate entries for the consultants). It's also a good idea to secure access to the folder containing the solution database using Windows Explorer. Now that you have a database to use, it's time to look at common administration tasks.

NOTE Whenever you change a VSS option, it's a good idea to ask users to log out and then log back in to see the change. Make sure the users also close and reopen Visual Studio. Otherwise, users could have unexpected results when working with VSS due to the change in options that their local setup won't show. It's also important to close and reopen Visual SourceSafe Administrator to ensure you see the changes correctly.

WORKING WITH USERS

The Users menu options show everything you can do with users. You can add, delete, and edit users. It's also possible to change a user's password.

When adding a user, you set the username, password, and permission, as shown in Figure 23.1. When you set a user for read-only permission, it means that they can see everything in the VSS database, but they can't change it. This setting affects the database only, not the Visual Studio solution. Consequently, you need to set the Windows folder to allow the user to read and change entries, but not to write them. In short, setting a user for read-only access means that the user can't add new items to VSS or to the Visual Studio solution—at least not if the user wants to place the new solution item under source control.

Editing a user lets you change the username and their VSS read only setting. The Edit User dialog box doesn't let you change the user password. To modify the user password you must select the Users ➤ Change Password command to display the Change Password dialog box. All that you need to do to change a password is enter the new password twice—VSS doesn't request the old password (a bonus when the user can't remember the old password).

Deleting a user removes that user's entry from the database. Theoretically, this should prevent the user from performing any tasks with VSS and it does work to an extent. However, the user still has access to the VSS database folder, so you need to use Windows Explorer to remove access to the folder as well as to VSS itself. The main Visual SourceSafe Administrator display shows the status of any users for the current solution, as shown in Figure 23.2.

FIGURE 23.1

Set the username, password, and permissions for the current Visual Studio solution.

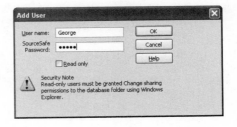

FIGURE 23.2
Monitor the status of
Visual Studio solution
developers using the
main display.

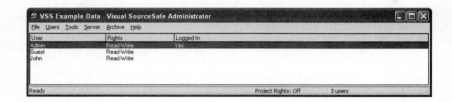

SETTING VSS OPTIONS

The Tools menu contains four options that affect the performance of VSS no matter which database
you have open. The Tools ➤ Fonts entry lets you change the font used to display information in
VSS, while the Tools ➤ Clean Up Temp Directory option removes temporary data from the user's
temporary folder. This second option is especially important when you want to maintain absolute
project security because the temporary folder can contains insightful bits of information about the
VSS database.

You use the Tools ➤ Lock SourceSafe Database option when you want to perform maintenance on
the current project. Selecting this option displays the Lock Visual SourceSafe Database dialog box.
Check the Lock All Users Out of Visual SourceSafe option and click Close to lock all users except the
administrator out of the database, which lets you work with the various project files without inter-
ruption. Imagine trying to archive a project with users logging in and out at will.

WARNING   Locking the VSS database will lock all users out—no matter what they are currently
doing. The Lock Visual SourceSafe Database dialog box shows a list of users logged into the system.
Make sure that this dialog box shows only the administrator as logged in to prevent potential
data loss.

The Tools ➤ Options command shows the SourceSafe Options dialog box shown in Figure 23.3.
You use this dialog box to set up various VSS project features such as the files that VSS recognizes and
defining how checkouts work. The following list provides an overview of the features you'll find on
each tab.

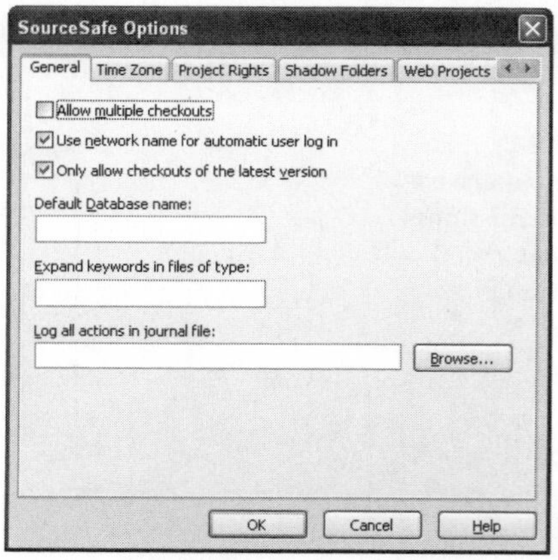

FIGURE 23.3
Change the VSS options
to meet user expecta-
tions and ensure every-
one follows company
policy.

General   Contains options that determine general VSS operation. The Allow Multiple Checkouts option lets multiple users check out the same file, which is generally a bad practice because it leads to data loss. Setting the Use Network Name for Automatic User Log In option is a good idea because it reduces the time and effort required to use VSS. Anything that reduces the effort of using VSS is a good idea because it encourages developers to use source control. The Only Allow Checkouts of the Latest Version option can be a two-edged sword. On the one hand, it prevents a developer from working with an old copy of the file. On the other hand, it also prevents developers from viewing old versions of the file for ideas on how to fix current problems (among other things). The Default Database Name option determines which database Visual SourceSafe Administrator opens when you start it. This option also affects the database displayed in Visual SourceSafe Explorer. Finally, when working in larger groups, you'll want to add an entry to Log All Actions in Journal File option to track individual actions as needed to correct team development problems.

Time Zone   You only need to use the Time Zone tab for projects that extend over multiple time zones. In short, this tab is for large projects. The Time Zone lets you set your time zone for the project so that VSS can synchronize entries from multiple locations.

Project Rights   Normally, VSS sets the Rights and Assignments feature off by default. Checking the Enable Rights and Assignments Commands option on this tab lets you set the rights individual users has to the project resources. The rights and assignments include read, check out/check in, add/rename/delete, and destroy. Each new right or assignment lets the user perform specific tasks. For example, although everyone involved in the project needs to read the files, you probably won't want to allow anyone but the administrator and project leader destroy files.

Shadow Folders   Setting up a shadow folder adds a level of insurance to your project. A shadow folder contains the most recently checked in files. It doesn't have all of the file versions—just the current one. If the main database becomes corrupted, you can at least get the current project files from the shadow folder. Although this setup isn't ideal, it's better than losing the entire project.

Web Projects   Web projects require special handling because VSS has to create special information for them. This information appears in the `SrcSafe.INI` file associated with the Web site. You'll see how this feature works in the "Working with VSS Projects" section of the chapter. The entries on this tab include the Web site's physical location and URL, the location of the site map, and the deployment path.

Web   This tab contains the settings for communicating over the Internet or an intranet. It includes settings for the FTP proxy and a list of servers that don't require use of the proxy. You can also set the name of default Web pages.

File Types   VSS has to recognize a file as being part of a project. The idea is to ensure that VSS provides full protection for your project, without becoming encumbered by temporary files that the project doesn't require. For example, VSS always recognizes binary files as including the DOC, DLL, EXE, and OCX extensions. However, you might decide to include other extensions. For example, you might want to include JPG files in this group. You work with the file types in three ways. First, if you want to add a new binary file type, simply add it to the Binary Files field by including a semicolon, the file specification (wildcards are acceptable), and the file extension like this: *.doc;*.dll;*.exe;*.ocx. When working with an existing file group, such as VB, add the new file extension to the list in the File Types Included in File Group field. Second, you can also add new file groups by clicking Add. Finally, you can remove file groups that you don't need by highlighting the group and clicking Delete.

SETTING SERVER OPTIONS

The server options control accessibility of a project database. The default setting makes the database accessible only to the local user. As shown in Figure 23.4, you can set options for both LAN and Web access. To set LAN access for VSS, check the Enable LAN Service for this Computer option on the LAN tab.

When working with an Internet or intranet setup, you must check the Enable SourceSafe Internet for this Computer option. Unless you want everyone in the world to know about your development efforts, you'll also want to check the Enable Secure Communication using SSL option. Using Secure Sockets Layer (SSL) encrypts communication to ensure that no one can eavesdrop on your project.

The second section of the SourceSafe Internet tab applies to projects individually—enabling Internet access for the computer doesn't provide access to the individual database. Check the Enable SourceSafe Internet for this Database option to make the database visible. You must also provide a DNS name or IP Address for the server.

FIGURE 23.4

Use the Server Configuration dialog box to change accessibility to the VSS database.

ARCHIVING PROJECTS

Most application development efforts don't go on forever. At some point, you reach a plateau and put the project away for a while. Of course, you don't want to lose the project database in the meantime. Archiving a project ensures that you have a compact means of storing it until you want to work on it again. The options on the Archive menu let you archive and restore projects as needed. The following steps show how to archive a project.

1. Select the Archive ➢ Archive Project command. You'll see a Choose Project to Archive dialog box.

2. Highlight the project you want to archive and click OK. You'll see the Archive Wizard dialog box shown in Figure 23.5. Notice that you can use this dialog box to add or remove projects from the archive list. Click Add to display the Choose Project to Archive dialog box again. Highlight a project and click Remove to delete it from the list.

3. Select the projects you want to archive and click Next. The wizard will ask how you want to archive the project, as shown in Figure 23.6. You have three options. The first option makes a backup of the project and you should use it regularly to backup your project as you work on it. The second option provides a final archive of your application. Use it when you want to put the project away for later use. The third option lets you remove project that you created by mistake from the database. Never delete a functional project without creating a backup of it first.

4. Select an archiving option. Type the name of an archive file as needed. Click Next. The wizard will ask whether you want to save all of the data or just the data for this version of the application. Generally, you want to save all of the data when creating a backup for any reason. Current version information is useful when you need to send a copy of the current version to another team or to another area of the company such as quality control.

5. Select a content option and click Finish. VSS will create the archive for you and display a completion message.

FIGURE 23.5
Use this dialog box to choose the projects you want to archive.

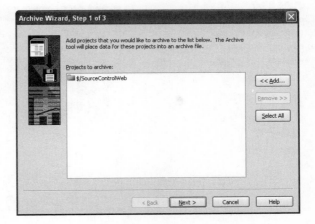

FIGURE 23.6
Select one of the three archiving options from the list to produce the kind of archive you want.

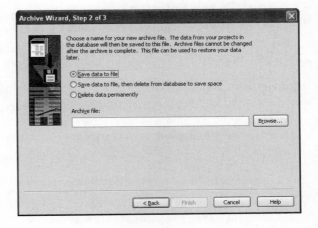

RESTORING PROJECTS

Eventually, you'll want to restore a project you stored away. The following steps show how to restore a project.

1. Select the Archive ➢ Restore Projects command. You'll see the Restore Wizard dialog box.

2. Click Browse to display the Open dialog box, locate the archive you want to restore, and click Open to select the file. Click Next. The restore wizard will show you a list of projects in the archive.

3. Highlight the projects you want to restore and click Next. The restore wizard will ask how you want to restore the project and let you provide a comment for the new project entry in the database, as shown in Figure 23.7.

4. Click Finish. The wizard will place the archived data into the database.

FIGURE 23.7
The restoration options let you place the project in its older folder or use a new folder for storage.

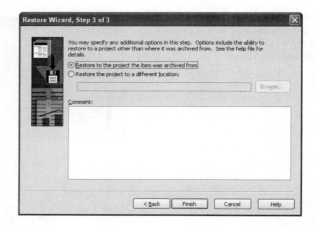

Adding VSS to a Solution

Using VSS with Visual Studio for Web-based applications is a two-step task. First, you must configure Visual Studio to use VSS. Second, you have to add the project to VSS manually. The following sections describe both tasks.

CONFIGURING VISUAL STUDIO

Before you can use VSS with Visual Studio, you must configure Visual Studio to use the VSS plug-in. The standard Visual Studio setup assumes that you're using the Visual Studio Team Foundation source control. Use these steps to change your configuration to use VSS.

1. Open Visual Studio. (Don't open any projects at this time.)

2. Choose the Tools ➢ Options command. You'll see the Options dialog box shown in Figure 23.8.

3. Select the `Source Control\Plug-in Selection` folder. Change the Current Source Control Plug-in setting to Microsoft Visual SourceSafe.

4. Select the `Source Control\Environment` folder. Choose the Visual SourceSafe (team development) or Independent Developer option in the Source Control Environment Settings drop-down list. As an alternative, you can set the individual fields to provide the level of source control you want. For example, as shown in Figure 23.9, I prefer to know when a file is checked in or out, so I set the On Save and On Edit fields to Prompt for Check Out. Many developers prefer complete automation and enable all of the automation features.

5. Select the `Source Control\Plug-in Settings` folder. Verify the Login ID (SourceSafe) field contains your VSS identifier, not your Windows login identifier.

6. Close Visual Studio and reopen it to ensure the settings work as anticipated.

ADDING A PROJECT TO SOURCE CONTROL

Using VSS for desktop applications is easy. Select the File ➢ New ➢ Project command and you'll see the entry for source control at the bottom of the New Project dialog box, as shown in Figure 23.10. All you need to do is check the Add to Source Control option to add the project to source control. VSS takes care of the rest for you automatically.

FIGURE 23.8
Open the Options dialog box to configure a new source control option.

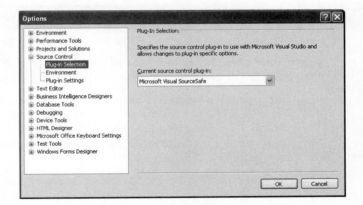

FIGURE 23.9
Set the source control environment as needed for your coding style.

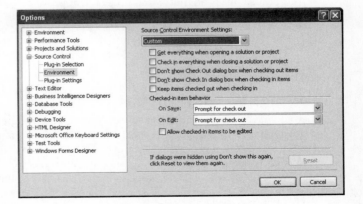

FIGURE 23.10
Using source control is a simple check away when working with desktop applications.

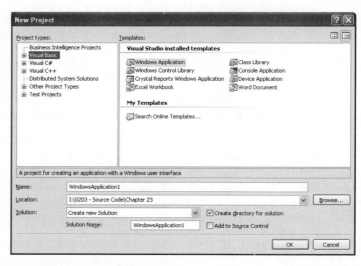

Unfortunately, you won't find this entry for a Web application, making it a lot more difficult to work with Web projects. The following steps tell you how to add VSS to a Web project.

1. Create a new project as usual. It doesn't matter which technique you use, the source control configure is the same. Make sure the project is open, but all of the files in it are closed.

2. Select the File ➢ Source Control ➢ Add Web Site to Source Control command. You'll see a Log On to Visual SourceSafe Database dialog box. If you set everything correctly using the procedure in the "Configuring Visual Studio" section and have set up a database correctly using the information in the "Administering VSS" section of the chapter, you should see your username and the default VSS database filled out.

3. Type your password in the SourceSafe Password field and click OK. You'll see the Add to Source Control dialog box shown in Figure 23.11. The dialog box will already contain the name of your project. When working with a solution, you'll want to select the solution folder. Because this is an individual project, it appears in the $ folder.

4. Click OK. VSS will warn you that the project doesn't exist. Click Yes to create it. VSS will create the project and set your code under source control. You can tell the process worked by the change of icon in Solution Explorer. Notice that each of the files now include a little lock next to it, as shown in Figure 23.12.

Working with VSS Projects

Once you have your project under source control, you'll want to begin writing some code. Depending on how your set up the source control options described in the "Configuring Visual Studio" section of the chapter, you might not notice much of a difference until disaster happens. VSS will work in the background saving the changes you make to your project. Only when you need to restore something from the database will you ever interact with VSS. On the other end of the spectrum, you can tell VSS to inform you about every action. The following sections describe the most common techniques when working with VSS. You'll see some of these events and use some techniques, but might not see others at all depending on your settings. For example, you can set VSS to check out files automatically, which means that you'll never need to worry about the material in the "Checking Files In" and "Checking Files Out" sections.

CHECKING FILES OUT

You can read any file in a project without checking it out. Try it on any project you create, opening the file doesn't cause VSS to react at all. The reason for this seeming lack of concern about open files is based on the idea that many developers will need to open a file for reference, but may never change it. Consequently, the first time you'll see the Check Out for Edit dialog box shown in Figure 23.13 is when you attempt to make a change. The simple act of dragging and dropping a control or typing text in the editor is enough to display this dialog box.

Notice the Comments field at the bottom of the dialog box. When working in a team environment, you want to provide a comment. You'll discover later in the "Using Visual SourceSafe Explorer" section of the chapter that the comment is accessible to other people on your team so they know why you have the file checked out. In many cases, this information is all someone needs to leave you to your coding and not bother you about checking the file back in immediately.

When you decide to check the file out, click Check Out. VSS will let you make the change to the file (assuming no one else has it open) and let everyone else know that the file is unavailable for editing.

FIGURE 23.11
Provide project information for VSS so it can set up a new source control project for you.

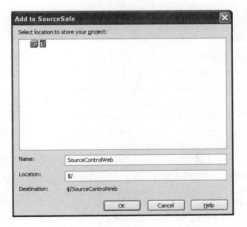

FIGURE 23.12
The Visual Studio IDE displays files under source control with a different icon.

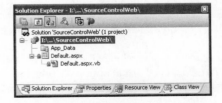

FIGURE 23.13
Checking files out automatically occurs when you attempt to make changes.

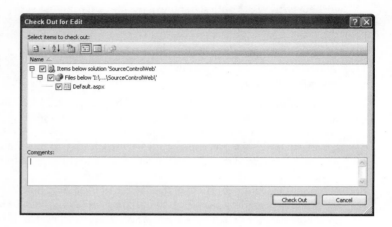

TIP The dialog box shown in Figure 23.13 shows why I normally set my system to tell me about every VSS action. Setting the IDE to check files out automatically could result in inadvertent edits to the file. Even if the automation doesn't create errors, you could check a file out accidentally, making it unavailable to someone else. By knowing precisely what VSS is doing, you can create a better work environment for everyone.

CHECKING FILES IN

At some point, you'll finish editing a file and want to check it in. You actually have two choices. First, you can make the changes permanent. Second, you can decide that the changes were a mistake and decide to revert to the original version. This second option is one of the safety features VSS provides. The act of deciding which check-in action to perform forces you to think about the changes you have made (and even when you weren't thinking very well—you can reverse the change later). The Pending Checkins window shown in Figure 23.14 provides several views of your open files and helps you determine which check-in to use.

TIP You can change the view that the Pending Checkins window provides. Selecting Flat View instead of Tree View will display just the checked out filenames in the list. Click Columns to see the list of columns that the Pending Checkins window can display.

When you decide that you want to save the changes that you made, simply highlight the file and click Check In. VSS will create a new version of that file and save it on disk. Likewise, if you decide that the changes were a mistake, highlight the file in question and click Undo Checkout. However, you might not know whether you want to save the changes. Click Compare Versions and you'll see a Difference Option dialog box like the one shown in Figure 23.15 where you can choose which versions of the file to compare.

You can choose any version of the file for comparison purposes by modifying the entries in the Compare and To fields. The Format options define how you see the comparison information, with the Visual format providing the best view of the data in most cases, as shown in Figure 23.16. Finally, you can choose how VSS performs the comparison. For example, you can choose to ignore case differences.

FIGURE 23.14
Use the Pending Check-ins window to manage open files.

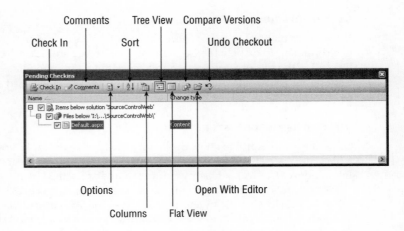

FIGURE 23.15
Check the differences between files as needed before a check-in to ensure you want to make the changes.

FIGURE 23.16
Use the Visual format for comparing differences when you want to see changes in context.

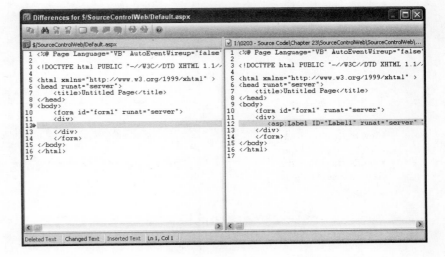

GETTING RESOURCES

Whenever you need to access more than one file, it's convenient to use the File ➤ Source Control ➤ Get command to display the Get window shown in Figure 23.17. Using this window, you can highlight all of the resources you want and check them out immediately, rather than one at a time. It's important to remember that checking a file out always blocks edit access to other developers, so you only want to check out the resources you actually need.

VIEWING RESOURCE HISTORY

Sometimes it's helpful to know the history of a file. For example, you might want to know who edited a file last. To see all of the versions for a particular resource, select it in Solution Explorer. Choose the File ➤ Source Control ➤ History command to display the History dialog box shown in Figure 23.18.

The controls along the right side of the History dialog box provide you with the capability of examining the file closely. Click View and you'll see the VSS copy of that version of the file. This can come in handy when you want to view a section of code to understand the changes made to the latest version. The Details button lets you view a properties window for the file that contains information such as the last date of edit and the person who performed the editing. Clicking Get will obtain the file for you. One of the options is already familiar—click Diff if you want compare this version of a file with another version (see the "Checking Files In" section of the chapter for details).

FIGURE 23.17
Obtain all of the resources you need at one time by using the Get window.

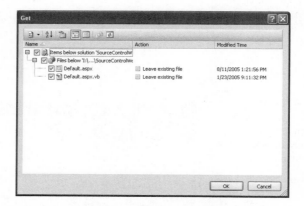

FIGURE 23.18
View the history of any resource in your project to understand how the resource has changed.

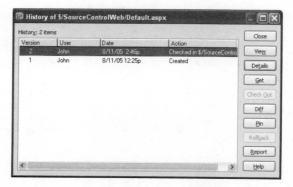

Some of the buttons perform maintenance or recovery tasks. For example, you can pin a file to ensure no one uses it. Pinning ensures you have exclusive access to the file to perform a maintenance task or simply to ensure you can completely recover from an error. Click Rollback when you want to recover the previous version of a file and use it, rather than the existing version of the file.

Using Visual SourceSafe Explorer

Visual SourceSafe Explorer doesn't add much to the capabilities provided by the Visual Studio IDE. It provides all of the Visual Studio features, but Visual SourceSafe Explorer often arranges them more conveniently. In addition, using Visual SourceSafe Explorer, you obtain a full view of any project, whereas, Visual Studio limits you to the current project. You access Visual SourceSafe Explorer using the Start ➢ Programs ➢ Microsoft Visual Studio 2005 ➢ Microsoft Visual SourceSafe ➢ Microsoft Visual SourceSafe command. Figure 23.19 shows a typical view of this utility.

Open files have a red box around them. You can also see the name of the person who has the file checked out and the time/date of the checkout. Generally, it's a bad idea to take any action on open files, but you can highlight a file and check it in using the Versions ➢ Check In command. Likewise, you can use the Versions ➢ Check Out command to check a file out for modification. Checking a file out using this method doesn't automatically open the correct application with the file loaded. You must select a working folder first and the file appears in that folder. Double-clicking the file will normally open it for editing. This technique does work well for files that you can't open in Visual Studio, such as graphics that might appear on your Web site. Use the File ➢ Set Working Folder command to set the working folder for Visual SourceSafe Explorer.

This utility does have a number of interesting features. One of the most interesting is that you can select a project entry, and then choose the Web ➢ Check Hyperlinks command to obtain a list of broken hyperlinks for the Web site. You can use the Web ➢ Deploy command to deploy your application, but it's generally better to use the command on the Web site menu of Visual Studio to perform this task.

FIGURE 23.19
Visual SourceSafe Explorer provides a convenient method for working with multiple projects.

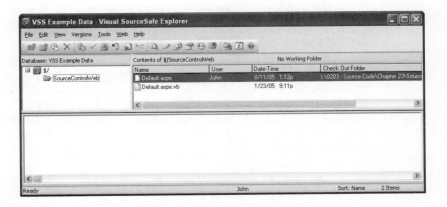

Working with Distributed System Designers

Visual Studio includes a new feature called Distributed System Designers (DSD) as part of their Dynamic Systems Initiative (DSI). The goal is to provide a design package, one that works with the operating system and installed services (such as BizTalk), yet reduces the developer's workload as well. This functionality ties in with the new features that Microsoft is adding into Windows to provide a Service-Oriented Architecture (SOA). The whole purpose of SOA is to provide application functionality as a service, rather than as a component. As you discovered in Chapter 13, a developer can connect to a Web service supported by any platform and use the services it provides. That's part of the goal of these designers. You can learn more about SOA in a number of places, including the overview at `http://www.service-architecture.com/`. In fact, you might want to go directly to the definition at `http://www.service-architecture.com/web-services/articles/service-oriented_architecture_soa_definition.html`.

Fortunately, the DSD tools that Microsoft provides help you design any application, not just those that work in a distributed environment. You can see Microsoft's original vision for this product at `http://msdn.microsoft.com/library/en-us/dnvsent/html/vsts-arch.asp`. The point is that you have new functionality that you can rely on to help you create better applications.

You can add the three diagrams used to implement DSD using options on the Add New Item dialog box (right-click the project entry in Solution Explorer and choose Add New Item from the context menu). Consequently, you don't have to create a special project to work with any of the diagrams—you can add them to an existing project. However, Visual Studio also provides two special projects just for working with DSD (one for a distributed system and a second for working with a logical datacenter). These projects appear in the Distribute System Solutions folder of the New Project dialog box that you access with the File ➢ New ➢ Project command.

NOTE   The diagrams you create with this technology provide an overview of what you want to do. The diagrams represent a complete picture using a few block diagrams. For a detailed picture of a particular piece such as a single application or a module within that application, you need another product such as Visio to perform the task.

Using the Application Connection Diagram

An application connection diagram is a convenient way of showing how software modules must communicate. For example, consider the simple application in Figure 23.20. This diagram shows that three kinds of client applications (desktop, Web, and Office) will connect to a Web service. The location of the Web service doesn't matter—all you need is an URL to access it using Visual Studio. The Web service, in turn, connects to the backend database. This particular model works for a number of Web service scenarios. For example, you might decide to create a connection to Amazon on your local intranet so developers can locate books they need more quickly. This model would work for that kind of application.

It's important to note a few items when you look at this diagram. The first, and most obvious, occurs when you create a connection between the database and the Web service. Visual Studio automatically presents a Connection Properties dialog box. You provide the connectivity information as you create the connections between the database and other parts of the application. Make sure you create a valid connection and test it out because this information becomes very important later.

The three code blocks include a `Template` property. You select the template that Visual Studio uses to create the solution modeled by the application diagram. Every application will include features that the template provides. For example, the Office block can be an Excel workbook, Excel template, Word document, or Word template. You can also rely on a custom template to perform the work.

Another feature that you should set as part of your application design is `Settings and Constraints`. Click the ellipses in this property and you'll see the Settings and Constraints window shown in Figure 23.21. You might decide that your application will only support some versions of Windows or that it might require a specific version of the .NET Framework on a given platform. Using the Settings and Constraints window makes it easy to configure all of these settings while you define the connectivity issues for the application.

Once you define the essential application design, you don't have to implement it yourself. Select the Diagram ➤ Implementation menu and you'll see two options. The Implement All Applications option will create a solution based on your entire diagram, while the Implement Application option will create a project based on the selected diagram element.

FIGURE 23.20
Application diagrams show the connectivity between pieces of software.

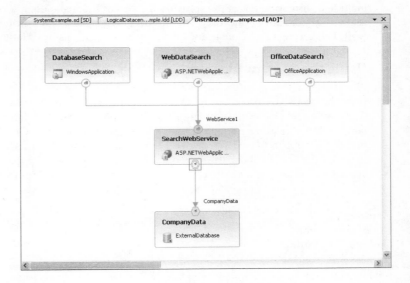

FIGURE 23.21
Define any constraints the application will have to operate under as part of the initial design.

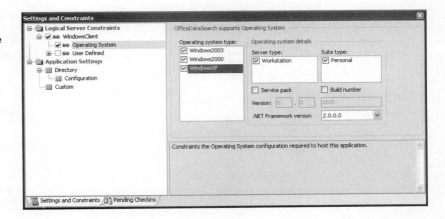

Using the Logical Datacenter Diagram

While the application connection diagram helps you design software connectivity, the logical datacenter diagram helps you create the hardware setup to run it on. All too often, developers create a piece of software without considering the hardware it will run on. Figure 23.22 shows a very simple hardware setup for the application in Figure 23.20.

Unlike the application diagram, Visual Studio won't generate the hardware you need. However, the Settings and Constraints property lets you describe the hardware and use that description when making decisions about software functionality. For example, one of the constraints might state that a particular client can support the application as a Web application, but not as a desktop application. All of these bits of information help you understand how the application you're considering will affect the hardware and, therefore, the application's ability to run.

Server constraints can convey a considerable about of information, too. For example, you can include information about the software the server has installed, the version of IIS, and other factors that will affect your application. You might consider issues such as the current security on a server as well. The Settings and Constraints include security entries by default.

Using the System Diagram

A system diagram considers a number of issues, but essentially, it combines the software and hardware diagrams you have created in such a way that you end up with a picture of the application deployment. For example, you might create a Web service and a database backend, but in a small system, these two features might reside on the same physical server. On the other hand, the database portion of the application might require several machines set up as a server farm when creating a large-scale application. In short, the system diagram helps you ensure that the software you create will appear in pieces that will work with your existing hardware. Figure 23.23 shows an example of the system diagram for the system described in Figure 23.20.

FIGURE 23.22
Create an accurate picture of the hardware you possess to run the application.

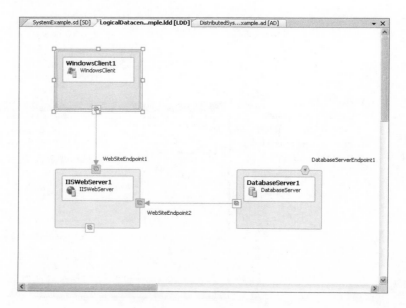

The system diagram might not look like much, but it acts as a basis for a fourth diagram. Once you complete this diagram, select Diagram ➤ Define Deployment command. You'll see the Define Deployment dialog box shown in Figure 23.24. Normally, you'll accept the default diagram (in this case, there's only one). However, you will have to select a specific diagram when you have more than one logical datacenter diagram in your project.

This is the point at which all of the planning pays off. Figure 23.25 shows a deployment diagram. You can't select this diagram from the Add New Item dialog box—you generate it as part of defining the deployment. Notice that all of the software items that appear in Figure 23.20 are now matched up with a physical device from the logical datacenter diagram. Not only do you know how all of the software items will communicate, you've designed a deployment diagram that ensures all of the software will run as intended.

FIGURE 23.23

Combine all of the pieces you have created to define the application deployment picture.

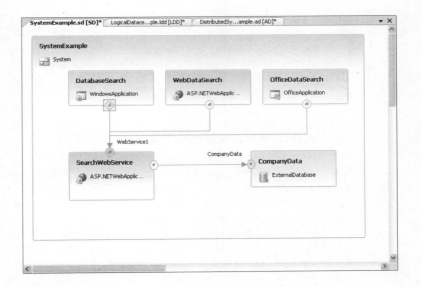

FIGURE 23.24

Choose a logical datacenter diagram to match with the software you have designed.

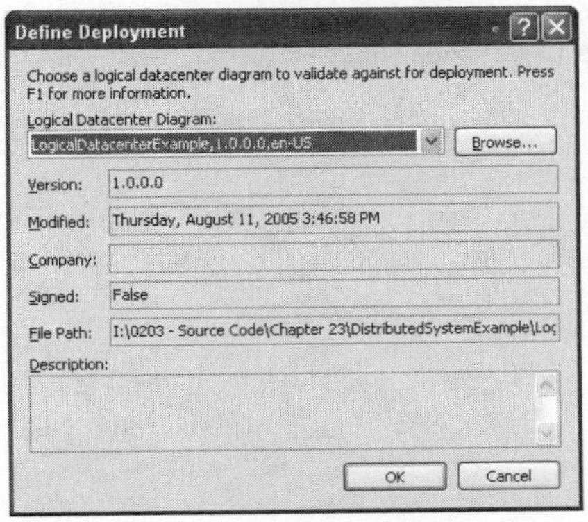

FIGURE 23.25
A deployment diagram matches software to hardware to endure everything will run.

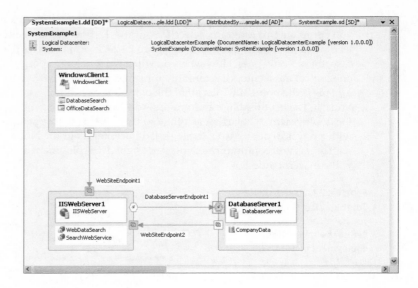

Defining Your Development Goals

This chapter has helped you discover the team development tools that Microsoft supplies with Visual Studio 2005. If you've used previous versions of the product, you'll know that Microsoft has made great strides in improving the team development environment. However, anyone who has worked on a large team project also understands that the supplied tools won't meet every possible need—they're a very big improvement, but there are still gaps in coverage.

The decision of how to use these team development tools is up to you. Some developers might decide to use an assortment of third party tools, rather than invest time in learning these new Microsoft tools. However, you should at least try them on a small project to see how they work for you—this is one area where Microsoft really has tried to improve Visual Studio 2005 to meet developer needs. Whether the tools will actually meet your needs depends on the kind of application you want to create and the team environment you need to maintain. The best policy is to determine which tools to use at the outset—before you write even one line of code and possibly as part of the application design process.

Chapter 24 helps you move your Visual Studio .NET 2003 applications to the Visual Studio .NET 2005 environment. Of course, this chapter applies only to Web applications since Visual Web Developer doesn't support desktop applications. However, many of the techniques you learn in this chapter apply equally well to desktop applications. In short, this is a good chapter for anyone to read who's performing an upgrade.

Chapter 24

Converting Visual Studio 2003 Applications

At some point, you'll decide that you no longer want to maintain two versions of your Web applications on your machine—you'll want to move your old projects to Visual Studio 2005. Unfortunately, like most moves, this one isn't painless. Microsoft has made progress in reducing the complexity of moving an application over the years, but you still have to do some of the work yourself. Sure, the IDE performs some tasks, such as converting the project file automatically, but you still have other issues to consider, such as replacing older code with new.

This chapter helps you perform application upgrades with a lot less pain. You can automate some tasks and eliminate others through careful planning. In some cases, you can get the IDE to help you perform the upgrade, even if the IDE won't perform the task automatically for you. These techniques help you get most applications converted, or at least, far enough along the way that you shouldn't run into problems. However, you might still run into a few applications that cause problems simply because of the unique environment in which they run. For example, this chapter won't help much if your application runs in a mixed .NET and Java environment.

After you convert an application, you also need to consider how to test it. A standard set of tests will check the application for user-related problems. For example, a standard test suite will ensure that the user actually ends up saving a file when using the File ➢ Save command. These test suites are also valuable when testing your updated code, but they won't test everything. This chapter also points out a few special tests you should run on your code to ensure it isn't hiding any odd version-related problems—issues that tend to sneak up on your when you least expect it.

Understanding the Process Is One Way

When you decide to move an application from Visual Studio .NET 2003 it's important to understand that the process is one way—at least to an extent. You can take the first step toward moving the application—converting the project file from its current version to the new Visual Studio 2005 version without any problem. The IDE saves the old project file and you can still use it to work with the application using Visual Studio .NET 2003. However, once you move beyond this first step, moving back becomes difficult because you would have to reverse any changes you make to the code. (Consequently, make sure you save a backup of your original Visual Studio .NET 2003 project.) The following sections describe the conversion process and examine some of the changes that you can expect to see as a result.

Deciding Whether You Want to Make a Change

Moving a personal application from one version of Visual Studio to another doesn't require much thought. Sure, you want to be sure you have a copy of the old code because you might decide that the upgrade really didn't work as expected. However, the decision to try the upgrade isn't very difficult because the code usually isn't too complex and the risks are relatively small. Contrast this with an enterprise application where the move between versions could require months, employment of a full development team, and massive changes to data structures. A move from one version of Visual Studio to another suddenly becomes a major decision. Consequently, before you do anything else in this chapter, consider whether you really want to make the move at all. Here are some concepts to consider as part of your decision.

Expense To obtain any benefit at all from the conversion process, you need to train the development staff to use the new product. In addition, you need to set up new quality assurance (QA) procedures to account for the updated features. All of the tests you used in the past now have to include checks for new features. In fact, the list of expensive pre-update changes is quite extensive. However, you can perform all of these tasks and still not make the expense worthwhile to the company's bottom line. The problem is that you still haven't identified the payoff. Before you start adding up the cost, you have to consider the payoff. You must answer the question of what value this new update provides and how long it will take to recover the expense.

Complexity It's possible to justify the expense of an update without considering whether the update is actually possible. Too many updates begin as nebulous ideas that have some goal in sight, but the developers involved never consider whether the light at the end of the tunnel is the sun or simply a train waiting to run them over. As complexity increases, so do the risks. At some point, the risks will become overwhelming and you're doomed to failure from the outset, even if you do everything else correctly. Sometimes, it's better to break the update into small pieces and perform updates on the application one piece at a time as finances and time permit. At least you'll have definite milestones you can achieve and successes you can point to when asked.

Hybrid Solutions At one time, developers had to make version moves an all or nothing choice. The all or nothing mind-set remains in many companies despite the fact that you no longer have an all or nothing choice to make. Using side-by-side execution lets you create some elements in Visual Studio 2003 and others in Visual Studio 2005 and let them execute side by side. Carefully using new components crafted in Visual Studio 2005 lets you update your old code with new technology without changing the old code very much. All you really need to consider is how to call the new components you create.

Source Control Projects under source control can prove problematic. The best idea is to export the project and work on it as a stand-alone item during the conversion process. If you want to keep the project in source control, make sure that no one else is using it or will use it. In addition, the IDE will check out the project during the conversion process, but tends not to check it back in—you'll have to perform this task manually. In addition, the IDE tends to assume that you're using a Microsoft source control solution and might not work well with other vendor products. Source control is a great way to work with projects, but the very tool that makes life easier as you work on your code can also cause problems during a conversion and you need to consider how to work through these problems.

Once you do decide to perform an update from Visual Studio .NET 2003 to Visual Studio 2005, make sure you create the required backup of all code and data for the existing project. Make a second copy on a test system and use the test system to make the update (rather than a production system). Take every precaution you normally would with a new application because, in many respects, you are creating a new application. The point is that enterprise developers have far more to consider before making a version upgrade than their single developer counterparts.

Performing the Conversion

The conversion process begins when you open the Visual Studio .NET 2003 project file using Visual Studio 2005. To perform this task, use the File ➢ Open ➢ Project/Solution command instead of opening a Web site as usual. Locate the SLN file for the project that you want to convert and click Open. The Visual Studio 2005 IDE automatically recognizes that the product is a Visual Studio .NET 2003 project and starts the Visual Studio Conversion Wizard. The following steps take you through the process of performing the conversion. You'll find this example in the `\Chapter 24\Convert` folder of the source code on the Sybex Web site.

1. Click Next to get past the Welcome dialog box. You'll see the Choose Whether to Create a Backup dialog box shown in Figure 24.1. It's always better to be safe than sorry, so creating a backup of your old project file is always a good idea.

2. Choose a backup option. I strongly recommend creating a backup. In most cases, you want to place the backup in a separate folder to make it easier to find later. The example uses the same project folder, but creates a `Backup` subfolder for the backup information.

3. Click Next. You'll see a Ready to Convert dialog box that contains a summary of the actions the Visual Studio Conversion Wizard will take. This is your last chance to change your mind.

> **WARNING** Make sure that you observe the source control warning on this last dialog box. Ensure that no one else is working on the project and that the Wizard can check out the project. Otherwise, you could experience odd problems with the project—everything from a failure to convert to damaged files.

FIGURE 24.1
Choose a backup option from this dialog box.

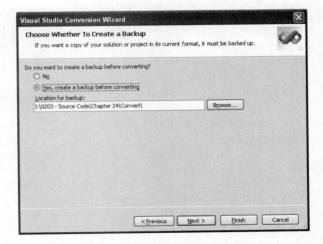

4. Click Finish. It's at this point that you could see any of a number of error messages. The most common error is going to be one where the IDE can't tell whether the server has the proper support installed. Remember that Visual Studio .NET 2003 relies on a separate IIS server to work with Web projects and that you've been using the built-in Web server for most of the projects in this book. Generally, you can still continue with the conversion process, but you'll have to address any errors the conversion program detects later.

5. Click OK after you record any error messages. Once the conversion process is complete, you'll see a Conversion Complete dialog box. This dialog box contains an option for displaying the conversion log when the wizard is closed.

6. Check the Show the Conversion Log When the Wizard is Closed option and click Close to close the Conversion Complete dialog box. Visual Studio 2005 displays a conversion report similar to the one shown in Figure 24.2.

You'll notice from Figure 24.2 that the conversion program experienced five warnings when converting the simple example. It's important to review these problems and correct any outstanding issues before you begin working with the project itself. Click the plus sign (+) next to the `Project: Convert.csproj` entry shown in Figure 24.2 and you'll see a list of actions that the conversion program performed, as shown in Figure 24.3.

In this case, none of the issues are major. The warnings deal with changes in the visibility of various methods within the application—these changes are normal for a conversion so you don't need to worry about them.

Understanding the Conversion Process

Converting your code produces a wealth of changes. The biggest change is the solution file. If you don't make a backup of this file, you have little chance of using the project from Visual Studio .NET 2003 if you change your mind later. This is the one change that's completely one way and you don't have any way to reverse it unless you make a backup of the requisite files.

FIGURE 24.2
Review the conversion log for errors before you try using the converted application.

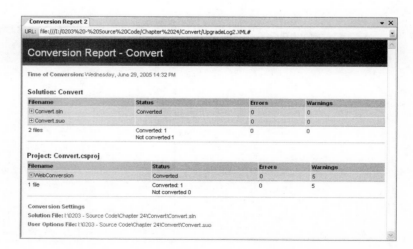

FIGURE 24.3
The Visual Studio
Conversion Wizard
performs a series of
complex steps to update
your application.

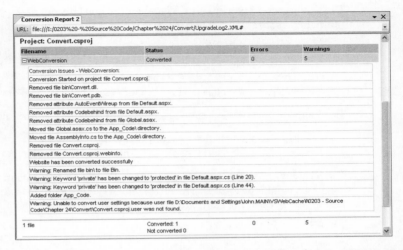

The changes are sometimes subtle. In fact, sometimes it's simply a different way of accomplishing the same task. Often, it pays to try various techniques using both IDEs so that you can see the differences and come up with a plan to work through them. In some cases, you might even consider continuing to perform some design work using Visual Studio 2003 just to ensure the code is compatible across the multiple development environments that you use. Consider the simple Web page described in Listing 24.1.

This page shows the Visual Studio .NET 2003 method of accomplishing the task. When you create the same page using Visual Studio 2005, you'll notice some differences. (You'll find the Visual Studio 2005 version of the example in the \Chapter 24\VWDExample folder of the source code on the Sybex Web site.) A few of the differences are easy to overcome and won't cause any problems for Visual Studio .NET 2003. For example, Visual Studio 2005 encases the page elements in a <Div> tag that Visual Studio .NET 2003 also supports, but doesn't use. The addition of this tag won't cause any problems.

However, some of the changes do present compatibility issues. For example, consider this code snippet for the <asp:Label> tag.

```
<asp:Label ID="lblGreeting" runat="server"
        Font-Bold="true" Font-Size="Large"
        Text="Project Conversion Example">
</asp:Label>
```

Notice that the code relies on a Text property that Visual Studio 2003 doesn't support. If you decide to move code from Visual Studio 2005 back to Visual Studio 2003, you would potentially need to change every label in the project—not a very appealing modification, but quite doable.

The <asp:Button> tag also changes somewhat. In this case, Visual Studio 2005 adds an attribute, OnClick, as shown here.

```
<asp:Button ID="btnTest" runat="server" Text="Test"
        ToolTip="Display the text you typed on screen."
        OnClick="btnTest_Click" />
```

The change won't work within Visual Studio 2003 properly, so you'd need to remove it in that environment. In short, you not only have to look for changes to existing programming code, but new code as well.

Another change is the <% @Page> directive. Here's the Visual Studio 2003 version.

```
<%@ Page language="c#" Codebehind="Default.aspx.cs"
    AutoEventWireup="false" Inherits="Convert.WebForm1" %>
```

The Visual Studio 2005 version is similar, but different. Here's the version for this project.

```
<%@ Page Language="C#" AutoEventWireup="true"
    CodeFile="Default.aspx.cs" Inherits="_Default" %>
```

The Visual Studio 2005 version uses a new `CodeFile` attribute in place of the `Codebehind` attribute used by Visual Studio 2003. The `AutoEventWireup` attribute is automatically set to true, rather than false. Finally, even the standard class definition is different, so you'd possibly need to change that as well.

LISTING 24.1:   A Simple Web Page in Visual Studio 2003

```
<form id="Form1" method="post" runat="server">
    <p>
        <asp:Label id="lblGreeting" runat="server"
                    Font-Bold="True" Font-Size="Large">
            Project Conversion Example
        </asp:Label>
    </p>
    <p>
        <asp:Label id="lblInput" runat="server"
                    AssociatedControlID="txtInput">
            Type Some Text:
        </asp:Label>
        <asp:TextBox id="txtInput" runat="server" accessKey="I"
                    ToolTip="Type some text to display on screen.">
        </asp:TextBox><br>
        <asp:Button id="btnTest" runat="server" Text="Test"
                    ToolTip="Display the text you typed on screen.">
        </asp:Button>
    </p>
    <p>
        <asp:Label id="lblOutput" runat="server" Visible="False">
        </asp:Label>
    </p>
</form>
```

Overcoming Potential Conversion Problems

You're going to run into a few problems with your converted code. The problems aren't insurmountable, but you must consider them nonetheless. The following sections help you understand a few of the more difficult conversion issues. Most of them don't have a right or wrong solution—simply a solution that works best for you. For example, when you upgrade, you might find that you have to upgrade custom components and controls as well. Maintaining two versions of these components and controls can be difficult, so you need to think about the conversion technique that will work in your particular environment. Sometimes the best solution is not making the upgrade at all when the work involved surpasses the benefits you gain.

Considering Deprecated Features

Even if you use just the .NET Framework and ASP.NET 1.1 for your Visual Studio 2003 application, Microsoft has made changes to the latest update and you'll find that not everything converts properly. For one thing, Microsoft has deprecated (gotten rid of) some of the features found in the older version of the .NET Framework. The techniques are different, so you have to make changes to your code.

Most of the changes are for the better. Microsoft has found ways of helping you accomplish a given task using fewer resources. Listing 24.2 shows an example of using a custom event source using Visual Studio 2003.

Notice that in this example, you must create an EventLog object to work with a custom event source. In addition, you provide standard strings as input to the CreateEventSource() method. Notice that there's an event registration process in this code as well. Listing 24.3 shows the same example using Visual Studio 2005.

In this case, you don't have to create an EventLog object because Microsoft marked the Event Log class methods as shared. Consequently, the application saves resources it would otherwise need to create the custom event log. You do need to create an object to register the custom event source. Instead of using strings, the CreateEventSource() method now requires you to define an EventSourceCreationData() object to hold the data. It's a small change, but one that you'd need to consider as part of the conversion process. This is one of the extreme examples of code rewriting, but it's an important example as well. You'll spend time working with the code once you perform a conversion because the conversion process doesn't accomplish everything for you.

Of course, the example code further points to the process of conversion being one way. Once you make these changes, you can't easily move the code back to Visual Studio 2003.

LISTING 24.2:   Using a Custom Event in Visual Studio 2003

```
Private Sub btnTest_Click(ByVal sender As System.Object, _
                ByVal e As System.EventArgs) _
                Handles btnTest.Click

    Dim eLog As EventLog              ' Holds the event log reference.
    Dim eLogEntry As EventLogEntry    ' A single entry.

    ' If you want to create a special log, then you need
    ' to register an event source first (as you already did in your
```

```
        ' example code).
        If (Not eLog.SourceExists("MyEventSource")) Then

            ' Create the new event source.
            eLog.CreateEventSource("MyEventSource", "MySpecialLog", ".")

        End If

        ' Register the new event source.
        eLog = New EventLog("MySpecialLog")
        eLog.Source = "MyEventSource"

        ' Create an entry.
        eLog.WriteEntry("MyEventSource", _
                        "Special Message", _
                        EventLogEntryType.Information, _
                        12, _
                        22)
    End Sub
```

LISTING 24.3:   Using a Custom Event in Visual Studio 2005

```
    Protected Sub btnTest_Click( _
        ByVal sender As Object, ByVal e As System.EventArgs)

        ' If you want to create a special log, then you need
        ' to register an event source first (as you already did in your
        ' example code).
        If (Not EventLog.SourceExists("MyEventSource")) Then

            ' Create the new event source.
            EventLog.CreateEventSource( _
                New EventSourceCreationData( _
                    "MyEventSource", "MySpecialLog"))

        End If

        ' Create an entry.
        EventLog.WriteEntry("MyEventSource", _
                            "Special Message", _
                            EventLogEntryType.Information, _
                            12, _
                            22)

    End Sub
```

Considering Difficult Conversion Issues

Generally, custom components and controls that you create yourself don't pose the problems that third party solutions do because you have the source code. The same holds true for any libraries you create. In both cases, you can choose to upgrade the code as needed to meet certain expectations for the converted application. However, now you have to consider what to do about the component, control, or source code library. You have a number of choices.

◆ Maintain the current code and live without the upgrade

◆ Upgrade the current code and all applications that rely on the external code (component, control, or library)

◆ Create two code bases—one for each version of the component, control, or library that you need to use

◆ Attempt to use the component or control as is from the latest version of the .NET application

There isn't a right answer in this list. All of these solutions work, but they work in specific conditions. When you have a huge code base consisting of applications that work well today and you don't see a pressing need to upgrade, then maintaining the current code might be the best solution. On the other hand, someone who has just a few applications and needs the features provided by Visual Studio 2005 might decide to upgrade all of their applications as well as the components and controls. The point is that you need to consider the problems that the conversion will present before you begin the conversion.

Something that many developers don't consider is how an upgrade will affect their code libraries. Code libraries aren't as isolated as components and controls, so often you can't attempt to use the current version of the code from the new application. Your ability to use the existing code is determined by how you created the code library. For example, you might have a better chance of using it when the code library hides the details of the code within classes.

Testing the Converted Application

At some point, you'll have a shiny new converted application. Of course, you don't even know whether the application will work. In many cases, you'll have to search through the code by hand looking for deprecated features and clean up any mysterious errors that suddenly appeared during the conversion process before you can do anything else.

During the examination process, when you're searching for errors and odd conversion problems, you should also make notes within the code. The Task List can become your best friend during this process. Make comments using the special keywords that appear in the task list. The default keywords include HACK, TODO, UNDONE, and UnresolvedMergeConflict. It's actually best to add new keywords to the list for the conversion process. To perform this task, select the Tools ➤ Options command to display the Options dialog box. Check Show All Settings in the Options dialog box. Select the Environment\Task List folder shown in Figure 24.4.

Beginning all of the keywords with the word, Convert, as shown in Figure 24.5 makes their purpose clear. You can create as many keywords as needed to define the tasks you need to perform clearly or to designate areas of the code that can cause problems so that you can find them with greater ease during testing.

FIGURE 24.4
Add task list keywords for the conversion process and use them to add items to your task list.

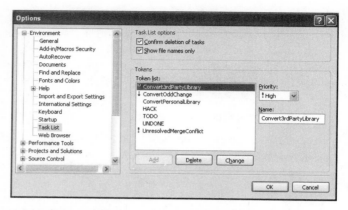

The test phase should begin with unit testing—just as you did when putting the application together initially. Performing unit testing helps you locate obvious problems quickly. Breaking the code up into pieces also helps you ascertain the effects of the conversion with greater accuracy. Because the point of conversion is to gain a benefit in flexibility, functionality, or performance, you want to be sure you can point out these differences and quantify them.

Perform integration testing next. Again, you're looking to put the application back together as you originally did. This is the point where good notes come into play. Notes can help you figure out the best way to put the application together and point out any problems that you had in the past. It's a good idea to know about these problems because you don't want to blame an existing condition on the conversion. Make sure you make a record of issues that you can definitely track now as a conversion issue. It's also important to continue looking for application differences and track any changes you notice. Track both positive and negative changes—both are important.

Some developers would stop when they had the application put together and call the application finished. However, you need to perform at least one additional step in the testing process—user testing. Users who have used the application every day are bound to notice differences that you don't see. It's not that they're any more adept than you are, but they work with the application continuously, so even small changes become obvious. Users also help you quantify the quality of the change—how it affected performance, reliability, usability, and other user-related issues.

Stress testing is a good addition to your repertoire if you don't already perform this task. It's not only important to determine what it takes to make the application fail but also to determine how it fails. The way in which the application fails can tell you a lot about the changes that the conversion has created. You can determine whether Microsoft really did fix the bugs that you had expected them to fix. It's also possible to see whether the application runs twice as fast, as you thought it would, or it has become a memory hog, which is an effect that you wanted to avoid. Using stress testing makes it possible to see how the application will fail so you know what to expect when the stress condition actually occurs.

Exporting Templates

Templates represent a type of conversion. You're converting a project or project item into a form that someone else can use. Fortunately, this process is a lot less error prone than converting an old .NET project into another form. The output works very reliably, and you'll find that it's a great way to share both projects and code.

To start the export process, you select the File ➢ Export Template command. You'll see the Export Template Wizard dialog box shown in Figure 24.5. This dialog box lets you choose the project you want to export (you must have the project loaded into the IDE) and the kind of export you want to perform. You must select the correct language from the list—this wizard won't translate a C# program into a Visual Basic program.

The following sections describe how to perform a project or an item template export. Both of these sections assume that you're starting at the Export Template Wizard dialog box shown in Figure 24.5.

NOTE   Pay close attention to how easy it is to export templates in the sections that follow. If you work in a team environment, you don't want developers to exchange templates freely and you will need to create a company policy regarding this feature. Otherwise, you could end up with a mix of rogue project types that developers use as freely as the carefully designed templates that you create.

FIGURE 24.5
Choose the kind of export that you want to perform from Visual Web Developer.

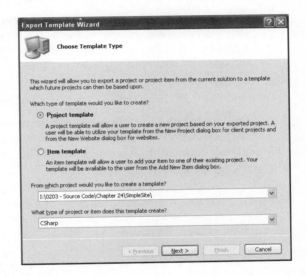

Creating a Project Template

A project template lets you share a project setup with someone else. The project template contains everything that your project contains. Consequently, if you built personal Web sites for a living and have a set of features that you always provide, you create the initial project and save it as a template. Using this technique saves time because you'll always start the project at the point where you're customizing it, rather than building the entire project from scratch every time.

The goal, then, is to build only part of an application—the common part that you'll use more than one time. If the application is already complete, then it's probably too late to build a good template from it because someone else would end up removing more material than they would use from the project. Of course, it isn't always easy to guess the point at which the template becomes the most usable, so you might have to try a few times before you get just the right setup. Use the following steps to export a project template. You'll find the export example in the `\Chapter 24\SimpleSite` folder of the source code on the Sybex Web site.

1. Select Project Template in the Export Template Wizard dialog box.

2. Choose the project from the project list and the language that the project uses from the list of available language choices.

3. Click Next. You'll see the Select Template Options dialog box shown in Figure 24.6. The figure shows the various entries filled out so you can see examples of what to enter.

4. Choose a template icon. Type a name for your project—make sure the name is descriptive because the user will have to select the project based on the name you provide. Type a description that tells the user of your template what to expect as output.

5. Choose the options you want to use for the template. Check the Automatically Import the Template into Visual Studio option when you want to make this template part of your personal setup. Check the Display an Explorer Window on the Output Files Folder if you want to see the output folder when the template is complete.

6. Note the location of the template output shown in the Output Location field. Highlight the content of the field and press Ctrl+C to save this information to the clipboard.

7. Click Finish. The Export Template Wizard creates a ZIP file containing all of the elements of your project. Depending on the options you selected, you might also see an Explorer window like the one shown in Figure 24.7 containing your project.

If you chose the Automatically Import the Template into Visual Studio option, you'll want to perform one additional check. Choose the File ➢ New ➢ Web Site command to display the New Web Site dialog box. Your template will appear in the My Templates section, as shown in Figure 24.8. Notice that the project uses the icon you selected, has the name you chose, and provides the description you typed into the wizard. Try creating a project using the template to verify that it works as anticipated.

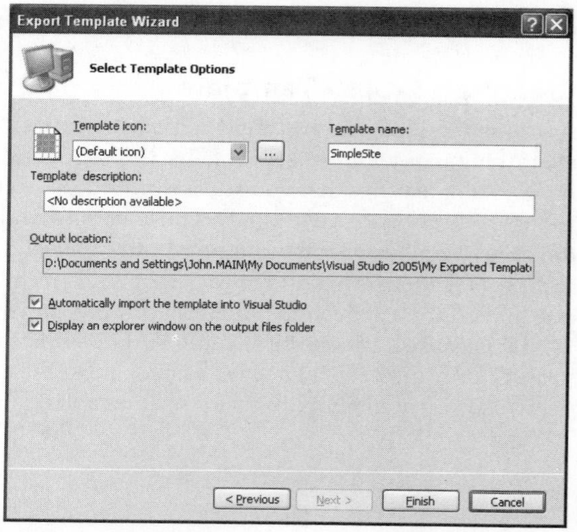

FIGURE 24.6
Determine the icon, template name, and description you want to use for the template.

FIGURE 24.7
The Explorer window displays the ZIP file containing your project template.

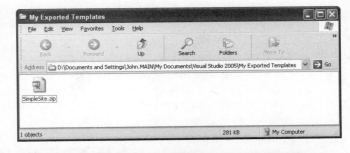

FIGURE 24.8
Verify that your template actually appears where you thought it would.

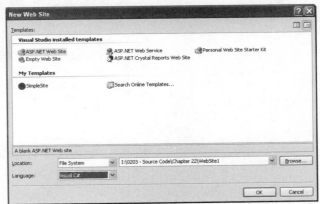

Of course, this entire process begs the question of what you should do with project templates that don't quite work as anticipated. Simply erase the ZIP file from your exported template folder (see Figure 24.7). In addition to the exported template folder, you'll need to remove the two entries for this project from the language folder for your Visual Web Developer installation. For example, when you create a Visual Basic project, you'll need to find the entries in the `\Documents and Settings\Your Name\My Documents\Visual Studio\ProjectTemplates\Visual Web Developer\VisualBasic` and `\Documents and Settings\Your Name\Application Data\Microsoft\VWDExpress\8.0\ProjectTemplatesCache\Visual Web Developer\VisualBasic` folders. Consequently, this change isn't permanent—it's merely inconvenient.

Creating an Item Template

Sometimes you don't need to save an entire project—all you need is an item from that project. For example, you might create a Cascading Style Sheet (CSS) file that you want to use with every project. You can save just this item as a template. The following steps show you how to create a new item template. You'll find the export example in the `\Chapter 24\SimpleSite` folder of the source code on the Sybex Web site.

1. Select Item Template in the Export Template Wizard dialog box.

2. Choose the project from the project list and the language that the project uses from the list of available language choices.

3. Click Next. You'll see the Select Item To Export dialog box shown in Figure 24.9. While it's possible to select more than one item to export, you'll generally get better results when you export one item at a time.

4. Click Next. You'll see the Select Item References dialog box shown in Figure 24.10. It's important to export all of the references that this item uses (which might not be any at all for an item such as a graphic). However, don't include any references that the item doesn't need. For example, even if your project uses the `System.XML.DLL`, don't export it unless the item actually uses it.

FIGURE 24.9
Choose the items that you want to export from the selected project.

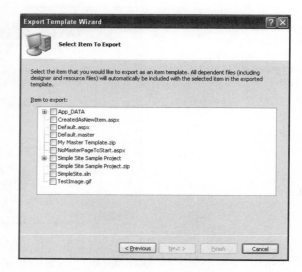

FIGURE 24.10
Select only the references that the item you want to export actually uses.

5. Click Next. You'll see the Item to Export dialog box shown in Figure 24.6. The wizard offers you the same choices for an item that it does for a project.

6. Choose a template icon. Type a descriptive name for the item. Type a description that tells the user of your template what to expect as output.

7. Choose the options you want to use for the template. Check the Automatically Import the Template into Visual Studio option when you want to make this template part of your personal setup. Check the Display an Explorer Window on the Output Files Folder if you want to see the output folder when the template is complete.

8. Note the location of the template output shown in the Output Location field. Highlight the content of the field and press Ctrl+C to save this information to the clipboard.

9. Click Finish. The Export Template Wizard creates a ZIP file containing all of the elements of your project. Depending on the options you selected, you might also see an Explorer window like the one shown in Figure 24.8 containing the item you exported.

As with the project template, you'll want to verify that the item template actually appears in the list of items that you can use. In this case, right-click the project in Solution Explorer and choose Add New Item from the context menu. You'll see the Add New Item dialog box shown in Figure 24.11. Notice that the template appears in the My Templates section.

You can remove an item template you no longer need using the same technique as for a project template. Begin by removing the template from your exported templates folder shown in Figure 24.8. In this case, you would remove the template entries from the `\Documents and Settings\Your Name\Application Data\Microsoft\VWDExpress\8.0\ItemTemplatesCache\Visual Web Developer\VisualBasic` and `\Documents and Settings\Your Name\My Documents\Visual Studio\ItemTemplates\Visual Web Developer\VisualBasic` folders.

FIGURE 24.11
Verify that the template you created is accessible from the Add New Item dialog box.

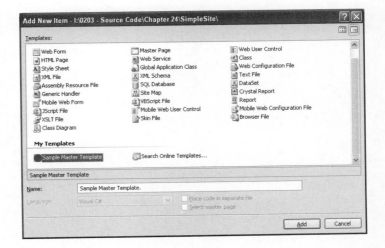

Defining Your Development Goals

This chapter has provided some guidelines for moving an application from Visual Studio .NET 2003 to Visual Studio 2005. You've discovered the pros and cons of such a move and learned about the pitfalls you'll encounter. Of course, planning helps reduce any potential problems that you might encounter. The biggest concept this chapter promotes is detailed testing after the application conversion to ensure you don't miss any hidden version-related problems with the converted application.

Before you do anything, consider the risks of moving your project to Visual Studio 2005. Defining what you expect and how you plan to achieve your goals will reduce the risk of failure when upgrading a project. Once you decide that the risks are low enough, it's time for you to plan your first application update. Start with a small project. In fact, you might want to start with a simple project you create in Visual Studio .NET 2003 for the sole purpose of testing. Don't make the test application too simple or you won't run into any significant problems that you need to consider as part of a real project upgrade, but don't spend a lot of time with this first application either. The point is to go through all of the steps defined in this chapter on a trial run to ensure you have a good process in place before you begin the real conversion process.

Some developers reading this book probably started working with Visual Web Developer Express. Chapter 25 provides help in getting that Express project moved to Visual Studio 2005—in essence, moving the project from the experimental stage to use within your organization. At some point, you'll want to move larger projects to the robust environment that Visual Studio 2005 can provide. Chapter 25 provides you with tips and hints on performing such an upgrade. More importantly, you'll discover where to look for potential upgrades to the application as a whole so it works more efficiently and reliably.

Chapter 25

Moving to Visual Studio 2005

Many developers use Visual Web Developer Express to begin learning about the new features that Microsoft included in the latest versions of the .NET Framework and ASP.NET. Because Visual Web Developer Express is very low cost and incurs little risk for you or your organization, it's a perfect way to start. Of course, you won't develop insignificant examples as part of your research, which means the code in Visual Web Developer has some value to both you and your organization. However, at some point, Visual Web Developer Express simply won't provide the tools you need, so the move to Visual Studio is essential.

This chapter addresses the code movement process from a little project to big project perspective. It assumes that you've experimented with Visual Web Developer Express and now need the full capabilities that Visual Studio can provide. The change in environment is a natural part of working with ASP.NET—you're moving from the learning to the using phase. Of course, it's not just physical size that determines the kind of programming environment you need—in many cases, you'll also need better functionality, access to additional tools, and an increased number of project templates. Moving your code can also buy all of these added features.

After you make the move from Visual Web Developer Express, you need to test your code in its new environment. You'll want to look for all of the normal usage problems, but it's also helpful to ensure your code is actually using all of those new features you needed. Consequently, you need to perform tests that check for code use within the application to ensure you're seeing the kinds of changes that you had expected.

Working with your code in the full version of Visual Web Developer also means it's far more likely that you'll also use a full version of IIS, rather than the built-in Web server. Consequently, you'll want to know how to compile the code before you check it to see how it really performs. This chapter also discusses how to use the new ASPNet_Compiler utility.

Finally, removing Visual Web Developer Express and replacing it with Visual Studio 2005 can produce some unwanted problems. The most critical of these problems is that your system might suddenly decide to ignore the ASP.NET file extensions. The code is correct, but it doesn't execute correctly. The final section of this chapter describes how to fix the problem.

Preserving Your Code

You've spent a lot of time putting the code together for your application, so it's important to preserve that investment as you move the application from Visual Web Developer Express to Visual Studio 2005. Fortunately, this process is a lot easier than converting a project from previous versions of Visual Studio .NET. All you really need to do is get the code onto Internet Information

Server (IIS), define it as an application, and create a solution (SLN) file for it. The following sections describe this process and help you make the big move without losing any code.

WARNING   Never assume that anything is going to work right the first time. If you haven't made a backup of your code already, make sure you do it before you move it to Visual Studio and IIS. Even though this process is relatively safe, you don't want to take any chances with the code you worked so hard to create.

Moving the Code to IIS

Moving the code to IIS isn't as simple as creating a folder for your application and hoping for the best. You need to create an application environment on IIS for the application. Of course, you'll begin by creating a folder within the `\Inetpub\wwwroot` folder and copying the code to it. Copy everything but the SLN and SUO files.

At this point, you need to change the folder into an application. The following steps show how to accomplish this task.

1. Open the Internet Information Services console found in the Administrative Tools folder of the Control Panel. You'll see a display similar to the one shown in Figure 25.1. The precise arrangement of folders and even Web sites on your system will differ from the one shown here, but the point of interest is the folder holding your code. This example relies on a new application called SimpleSite that you'll find in the `\Chapter 25\SimpleSite` folder of the source code on the Sybex Web site.

2. Right-click the folder containing the source code and choose Properties from the context menu. Select the Directory tab. You'll see a Properties dialog box like the one shown in Figure 25.2.

3. Click Create. IIS creates a new application with a name based on the folder name for the source code.

4. Select the Scripts and Executables option in the Execute Permissions field. Changing this option lets the ASP.NET executable code perform its task. Check the Write option. If you don't choose this option, the IDE won't be able to save code changes to the folder.

FIGURE 25.1
Locate the folder containing your application code in the Internet Information Services console.

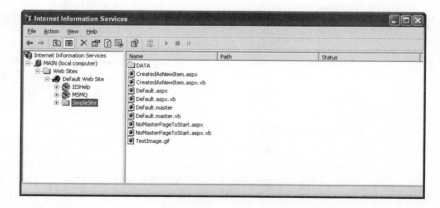

5. Choose the Documents tab. Remove the existing documents and add `Default.ASPX` to the list, as shown in Figure 25.3. Making this modification ensures that the user automatically sees the default page for your application when they open the Web site.

6. Select the ASP.NET tab. You'll see ASP.NET-specific information, as shown in Figure 25.4. Make sure you have the correct version selected for this application (IIS defaults to the latest version installed on your machine) and perform any required configuration editing.

At this point, your application is ready to use. You'll want to perform any required security and other standard setups that you would with any Web application. For example, you might want to create custom Web pages for the various error messages that your Web site can display.

FIGURE 25.2
Select the Directory tab to change your source folder into an application.

FIGURE 25.3
Set the default page so the user automatically sees the first page of your Web application.

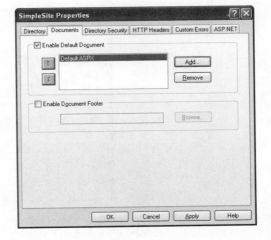

The ASP.NET configuration can become important depending on what you expect from the application. Figure 25.5 shows the ASP.NET Configuration Settings dialog box that appears when you click Edit Configuration on the ASP.NET tab of the Properties dialog box. This dialog box contains a wealth of settings that are only available to ASP.NET users. The settings only affect the current application, so you can easily set each application as needed.

FIGURE 25.4
Verify the ASP.NET information for your system and perform any required configuration.

FIGURE 25.5
Change the ASP.NET configuration as needed once you move the application to IIS.

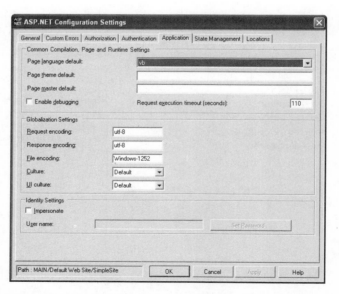

All of the tabs provide valuable settings. However, for the developer just moving the application to a server, the Application tab shown in Figure 25.5 is the most important. Notice that this tab lets you set a default master page and default theme for the application. When a page doesn't specify a master page or theme value, ASP.NET automatically applies these values. Check the Enable

Debugging option when you want to debug your new application. Make sure you adjust the timeout setting as needed, too. Otherwise, you'll experience timeouts whenever the server needs to use resources with a longer load time, such as a database.

Creating a Solution File

Moving the code to IIS and configuring IIS to use it correctly is actually the hardest part of the process. However, you still want to set up your IDE to work with the application you've moved to IIS. The first step is to make sure that you don't have an SLN file in that folder. Otherwise, Visual Studio .NET will attempt to use the old SLN, and you'll see some very odd results on screen. The following steps get you started.

1. Select the File ➤ Open ➤ Web Site command to display the Open Web Site dialog box. Start with Step 5 if you're using a remote connection.

WARNING   The Web server must have FrontPage Server Extensions installed when you use a remote connection. Otherwise, the Visual Studio .NET IDE displays an error message when it attempts to open the Web site. See the "Fixing FrontPage Server Extension Problems" section of the chapter for details on fixing this problem. You don't have to have FrontPage Extensions installed to use a Local IIS connection.

2. Choose the Local IIS option when using a local connection and you'll see the Local Internet Information Server display shown in Figure 25.6.

3. Highlight the project you want to use and click Open. The IDE opens the Web site for you.

4. Select the File ➤ Save All command. The IDE displays a Save File As dialog box where you can enter the name of the solution file. You can now access the solution as you would any other solution on your system.

5. Chose the Remote Sites option when using a remote connection, and you'll see the Remote Sites display shown in Figure 25.7.

FIGURE 25.6
The Local Internet Information Server display lets you choose local projects.

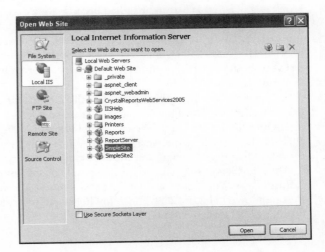

FIGURE 25.7
Use a remote site connection for Web applications on other machines.

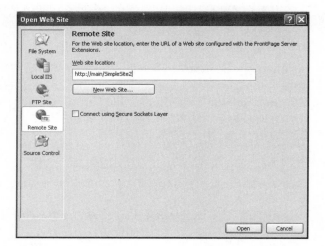

6. Type the location of the Web site you want to open. As an alternative, you can click browse and use the Select a Folder URL to Open dialog box to find the Web site.

7. Click Open. The IDE loads the project from the remote Web site. This process can require a few minutes when the project is large.

8. Select the File ➤ Save All command. The IDE displays a Save File As dialog box where you can enter the name of the solution file. You can now access the solution as you would any other solution on your system.

Fixing FrontPage Server Extension Problems

Remote Web sites can run into problems when you move an application from Visual Web Developer Express to IIS because a remote connection requires FrontPage Server Extensions. Some developers won't even have this feature installed because they don't need it in many cases. Begin by verifying you have the FrontPage Server Extensions installed by opening the Add or Remove Programs applet found in the Control Panel. Click Add/Remove Windows Components. Locate Internet Information Services (IIS) and click Details. The exact FrontPage version number can vary by Windows version, but you should have this option checked in the Internet Information Services (IIS) dialog box shown in Figure 25.8.

When you don't have this feature installed, check the option to install it as you would any other Windows feature. Once the new feature is installed, restart IIS by right-clicking the computer entry in the Internet Information Services console shown in Figure 25.1 and choosing All Tasks ➤ Restart IIS from the context menu. Adding FrontPage Server Extensions to IIS won't add them to your application, so you need to configure the application next.

Open the Server Extensions Administrator console found in the Administrative Tools folder of the Control Panel. You'll see a misnamed fpmmc (short for Server Extensions Administrator) window like the one shown in Figure 25.9. The following steps show you how to configure your application to use FrontPage Server Extensions.

FIGURE 25.8
Verify that you have
FrontPage Server
Extensions installed.

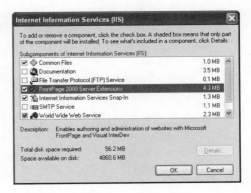

FIGURE 25.9
Use the Server Exten-
sions Administrator
to configure your
application.

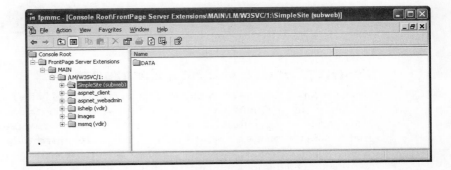

1. Locate your application in the left pane.

2. Right-click the application entry and choose All Tasks ➢ Configure Server Extensions from the
   context menu. You'll see the New Subweb Wizard dialog box.

3. Click Next. You'll see the Subweb Name dialog box.

4. Type a name for your application in the Title field. Generally, using your application name
   works fine.

5. Click Next. You'll see the Access Control dialog box. This dialog box contains two entries. The
   default entry uses the same administrator as the parent Web for this subweb. This is the only
   option you should choose unless you have a custom administrator that you want to use—most
   people don't because the default administrator works fine.

6. Click Next. You'll see a completion dialog box.

7. Click Finish. The Server Extensions Administrator configures your application to use
   FrontPage Extensions. It's easy to verify that the process worked as expected. Simply open the
   application in the Internet Information Services console and view its Properties page. You'll
   see a Server Extensions tab like the one shown in Figure 25.10.

FIGURE 25.10
Verify that your application now has FrontPage Server Extensions support.

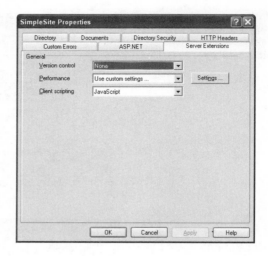

Testing Code in the New Environment

Moving an application to IIS, configuring, and creating an SLN file for it isn't the end of the road. Actually, it's the beginning of the real work for you as a developer. Before you do anything else, make sure you rebuild the entire solution. Keeping old files around is a sure way to cause yourself untold grief. Make sure you use the Build ➢ Rebuild Solution command, rather than just click the Build Solution button on the Build toolbar.

After you compile the solution completely, try accessing it from a browser. In many cases, the Web site runs just fine. However, even though things look fine, it doesn't mean they are fine. Make sure you test each page to ensure it loads and works as anticipated in the new environment.

Unfortunately, a move doesn't always go as anticipated. Finding even one page that doesn't work right is your signal that you might need to perform more extensive testing. The tips and techniques in the "Testing the Converted Application" section of Chapter 24 work just as well for applications that you have moved to a new location. Use these techniques to locate the sources of problems in your application and remedy them prior to making the application available to end users.

Compiling Your Code Using *ASPNet_Compiler.EXE*

One of the tasks you'll want to perform after changing versions of Visual Web Developer is to compile your code. The compilation process helps you assess your code in a number of ways. First, you can use this technique to develop a list of possible problems with your code. The compiler will output errors that you won't normally see, and you can simply send those errors to a text file for later analysis. Second, using the compiler helps you check your code more quickly. The pages will load at the same speed as they do for the user. Consequently, you can see how the Web pages perform in the new environment. You'll find the ASPNet_Compiler utility in the \WINDOWS\Microsoft.NET\Framework\ *Version* folder of your hard drive. It uses the command line syntax shown here.

```
ASPNet_Compiler [-?] [-m MetabasePath | -v VirtualPath [-p PhysicalDir]]
[TargetDir]
```

The compiler doesn't need very much information to get started. You must supply some information or the utility will display an error. For example, you must supply a path to the Web server folder. The following list tells you about the various command line options.

-?   Displays a list of options that you can use with this utility.

-m *MetabasePath*   Provides the full Internet Information Server (IIS) metabase path to the application. You can't use this switch with either the -v or -p switches.

NOTE   The metabase is essentially a database of information about IIS. Think of it as a kind of IIS registry. Microsoft moved the IIS settings out of the registry and into the metabase to allow developers to make changes to IIS without rebooting the system. Because the metabase is separate from the registry, you can also move the IIS settings to another machine with few problems. You can learn more about the metabase at `http://www.microsoft.com/technet/prodtechnol/ windows2000serv/technologies/iis/tips/metabase.mspx`. Another good article to read is the one on the WindowsNetworking.com site at `http://www.windowsnetworking.com/ kbase/WindowsTips/WindowsNT/AdminTips/IIS/IISMetabaseRegistry.html`.

-v *VirtualPath*   Provides the virtual path to the application you want to compile. The virtual path is the location of the application, as the user would see it. For example, if the user accesses the application using `http://myapp`, you would provide `/myapp` as the virtual path. You can't use this switch with the -m switch.

NOTE   If you omit both the -m and -v switches, the ASPNet_Compiler utility assumes that you want to compile the default application as listed in the IIS metabase.

-p *PhysicalDir*   Provides the physical location of the application on the hard drive. If you omit this switch, the ASPNet_Compiler utility uses the IIS metabase to locate the application. You must use this switch with the -v switch.

-nologo   Runs the ASPNet_Compiler utility without displaying a logo. You can use this switch with automated processing techniques.

The final optional argument is `TargetDir`. You use this argument to define the physical path of the compiled application. If you don't provide this argument, the ASPNet_Compiler utility compiles the application in place (within the same physical location as the application source code).

Fixing File Association Problems

You're going to run into problems with IIS file associations on your system. No matter what you do, IIS is going to suddenly forget it can process ASP.NET pages at some point unless you keep your machine going 24 hours a day and never change anything—an impractical setup for many people. Fortunately, Microsoft realized early on that you would need some method for repairing IIS and provided some utilities to do the job. The following sections describe the two utilities you need to keep your copy of IIS worry free.

Using the ASPNet_RegIIS Utility

One of the most common problems that you'll experience with IIS is that it forgets how to process the ASP.NET and associated pages. Your first cue that something is wrong is that IIS suddenly starts displaying error messages whenever someone requests an ASP.NET page. Of course, a good many other problems can occur to cause this problem, but don't rule out IIS as a source of the problem. You can verify IIS as a source of problems by looking in two areas.

The first source of problems occurs when the ASP.NET services don't startup correctly. You can verify this source of problems by opening the Services console found in the Administrative Tools folder of the Control Panel. Check the ASP.NET Admin Service and ASP.NET State Service entries shown in Figure 25.11. If these entries show Stopped status, even though the service is set for automatic startup, the problem is usually one where a registration problem has occurred and the service can't locate the resources it needs.

Another problem that occurs is that IIS actually loses the file extension support it requires. If IIS doesn't know what to do with a particular file extension, it usually displays an error message or does something unexpected (such as displaying your source code when available on screen).

You can verify a file extension problem by opening the Internet Information Services console located in the Administrative Tools folder of the Control Panel. Open the Web site that hosts your application. Right-click the application and choose Properties from the context menu. Select the Directory tab. You'll see the Properties dialog box shown in Figure 25.12. Click Configuration and you'll see the Application Configuration dialog box shown in Figure 25.12.

Notice that the Application Configuration dialog box contains entries for every file extension that this copy of IIS supports. The extensions appear in the first column of the Application Mappings table and, in this case, ASPX isn't one of them. The second column contains the path and name of the DLL that supports the file extension, while the third column shows which verbs (actions) the DLL can handle. An error in any of the three columns usually indicates a problem with the IIS setup.

NOTE   Always locate the ASPNet_RegIIS utility for the version of ASP.NET that you want to use with your Web application. Each version of the .NET Framework will have a separate folder in the \WINDOWS\Microsoft.NET\Framework folder. Select the folder that contains the version you want to use.

FIGURE 25.11
Determine whether
the ASP.NET services
can access the resources
they need.

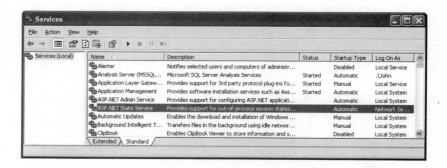

FIGURE 25.12
Set the default page so
the user automatically
sees the first page of your
Web application.

It's possible to fix some of these problems using manual techniques and you can certainly try a manual registration or fixing the file extensions if you think the error is minor. However, in most cases, you'll need to register ASP.NET again to ensure proper IIS operation. You use the ASPNet_RegIIS utility found in the \WINDOWS\Microsoft.NET\Framework*Version* folder of your system to perform this task. Here are the most commonly used command line options for this tool.

-i Install this version of ASP.NET on IIS. Using this option updates all of the script maps, updates the file extensions, registers any DLLs, and generally makes the same changes that a new Visual Studio .NET installation would make. This option also updates any existing features to the version of ASP.NET that you're installing. Use this option when you want to ensure the ASP.NET installation completely refreshes and fixes any major errors in the system.

NOTE Script mapping is the process of matching an application to a particular version of the .NET Framework for execution. ASP.NET supports the concept of maintaining multiple versions of the .NET Framework on a machine so that you can use the version that application relies on, rather than the latest version installed. This approach makes it less likely that your application will break because of an upgrade to ASP.NET. During an update, you must decide whether to maintain the current mapping—support for the current version of the .NET Framework—or update to the latest version of the .NET Framework. All of the options that discuss the script map (some sources use scriptmap) are referring to this process of maintaining the correct version of ASP.NET for each application. The ASP.NET Web site at http://www.asp.net/faq/SideBySide.aspx has an article that details the process for using more than one version of ASP.NET on a system.

-ir Perform all of the tasks required to register ASP.NET on IIS. This option doesn't perform any updates. Consequently, this option completes much faster than the -i option, but isn't as complete.

-iru Install this version of ASP.NET on IIS. This switch is the same as the -i option, but it verifies that no existing applications are using ASP.NET first. When the utility detects existing applications, it performs the installation and registration, but maintains any existing script maps so the existing applications don't break.

-enable   Enables ASP.NET in the IIS security console (IIS 6.0 or later) when used with the -i, -ir, or −r command line switches. You don't need to use this switch with older versions of IIS (including Windows XP, which is version 5.1 in most cases).

-disable   Disables ASP.NET in the IIS security console (IIS 6.0 or later) when used with the -i, -ir, or -r command line switches. You don't need to use this switch with older versions of IIS (including Windows XP, which is version 5.1 in most cases).

-s *Path*   Install the script maps for this version of ASP.NET at the specified path, rather than use the default path. This instruction follows the script map path recursively to install all subdirectories as well. Generally, you don't want to use this option unless you have a custom IIS setup.

-sn *Path*   Install the script maps for this version of ASP.NET at the specified path, rather than use the default path. This instruction doesn't use recursive installation, so you only obtain the script map at the top level. Generally, you don't want to use this option unless you have a custom IIS setup.

-r   Install this version of ASP.NET and update all of the script maps starting at the IIS metabase root for all of the script maps below the root. (See the note about the IIS metabase in the "Compiling Your Code Using *ASPNet_Compiler.EXE*" section of the chapter.) This switch updates all of the script maps regardless of the original version.

-u   Uninstall this version of ASP.NET. This switch automatically updates existing script maps to the highest version of ASP.NET still installed on the machine. If this is the last version of ASP.NET on the machine, then the application removes the existing script maps and your ASP.NET applications will no longer run.

-ua   Uninstall all versions of ASP.NET on the machine. This switch also removes all script maps—your ASP.NET applications will no longer run.

-k *Path*   Remove all script maps to any version of ASP.NET from the specified path. This switch removes the script maps recursively, so it removes all of the script maps for an entire application. Any subapplications will also stop working.

-kn *Path*   Remove all script maps to any version of ASP.NET from the specified path. This switch doesn't remove the script maps recursively, so other applications in a path are unaffected. Only the application specified by the path variable is affected by the change.

-lv   List all versions of ASP.NET installed on the machine. The output information includes the version status and installation path.

-lk   List the paths of the IIS metabase keys where the ASP.NET script map is defined, along with the ASP.NET version. Keys that inherit the ASP.NET script map from a parent don't appear in the listing.

-c   Install the client side scripts for this version of ASP.NET to the \aspnet_client subdirectory of each IIS site directory.

-e   Remove the client-side scripts for this version of ASP.NET from the \aspnet_client subdirectory of each IIS site directory.

-ea   Remove the client-side scripts for all versions of ASP.NET from the `\aspnet_client` subdirectory of each IIS site directory.

-w   Install the Web administrator tool.

-wu   Remove the Web administrator tool.

-wct *ConnectionType*   Change the connection type for the Web administrator tool. The `ConnectionType` value can include HF (hosted and forms authentication), HW (hosted and windows authentication), and L (local authentication).

-config+   Enable remote access to configuration information. This is a good option for team development on a private network, but an open invitation to cracker activity on a public system.

-config-   Disable remote system access to configuration information. Always use this option for public Web sites.

?   Display the complete list of help switches.

The `-i` command line switch is usually the only option you need when you want to fix errors in the ASP.NET setup. Start the utility at a command prompt so you can see the progress it makes. Figure 25.13 shows a typical installation sequence.

NOTE   Performing a fresh installation of ASP.NET can require several minutes to complete. Don't disturb the system during this process—go get a cup of coffee instead. Be patient—the process won't complete for several minutes even on a fast system.

Figure 25.13 has two important pieces of information in it. First, the utility completes by providing a success message. Second, it tells you there are errors. Check the error log in the folder specified. In most cases, you'll see an error message telling you that the W3SVC service didn't start in a timely manner. If this is the only error that you see (it will appear at least twice) and the Web service is currently operating as anticipated, you don't have to worry about the errors. In some cases, you will have to start the Web service manually, but in many cases you won't. Make sure you also check your ASP.NET services and manually start them if needed. Finally, check the Application Configuration dialog box again. Figure 25.14 shows that the dialog box on the test system now shows the correct entries for ASP.NET. Compare this dialog box to Figure 25.12 and you'll see that ASP.NET adds a lot of file extensions.

FIGURE 25.13
Verify that the installation takes place without error on your system.

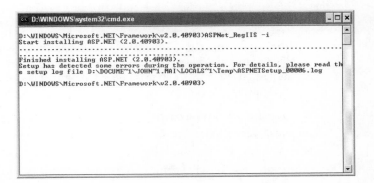

FIGURE 25.14
ASP.NET adds a lot of file
extensions to your Appli-
cation Configuration
dialog box.

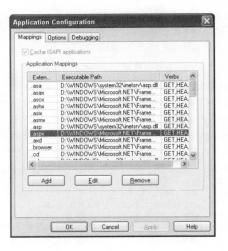

Using the ASPNet_RegSQL Utility

As with ASP.NET, sometimes you'll lose the SQL Server connection for your Web applications. The ASPNet_RegSQL utility helps you fix any connectivity problems without reinstalling SQL Server and ASP.NET. This utility operates separately from the ASPNet_RegIIS utility, so you might have to use both to restore application functionality completely when you rely on a database to implement certain features.

Unlike the ASPNet_RegIIS utility, the ASPNet_RegSQL utility comes with two interfaces. The first operates at the command line, while the second uses a wizard to accomplish its work. Because the ASPNet_RegSQL utility is more complex than the ASPNet_RegIIS utility, you'll want to use the wizard version of the utility whenever possible. The following sections describe both interfaces.

USING THE COMMAND LINE

You'll use the command line interface for the ASPNet_RegSQL utility when you work with scripts or when you don't feel the wizard provides sufficient access to a particular feature. Generally, the command line version is harder to use and error prone. That said, here are the connection-oriented command line switches for this utility.

WARNING   The command line switches are case sensitive. If you use the wrong case, the utility will fail in most cases, and might perform unanticipated and unwanted actions in other cases. You must use the dash (-) rather than a slash (/) when typing a command line switch. Failure to use the dash always results in an error.

-?   Displays a complete list of switches for this utility.

-W   Places the utility in wizard mode. This is the best mode to use for reconfiguring the SQL Server connection. See the "Working with the ASPNet_RegSQL Utility Wizard" section for details.

-S *Server*   Specifies the name of the server when creating a connection.

-U *Username*   Defines the name of the user when creating a connection.

-P *Password*   Defines the user password when creating a connection.

-E   Sets the utility to authenticate the user with Windows credentials, rather than a username and password when creating a connection.

-C *ConnectionString*   Contains the arguments required to create the connection. The connection string takes the place of the username, password, and server name command line switches. Don't include a database name as part of the connection string.

-sqlexportonly Filename   Sets the utility to generate a SQL script file for adding and removing the desired SQL Server features. The utility doesn't actually perform any changes when you specify this switch. You can use this switch with the -A, -R, −ssadd, and -ssremove switches.

Once you create a connection to SQL Server, you can perform various application service tasks. Here's a list of application service command line switches.

-A [all | m | r | p | s | c | w]   Use this switch with any of the optional keywords to add a feature to the SQL Server connection. You can use multiple switches together by specifying them as separate switches (-A m -A r) or by combining them into one switch (-A mr). The features include:

- **all**   All features
- **m**   Membership
- **r**   Role manager
- **p**   Profiles
- **s**   Site counters
- **c**   Personalization
- **w**   SQL Web event provider

-R [all | m | r | p | s | c | w]   Use this switch with any of the optional keywords to remove a feature from the SQL Server connection. You can use multiple switches together by specifying them as separate switches (-R m -R r) or by combining them into one switch (-R mr). The features include:

- **all**   All features, including all common tables and stored procedures
- **m**   Membership
- **r**   Role manager
- **p**   Profiles
- **s**   Site counters
- **c**   Personalization
- **w**   SQL Web event provider

-d *Database*   Contains the name of the database to use with application services. ASP.NET uses a default name of aspnetdb when you don't supply this value.

-Q   Sets the utility to perform all tasks quietly. You don't see confirmation or error messages. This is the mode to use with scripts and other forms of automation.

Besides application services tasks, you can also use the ASPNet_RegSQL utility to modify the cache dependency options. Here's a list of the command line switches you use to perform this task.

-d *Database*   Contains the name of the database to use for the cache dependency options. ASP.NET uses a default name of aspnetdb when you don't supply this value.

-ed   Enables the database for SQL cache dependency.

-dd   Disables the database for SQL cache dependency.

-et   Enables a particular table for SQL cache dependency. You must specify the -t command line switch to use this switch.

-et   Disables a particular table for SQL cache dependency. You must specify the -t command line switch to use this switch.

-t *Table*   Contains the name of the table to enable or disable for SQL cache dependency. You must also supply -et or -dt command line switch.

-lt   Lists all of the tables enabled for SQL cache dependency.

The final set of command line switches let you use the ASPNet_RegSQL utility to modify the session state options. Here's a list of the command line switches you use to perform this task.

-d *Database*   Contains the name of the database to use for the session state when the -sstype command line switch type is set to c (custom).

-ssadd   Adds support for the SQL Server mode session state.

-ssremove   Removes support for the SQL Server mode session state.

-sstype [t | p | c]   Defines the type of session state that SQL Server supports. These options include:

t   Defines a temporary session state. ASP.NET uses the tempdb database to store information. Stored procedures for managing the session appear in the ASPState database. ASP.NET doesn't persist any information when you start SQL Server. This is the default setting.

p   Defines a persisted session state. ASP.NET uses the ASPState database to store both state information and the stored procedures for managing the session. The information stays in place even after you restart SQL Server.

c   Defines a custom session state. ASP.NET stores both the state data and the stored procedures used to manage the session state in the custom database that you supply. You must combine this option with the -d command line switch.

Working with the ASPNet_RegSQL Utility Wizard

The command line version of the ASPNet_RegSQL utility works great for scripts, but you have a better option when making manual changes. Use the -W command line switch to place the ASPNet_RegSQL utility into wizard mode. When you use this switch, you'll see the ASP.NET SQL Server Setup Wizard appear. The following steps take you through the process of using this wizard.

1. Click Next to get past the Welcome dialog box. You'll see a Select a Setup Option dialog box. When you select the Remote Application Services Information from an Existing Database, the wizard takes you through a three-step process that removes SQL Server support from the system and then exits. The steps that follow assume that you're using the Configure SQL Server for Application Services option.

2. Select Configure SQL Server for Application Services and click Next. You'll see the Select Server and Database dialog box shown in Figure 25.15. This dialog box lets you choose the server and database that you want to work with, along with supplying your credentials for access to the server.

3. Choose the server and database you want to work with. Choose an authentication option. Click Next and you'll see a confirmation dialog box.

4. Click Next. The application will work for a few minutes as it configures the database. Eventually you'll see a completion dialog box.

5. Confirm that the configuration succeeded without error. Click Finish.

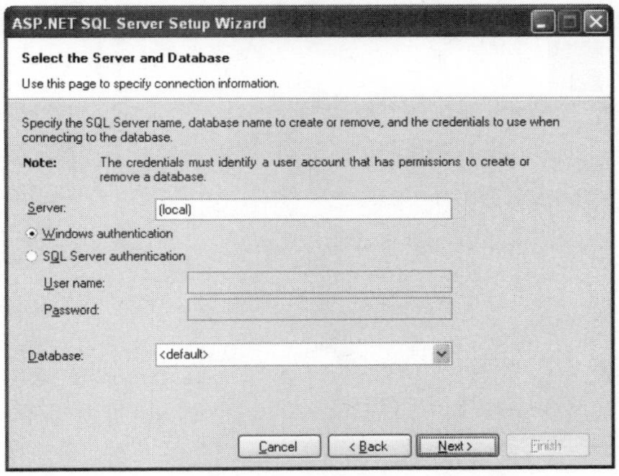

FIGURE 25.15
Choose the server and database that you want to configure.

Defining Your Development Goals

This chapter demonstrates the tasks you need to perform to move your application from Visual Web Developer Express to Visual Studio 2005. Most developers will begin trying out new ASP.NET 2.0 and .NET Framework 2.0 features using the Express products to determine whether a change even makes sense. However, once you get past that experimentation stage, you'll want to make the move to preserve your coding investment. You might not need to perform every task listed in this chapter, but make sure you take it step by step to ensure you don't miss anything critical either.

Now it's your turn to do some planning. You need to figure out when to make your move—changing development applications in the middle of a project is something you should avoid unless it's necessary. Make sure you have goals set for the upgrade. For example, consider what you expect to gain for every application and make those expectations part of a checklist you create. Ensure the testing regimen you create also verifies that the application actually makes use of the new functionality. In some cases, you might have to write new procedures and policies for working on code that considers these new features. For example, if you didn't have access to a testing utility before, such as the ActiveX Control Test Container, you'll want to add procedures for using it into your development process.

Congratulations! You've reached the last chapter of the book. However, your journey should also include the appendices for this book. Appendix A tells you how to avoid common development errors. None of these techniques appear in the book—I based them on a number of sources, so they do reflect real world problems. Appendix B describes how to work with character codes on Web pages. You might be surprised at the number of techniques you can use to get a special character to appear on screen. Appendix C provides 52 helpful tips you can use to optimize Windows better and faster. Try reading one at the start of every week and you'll find that you have a wealth of new ideas by the end of the year. Make sure you contact me at `JMueller@mwt.net` if you have any questions about this book. I'd also love to hear about your experiences working with Visual Studio 2005. Also, look on my Web site at `http://www.mwt.net/~jmueller/` for updates and additional information.

Appendix A

A Guide to Common Development Errors

All developers make mistakes. Part of the coding learning process is making mistakes and then learning from those mistakes. The difference between a good code writer and a great developer is often the willingness to make mistakes and learn from them. However, you don't always have to have a brick wall of bad code fall on you to learn a new technique or discover how to avoid errors. Sometimes, all you need to do is look at what someone else has done and obtain the lessons learned without making the same mistake. This appendix falls into the "learn from someone else's error" category—it contains a list of common errors that Web developers make and discusses how to avoid them.

Plan before You Write Code

It doesn't matter how small your project is, a failure to plan before you begin writing code is always an error. The problem is that these small projects tend to get bigger before you finish writing the application. Even personal projects can become labyrinthine in short order. Think about it this way—just as a builder needs a plan to construct a house, you need a plan to construct your application.

You could easily tell whether a builder decided to build a house without using a plan, and it's just as easy to determine when someone writes an application without one, as well. Application users can see that the application has design flaws because it doesn't work as anticipated. The plan that you use doesn't have to be very complicated, but you do need to think about these questions:

- What will the application do?
- How will the application accomplish its task?
- When will the application run?
- Who will use the application?
- Why is the application important?

Professional developers use a number of complex methods, such as the Unified Modeling Language (UML) (http://www.omg.org/gettingstarted/what_is_uml.htm), and applications, such as Microsoft Visio (http://office.microsoft.com/en-us/FX010857981033.aspx), to answer these questions. Because most Visual Web Developer applications are much smaller than these huge undertakings, you can normally answer the questions quite easily. Don't make this more complicated than you need to. You might answer the first question by saying that the application will display the pictures on your Web site.

The reason you want to go through this process is to ensure that you've thought about the application that you want to create. It's easier to answer the questions before you write any code instead of fixing the code later. Writing your answers down also helps you avoid making the application into something that you didn't intend. This is a common problem for everyone; even developers with a lot of experience write applications that quickly grow beyond the original intent.

Avoid Performance Bottlenecks

Web pages present all kinds of ways to waste resources and perform tasks more often than necessary. As the technology you use to create a Web page becomes more complex, the number of ways to create a performance bottleneck also increases. For this reason, you want to consider how to perform a specific task. Some developers feel obligated to use ASP.NET just because they're using Visual Web Developer to create their application. However, the smart way to develop the Web site is to rely on the least complex solution. Whenever possible, use standard HTML for static information to conserve resources. A help file doesn't change very often, so using HTML conserves resources. The following sections describe other ways to avoid performance bottlenecks.

Use *Page.IsPostBack* to Control Resource Use

When you need to use ASP.NET to create a Web page, you can avoid some common performance bottleneck issues through careful programming. For example, it's very likely that your Web page will contain one or more areas of initialization code. Letting this initialization code run every time the user calls the Web page can use resources inefficiently. Check whether the controls are already initialized using the `Page.IsPostback` property like this.

```
If (Not Page.IsPostback) Then
    ' Initialize the controls.
    MyControl.Text = "Hello"
    ... Other Controls ...
End If
```

Of course, this technique only works for static control initialization. A control that changes with every call will probably need initialization. In addition, remember that Web pages don't include the concept of state. ASP.NET pages keep track of the control state using various background techniques. Consequently, you might find that you do need to initialize some controls on each call. The point is to try the control using a static initialization whenever possible.

It's important to note that using `Page.IsPostback` can also help you avoid some difficult-to-find bugs in your Web page. For example, you might change the property value of a control programmatically in response to a user request. However, the change doesn't appear to stick—the control shows the old data on every call. The code to change the control looks fine, so you spend hours looking for the problem with a debugger. After a long search, you discover the problem occurs because the code re-initializes control's property on every call.

Perform Client-side Validation

Whenever possible, use client-side scripts to validate form entries for accuracy. Using server-side validation can result in a lot of extra network bandwidth usage, especially for large forms. When using server-side validation, the client sends the form to the server for approval every time the user moves to the next field on the form. Although you might not notice a large performance penalty when using a high-speed connection, the content back-and-forth validation traffic can cause significant performance problems when working on a low-speed connection such as dial-up.

Of course, you don't want to open a security breach in your setup and you must accommodate users that keep their scripting turned off. Consequently, you can't always use client-side validation, even if the performance hit of server-side validation is more than you'd like. When this situation occurs, try to divide the form into those elements that you must validate on the server and those that you can validate on the client. Using aggressive postprocessing can help a lot in this regard. Sometimes you can wait to catch the error when it first reaches the code behind for your application, rather than at the client or as part of a server-side validation control. However, make sure you do validate every entry the user makes.

Save the View State Only When Needed

All of the server-side controls that you use with Visual Web Developer set the `EnableViewState` property to `True` by default. What this means is that every control saves its state as part of the hidden `__VIEWSTATE` variable. The client and server send this information back and forth. Saving the view state information for a small control such as a text box isn't very resource intensive. However, when you start working with data grids, the price for saving that information increases dramatically. It's nothing for the variable to consume 10 KB or more of space, which means that you're transferring a lot of information for every call. Figure A.1 shows an example of a page that contains just a small data grid with eight entries on it.

Even this example is relatively resource intensive. The version of the page that saves the view state for the data grid consumes 5.6 KB, while a second version that doesn't use view state only requires 3.9 KB. (You'll find this example in the `\Appendix A\ViewState` folder of the source code on the Sybex Web site. The HTML sent to the browser with view state enabled appears in `Test1.HTM`, while the disabled version appears in `Test2.HTM`.) It's the same information, but in a smaller package. Add server-side validation to this example and you have a performance disaster in the making. Here's the best part. You can disable the view state and not lose any functionality. Because the data grid is rebuilt every time the client makes a request, saving the view state doesn't provide anything of value.

TIP You can always disable the view state of a control you can't see when the page is active. For example, the IDE will enable the view state for the `SqlDataSource` control, even though you can't see this control on screen. Controls that you can't see don't have a view state that you should save.

FIGURE A.1

Saving the view state makes sense when the control actually needs the information.

Don't get the idea that it's always a bad idea to enable the view state. Some controls, especially those with static data that the server won't recreate for every call, do need the view state enabled. However, using this feature only when you need it can make your application run a lot faster.

Set the Session State

The session state, like the view state, stores information about the application. However, the session state affects the application as a whole, rather than the status of a single control. Consequently, the session state has a larger effect on the functioning of your application. Unfortunately, as with the view state, the IDE always enables the session state. You can set the session state to one of three values: `True`, `False`, or `ReadOnly` using a page directive like this.

```
<%@ Page EnableSessionState="True" %>
<%@ Page EnableSessionState="ReadOnly" %>
<%@ Page EnableSessionState="False" %>
```

Setting the session state to `True` lets the application both read and write session state variables. Consequently, you can save session state information from one invocation of the page to another. However, this setting also consumes the most resources. Setting the session state to `ReadOnly` will let the application read the session state, but not change it. This setting is good when you need to work with the session state information because it uses fewer resources. Finally, set the session state to `False` to ensure that the application doesn't store the session state. Interestingly enough, this setting works more often than you might think.

Setting the session state to `ReadOnly` or `False` won't reduce the Web page size any (as demonstrated by `Test3.HTM`). However, you'll notice that the page loads significantly faster. In fact, the example page found in the `\Appendix A\ViewState` folder of the source code on the Sybex Web site is quite fast when you set the session state to `False` and noticeably faster when you set the session state to `ReadOnly`. The time savings come from the reduced preparation the server must perform to display the page. Even with the session state set to `False`, the example page, which displays the Categories table from the Northwind database, performs all standard tasks without a problem.

You also have several options for storing session state information in the `WeA.CONFIG` file. In this case, you can use the `<sessionState>` element to set the session state `Off` (no session state at all), `InProc` (the application stores the settings locally), `StateServer` (the settings appear on a remote server specifically designated for that task), `SQLServer` (the settings appear within a SQL Server database), or `Custom` (a custom configuration scenario that you create). A complete explanation of these options is outside the scope of this appendix, but generally, you'll want to use the `Off` option to get the best performance as shown here.

```
<configuration
 xmlns="http://schemas.microsoft.com/.NetConfiguration/v2.0">
    <system.web>
        <sessionState mode="Off" />
    </system.web>
</configuration>
```

Use Pure HTML Whenever Possible

Every time you drop an ASP.NET server control on the page, you're using processing cycles. The ASP.NET control requires server-side processing in all cases and additional client-side processing in some cases. Using pure HTML for the same task is far more efficient. Consequently, when you have a choice between an HTML tag and an ASP.NET control to implement a label, choose the HTML tag whenever possible.

Keep Your Data Safe

Security is the most talked about development issue today. It's true that better security will keep your data safer. In addition, well-designed security can reduce user confusion and frustration. However, security isn't the only consideration for data security. You also need to consider the reliability of adding, accessing, modifying, and deleting data as part of your application design. Underlying both of these issues is the code that you write. Using the development techniques in the following sections not only makes your data more secure but more reliable as well.

PUTTING THE TIME BACK INTO ACCESS

One of the biggest problems that developers face is time. Often, accountants, managers, and others who don't develop code for a living only understand the ticking of the clock and see how the expenditure time affects the bottom line. The outside world has tried to quantify developer productivity for years. In a race to deliver code within the time expectations of management, developers often cut corners and leave out the code that we all know should appear in the application.

Would it surprise you to know that most of the errors and security issues in code are there because of time issues? Even the best developers get flustered and fail to provide adequate checks in their code because it's easier to deliver the code now, rather than hear marketing whine one more time. Time is the enemy of security. Bowing to the demands of time, rather than exercising prudent programming practices, is the biggest mistake any developer can make.

Fortunately, the .NET Framework automatically adds code to perform many required security checks. The Common Language Runtime (CLR) uses these automatic code additions to perform security checks during runtime. Unless you trap the error, however, the user sees an ambiguous security error message, rather than a precise message stating how to fix the problem. The .NET Framework does improve the situation, but can't fix it completely.

Explaining the dichotomy of time versus quality to your boss isn't an easy undertaking and will be impossible if you can't quantify the argument in some way. It's important to put the science back into the art of programming by creating an underpinning of quality within your organization. For example, how many developers actually use a checklist to ensure they've met every programming need (such as the need to include security exception checking within the code)? A checklist requires validation, but once validated, it can provide the best means of quantifying your progress to those who need to know.

Checking Every Input

Relying on strong data typing, using all of the proper data transfer techniques, and keeping global variables to a minimum all help keep your data safe. However, it's far better to check the data every time you use it. Checking every input might seem like a waste of time, but it's the only way to ensure you have good data to work with. It's far better to find bad data before you use it, than to catch it as an exception or not catch it at all. With this in mind, the following list provides some items you need to check when working with incoming data.

Check the Data Range A data range defines the acceptable values for data input. For example, when you define a value in your code as Int32, it means that the user can enter any value from –2,147,483,648 through +2,147,483,647. However, your application might not find this range acceptable. When this happens, you must include special code in your application to check for potential error conditions. You might want to accept numbers from 0 to 40,000 in your code, which is outside the Int16 value range, but well within the Int32 value range. In short, a data range is specific to the need at hand. Generally, you'll find that value data types are the easiest to range check because they have predefined ranges. The .NET Framework supports more value types than you might think. For example, the .NET Framework considers a color used for drawing (System.Drawing.Color) a value type. You can see the full list of .NET Framework value types at http://msdn.microsoft.com/library/en-us/cpref/html/frlrfsystemvalue typeclasshierarchy.asp.

Check the Data Length Many of the exploits crackers use depend on the application not checking the length of the incoming data. For example, the buffer overrun technique has become so popular because few developers check the length of incoming data. Fortunately, for the .NET developer, CLR does much of the length checking automatically and raises an exception immediately after it detects data of the wrong length. Even so, CLR only checks for extreme cases—you still have to perform checks for your particular application. Data that's too short can be just as much a problem as data that's too long. For example, if your program needs a string that it will then parse for appropriate data, it could fail if it suddenly runs out of data before the parsing is complete. Ensuring the data is as long as you need before you begin any processing is the best way to avoid certain kinds of problems. Make sure you tell the user about these requirements (length limits) and present clear messages about the error when it does occur.

Control Unnecessary Characters Unnecessary characters are any characters that your application doesn't require as input. For example, if your application doesn't require any slashes, then you shouldn't accept them as input. Likewise, you should avoid any numeric or control character input unless you actually need them to make the application work properly. Crackers have devised a number of interesting exploits over the years to make use of extra characters. The problem is especially severe for Web applications where an application could actually end up combining several fields together if the cracker provides specific input. (It's easier to create combined fields in a Web application because form data isn't strongly typed and there's less direct separation of the data through use of individual variables.)

TIP You may think that checking individual characters in a string isn't worth the effort. Until you actually see some of the exploits that crackers use, it might seem that character checking is a solution in search of a problem. The Security Focus site articled titled, "Abusing poor programming techniques in webserver scripts V 1.0" at http://www.der-keiler.de/Mailing-Lists/ securityfocus/secprog/2001-07/0001.html shows that this is a significant problem.

PROVIDING PRECISE HELP

It always pays to provide good help with your application. A good help file can prevent many kinds of user input errors by showing the user precisely what your application expects to receive. Reducing input errors makes it possible to perform thorough analysis of the errors that remain, which reduces security risks from incorrect input in the end.

Some data types present special challenges that your application must handle to ensure data integrity, as well as address security concerns. For example, a date is a common data entry item that could present problems. First, you need to consider the format of the date. A user could type 1 June 2003, 06/01/2003, June 1, 2003, 2003/06/01, or any other acceptable variant. Desktop applications usually don't have many problems with dates, but they can become a problem with Web applications because the application must parse the date into an acceptable format. Allowing just one type of entry and telling the user about the precise data format will reduce the security problems—it's easier to determine when the data is correct.

Note that providing precise help won't eliminate all data entry errors. Some users will insist on attempting to enter data using whatever means they think best. In addition, there are biases to consider. A particular locale may use a specific date form, and the user will use that form out of habit. Even so, most users will get the point after a few tries, making good help beneficial. When you begin noticing patterns of constant abuse despite the help, your security screens should go up and you should consider the kind of user making the error.

Verifying Every Output

Just as you check every input, you also need to check every application output to provide maximum security. Although this application feature isn't quite as important as checking inputs, you should still consider adding it to your application. You don't know when a compromised system will modify the data between the time that your code receives the data as input and the time it sends it as output. A system is only as good as the security that the entire system provides and most systems have a number of security holes that you need to watch.

Use the same checks for data output as you do for data input. In other words, ensure that the data is of the correct type, the right size, contains only the characters you expect, and is within the correct range. Whenever these checks fail, you know that something is wrong. Security is going to be one of the main culprits, but also be willing to look for errors in your code. Output checks often help you locate bugs in your application by locating the source of the error more precisely.

Work Smarter, Not Harder

Computer languages generally provide more than one way to accomplish a task. In addition, the .NET Framework sometimes provides more than one class you can use for a given task. Add to this complexity the options that you have with a given technology, such as configuring your Web site, and you might think it impossible to use the best strategy all of the time. In fact, you probably won't use the best technique every time, but that's where the learning process comes into play. Maintaining an electronic notebook of what works and when is probably the best thing you can do for yourself. At some point, you'll have a whole book of pointers that will help you work smarter, rather than harder, to write great code. The following sections describe a few techniques you can try.

Try the *HttpServerUtility.Transfer* Method

Depending on what you're trying to accomplish, you don't always need to use the `HttpResponse.Redirect()` method to send the user to a new URL. Using this method incurs an extra round-trip between the client and the server, which produces a performance hit. In addition, the extra round-trip always invites unwanted introduced errors. When you don't plan to do anything but change the user's Web page, you can rely on the `HttpServerUtility.Transfer()` method instead. This method performs the transition at the server—the client sees the new Web page on the first trip.

Of course, using the `HttpServerUtility.Transfer()` method also means that you won't have an opportunity to perform client-side tasks before the new page appears. For example, when you rely on cookies to transfer certain kinds of data, you might find that the page doesn't work as expected. You want to test this method in various situations before you assume that the performance benefit is worth a coding change.

Use Exceptions Carefully

Exceptions are an essential part of good application design, so you need to use them as required. However, you should remember a simple rule about exceptions—they only occur under exceptional circumstances. Always use exceptions in controls or components to signal an error—don't display the error information from within the control or component. In addition, you might have to use exceptions to pass information to the next method in a call stack when a lower method can't handle the error. What you need to avoid is using an exception as a means of changing application flow or sending messages between application layers. The reason is simple: exceptions are very costly from a resource perspective. In addition, exceptions always produce a noticeable delay in execution.

Whenever possible, use standard coding techniques to change the execution path or pass data. For example, the server spends a lot less time processing an `If...Then` statement than it does unwinding the stack to process an exception. Likewise, passing a structure between methods is a lot faster than using an exception to create a complex message store.

The unfortunate part about exceptions is that they don't affect only one person or only your code. Every time the server processes an exception, it robs processing cycles from other applications. The exception generally runs at a higher priority than normal code does. Consequently, an application that uses enough exceptions in the wrong way can greatly reduce the work that a server can perform.

Use All Available Resources

You might be surprised to learn that most developers use only a small percentage of the resources available to them when writing code. In many cases, it's a problem of not knowing about a particular environment feature—it really is tough to keep all of those namespaces, classes, methods, events, and properties in your head. Because most projects today are on very short schedules, the developer has little reason to look for alternatives. Therefore, many developers continue to use inefficient programming techniques that result in less than optimal code because the technique is familiar—the developer doesn't have to do anything special to use a known technique. The following sections provide a few ideas of where to look for interesting new techniques that you can use to create better applications without a lot of work.

Rely on SQL Server Stored Procedures

SQL Server stored procedures can make your code run more efficiently in many cases. Whenever you can define a static query—one in which only the arguments change—use a stored procedure rather than a local command. Using a stored procedure lets SQL Server store the command locally—reducing network traffic. In addition, SQL Server compiles stored procedures, which means the request executes faster. The combination of all of these elements makes well-defined stored procedures execute faster and with fewer resources.

However, don't be afraid to use local commands as needed. Any ad hoc query requires a local command. When you can't define a query very well in advance, creating odd-looking stored procedures with convoluted logic can actually make the application run slower. When you need to choose between a stored procedure and a local command, decide whether you can state the query as a change in variables. If you can't, use a local command.

Using stored procedures can help you avoid some security issues. For example, stored procedures often resist script attacks when a local command won't. A script attack is one in which a cracker adds special coding to one, two, or more fields on a form to gain unauthorized access to an application. Of course, making sure you check every input reduces the problems of script attacks for local commands as well.

Precompile the Application

Precompiling your application makes the page load faster. This process occurs automatically the first time a user requests the page after you make a change. Unfortunately, if you change many pages, the load on the server can increase dramatically at precisely the wrong time—during peak server usage.

In the past, developers had two options for combating the performance and resource problems of compilation. They could use a third party utility to walk the Web site structure and request each Web page in turn, or they could perform the task manually. ASP.NET 2.0 comes with the AspNet_Compiler.EXE utility. You'll find it in the \WINDOWS\Microsoft.NET\Framework\v2.0.40607 folder of your hard drive. The advantage of using this utility is that you can perform a compilation of all Web pages in your application during nonpeak hours. Simply make all of the changes you want to make, upload them at one time, and run the compiler.

However, this utility has another significant advantage. You can compile the application on a development server and then upload just the compiled code to your production server. Using this technique means that the source code is no longer accessible on the Web site—only the compiled page is. Crackers have a lot harder time creating havoc on your Web site when they only have compiled versions of your Web pages to work with.

Appendix B

Working with Common Character Codes

Character codes are an important part of Web development because they help developers overcome various Web page display problems. For example, a greater than or less than sign normally signifies part of an HTML tag. To display these characters on screen, you must use a character code.

Developers commonly use two forms of character codes. First, you can replace the character directly using an entry from a chart. Second, you can replace the character programmatically using code. The technique you choose depends on how the Web page uses the character code. The direct replacement technique works best when you know the character at the time you develop the Web page. The programmatic approach works best for user entry or other runtime needs. This appendix describes both techniques.

Direct Replacement Using a Chart

Direct character replacement means providing an escaped (substituted) form of the character as part of the HTML so it appears on the page. In some cases, you can make the character more readable by using a special keyword. Here are five common examples to consider.

◆ > (greater than)

◆ < (less than)

◆ & (ampersand)

◆ " (double quote)

◆   (non-breaking space)

If you decide to use this approach, make sure you use the International Standards Organization (ISO) ISO-8559 standard. You can find a list of ISO-8559 characters at http://www.ramsch.org/martin/uni/fmi-hp/iso8859-1.html. Notice that all of these characters begin with an ampersand and end with a semicolon.

Another, perhaps more practical, method of replacing characters with an escaped character is to use the character's Unicode number. In this case, you create the escaped character by adding a number sign and the Unicode number to the escape sequence. For example,   is a space. Although this form is less readable than using the keywords, you can use it to create any character. You can find a list of Unicode characters and their associated numbers at http://www.unicode.org/charts/. Make sure you have the appropriate language support loaded when you use foreign language characters.

Because the number technique is so useful, you might want to create an application to display the numbers and their associated characters as a table. Listing B.1 shows one application you might try. You'll find this example in the \Appendix B\CharReplace folder of the source code on the Sybex Web site.

LISTING B.1:   Displaying Character Escape Sequences

```html
<form id="ShowChars" name="ShowChars" method="get">

    <h1>Direct Character Replacement</h1>

    <p>
        <label id="lblStart" for="txtStart">
            Starting Character Number:
        </label>
        <input id="txtStart"
               name="txtStart"
               type="text"
               title="Contains the beginning character number."
               value="32" /><br />
        <button id="btnSubmit"
                type="submit"
                title="Sends the request for processing.">
            Submit
        </button>
    </p>

    <table id="CommonChars"
           summary="Contains a list of common character replacements."
           title="Common Character List"
           border="2">
        <thead title="Table Heading">
            <tr>
                <th>Code</th>
                <th>Char</th>

                ... Additional Header Entries ...

            </tr>
        </thead>
        <tbody title="Table Data">
            <script language="javascript">
            //<!--
                var RowCount = 0;   // Counts the rows.
                var ColCount = 0;   // Counts the columns.
                var CharCount = 32; // Tracks the character number.
```

```
        // Process the input number, if any.
        var HREFValue = location.href.split("?");
        var StartValue;      // Holds the starting number.

        // When there is a query string to process.
        if (HREFValue.length > 1)
        {
            // Divide the first input into a name/value pair.
            StartValue = HREFValue[1].split("=");

            // Display the value and use it for the table.
            ShowChars.txtStart.value = StartValue[1];
            CharCount = StartValue[1];
        }

        // Display 9 rows.
        for (RowCount=0;RowCount<=8;RowCount++)
        {
            // Create a new row.
            document.writeln("<tr>");

            // Display 8 columns.
            for (ColCount=0;ColCount<=7;ColCount++)
            {
                // Write the character code.
                document.writeln(
                    '<td title="Code &amp;#"' + CharCount +
                    ';">&amp;#' + CharCount + ';</td>');

                // Write the character.
                document.writeln(
                    '<td title="Chararacter &#' + CharCount +
                    ';">&#' + CharCount + ';</td>');

                // Update the character count.
                CharCount++;
            }

            // End the current row.
            document.writeln("</tr>");
        }
        //-->
        </script>
    </tbody>
</table>

</form>
```

The code begins by displaying the text box you'll use to enter the starting character value and a button for submitting the new value. The page also includes a header for a table containing the escape character values. Figure B.1 shows a typical display. In this case, the output begins with the space character. However, you can begin with any legal Unicode value.

The table body relies on a script. The code begins by checking for a query string. The `HREFValue` array contains two entries when the HTML reference includes a query string. For the sake of clarity, the example leaves out some error trapping that you should include—it assumes that no one has tampered with the query string. When using this example in a production environment, you would add checks for the input values and possibly use the POST method in place of the GET method.

When the HTML reference contains a query string, the code splits it into a name value pair. Again, the code assumes the query string contains just one name value pair. The code assigns the result to `txtStart.value` so it displays the correct starting number on screen and `CharCount` so the character count starts at the correct number.

The example uses a hard-coded 9 row by 8 column table for display because this size fits well on most displays. However, you could easily change these values to suit any need. The table code begins by creating a new row with the opening `<tr>` tag. It then begins writing column values to the display. The columns include two kinds of values—the code used to create the character and the resulting character. The example is basically accessible because it includes the `title` attribute for both entries. The table entries end by adding the closing `</tr>` tag.

You might not want to go online to find the starting character number. Fortunately, you can also use the Character Map utility to locate this number. Figure B.2 shows what this utility looks like.

Simply select the character you want and look at the number that appears at the bottom of the dialog box. Unfortunately, this is a hexadecimal number. You can easily convert the hexadecimal number to a decimal number using the Calculator that comes with Windows.

FIGURE B.1
Displaying a list of escape character values can help you create difficult characters quickly.

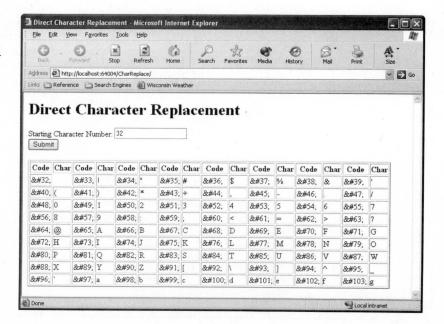

Code	Char	Code	Char	Code	Char	Code	Char	Code	Char	Code	Char	Code	Char	Code	Char
 		!	!	"	"	#	#	$	$	%	%	&	&	'	'
(	(	)	)	*	*	+	+	,	,	-	-	.	.	/	/
0	0	1	1	2	2	3	3	4	4	5	5	6	6	7	7
8	8	9	9	:	:	;	;	<	<	=	=	>	>	?	?
@	@	A	A	B	B	C	C	D	D	E	E	F	F	G	G
H	H	I	I	J	J	K	K	L	L	M	M	N	N	O	O
P	P	Q	Q	R	R	S	S	T	T	U	U	V	V	W	W
X	X	Y	Y	Z	Z	[	[	\	\	]	]	^	^	_	_
`	`	a	a	b	b	c	c	d	d	e	e	f	f	g	g

FIGURE B.2
Character Map makes it easy to learn the numbers associated with special characters.

Using Direct JavaScript Code

JavaScript provides a means of creating escaped output that is extremely simple. All you need to do is use the `escape()` function like this:

```
ResultVal.value = escape(InputVal.value);
```

In this case, the raw input appears in `InputVal.value`, while the output appears in `ResultVal.value`. The only requirement is that `InputVal.value` contain a string, which means you don't have to do anything special with the input except from a security standpoint (you still don't want someone to send a virus to your Web server). You'll find this example in the `\Appendix B\Direct` folder of the source code on the Sybex Web site.

The only problem with this technique is that it's standard—you have no control over the character replacement. In many cases, you won't care. You really do want to use the standard escaping technique for user input. The `unescape()` function removes the escaping from the string, so the entire process is very easy from beginning to end. However, sometimes you need better control over the output, which is where the technique shown in the "Using Indirect JavaScript Code" section comes into play.

Using Indirect JavaScript Code

For most people, working with Web sites is a unique experience because they encounter unexpected oddities that they haven't had to consider in the past. When you type a space into a word-processed document, nothing odd happens—the computer simply accepts the character. However, look at the word processor again. Notice how the word processor automatically looks at the space and uses it to determine where to split lines of text. The word processor does treat the space differently—it treats it as a delimiter (a fancy term that programmers use to mean a character that has a special meaning). Likewise, when you add a hyphen to a word, the computer could choose to split the sentence in the middle of the word. The hyphen acts as a delimiter.

The Internet also uses delimiters for a number of purposes, including URLs. When a Web server sees a space, it could assume that it has reached the end of the URL or the beginning of a new input parameter (or a number of other things). Consequently, you must replace spaces, question marks, and other characters with other characters that don't work as delimiters. You might have noticed this practice at work when you fill out a form on the Internet. The browser commonly replaces a space between two words with %20 or a plus sign (+). The Web server interprets these special character sequences as a space.

At first, you might think that the character replacement is random, but there's some method to the madness. In fact, it's relatively easy to write a JavaScript function that performs the character replacement so you don't need to worry about it. Listing B.2 shows this function. You'll find this example in the \Appendix B\Indirect folder of the source code on the Sybex Web site.

This might look like a lot of very complicated code, but it's actually an easy program. It uses a special technique called recursion to perform its work. In recursion, the programmer writes a program that solves the simplest form of a problem, and then has that program keep calling itself until it achieves that simple form. No matter how complex the input is, the program can solve it (given enough memory and time) because eventually the input will reach this simple solution.

In this instance, the program keeps calling itself until one of several conditions occurs. First, the program could run out of text to process. Second, the program might have some text left, but it might not contain the special character you want to replace (such as a space). If that's the case, then the program has already performed all of the required work, so it can stop.

Once the program determines there's data to process, it uses the substring() function to look for that character in the string. The substring() function returns just the first part of the string—the part that doesn't contain the special character. To this string, the code adds the replacement characters, such as %20 for a space.

It's at this point that the recursion process occurs. The code still has the other part of the string to consider—the last half. The first half of the string is free of the special character, but not the second half. When the code detects that there's still string to process, it calls itself again with the last half of the string. This process continues until the code has processed all of the input string. Figure B.3 shows typical output from this program.

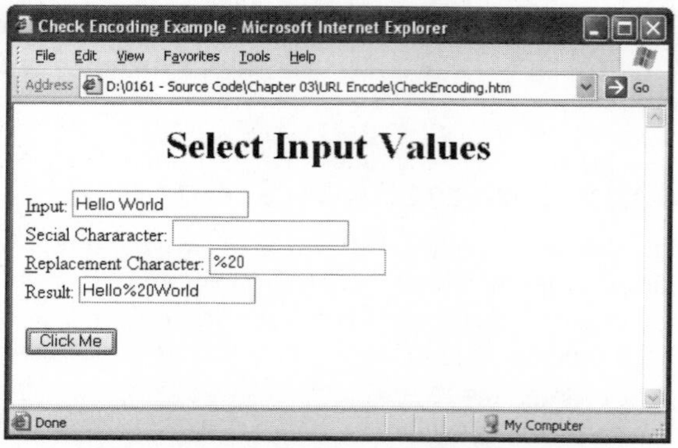

FIGURE B.3

The example program shows how you can perform URL encoding.

LISTING B.2:   Replacing Characters in a String

```javascript
function ReplaceCharacter(InputStr, Replace, UseInstead)
{
    // Define the length of the inputs.
    var InputLength = InputStr.length;
    var ReplaceLength = Replace.length;

    // Determine whether either input has a 0 length. If so,
    // the function can't succeed. However, because this is
    // a recursive function, the function does need to return
    // the original string.
    if ((InputLength == 0) || (ReplaceLength == 0))
        return InputStr;

    // Locate the first replacement value.
    var ReplaceIndex = InputStr.indexOf(Replace);

    // If the replacement value doesn't appear within the string,
    // then return. Again, keep the recursive nature of the
    // function in mind.
    if (ReplaceIndex == -1)
        return InputStr;

    // Create a string that includes the first part of the original
    // string and the replacement character, but not the rest of the
    // string.
    var Output = InputStr.substring(0, ReplaceIndex) + UseInstead;

    // Use recursion to process the string again if there is more data
    // to process.
    if (ReplaceIndex + ReplaceLength < InputLength)

        // Keep adding to the output string after each recursion.
        Output += ReplaceCharacter(
            InputStr.substring(ReplaceIndex + ReplaceLength, InputLength),
            Replace,
            UseInstead);

    // Return the output during each recursion.
    return Output;
}
```

The important consideration for this example is that you have complete control over the escaping process. You can escape any character, even those that JavaScript doesn't process using the `escape()` function. In addition, you can use any replacement that works. For example, you can choose to use something other than %20 to replace a space.

Appendix C

52 Indispensable Visual Studio Tricks and Techniques

This appendix contains 52 helpful hints that you can use to create better ASP.NET 2.0 applications. There's one tip for each week of the year. As you build applications using Visual Studio, you'll find new ways to get work done faster. Now that I've shared my tips with you, I'd love to hear about any tips you might have. Write me at JMueller@mwt.net to share them with me.

1. Always use HTML tags whenever possible to make your code run faster and with fewer compatibility problems. However, make sure you take advantage of the powerful features that ASP.NET provides. Whenever you can display complex data using one or two ASP.NET tags instead of a multitude of HTML tags, the ASP.NET tags are a better choice from a productivity perspective.

2. Don't be afraid to use the Class View window when working with Web services, controls, and components. This window displays important information that you can use to create classes faster and find the classes, methods, properties, and events you need in large projects. The Class View window doesn't appear by default, so many developers miss it. Use the View ➢ Other Windows ➢ Class View command to display the window.

3. Specifically release resource intensive objects, such as SQL Server connections and commands, using the Dispose() method. In some cases, the garbage collector won't release the resources fast enough for your application. The resulting resource error can hide in many forms. For example, in some situations, .NET will complain that a timeout occurred when the problem is really resource usage related. Yes, the code timed out, but it timed out because it was waiting for resources from the resource pool.

4. Whenever you create client-side scripts, try to create a server-side alternative that caters to users who don't have scripting enabled. Place the server-side code within a <NoScript> tag so only clients who lack the client-side functionality will see the server-side alternative.

5. The <Object> tag can introduce compatibility issues on your Web page—Internet Explorer is the only product that supports it completely. However, using this tag can also help you create flexible Web pages that have a robust interface.

6. Always remember that you can create database applications programmatically or using Server Explorer with Visual Studio. Using Server Explorer is generally faster and easier. However, the programmatic approach can provide better flexibility and is more tolerant of certain types of input errors.

7. Use the team development tools for all complex projects, even if you're the only one working on it. The team development tools can help you recover quickly from errors and provide a means of backing out of unsuccessful updates. Later, if you decide you do need help, it's easy to add someone to the project when you have used the team development tools from the outset.

8. Make your Web page easier to reconfigure and more accessible, as well, by using Cascading Style Sheets (CSS) to define all page formatting. All you need to do to format a new Web page after creating the CSS file is to add a reference to the CSS file. In some cases, you might also need to define a class for a particular page element to apply alternative formatting.

9. Use the Add New Online Template feature found in the various New dialog boxes to add functionality to Visual Studio. This feature lets you access both Microsoft and third party templates that add functionality to your working environment—potentially reducing the time required to complete tasks.

10. Rely on Crystal Reports or the Microsoft Reporting Technology features of Visual Studio to generate reports quickly, rather than attempt to create them by hand. Remember that Crystal Reports provides features that help you generate reports on Web site features, as well as company data. When you generate a lot of reports, you might want to get the full version of Crystal Reports or another third party product to gain the productivity benefits they provide.

11. Use the Object Browser as a means to explore the various namespaces, classes, methods, properties, and events in the .NET Framework. It's also easy to use this tool to work with COM components and any other code you can access. You can display this window using the View ➤ Object Browser command.

12. The standard Options dialog box displayed using the Tools ➤ Options command only displays a subset of the options at your disposal. Check the Show All Settings option to display a complete list of settings at your disposal.

13. The ASP.NET 2.0 page that you write isn't the HTML the client browser sees. In some cases, it helps to understand precisely how ASP.NET creates Web pages so you can create code that's more efficient. Use the View ➤ Source command in Internet Explorer to view the actual output of an ASP.NET page.

14. Microsoft is trying to make more resources available to developers who want to learn about the new Visual Studio features quickly. If you want just the basics, check out the 101 code samples at `http://lab.msdn.microsoft.com/vs2005/downloads/101samples/default .aspx`. For those developers who learn faster by viewing code examples, check out the starter kits that Microsoft has produced at `http://lab.msdn.microsoft.com/vs2005/downloads/ starterkits/`. Note that these starter kits are in addition to those that ship with the product. Finally, check out the video series for Visual Studio .NET 2005 at `http://lab.msdn .microsoft.com/express/beginner/default.aspx`.

15. Make sure you investigate the SmartTags provided with the Visual Studio controls. These SmartTags can greatly reduce development time by making configuration a lot easier. In most cases, the SmartTags let you configure common items—you'll still need to use the Properties window to perform complex setups using less common properties.

16. Select the WebParts controls that you use in an application with care. Although you must include a `WebPartManager` and `WebPartMenu` control, the other controls are optional and you should only use those controls that you actually need. Giving the user too much control over the appearance of a Web page can actually become more disruptive than helpful. Some users will tend to play with the display, rather than get useful work accomplished.

17. Visual Studio, along with ASP.NET 2.0, stores many application settings, including some user data, in the `ASPNetDB.MDF` file found in the `\App_Data` folder of any application you create. Studying the effects of application changes you make on this database can help you understand how ASP.NET works better. For example, you can demonstrate that ASP.NET 2.0 really does encrypt all user data.

18. If you have trouble seeing some of the highlighting that the Visual Studio IDE provides, you can change it using the options in the `Environment\Fonts and Colors` folder of the Options dialog box that you access using the Tools ➢ Options command. This folder also lets you change the font used to display code, information within windows, and other IDE features. Using a larger font often reduces eye fatigue and helps you see errors with greater ease.

19. Remember that you aren't limited to just one strategy when you must create an application that runs on multiple platforms. Among the most popular options are Web services, bridging, and cross-compilation. However, you have other choices and it's a good idea to explore them all. The time you spend looking for the right interoperability solution today can save you a significant amount of time tomorrow.

20. Performance counters are one of the most underused, yet abused, resources available to .NET developers for optimizing an application. A performance counter can count anything, so you need not employ it just to look for performance issues—you could check for errors or visitor usage patterns as well. Viewing these other sorts of data helps you create a comprehensive optimization plan. On the other hand, don't keep performance counters in place when you don't actually need them. Performance counters consume resources that you could use for other tasks. Provide a means of disabling non-critical performance counters to get the resources they use back when you don't need them.

21. The ASP.NET 2.0 `SiteMapPath` control provides the best method for presenting a path from the current page to the home page. This control appears in the Navigation tab of the Toolbox.

22. Don't assume that every component or control is a good candidate for use with the `<Object>` tag. Consider how the component or control will react to a Web environment and whether the control will display correctly. Components generally provide better overall functionality because they lack a visible interface.

23. Make sure you add validation controls to sensitive Web pages to ensure the user fills in all required information. The most common validation control, `RequiredFieldValidator`, ensures the user provides the requested information. Using this control reduces the risk of a user's leaving out important information that you need for contact or problem resolution. The most powerful validation control, `RegularExpressValidator`, ensures the data is in the correct format. Use this control to reduce the risk of users' providing unexpected information for highly formatted fields, such as telephone numbers.

24. Place application settings in the correct files. Use the `WEB.CONFIG` file to store application-specific settings. The `MACHINE.CONFIG` file is the place to store settings that affect your Web site as a whole. Using the correct configuration file reduces the amount of work you have to perform when your Web site requires configuration changes.

25. Create task entries in your code as needed by adding the appropriate keywords in comments. The common keywords include `HACK`, `TODO`, and `UNDONE`. You can add other keywords using the options in the `Environment\Task List` folder of the Options dialog box accessed using the Tools ➢ Options command.

26. Visit the Visual Studio Guided Tour Web site at `http://beta.asp.net/GuidedTour/default.aspx` for additional ideas on how to use this product. Microsoft will very likely add to the beginning tutorial and provide updates as necessary. Consequently, you could find new material over time.

27. Always test your ASP.NET applications using more than one browser if you plan to offer the Web page on a public Web site. For example, you might want to test the Web page using Internet Explorer and Firefox to ensure maximum compatibility. Despite Microsoft's claims, ASP.NET pages don't always display as anticipated in other browsers, so multiple browser testing helps reduce unpleasant surprises.

28. Server Explorer can help you create displays automatically in some cases—just drag and drop the table you want to view to the form. However, this technique performs formatting for you that you might not want. You can control this formatting using the options in the `Database Tools\Table Designer` folder of the Options dialog box that you can access using the Tools ➢ Options command.

29. Use the ASP.NET command line utilities found in the `\WINDOWS\Microsoft.NET\Framework\v2.0.40607` folder of your hard drive to your advantage. For example, the ASPNET_RegBrowsers utility lets you register the capabilities of the browsers you expect Web site users to use. The browser definitions appear in the `\WINDOWS\Microsoft.NET\Framework\v2.0.40607\CONFIG\Browsers` folder. Use the ASPNET_RegIIS utility to register or unregister a particular version of ASP.NET on a system. Likewise, you use the ASPNET_RegSQL utility to register a particular version of ASP.NET with SQL Server.

30. Never use the Data Encryption Standard (DES) to encrypt data on your Web site because this encryption technique is exceptionally easy to break with modern computers. Use Triple DES with care on Web pages and only for compatibility with older systems. Use the Advanced Encryption Standard (AES) whenever possible for maximum security.

31. The animated GIF is the most common and most compatible form of pizzazz you can add to a Web site. Most browsers support the animated GIF and you can find a wealth of tools to work with them. In fact, some Web sites offer predefined animated GIFs that you can use on your Web site without becoming an artist (make sure you use a trustworthy Web site so you don't download an animated GIF with a virus in it).

32. Database connections that you create using Server Explorer appear in the `Web.CONFIG` file associated with the project. You can find these settings as part of the `<connectionStrings>` element. In some cases, you can modify the settings manually to correct errors in the database entry.

33. It pays to visit the Channel 9 Web site at `http://channel9.msdn.com/` to learn more about various Microsoft projects. The Web site contains the latest information about various Microsoft projects including video. In addition, you can often find useful projects for Visual Studio you won't find in other places.

34. Many developers like to see a grid when designing forms. Other developers like to use a tighter (or looser) grid than the default settings allow. You can control the design of your forms better using the options found in the `Display\Display` folder of the Options dialog box that you can access using the Tools ➤ Options command.

35. ASP.NET 2.0 includes a number of new login controls that make working with users a lot easier. These controls appear under the Login tab of the Toolbox. Make sure you include the new `PasswordRecovery` control in your list of necessary tools to reduce support costs for your application.

36. Never assume that a Web site is secure simply because you implement Secure Sockets Layer (SSL) and verify the user's identity. Make sure you also check code privileges to ensure your security policy allows the code to perform the requested task under a given set of conditions. Many security breaches occur because a user executes code outside a safe environment.

37. Learn from the daily coding experiences of Brian Goldfarb, one of the Visual Studio developers, through his blog at `http://blogs.msdn.com/bgold/category/6057.aspx`.

38. Use the ASP.NET 2.0 `Menu` control to provide a path from the current page to other pages on your Web site. You can use this control to provide a means of accessing child pages, or simply as a means of finding other locations. The `Menu` control lets you define both dynamic (indexed) and static locations. This control appears on the Navigation tab of the Toolbox.

39. Visual Studio comes with a number of file extension mappings by default. For example, when you double-click an SLN (solution) file in Windows Explorer, the Visual Studio IDE loads the project for you. You can add new file extensions to the list by adding new file extensions using the features in the `Text Editor\File Extension` folder of the Options dialog box that you can access using the Tools ➤ Options command.

40. Find the latest tips and tricks for using ASP.NET 2.0 efficiently on the ASP.NET Tips and Tricks forum at `http://www.asp.net/Forums/ShowForum.aspx?tabindex=1&ForumID=134`.

41. SmartTags provide a wonderful way to add value to your Web pages. You can use the standard SmartTags, third party SmartTags, and even custom SmartTags to provide context-based functionality. However, because SmartTags rely on the `<Object>` tag, you'll find that some browsers won't support them. Consequently, while SmartTags offer a way to provide value-added content, you won't want to use them for essential content on a Web page.

42. Always provide a method to return a Web page to its default settings when using WebParts. Some users will change things so much that the page becomes a mess and it's easier to start the configuration from scratch. Make sure you tell the user the results of setting the Web page to its default state (that they will lose all of their settings).

43. Microsoft has increased the XML capabilities of ASP.NET 2.0. Make sure you use this new functionality to create robust applications that are easy to move to other locations. Generally, if you can use XML, rather than a database, to store information, the XML is easier to work with for simple data.

44. Always provide a written security policy. Even if you're a one-person shop, writing a policy down and using the written policy when writing code ensures that you apply the policy evenly and completely. As the size of a business grows, the need for a complete and comprehensive security policy increases. In addition, make sure you review the security policy annually, as a minimum, to ensure it covers new threats and business conditions.

45. If you program in more than one language, it's annoying to have the IDE behave one way when working with one language and another way when working with a second language. You can modify this behavior by setting generic settings for all languages. Make changes using the options in the `Text Editor\All Languages` folder of the Options dialog box that you can access using the Tools ➢ Options command.

46. Discover the Media Tracker sample application for Visual Studio at `http://channel9.msdn.com/ShowPost.aspx?PostID=23091`. This sample application performs the useful task of helping you track your media. However, it's also a very good way to learn more about Visual Studio coding techniques. You can download the application at `http://channel9.msdn.com/Photos/ZippedFiles/826da073-19ec-41a2-b20f-e9d81190ae1f.zip`.

47. Don't expect validation controls to perform all of the security work for your Web pages. Make sure you add code to your Web page to check for issues that the validation controls can't check. In addition, never assume that your method receives the data it needs from another method—always verify the data to reduce the risk of problems such as buffer overruns.

48. Using an XML file to hold the menu entries for a `Menu` control lets you update the entries without visiting each Web page manually. To keep the menus on your Web site updated, all you need to change is a single XML file. The Menu controls will update automatically during the next user visit.

49. Whenever you include the ability to remove (delete) content from a Web page using WebParts, include a `CatalogZone` control so the user can add the content back; otherwise, the user won't be able to add the content back onto the Web page. Because ASP.NET encrypts the user settings automatically, the administrator can't change the settings either. In short, the only way to change the settings back if you don't include the `CatalogZone` control is to remove the user settings from the database and instruct the user to start the configuration process from scratch.

50. Getting help is important. Sometimes the built-in help doesn't provide what you need, but using online help is extremely slow and cumbersome. You can strike a balance using the settings found in the `Help\Online` folder of the Options dialog box that you can access using the Tools ➢ Options command.

51. Although this book explores a lot of the new ASP.NET 2.0 functionality, you can learn more about ASP.NET 2.0 at `http://msdn.microsoft.com/asp.net/`.

52. Reduce your workload, whenever possible, by using Visual Studio automation. For example, you can create Web pages more quickly by defining master pages and themes. These two complementary technologies let you add all of the common formatting in one or two steps, and then concentrate solely on the content for that Web page.

Glossary

This book includes a glossary so that you can find terms and acronyms easily. It has several important features you need to know about. First, every acronym in the entire book appears here—even if there's a better than even chance you already know what the acronym stands for. (The book does exclude common acronyms such as units of measure and most file extensions because these terms are easy to find in other sources and most people know what they mean.) This way, there isn't any doubt that you'll always find everything you need to use the book properly.

Second, these definitions are specific to the book. In other words, when you look through this glossary, you're seeing the words defined in the context in which they're used in this the book. This might or might not always coincide with current industry usage since the computer industry changes the meaning of words so often.

Finally, I've used a conversational tone for the definitions in most cases. This means that the definitions might sacrifice a bit of puritanical accuracy for the sake of better understanding. The purpose of this glossary is to define the terms in such a way that there's less room for misunderstanding the intent of the book as a whole.

WHAT TO DO IF YOU DON'T FIND IT HERE

While this glossary is a complete view of the words and acronyms in the book, you'll run into situations when you need to know more. No matter how closely I look at terms throughout the book, there's always a chance I'll miss the one acronym or term that you really need to know. In addition to the technical information found in the book, I've directed your attention to numerous online sources of information throughout the book and few of the terms the Web site owners use will appear here unless I also chose to use them in the book. Fortunately, many sites on the Internet provide partial or complete glossaries to fill in the gaps:

Acronym Finder `http://www.acronymfinder.com/`

Free Online Dictionary Of Computing (FOLDOC) `http://nightflight.com/foldoc/`

Microsoft Business Users Glossary `http://www.microsoft.com/atwork/glossary.mspx`

Microsoft Encarta `http://encarta.msn.com/`

Microsoft Management Console (MMC) Glossary `http://msdn.microsoft.com/library/en-us/mmc/mmc/mmc_glossary_gly.asp`

Microsoft .NET Glossary `http://www.microsoft.com/NET/basics_glossary.aspx`

Microsoft Security Glossary `http://msdn.microsoft.com/library/en-us/dnanchor/html/securityanchor.asp`

TechEncyclopedia `http://www.techweb.com/encyclopedia/defineterm.jhtml?term=COM`

> **Webopedia** `http://webopedia.internet.com/`
>
> **yourDictionary.com** `http://www.yourdictionary.com/`
>
> Some entries in this list are quite specialized. For example, the Microsoft Management Console (MMC) Glossary provides definitions for terms that you'll encounter when using one of the Consoles found in the Administrative Tools folder of the Control Panel. You can find other Microsoft Glossaries listed at `http://www.microsoft.com/resources/glossary/default.mspx`. If you still don't find what you need, try the Microsoft Search page at `http://search.microsoft.com/`, type the word glossary, add a specific area such as network, and click Go.

A

Access Control Entry (ACE)

Defines the object rights for a single user or group. Every ACE has a header that defines the type, size, and flags for the ACE. Next comes an access mask that defines the rights a user or group has to the object. Finally, there's an entry for the user's or group's Security IDentifier (SID).

Access Control List (ACL)

Part of the Windows NT–based operating system security Application Programming Interface (API) used to determine both access and monitoring properties for an object. Each ACL contains one or more Access Control Entries (ACEs) that define the security properties for an individual or group. There are two major ACL groups: Security Access Control List (SACL) and Discretionary Access Control List (DACL). The SACL controls Windows auditing feature. The DACL controls access to the object.

Accessibility

A measure of a user's ability to interact with an application. For example, applications should provide both mouse and keyboard access to every control to ensure the user can reach the control for use. An application should support all devices without providing specialized support for a particular device unless necessary. A Braille input device should receive no special treatment beyond that required for a keyboard.

ACE

See Access Control Entry

ACL

See Access Control List

Active Server Pages (ASP)

A special type of scripting language environment used by Windows servers equipped with Internet Information Server (IIS). This specialized scripting language environment helps the developer create flexible Web applications that include server scripts written in a number of languages such as VBScript, JavaScript, JScript, and PerlScript. The use of variables and other features, such as access to server variables, helps the developer create scripts that can compensate for user and environmental needs as well as security concerns. ASP uses HTML to display content to the user. Recent extensions to ASP in the form of Active Server Pages eXtended (ASPX) provide a broader range of application support functionality, improved debugging, new features such as "code behind," and improved performance. Note that you need to install the .NET Framework to use ASPX pages.

Active Server Pages eXtended (ASPX)

An extension of Active Server Pages (ASP) that includes a number of new features such as the ability to use separate Web page and coding files. ASPX is normally associated with Microsoft's .NET Framework; a new tokenized application platform. Consequently, the technology relies on the objects that the .NET Framework provides, which includes additional functionality, ease of coding, and improved security.

Active Template Library (ATL)

A special set of header, source, object, and executable files created by Microsoft. The main purpose of ATL is to reduce the size and dependence of COM objects created for use in environments where memory and network bandwidth are a potential problem. For example, an ATL object won't normally rely on the Microsoft Foundation Classes (MFC). In many cases, the ATL executable is self-contained and doesn't rely on anything other than standard Windows core files. While ATL executable files are smaller than their MFC counterparts, they're also more complex to develop and often require the developer to write more code in order to obtain a similar result.

ActiveX Data Object (ADO)

A local and remote database access technology that relies on Object Linking and Embedding-Database (OLE-DB) to create the connection. ADO is a set of "wrapper" functions that make using OLE-DB and the underlying OLE-DB provider easier. ADO is designed as a replacement for Data Access Objects (DAO) and as an adjunct to Open Database Connectivity (ODBC).

ADO

See ActiveX Data Object

Advanced Encryption Standard (AES)

The mathematical basis for performing symmetric encryption and decryption of data. The algorithm originally appeared as the Rijndael algorithm, after it's inventors (Joan Daemen and Vincent Rijmen). This is a block cipher that can accept a number of data block sizes and key lengths. Many companies now use this algorithm as a replacement for the DES and Triple DES algorithms.

AES

See Advanced Encryption Standard

AJAX

See Asynchronous JavaScript And XML

Alpha Red Green Blue (ARGB)

The creation of a color based on the combination of red, green, and blue that defines it. Generally, each color can have a value between 0 and 255 on modern displays. The alpha component defines the transparency of the color where a color with a value of 255 is opaque and a color with a value of 0 is transparent.

American National Standards Institute (ANSI)

An organization dedicated to creating standard implementations of common technologies. For example, this group created the American Standard Code for Information Interchange (ASCII) character standard commonly used for application development.

American Standard Code for Information Interchange (ASCII)

A standard method of equating the numeric representations available in a computer to human-readable form. For example, the number 32 represents a space. The standard ASCII code contains 128 characters (7 bits). The extended ASCII code uses 8 bits for 256 characters. Display adapters from the same machine type usually use the same upper 128 characters. Printers, however, might reserve these upper 1 28 characters for nonstandard characters. For example, many older Epson printers use them for the italic representations of the lower 128 characters. This is the standard character set used by all Windows 9*x* implementations.

ANSI

See American National Standards Institute

API

See Application Programming Interface

Applet

A helper or utility application that normally performs a task within a specialized environment such as a browser or as part of an operating system. Java is one of the most commonly used languages for creating applets for browser applications. Another example is the Control Panel applications used to configure Windows. In both cases, the applications perform a limited task within a specialized environment.

Application

One or more executable files that include machine-readable code and specialized data. The complete program or group of programs. An application is a complete environment for performing one or more related tasks. Applications perform tasks for the user or system based on a specific need.

Application Programming Interface (API)

A method of defining a standard set of function or method calls and other interface elements. It usually defines the interface between a high-level language and the lower level elements used by a device driver or operating system. The ultimate goal is to provide some type of service to an application that requires access to the operating system or device feature set.

ARGB

See Alpha Red Green Blue

ASCII

See American Standard Code for Information Interchange

ASP

See Active Server Pages

ASPX

See Active Server Pages eXtended

Asynchronous JavaScript And XML (AJAX)

A technology that combines the JavaScript language and XML data storage to create a desktop application feel for Web applications. The technology works with most browsers, but the client must install a special AJAX engine to make the technology work. Besides the look and feel issues, the major feature of this technology is that it reduces network traffic by making requests only as needed. An application can replace part of a page, rather than request the entire page

from the server. In addition, requests occur asynchronously, which means both client and server can handle information as time permits, rather than immediately.

ATL

See Active Template Library

Attribute

An attribute expresses some feature peculiar to an object. When referring to a database, each field has an attribute that expresses what type of information it contains, the length of the field, the field name, and the number of decimals. When referring to a display, the attribute expresses pixel color, intensity, and position. In programming, an attribute can also specify some type of object functionality, such as the method used to implement security.

Audio Video Interleaved File Format (AVI)

A special file format that contains both audio and visual in digital format. AVI is one of the most popular methods for transmitting multimedia files across the Internet.

AVI

See Audio Video Interleaved File Format

AWT

Abstract Windowing Toolkit

B

Bandwidth

A measure of the amount of data a device can transfer in a given time. For example, the amount of data a processor can send to memory every second. In many cases, bandwidth also considers software limitations, such as the estimated bandwidth of an Internet connection.

Binary

1. A numbering system that only uses two digits: 0 and 1. 2. A method used to store worksheets, graphic

files, and other nontext information. The data store can appear in memory, but most often appears in a file on disk. While you can use the DOS TYPE command to send these files to the display, the contents of the file remain unreadable. Other binary files include programs with extensions of EXE, DLL, or COM.

Boolean

A method of determining whether a statement is true or false using rules of logic. Boolean values are often used to help a computer determine whether it needs to take a certain course of action based on current system or application conditions.

Bridging Interoperability

A technique for allowing two applications to communicate on different platforms that relies on an intermediate application. The intermediate application interprets and marshals data and communication between the two platforms.

Browser

A special application, such as Internet Explorer, Opera, FireFox, or Netscape, normally used to display data downloaded from the Internet. The most common form of Internet data is the HTML (Hyper-Text Markup Language) page. However, modern browsers can also display various types of graphics and even standard desktop application files such as Word for Windows documents directly. The actual capabilities provided by a browser vary widely depending on the software vendor and platform.

Buffer Overrun

A memory condition normally associated with a variable in which the application assigned more data to the variable than the variable is capable of holding. The excess data runs into other memory locations, which corrupts the information in those memory locations. In many cases, the buffer overrun affects other variables. However, when used maliciously, a buffer overrun can also overwrite other areas of memory such as code blocks or the application stack, causing the application to fail or perform tasks that the originator didn't intend.

C

CA

See Certificate Authority

CAB

See Cabinet File

Cabinet File (CAB)

1. A compressed-format file similar to the ZIP files used to transfer code and data from one location to another. Only developers who work with Microsoft language products normally use the CAB format, but anyone working in the Windows environment could use them by creating the file with the Compress utility. You can also decompress the file using the Expand utility. 2. A single file created to hold a number of compressed files. A related set of cabinet files can be contained in a folder. During installation of a program, the compressed files in a cabinet are decompressed and copied to an appropriate directory for the user.

Cache

A storage area for data, code, or other resources normally associated with memory or a special file on a hard drive. Both hardware and applications rely on the cache to improve performance.

Cascading Style Sheets (CSS)

A method for defining a standard Web page appearance using formatting information. The formatting may include headings, standard icons, backgrounds, and other features that would tend to give each page at a particular Web site the same appearance. The reason for using CSS includes speed of creating a Web site (it takes less time if the developer doesn't have to create an overall design for each page) and consistency. Changing the overall appearance of a Web site also becomes as easy as changing the style sheet instead of each page alone. CSS is also a standards supported technology, so it represents an easy method for developers to create Web pages that will work in standards-compliant browsers.

CD

Compact Disk

Certificate Authority (CA)

The originator of a digital credential. An organization or group that independently verifies the identity of a requestor and issues credentials that reflect that identity. The credentials are in the form of a certificate that the requestor can use for a number of purposes, such as identification of an email source or signing a component. To provide any value, both parties in an information exchange must trust the CA. In some cases, this means using a public CA such as VeriSign. However, in other cases, it means that third parties must trust the private company issuing the certificate. For example, some Windows server versions provide the means to issue private certificates.

cHTML

See Compact HyperText Markup Language

Class Identifier (CLSID)

A method of assigning a unique number to each object used by Windows. These numbers normally appear in the registry and Windows uses them for reference purposes. The number normally appears in the form {00000000-0000-0000-0000-000000000000}, but can take on other forms as well. This term also refers to various high-level language constructs used by programming languages.

Client

The requestor and recipient of data, services, or other resources from a file or other server type. This term can refer to a workstation or an application. Often used in conjunction with the term *server*, this is usually another PC or an application.

CLR

See Common Language Runtime

CLSID

See Class Identifier

CN

Context Name

Code Behind

A Web page coding technique where the display (user interface) code resides in a file separate from the file containing the code to make the Web page functional. This type of Web page scripting technology is most closely associated with Active Server Pages eXtended (ASPX). The advantage of this approach is that the developer spends less time looking for application code—reducing some task times such as debugging. Code behind helps promote code reuse by keeping code and user interface separate. The use of a separate code file also means that the same code file could serve multiple Web pages through the use of generic routines. The code behind portion contains all of the functions and methods that the Web page uses to control various display elements and to perform programming tasks in the background such as opening a database connection. The code behind file normally has the same name as the ASPX page, with the programming language suffix appended. For example, if the user interface portion of the application is `Default.ASPX`, the code behind portion might appear in the `Default.ASPX.CS` file when using C# as the coding language.

COM

See Component Object Model

COM+

See Component Object Model Plus

Common Language Runtime (CLR)

The engine used to interpret managed applications within the .NET Framework. All Visual Studio .NET languages that produce managed applications can use the same runtime engine. The major advantages of this approach include extensibility (you can add other languages) and reduced code size (you don't need a separate runtime for each language).

Common Object Request Broker Architecture (CORBA)

This protocol describes data and application code in the form of an object. This is the Object Management Group's (OMG) alternative to Microsoft's Component Object Model (COM). Although CORBA is incompatible with COM, it uses many of the same techniques as COM to create, manage, and define objects. CORBA was originally designed by IBM for inclusion with OS/2.

Compact HyperText Markup Language (cHTML)

A specialized form of the HyperText Markup Language (HTML) specially designed for mobile device use. Pages created with cHTML have the same appearance as HTML. However, cHTML doesn't support Joint Pictures Experts Group (JPEG) images, tables, image maps, multiple fonts or font styles, background colors or images, frames, Cascading Style Sheets (CSS), or more than two colors. All user tasks in cHTML rely on the use of four buttons, rather than on a full keyboard, including cursor forward, cursor backward, select, and back/stop. The Japan-based Access Company originated cHTML for use with i-mode devices. The protocol is used less now that most companies are developing around the eXtensible HyperText Markup Language (XHTML).

Compiler

A program that converts English-like statements into machine instructions in an executable or intermediate form. In some cases, the executable code can run without assistance on the host machine (called a native executable). In other cases, the intermediate code requires compilation into an executable form. This secondary form can rely on an interpreter, such as Beginner's All-Purpose Symbolic Instruction Code (BASIC), or runtime engine, such as Java, or it can use a secondary compiler or linker to change an object format into a standard native executable (C).

Component Object Model (COM)

A Microsoft specification for a binary-based, object-oriented code and data encapsulation method and transference technique. It's the basis for technologies such as OLE (Object Linking and Embedding) and ActiveX (compontents and controls). COM is limited to local connections.

Component Object Model Plus (COM+)

An updated version of both the Component Object Model (COM) and Distributed Component Object Model (DCOM) that includes features for modern remote and disconnected applications.

COM+ applications are registered on the server and client machines using standard installation programs and specialized administrative tools. The technology can use both standard connected and queued communication. Later versions of COM+ can even act as Web services with the proper configuration.

Connectivity

A measure of the interactions between clients and servers. In many cases, connectivity begins with the local machine and the interactions between applications and components. Local area networks (LANs) introduce another level of connectivity with machine-to-machine communications. Finally, wide area networks (WANs), metro area networks (MANs), intranets, and the Internet all introduce further levels of connectivity concerns.

Console

1. A type of character-mode application that normally runs at the DOS (command) prompt. A console application normally performs a simple or utilitarian task that doesn't require the Graphical User Interface (GUI) associated with most application development today. 2. The generic term for a workstation used to monitor server status information. In most cases, the workstation and server are the same device. Most people associate consoles with a character mode interface, but this isn't a requirement. 3. A short version of the longer term Microsoft Management Console (MMC). (See Microsoft Management Console for details.)

Constructor

An Object Oriented Programming (OOP) term that describes the special method the application operating environment calls during object instantiation. The constructor contains code that ensures the object is functional. Developers often use the constructor to initialize global variables, set operating environment conditions, and perform other object creation tasks.

Cookie

A value stored in one or more special files managed by a Web browser. The cookie can hold site-specific settings or other information specific to Web pages. In addition, the cookie can last just for the current session or the browser can hold it until some future expiration date. A developer always saves and restores the cookie as part of a Web page programming task using a programming language such as ASP, ASP.NET, JavaScript, Java, VBScript, or CGI. In most cases, this is the only file that a developer can access on the client site's hard drive. The cookie could appear in one or more files anywhere on the hard drive, depending on the browser currently in use. Microsoft Internet Explorer uses one file for each site storing a cookie. Netscape Navigator uses a single file named COOKIE.TXT to store all of the cookies from all sites.

CORBA

See Common Object Request Broker Architecture

Counter

1. An application designed to measure performance on a Windows system. The counter is part of a performance object. It's normally stored with other counters associated with the same performance object within a dynamic link library (DLL) on the host machine. A counter may allow monitoring of one or more instances of the same type of device or other object as individual performance statistics. 2. A specialized programming structure used to track application data. In some cases, the counter is a specialized object the developer adds to the application for the purpose for statistical data collection.

Cracker

A hacker (computer expert) who uses their skills for misdeeds on computer systems where they have little or no authorized access. A cracker normally possesses specialty software that allows easier access to the target network. In most cases, crackers require extensive amounts of time to break the security for a system before they can enter it. Some sources call a cracker a black hat hacker.

Cross-Compilation

The act of translating application code designed for one platform into executable output for another platform. Cross-compilation is one of the oldest techniques available on computer systems to ensure interoperability between different systems.

Cryptographic Service Provider (CSP)

A specialty company that deals in certifying the identity of companies, developers, or individuals on the Internet. This identification check allows the company to issue an electronic certificate, which can then be used to conduct transactions securely. Several levels of certification are normally provided within a specific group. For example, there are three levels of individual certification. The lowest merely verifies the individual's identity through an Internet mail address; the highest requires the individual to provide written proof along with a notarized statement. When you access a certified site or try to download a certified document such as a component, the browser will display the electronic certificate onscreen, allowing you to make a security determination based on fact.

CSP

See Cryptographic Service Provider

CSS

See Cascading Style Sheets

D

DAC

Dedicated Administrative Connection

Data Encryption Standard (DES)

An unsafe method of data encryption that relies on symmetric key encryption. This methodology was oringally introduced in 1975 and standardized by ANSI in 1981. As computer technology has improved, the encryption technique has become easier to crack, making it an unreliable means of protecting data.

Data Source Name (DSN)

A name assigned to a database connectivity description, such as an Open Database Connectivity (ODBC) connection. Applications use the DSN to make the connection to the database and gain access to specific database resources such as tables. The DSN always contains the name of the database server, the database, and (optionally) a resource like a query or table.

Many database technologies such as Object Linking and Embedding-Database (OLE-DB) rely on the use of DSN connection information.

Database

A data collection that consists of one or more storage elements and any associated objects. The organization of the database depends on the features and functionality of the Database Management System (DBMS) used to maintain it. A database normally uses a hierarchical or tabular format. A hierarchical database relies on nodes connected in any of a number of ways, such as record pointers. The tabular format relies on rows (records) made up of columns (fields). A database can appear as a single file, as part of a collection with the DBMS, as part of a worksheet for a spreadsheet, or any other organized disk format.

Database Management System (DBMS)

A method for storing and retrieving data based on tables, forms, queries, reports, fields, and other data elements. Each field represents a specific piece of data, such as an employee's last name. Records are made up of one or more fields. Each record is one complete entry in a table. A table contains one type of data, such as the names and addresses of all the employees in a company. It's composed of records (rows) and fields (columns), just like the tables you see in books. A database may contain one or more related tables. It may include a list of employees in one table, for example, and the pay records for each of those employees in a second table. Sometimes also referred to as a Relational Database Management System (RDBMS) that includes products such as SQL Server and Oracle.

DBMS

See Database Management System

DCOM

See Distributed Component Object Model

DCOMCnfg

Distributed Component Object Model Configuration Utility

DDoS

See Distributed Denial of Service

Delimiter

1. A special symbol or symbols used to separate text. For example, many programming languages use the single (') or double (") quote to separate text elements. 2. A boundary between two different objects. The boundary normally consists of a special symbol or group of symbols. A delimited file contains variable length records. Each field normally uses a comma as a delimiter. Each record normally uses a carriage return as a delimiter.

DES

See Data Encryption Standard

Digital Subscriber Line (DSL)

A term used to refer to any of a number of technologies that allow higher communication rates over standard telephone lines than normally allowed using standard modems. DSL is normally used between a remote location such as a home or office and the switching station or ISP. It isn't used between switching stations. Types of DSL include asynchronous DSL (ADSL), symmetric DSL (SDSL), and high bit-rate DSL (HDSL). The technologies vary by their ability to pack data onto the copper line, distance from the switching station, and other characteristics. ADSL allows communication from 1.5 Mbps to 9 Mbps downstream (to the remote connection) and 16 Kbps to 640 Kbps upstream (from the remote connection). SDSL allows communication up to 3 Mbps in both directions. HDSL allows communication up to 1.544 Mbps in both directions.

Digital Video Disk (DVD)

A high capacity optical storage media with capacities of 4.7 GB to 17 GB and data transfer rates of 600 KBps to 1.3 GBps. A single DVD can hold the contents of an entire movie or approximate 7.4 CD-ROMs. DVDs come in several formats including DVD-R, DVD-RW, DVD+R, DVD+RW, and DVD-RAM that allow read-only or read-write access. Newer dual-layer DVDs promise even greater storage capacities. All DVD drives include a second laser assembly used to read existing CD-ROMs. Some magazines will also use the term *digital versatile disk* for this storage media.

Directory

A storage unit description used with DOS, many character mode applications, and the Windows command prompt. Directories provide a means of separating files into different locations based on type or use. Using directories makes it easier to locate data and use applications.

DISCO

See Discovery of Web Services

DISCOMAP

Discovery of Web Services Map File

Discovery of Web Services (DISCO)

A service that's designed to make it easier to locate and use Web services. This particular service is a SOAP specific originally defined and supported by Microsoft. Other vendors, such as IBM, now use the technology as well. The DISCO service relies on a special protocol named SOAP Contract Language (SCL) to allow the discovery of services by remote computers.

Disk Operating System (DOS)

The underlying management software used by older PCs to provide basic system services and to allow the user to run application software. The operating system performs many low-level tasks through the basic input/output system (BIOS). The revision number determines the specifics of the services that DOS offers; check your user manual for details.

Distributed Application

An application that resides on more than one machine; normally a client and server, but not necessarily limited to this configuration. The application could include multiple levels of clients and servers, commonly referred to as tiers. The application is composed of multiple interchangeable elements. For example, a server component could service more than one application type. The application elements are loosely coupled (both systems only require access to self-describing messages) and the developer can replace each element with updates as needed as long as the new element provides the same interface to the client.

Distributed Component Object Model (DCOM)

A binary data transport protocol that interacts with the Component Object Model (COM), and is used for distributed application development. This protocol enables data transfers across the Internet or other non-local sources, but is usually limited to a local area network (LAN) or wide area network (WAN) environment. DCOM adds the capability to perform asynchronous, as well as synchronous, data transfers between machines. The use of asynchronous transfers prevents the client application from becoming blocked as it waits for the server to respond.

Distributed Denial of Service (DDoS)

A specialized form of denial of service attack where the cracker relies on a multitude of zombie (remotely controlled) machines to perform a denial of service attack on a target network. The cracker may not even know how many machines are involved in the attack since this technique often relies on virus programs to install the required software on an unsuspecting host.

DLL

See Dynamic Link Library

DOS

See Disk Operating System

DSD

Distributed System Designer

DSI

Dynamic Systems Initiative

DSL

See Digital Subscriber Line

DSN

See Data Source Name

DVD

See Digital Video Disk

Dynamic Link Library (DLL)

A specific form of application code loaded into memory by request. It's not executable by itself like an EXE is. A DLL does contain one or more discrete routines that an application may use to provide specific features. For example, a DLL could provide a common set of file dialogs used to access information on the hard drive. More than one application can use the functions provided by a DLL, reducing overall memory requirements when more than one application is running. DLLs have a number of purposes. For example, they can contain device-specific code in the form of a device driver. Some types of COM objects also rely on DLLs.

E

ECMA

See European Computer Manufacturer's Association

EJB

See Enterprise Java Beans

Element

1. A single data value within an array. 2. One node of an eXtensible Markup Language (XML) data structure. An element can contain values, other elements, or appear empty. Elements can also contain attributes that appear as name/value pairs. Properly formed elements appear as HTML tags with stricter usage rules. For example, the element must include a closing tag.

ELUA

See End User Licensing Agreement

Emulator

A specialized application that provides the same features and functionality as the target device. The device on which the emulator runs is normally more capable than the emulated device. For example, emulators commonly enable a developer to test applications designed for use on Personal Digital Assistants (PDAs) using the standard PC.

Encryption

The act of making data unreadable using a mathematical conversion. The data remains unreadable unless the reader provides a password or other key value. Encryption makes data safe for transport in unsecured environments like the Internet.

End User Licensing Agreement (ELUA)

The contract between the buyer and seller of products, especially computer software. The contract defines a license that allows the user to install and interact with the software application.

Enterprise Java Beans (EJB)

A component architecture developer by Sun that relies on the Java language. Developers commonly use EJB to create multi-tier and client/server applications. The EJB executes on a server. Developers commonly buy EJB components from third party vendors and simply connect the pieces they provide with code to create a working application.

Entity Relationship (ER)

A modeling language feature that provides a description of an object (such as a database table), as well as a list of the relationships between the object and all other entities in the model.

ER

See Entity Relationship

Error Trapping

The additional code required to detect, analyze, repair, report, and overcome errors in an application. An error trapping routine normally locates the precise origin of the error, determines the error type, and defines a course of action for repairing the error whenever possible. If the application can't recover, the error trapping routine helps the application fail gracefully after reporting the source and cause of the error to the application user.

European Computer Manufacturer's Association (ECMA)

A standards committee originally founded in 1961. ECMA is dedicated to standardizing information and communication systems. For example, it created the ECMAScript standard used for many Web page designs today. You can also find ECMA standards for product safety, security, networks, and storage media.

Event Handler

A special method or function that reacts to specific system or user events such as clicking a button on a form or the loss of focus for a text box.

Event Log File (EVT)

1. A file used to hold the event log entries for a particular aspect of system performance. For example, there are separate files for application, security, and system entries. Each log file can hold several different event types including audit, informational, warning, and error events. 2. An application event destination. The application never interacts with the EVT file itself since more than one application requires access to the EVT file at one time. A well-designed application will always use the Windows API to perform this task.

EVT

See Event Log File

EXE

See Executable File

Executable File (EXE)

1. A binary file that contains machine code (procedural steps the machine can understand), instructions, and data that an operating system can read to perform tasks. An executable file normally contains an application, but it can contain any form of code and resources. 2. A file containing tokenized data where a token relates to a specific instruction. A special runtime application reads the tokens, interprets them, and sends the results binary machine code to the operating system for execution. The use of tokens

lets a single executable work on more that one operating system or machine type, but slows application execution.

eXtensible Hypertext Markup Language (XHTML)

A cross between eXtensible Markup Language (XML) and HyperText Markup Language (HTML) specifically designed for Internet devices such as Personal Digital Assistants (PDAs) and cellular telephones, but also usable with desktop machine browsers. Since this language relies on XML, most developers classify it as an XML application builder. The language relies on several standardized namespaces to provide common data type and interface definitions. XHTML creates modules that are interpreted based on a specific platform's requirements. This means that a single document can serve the needs of many display devices.

eXtensible Markup Language (XML)

1. A method used to store information in an organized manner. The storage technique relies on hierarchical organization and uses special statements called tags to separate each storage element. Each tag defines a data attribute and can contain properties that further define each data element. 2. A standardized Web page design language used to incorporate data structuring within standard HTML documents. For example, you could use XML to display database information using something other than forms or tables. It's actually a lightweight version of Standard Generalized Markup Language (SGML) and is supported by the SGML community. XML also supports tag extensions that allow various parts of a Web-based application to exchange information. For example, once a user makes a choice within a catalog, that information could be added to an order entry form with a minimum of effort on the part of the developer. Since XML is easy to extend, some developers look at it as more of a base specification for other languages, rather than a complete language.

eXtensible Style Language Transformation (XSLT)

The language used within the eXtensible Style Language (XSL) to transform the content provided in an eXtensible Markup Language (XML) file into a form for display on screen or printing. An XSL processor combines XML content with the formatting instructions provided by XSLT and outputs a new document or document fragment. XSLT is a World Wide Web Consortium (W3C) standard.

F

FAQ
See Frequently Asked Question

File Transfer Protocol (FTP)
One of several common data transfer protocols for the Internet. This particular protocol specializes in data transfer in the form of a file download or upload. The site presents the user with a list of available files in a directory list format. An FTP site may choose DOS or UNIX formatting for the file listing, although the DOS format is extremely rare. Unlike HTTP sites, an FTP site provides a definite information hierarchy using directories and subdirectories, much like the file directory structure used on most workstation hard drives. Generally, FTP transfers require a special application, but some browsers now include this capability. FTP transfers occur without encryption, so security is an issue unless the owner of the FTP site encrypts the individual files.

Filter
An application, piece of hardware, or driver that accepts raw data as input, processes it in some way, and then outputs it as a finished product. Filters perform a variety of tasks including data translation, enhancement, and reduction. For example, a sound filter that changes Pulse-Code Modulation (PCM) data into Adaptive Differential Pulse-Code Modulation (ADPCM) data performs data translation. Another sound filter could perform data enhancement by adding a reverberation effect. A third sound filter could control the intensity of the sound by performing data reduction. Filters also affect data. For example, you can request that an application remove entries from a data stream provided by a Database Management System (DBMS).

Firewall
Hardware or software (or a combination of both) used to prevent unauthorized access to a private network. The firewall can use any of a number of techniques to detect unauthorized packets and deny access to them. Some firewalls not only check incoming packets but outgoing packets as well. There are many types of firewalls including packet filter, application gateway, proxy server, and circuit-level gateway. For maximum protection, the proxy server normally works best in a hardware configuration.

Folder
A specialized area for storing files on the hard drive. Folders help you manage both data and applications by breaking them up into smaller and easier to recognize groups. The folder acts as a storage receptacle. The DOS and command prompt equivalent term for folders is directories; the same term used by many other operating systems.

Frequently Asked Question (FAQ)
A document that contains answers to questions that many people ask. FAQs generally reduce support costs by providing answers to commonly asked questions that people can find in one place. Vendors use FAQs for many purposes including both hardware and software support.

FTP
See File Transfer Protocol

G

GAC
See Global Assembly Cache

GIF
See Graphics Interchange Format

Global Assembly Cache (GAC)
A central repository used by the .NET Framework for storing public managed components. The GAC contains only components with strong names, ensuring the integrity of the cache. In addition, the GAC can

hold multiple versions of the same component, which ensures that applications can access the version of a component that they need, rather than the single version accessible to all applications.

GACUtil

Global Assembly Cache Utility

Globally Unique Identifier (GUID)

A 128-bit number used to identify a Component Object Model (COM) object within the Windows registry. The GUID is used to find the object definition and allow applications to create instances of that object. GUIDs can include any kind of object, even nonvisual elements. In addition, some types of complex objects are actually aggregates of simple objects. For example, an object that implements a property page will normally have a minimum of two GUIDs: one for the property page and another for the object itself.

Graphical User Interface (GUI)

1. A method of displaying information that depends on both hardware capabilities and software instructions. A GUI uses the graphics capability of a display adapter to improve communication between the computer and its user. Using a GUI involves a large investment in both programming and hardware resources. 2. A system of icons and graphic images that replaces the character-mode menu system used by many older machines including "green screen" terminals that are connected to mainframes and sometimes to cash registers. The GUI can ride on top of another operating system (such as DOS, Linux, and UNIX) or reside as part of the operating system itself (such as the Macintosh and Windows). Advantages of a GUI are ease of use and high-resolution graphics. Disadvantages include cost, higher workstation hardware requirements, and lower performance over a similar system using a character mode interface.

Graphics Interchange Format (GIF)

One of several standard file formats used to transfer graphics over the Internet. There are several different standards for this file format—the latest of which is the GIF89a standard you'll find used on most Internet sites. CompuServe originally introduced the GIF standard as a method for reducing the time required to download a graphic and the impact of any single-bit errors that might occur. A secondary form of the GIF is the animated GIF. It allows the developer to store several images within one file. Between each image within the file are one or more control blocks that determine block boundaries, the display location of the next image in relation to the display area, and other display features. A browser or other specially designed application displays the graphic images one at a time in the order in which they appear within the file to create animation effects.

GUI

See Graphical User Interface

GUID

See Globally Unique Identifier

H

Hacker

An individual who works with computers at a low level (hardware or software), especially in the area of security. A hacker normally possesses specialty software or other tools that allows easier access to the target hardware or software application or network. The media defines two types of hackers that include those that break into systems for ethical purposes and those that do it to damage the system in some way. The proper term for the second group is *crackers* (see "Cracker" for details). Some people have started to call the first group "ethical hackers" or "white hat hackers" to prevent confusion. Ethical hackers normally work for security firms that specialize in finding holes in a company's security. However, hackers work in a wide range of computer arenas. For example, a person who writes low-level code (like that found in a device driver) after reverse engineering an existing driver is technically a hacker. The main emphasis of a hacker is to work for the benefit of others in the computer industry.

Handheld Device Markup Language (HDML)

A technology that predates most standardized efforts, such as the Wireless Access Protocol (WAP), for transmitting Internet content to cellular telephones. It's a proprietary language that users can only view using OpenWave browsers. The associated transport protocol is the Handheld Device Transport Protocol (HDTP). A user types a request into the phone, which is transferred to a gateway server using HDTP. The gateway server translates the request to HyperText Transport Protocol (HTTP), which it sends to the Web server. The Web server provides specialized HDML content, which the gateway server transfers to the cellular telephone using HDTP. To use this protocol, the Web server must understand the text/x-hdml Multipurpose Internet Mail Extensions (MIME) type.

HDML

See Handheld Device Markup Language

HTML

See HyperText Markup Language

HTTP

See HyperText Transfer Protocol

HTTPS

See HyperText Transfer Protocol Secure sockets

Hyperlink

A link within an electronic document to another location in the same document or to another document. The link normally appears as an underlined word, phrase, or sentence, but developers can also create hyperlinks from objects such as pushbuttons. The most common current use of hyperlinks is as part of Web pages, but any electronic document can contain hyperlinks.

HyperText Markup Language (HTML)

1. A data presentation and description (markup) language for the Internet that depends on the use of tags (keywords within angle brackets <>) to display formatted information on screen in a non-platform-specific manner. The non-platform-specific nature of this markup language makes it difficult to perform some basic tasks such as placement of a screen element at a specific location. However, the language does provide for the use of fonts, color, and various other enhancements on screen. There are also tags for displaying graphic images. Scripting tags for using scripting languages such as VBScript and JavaScript are available, although not all browsers support this addition. The <OBJECT> tag addition allows the use of ActiveX controls. 2. One method of displaying text, graphics, and sound on the Internet. HTML provides an ASCII-formatted page of information read by a special application called a browser. Depending on the browser's capabilities, some key words are translated into graphics elements, sounds, or text with special characteristics, such as color, font, or other attributes. Most browsers discard any keywords they don't understand, allowing browsers of various capabilities to explore the same page without problem. Obviously, there's a loss of capability if a browser doesn't support a specific keyword.

HyperText Transfer Protocol (HTTP)

One of several common data transfer protocols for the Internet. HTTP normally transfers textual data of some type. For example, the HyperText Markup Language (HTML) relies on HTTP to transfer the Web pages it defines from the server to the client. The eXtensible Markup Language and Simple Object Access Protocol (SOAP) also commonly rely on HTTP to transfer data between client and server. It's important to note that HTTP is separate from the data it transfers. For example, it's possible for SOAP to use the Simple Mail Transfer Protocol (SMTP) to perform data transfers between client and server.

HyperText Transfer Protocol Secure sockets (HTTPS)

A secure form of HTTP that relies on the secure sockets encryption technology to transfer data.

I

IDE

See Integrated Development Environment

Identifier (ID)

The name used to reference a function, procedure, object, or variable. An identifier generally begins with a character, followed by any number of characters and numbers. Some older systems place limits on identifier length, but most newer systems don't. In addition, some identifiers must appear in a specific format, such as the Globally Unique Identifer (GUID) Windows relies on to identify components and controls.

IIOP

See Internet Inter-ORB Protocol

IIS

See Internet Information Server

IL

See Intermediate Language

Infrastructure

The underlying base of an organization or system. One way to view infrastructure is a foundation on which all other elements of a system or organization are attached. Many vendors use this term to indicate the compatibility of their product with existing installations.

Integrated Development Environment (IDE)

The development environment used to write application code. An IDE provides all of the tools needed to write an application using one or more specialized editors. The IDE normally includes support for development language help, access to any tools required to support the language, a compiler, and a debugger. Some IDEs include support for advanced features such as automatic completion of language statements and balloon help showing the syntax for functions and other language elements. Many IDEs also use color or highlighting to emphasize specific language elements or constructs.

Intermediate Language (IL)

The common language that all .NET compilers output. The Common Language Runtime (CLR) interprets the tokens that reside in the IL. The use of a tokenized output ensures that all languages can share the functionality provided by the .NET Framework. Because CLR understands this one common language, any compiler that produces it is compatible with .NET.

Internet Information Server (IIS)

Microsoft's Web server that runs under the Windows Server operating system. IIS includes all of the standard Web server features including File Transfer Protocol (FTP) and HyperText Transfer Protocol (HTTP), along with both mail and news services.

Internet Inter-ORB Protocol (IIOP)

A binary protocol that the Open Management Group (OMG) designed for Internet use. This makes IIOP different than protocols such as DCOM and CORBA that are designed for LAN use only. IIOP does perform better on the Internet than DCOM or CORBA, but has the same problems as DCOM and CORBA in that it doesn't communicate well through firewalls.

Internet Protocol (IP)

The information exchange portion of the TCP/IP protocol used by the Internet. IP is an actual data transfer protocol that defines how the sender places information into packets and transmits from one place to another. TCP (Transmission Control Protocol) is the protocol that defines how the actual data transfer takes place.

Internet Server Application Programming Interface (ISAPI)

A set of function calls and interface elements designed to help developers create applications for Microsoft's Internet Information Server (IIS). Essentially, this set of API calls provides the programmer with access to the server itself. This technology makes it easier to provide full application access to the Internet server so the developer can perform tasks such as Web page redirection, security checks, and incoming data parsing. There are two forms of ISAPI: filters and extensions. An extension replaces script-based technologies like CGI. Its main purpose is to provide dynamic content to the user. A filter can extend the server itself by monitoring various events like user requests for access in the background. You can use a filter to create various types of new services like extended logging or specialized security schemes. Most developers use technologies such as Active Server Pages (ASP) in place of ISAPI because these technologies are easier to use. For example, ASP makes it easy to modify a file without the need to recompile it. However, ISAPI is still used for speed critical applications such as the Simple Object Access Protocol (SOAP) listener used by some SOAP implementations.

Internet Service Provider (ISP)

A vendor that provides one or more Internet-related services through a dial-up, Digital Subscriber Line (DSL), Integrated Services Digital Network (ISDN), cable television, or other outside connection. Normal services include email, newsgroup access, full Internet Web site access, and personal Web page hosting.

Interoperability

A measure of an application's ability to run in more than one environment, compatible or not. This term often refers to the ability of an application to run on more than one operating system or hardware platform. In some cases, this term refers to middleware's ability to overcome interoperability problems between platforms.

IP

See Internet Protocol

ISAPI

See Internet Server Application Programming Interface

ISO

International Standards Organization

ISP

See Internet Service Provider

J

JAR

See Java Archive File

Java Archive File (JAR)

A form of data storage that includes compression capability and provides an easy method of distributing all of the components for Java applets. To execute a Java applet, the host machine must have the Java Virtual Machine (JVM) installed.

Java API for XML Processing (JAXP)

A Java eXtensible Markup Language (XML) package that offers Simple Object Access Protocol (SOAP) support for applications. This technology is generally used with Web service applications.

Java DataBase Connectivity (JDBC)

A method of providing database interoperability similar to Open Database Connectivity (ODBC). This form of connectivity is Java specific and other applications require a JDBC-ODBC bridge to provide the necessary interoperability between the two systems. JDBC always uses SQL statements to request data from the database manager. Although ODBC is language independent, it has limited platform support. JDBC is language specific, but runs on any platform that supports Java.

Java Development Kit (JDK)

A special set of application development tools, re–sources, example code, help files, and other resources designed to help a programmer create Java applications. The JDK normally contains a full set of development tools and a copy of the Java Runtime Enviroment (JRE). However, most developers will require one or more third party solutions to create a complex Java application. For example, unlike many languages today, Java doesn't provide Simple Object Access Protocol (SOAP) support, so the developer would require a third party library to create an application that relies on SOAP.

Java Runtime Environment (JRE)

Another name for the Java Virtual Machine (JVM). This set of files provides Java support on the host machine allowing it to run Java applications.

Java Virtual Machine (JVM)

The application used to interpret the Java language originally developed by Sun Microsystems. This includes both text and byte code .CLASS files containing common routines. Java is similar to C++, but eliminates many of the complex programming constructs and uses a more restrictive security scheme. Many operating systems have a Java Virtual Machine including most versions of Windows, Mac OS, and Unix. The use of text files means that Java applets can run on any number of operating system platforms without modifications, but the use of an interpreter implies slower execution speed.

JavaScript (JS)

A file containing a program written in JavaScript; a language with a C-like syntax. Don't confuse Java and JavaScript; the two languages aren't the same. Most browsers support JavaScript and developers like to use it for local and remote applications alike. There are many versions of JavaScript, including Microsoft's JScript and the European Computer Manufacturer's Association (ECMA) ECMAScript.

JAXP

See Java API for XML Processing

JDBC

See Java DataBase Connectivity

JDK

See Java Development Kit

JIT Activation

See Just-in-Time Activation

JIT Compiler

See Just-in-Time Compiler

Joint Photographic Experts Group File Format (JPEG)

A standard graphics file format used on the Internet. This is a vector file format normally used to render high-resolution images or pictures. (The current version of the file standard supports 16.7 million colors.) JPEG provides lossy graphic compression that makes the image file considerably smaller. However, the image loses detail as the amount of compression increases. The file extension also appears as JPG. Other standard Internet graphics formats include Graphics Interchange Format (GIF) and Portable Network Graphics (PNG).

JPEG

See Joint Photographic Experts Group File Format

JRE

See Java Runtime Environment

JS

See JavaScript

Just-in-Time Activation (JIT Activation)

An application, component, control, or service execution method that starts executing the code only as needed, rather than allowing it to remain in memory. Server resources are always scarce, so good resource management techniques are essential. The latest component resource management techniques normally include gaining access to resources only when needed, then releasing them immediately. However, older components were designed to gain access to all of the resources required to perform a task early, then hold onto those resources until no longer needed. Using JIT activation means that even if a client holds onto a component reference, Windows can still use physical resources required by that component until they're needed again by the application. Windows monitors all of the components that are marked as JIT enabled. When a certain time period has elapsed without any method calls, the component deactivates, and the resources that it's using are returned to the resource pool. As far as the application is concerned, the component is still active and the reference to it is still valid. The next time the application makes a method call to the deactivated component, Windows reactivates it and allocates the resources that it requires. This entire process occurs in the background without any programmer input. Newer technologies, such as .NET, have extended JIT to include every aspect of the application.

Just-in-Time Compiler (JIT Compiler)

A specialized applications that transforms code into executable form with Just-in-Time activation in mind.

JVM

See Java Virtual Machine

L

LAN

See Local Area Network

Local Area Network (LAN)

Two or more devices located in a relatively small physical area connected together using a combination of hardware and software. The devices, normally computers and peripheral equipment such as printers, are called nodes. An NIC (network interface card) provides the hardware communication between nodes through an appropriate medium (cable or microwave transmission). The actual connection is provided through cables, in many cases, but can also rely on radio waves, infrared, and other technologies. There are two common types of LANs (also called networks). Peer-to-peer networks allow each node to connect to any other node on the network with shareable resources. This is a distributed method of files and peripheral devices. A client-server network uses one or more servers to share resources. This is a centralized method of sharing files and peripheral devices. A server provides resources to clients (usually workstations).

M

Master Page

A document that acts as a template for other documents. The master page does include common content such as pictures and text that will appear on all pages created using it. However, it doesn't contain any unique data. Instead, the page created with the master page contains unique data for that page.

MBSA

Microsoft Baseline Security Analyzer

MD5

See Message Digest 5

Message Digest 5 (MD5)

The mathematical basis for creating a message digest (a value) based on the content of the message. The basis of this technology is that no two messages will produce the same message digest. Consequently, the recipient can validate the content of a message by performing the calculation and comparing it to the message digest value. MD5 is a one-way hash, which means that it isn't used for encrypting and decrypting the data. Professor Ronal Rivest created MD5 in 1991 to verify the authenticity of digital signatures.

MFC

See Microsoft Foundation Classes

Microsoft Foundation Classes (MFC)

The set of code libraries required to make many Microsoft applications work. These files contain the shared classes used as a basis for creating the application. For example, a push-button is a separate class within these files. Normally, you'll find the MFC files in the Windows SYSTEM folder; they use MFC as the starting letters of the filename.

Microsoft Database Engine (MSDE)

This term also appears as Microsoft Desktop Engine and Microsoft Data Engine in various publications. MSDE is a miniature form of SQL Server that enables developers to create test database applications. Microsoft designed this engine for use by one person, usually the developer; although, you can potentially use it for up to five people. The developer accesses MSDE through a programming language Integrated Development Environment (IDE) or using command line utilities. In some cases, MSDE is also used to provide access to a remote copy of SQL Server. Some third party products, such as MSDE Query, provide a graphical user interface (GUI) for MSDE.

Microsoft Installer (MSI)

1. A technique for installing applications within Windows that allows later removal even if the system configuration has changed. This technique also provides support for additional vendor information, partial installations, multiple configurations, and installation recovery. 2. A file format containing instructions for installing Windows applications. The file is actually a database that contains specialized instructions and data in a specific format that's read by the Microsoft installer application.

Microsoft Intermediate Lanuage (MSIL)

The tokenized output of all .NET language compilers. The Common Language Runtime (CLR) reads the MSIL output and converts it to platform-specific code, which the platform then executes.

Microsoft Management Console (MMC)

A special application that displays special programs called snap-ins that help the user manage Windows, a device, or an application. MMC acts as an object container for Windows management objects like Component Services and Computer Management. The management objects are actually special components that provide interfaces that allow the user to access them within MMC to maintain and control the operation of Windows. A developer can create special versions of these objects for application management or other tasks. Using a single application like MMC helps maintain the same user interface across all management applications.

Microsoft Message Queuing Services (MSMQ)

A technology that enables a developer to create applications that rely on asynchronous data transfer. The data passed between client and server is recorded in a message and stored in a local or remote queue until the recipient can process it. A local listener alerts the affected application component to the presence of the message in the queue. A player interprets the content of the message for the application component so that the application component can react to it. The asynchronous application support provided by MSMQ has a number of useful applications including disconnected application support and load balancing.

MIME

See Multipurpose Internet Mail Extensions

MMC

See Microsoft Management Console

MSDE

See Microsoft Database Engine

MSDN

Microsoft Developer Network

MSI

See Microsoft Installer

MSIL

See Microsoft Intermediate Lanuage

MSMQ

See Microsoft Message Queuing Services

Multipurpose Internet Mail Extensions (MIME)

The standard method for defining the content of Internet messages. This standard allows computers to exchange objects, character sets, and multimedia using email without regard to the computer's underlying operating system. MIME is defined in the Internet Engineering Task Force (IETF) Request for Comment (RFC) 1521 standard.

N

National Institute of Standards and Technology (NIST)

A government agency that helps business develop and apply technology, measurements, and standards. In some cases, NIST also performs independent research and shares the finding with business.

NIST

See National Institute of Standards and Technology

O

Object Library File (OLB)

This file contains interface information for an object of any type (usually with the same filename). The OLB file lets the developer to see the various interfaces provided by a component. In addition to interfaces, the developer will also see the methods, properties, and list of acceptable property values (when available) associated with the object.

Object Linking and Embedding-Database (OLE-DB)

A low-level database access technology that relies on COM and a vendor supplied OLE-DB provider rather than the SQL used by Open DataBase Connectivity (ODBC). OLE-DB is designed to work with both remote and local databases. In addition, it can access database managers that don't rely on SQL such as those found on mainframe computers. OLE-DB and ODBC are cooperative, rather than competing data access technologies. OLE-DB, when coupled with ActiveX Data Objects (ADO), is designed to replace older database technologies such as Remote Data Objects (RDO) and Data Access Objects (DAO).

ODBC

See Open Database Connectivity

OLB

See Object Library File

OLE-DB

See Object Linking and Embedding–Database

OMA

Open Mobile Alliance

Open Database Connectivity (ODBC)

One of several methods for exchanging data between DBMSs. In most cases, this involves three steps: installing an appropriate driver, adding a source to the Data Sources (ODBC) applet in the Control Panel, and using specialized statements, such as Structured Query Language (SQL), to access the database.

Optimization

The configuration and organization of an operating system such that it provides specific functionality and performance in any of several areas including speed, reliability, usability, stability, security, and resource usage. Improving one area generally degrades one or more other areas so that the act of optimization also requires balancing the goals so that the optimization meets specific needs. For example, optimizing a system to provide better security generally reduces usability and speed, and increases resource usage. In some cases, a security update could even affect system reliability and stability.

P

P3P

See Platform for Privacy Preferences

Parameter

A value received by a function or procedure from another function or procedure, the command line, or some other source.

PDA

See Personal Digital Assistant

PDF

See Portable Document Format

Personal Digital Assistant (PDA)

A small handheld computing device such as a Palm Pilot or Pocket PC. People normally rely on these devices to accomplish personal tasks such as taking notes and maintaining an itinerary during business trips. Some PDAs rely on special operating systems and lack any standard application support. However, newer PDAs include some level of standard application support because vendors are supplying specialized compilers for them. In addition, you'll find common applications included, such as browsers and application office suites that include word processing and spreadsheet support.

PHP

PHP Hypertext Processor

Platform

A description of the combination of software and hardware used to create a computing system. For example, many users use a combination of the Windows operating system and an Intel processor. The combination often appears as the Wintel platform. In some cases, a discussion will only use the operating system as the basis for a platform. A developer might create applications only for the Windows platform. The use of the term *platform* is often ambiguous and requires the actual platform type to make the meaning clear.

Platform for Privacy Preferences (P3P)

A Worldwide Web Consortium (W3C) sponsored technique for ensuring privacy through specialized programming techniques. The specification defines methods of communicating information requests, use, storage technique, and requirements to the requestor. The requestor then decides whether the requirements are acceptable and optionally transfers the necessary information.

Plug-in

A descriptive term for helper applications, components, or controls that a container (host) application uses to provide optional functionality. Plug-ins appear in a number of forms such as a sound processing system for playing streaming audio normally downloaded as a separate item for container applications such as browsers. The container application provides an environment in which the plug-in can operate. The container application calls on the plug-in to perform specialized tasks that the developer of the container application chose not to include.

PNG

See Portable Network Graphic

Portable Document Format (PDF)

A formatted, book-like document format originally created by Adobe. This document format initially captured the output of desktop publishing applications. Many other applications, especially graphics applications, now output to the PDF format. Users can view PDF files using the free Acrobat Reader utility.

Portable Network Graphic (PNG)

A graphics file format (pronounced ping) similar to the Graphics Interchange Format (GIF) used for Internet graphics. This graphics format is newer than the GIF and many developers consider it superior because it uses a newer compression mechanism. Many developers use the PNG file format because it doesn't rely on patented technology as the GIF format does.

Private Key File (PVK)

A file containing the private key used to encrypt data or other content sent from one location to another.

Protocol

A set of rules used to define a specific behavior. For example, protocols define how networks and the Internet transfer data. Other protocols define how data is formatted within files. Most protocols rely on some type of standardization process to achieve development community support.

PVK

See Private Key File

Q

Query

A request or question made by a user of an application program using an interface. The query can appear as part of a form or other type of input, or the user can make the query as part of a script when using automation. Common queries include search requests for documents or a request to perform a task such as checking the status of the computer hardware. The data returned by the query can appear in a number of locations, including databases and flat file storage.

R

RAM

See Random Access Memory

Random Access Memory (RAM)

The basic term used to describe volatile data storage within a computer system. RAM comes in a variety of types such as Direct Rambus Dynamic Random Access Memory (DRDRAM), Double Data Rate Synchronous Dynamic Random Access Memory (DDR SDRAM), Dual-Ported Video RAM (VRAM), Extended Data Out Dynamic Random Access Memory (EDO DRAM), and Static Random Access Memory (SRAM). Each of these RAM types has specialized features. These special features make some kinds of RAM more acceptable for some storage tasks than others.

Registry

A specialized hierarchical database used to hold settings, configuration, file associations, and other information for Windows. The registry is a hierarchy or tree consisting of keys and associated values. The operating system searches the registry tree for keys that it requires, then requests values for those keys in order to perform tasks such as configure an application. The registry is organized into hives. Each hive contains settings for a particular operating system element such as user information and hardware configuration. Users share common hives such as those

used for hardware, but have separate hives for their information as long as Windows is configured to provide separate desktops for each user.

Registry Key

A registry entry; a method of organizing registry data. It provides the structure required to hold configuration values and other information required by both Windows and the applications it runs. Each registry key resides within a hive and can contain zero or more values. Children of registry keys are called subkeys.

Registry Setting

The combination of a registry key and one or more registry values that describe an option such as an application configuration value. A registry setting could describe where to find additional values for an executable file. The setting provides a complete description of a single data element.

Registry Value

An individual piece of data within the Windows registry database. Each value provides some type of information associated with a registry key, such as configuration information, a globally unique identifier (GUID), human readable value, numeric value, binary sequence, or other appropriate data. The common registry data types include string, DWORD, binary, multi-string, and expandable string. Of these values, the string data types are easiest to read and understand.

Remote Method Invocation (RMI)

A relatively simple wire protocol designed to support Java. RMI is a binary protocol like DCOM and CORBA and is built on a CORBA base. This protocol won't support platforms other than Java.

Remote Procedure Call (RPC)

One of several methods for accessing data within another application. RPC is designed to look for the application first on the local workstation, and then across the network at the applications stored on other workstations.

Report File (RPT File)

A file containing the definitions required to connect with a database, obtain requested data, interpret and manipulate the data, and provide output in any of a number of formats including visual and printed. The most common application for creating and modifying RPT files is Crystal Reports.

Rivest Shamir Adleman algorithm (RSA)

An authentication technology named after its creators that relies on a private-public key pair to create a set of credentials. The credentials are then used as a means of identification for logging into various network resources. Using this methodology allows for secure data transmission as well as user-oriented features like one password login to the network.

RMI

See Remote Method Invocation

RPC

See Remote Procedure Call

RPT File

See Report File

RSA

See Rivest Shamir Adleman algorithm

Runtime Error

A fault that occurs while an application executes, which usually generates a message describing the problem and can cause the application to terminate prematurely.

S

Scalable Vector Graphics (SVG)

A vector-based method of describing a graphic using XML. Vector graphics are infinitely scalable because they rely on math definitions, rather than bitmaps. They also require less storage space than bitmap graphics. Unfortunately, SVG requires more display time, processing power, and resources. It also requires a special XML parser and display application.

Script

Usually associated with an interpreted macro language used to create simple applications, productivity enhancers, or automated data manipulators. Most operating systems support at least one scripting language. You'll also find scripting capability in many higher end applications such as Web browsers and word processors. Scripts are normally used to write small utility-type applications rather than large-scale applications that require the use of a compiled language. In addition, many scripting languages are limited in their access of the full set of operating system features.

SDK

See Software Development Kit

Secure Hashing Algorithm 1 (SHA-1)

The mathematical basis for encrypting and decrypting data used with the Digital Signature Standard (DSS) introduced by the National Institute of Standards and Technology (NIST). DSS also relies on Digital Signature Algorithm (DSA) to provide the digital signature functionality.

Secure Socket Layer (SSL)

A digital signature technology used for exchanging information between a client and a server. Essentially an SSL-compliant server will request a digital certificate from the client machine. The client can likewise request a digital certificate from the server. Companies or individuals obtain these digital certificates from a third party vendor like VeriSign or other trusted source that can vouch for the identity of both parties.

Security Identifier (SID)

The part of an access token that identifies the object throughout the network; it's like having an account number. The access token that the SID identifies tells what groups the object belongs to and what privileges the object has.

Server

1. A specialized computer designed to answer client requests for services such as printing and centralized

file storage. 2. An application or workstation that provides services, resources, or data to a client application or workstation. The client usually makes requests in the form of Object Linking and Embedding (OLE), Dynamic Data Exchange (DDE), Distributed Component Object Model (DCOM), Component Object Model Plus (COM+), HyperText Markup Language (HTML), or other command formats. The server response to a request is service, resource, data, error message, or an access denied message.

SHA-1

See Secure Hashing Algorithm 1

SID

See Security Identifier

Simple Object Access Protocol (SOAP)

A protocol that provides the means for exchanging data between a requestor and a server. Originally, SOAP provided the means for binary technologies such as Component Object Model (COM) to exchange data with other binary technologies such as Common Object Request Broker Architecture (CORBA) using eXtensible Markup Language (XML) as an intermediary. However, SOAP is often used as the basis for Web services communication today. A developer could also use SOAP on a local area network (LAN) or in any other environment that requires machine-to-machine communication and the two target machines provide the required infrastructure.

SLN

See Solution File

SmartTag

A specialized menu attached to an object. In some cases, an application creates the object in an ad hoc fashion when it detects the presence of specific data such as an address, name, or stock symbol. The menu contains a list of tasks that the user can perform with the object. In many cases, the contents of the menu change based on the object data or status.

SOAP

See Simple Object Access Protocol

Software Development Kit (SDK)

A special add-on for developers to an operating system or an application that describes how to access its internal features. For example, an SDK for Windows would show how to create a File Open dialog box. Programmers use an SDK to learn how to access special Windows components such as the Component Object Model (COM) or the Media Player.

Solution File (SLN)

The file used by Visual Studio and other development environments to store application settings such as special file views and a list of the files contained within the application. The solution file is the central storage location for application-specific information that doesn't affect the actual application code.

SPC

Software Publisher Certificate

SQL

See Structured Query Language

SSL

See Secure Socket Layer

String

Two or more characters connected to form a word or other character-based information. Strings normally provide human readable data, but you can find non-human (machine) readable forms. For example, even though a path and filename normally appear in a string, you have to know how to read the string to interpret it correctly.

Structured Query Language (SQL)

Most Database Management Systems (DBMSs) use this language to exchange information; many also use it as their native language. SQL provides a method for manipulating data controlled by the DBMS. It defines which table or tables to use, determines what information to get from the table, and resolves how to sort the information. A typical request will include the name of the database, table, and columns needed for display or editing purposes. SQL can filter a request and limit the number of rows using special features.

Developers also use SQL to manipulate database information by adding, deleting, modifying, or searching records. IBM research center designed SQL between 1974 and 1975. Oracle introduced the first product to use SQL in 1979. SQL originally appeared on mainframe and minicomputers. Today it's a favorite language for most PC DBMS as well. There are many versions of SQL.

SVG

See Scalable Vector Graphics

T

T-SQL

See Transact Structured Query Language

Tagged Image File Format (TIFF)

A bit-mapped (raster) graphics file format used on the PC and Macintosh. The TIFF file format offers a broad range of color formats including black and white, gray scale, and color. One of the advantages of using TIF is that it provides a variety of compression methods and offers smaller storage form factor. Files on the PC often use a TIF extension.

TCP/IP

See Transmission Control Protocol/Internet Protocol

TIFF

See Tagged Image File Format

TLB

See Type Library File

Transact-Structured Query Language (T-SQL)

A Microsoft variant of the Structured Query Language (SQL) designed for use with SQL Server.

Transmission Control Protocol/Internet Protocol (TCP/IP)

A standard communication line protocol (set of rules) developed by the U.S. Department of Defense. The protocol defines how two devices talk to each other. TCP defines a communication methodology where it guarantees packet delivery and also ensures the packets appear at the recipient in the same order they were sent. IP defines the packet characteristics.

Type Library File (TLB)

This file contains interface information for a specific component (usually with the same filename). The TLB file lets the developer to see the various interfaces provided by a component. In addition to interfaces, the developer will also see the methods, properties, and a list of acceptable property values (when available) associated with the component.

U

UDDI

See Universal Description, Discovery, and Integration

UI

See User Interface

UML

See Unified Modeling Language

Unicode Character

A double byte (16-bit) character used to represent more than the character set used by the English language. Unicode character sets are standardized by international convention. Advanced operating systems normally rely on Unicode for enhanced language support and consistent data handling. This is the standard character set used by newer versions of Windows; although, all versions of Windows can still use ASCII characters when needed for compatibility purposes.

Unified Modeling Language (UML)

A specialized form of presentation used to express the design of an application.

Uniform Resource Identifier (URI)

A generic term for all names and addresses that reference objects on the Internet. A URL is a specific type of URI. See Uniform Resource Locator (URL).

Uniform Resource Locator (URL)

A text representation of a specific location on the Internet. URLs normally include the protocol (`http://` for example), the target location (World Wide Web or `www`), the domain or server name (`mycompany`), and a domain type (`com` for commercial). (Many URLs don't include the www portion of the address anymore.) It can also include a hierarchical location within that Web site. The URL usually specifies a particular file on the Web server, although there are some situations when a Web server will use a default filename. For example, asking the browser to find `http://www.mycompany.com`, would probably display the `DEFAULT.HTM` or `INDEX.HTM` file at that location. The actual default filename depends on the Web server used. In some cases, the default filename is configurable and could be any of a number of files. For example, Internet Information Server (IIS) offers this feature, so the developer can use anything from an HTM, to an ASP, to an XML file as the default.

Uniform Resource Name (URN)

A managed resource identifier. Being a managed resource means that a URN is guaranteed to be unique. Companies that want to use a URN must apply for a Namespace Identifier (NID) from an authority such as the Internet Assigned Numbers Authority (IANA). The NID appears as part of every resource reference that the company creates.

Universal Description, Discovery, and Integration (UDDI)

A standard method of advertising application and other software-related services online. The vendor offering the service registers at one or more centralized locations. Clients wishing to use the service add pointers to the service to their application.

UTC

Universal Time Code

Unmanaged Code

A .NET programming term for natively compiled code that runs directly under DOS or Windows. Native code executes without the benefit of the Common Language Runtime (CLR).

URI

See Uniform Resource Identifier

URL

See Uniform Resource Locator

URN

See Uniform Resource Name

US-CERT

United States Computer Emergency Response Team

User Interface (UI)

The portion of an application that contains user accessible controls and data manipulation elements. The user interface for a Windows application is commonly composed of buttons, text boxes, static text, graphics, and other design elements.

V

VBE

See Visual Basic Editor

VBS

See Visual Basic Script

Virtual Private Network (VPN)

A special form of network connection that relies on the Internet to provide required connectivity. The connection is virtual because the user can make or break it as needed. The reason that this connection has to be private is to deny access to either the client machine or remote server by outside parties. A user gains initial access to the server through an ISP. After initiating access to the Internet, the user employs a second connection to the server using Point-to-Point Tunneling Protocol (PPTP) or other security connection technology. The setup is extremely secure because it actually uses two levels of data encryption: digital signing of packets and encrypted passwords.

Visual Basic Editor (VBE)

A development environment normally used to create and edit Visual Basic Script (VBS) or Visual Basic for

Applications (VBA) code. VBE is also the extension used for many modern script files. The VBE extension replaces the Visual Basic Script (VBS) extension used in the past.

Visual Basic Script (VBS)

A file containing a program that relies on a subset of the full Visual Basic language. Users normally rely on VBS to create small applications and macros. Visual Basic Script or VBScript works well as a stand-alone language. Many developers also use it within Web pages and as part of Internet Information Server (IIS) Active Server Pages (ASP).

VPN

See Virtual Private Network

W

W3C

See World Wide Web Consortium

WAN

See Wide Area Network

WAP

See Wireless Access Protocol

Web Services Description Language (WSDL)

A method of describing a Web-based application (Web service) that's accessible through an Internet or intranet connection. The file associated with this description contains the service description, port type, interface description, individual method names, and parameter types. A WSDL file relies on namespace support to provide descriptions of common elements such as data types. Most WSDL files include references to two or more resources maintained by standards organizations to ensure compatibility across implementations.

WebSAT

Web Static Analyzer Tool

WebVIP

Web Variable Instrumenter Program

Wide Area Network (WAN)

An extension of the local area network (LAN), a WAN connects two or more LANs together using a variety of methods. A WAN usually encompasses more than one physical site, such as a building. Most WANs rely on microwave communications, fiber optic connections, or leased telephone lines to provide the internetwork connections to keep all nodes in the network talking with each other.

Windows Scripting Host (WSH)

The Windows capability to write and execute scripts at the system level. This service allows the user to reduce the number of repetitive tasks required to get applications to work together. A user can use a script, for example, that scans their hard drive for errors, backs it up, then optimizes it; all without any work on the user's part except for the initial script execution. The user may have to perform additional work if the script encounters an error, but nothing more than the user would normally do. Scripts can employ one of two default languages, JavaScript or VBScript. The user can also create scripts via languages such as REXX and Perl when working with a third party add-in product.

Wireless Access Protocol (WAP)

A method of providing secure access for mobile devices of all types to Web-based application content through a gateway. The underlying technology works much like Handheld Device Markup Language (HDML), but using standardized and secure access techniques. This technology supports most mobile networks including Cellular Digital Packet Data (CDPD), Code-Division Multiple Access (CDMA), Global System for Mobile Communications (GSM), and Time Division Multiple Access (TDMA). Supported mobile device operating systems include PalmOS, EPOC, Windows CE, FLEXOS, OS/9, and JavaOS. The technology can support pages in either Wireless Markup Language (WML) or HyperText Markup Language (HTML) format although WML is preferred because it better supports mobile device requirements.

Wireless Markup Language (WML)

An XML-based language used to communicate with Wireless Access Protocol (WAP) devices such as cellular telephones or personal digital assistants (PDAs). Most cellular telephones provide support for WML. The pages are served in a manner similar to the used by the Handheld Device Markup Language (HDML).

Wizard

A specialized application or application module that reduces the complexity of using or configuring an operating system, application, or other component. A wizard normally relies on procedural steps and simple questions to obtain the information needed to perform a complex task.

WML

See Wireless Markup Language

World Wide Web Consortium (W3C)

A standards organization devoted to Internet standards, especially security issues. This organization is also involved in other issues such as defining the special <OBJECT> tag used to implement ActiveX technology. The W3C also defines a wealth of other HTML and XML standards. The W3C first appeared in December 1994, when it endorsed the SSL (Secure Sockets Layer) standard. In February 1995, it also endorsed application-level security for the Internet.

WSDL

See Web Services Description Language

WSH

See Windows Scripting Host

X

XHTML

See eXtensible Hypertext Markup Language

XML

See eXtensible Markup Language

XSLT

See eXtensible Style Language Transformation

Z

ZIP

A file that acts as a container for other files. The ZIP normally provides some level of data compression to make the resulting package smaller than the individual files. Some operating systems such as Windows XP provide built-in support for the ZIP file. However, in many cases, you need to buy or download an application that provides the ZIP file functionality.

Index

Note to the reader: Throughout this index **boldfaced** page numbers indicate primary discussions of a topic. *Italicized* page numbers indicate illustrations.

P